T0212781

Lecture Notes in Computer Science   9660

Commenced Publication in 1973
Founding and Former Series Editors:
Gerhard Goos, Juris Hartmanis, and Jan van Leeuwen

More information about this series at http://www.springer.com/series/7407

Erika Ábrahám · Marcello Bonsangue
Einar Broch Johnsen (Eds.)

Theory and Practice
of Formal Methods

Essays Dedicated to Frank de Boer
on the Occasion of His 60th Birthday

 Springer

Editors
Erika Ábrahám
RWTH Aachen University
Aachen
Germany

Marcello Bonsangue
Leiden University
Leiden
The Netherlands

Einar Broch Johnsen
University of Oslo
Oslo
Norway

ISSN 0302-9743 ISSN 1611-3349 (electronic)
Lecture Notes in Computer Science
ISBN 978-3-319-30733-6 ISBN 978-3-319-30734-3 (eBook)
DOI 10.1007/978-3-319-30734-3

Library of Congress Control Number: 2016932347

LNCS Sublibrary: SL1 – Theoretical Computer Science and General Issues

Printed on acid-free paper

This Springer imprint is published by SpringerNature
The registered company is Springer International Publishing AG Switzerland

Frank de Boer

(Photo taken by Einar Broch Johnsen)

Preface

This festschrift celebrates the 60th anniversary of Professor Frank S. de Boer. Frank is a prominent member of the research community in formal methods and theoretical computer science. A brief look through his lengthy publication list reveals a broad area of interest and a versatile modus operandi compared with many of his colleagues: logic and constraint programming; deductive proof systems, soundness, and completeness; semantics, compositionality, and full abstraction; process algebra and decidability; multithreading and actor-based concurrency; agent programming, ontologies, and modal logic; real-time systems, timed automata, and schedulability; enterprise architectures, choreography, and coordination; testing and runtime monitoring; and cloud computing and service-level agreements. For a while, he also liked failures, especially in semantics, and optimistically concluded with the failure of failures. In fact, Frank has an opportunistic approach to research. Rather than seeing obstacles, he finds opportunities.

In the shadow of Frank's research achievements, there is the "deboerian myth." In this short preface, we will not dwell further on his scientific accomplishments. Instead, we seek to cement this myth. Not the man behind the myth, but the myth behind the man. It has been said that when Frank started his PhD in computer science, the world lost a skilled classical guitarist. Rumor has it that he was even playing professionally for a while. From his former hippie life as a guitar player, Frank has retained a relaxed attitude to life and a certain *joie de vivre* which he effectively combines with his research. Marjan Sirjani explains: "Frank is a philosopher, a logician, and a computer scientist. He has novel ideas in many diverse fields, from Hoare logic to timed actors to Java threads. Frank is fun and frustration! He may not be always politically correct, but he rarely offends people, as he is just who he is, he is just Frank. He is full of energy and he loves sunny days, for him it's a sin to work on a sunny day." Ernst-Rüdiger Olderog remembers working with Frank and Krzysztof Apt after Frank's paragliding accident in Malaysia: "While Frank was well on his way of recovery, but still in need of crutches, we three authors met in December 2008 and January 2009 in the spacy kitchen of his home in Amsterdam to work on our book. This 'kitchen informatics' created a nice and intense working atmosphere despite Frank's hardship." Alexandra Silva recounts meeting Frank after his first experience preparing meat on his newly acquired, high-tech grill at his summer house: "I will never forget the passion with which he described this and all the adjectives he used. In life, as in research, passion is the key to happiness and a great steak and wine are one step towards perfection! A lesson learned from Frank de Boer!" Lara Astefanoaei recalls Frank's good humor and witty remark: "I remember one of my first Dutch storms, I was... impressed :). Frank, not quite: cows and trees weren't flying yet, he observed, calmly. And with a laughter."

Several stories touch on Frank's ability to improvise. Davide Ancona observes that Frank is a very relaxed traveler: "Some years ago Frank and I happened to attend a conference at Riva del Garda (a nice Italian town on the Garda lake); we both agreed that the venue was very pleasant, but Frank was a bit disappointed since Verona was not so close as he had expected; he knew that Verona was not so far away from the Garda lake (about 30 km) therefore he had decided to fly to Verona to get to the conference venue. After he arrived at Verona airport he got on a taxi to reach Riva del Garda; Frank did not mention anything about the reaction of the taxi driver, but told me placidly: Actually, the drive was longer than expected". In fact, Riva del Garda is more than 80 km from Verona (and more than 1 hour away by car). Reiner Hähnle points out that this ability to improvise also carries over to Frank's scientific abilities: "I've always been immensely impressed by Frank's capability to come up with a really good impromptu presentation without any preparation time whatsoever. This is how it goes: assume you had agreed with Frank that he gives a presentation at your project gathering a few weeks ago and that he actually made it to the meeting (but that's another story …). Now you ask him whether this or that time slot is ok. The reply, almost inevitably, is an incredulous 'Indeed? I really agreed to give a talk – now?'. Your heart sinks, but you don't worry, because: 'All right, I'll improvise something on the topic.' And he proceeds to give a really convincing talk, not necessarily about what you had originally agreed upon, but nevertheless the audience/reviewers/students are impressed and happy!"

One of the editors of this volume can confirm Frank's ability to improvise. After we had planned the EU project CREDO while driving around Beijing in a taxi looking for whisky, and had written the project proposal while escaping polar bears in Spitsbergen some months later, we were invited for contract negotiations in Brussels. Owing to certain misunderstandings, we were sent back and forth between the buildings of the European Commission for a while and arrived 20 minutes late for the negotiation meeting. The project officers clearly expressed their lack of appreciation for this delay and then asked Frank as coordinator to give his presentation of the project. "What, am I expected to present something? Sure, … I hope it is ok that I don't use slides?" Frank, of course, gave an excellent 20-minute presentation; the project officers completely forgot how annoyed they were and we got the funding.

This volume collects a number of papers by Frank's collaborators over the years. Their broad range of topics reflects Frank's versatility. On behalf of all your friends in science: Happy birthday, Frank!

January 2016

Erika Ábrahám
Marcello Bonsangue
Einar Broch Johnsen

Organization

This festschrift was organized by Frank's colleagues and friends Erika Ábrahám, Marcello Bonsangue, and Einar Broch Johnsen.

Reviewers

Aichernig, Bernhard K.
Albert, Elvira
Ancona, Davide
Arbab, Farhad
Astefanoaei, Lacramioara
Baier, Christel
Clarke, Dave
Correas, Jesús
Drossopoulou, Sophia
Gabbrielli, Maurizio
de Gouw, Stijn
Helvensteijn, Michiel
Hooman, Jozef
Hähnle, Reiner
Svetlana, Jaksic
Khamespanah, Ehsan

Kyas, Marcel
Laneve, Cosimo
Lucanu, Dorel
Meyer, John-Jules
Nobakht, Behrooz
Olderog, Ernst-Ruediger
Pantovic, Jovanka Vanja
Roman-Díez, Guillermo
Rot, Jurriaan
Silva, Alexandra
Sirjani, Marjan
Steffen, Martin
de Vink, Erik
Yi, Wang
Yoshida, Nobuko
Zavattaro, Gianluigi

Contents

Personal Notes

Program Verification: To Err is Human

Krzysztof R. Apt[✉]

CWI, Science Park 123, 1098 XG Amsterdam, The Netherlands
apt@cwi.nl

Frank de Boer devoted a large part of his scientific career to program verification. As a result our scientific roads crossed a number of times, occasionally in an unexpected way.

One would expect that researchers studying program verification are careful in checking their arguments and don't publish papers with erroneous arguments. Unfortunately, it is easier said than done. In what follows I shall present some evidence for it in the form of four small stories. In two of them Frank has played a crucial role.

Error Number 1. I got interested in program verification in 1975, soon after joining Mathematisch Centrum (now Centrum Wiskunde en Informatica). Thanks to Jaco de Bakker I stumbled upon the influential paper [7] of Stephen Cook. Cook introduced the important notion, now called *Cook's completeness*, and proved that a certain Hoare-like proof system for programs without recursion is complete in his sense. After having studied this paper for some time I came to an astonishing conclusion that its main result is false. I checked my argument several times but found no flaw in my reasoning. Here it is.

Cook allowed in his mini programming language local variables introduced by means of a block statement. In particular, the program

$$\textbf{begin new } x; z := x \textbf{ end}; \textbf{begin new } y; v := y \textbf{ end}$$

that introduced two local variables, x and y, was a legal one, no matter that both assignments in it referred to uninitialized variables.

Now, according to Cook's semantics local variables were implicitly initialized to the value present at the top of the stack after the push instruction. As a result in the above program both x and y got initialized to the same value. Consequently, after the execution of this program the assertion $z = v$ was true, but there was no way to prove it!

I wrote a letter to Cook pointing out this error and suggested how it could be avoided. Cook agreed with my observations and published an erratum as [8] in which he presented my observations.

Error Number 2. My interest in program verification eventually led to a publication of a survey paper, [2], that appeared in 1981. One of the topics I discussed was termination of recursive procedures. In the paper I presented a completeness proof of an appropriate Hoare-like proof system for total correctness.

Now it was Frank's turn. A couple of years later he made me aware that a subtle interaction between various proof rules present in the system made it is possible to deduce incorrect conclusions in it. In other words, the system I

© Springer International Publishing Switzerland 2016
E. Ábrahám et al. (Eds.): de Boer Festschrift, LNCS 9660, pp. 3–5, 2016.
DOI: 10.1007/978-3-319-30734-3_1

presented was unsound. Frank and myself tried to publish in the ACM Toplas, the journal in which [2] appeared, a letter clarifying the error. Unfortunately, we never got any reply from the Editor-in-Chief for the reasons that remained obscure for us.

Sometime later Frank, jointly with Pierre America, analyzed in detail in [1] the source of my error and proposed a correction in the form of additional restrictions on the proof rules used. This restriction was so devised that the proposed system remained complete.

Error Number 3. During the late eighties I embarked with Ernst-Rüdiger Olderog upon a project of writing a book on program verification. One of the topics we planned to cover was verification of parallel programs. The most influential paper in this area was the seminal [9] that introduced the so-called Owicki-Gries method. Owicki and Gries considered both partial correctness and termination, though the main emphasis of their paper was on partial correctness.

When studying their paper we came to a conclusion that their argument showing soundness of their method of proving termination of parallel programs was incorrect. This did not yet mean that the method *itself* was incorrect, though we were convinced that in fact it *was*. It remained to find a counterexample, so a program that did not terminate but the termination of which could be established using Owicki and Gries method. After some time we involved Frank. Soon he found a counterexample. This led to [3], my first joint publication with Frank. (A curious meta-feature of this paper was that it started on page 0. The reason was that it was the first paper in a book dedicated to Edsger Wybe Dijkstra.) In the paper we presented the counterexample and proposed a way to repair the method. The results were incorporated in the book Ernst-Rüdiger and myself published as [6].

Small Errors. The second edition of the book appeared in 1997. In 2007 Springer approached Ernst-Rüdiger and me suggesting to publish the third edition. After some deliberation we approached Frank, who —much to our delight— agreed to get involved. The idea was to extend the book by incorporating his work on verification of object-oriented programs into it. This would call for an addition of some new preparatory material on recursive procedures and a revision of one or two earlier chapters.

Our joint work on the book took an unexpected turn when Frank had a serious parasailing accident during his stay in Malaysia. He misunderstood the instructions and fell from the height of some 10 m to the beach, crushing three vertebra and breaking a couple of bones in both feet. After a repatriation to the Netherlands he was immobilized for several months at home.

One would think that Frank's accident had an adverse effect on our work. Nothing could be farther from truth. Thanks to his stay at home Frank could focus on research, leaving administrative tasks to others. During this period I worked with Frank often at his apartment, once with Ernst-Rüdiger who came to visit us from Oldenburg. As a result our work on the third edition proceeded smoothly.

After a huge effort we succeeded to deliver the files to Springer on time in May 2009. I still remember processing the final overfulls during the Queen's Day, listening to a deafening music from a boat moored close to our house at a canal in the center of Amsterdam.

This rush to meet Springer's deadline was hardly appreciated by Springer. It took them another five months (sic!) to publish the book as [4]. Regrettably, we did not appreciate the quality of print and after tedious discussions convinced Springer that they should produce a higher quality printout.

Additionally, because of this (in retrospect totally unneeded) rush, some small errors slipped into the chapter on object-oriented programming. Nothing serious, but still. A corrected version of the book appeared early in 2011.

My (so far) last publication with Frank is an expanded account of the above chapter that appeared as [5], with Stijn de Gouw as the fourth author.

The conclusion one can draw from the above small accounts is that not only program verification but also *reasoning about* program verification can be tricky. Interaction between variables used in assertions and in the programs can be extremely subtle and even if one is aware of it, one can still occasionally err. Fortunately, in research, in contrast to chess, errors can often be corrected.

Frank, many happy returns on your 60th birthday!

References

1. America, P., de Boer, F.S.: Proving total correctness of recursive procedures. Inf. Comput. **84**(2), 129–162 (1990)
2. Apt, K.R.: Ten years of Hoare's logic, a survey, part I. ACM Trans. Prog. Lang. Syst. **3**, 431–483 (1981)
3. Apt, K.R., de Boer, F.S., Olderog, E.R.: Proving termination of parallel programs. In: Feijen, W.H.J., van Gasteren, A.J.M., Gries, D., Misra, J. (eds.) Beauty is Our Business, A Birthday Salute to Edsger W. Dijkstra, pp. 0–6. Springer-Verlag, New York (1990)
4. Apt, K.R., de Boer, F.S., Olderog, E.R.: Verification of Sequential and Concurrent Programs, 3rd edn. Springer-Verlag, New York (2009)
5. Apt, K.R., de Boer, F.S., Olderog, E.-R., de Gouw, S.: Verification of object-oriented programs: a transformational approach. J. Comput. Syst. Sci. **78**(3), 823–852 (2012)
6. Apt, K.R., Olderog, E.R.: Verification of Sequential and Concurrent Programs. Springer-Verlag, New York (1991)
7. Cook, S.A.: Soundness and completeness of an axiom system for program verification. SIAM J. Comput. **7**(1), 70–90 (1978)
8. Cook, S.A.: Corrigendum: Soundness and completeness of an axiom system for program verification. SIAM J. Comput. **10**(3), 612 (1981)
9. Owicki, S., Gries, D.: An axiomatic proof technique for parallel programs. Acta Inf. **6**, 319–340 (1976)

Fond (and Frank) Memories of Frank

Prakash Panangaden[✉]

School of Computer Science, McGill University, 3480 Rue University, Room 318,
Montréal, QC H3A 0E9, Canada
prakash@cs.mcgill.ca

How can Frank be 60? I'm only, oh yeah wait, it all comes back to me
now! Frank is so youthful and vigorous that it seems hard to believe that he is
approaching 60; the new 40 as the popular saying goes. I met Frank long ago
at some now forgotten conference. However, it was in 1990 that I spent a week
in Amsterdam visiting the CWI and again in 1992, when I spent a month at
CWI that I really got to know him well. We were friendly rivals over concurrent
constraint programming and friends on all topics in semantics of concurrency.
Of course, we were bitter enemies on the squash court where I consistently
thrashed him, but perhaps he remembers it differently! Sadly in the late 1990s
our interests diverged when I pursued probabilistic systems and Frank continued
with different directions in concurrency theory.

Let me describe our work in concurrent constraint programming. In the
late 1980's there was much excitement about the "Japanese Fifth Generation
Project" which aimed to build massively parallel machines that were geared
towards symbolic computing rather than numerical computation. The language
of choice was concurrent logic programming of which there were several variations. Some order was brought to this world by Vijay Saraswat with his pioneering thesis on Concurrent Constraint Programming [Sar87, Sar90]. This was
quickly followed by denotational semantics for this family of languages developed
in [SRP91] and independently in [dBP90]. The work in [SRP91] built on ideas
from [JPP89] whereas the ideas in [dBP90] were a remarkable precursor to the
later proliferation of game semantics.

What was striking about concurrent constraint programming was that it
allowed "side effects" but in a graceful way. One could update data structures by
adding information, but one could not take away information as with the brutal
assignment statement of imperative programming languages. The conceptual
model was as follows. There is a repository of "information" called the store.
The store is just a first-order formula in some logical language. This logic is
equipped with a notion of entailment; how entailment queries are answered is
abstracted away. Several processes are allowed to run concurrently and interact
with the store by either adding information to the store, a so-called **tell** operation
or they can **ask** whether a formula is entailed by the store. Syntactically one can
write tell(f) and ask(f) ---> P. The former just adds the formula f to the
store and the latter asks whether the store entails the formula f. If it does the
process continues by executing P, otherwise it suspends. Note that this is not an
if-then-else; an **ask** never returns false. A suspended process may wake up later
on if and when some other process adds information to the store which makes

© Springer International Publishing Switzerland 2016
E. Ábrahám et al. (Eds.): de Boer Festschrift, LNCS 9660, pp. 6–8, 2016.
DOI: 10.1007/978-3-319-30734-3_2

it strong enough to imply the guard. Thus the "ask" is really a synchronization mechanism.

The insight of de Boer and Palamidessi was to model this as a dialogue between processes. Each process was viewed as a sequence alternately posing questions and answering other questions. They imposed clever closure conditions on these interaction sequences and came up with a fully abstract model for concurrent constraint programming. Essentially the same ideas appear in the Saraswat *et al.* paper but with the added twist that the interactions were modelled with closure operators so the way that the closure conditions were expressed were different. Later it was realized that this kind of model has exactly the same algebra as the existential fragment of first-order logic [MPSS95]: ask was a weak form of implication, parallel composition was "and" and block structuring was existential quantification. Concurrent constraint programming evolved many interesting variations later involving time [SJG94,SJG96], continuous change [GJS98] probability [GJS97,GJP99] and so forth. Indeed there has been recent work on adding epistemic modalities to the logic [CKP09].

It was an exciting time for concurrency and I am happy to say concurrency theory continues as vibrant as ever and Frank continues to do pioneering work in the area. So here's to you Frank, many happy returns of the day.

References

[CKP09] Chatzikokolakis, K., Knight, S., Panangaden, P.: Epistemic strategies and games on concurrent processes. In: Nielsen, M., Kučera, A., Miltersen, P.B., Palamidessi, C., Tůma, P., Valencia, F. (eds.) SOFSEM 2009. LNCS, vol. 5404, pp. 153–166. Springer, Heidelberg (2009)

[dBP90] de Boer, F.S., Palamidessi, C.: On the asynchronous nature of communication in concurrent logic languages: a fully abstract model based on sequences. In: Baeten, J.C.M., Klop, J.W. (eds.) CONCUR 1990. LNCS, vol. 458, pp. 99–114. Springer, Heidelberg (1990)

[GJP99] Gupta, V., Jagadeesan, R., Panangaden, P.: Stochastic processes as concurrent constraint programs. In: Proceedings of the 26th Proceedings Of The Annual ACM Symposium On Principles Of Programming Languages, pp. 189–202 (1999)

[GJS97] Gupta, V., Jagadeesan, R., Saraswat, V.: Probabilistic concurrent constraint programming. In: Mazurkiewicz, A., Winkowski, J. (eds.) CONCUR 1997. LNCS, vol. 1243, pp. 243–257. Springer, Heidelberg (1997)

[GJS98] Gupta, V., Jagadeesan, R., Saraswat, V.A.: Computing with continuous change. Sci. Comput. Program. **30**(1), 3–49 (1998)

[JPP89] Jagadeesan, R., Panangaden, P., Pingali, K.: A fully abstract semantics for a functional language with logic variables. In: Proceedings of IEEE Symposium on Logic in Computer Science, pp. 294–303 (1989)

[MPSS95] Mendler, N.P., Panangaden, P., Scott, P.J., Seely, R.A.G.: A logical view of concurrent constraint programming. Nord. J. Comput. **2**, 182–221 (1995)

[Sar87] Saraswat, V.A.: The concurrent logic programming language cp: definition and operational semantics. In Proceedings of the SIGACT-SIGPLAN Symposium on Principles of Programming Languages, pp. 49–62. ACM, January 1987

[Sar90] Saraswat, V.A.: Concurrent Constraint Programming Languages. Doctoral Dissertation Award and Logic Programming Series. MIT Press, Cambridge (1990)

[SJG94] Saraswat, V.A., Jagadeesan, R., Gupta, V.: Foundations of timed concurrent constraint programming. In: Proceedings of the Ninth Annual IEEE Symposium On Logic In Computer Science, Paris, 1994, pp. 71–80. IEEE Press (1994)

[SJG96] Saraswat, V., Jagadeesan, R., Gupta, V.: Timed default concurrent constraint programming. J. Symbolic Comput. **22**(5), 475–520 (1996)

[SRP91] Saraswat, V.A., Rinard, M., Panangaden, P.: Semantic foundations of concurrent constraint programming. In: Proceedings of the Eighteenth Annual ACM Symposium on Principles of Programming Languages (1991)

Warmest Congratulations, Frank!

Willem-Paul de Roever[1,2(✉)]

[1] Christian-Albrechts-Universität Zu Kiel, Kiel, Germany
[2] Ebereschenweg 70, 24161 Altenholz, Germany
wpr@informatik.uni-kiel.de

© Springer International Publishing Switzerland 2016
E. Ábrahám et al. (Eds.): de Boer Festschrift, LNCS 9660, pp. 9–11, 2016.
DOI: 10.1007/978-3-319-30734-3_3

Dear Frank,

Corinne and I congratulate you warmly with the many successful and fulfilled years you have behind you, and wish you and Hilda dearly a lot of more of such happy years to come!

In this contribution, I would like to focus on my gratitude to you for our long and close professional collaboration and for our friendship.

My immediately very high opinion of you as a researcher was, amongst others, based upon your revolutionary work on Hoare logics for process creation, constituting the main part of your dissertation, extending the techniques which Krzysztof Apt, Nissim Francez and I had developed for obtaining a Hoare logic for Hoare's language CSP (Communicating Sequential Processes). This has been one of the main themes in your research, e.g., judging by your many publications on object orientation in various settings. You started this work in the context of ESPRIT Project 415 at the CWI under Jaco de Bakker, your thesis advisor, from 1985 to 1989. Doing research at the CWI remained one of the passions throughout your working life! Jaco had been also my thesis adviser and was a close colleague, who launched the NFI-funded REX project (1983–1993) together with Grzegorz Rozenberg and me. This project became our main basis to further the academic study of Concurrency in Computer Science in the Netherlands. On a position financed by REX and allotted to my chair, you worked in 1989–1993 at the Eindhoven University of Technology.

In the first half of the 90 s, it became evident to you that it would not be easy to fulfill your hopeful expectations about your professional life. For ideally, you would love to do and lead research at the CWI, combined with a professorate.

I remember a meal the two of us had in an Asiatic restaurant in the Oosterpark buurt, in Amsterdam, in that period, during which you expressed your insecurity about your future career. Since I had been in a very similar situation, before, and had shared my professional doubts with some of my trusted professors, I in fact told you little more than the advice they had given to me. Namely, that you should establish your name as a brilliant researcher in an international setting, and, that, once you were recognized as such internationally, you would be able to realize your professional goals in the Netherlands because of sheer peer pressure; e.g., a position at the CWI might become a possibility! Note that this is far easier said than done, because it touches upon the very essence of one's professional life, but at least it sketches the way ahead! And I told you also that I would do my best to support you in this respect, since in the meantime I had found out myself how this could be done in my own situation by creating a trusted international circle of friends and colleagues whose support and help I could enlist when doing research and, later, when composing international (EU/ESPRIT, at that time) projects, the latter being one of the passions in my own professional career!

And indeed, when consulting your professional history, I see this support confirmed. From 1990 onwards, you participated in most of my ESPRIT/EU projects (SPEC, REACT, OMEGA and CREDO), first as a participant, then as a partner, and finally, as a Coordinator! The term "support" is here rather blurred, because, as you will realize immediately, very soon we supported each other.

Certainly, you, as coordinator of the EU-project CREDO, and as supervisor of my last "Kieler" Ph.D. students Ulrich Hannemann, who obtained his degree at the University of Utrecht, and Erika Ábrahám, Marcel Kyas, Immo Grabe and Andreas Grüner, in your position as Professor at the University of Leiden, are without any doubt the one who helped me scientifically in the later years of my professional life. For to a considerable degree due to your participation and supervision, my Ph.D. students were able to do research at the cutting edge of the frontier of research in our field of Semantics, Specification and Verification of Concurrent Programs!

I would like to express here my gratitude to the CWI and the LIACS-institute of the University of Leiden, for their generous support of these students from Kiel! Erika Ábrahám (now Associate Professor at the RWTH, Aachen) was supported in the two phases of the Moby-J project, a bilateral NWO/DFG research project between the Netherlands and Germany, which Marcello Bonsangue and you initiated at the University of Leiden and I at the University of Kiel. Moby-J led in 2003 to the well-known FMCO Symposia (FMCO stands for Formal Methods for Components and Objects), lastly organized in 2012, with 10 corresponding proceedings in Springer's LNCS series.

I count 24 publications in which both our names occur in the list of co-authors. And, indeed, in scientific respect I consider you as my direct successor. This is one of the reasons why I didn't feel any remorse when I was succeeded, when pensioned in 2008 at the University of Kiel, by a professor in Software-Engineering–for that position my Institute at the University of Kiel needed first of all, especially to obtain accreditation for its Bachelor and Master Degree programs! But research is international, and in that context I am glad that I had passed my torch on to you!

Here, I want mention in particular your semantic insights in the foundations of Floyd's Inductive Assertion method which you have shared with me when we started to write our book on Concurrency Verification (together with Ulrich Hannemann, Jozef Hooman, Yassine Lakhnech, Mannes Poel and Job Zwiers). I am quite sure, that, without your crystal-clear insights, I would not have succeeded to unify the various approaches discussed in that book successfully; what's more, without your insights it wouldn't have been written!

But, what is far more important to me now, what a massive amount of fun we have had through all these years! I remember all those dinner parties Marcello Bonsangue and you have organized in Leiden, and you in Amsterdam (here, I remember in particular some Italian restaurants) and abroad, and how our pleasure and enjoyment still increased when Einar Broch Johnsen (from the University of Oslo) joined our innermost project circle! Especially last time, at August 2nd, comes to my mind, when Einar just popped up as a surprise guest out of thin air at your weekend home in Voorthuizen, where Hilda and you staged a party for us! That is the stuff happy memories are made out of!

When discussing this contribution to your Festschrift with Corinne, she recalled with pleasure how through the years we have felt truly at home in each other's company. Sometimes, this concerned the three of us, and, when Hilda had no professional obligations, the four of us. So, from the bottom of our hearts, we thank you for our year-long friendship and collaboration, Frank! Hopefully, in future some more occasions may arise where we can enjoy each other's company!

Your friends,

Corinne and Willem-Paul de Roever.

Scientific Contributions

Conformance Checking of Real-Time Models
Symbolic Execution vs. Bounded Model Checking

Bernhard K. Aichernig$^{(\boxtimes)}$, Florian Lorber, and Martin Tappler

Institute for Software Technology, Graz University of Technology, Graz, Austria
{aichernig,florber}@ist.tugraz.at

Abstract. We compare conformance checking based on symbolic execution to conformance checking via bounded model checking. The application context is fault-based test case generation, focusing on real-time faults. The existing bounded model checking approach is performed on timed automata. It supports time-relevant mutation operators and a preprocessing functionality for removing silent transitions and non-determinism. The new symbolic execution approach is performed on timed action systems, which are a novel variant of Back's action systems augmented by clock variables and real-time semantics. It supports the same set of mutation operators, silent transitions, non-determinism and data variables. We show how to encode timed automata as timed action systems and perform experiments on three variants of a car alarm system, to investigate the influence of silent transitions, non-determinism and data variables. Both approaches rely on the SMT solver Z3.

1 Introduction

Time-critical systems can often be far more complex than their untimed counterparts. Due to this raised complexity, they require an especially thorough verification and validation. For example, in the automotive domain, companies rely heavily on testing to ensure the quality of their systems. Manual test generation is a tedious and error-prone process, without guarantee of capturing all relevant parts of the system. Model-based test-case generation deals with these problems by automatically generating test cases on the basis of a test model. The tests are usually generated based on coverage criteria, like e.g., state or transition coverage of the test model. Model-based mutation testing is a fault-based approach: we define a set of fault models, so called mutation operators, that are systematically applied to the test model, creating a set of faulty models, called mutants. The main part of the test-case generation consists of performing a conformance check between the original test model and its mutants. In case of non-conformance, we build a test case covering the shortest path from the initial state to the conformance violation. Thus, we gain a test suite covering all non-equivalent mutants, able to detect every faulty implementation that implements any of the specified fault models. In this paper we present two methods for this conformance check, based on two types of timed models: the first approach is done via bounded model checking and performed on timed automata.

© Springer International Publishing Switzerland 2016
E. Ábrahám et al. (Eds.): de Boer Festschrift, LNCS 9660, pp. 15–32, 2016.
DOI: 10.1007/978-3-319-30734-3_4

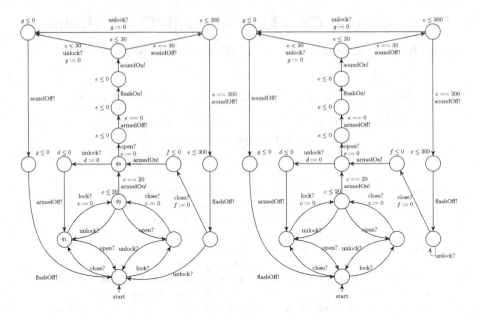

Fig. 1. Car alarm system: correct specification (left) and a mutant (right).

This approach was already published [5]. The second new one is based on symbolic execution and works on timed action systems. We define a novel variant of timed action systems closely related to timed automata, giving them a trace based semantics. We compare both approaches in terms of runtime, applied to different models of a car alarm system. Given that the mutation operators might yield hundreds of mutants, the performance of the conformance check is crucial.

The present paper, written for the Festschrift in honour of *Frank S. de Boer*, touches upon three of his active research topics: symbolic execution [1,30], real-time behaviour [8,12,18], and testing [23,24,30]. Our study indicates that symbolic execution is a promising candidate for automatically analysing real-time behaviour. As it has been pointed out [7], this is especially relevant to expressive modelling languages, like e.g. Real-Time ABS [8,12].

Running Example. We will illustrate the different approaches on a car alarm system, that was provided by Ford as a use case for the past EU FP7 project MOGENTES (http://www.mogentes.eu), and was since used as an internal benchmark for various publications [3,5]. The car alarm system is illustrated as a timed automata in Fig. 1: it provides the user with the options to open, close, lock and unlock the doors. If the doors stay locked and closed for 20 s, the system is armed. Forcing the doors open, without unlocking them first, will cause the activation of the sound and flash alarm. The alarms will deactivate either if the doors are unlocked, or after 30 and 300 s, respectively.

The remainder of the paper is structured as follows: first, in Sect. 2 we will give some preliminaries, covering timed automata, model-based mutation testing and bounded model checking. Then, in Sect. 3 we will introduce timed action systems, giving them symbolic trace semantics and explaining how to apply a symbolic conformance check based on the Symbolic Timed Input Output Conformance (**stioco**) relation. In Sect. 4 we will present our experimental results, comparing symbolic execution to the bounded model checking approach. Finally, in Sect. 5 we discuss related work and conclude the paper in Sect. 6.

2   Preliminaries

2.1   Timed Automata

Timed Automata (TA) [9] are a widely used formalism for specifying time critical systems. They are used in several areas, as for instance schedulability analysis [18]. Basic TA are finite state machines, augmented by clocks to measure the passage of time. Time is considered to only pass in states, and may be restricted by invariants, enforcing that the states are left before the invariants are broken. Transitions are considered to take zero time. They can be restricted by clock constraints in their guard, and each transition may be linked to a set of clocks that are reset upon passage of the transition. The automaton in Fig. 1 (left) contains 5 clocks. The transition from q_1 to q_2 resets the clock c. In q_2 the passage of time is restricted by the invariant $c \leq 20$ and the transition from q_2 to q_3 is restricted by the time guard $c == 20$.

The experiments conducted for this work were applied on three classes of *Timed Automata with Inputs and Outputs*, meaning that the set of observable actions is spilt into two disjoint sets of inputs (denoted by a question mark) and outputs (denoted by an exclamation mark):

1. **Deterministic Timed Automata.** We consider a TA to be deterministic, if it does not contain silent transitions and for all transitions with same source state and same action label, their guards cannot be satisfied simultaneously.
2. **Non-Deterministic Timed Automata with Silent Transitions.** Silent transitions are considered internal actions, that are not observable to the user. Both, non-determinism and silent transitions cannot be removed in general [11]. Recently, we presented a bounded approach for silent transition removal and determinization [22]: it unfolds the automaton up to a certain depth and determinizes it, creating a deterministic tree-shaped TA.
3. **Timed Automata with Data Variables.** Another extension to timed automata is the support for data variables. These are integer variables, that can be used both in guards and assignments of transitions. They can also be used as parameters for transitions, where the parameters for input transitions are chosen by the user, and all other parameters are chosen by the system.

2.2   Model-Based Mutation Testing

As already stated by Dijkstra [14], one of the main downsides of testing is the fact that it can never prove the complete absence of bugs in a system under

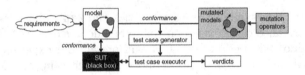

Fig. 2. Model-based mutation testing [4]

test (SUT). Model-based mutation testing addresses this problem, by generating tests able to prove the absence of certain kinds of bugs in deterministic SUTs.

The workflow of model-based mutation testing is illustrated in Fig. 2. It starts from the requirements to produce a test model (top left corner), that is processed by the mutation tool (according to a set of mutation operators), to create a set of mutated models (top right corner). For a mutant example see Fig. 1. Next, each of the model mutants is checked for conformance to the test model. If no conformance violation is detected, the mutant is considered equivalent, indicating that the concrete mutation did not propagate to any visible failure. However, if non-conformance is detected, the mutation introduced a fault with observable consequences. In that case, we produce an abstract test case, covering the shortest path to the observed conformance violation. The test suite consisting of all produced abstract test cases is then passed on to the test case executer. There, the test cases are concretized and executed on the SUT. If a deterministic SUT shows the same faulty behaviour as any of the mutants, the corresponding test case is guaranteed to detect the fault and returns the verdict *fail*. If the SUT conforms to the test model, a *pass* verdict is issued.

The conformance relation may vary: in untimed systems, the Input Output Conformance (**ioco**) by Tretmans [25] is widely used. The intuition behind **ioco** is that for all traces of the specification, the outputs of the implementation (in our case, the mutants) must be a subset of the outputs of the specification. Several extensions of **ioco** to real-time exist. For our bounded-model checking of TAs, we use the Timed Input Output Conformance (**tioco**) introduced by Krichen & Tripakis [19]. Here, time is seen as output. For the theory and first experimental results on model-based mutation testing with TA we refer to [5].

For the symbolic execution approach on timed action systems, we rely on a symbolic conformance relation. The first Symbolic Input Output Conformance (**sioco**) relation was introduced by Frantzen et al. [16]. Von Styp et al. [26] expanded the relation by adding support for time, defining the **sioco** relation for Symbolic Timed Automata (STA). We use a very similar conformance relation to **stioco**, based on timed action systems. Additionally we also support silent transitions, which are not handled by Von Styp. et al. The symbolic conformance check for untimed action systems was recently published [6].

Together with the Austrian Institute of Technology, we developed a model-based mutation testing tool-chain working on UML-models, Action Systems and TA (www.momut.org). Timed action systems are not yet officially supported.

2.3   Bounded Model Checking

In our first work on model-based mutation testing for TA [5], we proposed a conformance check via bounded model checking. We used *tioco* as a conformance relation and showed how to encode the conformance-check as a language inclusion problem. Via bounded model checking, we searched for a state where the mutant can perform an output (since we check *tioco* conformance, this includes the passage of time) that is not allowed by the specification.

We bounded the language inclusion by a bound k, and encoded it as an SMT-formula. This formula is split into two parts: the first part is the reachability check, which contains the correct step relation for k steps, of both the specification and the mutants. It calculates all states that are reachable within k steps. The second part performs the conformance check for all states that are found by the reachability. The conformance formula is a conjunction of a valid step in the mutant (taking only the outputs into account) and the negation of all valid steps of the specification. Thus, the formula is satisfiable, if the mutant is at some point able to generate an output that is not allowed by the specification. If that happens, the SMT solver returns a concrete model that serves as a counter example for the conformance.

This counter example can then be transformed into a real test case by adding verdicts and symbolic time constraints. We use the SMT solver Z3 and its feature for incremental solving.

2.4   Conventions

Generally, we assume the usage of two-sorted logic, where one sort d is defined for discrete data and the other sort t for time-related formulas and terms. We further require that the constant 0_t of sort t and the binary addition $+_t$ for pairs of sort t must be defined. In addition, the relations $\leq, <, =, >\geq$ must be defined for all pairs of sorts d and t, i.e. any comparison between time and data must be possible. Note that in practise, we allow for more sorts in our models, such as user-defined enumeration sorts, but we use a type checker to ensure that only meaningful comparisons are performed.

We will denote the set of terms containing variables from a set X by $Te(X)$ and first-order formulas containing free variables from the same set by $Fr(X)$. The function $free(\varphi)$ maps a formula φ to the set of all free variables in φ.

The set $CC(X, Y)$ denotes the set of clock constraints, with clock variables in X and constraint operands in $Y \cup Te(\emptyset)$. A clock constraint is of the form $x \otimes y$, with $x \in X$, $y \in Y \cup Te(\emptyset)$ and $\otimes \in \{\leq, <, =, >\geq\}$, i.e. it is comparison between a clock variable and a variable or a constant term.

The set of all total functions from A to B shall be denoted by B^A. The substitution of variables shall be denoted by $g[\sigma]$, where σ is a function from variables to terms and g is some formula or term. Hence, the signature of $[\sigma]$ is given by $[\sigma] : Te(X) \cup Fr(X) \to Te(X) \cup Fr(X)$, where X is a set of variables. The term f_X denotes the domain restriction of a function f to the set X.

Sequences containing $e_1, e_2, \ldots, e_n$ will be denoted by $\langle e_1 \cdot e_2 \cdots e_n \rangle$ and the concatenation of two sequences σ_1 and σ_2 will be denoted by $\sigma_1 \hat{\ } \sigma_2$.

3   Timed Action Systems

Action Systems (ASs) were introduced by Back and Kurkio-Suonio [10] for modelling distributed systems. In more recent work, ASs have been used as a modelling formalism for mutation-based test-case generation for reactive systems [2,4]. An event-centred view of ASs has been taken in this context, for deriving test cases and for checking of **ioco** conformance between ASs. More concretely, for model-based mutation testing each action is assigned a label and an action type, which identifies the action as being an output, input or internal action.

For the definition of Timed Action Systems (TASs), we also follow this approach. However, the modelling formalism discussed in the following is more restricted with respect to discrete actions than other variants of the AS formalism. Nevertheless, we also extend traditional ASs by explicitly accounting for time, which is inspired by TA.

In our approach, an AS defines a set of actions and corresponding guarded commands, a set of state variables and an initialisation for these variables. An action defines a set of parameters and has an action type. For each action, the corresponding guarded command defines the conditions in which the action may be executed and the effect of the action execution. The guarded commands may access state variables and the parameters of the corresponding action. There may be several actions with the same label and if multiple action share the same label, they must also have the same parameters and action type.

During the execution of an AS, at each step an enabled action is chosen non-deterministically and executed. Through this the state is continuously updated until the execution terminates, when none of the actions is enabled. An action is enabled if the guard of its corresponding guarded command is satisfiable.

In order to allow for the modelling of time, we extend ASs by adding clock variables as in TA. In between the execution of two discrete actions, the system may wait for certain amounts of time, which increases the values of the clock variables. This act of waiting will also be referred to as delay in the following. To be able to define the conditions for the actual waiting time, we add time invariants to ASs. The time invariant of an AS must hold in all states and consists of several clauses. A clause defines a time constraint which must hold if the state variables satisfy the condition defined by the clause. Finally, guarded commands may define conditions using clocks and may reset clocks.

In the following, we define the syntax and a trace-based semantics for TASs. Both are inspired by the work of Frantzen et al. [16] and von Styp et al. [26], who use STA. Since STA are similar to TA, our version of **stioco** can be seen as an extension of the original definition [26], as we also allow internal actions.

3.1   Syntax

Figure 3 illustrates the structure of the concrete syntax of TASs and models a part of the CAS. It specifies 5 real-valued clocks, that the initial state of the system shall be OpenAndUnlocked, that the system must not wait longer than 20 time units in state ClosedAndLocked and defines the actions. The actions are labelled with

```
clocks[Real]{ c;d;e;f;g }
init{
   location := OpenAndUnlocked;}
invariant{
   if location == ClosedAndLocked then c <= 20;
   ... }
actions{
   !armedOn() if location == ClosedAndLocked and c == 20 then {
      location := Armed; };

   ?open() resets e if location == Armed then {
      location := BeforeAlarm; };
   ... }
```

Fig. 3. A snippet of the TAS model of the CAS.

armedOn and open. These two events are fully defined through two and three actions respectively. In the following, we present the abstract syntax of TASs.

Definition 1 (Abstract Syntax of Timed Action Systems). *A timed action system is a tuple* $\mathcal{TAS} = \langle \mathcal{V}, \mathcal{I}, \mathcal{C}, \Lambda_I, \Lambda_U, \iota, Inv, A \rangle$*, where* $\mathcal{V}$ *is the set of state variables,* $\mathcal{I}$ *is the set of parameter variables and* $\mathcal{C}$ *is the set of clock variables , with* $\mathcal{V}, \mathcal{I}, \mathcal{C}$ *being mutually disjoint.* $\Lambda = \Lambda_I \cup \Lambda_U$ *is the set of action labels, with* Λ_I *being the set of input action labels and* Λ_U *being the set of output action labels. The constant* $\tau \notin \Lambda$ *denotes an internal action and we set* $\Lambda_\tau = \Lambda \cup \{\tau\}$*. The initialisation of the action system is* $\iota \in Te(\emptyset)^{\mathcal{V}}$*. Inv is the time invariant of* $\mathcal{TAS}$*, which is of the form* $\bigwedge_i dc_i \rightarrow cc_i$*, with* $dc_i \in Fr(\mathcal{V})$ *and* $cc_i \in CC(\mathcal{C}, \mathcal{V})$ *for all i. The set* $A \subseteq \Lambda_\tau \times Fr(\mathcal{V} \cup \mathcal{I}) \times CC(\mathcal{C}, \mathcal{V}) \times Te(\mathcal{V} \cup \mathcal{I})^{\mathcal{V}} \times \mathcal{P}(\mathcal{C})$ *is the set of all actions. For* $a = (\lambda, g, g_c, up, r) \in A$*,* λ *is called label, g is called guard,* g_c *is the clock guard, up is the update mapping, defined by assignments in the guarded command and r is a set of clocks, which are reset by executing a.*

Before we define semantics for TASs, we introduce two requirements and two auxiliary functions. These are similar to the requirements defined for Symbolic Transition Systems (STSs) by Frantzen et al. [16]. The functions *arity* and *para* associate each action with its number of parameters and a tuple containing its parameters respectively.

1. For all actions λ, *para* maps λ to a tuple of distinct parameter variables and for $(\lambda, g, g_c, up, r) \in A$ it holds that $free(g) \subseteq \mathcal{V} \cup para(\lambda)$ and $up \in Te(\mathcal{V} \cup para(\lambda))^{\mathcal{V}}$.
2. As for τ-edges of STSs, we disallow the definition of parameter variables for internal actions of TASs, i.e. for all τ-actions, it must hold that $arity(\tau) = 0$.

Example 1 (Abstract Syntactical Representation of the CAS). The CAS defined in Fig. 3 is a TAS $\langle \mathcal{V}, \mathcal{I}, \mathcal{C}, \Lambda_I, \Lambda_U, \iota, Inv, A \rangle$, where $\mathcal{V} = \{location\}$, $\mathcal{I} = \{\}$, $\mathcal{C} = \{c, d, e, f, g\}$, $\Lambda_I = \{open, \ldots\}$, $\Lambda_U = \{armedOn, \ldots\}$, $\iota = \{location \mapsto OpenAndUnlocked\}$, $Inv = (location = ClosedAndLocked) \rightarrow c \leq 20 \wedge \ldots$ and $A = \{o, a, \ldots\}$. With actions $o = (open, location = Armed, \top, \{location \mapsto BeforeAlarm\}, \{e\})$ and $a = (armedOn, location = ClosedAndLocked, c = 20, \{location \mapsto Armed\}, \{\})$. Parts omitted in Fig. 3 are represented by dots.

3.2 Semantics and Stioco

In this subsection, we give a symbolic trace semantics for TASs and discuss **stioco** checking. A symbolic trace represents one (sequential) run of the symbolic execution of a TAS. This symbolic trace semantics forms the basis for our implementation of the symbolic executor and the **stioco** conformance checker.

The trace-based semantics must fulfil four requirements: a trace must (1) start with a delay, (2) consist of alternating sequences of discrete actions and delays, and (3) end in a delay. The first two requirements are placed on the semantics in correspondence to the definition of traces by von Styp et al. [26]. Conversely, the third requirement serves to simplify conformance checking while it does not limit generality as zero delays are possible. Additionally, (4) a trace should handle internal actions appropriately: consider the concrete timed trace $ct = \langle 1 \cdot !a \cdot 2 \cdot \tau \cdot 3 \cdot ?b \cdot 0 \rangle$. For checking **tioco** conformance one is only interested in observable traces of the specification [19]. Thus, we would project ct to the set of observable input and output actions, erasing the τ-action and summing up the two consecutive delays: $ct' = \langle 1 \cdot !a \cdot 5 \cdot ?b \cdot 0 \rangle$.

In the symbolic setting, we use symbolic traces where constant time delays are replaced by symbolic delay variables. As common in symbolic execution, these symbolic delays are defined via constraints. We distinguish between two kinds of delay variables: observable delays t_i, which are part of the observable trace and unobservable delays $d_{i,j}$ that appear only in constraints. Observable delays are always defined in terms of unobservable delays. For example, the symbolic trace $st = \langle d_1 \cdot !a \cdot d_{2,1} \cdot \tau \cdot d_{2,2} \cdot ?b \cdot d_3 \rangle$ including an unobservable τ-action would be projected to an observable trace $st' = \langle t_1 \cdot !a \cdot t_2 \cdot ?b \cdot t_3 \rangle$ with the constraints $t_1 = d_1$, $t_2 = d_{2,1} + d_{2,2}$ and $t_3 = d_3$. Note that while observing the delay t_2, it is not possible to distinguish between the internal delays $d_{2,1}$ and $d_{2,2}$.

So far, we only considered delays. For the trace-based semantics we need to update the state of variables and clocks along a trace and collect the constraints: discrete and time guards of actions, time invariants and constraints which express that consecutive unobservable delays sum up to observable delays. In addition, it is necessary to keep track of the set of unobservable delays along a trace, because we will hide these via existential quantification for the conformance check.

In order to define the formal semantics, we introduce concepts similar to those used for the original definition of **stioco** [26]. For elegant clock update definitions, we introduce the singleton sets $\mathcal{D} = \{d\}$ and $\mathcal{T} = \{t\}$ containing an unobservable and an observable delay, respectively. Since we need to distinguish between different occurrences of variables in a trace we introduce the disjoint indexed sets for observable delays $\mathcal{T}_i$, unobservable delays $\mathcal{D}_{i,j}$ and parameters $\mathcal{I}_i$ with $i, j \in \mathbb{N}$. The index i corresponds to the position in the trace and j corresponds to the number of delays since the last observable action.

Furthermore we assume that there exists a bijective variable-renaming $r_i :$ $\mathcal{I} \cup \mathcal{T} \to \mathcal{I}_i \cup \mathcal{T}_i$, which adds an index i to non-indexed variables and there exists a bijective variable-renaming $dr_{i,j} : \mathcal{D} \to \mathcal{D}_{i,j}$, which adds indexes i and j to unobservable delay variables. We set $\widehat{\mathcal{T}} = \bigcup_i \mathcal{T}_i$, $\widehat{\mathcal{I}} = \bigcup_i \mathcal{I}_i$ and $\widehat{\mathcal{D}} = \bigcup_i \bigcup_j \mathcal{D}_{i,j}$.

We model symbolic clock updates with a function $\varrho \in Te(\mathcal{C} \cup \mathcal{D})^{\mathcal{C}}$, with $\varrho(c) = c + d$ for all $c \in \mathcal{C}$ and $d \in \mathcal{D}$. With this machinery we can now elegantly define clock updates in step i, j as a composed substitution function $[dr_{i,j}] \circ \varrho$, first replacing the clocks with the term $c + d$ and then indexing d appropriately.

For clock resets of all clocks in a set r, we define a term-mapping $FO(r)$, such that $FO(r)(c) = 0_t$ for $c \in r$ and $FO(r)(c) = c$ otherwise, i.e. it sets clocks in r to zero. Finally, we define the set of all variables as $\widehat{Var} = \mathcal{V} \cup \widehat{\mathcal{I}} \cup \widehat{\mathcal{D}} \cup \widehat{\mathcal{T}} \cup \mathcal{C}$.

Symbolic Trace Semantics. The symbolic trace semantics of a TAS representing its symbolic execution is then given by the generalised transition relation $\Rightarrow \subseteq ((\widehat{\mathcal{T}} \cdot \Lambda)^* \cdot \widehat{\mathcal{T}}) \times Fr(\widehat{Var}) \times Te(\mathcal{V} \cup \widehat{\mathcal{I}})^{\mathcal{V}} \times Te(\mathcal{C} \cup \widehat{\mathcal{D}})^{\mathcal{C}} \times \mathcal{P}(\widehat{\mathcal{D}})$, which is defined below. It is a set of 5-tuples (σ, pc, q, q_c, D), where σ is an alternating sequence of delays and actions; pc is the path condition, i.e. the conditions which need to be satisfied for σ to be executable; q is the discrete symbolic state of the variables $\mathcal{V}$, i.e. a mapping from state variables to terms over state variables and parameters $\widehat{\mathcal{I}}$; q_c is the symbolic state of the clocks $\mathcal{C}$, i.e. a mapping from clocks to sums of unobservable delays, and D contains the set of unobservable delays $d_{i,j}$ collected along the observable symbolic trace σ.

Definition 2 (Generalized Transition Relation). *Given a timed action system* $\mathcal{TAS} = \langle \mathcal{V}, \mathcal{I}, \mathcal{C}, \Lambda_I, \Lambda_U, \iota, Inv, A \rangle$, *its generalised transition relation* $\Rightarrow$ *is defined to be the smallest set, which satisfies the following three rules:*

$$\frac{}{(\langle t_1 \rangle, Inv \wedge Inv[[dr_{1,1}] \circ \varrho] \wedge t_1 = d_{1,1}, id, ([dr_{1,1}] \circ \varrho)_\mathcal{C}, \{d_{1,1}\}) \in \Rightarrow} \quad (\mathbf{T}\epsilon)$$

$$\frac{(\sigma \hat{~} \langle t_i \rangle, pc, q, q_c, D) \in \Rightarrow \qquad (\lambda, g, g_c, up, r) \in A \qquad \lambda \neq \tau}{(\sigma \hat{~} \langle t_i \cdot \lambda \cdot t_{i+1} \rangle, pc \wedge t_{i+1} = d_{i+1,1} \wedge dc \wedge tc, q', q_c', D \cup \{d_{i+1,1}\}) \in \Rightarrow} \quad (\mathbf{T}\lambda)$$

where
$q' = ([q] \circ ([r_{i+1}] \circ up))_\mathcal{V},$
$q_c' = ([q_c] \circ ([FO(r)] \circ ([dr_{i+1,1}] \circ \varrho)))_\mathcal{C},$
$dc = (g[r_{i+1}])[q] \wedge (g_c[q])[q_c] \wedge (Inv[q'])[[q_c] \circ FO(r)]$ *and*
$tc = (Inv[q'])[q_c']$

$$\frac{(\sigma \hat{~} \langle t_i \rangle, pc \wedge t_i = \sum_{j=1}^{k} d_{i,j}, q, q_c, D) \in \Rightarrow \qquad (\tau, g, g_c, up, r) \in A}{(\sigma \hat{~} \langle t_i \rangle, pc \wedge t_i = \sum_{j=1}^{k+1} d_{i,j} \wedge dc \wedge tc, q', q_c', D \cup \{d_{i,k+1}\}) \in \Rightarrow} \quad (\mathbf{T}\tau)$$

where
$q' = [q] \circ up,$
$q_c' = ([q_c] \circ ([FO(r)] \circ ([dr_{i,k+1}] \circ \varrho)))_\mathcal{C},$
$dc = g[q] \wedge (g_c[q])[q_c] \wedge (Inv[q'])[[q_c] \circ FO(r)]$ *and*
$tc = (Inv[q'])[q_c']$

Rule $\mathbf{T}\epsilon$ is the base case expressing the initial delay t_1 before the first action, if any. It states that the time invariant must hold before and after this delay. The identity function id expresses the unchanging of the discrete state. The clocks $\mathcal{C}$ are updated accordingly.

Rule $\mathbf{T}\lambda$ expresses that the symbolic execution of an observable action extends the observable trace by a sequence $\langle \lambda \cdot t_{i+1} \rangle$, where λ is the corresponding action label and t_{i+1} is an observable delay. A new unobservable delay in step $i+1, 1$ is added to the set of unobservable delays and set to be equal to the observable delay in the path condition. Additionally, the discrete (dc) and time constraints (tc) are added to the path condition as well. Furthermore, the discrete state q is updated to q' according to the update function up of the action. This discrete state update takes also care of the proper variable renaming (or variable indexing) via function r_{i+1}. The clocks are partially reset according to the reset set r and then delayed.

Rule $\mathbf{T}\tau$ expresses that the symbolic execution of an internal action (with a τ label) does not change the observable trace $\sigma^\wedge \langle t_i \rangle$, but adds a new delay $d_{i,k+1}$ to the set of unobservable delays D. The new delay in step $i, k+1$ is added to the path condition, together with the discrete (dc) and time constraints (tc). Furthermore, the discrete state q is updated to q' according to the update function up of the action. The clocks are partially reset according to r and then delayed according to $d_{i,k+1}$.

The discrete constraint dc mentioned in both rules $\mathbf{T}\lambda$ and $\mathbf{T}\tau$ contains not only discrete conditions but constrains the execution of discrete actions. For a discrete action to be executable, the guard g and the clock guard g_c must be satisfied in the pre state and the time invariant must be satisfied after updating the discrete state and resetting the clocks. The time constraint tc analogously constrains the length of the delay, by specifying that the time invariant must hold after executing the discrete action, resetting and updating clocks.

Example 2 (Generalized Transition Relation of the CAS). In this example, we list two elements of the generalised transition relation of the CAS. It contains by definition through rule $\mathbf{T}\epsilon$ the element $(\langle t_1 \rangle, I \wedge I' \wedge t_1 = d_{1,1}, \{location \mapsto location\}, \bigcup_{x \in \mathcal{C}} \{x \mapsto x + d_{1,1}\}, \{d_{1,1}\})$, where $I = (location = ClosedAndLocked) \rightarrow c \leq 20 \wedge \dots$ and $I' = (location = ClosedAndLocked) \rightarrow c + d_{1,1} \leq 20 \wedge \dots$. A trace consisting of only the open-action, which executes the open-action as defined in Fig. 3 corresponds to the tuple $(\langle t_1 \cdot ?open \cdot t_2 \rangle, pc, q, q_c, \{d_{1,1}, d_{2,1}\})$, where $q = \{location \mapsto BeforeAlarm\}$, $q_c = \{e \mapsto d_{2,1}\} \cup \bigcup_{x \in \mathcal{C} \setminus \{e\}} \{x \mapsto x + d_{1,1} + d_{2,1}\}$ $pc = I \wedge I' \wedge t_1 = d_{1,1} \wedge t_2 = d_{2,1} \wedge dc \wedge tc$, with $dc = (location = Armed) \wedge (BeforeAlarm = ClosedAndLocked) \rightarrow c + d_{1,1} \leq 20 \wedge \dots$ and $tc = (BeforeAlarm = ClosedAndLocked) \rightarrow c + d_{1,1} + d_{2,1} \leq 20 \wedge \dots$

Conformance Checking. Since the **stiocos** conformance relation for TASs is very similar to the definition of **stioco** of von Styp et al. [26], we will not give the full definition, but rather list the three most important differences:

– We use the semantics discussed above. As unobservable delays along a trace are relevant for conformance, symbolic states and symbolic observations consider these as well. Hence, states and observations are tuples, where one tuple element contains the unobservable delays which have been collected before reaching a symbolic state or before observing some symbolic observation.

- The symbolic observation of delays needs to be adapted as well, i.e. a symbolic counterpart of the $elapse(s)$-function [19] must be defined, which maps a state s to the set of delays, which can be executed without executing an observable action. Hence, a symbolic $elapse(s)$-function could be defined as a trace, which consists of only one delay, executed in state s. More concretely, it could be defined as $(t_1, pc, q, q_c, D) \in \Rightarrow$, but with shifted indexes and a substitution of the actual state into pc, q and q_c.
- The original **stioco** definition uses a function Φ, which gives a condition for observing some observation after a given trace σ. To account for internal actions, this function needs to existentially quantify over the sets of unobservable delays collected along σ.

The conformance check is implemented in the same fashion as the **sioco** conformance check for untimed action systems [6], which is itself inspired by the **ioco** conformance checker used in [2,3]. More concretely, it performs a bounded depth-first search for *unsafe states*, which are states in which non-conformance may be observed. For this purpose, both mutant and specification are symbolically executed in parallel, such that they synchronise on observable actions, but execute internal actions independently from each other. In order to ensure input-enabledness of the mutant, which is a requirement for **stioco**, we perform an angelic completion for the mutant. Hence, we implicitly add self-loops to states for all non-specified inputs. At each step, a conformance check is performed and if non-conformance is detected, the trace leading to the current state and the satisfiable non-conformance condition are returned.

However, a naive implementation of this procedure would suffer from problems such as path explosion [13] and thus be far too slow to be useful. Consequently, several optimisations have been implemented, which can roughly be grouped into three categories:

Pruning of search tree. If during the search for unsafe states, we reach a symbolic state which has already been visited, we prune the search tree. For this purpose, we implemented symbolic checks for equivalence of states, which are based on the state inclusion condition defined by Gaston et al. [17]. These checks deem two symbolic states to be equivalent, if they correspond to the same sets of concrete states.

Precomputation. We precompute symbolic execution graphs, which encode all executable traces for the specification. This information can be reused during the conformance check and results in a performance gain, as we check conformance for hundreds of different mutants with the same specification.

Syntactic mutation analysis. As long as the mutation has not been executed, the number of satisfiability checks can be reduced drastically, e.g. by using the precomputed execution graph for the mutant as well.

3.3   Encoding Timed Automata Using Timed Action Systems

In order to encode a Timed Automaton (TA) as a TAS, we essentially create a TAS having the same set of state variables plus one additional state variable representing the current location and having the same set of transitions. The procedure for translating TA into TASs can be structured as follows:

1. Create a TAS with the same set of state variables, clocks and action labels.
2. Create a set of constants *Loc*, where each constant represents a location in the TA. Define a function *rep*, which maps locations to their respective constants.
3. Add an additional state variable called *location*, which takes values in *Loc*, and rename an existing variable with the same name, if such a variable exists. Initialise *location* with $rep(l_0)$, where l_0 is the initial location of the TA.
4. For each transition of the TA with source location l and target location l':
   4.1 Create an action with same guards, clock resets, state updates and label.
   4.2 Add $location = rep(l)$ to the guard and add $location \mapsto rep(l')$ to the state update.
5. Initialise the time invariant to $\top$, then for each invariant i of a location l: Conjunct the clause $rep(l) = location \to i$ to the time invariant of the TAS.

Any TAS that was built according to this structure, can also be encoded as a TA, by reverting the steps above.

4   Experimental Results

To give a first comparison of the two approaches we use the car alarm system that was introduced in Sect. 1. We defined different variants, containing model elements such as silent transitions and data variables, that can be challenging for the conformance checks. In all the experiments we use the following settings: we translated from timed automata to timed action systems as closely as possible: The different models contain the same number of states and transitions and the same sets of clocks and variables. We used eight different mutation operators (similar to those in [5], excluding the changing of action labels, that would have been problematic to implement for the TAs), that were implemented equally for both types of models. However, due to the different modelling styles, the amount of mutants did vary slightly in some cases. All experiments were run on a MacBook Pro with a 2.8 GHz Intel Core i7 and 8 GB RAM.

Table 1. Computation time for the different conformance checks on the deterministic version of the car alarm system.

Depth	Bounded model checking				Symbolic execution			
	Mean	Median	Max	Min	Mean	Median	Max	Min
12	1.4 s	1.1 s	33 s	0.07 s	1.7 s	0.02 s	38.83 s	~ 0 s

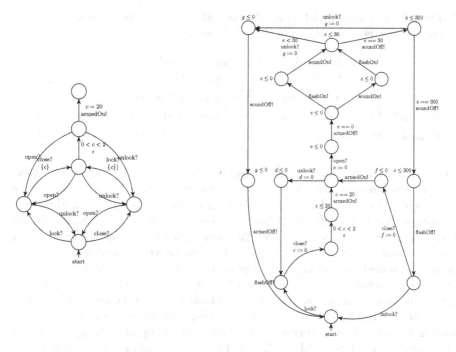

Fig. 4. Partial models of the car alarm system with silent transitions.

4.1 Deterministic Car Alarm System

We first investigate the model in Fig. 1. It is deterministic and has 5 clocks, 16 locations and 25 transitions. The results of applying both approaches are displayed in Table 1. The bounded model checking performed slightly faster and at a very constant rate, without many statistical outliers. The symbolic execution, with the median far below the mean value, was very fast for most of the mutants, however there were some that took significantly longer than the rest, and increased the average processing time. The overall runtime of the bounded model checking was 30.0 min for 1,320 mutants, compared to 27.5 min for 968 mutants in the symbolic execution.

4.2 Non-deterministic Car Alarm System

The next model contains a silent transition that non-deterministically delays the 20 s timer responsible for arming the system by up to two seconds. This changes the time constraints for the arming of the system and adds non-determinism for the *unlock* and *open* transitions leaving the locations. We used this model previously [22]. Besides the non-determinism, it differs from the original car alarm system, by underspecifying whether the sound alarm or the flash alarm is activated first. The bounded model checking approach can neither deal with non-determinism, as it might lead to spurious counterexamples, nor with silent transitions. As already described in Sect. 2, this can be tackled,

Table 2. Computation time for the different conformance checks on the partial models of the *non-deterministic* version of the car alarm system.

Model	Depth	Bounded model checking				Symbolic execution			
		Mean	Median	Max	Min	Mean	Median	Max	Min
Partial 1	8	9.7 s	8.0 s	85.1 s	0.3 s	0.28 s	0.04 s	16.78 s	~0 s
Partial 2	12	1.6 s	1.63 s	37.3 s	0.08 s	0.08 s	0.03 s	2.28 s	~0 s
Complete	12	x	x	x	x	0.79 s	0.06 s	360.84 s	~0 s

by a bounded determination of the automaton in a preprocessing step. However, this preprocessing leads to a severe state space explosion. If applied to the non-deterministic car alarm system, with a maximum depth of 12, the deterministic automaton contains 13,545 locations, and can not be processed by the test case generation tool anymore. We thus split the original model into two *tioco*-conform partial models, where the first one captures the different variants of locking, unlocking, closing and opening the doors, up to the first arming transition. The second one only contains one direct path to the armed state, but covers the rest of the system. Both partial models are illustrated in Fig. 4. This keeps most of the branching in the first smaller system, and the main functionality in the second and larger system. The results of applying the approaches to these models are illustrated in Table 2. The overall runtime for the first partial model was 32.8 min for 220 mutants for applying the bounded model checking and 48.1 s for 168 mutants for the symbolic execution. For the second partial model, the bounded model checking took 34.1 min for 1,263 mutants and the symbolic execution only needed 68.1 s for 832 mutants.

The ability of the symbolic approach, to process the models without unfolding them first, clearly gives it an advantage here. Not only is it a lot faster on the partial models, it was also able to process the complete model. Additionally, it has on average even been faster than in the deterministic case. There are two main reasons for this behaviour. Firstly, three mutants have not been checked for conformance automatically, because they ran into a timeout (ten minutes), and were excluded from the experiments. However, manual inspection revealed that these mutants conform to the specification. Secondly, the introduction of a silent transition led to a much larger portion of nonequivalent mutants. Aichernig et al. showed that **ioco** checking of equivalent mutants takes significantly longer than **ioco** checking of non-equivalent mutants [3], thus a lower number of equivalent mutants can explain the reduction in average runtime from 1.7 s to 0.79 s.

4.3 Car Alarm System with PIN Code

This final model treats the ability of processing data variables. The unlock and lock transitions of the car alarm system are augmented by a PIN code. If the code is entered correctly, the system acknowledges it with a new *ack*-output, and continues as before. If it was entered incorrectly, the system will start the alarms, after a *nack*- output. This model only uses one clock, whereas five clocks were used in the original car alarm system.

Table 3. Computation time for the different conformance checks on the deterministic version of the car alarm system, augmented by a *PIN code*.

Depth	Bounded model checking				Symbolic execution			
	Mean	Median	Max	Min	Mean	Median	Max	Min
8	1.46 s	0.28 s	59.41 s	0.12 s	0.07 s	0.05 s	0.82 s	$\sim 0s$
12	4.12 s	0.35 s	35.41 s	0.13 s	0.24 s	0.05 s	3.67 s	$\sim 0s$

The PIN code did not have any negative influence on both approaches, as illustrated in Table 3. For the symbolic execution, the mean conformance check time was even reduced. This was most likely caused by the fact that only one clock was used in this model. Furthermore, there were several more mutants, most of which were non-equivalent.

Altogether, the bounded model checking was applied to 1,702 mutants and needed 41.4 min on depth 8 and 116.8 min on depth 12. The symbolic execution was again faster, needing 143.0 (depth 8) and 460.8 (depth 12) s for 1,918 mutants. For the reported numbers, we restricted the PIN code to three digits. However, we also applied the experiments with higher values (four and five digits), without any negative consequences.

4.4 Lessons Learned

During the experiments, we found several model elements that influence the presented approaches in different ways:

1. **The number of clocks** has a big influence on the runtime of the symbolic execution approach. Adding clock variables slows the check down, whereas merging two independent clocks reduces the runtime noticeably. In contrast, for the bounded model checking, the number of clocks does not have a significant influence on the runtime.
2. **Non-determinism** is an obstacle for conformance checking. For the bounded model checking, where determination has to be done beforehand, this leads to a state-space explosion and the complete model even became infeasible. The symbolic execution, however, only experienced a reduction in performance for some problematic mutants such as the two mutants which had to be excluded from the experiments. Nevertheless, it was still able to process the remaining mutants in reasonable time, though it should be noted that the maximum runtime increased from about 40 s in the deterministic case to about six minutes. This can be attributed to the fact that multiple symbolic states can be reached by executing observable traces if non-determinism is involved, which in turn increases the complexity for satisfiability checking of the non-conformance condition.
3. **Statistical outliers** with respect to runtime are more frequent and more extreme in symbolic execution, than on bounded model checking. In bounded model checking, the processing time of different equivalent mutants is usually the same. For symbolic execution, some mutants are harder to check than others. Usually, these are equivalent mutants, which contain mutations that are

executed early during the search for conformance violations, while mutations that are executed at higher depths generally cause a much lower performance penalty. This is due to the fact, that in the latter situation, optimisations based on syntactic mutation analysis have a larger impact.

5   Related Work

Several time extensions for action systems have already been proposed: Fidge and Wellings [15] proposed timed action systems, assuming time-consuming actions and discrete time. Westerlund and Plosila [29] proposed action systems based on continuous time, where each action system contains a clock to measure the time since start of the system. Again, time is considered to be consumed by actions, and may not pass between them. Wabenhorst [27] proposes a formalism combining time-consuming actions and an additional wait action executed if none of the other actions are enabled. In contrast to these proposals, we consider actions that take zero time, followed by delays. This keeps our definition of timed action systems very close to timed automata.

Kurki-Suonio [20] proposed a time extension to action systems, using, equal to our approach, zero time actions, but using only one global variable to track time. Each action has a parameter specifying its time of execution. They can only be executed if the global time is smaller or equal to their time of execution. If an action is chosen, it raises the global time to its time of execution. Contrary to this approach, we use invariants instead of deadlines for limiting time progress and we support multiple clocks, allowing for more complex time constraints.

We also encoded the language inclusion problem within UPPAAL [21], by adding a trap-property to the product of the specification and a mutant. First experiments showed that UPPAAL is very fast in detecting non-conformance in the deterministic case. In the non-deterministic case, the encoding we used suffered from the same problem as the bounded-model checking: it lead to spurious counter examples. Adding a PIN code with a range of $0 - 500$ to the deterministic model already slowed the conformance check down and expanding it to 5000 made the whole approach infeasible.

Wang et al. [28] presented a zone-based language inclusion check for timed automata. It seems to be faster then ours, however it does not support silent transitions, and only terminates for determinizable classes of timed automata.

6   Conclusion

We have introduced timed action systems in a fashion as close to timed automata as possible. We showed how to translate timed automata into timed action systems and defined a symbolic trace semantics for them. Using this semantics, we applied a symbolic conformance check based on the **stioco** conformance relation. We then compared bounded model checking and symbolic execution in the context of test-case generation, applied to different models of a car alarm system. The results showed that symbolic execution was able to handle non-determinism very well, and that data variables did have no negative influence on both approaches.

Acknowledgement. The research leading to these results has received funding from the ARTEMIS Joint Undertaking under grant agreement N° 332830 and from the Austrian Research Promotion Agency (FFG) under grant agreements N° 838498 for the implementation of the project CRYSTAL, Critical System Engineering Acceleration and N° 845582 for the project TRUCONF, Trust via cost function driven model based test case generation for non-functional properties of systems of systems.

References

1. Ahrendt, W., de Boer, F.S., Grabe, I.: Abstract object creation in dynamic logic. In: Cavalcanti, A., Dams, D.R. (eds.) FM 2009. LNCS, vol. 5850, pp. 612–627. Springer, Heidelberg (2009)
2. Aichernig, B.K., Brandl, H., Jöbstl, E., Krenn, W.: Model-based mutation testing of hybrid systems. In: de Boer, F.S., Bonsangue, M.M., Hallerstede, S., Leuschel, M. (eds.) FMCO 2009. LNCS, vol. 6286, pp. 228–249. Springer, Heidelberg (2010)
3. Aichernig, B.K., Brandl, H., Jöbstl, E., Krenn, W., Schlick, R., Tiran, S.: Killing strategies for model-based mutation testing. Softw. Test. Verification Reliab. **25**, 716–748 (2014)
4. Aichernig, B.K., Jöbstl, E., Tiran, S.: Model-based mutation testing via symbolic refinement checking. Sci. Comput. Program. **97**, 383–404 (2015)
5. Aichernig, B.K., Lorber, F., Ničković, D.: Time for mutants — Model-based mutation testing with timed automata. In: Veanes, M., Viganò, L. (eds.) TAP 2013. LNCS, vol. 7942, pp. 20–38. Springer, Heidelberg (2013)
6. Aichernig, B.K., Tappler, M.: Symbolic input-output conformance checking for model-based mutation testing. In: USE (2015)
7. Albert, E., de Boer, F.S., Hähnle, R., Johnsen, E.B., Laneve, C.: Engineering virtualized services. In: Second Nordic Symposium on Cloud Computing & Internet Technologies, NordiCloud 2013, Oslo, Norway, 1–3 September 2013, pp. 59–63 (2013)
8. Albert, E., de Boer, F.S., Hähnle, R., Johnsen, E.B., Schlatte, R., Tarifa, S.L.T., Wong, Y.H.: Formal modeling and analysis of resource management for cloud architectures: an industrial case study using real-time ABS. Serv. Oriented Comput. Appl. **8**(4), 323–339 (2014)
9. Alur, R., Dill, D.L.: A theory of timed automata. Theor. Comput. Sci. **126**(2), 183–235 (1994)
10. Back, R.-J., Kurki-Suonio, R.: Decentralization of process nets withcentralized control. In: Proceedings of the Second Annual ACM SIGACT-SIGOPS Symposium on Principles of Distributed Computing, Montreal, Quebec, Canada, 17-19 August 1983, pp. 131–142 (1983)
11. Bérard, B., Petit, A., Diekert, V., Gastin, P.: Characterization of the expressive power of silent transitions in timed automata. Fundam. Inform. **36**(2–3), 145–182 (1998)
12. Bjørk, J., de Boer, F.S., Johnsen, E.B., Schlatte, R., Tarifa, S.L.T.: User-defined schedulers for real-time concurrent objects. Innovations Syst. Softw. Eng. (ISSE) **9**(1), 29–43 (2013)

13. Cadar, C., Sen, K.: Symbolic execution for software testing: three decades later. Commun. ACM **56**(2), 82–90 (2013)
14. Dijkstra, E.W.: Information streams sharing a finite buffer. Inf. Process. Lett. **1**(5), 179–180 (1972)
15. Fidge, C.J., Wellings, A.J.: An action-based formal model for concurrent real-time systems. Formal Aspects Comput. **9**(2), 175–207 (1997)
16. Frantzen, L., Tretmans, J., Willemse, T.A.C.: A symbolic framework for model-based testing. In: Havelund, K., Núñez, M., Roşu, G., Wolff, B. (eds.) FATES 2006 and RV 2006. LNCS, vol. 4262, pp. 40–54. Springer, Heidelberg (2006)
17. Gaston, C., Le Gall, P., Rapin, N., Touil, A.: Symbolic execution techniques for test purpose definition. In: Uyar, M.U., Duale, A.Y., Fecko, M.A. (eds.) TestCom 2006. LNCS, vol. 3964, pp. 1–18. Springer, Heidelberg (2006)
18. Jaghoori, M.M., Longuet, D., de Boer, F.S., Chothia, T.: Schedulability and compatibility of real time asynchronous objects. In: Real-Time Systems Symposium 2008, pp. 70–79, November 2008
19. Krichen, M., Tripakis, S.: Conformance testing for real-time systems. Formal Methods Syst. Des. **34**(3), 238–304 (2009)
20. Kurki-Suonio, R.: Action systems in incremental and aspect-oriented modeling. Distrib. Comput. **16**(2–3), 201–217 (2003)
21. Larsen, K.G., Pettersson, P., Yi, W.: UPPAAL in a nutshell. STTT **1**(1–2), 134–152 (1997)
22. Lorber, F., Rosenmann, A., Ničković, D., Aichernig, B.K.: Bounded determinization of timed automata with silent transitions. In: Sankaranarayanan, S., Vicario, E. (eds.) FORMATS 2015. LNCS, vol. 9268, pp. 288–304. Springer, Heidelberg (2015)
23. Meng, S., Arbab, F., Aichernig, B.K., Astefanoaei, L., de Boer, F.S., Rutten, J.J.M.M.: Connectors as designs: Modeling, refinement and test case generation. Sci. Comput. Program. **77**(7–8), 799–822 (2012)
24. Schlatte, R., Aichernig, B.K., de Boer, F.S., Griesmayer, A., Johnsen, E.B.: Testing concurrent objects with application-specific schedulers. In: Fitzgerald, J.S., Haxthausen, A.E., Yenigun, H. (eds.) ICTAC 2008. LNCS, vol. 5160, pp. 319–333. Springer, Heidelberg (2008)
25. Tretmans, J.: Model based testing with labelled transition systems. In: Hierons, R.M., Bowen, J.P., Harman, M. (eds.) FORTEST. LNCS, vol. 4949, pp. 1–38. Springer, Heidelberg (2008)
26. von Styp, S., Bohnenkamp, H., Schmaltz, J.: A conformance testing relation for symbolic timed automata. In: Chatterjee, K., Henzinger, T.A. (eds.) FORMATS 2010. LNCS, vol. 6246, pp. 243–255. Springer, Heidelberg (2010)
27. Wabenhorst, A.: A model of real-time distributed systems. In: PROCOMET 1998, pp. 462–481. Chapman and Hall (1998)
28. Wang, T., Sun, J., Liu, Y., Wang, X., Li, S.: Are timed automata bad for a specification language? Language inclusion checking for timed automata. In: Ábrahám, E., Havelund, K. (eds.) TACAS 2014 (ETAPS). LNCS, vol. 8413, pp. 310–325. Springer, Heidelberg (2014)
29. Westerlund, T., Plosila, J.: Formal timing model for hardware components. In: Norchip Conference, 2004. Proceedings, pp. 293–296, November 2004
30. Wong, P.Y.H., Bubel, R., de Boer, F.S., Gómez-Zamalloa, M., de Gouw, S., Hähnle, R., Meinke, K., Sindhu, M.A.: Testing abstract behavioral specifications. Int. J. Softw. Tools Technol. (STTT) **17**(1), 107–119 (2015)

Resource Analysis of Distributed Systems

Elvira Albert[1]([✉]), Jesús Correas[1], and Guillermo Román-Díez[2]

[1] DSIC, Complutense University of Madrid, Madrid, Spain
elvira@sip.ucm.es
[2] DLSIIS, Technical University of Madrid, Madrid, Spain

Abstract. Distributed systems are composed of nodes that communicate and coordinate their actions by passing messages. The nodes interact with each other in order to achieve a common goal. Resource analysis of distributed systems needs to consider the distribution, communication and interaction aspects of the systems as well. We sketch the basic framework proposed for the resource analysis of distributed systems, together with the new notions of cost that arise in such distributed context. In particular, we will discuss the notions of: *peak cost* that captures the maximum amount of resources that each distributed node might require along the whole execution; and *parallel cost* which corresponds to the maximum cost of the execution by taking into account that, when distributed tasks run in parallel, we need to account only for the cost of the most expensive one. The framework is developed for a concurrent objects language with futures, a formalism that is based on Frank's work.

1 Introduction

Static resource analysis [18] aims at inferring an *upper bound* on the amount of resources required along any execution of a software system by only inspecting its code and without executing it [3,11,12,19]. We rely on a *generic* resource analysis framework [2,3] that is parametric w.r.t. the type of resource that one wants to measure. Traditional resources include the number of steps executed, the amount of memory allocated, or the number of calls to a specific method.

Distributed systems pose new challenges to resource analysis [17]. The fact that they are composed of a number of distributed nodes that communicate by exchanging messages needs to be considered by the analysis. We consider a simple class-based programming language with four instructions to define the distributed execution model: (1) new C creates a new distributed component, referred to as a *location*, that executes methods of class C, (2) f=a.m($\bar{x}$) spawns an asynchronous task m($\bar{x}$) on the location a, and f is a future variable that allows us to check whether the asynchronous task has been completed, (3) the instruction await f? allows us to synchronize with the termination of the task associated to the future variable f, and (4) the instruction f.get returns the value computed by the task associated to the future variable f (or blocks if the task has not terminated yet). We omit class definitions when they are not relevant

© Springer International Publishing Switzerland 2016
E. Ábrahám et al. (Eds.): de Boer Festschrift, LNCS 9660, pp. 33–46, 2016.
DOI: 10.1007/978-3-319-30734-3_5

for the examples. This language is the core of ABS [14], a concurrent objects language with *futures*. A formal semantics for such language can be found in Frank's work [10].

The notion of *cost center* [1] is fundamental to define the framework of resource analysis for distributed systems. The main idea is that it allows splitting the cost of executing the whole system at the granularity of interest. For instance, one can observe the cost associated to each distributed component. And it allows observing the cost associated to executing a certain task within a distributed component. Using cost centers, we can define new performance indicators for distributed systems [6]. Consider the distributed system depicted in Fig. 1 which is composed of four distributed components. Our interest is in inferring performance indicators that allow us to estimate the overall performance of the distributed system. One of the main indicators will be the one that determines whether the load is well balanced among the distributed nodes. For this purpose, we infer the resource usage for each of the distributed nodes (in the figure it appears in blue over the node). Note that since the computation depends on input variables n and m, the resource usage is given by means of cost expressions that can be evaluated for concrete input values for n and m. By comparing such cost expressions, we can identify whether there is a bottle neck in the system (for instance the resource usage of the upper component is exponential and this might be too expensive). Another essential performance indicator is the one that estimates the sizes of the communication among the distributed components. This is depicted in the figure by arrows whose labels indicate the amount of data sent from one component to another. Again, since this might depend on the input data, it is expressed by means of cost expressions in terms of the input values. This way we are able to approximate communication costs.

Besides defining new performance indicators, there are new notions of cost that arise in the context of distributed systems. In particular, we pursue the notion of *peak cost* [7] which corresponds to the maximum amount of resources that the location might require along any execution. Inferring the peak cost is not trivial, since we need to infer: (1) the amount of tasks posted to its queue, (2) their respective costs, and (3) knowledge on whether the tasks may be posted in parallel and thus be pending to execute simultaneously.

The other notion of cost that we are able to infer is the *parallel cost* [4], which differs from the standard notion of serial cost because when tasks execute in parallel it only considers the cost of the most expensive one. Thus, it is different from the standard notion of cost because it exploits the truly concurrent execution model of distributed processing to capture the cost of synchronized tasks executing in parallel. It is also different to the peak cost since the peak cost is serial, i.e., it accumulates the resource consumption in each component and does not exploit the overall parallelism as it is required for inferring the parallel cost. The main challenge to infer the parallel cost is to infer the parallelism between tasks while accounting for waiting and idle processor times at the different locations.

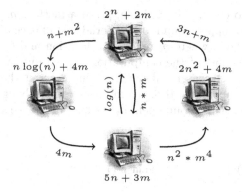

Fig. 1. Performance indicators in a distributed system

The contribution of this paper is putting within the same setting different analyses that have been published in the following venues: the analysis that underlie performance indicators is developed in [5,6], the peak cost analysis puts together work published at [7,8], and the parallel cost analysis was introduced at [4]. The rest of the paper is structured as follows: Sect. 2 describes the basics of the resource analysis framework. Section 3 introduces the indicators that can be considered to estimate the performance of a distributed system. In Sect. 4 we overview the main ideas of the peak cost analysis. Section 5 intuitively explains the notion of parallel cost and an analysis that overapproximates it. Finally, Sect. 6 concludes and points out some directions for future work.

2   Resource Analysis with Cost Centers

The notion of cost center is an artifact used to define the granularity of a cost analyzer. In [1], the proposal is to define a cost center for each distributed component; i.e., cost centers are of the form $c(o)$ where o is a location identifier and $c(\_)$ is the artifact used in the cost expressions to attribute the cost to the different components. Every time the analyzer accounts for the cost of executing an instruction $inst$ at program point pp, it also checks at which location the instruction is executing, since the instruction might be reached from executions on different distributed components. This information can be approximated by an analysis that is called points-to, and different levels of precision can be achieved (see e.g. [15,16]). In particular, given a program point pp and the current distributed location $this$, points-to analysis returns the set of locations $O_{pp} = pt(pp, this)$ which along the execution $this$ can be instantiated to. The cost of the instruction is accumulated in the cost centers of all elements in O_{pp} as

$$\sum_{\forall o \in O_{pp}} c(o) * cost(inst),$$

where $cost(inst)$ expresses in an abstract way the cost of executing the instruction. If we are counting steps, then $cost(inst) = 1$. If we measure time, $cost(inst)$

refers to the time to execute *inst*. Then, given a method $m(\bar{x})$, the cost analyzer will compute an upper bound for the serial cost of executing m of the form $m^+(\bar{x}) = \sum_{i=1}^n c(o_i) * C_i$, where o_i refers to a location and C_i is a cost expression that bounds the cost of the computation carried out by location o_i when executing m. Thus, cost centers allow computing costs at the granularity level of the distributed components. If one is interested in studying the computation performed by one particular component o_j, we simply replace all $c(o_i)$ with $i \neq j$ by 0 and $c(o_j)$ by 1.

```
1 void m (int n) {          8 void p () {              13 void q () {
2   ...                      9   ...                    14   ...
3   x. p();                 10   y. s();                 15 }
4   ...                     11   ...                     16 void s () {
5   y. q();                 12 }                         17   ...
6   ...                                                  18 }
7 }
```

Fig. 2. Example of resource analysis with cost centers

Example 1. For the code excerpt in Fig. 2, we have three cost centers for the three locations that accumulate the costs of the code they execute: the cost center for the location executing m, namely o, and the cost centers for the locations referenced by x and y, that we suppose already created. Therefore, we have that the cost of executing m is $m^+(n) = c(o) * \widehat{m} + c(x) * \widehat{p} + c(y) * \widehat{s} + c(y) * \widehat{q}$, where we represent with $\widehat{z}$ the cost of the instructions in method z. ∎

Other Types of Granularity. But, besides the original idea of using the cost centers to represent the distributed components, they can be used to achieve other kinds of granularity in the analysis. In particular, in the peak cost analysis (Sect. 4), they will allow us to achieve *task-level* granularity; and in the parallel cost analysis (Sect. 5), to achieve *block-level* granularity, as explained below.

As for task-level granularity, one wants to obtain the cost associated to the execution of each task m when executed on each distributed component o. To this purpose, we define cost centers of the form $c(o{:}m)$ which contain the location identifier o and the task m running on it. Then, every time the analyzer accounts for the cost of executing an instruction *inst*, it checks at which location *inst* is executing (e.g., o) and to which method it belongs (e.g., m), and accumulates $c(o{:}m) * cost(inst)$. As for the block-level granularity, we define block-level cost centers $c(o{:}b)$ which contain the location identifier o and the block b running on it.

Let $\mathcal{M}$ be a set that contains all method names combined with all location identifiers where they can be executed. Given a method $m(\bar{x})$, the cost analyzer now computes a *task-level upper bound* for the cost of executing m. This upper bound is of the form $m^+(\bar{x}) = \sum_{i=1}^n c(o_i{:}m_i) * C_i$, where $o_i{:}m_i \in \mathcal{M}$, and C_i is a cost expression that bounds the cost of the computation carried out by location o_i while executing block m_i. Let $\overline{\mathcal{B}}$ be a set that contains all blocks combined with all location identifiers where they can be executed. Given a method $m(\bar{x})$, the cost analyzer now computes a *block-level upper bound* for the cost of executing m. This upper bound is of the form $m^+(\bar{x}) = \sum_{i=1}^{n} c(o_i{:}b_i) * C_i$, where $o_i{:}b_i \in \overline{\mathcal{B}}$, and C_i is a cost expression that bounds the cost of the computation carried out by location o_i while executing block b_i. Observe that b_i need not be a block of m because we can have transitive calls from m to other methods; the cost of executing these calls accumulates in $m^+(\bar{x})$.

As we have seen, resource analysis allows different levels of granularity, thus we can have different types of cost center artifacts. For any kind of granularity, the notation $m^+(\bar{x})|_{cc}$ is used to express the cost associated to the cost center $c(cc)$ within the cost expression $m^+(\bar{x})$, i.e., the cost obtained by setting all $c(cc_i)$ to 1 when $cc' = cc$ and to 0 otherwise. Given a set of cost centers $N = \{cc_1, \ldots, cc_n\}$, we let $m^+(\bar{x})|_N$ refer to the cost obtained by setting to one the cost centers $c(cc_i)$ such that $cc_i \in N$.

3 Performance Indicators

In this section we define indicators that can be considered to estimate the performance of a distributed system [6]. In particular, we are interested in predicting the load balance of the distributed locations, the number of communications between nodes and the amount of data transferred among them.

3.1 Load Balance

Using the cost centers described in Sect. 2, we define an indicator to assess how balanced the load of the distributed nodes that compose the system is. By attributing the cost of each instruction to the location responsible of executing it, upper bounds can help during the development process to take better design decisions for obtaining an optimal load balancing.

Example 2. In the source code shown in Fig. 3(left and center), method m creates a new location using new at L2, pointed by variable a, and then a while loop spawns n tasks executing method p (L4). Besides, method p contains another loop that calls q n times (L10). Observe that the second argument of the call to p at L4 causes method q be executed at location a. If we replace the second argument by this at L4, that is a.p(n,this), method q will be executed at the location executing m. We refer to this location as o. The upper bound expressions for the number of steps are the same for both cases, but such decision is crucial for properly balancing the system. By using the resource analysis of Sect. 2, for a.p(n,a) at L4, the cost attributed to o is $m^+(n)|_o = 9 + 7 * n$ and the cost attributed to a is $m^+(n)|_a = 1 + n * (6 + 14 * n)$. It can be seen that the program is not properly balanced, since $m^+(n)|_o$ is a linear expression w.r.t. the value of n, while $m^+(n)|_a$ is a quadratic expression. On the other hand,

```
1 void m (int n) {              8 void p (int n, loc x) {       15 void m2 (int n) {
2   loc a = new Obj();          9   while (n > 0) {             16   while (n > 0) {
3   while (n > 0) {            10     x. q();                  17     loc a = new Obj();
4     a. p(n,a);              11     n = n − 1;                18     a. p(n,a);
5     n = n − 1;             12   }                           19     n = n − 1;
6   }                        13 }                             20   }
7 }                          14 q () { 10 instr }             21 }
```

Fig. 3. Example of performance indicators

by using a.p(n,this) at L4, we have that $m^+(n)|_a = 1 + n * (6 + 7 * n)$ and $m^+(n)|_o = 9 + n * (7 + 7 * n)$. In this case we can see that the program is more evenly balanced, as both expressions are quadratic w.r.t. n.

When reasoning about distributed systems, it is essential to have information about their configuration, i.e., the sorts and quantities of nodes that compose the system. As we have seen in the previous example, configurations may be straightforward in simple applications, but the tendency is to have rather complex and dynamically changing configurations (cloud computing is an example of this). To this end, in addition to the upper bound on the number of instructions executed by each location, it is required to have information about how many instances of each location might exist. Resource analysis described at Sect. 2 can also be extended to provide such information.

Example 3. As we have seen in Example 2, method m only uses two locations, o and a. In contrast, method m2 shown in Fig. 3(right) creates locations within a loop and, by means of the resource analysis, we can infer that the number of locations created at m2 is bounded by the value of n.

If we consider that a system is optimally balanced when all its components execute the same number of instructions, we can use the upper bounds on the number of instructions and the upper bounds on the number of distributed components to reason about how balanced the load of the distributed nodes that compose the system is. As regards the number of instructions executed by each location in the system, we have to take into account that an abstract location might represent multiple concrete locations. This means that the number of instructions executed by an abstract location actually accounts for the instructions executed by all locations it represents.

Example 4. The analysis of m2 returns that $m2^+(n)|_o = 6 + 10 * n$ and that the number of instructions executed by all locations created within the loop is $m2^+(n)|_a = n * (7 + 14 * n)$. As we have seen in Example 3, the number of locations created within the loop is bounded by the value of the input argument n. Therefore, we have n locations that execute $n * (7 + 14 * n)$ instructions, and another location o that executes $6 + 10 * n$ steps, which implies that the system is properly balanced.

3.2   Number of Transmissions and Transmission Data Sizes

Knowledge of the number of communications and the transmission data sizes is essential, among other things, to predict the bandwidth required to achieve a certain response time, or conversely, to estimate the response time for a given bandwidth. The different locations of a distributed system communicate and coordinate their actions by posting tasks among them. A task is posted by building a message with the task name and the data on which such task has to be executed. When the task completes, the result can be retrieved by means of another message from which the result of the computation can be obtained. Thus, the transmission data size of a distributed system mainly depends on the amount of messages posted among the locations of the system, and the sizes of the data transferred in the messages. In order to estimate the transmission data sizes, we need to keep track of the amount of data transmitted in two ways:

1. By posting asynchronous tasks among the locations. This requires building a message in which the name of the task to execute and the data on which it executes are included.
2. By retrieving the results of executing the tasks. In our setting, future variables are used to synchronize with the completion of a task and retrieve the result.

Our analysis infers a safe over-approximation of the transmission data sizes required by both sources of communications in a distributed system. Our method infers two different pieces of information: the number of tasks spawned at a given location, and the data sizes transmitted as a result of the task spawned.

Since we are considering an abstract representation of data by means of functional types, we will focus on *units of data* transmitted instead of bits, which depends on the actual implementation and is highly platform-dependent. Concretely, we assume that the cost of transmitting a basic value or a data type constructor is one unit of data. This size measure is known as *term size*. However, our static analysis would work also with any other mapping from data types to corresponding sizes (given by means of a function α).

Example 5. The example program showed in Fig. 4 creates locations s and m at L6 and L7, respectively, to perform some processing on a list. The list l has an initial content set at L5 (not relevant for the example) that is passed as a parameter of the call to method work at location m, and thus there is data transmission at this point. Method work extends the list with n values, and calls method process at location s (L23) after adding each element to the list, passing the list as argument. Method process does some processing to the list passed as argument. There are two program points in method work where data is transmitted between locations m and s: L23 and L24, that correspond to the call to process and the retrieval of the returned value, respectively.

Data structures are defined by means of data constructs, as it is showed in L1 with the data type definition for representing lists of integers. We consider the term size of data structures as the size measure. For example, a list defined as l = Cons(1, Cons(2, Cons(3,Nil))) has size $\alpha(l) = 7$, as it counts 2 for each

```
1  data List = Nil | Cons(Int, List );        15  class Master {
2  // main method                             16   Slave s;
3  Unit main (Int n) {                         17   work(List l , Int n) {
4   Slave s; Master m; List l ;               18    Int x;
5   l = . . .;                                 19    Int n;
6   s = new Slave();                           20    fut <Int> y;
7   m = new Master(s);                         21    while (n>0){
8   m.work(l, n);                              22     l = Cons(n,l);
9  }                                           23     y = s.process (l );
10  class Slave {                              24     x = y.get;
11   Int process (List le ) {                  25     n−−;
12    . . .                                    26    }
13    return h;                                27   }
14  }}// end class                             28  }// end class
```

Fig. 4. Example of transmission data sizes

element in the list (the Cons constructor and the element itself), plus 1 for the Nil constructor.

For inferring an upper bound on the number of tasks spawned between all pairs of distributed locations, we use the cost analysis framework described in Sect. 2. In particular, we need to use a *symbolic* cost center that allows us to annotate the caller and callee locations when a task is spawned in the program. In essence, if we find an instruction a.m(x) which spawns a task m at location a, the cost model symbolically counts $c(this, a, m) * 1$, i.e., it counts that 1 task executing m is spawned from the current location this at a. If the task is spawned within a loop that performs n iterations, the analysis will infer $c(this, a, m) * n$.

Example 6. For the code in Fig. 4, cost analysis infers that the number of iterations of the loop in work (at L21) is bounded by the expression $nat(n)$. Function $nat(x) = max(x, 0)$ is used to avoid negative evaluations of the cost expressions. Then, by applying the number of tasks cost model we obtain the following expression that bounds the number of tasks spawned at L23: $c(m, s, process) * nat(n)$.

The second piece of information obtained by our analysis is the data sizes transmitted as a result of spawning a task. To this end, we need to infer the sizes of the arguments in the task invocations. Typically, size analysis [9] infers upper bounds on the data sizes at the end of the program execution. Here, we are interested in inferring the sizes at the points in which tasks are spawned. In particular, given an instruction a.m(x), we aim at over-approximating the size of x when the program reaches the above instruction. If the above instruction can be executed several times, we aim at inferring the largest size of x, denoted $\alpha(x)$, in all executions of the instruction. Altogether, $c(this, a, m) * \alpha(x)$ is a safe over-approximation of the data size transmission contributed by this instruction. The analysis will infer such information for each pair of locations in the system that communicate, annotating also the task that was spawned.

Example 7. Since in method work the size of l is increased within the loop at L22, the maximum size of l is produced in the last call to process. Recall that the term size of the list l counts 2 units for each element in the list. Therefore, each iteration of the loop at L21 increments the term size of the list in 2 units and, consequently, the last call to process is done with a list of size $l_0 + 2*n$, where l_0 is the term size of the initial list, created at L5. In addition, the value returned by the call to process is retrieved at L24. Since the data retrieved is of type Int, its size is 1. Then, the data transmitted between locations m and s is bounded by the following expression, where the constant $\mathcal{I}$ is the size of establishing the communication:

$$c(\mathsf{m}, \mathsf{s}, \mathsf{process}) * \mathsf{nat}(n) * (\mathcal{I} + \mathsf{nat}(l + n * 2)) + c(\mathsf{s}, \mathsf{m}, \mathsf{process}) * \mathsf{nat}(n) * (\mathcal{I} + 1).$$

4   Peak Cost Analysis

The framework presented so far allows us to infer the total number of instructions that it needs to execute, the total amount of memory that it will need to allocate, or the total number of tasks that will be added to its queue. This is a too pessimistic estimation of the amount of resources actually required in the real execution. The amount of work that each location has to perform can greatly vary along the execution depending on: (1) the amount of tasks posted to its queue, (2) their respective costs, and (3) the fact that they may be posted in parallel and thus be pending to execute *simultaneously*. In order to obtain a more accurate measure of the resources required by a location, the *peak* of the resource consumption can be inferred instead [7], which captures the maximum amount of resources that the location might require along any execution. In addition to its application to verification, this information is crucial to dimensioning the distributed system: it will allow us to determine the size of each location *task queue*; the required size of the location's memory; and the processor execution speed required to execute the peak of instructions and provide a certain response time. It is also of great relevance in the context of software *virtualization* as used in cloud computing, as the peak cost allows estimating how much processing/storage capacity one needs to buy in the host machine, and thus can greatly reduce costs.

Inferring the peak cost is challenging because it increases and decreases along the execution, unlike the standard notion of *total cost* which is cumulative. To this end, it is very relevant to infer, for each distributed component, its *abstract queue configuration*, which captures all possible configurations that its queue can take along the execution. A particular queue configuration is given as the sets of tasks that the location may have pending to execute at a moment of time. For instance, let us see the following example program, which has as entry method ex1:

```
1 void ex1() {          6 void m1() {          12 void m2() {
2   ff  = this.m1();     7   fa  = x.a();        13   x.d();
3   await ff ?;          8   await fa ?;         14   x.e();
4   this . m2();         9   fb  = x.b();        15 }
5 }                     10   await fb?;
                        11 }
```

It first invokes method m1, which spawns tasks a and b at location x. Method m1 guarantees that a and b are completed when it finishes. Besides, we know that the await instruction in L8 ensures that a and b cannot happen in parallel. Method m2 spawns tasks d and e and does not await for their termination. We can observe that the await instructions in m1 guarantee that the queue is empty before launching m2. We can represent the tasks in the queue of location x by the tasks queue graph by means of the following queue configurations: $\{\{a\}, \{b\}, \{d, e\}\}$.

In order to quantify queue configurations and obtain the peak cost, we need to over-approximate: (1) the number of instances that we might have running simultaneously for each task and (2) the worst-case cost of such instances. The main extension has been to define cost centers of the form $c(o{:}m)$ which contain the location identifier o and the task m running on it, as explained in Sect. 2. Now, using the upper bounds on the total cost we already gather both types of information. This is because the cost attached to the cost center $c(o{:}m)$ accounts for the accumulation of the resource consumption of *all* tasks running method m at location o. We therefore can safely use the total cost of the entry method $ex1(\bar{x})$ restricted to $o{:}m$, denoted $ex1^+(\bar{x})|_{\{o:m\}}$, as the upper bound of the cost associated with the execution of method m at location o which sets up to 0 the cost centers different from $c(o{:}m)$. The key idea to infer the *quantified queue configuration*, or simply *peak cost*, of each location is to compute the total cost for each element in the set of abstract configurations and stay with the maximum of all of them. In the previous example, the peak cost of location x in ex1 is $max\{ex1^+(n)|_{c_1}, ex1^+(n)|_{c_2}, ex1^+(n)|_{c_3}\}$, where $c_1 = \{x{:}a\}$, $c_2 = \{x{:}b\}$ and $c_3 = \{x{:}d, x{:}e\}$.

5   Parallel Cost Analysis

Parallel cost differs from the standard notion of *serial cost* by exploiting the truly concurrent execution model of distributed processing to capture the cost of synchronized tasks executing in parallel. It is also different to the peak cost since this one is still serial; i.e., it accumulates the resource consumption in each component and does not exploit the overall parallelism as it is required for inferring the parallel cost [13]. It is challenging to infer parallel cost because one needs to soundly infer the parallelism between tasks while accounting for waiting and idle processor times at the different locations. Let us see an example.

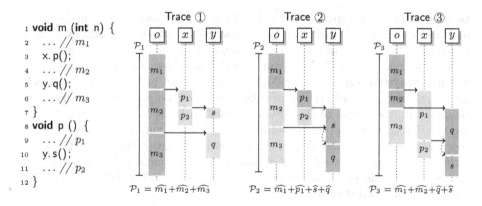

Fig. 5. Example of parallel cost

Example 8. Figure 5(left) shows a simple method m that spawns two tasks by calling p and q at locations x and y, resp. In turn, p spawns a task by calling s at location y. This program only features distributed execution, concurrent behaviours within the locations are ignored for now. In the sequel we denote by $\widehat{m}$ the cost of block m. $\widehat{m_1}$, $\widehat{m_2}$ and $\widehat{m_3}$ denote, resp., the cost from the beginning of m to the call x.p(), the cost between x.p() and y.q(), and the remaining cost of m. $\widehat{p_1}$ and $\widehat{p_2}$ are analogous. The resource analysis described in Sect. 2 can be used for obtaining an upper bound of the cost of each block.

The notion of parallel cost $\mathcal{P}$ corresponds to the cost consumed between the first instruction executed by the program at the initial location and the last instruction executed at any location by taking into account the parallel execution of instructions and idle times at the different locations.

Example 9. Figure 5(right) shows three possible traces of the execution of this example (more traces are feasible). Below the traces, the expressions $\mathcal{P}_1$, $\mathcal{P}_2$ and $\mathcal{P}_3$ show the parallel cost for each trace. The main observation here is that the parallel cost varies depending on the duration of the tasks. It will be the worst (maximum) value of such expressions, that is, $\mathcal{P}=max(\mathcal{P}_1, \mathcal{P}_2, \mathcal{P}_3, \dots)$. In ② p_1 is shorter than m_2, and s executes before q. In ③, q is scheduled before s, resulting in different parallel cost expressions. In ①, the processor of location y becomes idle after executing s and must wait for task q to arrive.

In the general case, the inference of parallel cost is complicated because: (1) It is unknown if the processor is available when we spawn a task, as this depends on the duration of the tasks that were already in the queue; e.g., when task q is spawned we do not know if the processor is idle (trace ①) or if it is taken (trace ②). Thus, all scenarios must be considered; (2) Locations can be dynamically created, and tasks can be dynamically spawned among the different locations (e.g., from location o we spawn tasks at two other locations).

Besides, tasks can be spawned in a circular way; e.g., task s could make a call back to location x; (3) Tasks can be spawned inside loops, we might even have non-terminating loops that create an unbounded number of tasks. We use a *distributed flow graph* (DFG) to capture the different flows of execution that the distributed system can perform. We use the standard partitioning of methods into blocks used to build the control flow graph of the program. The nodes in the DFG are the blocks of the CFG combined with the location's identity and are used as cost centers when obtaining the upper bound as in Sect. 2. The edges represent the control flow in the sequential execution (drawn with normal arrows) and all possible orderings of tasks in the location's queues (drawn with dashed arrows) since, when the processor is released, any pending task of the same location could start executing.

Example 10. Figure 6 shows the DFG for the program in Fig. 5. Nodes in gray are the exit nodes of the methods, and it implies that the execution can terminate executing $o{:}m_3$, $x{:}p_2$, $y{:}s$ or $y{:}q$. Solid edges include those existing in the CFG of the sequential program but combined with the location's identity and those derived from calls. The dashed edges model that the execution order of s and q at location y is unknown.

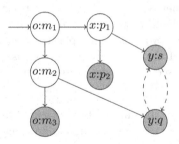

Fig. 6. DFG for Fig. 5

Our analysis consists of obtaining the maximal parallel cost from all possible executions of the program, based on the DFG. The execution paths in the DFG start in the initial node that corresponds to the entry method of the program, and finish in any exit node of a method. The key idea to obtain the parallel cost from paths in the graph is that the cost of each block contains not only the cost of the block itself but this cost is multiplied by the number of times the block is visited. As the order in which blocks are executed is not relevant for the resource analysis, we use sets instead of sequences. The parallel cost of the distributed system can be over-approximated by the maximum cost for all paths to nodes that correspond to method exit blocks.

Example 11. Given the DFG in Example 10, we have the following sets:

$$\underbrace{\{o{:}m_1, o{:}m_2, o{:}m_3\}}_{N_1}, \quad \underbrace{\{o{:}m_1, x{:}p_1, x{:}p_2\}}_{N_2}, \quad \underbrace{\{o{:}m_1, x{:}p_1, y{:}s, y{:}q\}}_{N_3}, \quad \underbrace{\{o{:}m_1, o{:}m_2, y{:}s, y{:}q\}}_{N_4}$$

Observe that these sets represent traces of the program. The execution captured by N_1 corresponds to trace ① of Fig. 5. In this trace, the code executed at location o leads to the maximal cost. Similarly, the set N_3 corresponds to trace ② and N_4 corresponds to trace ③. The set N_2 corresponds to a trace where $x{:}p_2$ leads to the maximal cost (not shown in Fig. 5). The cost is obtained by using the block-level costs for all nodes that compose the sets above. The overall parallel cost is computed as: $\widehat{\mathcal{P}}(\mathsf{m}(n)) = max(\mathsf{m}^+(n)|_{N_1}, \mathsf{m}^+(n)|_{N_2}, \mathsf{m}^+(n)|_{N_3}, \mathsf{m}^+(n)|_{N_4})$. Importantly, $\widehat{\mathcal{P}}$ is more precise than the serial cost because all paths have at least one missing node. For instance, N_1 does not contain the cost of $x{:}p_1$, $x{:}p_2$, $y{:}s$, $y{:}q$ and N_3 does not contain the cost of $o{:}m_2$, $o{:}m_3$, $x{:}p_2$.

6   Conclusions and Future Work

We have presented the basic concepts underlying the resource analysis of distributed systems. The overall framework is based on the idea of having cost centers which allow defining the required level of granularity. We have seen how, using cost centers, performance indicators can be defined to assess the overall performance of the distributed system, e.g., whether the load is well-balanced among the nodes, the communication costs, etc. Also, new notions of cost can be defined to estimate the peak cost required by each distributed node, and the parallel cost which exploits the parallelism in the execution.

In future work, we are investigating the new challenges that arise in the resource analysis of concurrent systems. In particular, new technique are required to infer the cost when each distributed component allows interleaving among the tasks that it has to execute. Also, we are improving the precision of the *may-happen-in-parallel* analysis which is used to infer the cost of the tasks running concurrently.

Acknowledgments. We are grateful to all members of the COSTA group and Einar Broch Johnsen for their collaborations to develop some of the analyses that underlie our basic framework and their contributions to the SACO system. This work was funded partially by the EU project FP7-ICT-610582 ENVISAGE: Engineering Virtualized Services (http://www.envisage-project.eu), by the Spanish MINECO project TIN2012-38137, and by the CM project S2013/ICE-3006.

References

1. Albert, E., Arenas, P., Correas, J., Genaim, S., Gómez-Zamalloa, M., Puebla, G., Román-Díez, G.: Object-sensitive cost analysis for concurrent objects. Softw. Test. Verification Reliab. **25**(3), 218–271 (2015)
2. Albert, E., Arenas, P., Genaim, S., Puebla, G.: Closed-form upper bounds in static cost analysis. J. Autom. Reasoning **46**(2), 161–203 (2011)
3. Albert, E., Arenas, P., Genaim, S., Puebla, G., Zanardini, D.: Cost analysis of object-oriented bytecode programs. Theoret. Comput. Sci. Spec. Issue Quant. Aspects Program. Lang. **413**(1), 142–159 (2012)
4. Albert, E., Correas, J., Johnsen, E.B., Román-Díez, G.: Parallel cost analysis of distributed systems. In: Blazy, S., Jensen, T. (eds.) SAS 2015. LNCS, vol. 9291, pp. 275–292. Springer, Heidelberg (2015)
5. Albert, E., Correas, J., Puebla, G., Román-Díez, G.: Quantified abstractions of distributed systems. In: Johnsen, E.B., Petre, L. (eds.) IFM 2013. LNCS, vol. 7940, pp. 285–300. Springer, Heidelberg (2013)

6. Albert, E., Correas, J., Puebla, G., Román-Díez, G.: Quantified abstract configurations of distributed systems. Formal aspects Comput. **27**(4), 665–699 (2015)
7. Albert, E., Correas, J., Román-Díez, G.: Peak cost analysis of distributed systems. In: Müller-Olm, M., Seidl, H. (eds.) Static Analysis. LNCS, vol. 8723, pp. 18–33. Springer, Heidelberg (2014)
8. Albert, E., Fernández, J.C., Román-Díez, G.: Non-cumulative resource analysis. In: Baier, C., Tinelli, C. (eds.) TACAS 2015. LNCS, vol. 9035, pp. 85–100. Springer, Heidelberg (2015)
9. Cousot, P., Halbwachs, N.: Automatic discovery of linear restraints among variables of a program. In: Proceedings of the POPL 1978, pp. 84–96 (1978)
10. de Boer, F.S., Clarke, D., Johnsen, E.B.: A complete guide to the future. In: De Nicola, R. (ed.) ESOP 2007. LNCS, vol. 4421, pp. 316–330. Springer, Heidelberg (2007)
11. Gulwani, S., Mehra, K.K., Chilimbi, T.M.: Speed: precise and efficient static estimation of program computational complexity. In: Proceedings of POPL 2009, pp. 127–139. ACM (2009)
12. Hoffmann, J., Aehlig, K., Hofmannn, M.: Multivariate amortized resource analysis. ACM Trans. Program. Lang. Syst. **34**(3), 14:1–14:62 (2012)
13. Hoffmann, J., Shao, Z.: Automatic static cost analysis for parallel programs. In: Vitek, J. (ed.) ESOP 2015. LNCS, vol. 9032, pp. 132–157. Springer, Heidelberg (2015)
14. Johnsen, E.B., Hähnle, R., Schäfer, J., Schlatte, R., Steffen, M.: ABS: a core language for abstract behavioral specification. In: Aichernig, B.K., de Boer, F.S., Bonsangue, M.M. (eds.) Formal Methods for Components and Objects. LNCS, vol. 6957, pp. 142–164. Springer, Heidelberg (2011)
15. Milanova, A., Rountev, A., Ryder, B.G.: Parameterized object sensitivity for points-to analysis for java. ACM Trans. Softw. Eng. Methodol. **14**, 1–41 (2005)
16. Smaragdakis, Y., Bravenboer, M., Lhoták, O.: Pick your contexts well: understanding object-sensitivity. In: Proceedings of the POPL 2011, pp. 17–30. ACM (2011)
17. Sutter, H., Larus, J.R.: Software and the concurrency revolution. ACM Queue **3**(7), 54–62 (2005)
18. Wegbreit, B.: Mechanical program analysis. Commun. ACM **18**(9), 528–539 (1975)
19. Zuleger, F., Gulwani, S., Sinn, M., Veith, H.: Bound analysis of imperative programs with the size-change abstraction. In: Yahav, E. (ed.) Static Analysis. LNCS, vol. 6887, pp. 280–297. Springer, Heidelberg (2011)

Comparing Trace Expressions and Linear Temporal Logic for Runtime Verification

Davide Ancona[✉], Angelo Ferrando, and Viviana Mascardi

DIBRIS, Università di Genova, Genova, Italy
{davide.ancona,viviana.mascardi}@unige.it,
angelo.ferrando@dibris.unige.it

Abstract. Trace expressions are a compact and expressive formalism, initially devised for runtime verification of agent interactions in multiagent systems, which has been successfully employed to model real protocols, and to generate monitors for mainstream multiagent system platforms, and generalized to support runtime verification of different kinds of properties and systems.

In this paper we formally compare the expressive power of trace expressions with the Linear Temporal Logic (LTL), a formalism widely adopted in runtime verification. We show that any LTL formula can be translated into a trace expression which is equivalent from the point of view of runtime verification. Since trace expressions are able to express and verify sets of traces that are not context-free, we can derive that in the context of runtime verification trace expressions are more expressive than LTL.

1 Introduction

Runtime verification (RV) is a software verification technique that complements formal static verification (as model checking), and testing. In RV dynamic checking of the correct behavior of a system is performed by a monitor which is generated from a formal specification of the properties to be verified.

As happens for formal static verification, RV relies on a high level specification formalism to specify the expected properties of a system; similarly to testing, RV is a lightweight, effective but non exhaustive technique to verify complex properties of a system at runtime.

In contrast to formal static verification and testing, RV offers opportunities for error recovery which make this approach more attractive for the development of reliable software: not only a system can be constantly monitored for its whole lifetime to detect possible misbehavior, but also appropriate handlers can be executed for error recovery.

There are several specification formalisms employed by RV; some of them are well-known formalisms that have been originally introduced for other aims, as regular expressions, context free grammars, and LTL, while others have been expressly devised for RV.

Partly funded by "Progetto MIUR PRIN CINA Prot. 2010LHT4KM".

E. Ábrahám et al. (Eds.): de Boer Festschrift, LNCS 9660, pp. 47–64, 2016.
DOI: 10.1007/978-3-319-30734-3_6

Trace expressions belong to this latter group; they are an evolution of global types [2], which have been initially proposed for RV of agent interactions in multiagent systems. Trace expressions are an expressive formalism based on a set of operators (including prefixing, concatenation, shuffle, union, and intersection) to denote finite and infinite traces of events. Their semantics is based on a labeled transition system defined by a simple set of rewriting rules which directly drive the behavior of monitors generated from trace expressions.

In this paper we formally compare trace expressions with LTL, a formalism to specify infinite traces of events that is widely used for RV, even though it was initially introduced for model checking.

When used for RV, the expressive power of LTL is reduced, because at runtime only finite traces can be checked. For instance, the formula Fp (finally p) which states that an event satisfying the predicate p will eventually occur after a finite trace of other occurred events, can only be partially verified at runtime, because no monitor is able to reject an infinite trace of events that do not satisfy p, which, of course, is not a model for Fp.

To provide a formal account for this limitation, a three-valued semantics for LTL, called LTL_3 has been proposed [3]. A third truth value "?" is introduced to specify that after a finite trace of events has occurred, the outcome of a monitor can be inconclusive. For instance, if we consider the formula Fp, and the event e which does not satisfy p, then no monitor generated from Fp is able to decide whether Fp is satisfied or not after the trace eee.

In trace expressions this limitation of RV is naturally modeled by the standard semantics: if the semantics of a trace expression τ contains all finite traces e, ee, eee, ..., then it must also contain the infinite trace $e \dots e \dots$ because no monitor generated from τ will be able to reject it. This corresponds to the more formal claim stating that the semantics of any trace expression is a complete metric space of traces, when the standard distance between traces is considered.

As a consequence, when the standard semantics is considered, one can conclude that LTL and trace expressions are not comparable: neither is more expressive than the other. However, since the two formalisms are considered in the context of RV, if the more appropriate three-valued semantics is considered, then trace expressions are strictly more expressive than LTL: every LTL formula can be encoded into a trace expression with an equivalent three-valued semantics, whereas the opposite property does not hold, since trace expressions are also able to specify context-free and non context-free languages.

The paper is organized in the following way: Sect. 2 introduces trace expressions, whereas Sect. 3 is concerned with their expressive power; examples show that trace expressions can specify context-free and non context-free languages. Section 4 introduces LTL and the corresponding three-valued semantics, and formally compares this logic with trace expressions, while Sect. 5 provides a brief survey of related work. Conclusions are drawn in Sect. 6.

2   Trace Expressions

Trace expressions are a specification formalism expressly designed for RV; they are an evolution of global types, which have been initially proposed by Ancona, Drossopoulou and Mascardi [2] for RV of agent interactions in multiagent systems.

Trace expressions introduce three novelties:

- while global types are strongly based on the notion of agent interaction, because they have been expressly conceived for RV of protocol compliance in multiagent systems, trace expressions support a general notion of event, and can be exploited for RV in more general scenarios; for instance, besides agent interactions, trace expressions can be used for monitoring events as method invocations, or resource acquisition and release by threads;
- as a further generalization, trace expressions support the notion of *event type*: sets of events can be simply represented by predicates;
- besides the union (a.k.a. choice), concatenation, and shuffle (a.k.a. fork) operators, trace expressions support intersection as well. Intersection replaces the constrained shuffle operator [1, 9], an extension of the shuffle operator introduced for making global types more expressive. Constrained shuffle imposes synchronization constraints on the events inside a shuffle, thus making global types and their semantics more complex; furthermore, constrained shuffle is not compositional: it cannot be expressed as an operation between sets of event traces (that is, the mathematical entities denoted by trace expressions). In contrast, the intersection operator has a simple, intuitive, and compositional semantics (as suggested by the name itself) and yet is very expressive; for instance, as shown in Sect. 3, it can be used for specifying non context-free sets of event traces.

Events. In the following we denote by $\mathcal{E}$ a fixed universe of events. An event trace over $\mathcal{E}$ is a possibly infinite sequence of events in $\mathcal{E}$. In the rest of the paper the meta-variables e, w, σ and u will range over the sets $\mathcal{E}$, $\mathcal{E}^\omega$, $\mathcal{E}^*$, and $\mathcal{E}^\omega \cup \mathcal{E}^*$, respectively; juxtaposition $e\,u$ denotes the trace where e is the first event, and u is the rest of the trace. A trace expression over $\mathcal{E}$ denotes a set of event traces over $\mathcal{E}$.

As a possible example, we might have

$$\mathcal{E} = \{o.m \mid o \text{ object identity}, m \text{ method name}\}$$

where the event $o.m$ corresponds to an invocation of method named[1] m on the target object o. This is a typical example of set of events arising when monitoring object-oriented systems (we will show an example later on).

---

[1] Here, for simplicity, an event does not include the signature of the method as it should be the case for those languages supporting static overloading.

Event Types. To be more general, trace expressions are built on top of event types (chosen from a set $\mathcal{ET}$), rather than of single events; an event type denotes a subset of $\mathcal{E}$, and corresponds to a predicate of arity $k \geq 1$, where the first implicit argument corresponds to the event e under consideration; referring to the example where events are method invocations, we may introduce the type *safe(o)* of all safe method invocations for a given object o, defined by the predicate *safe* of arity 2 s.t. *safe(e, o)* holds iff $e = o.isEmpty$.

The first argument of the predicate is left implicit in the event type, and we write $e \in safe(o)$ to mean that *safe(e, o)* holds. Similarly, the set of events specified by an event type ϑ is denoted by $[\![\vartheta]\!]$; for instance, $[\![safe(o)]\!] = \{e \mid e \in safe(o)\}$.

For generality, we leave unspecified the formalism used for defining event types; however, in practice we do not expect that much expressive power is required. For instance, for all examples presented in this paper a formalism less powerful than regular expressions is sufficient.

Trace Expressions. A trace expression τ represents a set of possibly infinite event traces, and is defined on top of the following operators:[2]

- ϵ (empty trace), denoting the singleton set $\{\epsilon\}$ containing the empty event trace ϵ.
- $\vartheta{:}\tau$ (*prefix*), denoting the set of all traces whose first event e matches the event type ϑ ($e \in \vartheta$), and the remaining part is a trace of τ.
- $\tau_1{\cdot}\tau_2$ (*concatenation*), denoting the set of all traces obtained by concatenating the traces of τ_1 with those of τ_2.
- $\tau_1{\wedge}\tau_2$ (*intersection*), denoting the intersection of the traces of τ_1 and τ_2.
- $\tau_1{\vee}\tau_2$ (*union*), denoting the union of the traces of τ_1 and τ_2.
- $\tau_1{|}\tau_2$ (*shuffle*), denoting the set obtained by shuffling the traces of τ_1 with the traces of τ_2.

To support recursion without introducing an explicit construct, trace expressions are regular (a.k.a. rational or cyclic) terms: they correspond to trees where nodes are either the leaf ϵ, or the node (corresponding to the prefix operator) ϑ with one child, or the nodes $\cdot$, $\wedge$, $\vee$, and $|$ all having two children. According to the standard definition of rational trees, their depth is allowed to be infinite, but the number of their subtrees must be finite. As originally proposed by Courcelle [8], such regular trees can be modeled as partial functions from $\{0, 1\}^*$ to the set of nodes (in our case $\{\epsilon, \cdot, \wedge, \vee, |\} \cup \mathcal{ET}$) satisfying certain conditions.

A regular term can be represented by a finite set of syntactic equations, as happens, for instance, in most modern Prolog implementations where unification supports cyclic terms.

As an example of non recursive trace expression, let $\mathcal{E}$ be the set $\{e_1, \ldots, e_7\}$, and ϑ_i, $i = 1, \ldots, 7$, be the event types such that $e \in \vartheta_i$ iff $e = e_i$ (that is,

---

[2] Binary operators associate from left, and are listed in decreasing order of precedence, that is, the first operator has the highest precedence.

$\llbracket \vartheta_i \rrbracket = \{e_i\}$); then the trace expression

$$TE_1 = ((\vartheta_1 : \epsilon | \vartheta_2 : \epsilon) \vee (\vartheta_3 : \epsilon | \vartheta_4 : \epsilon)) \cdot (\vartheta_5 : \vartheta_6 : \epsilon | \vartheta_7 : \epsilon)$$

denotes the following set of event traces:

$$\left\{ \begin{array}{l} e_1 e_2 e_5 e_6 e_7, e_1 e_2 e_5 e_7 e_6, e_1 e_2 e_7 e_5 e_6, e_2 e_1 e_5 e_6 e_7, e_2 e_1 e_5 e_7 e_6, e_2 e_1 e_7 e_5 e_6, \\ e_3 e_4 e_5 e_6 e_7, e_3 e_4 e_5 e_7 e_6, e_3 e_4 e_7 e_5 e_6, e_4 e_3 e_5 e_6 e_7, e_4 e_3 e_5 e_7 e_6, e_4 e_3 e_7 e_5 e_6 \end{array} \right\}$$

As an example of recursive trace expression, if ϑ_i denotes the same event type defined above for $i = 1, \ldots, 7$, and $\llbracket \vartheta \rrbracket = \{e_4, e_5, e_6, e_7\}$, $\llbracket \vartheta' \rrbracket = \{e_1, e_2, e_6, e_7\}$, and $\llbracket \vartheta'' \rrbracket = \{e_1, e_2, e_3, e_4\}$, then the trace expression

$$TE_2 = (E | \vartheta_1 : \vartheta_2 : \vartheta_3 : \epsilon) \wedge (E' | \vartheta_3 : \vartheta_4 : \vartheta_5 : \epsilon) \wedge (E'' | \vartheta_5 : \vartheta_6 : \vartheta_7 : \epsilon)$$
$$E = \epsilon \vee \vartheta : E \qquad E' = \epsilon \vee \vartheta' : E' \qquad E'' = \epsilon \vee \vartheta'' : E''$$

denotes the set $\{e_1 e_2 e_3 e_4 e_5 e_6 e_7\}$.

Finally, the recursive trace expressions $T_1 = (\epsilon \vee \vartheta_1 : T_1) \cdot T_2$, $T_2 = (\epsilon \vee \vartheta_2 : T_2)$ represent the infinite but regular terms $(\epsilon \vee \vartheta_1 : (\epsilon \vee \vartheta_1 : \ldots)) \cdot (\epsilon \vee \vartheta_2 : (\epsilon \vee \vartheta_2 : \ldots))$ and $(\epsilon \vee (\vartheta_2 : (\epsilon \vee (\vartheta_2 : \ldots))))$, respectively.

In the rest of the paper we will limit our investigation to *contractive* (a.k.a. *guarded*) trace expressions.

Definition 1. *A trace expression τ is* contractive *if all its infinite paths contain the prefix operator.*

In contractive trace expressions all recursive subexpressions must be guarded by the prefix operator; for instance, the trace expression defined by $T_1 = (\epsilon \vee (\vartheta : T_1))$ is contractive: its infinite path contains infinite occurrences of $\vee$, but also of the : operator; conversely, the trace expression $T_2 = (\vartheta : T_2) | T_2$ is not contractive.

Trivially, every trace expression corresponding to a finite tree (that is, a non cyclic term) is contractive.

For all contractive trace expressions, any path from their root must always reach either a ϵ or a : node in a finite number of steps. Since in this paper all definitions over trace expressions treat $\vartheta : \tau$ as a base case (that is, the definition is not propagated to the subexpression τ), restricting trace expressions to contractive ones has the advantage that most of the definitions and proofs requires induction, rather than coinduction, despite trace expressions can be cyclic. As a consequence, the implementation of trace expressions becomes considerably simpler. For this reason, in the rest of the paper we will only consider contractive trace expressions.

The semantics of trace expressions is specified by the transition relation $\delta \subseteq \mathcal{T} \times \mathcal{E} \times \mathcal{T}$, where $\mathcal{T}$ and $\mathcal{E}$ denote the set of trace expressions and of events, respectively. As it is customary, we write $\tau_1 \xrightarrow{e} \tau_2$ to mean $(\tau_1, e, \tau_2) \in \delta$. If the trace expression τ_1 specifies the current valid state of the system, then an event e is considered valid iff there exists a transition $\tau_1 \xrightarrow{e} \tau_2$; in such a case, τ_2 will specify the next valid state of the system after event e. Otherwise, the event e is

$$(\text{prefix}) \frac{}{\vartheta{:}\tau \xrightarrow{e} \tau} \; e \in \vartheta \qquad (\text{or-l}) \frac{\tau_1 \xrightarrow{e} \tau_1'}{\tau_1 \vee \tau_2 \xrightarrow{e} \tau_1'} \qquad (\text{or-r}) \frac{\tau_2 \xrightarrow{e} \tau_2'}{\tau_1 \vee \tau_2 \xrightarrow{e} \tau_2'}$$

$$(\text{and}) \frac{\tau_1 \xrightarrow{e} \tau_1' \quad \tau_2 \xrightarrow{e} \tau_2'}{\tau_1 \wedge \tau_2 \xrightarrow{e} \tau_1' \wedge \tau_2'} \qquad (\text{shuffle-l}) \frac{\tau_1 \xrightarrow{e} \tau_1'}{\tau_1 | \tau_2 \xrightarrow{e} \tau_1' | \tau_2} \qquad (\text{shuffle-r}) \frac{\tau_2 \xrightarrow{e} \tau_2'}{\tau_1 | \tau_2 \xrightarrow{e} \tau_1 | \tau_2'}$$

$$(\text{cat-l}) \frac{\tau_1 \xrightarrow{e} \tau_1'}{\tau_1 {\cdot} \tau_2 \xrightarrow{e} \tau_1' {\cdot} \tau_2} \qquad (\text{cat-r}) \frac{\tau_2 \xrightarrow{e} \tau_2'}{\tau_1 {\cdot} \tau_2 \xrightarrow{e} \tau_2'} \; \epsilon(\tau_1)$$

Fig. 1. Operational semantics of trace expressions

$$(\epsilon\text{-empty}) \frac{}{\epsilon(\epsilon)} \qquad (\epsilon\text{-or-l}) \frac{\epsilon(\tau_1)}{\epsilon(\tau_1 \vee \tau_2)} \qquad (\epsilon\text{-or-r}) \frac{\epsilon(\tau_2)}{\epsilon(\tau_1 \vee \tau_2)} \qquad (\epsilon\text{-shuffle}) \frac{\epsilon(\tau_1) \quad \epsilon(\tau_2)}{\epsilon(\tau_1 | \tau_2)}$$

$$(\epsilon\text{-cat}) \frac{\epsilon(\tau_1) \quad \epsilon(\tau_2)}{\epsilon(\tau_1 {\cdot} \tau_2)} \qquad (\epsilon\text{-and}) \frac{\epsilon(\tau_1) \quad \epsilon(\tau_2)}{\epsilon(\tau_1 \wedge \tau_2)}$$

Fig. 2. Empty trace containment

not considered to be valid in the current state represented by τ_1. Figure 1 defines the inductive rules for the transition function.

While the transition relation δ with its corresponding rules in Fig. 1 defines the non empty traces of a trace expression, the predicate $\epsilon(\_)$, inductively defined by the rules in Fig. 2, defines the trace expressions that contain the empty trace ϵ. If $\epsilon(\tau)$ holds, then the empty trace is a valid trace for τ.

Rule (prefix) states that valid traces of $\vartheta{:}\tau$ can only start with an event e of type ϑ (side condition $e \in \vartheta$), and continue with traces in τ.

Rules (or-l) and (or-r) state that the only valid traces of $\tau_1 \vee \tau_2$ have shape $e\,u$, where either $e\,u$ is valid for τ_1 (rule (or-l)), or $e\,u$ is valid for τ_2 (rule (or-r)).

Rule (and) states that the only valid traces of $\tau_1 \wedge \tau_2$ have shape $e\,u$, where $e\,u$ is valid for both τ_1 and τ_2.

Rules (shuffle-l) and (shuffle-r) state that the only valid traces of $\tau_1 | \tau_2$ have shape $e\,u$, where either $e\,u_1'$ and u_2 are valid traces for τ_1 and τ_2, respectively, and u can be obtained as the shuffle of u_1' with u_2 (rule (shuffle-l)), or u_1 and $e\,u_2'$ are valid traces for τ_1 and τ_2, respectively, and u can be obtained as the shuffle of u_1 with u_2' (rule (shuffle-r)).

Rules (cat-l) and (cat-r) state that the only valid traces of $\tau_1 {\cdot} \tau_2$ have shape $e\,u$, where either $e\,u_1'$ and u_2 are valid traces for τ_1 and τ_2, respectively, and u can be obtained as the concatenation of u_1' to u_2 (rule (cat-l)), or ϵ is a valid trace for τ_1 (side condition $\epsilon(\tau_1)$) and $e\,u$ is a valid trace for τ_2 (rule (cat-r)).

For what concerns Fig. 2, rules (ϵ-shuffle), (ϵ-cat) and (ϵ-and) require the empty trace to be contained in both subexpressions τ_1 and τ_2, whereas for the union operator it suffices that the empty trace is contained in either τ_1 (rule (ϵ-or-l)) or τ_2 (rule (ϵ-or-r)). Trace expressions built with the prefix operator can never contain the empty trace, whereas ϵ contains just the empty trace (rule (ϵ-empty)).

The set of traces $[\![\tau]\!]$ denoted by a trace expression τ is defined in terms of the transition relation δ, and the predicate $\epsilon(\_)$. Since $[\![\tau]\!]$ may contain infinite traces, the definition of $[\![\tau]\!]$ is coinductive.

Definition 2. *For all possibly infinite event traces u and trace expressions τ, $u \in [\![\tau]\!]$ is coinductively defined as follows:*

- *either $u = \epsilon$ and $\epsilon(\tau)$ holds,*
- *or $u = e\,u'$, and there exists τ' s.t. $\tau \xrightarrow{e} \tau'$ and $u' \in [\![\tau']\!]$ hold.*

In the following we will need to consider the reflexive and transitive closure of the transition relation: if σ is a finite (possibly empty) event trace, then the relation $\tau \xrightarrow{\sigma} \tau'$ is inductively defined as follows: $\tau \xrightarrow{\sigma} \tau'$ holds iff

- $\sigma = \epsilon$, and $\tau' = \tau$;
- or $\sigma = e\,\sigma'$, and there exists τ'' s.t. $\tau \xrightarrow{e} \tau''$, and $\tau'' \xrightarrow{\sigma'} \tau'$.

Let us consider again the previous examples of trace expressions:

$$TE_1 = ((\vartheta_1{:}\epsilon|\vartheta_2{:}\epsilon)\vee(\vartheta_3{:}\epsilon|\vartheta_4{:}\epsilon))\cdot(\vartheta_5{:}\vartheta_6{:}\epsilon|\vartheta_7{:}\epsilon)$$
$$TE_2 = (E|\vartheta_1{:}\vartheta_2{:}\vartheta_3{:}\epsilon)\wedge(E'|\vartheta_3{:}\vartheta_4{:}\vartheta_5{:}\epsilon)\wedge(E''|\vartheta_5{:}\vartheta_6{:}\vartheta_7{:}\epsilon)$$
$$E = \epsilon\vee\vartheta{:}E \qquad E' = \epsilon\vee\vartheta'{:}E' \qquad E'' = \epsilon\vee\vartheta''{:}E''$$
$$\forall i \in \{1..7\}\;\; [\![\vartheta_i]\!] = \{e_i\} \qquad [\![\vartheta]\!] = \{e_4, e_5, e_6, e_7\}$$
$$[\![\vartheta']\!] = \{e_1, e_2, e_6, e_7\} \quad [\![\vartheta'']\!] = \{e_1, e_2, e_3, e_4\}$$

We show that there exist τ_1, τ_2 s.t. $TE_1 \xrightarrow{\sigma_1} \tau_1$, with $\sigma_1 = e_1e_2e_5e_6e_7$, $\epsilon(\tau_1)$, $TE_2 \xrightarrow{\sigma_2} \tau_2$, with $\sigma_2 = e_1e_2e_3e_4e_5e_6e_7$, and $\epsilon(\tau_2)$.

For $TE_1 \xrightarrow{\sigma_1} \tau_1$ we have $\vartheta_1{:}\epsilon|\vartheta_2{:}\epsilon \xrightarrow{e_1} \epsilon|\vartheta_2{:}\epsilon \xrightarrow{e_2} \epsilon|\epsilon$, $(\vartheta_1{:}\epsilon|\vartheta_2{:}\epsilon)\vee(\vartheta_3{:}\epsilon|\vartheta_4{:}\epsilon) \xrightarrow{e_1e_2} \epsilon|\epsilon$, and $TE_1 \xrightarrow{e_1e_2} (\epsilon|\epsilon)\cdot(\vartheta_5{:}\vartheta_6{:}\epsilon|\vartheta_7{:}\epsilon)$. Furthermore, $\vartheta_5{:}\vartheta_6{:}\epsilon|\vartheta_7{:}\epsilon \xrightarrow{e_5} \vartheta_6{:}\epsilon|\vartheta_7{:}\epsilon \xrightarrow{e_6} \epsilon|\vartheta_7{:}\epsilon \xrightarrow{e_7} \epsilon|\epsilon$, hence $\vartheta_5{:}\vartheta_6{:}\epsilon|\vartheta_7{:}\epsilon \xrightarrow{e_5e_6e_7} \epsilon|\epsilon$, and, because $\epsilon(\epsilon|\epsilon)$, we can conclude $(\epsilon|\epsilon)\cdot(\vartheta_5{:}\vartheta_6{:}\epsilon|\vartheta_7{:}\epsilon) \xrightarrow{e_5e_6e_7} \epsilon|\epsilon$, hence, $TE_1 \xrightarrow{e_1e_2e_5e_6e_7} \epsilon|\epsilon$.

For $TE_2 \xrightarrow{\sigma_2} \tau_2$ we have $E|\vartheta_1{:}\vartheta_2{:}\vartheta_3{:}\epsilon \xrightarrow{e_1e_2e_3} E|\epsilon \xrightarrow{e_4e_5e_6e_7} E|\epsilon$, $E'|\vartheta_3{:}\vartheta_4{:}\vartheta_5{:}\epsilon \xrightarrow{e_1e_2} E'|\vartheta_3{:}\vartheta_4{:}\vartheta_5{:}\epsilon \xrightarrow{e_3e_4e_5} E'|\epsilon \xrightarrow{e_6e_7} E'|\epsilon$, $E''|\vartheta_5{:}\vartheta_6{:}\vartheta_7{:}\epsilon \xrightarrow{e_1e_2e_3e_4} E''|\vartheta_5{:}\vartheta_6{:}\vartheta_7{:}\epsilon \xrightarrow{e_5e_6e_7} E''|\epsilon$. Therefore $TE_2 \xrightarrow{e_1e_2e_3e_4e_5e_6e_7} (E|\epsilon)\wedge(E'|\epsilon)\wedge(E''|\epsilon)$ and $\epsilon(E|\epsilon)$, $\epsilon(E'|\epsilon)$, and $\epsilon(E''|\epsilon)$, hence $\epsilon((E|\epsilon)\wedge(E'|\epsilon)\wedge(E''|\epsilon))$.

Since the semantics of trace expressions is coinductive, they can specify non terminating behavior; for instance, the trace expression defined by $T = \vartheta_1{:}T$ denotes the set with just the infinite trace $e_1 e_1 \ldots e_1 \ldots$ containing infinite occurrences of e_1; had we considered an inductive semantics, T would have denoted the empty set. For the very same reason, the trace expression defined by $T' = \epsilon\vee\vartheta_1{:}T'$ denotes the set containing all finite traces of the event e_1, but also the infinite trace $e_1 e_1 \ldots e_1 \ldots$. From the point of view of RV, the only difference between the two types is that for T' the monitored system is allowed to halt at any time, whereas for T the system can never stop.

Since at runtime it is not possible to check that a given monitored system will always eventually stop, trace expressions cannot denote sets of traces which are not complete metric spaces, with the standard distance between traces: $d(u_1, u_2) = 2^{-n}$, where n denotes the smallest index (starting from 0) at which the two traces are different; by convention, if the two traces are equal, than $n = \infty$, and $2^{-n} = 0$. For instance, if the semantics of a trace expression τ contains traces of arbitrarily large length of the event e_1, then it also contains the infinite trace $e_1 e_1 \ldots e_1 \ldots$; indeed, the monitor associated with τ will not be able to reject it.

Such a limitation is independent of the used formalism, but it is intimately related to RV; as pointed out in Sect. 4, similar issues arise when LTL is used for RV: its semantics has to be revisited to take into account the fact that at runtime only finite traces can be monitored and checked.

Deterministic Trace Expressions. There are trace expressions τ for which the problem of word recognition is less efficient because of non determinism. Non determinism originates from the union, shuffle, and concatenation operators, because for each of them two possibly overlapping transition rules are defined.

Let us consider the trace expression $\tau = (\vartheta_1{:}\vartheta_2{:}\epsilon) \vee (\vartheta_1{:}\vartheta_3{:}\epsilon)$, where $\llbracket \vartheta_i \rrbracket = \{e_i\}$ for $i = 1, \ldots, 3$. Both transitions $\tau \xrightarrow{e_1} \vartheta_2{:}\epsilon$ and $\tau \xrightarrow{e_1} \vartheta_3{:}\epsilon$ are valid, but $\llbracket \vartheta_2{:}\epsilon \rrbracket \neq \llbracket \vartheta_3{:}\epsilon \rrbracket$; therefore, to correctly accept the trace $e_1 e_3$, both rules have to be applied simultaneously, and the set of trace expressions $\{\vartheta_2{:}\epsilon, \vartheta_3{:}\epsilon\}$ has to be considered, as it is done for non deterministic automata.

Similarly, for the trace expression $\tau' = (\vartheta_1{:}\vartheta_2{:}\epsilon) | (\vartheta_1{:}\vartheta_3{:}\epsilon)$, both transitions $\tau' \xrightarrow{e_1} (\vartheta_2{:}\epsilon) | (\vartheta_1{:}\vartheta_3{:}\epsilon)$ and $\tau' \xrightarrow{e_1} (\vartheta_1{:}\vartheta_2{:}\epsilon) | (\vartheta_3{:}\epsilon)$ are valid, but $\llbracket (\vartheta_2{:}\epsilon) | (\vartheta_1{:}\vartheta_3{:}\epsilon) \rrbracket \neq \llbracket (\vartheta_1{:}\vartheta_2{:}\epsilon) | (\vartheta_3{:}\epsilon) \rrbracket$.

Finally, for the trace expression $\tau'' = (\epsilon \vee \vartheta_1{:}\vartheta_2{:}\epsilon) \cdot (\vartheta_1{:}\epsilon)$ both transitions $\tau'' \xrightarrow{e_1} (\vartheta_2{:}\epsilon) \cdot (\vartheta_1{:}\epsilon)$ and $\tau'' \xrightarrow{e_1} \epsilon$ are valid, but $\llbracket (\vartheta_2{:}\epsilon) \cdot (\vartheta_1{:}\epsilon) \rrbracket \neq \llbracket \epsilon \rrbracket$.

In the rest of this paper we will focus on deterministic trace expressions: indeed, the problem of word recognition is simpler and more efficient in the deterministic case.

Deterministic trace expressions are defined as follows.

Definition 3. *Let τ be a trace expression; τ is* deterministic *if for all finite event traces σ, if $\tau \xrightarrow{\sigma} \tau'$ and $\tau \xrightarrow{\sigma} \tau''$ are valid, then $\llbracket \tau' \rrbracket = \llbracket \tau'' \rrbracket$.*

The trace expressions τ, τ', and τ'', as defined above, are not deterministic, while the respectively equivalent trace expressions $\vartheta_1{:}(\vartheta_2{:}\epsilon \vee \vartheta_3{:}\epsilon)$, $\vartheta_1{:} (((\vartheta_2{:}\epsilon) | (\vartheta_1{:}\vartheta_3{:}\epsilon)) \vee ((\vartheta_1{:}\vartheta_2{:}\epsilon) | (\vartheta_3{:}\epsilon)))$, and $\vartheta_1{:}(\epsilon \vee \vartheta_2{:}\vartheta_1{:}\epsilon)$ are deterministic.

3 Examples of Specifications with Trace Expressions

In this section we provide some examples to show the expressive power of trace expressions. Unless specified otherwise, for simplicity in the rest of the paper we will consider singleton event types, that is, event types representing a single event; with abuse of notation, we will abbreviate events with their corresponding singleton event types.

3.1 Derived Operators

We first introduce some useful operators that will be used in the rest of the paper.

Constants. The constants 1 and 0 denote the set of all possible traces over $\mathcal{E}$ and the empty set, respectively. Constant 1 is equivalent to the expression $T = \epsilon \vee any{:}T$, where *any* is the event type s.t. $[\![any]\!] = \mathcal{E}$; constant 0 is equivalent to the expression *none*:ϵ, where *none* is the event type s.t. $[\![none]\!] = \emptyset$.

Filter Operator. The filter operator is useful for making trace expressions more compact and readable. The expression $\vartheta \gg \tau$ denotes the set of all traces contained in τ, when deprived of all events that do not match ϑ. Assuming that event types are closed by complementation, the expression above is a convenient syntactic shortcut for $T|\tau$, where $T = \epsilon \vee \overline{\vartheta}{:}T$, and $\overline{\vartheta}$ is the complement event type of ϑ, that is, $[\![\overline{\vartheta}]\!] = \mathcal{E} \setminus [\![\vartheta]\!]$.

The corresponding rules for the transition relation and the auxiliary function $\epsilon(\_)$ can be easily derived:

$$\text{(cond-t)}\ \frac{\tau \xrightarrow{e} \tau'}{\vartheta \gg \tau \xrightarrow{e} \vartheta \gg \tau'}\ e \in \vartheta \qquad \text{(cond-f)}\ \frac{}{\vartheta \gg \tau \xrightarrow{e} \vartheta \gg \tau}\ e \notin \vartheta \qquad \text{(ϵ-cond)}\ \frac{\epsilon(\tau)}{\epsilon(\vartheta \gg \tau)}$$

Stack Objects. We expand the example where events correspond to method invocations on objects; besides the already introduced event type $safe(o)$ s.t. $e \in safe(o)$ iff $e = o.isEmpty$, we define the following other event types:

$[\![pop(o)]\!] = \{o.pop\}$, $[\![top(o)]\!] = \{o.top\}$, $[\![push(o)]\!] = \{o.push\}$,
$[\![stack(o)]\!] = \{o.pop, o.top, o.push, o.isEmpty\}$,
$[\![unsafe(o)]\!] = \{o.pop, o.top, o.push\}$.

Our purpose is to specify through a trace expression *Stack* all safe traces of method invocations on a stack object o which we assume to be initially empty. Safety requires that methods *top* and *pop* can never be invoked on o when o represents the empty stack.

More in details, a trace of method invocations on a given object having identity o is correct iff any finite prefix does not contain more $pop(o)$ event types than $push(o)$, and the event type $top(o)$ can appear only if the number of $pop(o)$ event types is strictly less than the number of $push(o)$ event types occurring before $top(o)$.

The trace expression *Stack* is defined as follows:

$$Stack = Any \wedge unsafe(o) \gg Unsafe \qquad\qquad Any = \epsilon \vee stack(o){:}Any$$
$$Unsafe = \epsilon \vee (push(o){:}(Unsafe|(Tops \cdot (pop(o){:}\epsilon \vee \epsilon)))) \quad Tops = \epsilon \vee top(o){:}Tops$$

A correct stack trace is specified by *Stack* which is the intersection of *Any* and $unsafe(o) \gg Unsafe$; *Any* specifies any possible trace of method invocations on stack objects, whereas if an event has type $unsafe(o)$, then it has to verify the trace expression *Unsafe*, which requires that a *push* event must precede a possible empty trace of *top* events, which, in turn, must precede an optional event *pop*; the expression is recursively shuffled with itself, since any *push* event can be safely shuffled with a *top* or a *pop* event.

The specification is deterministic. To make an example, we can consider $Stack \xrightarrow{\sigma} \tau$ with $\sigma = push(o)\, push(o)$, and

$$\tau = Any \wedge unsafe(o) \gg (Unsafe \,|\, Tops \cdot ((pop(o):\epsilon) \vee \epsilon) \,|\, Tops \cdot ((pop(o):\epsilon) \vee \epsilon)).$$

We may observe that $\tau \xrightarrow{e} \tau_1$ and $\tau \xrightarrow{e} \tau_2$, with[3] $e = pop(o)$, and

$$\tau_1 = Any \wedge unsafe(o) \gg (Unsafe \,|\, \epsilon \,|\, Tops \cdot ((pop(o):\epsilon) \vee \epsilon))$$
$$\tau_2 = Any \wedge unsafe(o) \gg (Unsafe \,|\, Tops \cdot ((pop(o):\epsilon) \vee \epsilon) \,|\, \epsilon),$$

but $[\![\tau_1]\!] = [\![\tau_2]\!]$.

3.2 Alternating Bit Protocol

A more complex example concerning interactions is the alternating bit protocol (ABP), as defined by Deniélou and Yoshida [11], where two parties, Alice and Bob, are involved, and four different types of events can occur: Alice sends a first kind of message to Bob (event type msg_1), Alice sends a second kind of message to Bob (event type msg_2), Bob replies to Alice with an acknowledge to the first kind of message (event type ack_1), Bob replies to Alice with an acknowledge to the second kind of message (event type ack_2). The protocol has to satisfy the following constraints for all event occurrences:

- The n-th occurrence of the event of type msg_1 must precede the n-th occurrence of the event of type msg_2, which, in turn, must precede the $(n+1)$-th occurrence of the event of type msg_1.
- The n-th occurrence of the event of type msg_1 must precede the n-th occurrence of the event of type ack_1, which, in turn, must precede the $(n+1)$-th occurrence of the event of type msg_1.
- The n-th occurrence of the event of type msg_2 must precede the n-th occurrence of the event of type ack_2, which, in turn, must precede the $(n+1)$-th occurrence of the event of type msg_2.

The protocol can be specified by the following trace expression (starting from variable $AltBit_1$):

$$AltBit_1 = msg_1 : M_2 \qquad\qquad AltBit_2 = msg_2 : M_1$$
$$M_1 = msg_1 : A_2 \vee ack_2 : AltBit_1 \qquad M_2 = msg_2 : A_1 \vee ack_1 : AltBit_2$$
$$A_1 = ack_1 : M_1 \vee ack_2 : ack_1 : AltBit_1 \quad A_2 = ack_2 : M_2 \vee ack_1 : ack_2 : AltBit_2$$

---

[3] For efficiency reasons, our implementation exploits simplification opportunities after each transition step, therefore in practice for this example the two transitions would lead to the same expression.

In this case the prefix and union operators are sufficient for specifying the correct behavior of the system, however, the corresponding trace expression is not very readable. More importantly, if only the prefix and union operators are employed, the size of the expressions grows exponentially with the number of different involved event types.

This problem can be avoided by the use of the intersection and filter operators.

Let $msg\_ack(i)$, $i = 1, 2$, and msg denote the event types s.t. $[\![msg\_ack(i)]\!] = [\![msg_i]\!] \cup [\![ack_i]\!]$, $i = 1, 2$, and $[\![msg]\!] = [\![msg_1]\!] \cup [\![msg_2]\!]$. Then the ABP can be specified by the following deterministic trace expression:

$$AltBit = (msg \gg MM) \wedge (msg\_ack(1) \gg MA_1) \wedge (msg\_ack(2) \gg MA_2)$$
$$MM = msg_1{:}msg_2{:}MM \quad MA_1 = msg_1{:}ack_1{:}MA_1 \quad MA_2 = msg_2{:}ack_2{:}MA_2$$

The three trace expressions defined by MM, MA_1, and MA_2 correspond to the three constraints informally stated above. The main trace expression $AltBit$ can be easily read as follows: if an event has type msg_1 or msg_2, then it must verify MM, and if an event has type msg_1 or ack_1, then it must verify MA_1, and if an event has type msg_2 or ack_2, then it must verify MA_2.

The trace expression can be easily generalized to k different kinds of messages (with $k \geq 2$), with the size of the expression growing linearly with the number of different involved event types. For instance, for $k = 3$ we have the following trace expression:

$$AltBit =$$
$$(msg \gg MM) \wedge (msg\_ack(1) \gg MA_1) \wedge (msg\_ack(2) \gg MA_2) \wedge (msg\_ack(3) \gg MA_3)$$
$$MM = msg_1{:}msg_2{:}msg_3{:}MM \quad MA_1 = msg_1{:}ack_1{:}MA_1$$
$$MA_2 = msg_2{:}ack_2{:}MA_2 \qquad MA_3 = msg_3{:}ack_3{:}MA_2.$$

3.3 Non Context Free Languages

Trace expressions allow the specification of non context free languages; let us consider for instance the typical example of non context free language $\{a^n b^n c^n \mid n \geq 0\}$. This language can be specified by the following trace expression (defined by T)

$$T = (a\_or\_b \gg AB) \wedge (b\_or\_c \gg BC) \qquad AB = \epsilon \vee (a{:}(AB \cdot (b{:}\epsilon)))$$
$$BC = \epsilon \vee (b{:}(BC \cdot (c{:}\epsilon)))$$

where $[\![a]\!] = \{a\}$, $[\![b]\!] = \{b\}$, $[\![c]\!] = \{c\}$, $[\![a\_or\_b]\!] = \{a, b\}$, and $[\![b\_or\_c]\!] = \{b, c\}$.

Assuming the universe of events $\mathcal{E} = \{a, b, c\}$, the expression $a\_or\_b \gg AB$ denotes all traces of events over $\mathcal{E}$ that, when restricted to finite length[4] and to events a or b, correspond to the sequence $a^n b^n$ for some $n \in \mathbb{N}$; similarly, the

---

[4] Recall that for a comparison with context-free languages we need to disregard infinite traces; for instance, $a\_or\_b \gg AB$ and $b\_or\_c \gg BC$ contain also the infinite traces a^ω and b^ω, respectively.

expression $b\_or\_c \gg BC$ denotes all traces of events over $\mathcal{E}$ that, when restricted to finite length and to events b or c, correspond to the sequence $b^n c^n$ for some $n \in \mathbb{N}$. Hence the finite traces of T, which is the intersection of $a\_or\_b \gg AB$ and $b\_or\_c \gg BC$, are the non-context free language $\{a^n b^n c^n \mid n \geq 0\}$.

Although T is deterministic, it has the drawback that non correct traces can be detected with a certain latency. For instance the transition $T \xrightarrow{aabc} T'$ holds, with $T' = (a\_or\_b \gg (b{:}\epsilon)) \wedge (b\_or\_c \gg \epsilon)$, and clearly $aabc$ is not a valid prefix for the language; however, $[\![T']\!] = \emptyset$, and T' is not able to accept any further event, that is, recognition fails, independently from the next event.

To avoid this problem, the following equivalent (assuming that $\mathcal{E} = \{a, b, c\}$) deterministic trace expression can be employed:

$$T_2 = (AB{\cdot}C) \wedge (b\_or\_c \gg BC) \quad AB = \epsilon \vee (a{:}(AB{\cdot}(b{:}\epsilon)))$$
$$BC = \epsilon \vee (b{:}(BC{\cdot}(c{:}\epsilon))) \qquad C = \epsilon \vee c{:}C$$

In this case, $AB{\cdot}C$ forces events of type c to occur only after all required events of type b have been already occurred. In this case there is no T_2'' s.t. $T_2 \xrightarrow{aabc} T_2''$ holds; indeed, $T_2 \xrightarrow{aab} T_2'$ with $T_2' = ((b{:}\epsilon){\cdot}(\epsilon \vee (c{:}C))) \wedge (b\_or\_c \gg (BC{\cdot}(c{:}\epsilon)))$, and there exists no T_2'' s.t. $T_2' \xrightarrow{c} T_2''$, since the only possible transition from T_2' is $T_2' \xrightarrow{b} T_2''$, with $T_2'' = (\epsilon \vee (c{:}C)) \wedge (b\_or\_c \gg ((\epsilon \vee (b{:}BC{\cdot}(c{:}\epsilon))){\cdot}((c{:}\epsilon){\cdot}(c{:}\epsilon))))$, and $[\![T_2'']\!] = \{cc\}$.

4 Comparison with LTL

In this section we formally prove that trace expressions are more expressive than LTL, when both formalisms are used for RV. To this purpose we consider the LTL$_3$ semantics [3], an adaptation of the standard semantics of LTL formulas expressly introduced to take into account the limitations of RV due to its inability to check infinite traces. Despite there are LTL formulas which do not have an equivalent trace expression according to the standard LTL semantics, when LTL$_3$ is considered such a difference is no longer exhibited: for any LTL formula φ it is possible to build a contractive and deterministic trace expression τ such that the monitors generated by φ and τ, respectively, are behaviorally equivalent.

4.1 Background

LTL is a modal logic which has been introduced for specifying temporal properties of systems; despite its original main application is static verification through model checking, more recently it has been adopted as a specification formalism for RV, and some RV tools support it [6,12].

LTL Syntax and Semantics. Given a finite set of atomic propositions AP, the set of LTL formulas over AP is inductively defined as follows:

- *true* is an LTL formula;

- if $p \in AP$ then p is an LTL formula;
- if φ and ψ are LTL formulas then $\neg\psi$, $\varphi\lor\psi$, $X\psi$, and $\varphi U\psi$ are LTL formulas.

Additional operators can be derived in the standard way: $\varphi\land\psi = \neg(\neg\varphi\lor\neg\psi)$, $\varphi \Rightarrow \psi = \neg\varphi\lor\psi$, $F\varphi$ (or $\Diamond\varphi$) = $true\,U\varphi$, and $G\varphi$ (or $\Box\varphi$) $= \neg(true\,U\neg\varphi)$.

Let $\Sigma = 2^{AP}$ be the set of all possible subsets of AP; if $p \in AP$ and $a \in \Sigma$, then p holds in a iff $p \in a$. An LTL model is an infinite trace $w \in \Sigma^\omega$; $w(i)$ denotes the element $a \in \Sigma$ at position i in trace w; more formally, if $w = aw'$, then $w(0) = a$, and $w(i) = w'(i-1)$ if $i > 0$.

The semantics of a formula φ depends on the satisfaction relation $w, i \vDash \varphi$ (w satisfies φ in i) defined as follows:

- $w, i \vDash p$ iff $p \in w(i)$;
- $w, i \vDash \neg\phi$ iff $w, i \nvDash \phi$;
- $w, i \vDash \varphi \lor \psi$ iff $w, i \vDash \varphi$ or $w, i \vDash \psi$;
- $w, i \vDash X\varphi$ iff $w, i+1 \vDash \varphi$ (next operator);
- $w, i \vDash \varphi U\psi$ iff $\exists j \geq 0\;\; w, j \vDash \psi$ and $\forall 0 \leq k < j\;\; w, k \vDash \varphi$ (until operator).

Finally, $w \vDash \varphi$ (w satisfies φ) holds iff $w, 0 \vDash \varphi$ holds.

We recall that the set of all models of LTL formulas is the language of star-free ω-regular languages over Σ [7].

In order to encode an LTL formula into an equivalent trace expression we exploit the result stating that an LTL formula can be translated into an equivalent non deterministic Büchi automaton [3,14].

Non Deterministic Büchi Automata. A Büchi automaton is a type of ω-automaton which extends a finite automaton to infinite inputs. It accepts an infinite input sequence if there exists a run of the automaton that visits (at least) one of the final states infinitely often.

A (non deterministic) Büchi automaton (NBA) is a tuple $(\Sigma, Q, Q_0, \delta, F)$, where

- Σ is a finite alphabet;
- Q is a finite non-empty set of states;
- $Q_0 \subseteq Q$ is a set of initial states;
- $\delta{:}Q \times \Sigma \to 2^Q$ is a transition function;
- $F \subseteq Q$ is a set of accepting states.

A run of an automaton $(\Sigma, Q, Q_0, \delta, F)$ on a word $w \in \Sigma^\omega$ is an infinite trace $\rho = q_0 w(0) q_1 w(1) q_2 \ldots$, s.t. $q_0 \in Q_0$, and for all $i \geq 0$ $q_{i+1} \in \delta(q_i, w(i))$. A run ρ is called accepting iff $Inf(\rho) \cap F \neq \emptyset$, where $Inf(\rho)$ denotes the states visited infinitely often.

LTL$_3$. LTL$_3$ is a three-valued semantics [3] for LTL formulas, devised to adapt the standard semantics to RV, to correctly consider the limitation that at run-time only finite traces can be checked.

Given a finite trace $\sigma \in \Sigma^*$ of length $|\sigma| = n$, a continuation of σ is an infinite trace $w \in \Sigma^\omega$ s.t. for all $0 \leq i < n$ $w(i) = \sigma(i)$.

Given a finite trace $\sigma \in \Sigma^*$, and an LTL formula φ, the LTL$_3$ semantics of φ, denoted by $\sigma \vDash_3 \varphi$, is defined as follows:

$$\sigma \vDash_3 \varphi = \begin{cases} \top & \text{iff } w \vDash \varphi \text{ for all continuations } w \text{ of } \sigma \\ \bot & \text{iff } w \nvDash \varphi \text{ for all continuations } w \text{ of } \sigma \\ ? & \text{iff neither of the two conditions above holds} \end{cases}$$

As an example, let us consider the formula $\varphi = p\,U\,q$, where $p, q \in AP$; according to the definition above, $\{p\}\{p\}\{q\} \vDash_3 \varphi = \top$, that is, φ is satisfied by the finite trace $\{p\}\{p\}\{q\}$, and monitoring succeeds; $\{p\}\{p\}\emptyset \vDash_3 \varphi = \bot$, that is, φ is not satisfied by the finite trace $\{p\}\{p\}\emptyset$, and monitoring fails; finally, $\{p\}\{p\}\{p\} \vDash_3 \varphi = ?$, that is, at this stage monitoring is inconclusive, and the monitor has to keep monitoring the property expressed by φ. Assuming that $AP = \{p, q\}$, the LTL$_3$ semantics of $p\,U\,q$ corresponds to the finite state machine (FSM) defined in Fig. 3, which fully determines the expected behavior of a monitor for the RV of $p\,U\,q$.

More in general, for all LTL formulas φ, it is possible to build an FSM which is a deterministic finite automaton (DFA) where the alphabet is Σ (that is, 2^{AP}), all states are final, each state returns either $\top$ (successful), or $\bot$ (failure), or ? (inconclusive), and the behavior of the FSM respects the LTL$_3$ semantics of φ: for all finite traces $\sigma \in \Sigma^*$, the FSM accepts σ with final state that returns $v \in \{\top, \bot, ?\}$ iff $\sigma \vDash_3 \varphi = v$.

The sequence of steps required to generate from an LTL formula φ an FSM that respects the LTL$_3$ semantics of φ [3] is summarized in Fig. 4.

For each LTL formula φ and $\neg\varphi$ (1), the equivalent NBAs $\mathcal{A}^\varphi$, and $\mathcal{A}^{\neg\varphi}$ are built (2), all states that generate a non empty language are identified (3) and made final and the NBAs are transformed into the corresponding NFAs $\hat{\mathcal{A}}^\varphi$, and $\hat{\mathcal{A}}^{\neg\varphi}$ (4), and, then, into the equivalent DFAs $\tilde{\mathcal{A}}^\varphi$ and $\tilde{\mathcal{A}}^{\neg\varphi}$ (5). Finally, the product of $\tilde{\mathcal{A}}^\varphi$ and $\tilde{\mathcal{A}}^{\neg\varphi}$ is computed, and from it the final FSM $\mathcal{M}^\varphi$ is derived by minimization, and by classifying the states in the following way: (q, q') returns

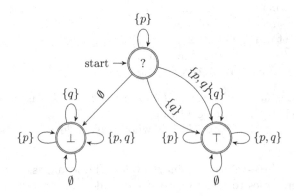

Fig. 3. FSM of the monitor for $p\,U\,q$, with $AP = \{p, q\}$

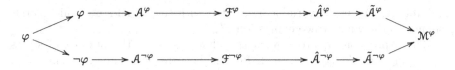

Fig. 4. Steps required to generate an FSM from an LTL formula φ

$\top$ iff q' is not final in $\tilde{A}^{\neg\varphi}$, $\bot$ iff q is not final in $\tilde{A}^\varphi$, and ? if both q and q' are final in $\tilde{A}^\varphi$, and $\tilde{A}^{\neg\varphi}$, respectively.

4.2 Comparing Trace Expressions with LTL

We have shown that LTL formulas as pUq cannot be fully verified at runtime, therefore a three-valued semantics LTL_3 has been introduced. To be able to compare LTL formulas with trace expressions, the same three-valued semantics is considered for trace expressions as well.

Given a finite trace $\sigma \in \Sigma^*$ of length $|\sigma| = n$, a continuation of σ is an finite or infinite trace $u \in \Sigma^* \cup \Sigma^\omega$ s.t. for all $0 \le i < n$ $u(i) = \sigma(i)$.

The three-valued semantics of a trace expression τ is defined as follows:

$$\sigma \in [\![\tau]\!]_3 = \begin{cases} \top \text{ iff } u \in [\![\tau]\!] \text{ for all continuations } u \text{ of } \sigma \\ \bot \text{ iff } u \notin [\![\tau]\!] \text{ for all continuations } u \text{ of } \sigma \\ ? \text{ iff neither of the two conditions above holds} \end{cases}$$

Let us consider again the formula $\varphi = pUq$; if we assume that each atomic predicate in AP has a corresponding event type denoted in the same way, then the closest trace expression τ into which φ can be translated is defined by $T = p{:}T \vee q{:}1$, where 1 is the derivable constant introduced in Sect. 3 denoting all possible traces. If we consider the standard semantics we have that, since $\{p\}$ is an event that satisfies p, $\{p\}^\omega \in [\![\tau]\!]$, but $\{p\}^\omega \nvDash \varphi$. However, when considering the three-valued semantics we have that for all $v \in \{\top, \bot, ?\}$ and $\sigma \in \Sigma^*$, $\sigma \vDash \varphi = v$ iff $\sigma \in [\![\tau]\!]_3 = v$. In particular, for all $n \ge 0$, $\{p\}^n \vDash \varphi =?$ and $\{p\}^n \in [\![\tau]\!]_3 =?$.

To translate an LTL formula φ into a trace expression τ s.t. the three-valued semantics is preserved, we exploit the result presented in Sect. 4.1. First, φ is translated into an equivalent FSM $\mathcal{M}^\varphi$, then $\mathcal{M}^\varphi$ is translated into an equivalent contractive and deterministic trace expression τ^φ. The latter translation is defined as follows:

- if the initial state returns $\top$, then φ is a tautology, and the corresponding trace expression is the constant 1;
- if the initial state returns $\bot$, then φ is a unsatisfiable, and the corresponding trace expression is the constant 0;
- if the initial state returns ?, then the corresponding trace expression is defined by a finite set of equations $X_1 = \tau_1, \ldots, X_n = \tau_n$, where n is the number of states in $\mathcal{M}^\varphi$ that return ?, each of such states is associated with a distinct

variable X_i, X_1 is the variable associated with the initial state which corresponds to the whole trace expression τ^φ.

The expressions τ_i are defined as follows: let k be the number of states $q_1, \ldots, q_k$ that do not return $\perp$ for which there exists an incoming edge, labeled with the element $a_i \in 2^{AP}$, from the node associated with X_i; we know that $k > 0$, because the node associated with X_i returns ?. Then $\tau_i = a_1{:}f(q_1) \vee \ldots \vee a_k{:}f(q_k)$, where $f(q)$ is defined as follows: if q returns $\top$, then $f(q) = 1$, otherwise (that is, q returns ?), $f(q) = X_q$ (that is, the variable uniquely associated with q is returned).

Since all variables in the expressions $\tau_1, \ldots, \tau_n$ are guarded by the prefix operator, τ^φ is contractive; furthermore, it is deterministic because $\mathcal{M}^\varphi$ is deterministic.

Theorem 1. *Let $\mathcal{M}^\varphi$ be the FSM equivalent to φ generated by the procedure described in Sect. 4.1. Then, the trace expression τ^φ generated from $\mathcal{M}^\varphi$ as specified in Sect. 4.2 preserves the semantics of $\mathcal{M}^\varphi$: for all $\sigma \in \Sigma^*$ $\mathcal{M}^\varphi$ accepts σ with output $v \in \{\top, \perp, ?\}$ iff $\sigma \in [\![\tau^\varphi]\!]_3 = v$.*

Proof Sketch: the proof proceeds by induction on the length of σ. The cases where the initial state of the FSM returns $\top$ or $\perp$ are immediate to be proved. The proof when the initial state returns ? is based on the fact that, in this case, by construction $[\![\tau^\varphi]\!] \neq \emptyset$ and there always exists a trace u s.t. $u \notin [\![\tau^\varphi]\!]$, therefore $\epsilon \in [\![\tau^\varphi]\!]_3 = ?$.   □

In Sect. 3.3 we have shown a trace expression τ that specifies a non context free language of traces (when only finite traces are considered). More formally, $\sigma \in [\![\tau \cdot 1]\!]_3 = \top$ iff $\sigma \in \{a^n b^n c^n \mid n \geq 0\}$.

This means that for RV (that is, when the three-values semantics is considered) trace expressions are strictly more expressive than LTL logic, since the LTL logic is less expressive than ω-regular languages.

5   Related Work

In this section we briefly survey work related to runtime verification, and to formalisms, other than LTL, for specifying event traces.

Global Types and Multi-party Sessions. Though trace expressions and global types [5] are rather similar (indeed, global types correspond to trace expressions without the concatenation and the intersection operators), the aim of trace expressions diverges from that of Castagna et al.'s behavioral types for many reasons:

– trace expressions are not intended to be used for annotating and statically checking programs, but rather, for specifying properties that have to be verified at runtime;

- while Castagna et al.'s types are expressly designed for describing multiparty interactions between distributed components, trace expressions are meant as a more general formalism which can be used for runtime verification of different kinds of properties and systems;
- finally, trace expressions have a coinductive, rather than inductive, semantics, hence they can denote sets containing infinite traces; this is important for being able to verify systems that must not terminate.

Object-Oriented Languages. In the context of runtime verification of object-oriented languages, there exist several formalisms for specifying valid or invalid traces of method invocations, as done in the stack objects example in Sect. 3.1.

Program Query Language (PQL) [13] allows developers to express a large class of application specific code patterns. PQL is more expressive than context-free languages, since its class of languages is that of the closure of context-free languages combined with intersection, hence, the formalism seems to be as expressive as trace expressions. However, no formal semantics is defined for PQL, and it is not clear whether PQL queries can denote infinite traces.

The jassda [4] framework and tool enable runtime checking of Java programs against a CSP-like specification. Like in trace expressions, the trace semantics of a process is defined by collecting all event sequences that are possible with respect to the operational semantics. Processes are built with operators similar to those of trace expressions, except for concatenation and intersection, which are not supported by jassda.

SAGA [10] is a tool for runtime verification of properties of Java programs specified with attribute grammars. The implementation is based on four different components: a state-based assertion checker, a parser generator, a debugger and a general tool for meta-programming. The tool is extremely powerful and has been successfully applied to an industrial case from the e-commerce with multi-threaded Java. The main difference w.r.t. our approach is that SAGA has been developed for runtime checking of a combination of protocol- and data-oriented properties of object-oriented programs, whereas, at the moment, trace expressions have been successfully employed for runtime verification of multiagent systems.

6 Conclusion

Trace expressions are a compact and expressive formalism that has been used for RV of interaction protocols in multiagent systems.

In this paper we have formally compared trace expressions with LTL, a formalism widely adopted in RV. To this aim we have employed the three-valued semantics [3] proposed for LTL in the context of RV, and we have proved that for the purpose of RV, trace expressions are strictly more expressive than LTL: every LTL formula can be encoded into a trace expression which preserves its three-valued semantics, but the opposite property does not hold, since trace expressions are able to specify context-free and non context-free languages.

Anyway, the benefits of trace expressions over LTL in the context of runtime verification needs to be studied on the basis of an implementation and case studies.

Another interesting subject for further investigation would consists in the study of the class of language that is covered by trace expressions, and by contractive and/or deterministic trace expressions.

References

1. Ancona, D., Briola, D., Ferrando, A., Mascardi, V.: Global protocols as first class entities for self-adaptive agents. In: Proceedings of the International Conference on Autonomous Agents and Multiagent Systems, AAMAS 2015, pp. 1019–1029 (2015)
2. Ancona, D., Drossopoulou, S., Mascardi, V.: Automatic generation of self-monitoring MASs from multiparty global session types in Jason. In: Baldoni, M., Dennis, L., Mascardi, V., Vasconcelos, W. (eds.) DALT 2012. LNCS, vol. 7784, pp. 76–95. Springer, Heidelberg (2013)
3. Bauer, A., Leucker, M., Schallhart, C.: Runtime verification for LTL and TLTL. ACM Trans. Softw. Eng. Methodol. (TOSEM) **20**, 1–64 (2009)
4. Brörkens, M., Möller, M.: Dynamic event generation for runtime checking using the JDI. Electr. Notes Theor. Comput. Sci. **70**(4), 21–35 (2002)
5. Castagna, G., Dezani-Ciancaglini, M., Padovani, L.: On global types and multiparty session. Logical Methods Comput. Sci. **8**(1), 1–45 (2012)
6. Chen, F., Rosu, G.: Mop: an efficient and generic runtime verification framework. In: OOPSLA 2007, pp. 569–588 (2007)
7. Cohen, J., Perrin, D., Pin, J.-E.: On the expressive power of temporal logic. J. Comput. Syst. Sci. **46**, 271–294 (1993)
8. Courcelle, B.: Fundamental properties of infinite trees. Theoret. Comput. Sci. **25**, 95–169 (1983)
9. Ancona D., Barbieri, M., Mascardi, V.: Constrained global types for dynamic checking of protocol conformance in multi-agent systems. In: Proceedings of the 28th Annual ACM Symposium on Applied Computing, SAC 2013, pp. 1377–1379 (2013)
10. de Boer, F.S., de Gouw, S.: Combining monitoring with run-time assertion checking. In: Bernardo, M., Damiani, F., Hähnle, R., Johnsen, E.B., Schaefer, I. (eds.) SFM 2014. LNCS, vol. 8483, pp. 217–262. Springer, Heidelberg (2014)
11. Deniélou, P.-M., Yoshida, N.: Multiparty session types meet communicating automata. In: Seidl, H. (ed.) ESOP 2012. LNCS, vol. 7211, pp. 194–213. Springer, Heidelberg (2012)
12. Luo, Q., Zhang, Y., Lee, C., Jin, D., Meredith, P.O.N., Şerbănuţă, T.F., Roşu, G.: RV-Monitor: efficient parametric runtime verification with simultaneous properties. In: Bonakdarpour, B., Smolka, S.A. (eds.) RV 2014. LNCS, vol. 8734, pp. 285–300. Springer, Heidelberg (2014)
13. Martin, M.C., Livshits, V.B., Lam, M.S.: Finding application errors and security flaws using PQL: a program query language. OOPSLA **2005**, 365–383 (2005)
14. Sistla, A.P., Vardi, M.Y., Wolper, P.: The complementation problem for büchi automata with appplications to temporal logic. Theor. Comput. Sci. **49**, 217–237 (1987)

Proper Protocol

Farhad Arbab[1,2(✉)]

[1] Formal Methods, CWI, Science Park 123, 1098 XG Amsterdam, The Netherlands
`farhad@cwi.nl`
[2] Leiden Institute for Advanced Computer Science,
Leiden University, Leiden, The Netherlands

Abstract. Treating interaction as an explicit first-class concept, complete with its own composition operators, leads to a model of concurrency that allows direct specification and manipulation of protocols as proper mathematical objects. Reo [2,5,6,8] serves as a premier example of such an interaction-centric model of concurrency.

In this paper, we peruse Reo and explain how its model of protocols as encapsulated, reusable constructs facilitates their fulfilling of the more prominent role slated for them in engineering of modular, verifiable, scalable concurrent software. We also explore clues enlaced with some recent results of our ongoing work on compiling Reo protocol specifications into efficient executable code, which sketch a promising perspective for future work on high-level protocol specification languages.

1 Preamble

For the bulk of the time that Frank de Boer and I have been colleagues at CWI and Leiden, my work has focused on concurrency, coordination, and Reo, and Frank has been working on concurrency, object orientation, formal verification, and many other topics. Nevertheless, Frank's impact on Reo goes beyond his direct contributions through formal collaborations on projects and his coauthorship of papers. Through discussions and by his interest and his questions, Frank has helped me—as well as many of our colleagues—to focus and refine our understanding, and even chart our course into new projects.

2 Introduction

Today's low-cost multicore commodity hardware has made scalable parallel computing platforms affordable. Offering many processor cores on the same chip, cheap threading with fast communication and shared memory, these platforms can potentially accommodate applications that requires massively concurrent computing. Nevertheless, full utilization of the enormous potential offered by such platforms in real-life applications seems to lag dramatically behind. The striking gap between the potential massive concurrency offered by these platforms and their practical uptake raises a perhaps heretical question: do we even

E. Ábrahám et al. (Eds.): de Boer Festschrift, LNCS 9660, pp. 65–87, 2016.
DOI: 10.1007/978-3-319-30734-3_7

need such massively concurrent platforms? More specifically, what types of applications can actually benefit from such massively concurrent platforms, and by how much?

A most emphatically positive answer to the first question may provide an answer to the second by identifying an auspiciously significant class of important applications that can benefit by a substantial factor. However, such a propitious outcome of this inquiry, in turn, raises another question: if massively concurrent systems have important practical applications and computing platforms do exist to provide them, then what has hindered extensive uptake of these platforms to accommodate those applications?

We argue that an emphatically positive answer to the first question is indeed justified. A vast number of important problems can indeed use large-scale coarse grain concurrency, at least in principle. However, conspicuously missing are effective techniques for developing scalable concurrent software that turns the raw computing power of massively concurrent multicore platforms into effective applications that solve those problems.

The growing importance of applications that involve huge volumes of data and peta-scale graphs of their inter-relations, make the need for programming techniques to harness the massive concurrency offered by multicore platforms ever more vivid. To find what has hindered extensive development of massively concurrent applications we must look into the inadequacies of contemporary programming constructs and models for concurrency. These inadequacies stem from the fact that, ironically, *concurrency protocols* have not received the proper attention that they deserve in the classical work on concurrency.

In spite of the fact that *interaction* constitutes the most challenging aspect of concurrency, traditional models of concurrency predominantly treat interaction as a secondary or derived concept. Shared memory, message passing, calculi such as CSP [30], CCS [49], the π-calculus [50,53], further process algebras [11,16,23], and the actor model [3] represent popular approaches to tackle the complexities of constructing concurrent systems. Beneath their significant differences, all these models share one common characteristic, inherited from the world of sequential programming: they all constitute *action-centric* models of concurrency. All these models provide constructs for the direct specification of *things that interact*, rather than a direct specification of *interaction* (protocols). Consequently, in these formalisms (a protocol that specifies an intended) interaction becomes a derived or secondary concept whose properties can be studied only indirectly, as the side-effects of the (intended or coincidental) couplings or clashes of the *actions* whose compositions comprise a model.

Our work on Reo shows that one can formally treat interaction as an explicit first-class concept, complete with its own composition operators. Several significant advantages ensue from such an *interaction-centric* model of concurrency. Treating protocols as proper mathematical objects expressed as encapsulated syntactic constructs, explicitly separates them from computation code of applications, which simplifies software development by adhering to the principle of separation of concerns. Separation of protocols from computation allows formal verification and analysis of protocols in isolation from any application code. As concrete encapsulated formal constructs, one can reuse such formally verified protocols, verbatim—perhaps out of a library—in different applications. Moreover, one can directly compose simpler (verified) protocols into arbitrarily more complex protocols, which allows compositional verification of the resulting more complex protocols. Finally, although it may superficially seem counter-intuitive, an interaction-centric model of concurrency, such as Reo, opens up a vast field of opportunities to refine information-rich, high-level models of protocols into efficient executable code whose performance can compete with and even beat that of carefully hand-crafted code.

3   The Bounty of Concurrency

The extent to which a solution to a problem can benefit from concurrency depends on the amount of concurrency inherent in that problem. The famous computer architect Gene Amdahl[1], had quantified this message in what has become known as Amdahl's law [4].

Amdahl's Law. An application consists of an inherently sequential part and a potentially concurrent part. Let a designate the time that it takes to execute the sequential part on a single processor, and b the time that it takes to execute the potentially concurrent part on a single processor. Thus the total execution time of this application on a single processor is $T(1) = a + b$. Generously ignoring all overhead, throwing n processors at this application can speed up only its potentially concurrent part by a factor of n. Thus, the total execution time of this application on an n-processor machine is $T(n) = a + b/n$. Therefore, the speedup that we can expect from running this application on an n-processor machine compared to running it on a single processor is bound by $S_{Amdahl}(n) = \frac{T(1)}{T(n)}$. Define $\alpha = a/(a+b)$ and we obtain Amdahl's law expressing the upper-bound for the speedup of an application running on n processors compared to its execution time on a single processor, in terms of its inherently sequential fraction, α:

$$S_{Amdahl}(n, \alpha) = \frac{1}{\alpha + \frac{1-\alpha}{n}} \qquad (1)$$

Figure 1(a) shows the graph of speedup (on logarithmic scale) according to Amdahl's law as a function of number of processors, for a range of α values from 0.01 to 0.9. This graph puts a discouraging damper on the enthusiasm about the speedup of applications on parallel machines. If 50 % of an application is inherently sequential, its execution on a 2-processor machine speeds up by a factor of 1.33 and this "linear" speedup tapers off quickly to 1.66 on a 5-processor machine, improving to nearly 2 only on a 100-processor machine. If only 10 % of an application is inherently sequential, its execution improves almost linearly by

---

[1] While this paper was under review, Gene Amdahl [16 November 1922 – 10 November 2015] passed away.

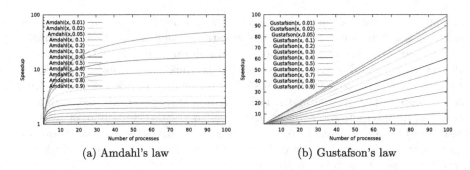

(a) Amdahl's law   (b) Gustafson's law

Fig. 1. Amdahl's and Gustafson's laws

adding up to 5 processors, but this improvement tapers off to a speedup of only 5.26 with 10 processors, 6.89 with 20, and 9.17 with 100 processors. Even with an infinite number of processors, this application speeds up by only a depressing factor of 10! For an application 99 % of which is inherently concurrent, nearly-linear speed up lasts only up to about a dozen processors; 20 processors yield a 16.80 speedup, which tapers off to only 50.25 with 100 processors.

Amdahl's law is in fact not as depressing as it may seem, because it simply states an obvious fact: that there is just so much juice that you can extract out of an orange, no matter how long and hard you press it (even if we ignore the overhead of the juice that gets trapped and goes to waste in the pulp). An application that spends only 10 % of its time executing its inherently sequential part has no more than a ten-fold juice of speedup to extract, even if you press it by the computational force of an infinite number of processors. In practice, you may be happy with a 9-fold speedup of this application on a 100-processor machine, or settle for a 5-fold speedup with only 10 processors, and let the remaining speedup juice go to waste with the pulp, because obtaining this remaining speedup is simply not worth the cost of its extraction.

Is this the best we can hope to reap from the bounty bestowed by massively concurrent hardware?

Gustafson's Law. Amdahl's law gives a bound for how much juice we can extract from a specific individual orange, i.e., how much faster we can run an application that solves a *fixed-size* problem on a multiprocessor machine. Amdahl's law, however, does not limit our ability to quench our thirst for more orange juice: we can simply juice bigger (amounts of) oranges!

A very important class of applications in concurrency involves solving problems whose sizes can increase arbitrarily. What matters in these applications is not so much speeding up the solution of a specific instance of such a problem (e.g., mining graphs of a given size) on a multiprocessor machine. We may already be content (if not happy) with the execution speed of this solution on a k-processor machine. The purpose of employing more than k processors in such applications is to solve larger-sized instances of the same problem (e.g., mining proportionally larger graphs) in still reasonable time. Bigger-size problems, thus, provide arbitrarily bigger (amounts of) oranges to juice!

Gustafson revisited Amdahl's law to accommodate precisely this class of applications [26], which we call *scalable*. Let $T_k(n)$ denote the execution time of a scalable problem of size n on a k processor machine. A scalable application also contains an inherently sequential part, whose execution on a single processor takes a time units. The potentially concurrent part of such an application has a repetitive structure that scales directly with the size of the problem. Let b be the sequential execution time of the potentially concurrent part of this application, solving the size-1 instance of the problem. The total execution time of the application for the size-1 instance of the problem on a single processor, then, is $T_1(1) = a + b$, and the execution time of a size-n instance of the problem on a single processor machine is $T_1(n) = a + n \times b$.

With more processors, we can parallelize the potentially concurrent part of solving a larger instance of the problem. Thus, ignoring all overhead, the execution time of a size-n instance of the problem on an n-processor machine is $T_n(n) = a + b$, which means $T_n(n) = T_1(1)$. Defining $\alpha = a/(a + b)$, as before, we get Gustafson's law for speedup:

$$S_{Gustafson}(n, \alpha) = n - \alpha \times (n - 1) \qquad (2)$$

Figure 1(b) shows the graph of speedup for scalable problems according to Gustafson's law as a function of number of processors, for a range of α values from 0.01 to 0.9. It seems that at least for scalable problems, Gustafson's law rescues usefulness of concurrency from the grim grip of Amdahl's law.

Superficially, the two graphs in Fig. 1 seem to contradict each other: for every value of α, Fig. 1(a) establishes a strict asymptotic limit less than n for speedup, whereas Fig. 1(b) shows that speedup increases linearly in n, without bounds, at an α-dependent slope. In fact, far from contradicting Amdahl's law, Gustafson's law complements it. For scalable applications, as we increase n, we change the application by increasing the size of the problem that it solves and thereby increase the amount of concurrent juice that it contains. As a result, the ratio of the inherently sequential part of the application to its total execution time on a single processor shrinks, and the application moves up the rungs of the ladder of α curves in Fig. 1(a).

Let $\delta(n) = a/(a + n \times b)$ designate the fraction of the inherently sequential part of a scalable application of size n. Rewriting $\delta(n)$ in terms of α, we get:

$$\delta(n) = \frac{\alpha}{\alpha + (1 - \alpha) \times n} \qquad (3)$$

Equation 3 shows that for a fixed α, as n grows, $\delta(n)$ diminishes, endowing more concurrency juice to the application, which moves the application up the ladder of the curves in the graph of Amdah's law in Fig. 1(a). In fact, substituting $\delta(n)$ for α in Eq. 1, Amdahl's law yields $S_{Amdahl}(n, \delta(n)) = 1$, which shows that for scalable problems, as we increase the number of processors from n to $n + k$ to match the increase of the problem size from n to $n + k$, the quantity $\delta(n)$

diminishes exactly such that we obtain no "real speedup" gain by Amdahl's law: *all* extra concurrency provided by the additional k processors goes to solving the k-size larger problem. This observation suggests that perhaps more usefully, we can think of Gustafson's law not so much as a measure of speedup, but rather a measure of *scalability* of a scalable application.

Communication Overhead. Both Amdahl's and Gustafson's laws mean to express upper bounds, and thus they ignore all overhead. Obviously, the interaction protocol that enables communications among concurrent chunks of the application greatly influences this overhead. To account for protocol overhead, we revise Gustafson's equation for the execution time of a size-n scalable problem on an n-processor machine as $T_n(n) = a + b + c$ where c is the extra time that the application takes to complete because of protocol overhead.

For $n > 1$, every parallel computation fragment executes a number of communication operations. The extra delays required to complete these operations collectively comprise $c = f(n)$, which means speedup of a scalable application is:

$$S(n, \alpha) = \frac{n - \alpha \times (n - 1)}{1 + \frac{f(n)}{T_1(1)}} \tag{4}$$

For any application, α and $T_1(1)$ are constants. The nominator in Eq. 4 is linear in n. The effectiveness of the speedup (or, scalability) of an application, then crucially depends on the nature of its protocol overhead function $f(n)$. A good linear protocol yields only a constant speedup (i.e., no scalability), and even a quadratic $f(n)$ quickly dampens scalability by $1/n$ as n increases.

So, where exactly in a concurrent application can we find its communication protocol that has such a significant impact on its performance and scalability?

4   Where's Waldo?

In a modern well-structured program, we can easily locate a segment of code that implements some computation function, e.g., *FourierTransform*, or a computation construct such as the abstract data type *stack*. These implementations, of course, use concrete algorithms and data structures. For instance, the implementation of *stack* may use a linked list data structure. Because they are so easy to locate, if desired, we can readily replace the implementation code for *FourierTransform* or *stack* with the piece of code for some alternative implementation of these computation constructs. For instance, we can easily replace the linked-list implementation of *stack* with an array implementation of *stack* to improve the performance of an application. If the application software is indeed well-structured (e.g., *stack* is implemented as a class in an object-oriented language), this implementation code swapping will be completely invisible to the rest of the software, regardless of how often or intensively it uses various incarnations of *stack*. A more efficient implementation of an abstract data type or a computation function simply improves the overall performance of the application, without requiring any modification to the rest of the software. Moreover, to scale up a well-structured program using a stack of size k to one that needs a stack of size $2k$, all we need to do is change the value assigned to some identifier from k to $2k$.

Programming language constructs and abstractions, along with techniques for their efficient compilation, have dramatically advanced in the last half-century, to the extent that we can now program at the level of (parametric) types, classes, objects, mathematical functions, monads, or Horn clauses, when appropriate, and obtain executable code whose performance competes with—indeed often beats—that of code written by even better-than-average programmers in some low-level language. It is precisely these advances that, among other things, make it easy to carry out the above mentioned software modifications so painlessly.

Protocols constitute no less significant a concept in concurrent applications than functions, types, and other computational constructs, and variants of concrete implementations of protocols have an least equally significant impact on the performance of a concurrent application. Moreover, as we saw in Sect. 3, protocol (overhead) plays a crucial role in the scale-up of scalable problems. Given the significance of protocols and the long history of concurrency, one would expect—rather naively—to find in modern software high-level *protocol constructs* (as counterparts to constructs for types, classes, etc.), that make, e.g., scaling up a two-producer-one-consumer protocol to a k-producer-one-consumer protocol as easy as changing the value assigned to some identifier in its implementation code from 2 to k. Or—even more naively—that to change one implementation of a two-producer-one-consumer protocol with another, all that should be necessary is to swap the two pieces of code for their respective implementations, without any change to the rest of the software. Perplexingly, neither of these software modifications is so painless today!

Programming constructs and models for concurrency have essentially stagnated in the past half-century. Algorithmic skeletons [25] represent an attempt to facilitate development of better structured concurrent programs by offering encapsulated protocol skeletons that programmers can flesh out to suit the specifics of their applications. Several skeleton libraries exist. However, although useful in practice when a problem readily fits the design patterns of available skeletons, algorithmic skeletons have not given rise to a formal model of encapsulated, composable protocols analogous to types, objects, and classes. Transactional memory [29,47,54] represents another attempt to simplify concurrent programming by providing *transaction* as a syntactic construct for high-level mutual exclusion. Although a transaction can qualify as a protocol, transactions often necessarily contain application specific computation code, which makes them *impure* (non-reusable). Moreover, treating every protocol as a transaction can lead to over-sequentialization, and this model does not provide adequate means to derive more complex (than single transaction) protocols through structural composition of other protocols (transactions). In contrast to advances in abstractions and constructs for sequential programming, no real abstract *protocol constructs* have evolved. Processes, threads, locks, semaphores, contrivances for mutual exclusion, monitors, rendezvous, etc., of roughly 50 years ago comprise all programming constructs we have to express protocols in our modern software.

The pervasive integration of computing and interaction in so many aspects of our lives today has vastly expanded the number of applications that require scalable complex protocols. Meanwhile, advances in processor, memory, and communication hardware have made leaps and bounds in the past 50 years to provide suitable hardware to accommodate these applications. Software technology must develop code that transforms the raw power of available hardware into concurrent applications that embody those required scalable complex protocols. Stagnation of programming constructs and models for concurrency has created a stifling bottleneck in development of these applications. Between the two expanding domains of *necessity* and *possibility*, software engineers are left stranded to fend for themselves, armed with nothing more than the same 50-year-old cumbersome concurrency constructs, and their own wits. In this sense, our arsenal of 50-year-old concurrency programming constructs is dramatically less adequate for our software engineering needs of today than it was 50 years ago.

Finding what constituted a *stack* (just as an example) in a typical "well-structured" Fortran IV or PL/I code of early 1970's required as much time and mental effort as finding Waldo[2]—and it was far less entertaining. The mere act of locating what constitutes a protocol in a typical well-structured concurrent application of today often requires substantially more time, effort, and expertise than was required to find a *stack* in a Frotran IV or PL/I application of the 1970's; and replacing the implementation of this protocol or scaling it up often cascades numerous prohibitively intrusive intricate changes throughout the entire software.

5   Interaction-Centric Concurrency

Traditional action-centric models for concurrent programming embed within the sequential programming paradigm a befitting selection of primitives such as locks, semaphores, monitors, send/receive, message passing, rendezvous, etc., for programmers to manifest an interaction protocol contingent on the control flows of disparate sequential threads, that run under an implied nondeterminism on the order of their execution. This dispersion of interaction-inducing actions makes protocols nebulous, intangible, and ephemeral, which explains why even identifying the constructs that constitute a protocol in an application programmed in such models often becomes a non-trivial challenge.

The dataflow paradigm provides an alternative perspective on concurrent programming. It liberates the manifestation of interaction protocols from the control flows of sequential threads, expressing them instead as concrete graphs that make the nondeterminism of their execution explicitly evident. The classical works on dataflow programming pioneered by Kahn [45, 46], Dennis [22],

---

[2] In Martin Handford's 1980's popular books of double-page illustrations, that challenged readers to locate a certain Waldo character "hidden" in plain sight in a crowd.

and Arvind [9] serve as inspiring early examples of interaction-centric models of concurrency: abstracting away the semantic content of computation nodes in such a dataflow graph leaves a structure behind that explicitly represents a concrete interaction protocol. One can easily compose protocols by splicing their graphs together. Because the edges in these specific dataflow graphs represent FIFO communication links, these protocols cannot directly express synchrony. The need for synchrony in concurrency, especially in real-time and embedded systems, led to the development of synchronous languages [15,17,21,24], where edges represent synchronous communication. Ptolemy [19,48] allows hierarchical composition of graphs each representing a synchronous or asynchronous interaction among actors, to model heterogeneous systems.

In the world of sequential programs, with the formal semantics of a function as a black-box that transforms its input to its output, the semantic equivalence of two functions is a congruence, i.e., given two equivalent functions, one can always replace the other. In the world of concurrent programs, such semantic equivalence is not a congruence, i.e., given two concurrent computation units whose functions are equivalent, one cannot always replace the other [18]. This observation, known as the Brock-Ackerman anomaly, shows that interaction requires a more expressive formal semantics enriched by a notion of time, to discern differences between otherwise equivalent units of computation that arise out of alternative orders of their execution. Some dataflow models suffer from this anomaly, and some avoid it by imposing restrictions.

Such earlier work as above has inspired our notion of interaction-centric concurrency, and our work on Reo builds upon and extends this work. More recent work on BIP [10,14], multiparty session types [20,32], Scribble [31,55], and Pabble [51,52] represent other examples of interaction-centric models that to various degrees of expressiveness and generality make protocols concrete central objects of discourse.

Treating interaction as a full-fledged first-class concept requires a model that offers (1) an explicit, direct, concrete representation of interaction among actors, independent of their (communication) actions; (2) a set of primitive interactions; and (3) composition operators to combine (primitive) interactions into more complex interactions. A most primitive interaction specifies a *relation* between two communication actions, e.g., a send and a receive. For instance, such a relation may state that the two actions must happen synchronously, or that one (e.g., the read) must necessarily happen strictly some time after the other has completed. This specification is oblivious to the actor entities that perform such communication operations; all that matters is that the specified relation holds on the timing and the contents of the data exchanged by those operations. Such specifications quite naturally accede a formal representation as *constraints*, which come equipped with *relational composition* that allows constructing more complex constraints out of simpler ones.

Protocols as Connectors. Concretely, we regard a protocol simply as a constraint, which declaratively specifies *what* must hold in terms of a relation, disregarding *how* it can hold. Expressed as constraints, pure protocols become first-class, tangible, reusable encapsulated constructs in their own right. As concrete software constructs, such protocols can manifest as architecturally meaningful *connectors* that portrayed graphically, resemble a generalization of dataflow graphs where nodes have fixed semantics but each edge represents an arbitrary interaction relation.

Components. In an interaction-centric model of concurrency, a computational process (or thread), or *component* is written in any conventional programming language, such as C, C++, Java, etc. The only means of communication of a component with its outside world is through *blocking I/O operations* that it may perform exclusively on its own *ports*. Inter-component communication is possible only by mediation of connectors, which implement interaction protocols, outside of the components.

If i is an input port of a component, C, there are only two operations that C can perform on i: (1) blocking input get(i, v) waits indefinitely or until it succeeds to obtain a value through i and assigns it to variable v; or (2) input with time-out get(i, v, t) behaves similarly, except that it unblocks and returns false if the specified time-out t expires before it obtains a value to assign to v. Analogously, if o is an output port of a component, there are only two operations that the component can perform on o: (1) blocking output put(o, v) waits indefinitely or until it succeeds to dispense the value in variable v through o; or (2) output with time-out put(o, v, t) behaves similarly, except that it unblocks and returns false if the specified time-out t expires before it dispenses the value in v.

6   Overview of Reo

We have used the interaction-as-constraint perspective described above to formalize an interaction-centric model of concurrency wherein every interaction protocol is a constraint obtained as a (relational) composition of a small set of simple binary constraints. This model serves as the formal foundation of a domain-specific language (DSL), called Reo [2,5–8], for programming concurrency protocols that manifest as connectors. Complex connectors in Reo are constructed as a network of primitive binary connectors, called *channels*.

We summarize only the main concepts in Reo here. Further details about Reo and its semantics can be found in cited references. Tool support for Reo consists of a set of Eclipse plug-ins that together comprise the Extensible Coordination Tools (ECT) visual programming environment [1].

Channels. A channel is a medium of communication that consists of two ends and a constraint on the dataflows observed at those ends. There are two types of channel ends: *source* and *sink*. A source channel end accepts data into its channel, and a sink channel end dispenses data out of its channel. Every channel (type) specifies its own particular behavior as constraints on the flow of data through its ends. These constraints relate, for example, the content, the conditions for

Fig. 2. A typical set of Reo channels

loss, and/or creation of data that pass through the ends of a channel, as well as the atomicity, exclusion, order, and/or timing of their passage. Reo places no restriction on the behavior of a channel and thus allows an open-ended set of different channel types to be used simultaneously together.

A very small set of channels, each with very simple behavior, suffices to construct useful Reo connectors with significantly complex behavior. Figure 2 shows a common set of primitive channels often used to build Reo connectors. Readers can find intuitive and formal definitions of the behavior of these channels in various Reo literature, e.g. [7].

Nodes. Complex connectors are constructed by composing simpler ones by *joining* channel ends together in *nodes*. A Reo node is a logical place where channel ends coincide and coordinate their dataflows as prescribed by the *type* of the node. Figure 3 shows the three possible node types in Reo. A node is either *source*, *sink*, or *mixed*, depending on whether all its coincident channel ends consist of source ends, sink ends, or a combination of the two. Unlike channels, Reo defines a fixed semantics for (i.e., the constraints on the dataflow through) its nodes.

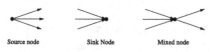

Fig. 3. Reo nodes

The source and sink nodes of a connector are collectively called its *boundary nodes*. Boundary nodes define the interface of a connector. Components attach to the boundary nodes of a connector and interact anonymously via the `get` and `put` operations mentioned in Sect. 5 with each other through this interface.

Semantics. Reo allows arbitrary user-defined channels as primitives; arbitrary mix of synchrony and asynchrony; and relational constraints between input and output. This makes Reo more expressive than, e.g., dataflow models, Kahn networks, synchronous languages, stream processing languages, workflow models, and Petri nets. On the other hand, it makes the semantics of Reo quite nontrivial. Various models for the formal semantics of Reo have been developed (most, variants that fall within a small number of main families), each to serve some specific purpose, e.g., animation, verification, and code generation; a comprehensive overview of these semantic models appears elsewhere [34].

7   Examples

Consider a simple concurrent application with two producers, which we designate as Green and Red, and one consumer. We want the consumer to repeatedly obtain and display the data made available by the Green and the Red producers, alternately. In spite of its apparent conciseness, the last sentence does *not* precisely specify a single concrete protocol. In this section, we present a number of protocols to implement different versions of the alternating producers and consumer example. These examples illustrate that using Reo it is trivial to (1) change the protocol of an application, without altering any of its processes, or (2) scale the specification of a protocol to accommodate $k > 2$ producers.

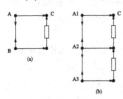

The connector in Fig. 4(a) is an *alternator* that imposes an ordering on the flow of the data from its input nodes A and B to its output node C. Subsequent take operations at C obtain the data items written to $A, B, A, B, ...$ The connector in Fig. 4(b) is obtained by replicating the one in Fig. 4(a). It delivers the data items obtained from $A1$, $A2$, and $A3$, through C, in that order.

Fig. 4. Alternators

We can compose a version of our alternating producers and consumer example by attaching the output ports of the Green and Red producers to nodes A and B of the connector in Fig. 4(a), respectively, and the input port of the consumer to its node C. The protocols of the connectors in Fig. 4 synchronize their producers in each round. Whether or not this is a desirable property, of course, depends on the application. Our original specification of this example allows this protocol, as well as many other alternatives.

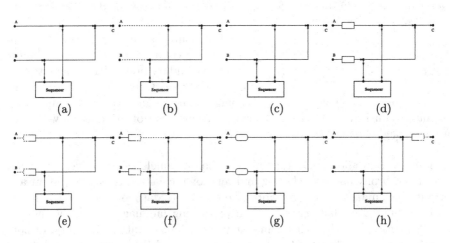

Fig. 5. Variants of alternating producers protocol

We can obtain new versions of our alternating producers and consumer example by attaching the ports of our producers and consumer to nodes A, B, and C of every connector in Fig. 5. All connectors in this figure share the same skeleton structure, based on a two-node version of a *sequencer* connector. Detailed description of the sequencer and these connectors is beyond the scope of this paper. What matters for our discussion is that there are at least these other 8 different concrete protocols each of which with its own properties, that can serve as a suitable solution for an alternating producers and consumer application. We can easily parameterize any of these connectors to scale up the number of their producers.

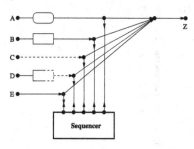

Fig. 6. Mix and match

Applications with many producers may indeed require somewhat different treatment of the output of some of their producers. It is trivial to mix-and-match the necessary interaction (sub-)protocols in Fig. 5, to tailor-make such a protocol, e.g., as in the example in Fig. 6. Such mix-and-match is generally unthinkable when protocols are expressed in terms of action-centric constructs of traditional models of concurrency.

8 Compilation

The examples in Sect. 7 exhibit the advantages of an interaction-centric model of concurrency that regards protocols as constraints. A high-level language like Reo that supports this form of protocol specification offers clear software engineering advantages (e.g., programmability, maintainability, verbatim-reusability, verifiability, etc.). However, as in constraint programming, it seems far less obvious that protocol specifications expressed in such a high-level language can be compiled into efficient and scalable executable code.

Recent results of our on-going work suggest that in time, sufficiently smart compilers for high-level protocol languages can generate executable code with better performance than hand-crafted code produced by programmers written in contemporary general-purpose languages with constructs of traditional models of concurrency. Superficially, our promising results may seem surprising and this claim, outlandish. Most of our results have already appeared in the literature [33, 35–43] and comprise the bulk of the work by Jongmans in his recently submitted PhD thesis [44]. Without getting into the technical details of how we obtained these results or the challenges that remain ahead, in this section, we summarize some of our results, and in the next section, describe a perspective on concurrent programming that "anticipates" our promising results and justifies the optimism of our claim.

Our compiler uses the constraint automata semantics of Reo [12]. It maps every node and every channel in a Reo connector to its corresponding constraint automaton. This yields a set of "small" automata that collectively represent the connector's semantics. The compiler then translates this set of small automata into Java/C and merges the code so generated with the Java/C code that invoke the components. An external compiler for Java/C subsequently translates the full code base into a binary. Our Reo compiler currently applies a set of high-level optimization techniques on the intermediate constraint automata it produces. Some basic optimization methods identify groups of loosely- and tightly-coupled small automata in order to improve scalability and strike a balance between low latency (sequentiality) and high throughput (parallelism) in the resulting executable code.

For some protocols, these optimizations already allow our compiler to generate code that can compete with code written by a competent programmer [39]. Figure 7 shows one of our most promising results. It shows the performance of three implementations of a k-producers-single-consumer protocol, for $k \in \{2^i \mid 2 \leq i \leq 9\}$: one naive hand-written implementation in C (blue, solid line), one hand-crafted optimized implementation in C (yellow, dashed line), and one implementation expressed in Reo and compiled into C (red, dotted line). In every round of this protocol, every producer sends one datum to the consumer. Once the consumer has received a datum from every producer, in any order, it sends an acknowledgment to the producers, thereby signaling that the consumer is ready for the next round. To measure just the performance of the protocol, we did not give the producers and the consumers real computational tasks (i.e., the producers sent only dummy data).

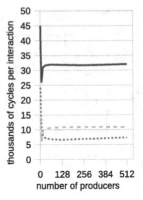

Fig. 7. Performance (Color figure online)

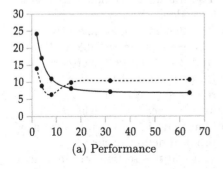

(a) Performance

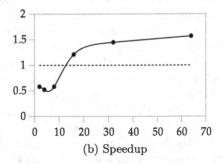

(b) Speedup

Fig. 8. Comparing hand-crafted (dashed) and Reo compiler generated (solid) protocol code: (a) thousands of CPU-cycles per protocol iteration vs. number of producers; (b) relative performance vs. number of producers.

In fact, this version of our compiler generates code that runs on the *Proto Runtime Toolkit* (PRT) [27,28]. PRT offers a run-time system for C code and a set of APIs. On its start-up, the PRT run-time system seizes control of the available cores from the operating system, thereby gaining full responsibility for scheduling instructions onto those cores. Software engineers use these cores through an API for managing PRT threads and a separate API for imposing custom scheduling policies. PRT-aware C code invokes the former API to instantiate units of parallelism, which the PRT run-time system subsequently schedules onto cores, without interference by the operating system. Bypassing the operating system (and its rather heavy-weight scheduler) in this way, contributes to better performance. However, programming efficiently, directly at the level of PRT requires special skills. The PRT back-end of our Reo compiler shields programmers from PRT and its details, but reaps the benefits of improved performance that it provides, through a PRT API custom-made for Reo.

Figure 8 shows at a finer scale the performance and speedup of our Reo compiler generated code with that of a carefully optimized hand-written code using p-threads in C, for the above mentioned k-producers-single-consumer protocol. Figure 8(a) shows performance (in thousands of CPU-cycles per iteration of protocol, averaged over 10 runs) of the compiler generated (solid line) and the hand-crafted (dashed line) code as a function of the number of producers in this application. Figure 8(b) shows speedup of the compiler generated relative to the hand-crafted code as a function of number of producers.

These results show that already our current compilation technology is capable of generating code that can compete with—and in this case even outperform—carefully hand-crafted code. Surely, our technology is not yet mature enough to always achieve such positive results. The PhD thesis of Jongmans [44] discusses a number of formally sound high-level automata optimization techniques and contains extensive comparisons of our Reo compiler technology using the NAS Parallel Benchmarks [13]. His results demonstrate practical utility of verbatim reuse of protocols. They also show that in 37 % of cases our Reo compiler generated code is no worse than 10 % slower than the reference hand-crafted code of these benchmarks. In another 38 % of cases, our Reo compiler generated code is faster than their reference hand-crafted code. In the remaining 25 % of the cases, our Reo compiler generated code is between 10 % and 40 % slower. Some of these cases may improve by one or more of the many other high-level optimization techniques that we have not investigated yet. Nevertheless, these results offer preliminary evidence that programming concurrency protocols using high-level, interaction-centric constructs and abstractions can result in equally good—or better—performance as compared to hand-crafted code using conventional action-centric models of concurrency. Superficially, these results seem counter-intuitive. In the next section, we explain why, in fact, they are not.

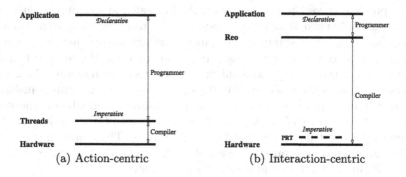

(a) Action-centric   (b) Interaction-centric

Fig. 9. Action-centric vs. interaction-centric protocol programming

9   Mind the Gap

Figure 9(a) shows three levels of abstraction of the protocol of a concurrent program. At the application level a protocol primarily expresses *what* it needs to accomplish, which essentially has a declarative nature. As an implementation in a conventional action-centric model of concurrency in a modern programming language, this protocol, for instance, turns into imperatives that control the scheduling of threads. Obviously, these imperatives must be refined into finer-grained imperatives of machine instructions before the application can actually execute on some hardware.

Figure 9(a), thus, shows that two transformations must take place before a specification of what a protocol needs to accomplish can actually run on some hardware: (1) translation by the programmer from the specification of *what* into the imperatives of *how*, e.g., expressed using the API of some threading library, and (2) translation by the compiler (of a conventional language) from the resulting threading API calls into executable machine instructions.

The distance between a pair of levels of abstraction in this figure suggests the complexity of abstraction/refinement transformation between them. One can, for instance, use the ratio of the number of lines of "code" that it takes to specify a protocol at each level of abstraction, and the mutual interdependence of these lines as a crude measure for this complexity. For example, the translation of an API call by the compiler of a conventional programming language into executable code may produce many lines of low-level code, but each such translation is quite straight-forward and the lines of code that result from two API calls essentially do not depend on each other (any more than the original two API calls did). As such, for instance, a C compiler contributes relatively little to the refinement into executable code of the protocol part of an application that is already expressed in terms of some threading API calls, as compared with the complexity of the refinement that the programmer performs, in order to transform the application-level specification of the protocol into precisely those specific threading API calls.

Programming of concurrency protocols is notoriously difficult precisely because the gap between the two levels of abstraction that specify what a protocol must accomplish and the imperatives that state how, represents a chasm of complexity. Programmers must navigate through this chasm essentially on their own, to produce *correct* imperative code. Additionally, programmers must also strive to manually make their correct code *efficient* too. And to reap the benefits of Gustafson's law, increasingly, programmers must also ensure that their correct, efficient code is *scalable* as well. These requirements make the manual translation of what a protocol must accomplish into how to do so imperatively, a very tall order that often frazzles even expert programmers. Because this translation substantially takes place in the mind of a programmer, even when it succeeds, it leaves no formal trace of its steps in the resulting code, from which a tool can subsequently reconstruct this translation or its inverse. Thus, the *intention* contained in *what* a protocol must achieve and the information about its translation into *how* its implementation does so are irrecoverably lost.

Imagine for a moment that instead of concurrency protocols we deal with our more familiar sequential programs, and consider an example of sorting an array of integers. A programmer may take this requirement (sort an array of integers) and produce a correct piece of code, written in a sequential language X. Assume that this code in fact implements a bubble-sort algorithm, perhaps because the programmer does not know any better sort algorithms. A compiler for X can do its best to generate optimized code for this program. However, can such a compiler look at all assignment, if-then-else, and for-loop constructs in its input, to divine from this jumble of source code that its programmer really intended to sort this array, and thus "compile" the bubble-sort algorithm that it finds in its input into the machine code for a quick-sort algorithm? Even if this transformation were theoretically possible, would it be desirable for a compiler to do so? After all, perhaps our programmer *did* actually know better and had a very good reason—unknowable to the compiler—to want a bubble-sort algorithm in this application.

Back to our concurrency protocol in Fig. 9(a), the fact that the programmer manually endeavors to translate what a protocol must accomplish into how to do so utilizing the low-level imperatives of an action-centric model, leaves relatively little wiggle room for the compiler to do significantly meaningful optimization *of the protocol*: following our sort analogy, above, it can optimize the implementation of each imperative, but it cannot compile its input imperatives of a "bubble-sort protocol" into the machine code for a "quick-sort" alternative protocol. Doing so requires a compiler to trace back the irrecoverable mental translation steps that the programmer took to produce its source code in the opposite direction, to divine the application level intention of the protocol; something of questionable desirability, even if theoretically possible.

Figure 9(b) shows the three levels of abstraction of the protocol of a concurrent program using an interaction-centric model of concurrency, such as Reo. The declarative, compositional constraint-programming style of protocol specification in Reo shrinks the gap between *what* a protocol must accomplish and its formal specification. As our examples demonstrate, this smaller gap makes it easier for a programmer to construct modular, verifiable, reusable, and scalable protocol specifications by composition. The programmer can now merely specify *what* (i.e., "sort") formally, instead of over-specifying *how* (i.e., "bubble-sort"), imperatively.[3] Shrinking the first gap also leaves much larger room in the second gap for a compiler to perform meaningful protocol optimization. In spite of its infancy, our compiler technology for Reo already demonstrates the practical feasibility of such meaningful optimization in our current results.

The specific version of the Reo compiler used in the benchmarks depicted in Figs. 7 and 8, generates C code that uses the API provided by the PRT system mentioned in Sect. 8. Thus, although this version of our Reo compiler does not generate object code that directly runs on the bare hardware, it indirectly does so assisted by the C compiler and the PRT run-time. We ignore this technical

---

[3] Of course, by adding extra "redundant" constraints, a programmer can also "specify" a bubble-sort, when and if desired.

detail in Fig. 9(b), because whether "compiler" in this figure designates a single Reo compiler or consists of a chain of automated tools does not change the point of our current discussion. However, for clarity, the dashed line in Fig. 9(b) shows the actual target level of abstraction of the concurrency constructs used in the C code generated by the version of our Reo compiler used in the above benchmarks: the PRT API. With respect to the other main levels of abstraction in this figure, PRT sits below the operating system, closer to the hardware, and offers concurrency constructs at a lower level of abstraction than that of operating system supported threading and scheduling facilities.

Fair Gain. A superficial reading of the "performance comparison" depicted in Figs. 7 and 8 may seem to reveal as much about the effectiveness of our optimization techniques, as it does about the competency of the C programmer who produced the hand-crafted version of the protocol code of this application. However, below this surface, lies a more crucial fundamental point that is independent of the competency of any individual programmer, or the precise factor by which our optimization techniques potentially can or currently do outperform hand-crafted code that a programmer can (even hypothetically) produce.

Crucial to this benchmark is the fact that the task assigned to the programmer restricted him to use concurrency constructs available in contemporary programming languages, such as Java or C (in this case p-threads). On the other hand, our Reo compiler in this case bypasses this level of abstraction (and the coarser-grained, OS-level scheduling inefficiencies that it entails) and generates code using finer-grained constructs *below* the OS-level and the concurrency constructs that it supports. From this perspective, comparing the performance of the two versions of the code is even unfair, because the statement of the task assignment prevents the programmer from using lower-level constructs to directly hand-craft code similar to (or perhaps better than) what our Reo compiler produces. But precisely this *unfairness* constitutes the crux of our argument in this section.

There are two conceivable ways to make such a comparison fair, i.e., produce code using constructs that are "fairly comparable" to the constructs that our Reo compiler uses to produces its code: (1) develop tools that take p-threads level code written by a programmer and produce more optimized code; or (2) allow the programmer to directly code below the level of p-threads and OS.

Option 1 requires developing tools that can reconstruct the intentions behind the p-threads constructs used to encode a protocol (fragment); i.e., divine programmer's intention of "sort" from an imperative "bubble-sort" implementation code. Generally, this is impossible because the information about the mental transformation of *what* a protocol does into *how* it does it is irrecoverably lost. For instance, consider the piece of C code on the left. If its programmer intended *just* to assign the output of some_function to every a[i], for random inputs x, a compiler can parallelize the loop. However, if the programmer *additionally* intended the resulting array to have the same content, with the same random seed, in different executions (e.g., to reproduce bugs), a compiler cannot parallelize the loop: in that case, the order of generating random numbers matters. Observe that from this code alone, neither a compiler *nor a human* can judiciously decide about loop parallelization; making such a decision requires *intention* information irrecoverable from this code.

```
int x;
for (int i = 0; i < 10; i++) {
    x = rand();
    a[i] = some_function(x);
    // without side effects
}
```

Option 2, i.e., removing the artificial barrier of programming at the level of p-threads, is certainly possible. However, manually programming below p-threads and OS-level sharply raises the level of expertise required by a programmer to code directly at such a low level, and dramatically increases the size and the complexity of the resulting code. Higher competency requirements and increased size and complexity of the resulting code, in turn, sharply reduce the number of individuals who qualify to perform such programming assignments, and dramatically lower the likelihood of success of those who undertake such daunting tasks. Besides, applications that directly use constructs below p-threads or OS abstractions become highly brittle and non-portable, as they rely on constructs that most likely do not exist verbatim on other platforms, or even on a future upgrade of their original platforms. Of course, the above drawbacks of producing programs at a level below p-threads and OS abstractions become moot if instead of a human programmer, a compiler performs this programming, starting with some high-level protocol specification.

While option 1, in principle, involves divining lost information, option 2 does not involve theoretical impossibilities; the difficulties in option 2 are "merely" technical and pragmatic. Our Reo compiler automates some of the technicalities involved in bypassing conventional concurrency constructs, making it more pragmatic to go from a high-level declarative specification of a *what* to a very efficient *how*-implementation below the level of p-threads or OS.

10   Concluding Remarks

Protocols constitute the most challenging aspect of concurrent applications. Specification of a protocol in action-centric models of concurrency invariably obscures what the protocol must achieve, because they lack mechanisms to forbid or even discourage dispersing constituent constructs of a protocol throughout an application software. Such dispersion intertwines protocol constructs with other data- and control-flow constructs of the application, which obfuscates the protocol, making it only an intangible by-product, implied by some sets of nebulous, logically-related-but-physically-scattered communication actions.

An increasingly important class of concurrent applications demand analysis, verification, reuse, composition, and scaling of protocols. Meeting the software engineering challenges of these applications requires definition and manipulation of protocols as proper mathematical objects, with composition and other operators to work with them. As a prime example of an interaction-centric model of concurrency, Reo can meet these challenges. Specification of protocols as declarative constraints in Reo makes them easier to manipulate and analyze directly, and makes it possible to compose protocols, scale, and reuse them verbatim.

The results of our ongoing work on compiling Reo suggest that, in addition to software engineering advantages, a high-level protocol language, such as Reo, can have advantages with respect to performance as well. Superficially, obtaining executable code that outperforms hand-crafted code, from the compiler of such a high-level protocol language seems counter-intuitive: one expects to pay the price of easier specification at a higher-level of abstraction, plus the software engineering benefits that it entails, by accepting a heavy penalty in performance. The perspective we described in this paper explains why avoiding such a performance penalty seems possible: compilers for such high-level languages can use formal information about what a protocol must achieve, to perform optimizations that compilers for lower-level languages cannot apply, simply because manual transformation by programmers irrecoverably loses such intention information.

References

1. Extensible Coordination Tools home page. http://reo.project.cwi.nl/cgibin/trac. cgi/reo/wiki/Tools
2. Reo home page. http://reo.project.cwi.nl
3. Agha, G.: Actors: A Model of Concurrent Computation in Distributed Systems. MIT Press, Cambridge (1986)
4. Amdahl, G.M.: Validity of the single processor approach to achieving large scale computing capabilities. In: American Federation of Information Processing Societies: Proceedings of the AFIPS 1967 Spring Joint Computer Conference, 18–20 April 1967, Atlantic City, New Jersey, USA. AFIPS Conference Proceedings, vol. 30, pp. 483–485. AFIPS/ACM/Thomson Book Company, Washington D.C. (1967)
5. Arbab, F.: Reo: a channel-based coordination model for component composition. Math. Struct. Comput. Sci. 14(3), 329–366 (2004)
6. Arbab, F.: Abstract behavior types: a foundation model for components and their composition. Sci. Comput. Program. 55(1–3), 3–52 (2005)
7. Arbab, F.: Puff, the magic protocol. In: Agha, G., Danvy, O., Meseguer, J. (eds.) Formal Modeling: Actors, Open Systems, Biological Systems. LNCS, vol. 7000, pp. 169–206. Springer, Heidelberg (2011)
8. Arbab, F., Mavaddat, F.: Coordination through channel composition. In: Arbab, F., Talcott, C. (eds.) COORDINATION 2002. LNCS, vol. 2315, pp. 22–39. Springer, Heidelberg (2002)
9. Arvind, Gostelow, K.P., Plouffe, W.: Indeterminacy, monitors, and dataflow. In: Rosen, S., Denning, P.J. (eds.) Proceedings of the Sixth Symposium on Operating System Principles, SOSP 1977, Purdue University, West Lafayette, Indiana, USA, 16–18 November 1977, pp. 159–169. ACM (1977)
10. Attie, P., Baranov, E., Bliudze, S., Jaber, M., Sifakis, J.: A general framework for architecture composability. In: Giannakopoulou, D., Salaün, G. (eds.) SEFM 2014. LNCS, vol. 8702, pp. 128–143. Springer, Heidelberg (2014)
11. Baeten, J.C.M., Weijland, W.P.: Process Algebra. Cambridge University Press, New York (1990)
12. Baier, C., Sirjani, M., Arbab, F., Rutten, J.: Modeling component connectors in Reo by constraint automata. Sci. Comput. Program. 61(2), 75–113 (2006)

13. Bailey, D.H., Barszcz, E., Barton, J.T., Browning, D.S., Carter, R.L., Dagum, L., Fatoohi, R.A., Frederickson, P.O., Lasinski, T.A., Schreiber, R., Simon, H.D., Venkatakrishnan, V., Weeratunga, S.: The NAS parallel benchmarks. IJHPCA 5(3), 63–73 (1991)

14. Basu, A., Bozga, M., Sifakis, J.: Modeling heterogeneous real-time components in BIP. In: Proceedings of SEFM 2006, pp. 3–12. IEEE (2006)

15. Benveniste, A., Caspi, P., Le Guernic, P., Halbwachs, N.: Data-flow synchronous languages. In: de Bakker, J.W., de Roever, W.-P., Rozenberg, G. (eds.) REX 1993. LNCS, vol. 803, pp. 1–45. Springer, Heidelberg (1994)

16. Bergstra, J.A., Klop, J.W.: Process algebra for synchronous communication. Inf. Control 60, 109–137 (1984)

17. Berry, G.: Esterel and Jazz: two synchronous languages for circuit design. In: Pierre, L., Kropf, T. (eds.) CHARME 1999. LNCS, vol. 1703, p. 1. Springer, Heidelberg (1999)

18. Dean Brock, J., Ackerman, W.B.: Scenarios: a model of non-determinate computation. In: Díaz, J., Ramos, I. (eds.) Formalization of Programming Concepts. LNCS, vol. 107, pp. 252–259. Springer, Heidelberg (1981)

19. Buck, J.T., Ha, S., Lee, E.A., Messerschmitt, D.G.: Ptolemy: a framework for simulating and prototyping heterogenous systems. Int. J. Comput. Simul. 4(2), 155–182 (1994)

20. Carbone, M., Yoshida, N., Honda, K.: Asynchronous session types: exceptions and multiparty interactions. In: Bernardo, M., Padovani, L., Zavattaro, G. (eds.) SFM 2009. LNCS, vol. 5569, pp. 187–212. Springer, Heidelberg (2009)

21. Caspi, P., Pilaud, D., Halbwachs, N., Plaice, J.: Lustre: a declarative language for programming synchronous systems. In: Conference Record of the Fourteenth Annual ACM Symposium on Principles of Programming Languages, Munich, Germany, 21–23 January 1987, pp. 178–188. ACM Press (1987)

22. Dennis, J.B., Gao, G.R.: An efficient pipelined dataflow processor architecture. In: Michael, G.A. (ed.) Proceedings Supercomputing 1988, Orlando, FL, USA, 12–17 November 1988, pp. 368–373. IEEE Computer Society (1988)

23. Fokkink, W.: Introduction to Process Algebra. Texts in Theoretical Computer Science, An EATCS Series. Springer, Heidelberg (1999)

24. Gautier, T., Le Guernic, P., Besnard, L.: SIGNAL: a declarative language for synchronous programming of real-time systems. In: Kahn, G. (ed.) Functional Programming Languages and Computer Architecture. LNCS, vol. 274, pp. 257–277. Springer, Heidelberg (1987)

25. González-Vélez, H., Leyton, M.: A survey of algorithmic skeleton frameworks: high-level structured parallel programming enablers. Softw. Pract. Exper. 40(12), 1135–1160 (2010)

26. Gustafson, J.L.: Reevaluating Amdahl's law. Commun. ACM 31(5), 532–533 (1988)

27. Halle, S.: A Study of Frameworks for Collectively Meeting the Productivity, Portability, and Adoptability Goals for Parallel Software. Ph.D. thesis, University of California, Santa Cruz (2011)

28. Halle, S., Cohen, A.: A mutable hardware abstraction to replace threads. In: Rajopadhye, S., Mills Strout, M. (eds.) LCPC 2011. LNCS, vol. 7146, pp. 185–202. Springer, Heidelberg (2013)

29. Herlihy, M., Moss, J.E.B.: Transactional memory: architectural support for lock-free data structures. SIGARCH Comput. Archit. News 21(2), 289–300 (1993)

30. Hoare, C.A.R.: Communicating Sequential Processes. Prentice-Hall, Upper Saddle River (1985)

31. Honda, K., Mukhamedov, A., Brown, G., Chen, T.-C., Yoshida, N.: Scribbling interactions with a formal foundation. In: Natarajan, R., Ojo, A. (eds.) ICDCIT 2011. LNCS, vol. 6536, pp. 55–75. Springer, Heidelberg (2011)

32. Honda, K., Yoshida, N., Carbone, M.: Multiparty asynchronous session types. In: Necula, G.C., Wadler, P. (eds.) Proceedings of the 35th ACM SIGPLAN-SIGACT Symposium on Principles of Programming Languages, POPL 2008, San Francisco, California, USA, 7–12 January 2008, pp. 273–284. ACM (2008)

33. Jongmans, S.-S., Arbab, F.: Global consensus through local synchronization: a formal basis for partially-distributed coordination. Sci. Comput. Program. **115–116**, 199–224 (2016)

34. Jongmans, S.-S., Arbab, F.: Overview of thirty semantic formalisms for Reo. Sci. Ann. Comput. Sci. **22**(1), 201–251 (2012)

35. Jongmans, S.-S.T.Q., Arbab, F.: Global consensus through local synchronization. In: Canal, C., Villari, M. (eds.) ESOCC 2013. CCIS, vol. 393, pp. 174–188. Springer, Heidelberg (2013)

36. Jongmans, S.-S., Arbab, F.: Modularizing and specifying protocols among threads. In: Proceedings of PLACES 2012. EPTCS, vol. 109, pp. 34–45. CoRR (2013)

37. Jongmans, S.-S., Arbab, F.: Toward sequentializing overparallelized protocol code. In: Proceedings of ICE 2014, EPTCS, vol. 166, pp. 38–44. CoRR (2014)

38. Jongmans, S.-S.T.Q., Halle, S., Arbab, F.: Automata-based optimization of interaction protocols for scalable multicore platforms. In: Kühn, E., Pugliese, R. (eds.) COORDINATION 2014. LNCS, vol. 8459, pp. 65–82. Springer, Heidelberg (2014)

39. Jongmans, S.-S., Halle, S., Arbab, F.: Reo: a dataflow inspired language for multicore. In: Proceedings of DFM 2013, pp. 42–50. IEEE (2014)

40. Jongmans, S.-S., Santini, F., Arbab, F.: Partially-distributed coordination with Reo. In: Proceedings of PDP 2014, pp. 697–706. IEEE (2014)

41. Jongmans, S.-S., Santini, F., Sargolzaei, M., Arbab, F., Afsarmanesh, H.: Orchestrating web services using Reo: from circuits and behaviors to automatically generated code. SOCA **8**(4), 277–297 (2014)

42. Jongmans, S.-S.T.Q., Arbab, F.: Can high throughput atone for high latency in compiler-generated protocol code? In: Dastani, M., Sirjani, M. (eds.) FSEN 2015. LNCS, vol. 9392, pp. 238–258. Springer, Heidelberg (2015)

43. Jongmans, S.-S.T.Q., Santini, F., Arbab, F.: Partially distributed coordination with Reo and constraint automata. SOCA **9**(3–4), 311–339 (2015)

44. Jongmans, S.-S.T.Q.: Automata-Theoretic Protocol Programming: Parallel Computation, Threads and Their Interaction, Optimized Compilation, [at a] High Level of Abstraction. Ph.D. thesis, Leiden University (2015, submitted)

45. Kahn, G.: The semantics of a simple language for parallel programming. In: Rosenfeld, J.L. (ed.) Information Processing, pp. 471–475. North Holland, Amsterdam (1974)

46. Kahn, G., MacQueen, D.B.: Coroutines and networks of parallel processes. In: IFIP Congress, pp. 993–998 (1977)

47. Knight, T.: An architecture for mostly functional languages. In: Proceedings of the 1986 ACM Conference on LISP and Functional Programming, LFP 1986, pp. 105–112. ACM, New York (1986)

48. Liu, X., Xiong, Y., Lee, E.A.: The ptolemy II framework for visual languages. In: 2002 IEEE CS International Symposium on Human-Centric Computing Languages and Environments (HCC 2001), 5–7 September 2001, Stresa, Italy, p. 50. IEEE Computer Society (2001)

49. Milner, R.: A Calculus of Communicating Systems. LNCS, vol. 92. Springer, Heidelberg (1980)

50. Milner, R.: Elements of interaction - turing award lecture. Commun. ACM **36**(1), 78–89 (1993)
51. Ng, N., de Figueiredo Coutinho, J.G., Yoshida, N.: Protocols by default - safe MPI code generation based on session types. In: Franke, B. (ed.) CC 2015. LNCS, vol. 9031, pp. 212–232. Springer, Heidelberg (2015)
52. Ng, N., Yoshida, N.: Pabble: parameterised scribble for parallel programming. In: 22nd Euromicro International Conference on Parallel, Distributed, and Network-Based Processing, PDP 2014, Torino, Italy, 12–14 February 2014, pp. 707–714. IEEE Computer Society (2014)
53. Sangiorgi, D., Walker, D.: Pi-Calculus: A Theory of Mobile Processes. Cambridge University Press, New York (2001)
54. Shavit, N., Touitou, D.: Software transactional memory. In: Proceedings of the Fourteenth Annual ACM Symposium on Principles of Distributed Computing, PODC 1995, pp. 204–213. ACM, New York (1995)
55. Yoshida, N., Hu, R., Neykova, R., Ng, N.: The scribble protocol language. In: Abadi, M., Lluch Lafuente, A. (eds.) TGC 2013. LNCS, vol. 8358, pp. 22–41. Springer, Heidelberg (2014)

A Compositional Approach to the Verification of Hybrid Systems

Lăcrămioara Aştefănoaei[1]([⊠]), Saddek Bensalem[2], and Marius Bozga[2]

[1] fortiss - An-Institut TUM, Guerickestr. 25, 80805 München, Germany
astefanoaei@fortiss.org
[2] UJF-Grenoble, CNRS VERIMAG UMR 5104, 38041 Grenoble, France

Abstract. The increase of complexity in modelling systems and the chances of success when model-checking them tend to be inversely proportional. This mere observation justifies plainly the need to investigate alternative ways for verification. In this paper we present such an alternative which uses a compositional verification rule. The basic idea is to automatically compute local properties and combine them such that together they are strong enough to prove global safety properties of systems. In [2] we showed how such a rule works in the framework of timed systems with a fixed number of components and in [3] how the whole approach can be extended to the parameterised case. The application of the compositional verification rule can be pushed even further with respect to two directions: (1) hybrid and (2) parametric systems. This is the subject of the present paper.

1 Introduction

This paper spiraled from three concepts: *compositionality, safety* and *hybrid systems*. On compositionality, we would like to recall a short text from Dijkstra's "On Understanding Programs":

> *On a number of occasions I have stated the requirement that if we ever want to be able to compose really large programs reliably, we need a discipline such that the intellectual effort E (measured in some loose sense) needed to understand a program does not grow more rapidly than proportional to the program length L (measured in an equally loose sense) and that if the best we can attain is a growth of E proportional to, say L^2, we had better admit defeat. As an aside I used to express my fear that many programs were written in such a fashion that the functional dependence was more like an exponential growth.*

Despite being frequently used over the years, we feel that the fragment in particular and Dijkstra's remarks in general have not lost their savoury and charm.

Compositionality and safety, together with time, have already been the main characters in our previous work [2,3] where we orchestrated a compositional method for verifying timed automata. *Timed automata* is an expressive formalism for modelling timing constraints. It would be not an easy task to ignore

E. Ábrahám et al. (Eds.): de Boer Festschrift, LNCS 9660, pp. 88–103, 2016.
DOI: 10.1007/978-3-319-30734-3_8

"time" as a less important concept. Deadlines, delays... are everywhere. Correct scheduling, to name but one time related application, is crucial for critical systems. In this paper we propose to go a bit further, to the "realm of hybridity" and show how our method scales to the verification of state safety properties in the context of *(parametric) hybrid systems* interacting by means of multi-party interactions. This is just but a first step in a more ambitious project on verifying programable controller programs (PLCs) in the context of cyber-physical systems in the domain of industrial automation. "Cyber-physical systems" is all about interconnecting devices, sensors, actuators, all of these being distributed. Such dynamic systems with both discrete and continuous components fit well the class of hybrid systems: PLCs play the role of discrete components while the external environment sensed or impacted by devices such as valves, sensors, or activators exhibits a continuous behaviour. Lately, results on the application of hybrid systems are documented in projects such as COMPASS[1], Veriware[2], or in CPS-VO groups such as ARCH[3] and UncoVerCPS[4] to name but a few. These recent successes suggest that the use of the formalism in industry is growing and this brings opportunities for verification to be put into practice especially in domains where safety is a most critical aspect. We note that, in academia, the verification of hybrid systems has been studied since the early nineties. Central to verification, the reachability problem has been shown to be undecidable for hybrid automata except for few cases such as variations on timed automata and we refer to [23] as a classical reference. Nevertheless, this is not a reason to discourage as by means of abstraction, the fixpoint computation behind reachability converges and in fact there is quite a variety of approaches and tools for model-checking [8–10,12,15–17,19,21,30–32,37,41,42], to cite the most recent results. Compositional approaches are fewer. The relevant references we are aware of are [6,14,18,24,26,29,39] and they are either based on assume guarantee or rely on user interaction as it is the case with the interactive prover KeYmaera [29,39]. Consequently, we find that it is worth-while investigating *automatic* compositional approaches and this offers us enough justification to motivate our work. Our methodology follows the one introduced in [2]. The building blocks can be summed up as the following steps:

- generate local invariants for individual components as over approximations of their symbolic state space (possibly in a property-driven manner *à la* IC3 [40])
- generate interaction invariants to express relations between the different components and/or auxiliary variables
- assemble all invariants into one formula (possibly quantify it existentially on unknown parameters), and feed it to the SMT-solver Z3 [35].

We emphasise that all the computations are completely automatic. We note that these basic building blocks are not new. The novelty is more in bringing them

---

[1] compass.informatik.rwth-aachen.de.

[2] veriware.org.

[3] cps-vo.org/group/ARCH.

[4] cps-vo.org/group/UnCoVerCPS.

together in a coherent methodology. Its simplicity should encourage its use as especially a preliminary step in verification. Behind "preliminary" is the fact that our method is sound, but not complete. Consequently, if Z3, when given as input the formula corresponding to our verification rule, yields "no solution", or in other words, that the "bad" states are not reachable, then we are done. Otherwise, auxiliary techniques, as for instance, counterexample refinement, are needed to prove the system safe.

Organisation of the Paper. Section 2 recalls the classical definitions used in our framework. Section 3 presents how to effectively verify linear hybrid systems compositionally. Section 4 discusses extensions and Sect. 5 concludes.

2   Model

In our setup, components are linear hybrid automata and systems are compositions of components with respect to multi-party interactions. The definitions for hybrid automata are adopted from [1,21]. Before recalling them, we first fix some notation.

We use $\mathcal{X}$ to denote real-valued variables. A valuation $\mathbf{v}$ is a function that assigns a real-value $\mathbf{v}(x) \in \mathbb{R}$ to each variable $x \in \mathcal{X}$. It is useful to note that a valuation $\mathbf{v}$ can be identified with the point $(\mathbf{v}(x_1), \ldots, \mathbf{v}(x_n)) \in \mathbb{R}^n$. We denote by $\mathbf{V}$ the set of valuations. Given a set of variables $\mathcal{X}$, a linear inequality has the form $\sum_{i=1}^{n} \alpha_i x_i \# \beta_i$ with $x_i \in \mathcal{X}$, $\alpha_i, \beta \in \mathbb{Z}$, $\# \in \{<, \leq, =, \geq, >\}$. A convex linear constraint is a finite conjunction of linear inequalities. The set of convex linear constraints over $\mathcal{X}$ is denoted by $\mathcal{L}(\mathcal{X})$. The geometrical interpretation of a convex linear constraint is that of as a convex polyhedron.

Definition 1. *A component is a hybrid automaton $(L, l_0, \mathcal{X}, A, T, \mathsf{tpc}, \mathcal{D})$ where:*

- *L is a finite set of locations and l_0 is an initial location;*
- *$\mathcal{X}$ is a finite set of real-valued variables;*
- *A a finite set of actions;*
- *T is a set of transitions: each transition $\tau = (l, a, g, \mu, l')$ consists of a source location $l \in L$, a target location $l' \in L$, an action $a \in A$, g is a guard condition in $\mathcal{L}(\mathcal{X})$, and a jump relation $\mu \in \mathcal{L}(\mathcal{X} \cup \mathcal{X}')$ with $\mathcal{X}'$ denoting the variables at l';*
- *$\mathsf{tpc} : L \to \mathcal{L}(\mathcal{X})$ assigns a convex linear time progress condition to each location;*
- *$\mathcal{D} : L \to (\mathbb{R}^n \to \mathbb{R}^n)$ assigns activities to each location. The activities D_l describe how the continuous variables evolve within each location l.*

The class of hybrid automata with linear dynamics is called *linear* hybrid automata (LHA). By linear dynamics it is meant that the activities are given by convex linear constraints over the time derivatives of the variables, that is, $\mathcal{D}_l$ is in $\mathcal{L}(\dot{\mathcal{X}})$ for each l in L.

We restrict to linear dynamics for two reasons. The first one is to simplify the presentation: technically, it makes little difference had the dynamics been more complicated. Our second reason is of a more pragmatic type: after investigating the existing tools, the ones answering best our needs handle only LHAs. As a side remark, we note also that though there has been a considerable amount of work and advancement on SMT solvers for nonlinear arithmetics (Z3, SMT-RAT, CVC3, miniSMT, RAHD, hydlogic, dReal, iSAT to name a few cited in [10]), their current performance is still not satisfactory and their scalability is problematic [36].

The semantics of a component B modelled as an LHA $(L, l_0, \mathcal{X}, A, T, \text{tpc}, \mathcal{D})$ is given as a labelled transition system $(Q, A, \rightarrow)$ where $Q \subseteq \{(l, \mathbf{v}) \in L \times \mathbf{V} \mid \mathbf{v} \in \text{tpc}(l)\}$ denotes the states of B and $\rightarrow \subseteq Q \times (A \cup \mathbb{R}_{\geq 0}) \times Q$ denotes the transitions according to the rules:

- $(l, \mathbf{v}) \xrightarrow{\delta} (l, \mathbf{v}')$ if $\exists k \in \mathcal{D}(l).\mathbf{v}' = \mathbf{v} + \delta k$ (time progress);
- $(l, \mathbf{v}) \xrightarrow{a} (l', \mathbf{v}')$ if $(l, (a, g, \mu), l') \in T$, $\mathbf{v} \in g$ and $(\mathbf{v}, \mathbf{v}') \in \mu$ (action step).

Since this semantics yields an infinite state space, to effectively compute the states of a component, symbolic representations are used instead. A symbolic state is a pair (l, ζ) of a location l and a constraint ζ over variables. It has been shown that the reachable states of an LHA can be effectively represented by convex polyhedra [1]. Consequently, the operations corresponding to the delay and action transitions are performed on convex polyhedra rather than on concrete valuations. As discussed in [18], what is crucial is implementing them efficiently. Here, we only recall their definitions from [27] however adapted slightly as in [21]. The operation time_succ for letting time progress within a symbolic state is defined as time_succ$((l, \zeta)) = (l, \zeta \uparrow_q)$ where $\uparrow_q$ is the time-elapse operator defined in turn as follows:

$$\mathbf{v}' \in \zeta \uparrow_q \text{ iff } \exists \mathbf{v} \in \zeta, \delta \in \mathbb{R}_{\geq 0}, k \in \mathcal{D}(l).\mathbf{v}' = \mathbf{v} + \delta k \wedge \mathbf{v}' \in \text{tpc}(l).$$

The successor with respect to a discrete transition $t = (l, (\_, g, \mu), l')$ is defined as disc_succ$(t, (l, \zeta)) = (l', \zeta')$ where

$$\mathbf{v}' \in \zeta' \text{ iff } \exists \mathbf{v} \in \zeta \cap \text{tpc}(l) \cap g.(\mathbf{v}, \mathbf{v}') \in \mu \wedge \mathbf{v}' \in \text{tpc}(l').$$

With these two operations, the successor operator, succ, is defined simply as succ$(t, (l, \zeta)) = \text{time\_succ}(\text{disc\_succ}(t, (l, \zeta)))$.

A symbolic execution of a component starting from a symbolic state s_0 is a sequence of symbolic states $s_0, s_1, \ldots, s_n, \ldots$ such that for any $i > 0$ there exists a transition t for which s_i is succ(t, s_{i-1}).

Given a component B with initial symbolic state s_0 and transitions T, the set of reachable symbolic states $Reach(B)$ is $Reach(s_0)$ where $Reach$ is defined recursively for an arbitrary s as $\{s\} \cup \bigcup_{t \in T} Reach(\text{succ}(t, s))$.

In our framework, components communicate by means of *interactions*, which are synchronisations between their actions. Given n components B_i, $1 \leq i \leq n$, with disjoint sets of actions A_i, an interaction is a subset of actions $\alpha \subseteq \cup_i A_i$ containing at most one action per component, that is, of the form $\alpha = \{a_i\}_{i \in I}$, with $a_i \in A_i$ for all $i \in I \subseteq \{1, \ldots, n\}$. Given a set of interactions $\gamma \subseteq 2^{\cup_i A_i}$, we denote by $Act(\gamma)$ the set of actions involved in γ, that is, $Act(\gamma) = \cup_{\alpha \in \gamma} \alpha$. A *hybrid system* is the composition of components B_i for a set of interactions γ such that $Act(\gamma) = \cup_i A_i$. For n components $B_i = (L_i, l_0^i, \mathcal{X}_i, A_i, T_i, \mathsf{tpc}_i, \mathcal{D}_i)$ with $A_i \cap A_j = \emptyset$, $\mathcal{X}_i \cap \mathcal{X}_j = \emptyset$, for any $i \neq j$, the *composition* $\|_\gamma B_i$ with respect to a set of interactions γ is defined by an LHA $(L, \bar{l}_0, \mathcal{X}, \gamma, T_\gamma, \mathsf{tpc}, \mathcal{D})$ where $\bar{l}_0 = (l_0^1, \ldots, l_0^n)$, $\mathcal{X} = \cup_i \mathcal{X}_i$, $L = \times_i L_i$, $\mathsf{tpc}(\bar{l}) = \cap_i \mathsf{tpc}_i(l_i)$, $\mathcal{D}(l) = \cap_i \mathcal{D}_i(l_i)$ and T_γ is such that for any interaction $\alpha = \{a_i\}_{i \in I}$ we have that $\bar{l} \xrightarrow{\alpha, g, \mu} \bar{l}'$ where $\bar{l} = (l_1, \ldots, l_n)$, $g = \cap_{i \in I} g_i$, $\mu = \cap_{i \in I} \mu_i$, and $\bar{l}'(i) = $ if $(i \notin I)$ l_i else l_i' for $l_i \xrightarrow{a_i, g_i, r_i} l_i'$. In a system $\|_\gamma B_i$ a component B_i can execute action a_i only as part of an interaction α containing it, that is, along with the execution of all other actions from α. This corresponds to the usual notion of multi-party interaction.

Remark 1. Our method being compositional, allowing shared variables is error-prone. Consequently, we require that the sets of local variables are disjoint. However, we note that, in principle, we could deal with a certain "amount" of sharing by adopting a strategy as follows: components share variables in a read-only fashion, while updates can take place in the "owner" component.

Example 1. As a working example we take a classic one, that of a temperature control system which was described first in [28]. We, however, use the model from [1]. The system maintains the coolant temperature inside a reactor tank within given bounds 3 and 15 by moving two rods. When the temperature reaches 15, the controller uses a rod to refrigerate the tank. The temperature rises and decreases at the rate of 6, respectively 2. A rod can be reused only after 6 time units. If the temperature cannot decrease because no rod is available the system is shutdown. Figure 1 shows the corresponding hybrid system with t measuring the temperature and x_0, x_1 the clocks counting the time elapsed since the last use of rod 0 and 1. The set of interactions γ is $\{heat \mid rest_i, cool \mid cool_i\}$ with $i \in \{0, 1\}$. For clarity, the activities and the time progress conditions associated with the locations of the controller are depicted in blue. We denote the trigger for shutdown as $shutdown := (t = 15 \wedge_i x_i < 6)$. We say that the system is *safe* when it is not shutdown and, for the ease of reference, we denote this property by Ψ, i.e., $\Psi := \neg shutdown$.

Remark 2. We note that in [1] the system is presented as one component (representing the composition of the controller and the two rods) while we manually decomposed it into three components. At what extent can such decompositions be automated is a research topic on its own.

The separate executions of the controller and of the rods respectively are as follows:

$$(lc_0, 15 \geq t \geq 0) \xrightarrow{cool} (lc_1, 15 \geq t \geq 3) \xrightarrow{heat} (lc_0, 15 \geq t \geq 3) \qquad (l_{0i}, x_i \geq 6) \xrightarrow{cool_i} (l_{1i}, x_i \geq 6) \xrightarrow{rest_i} (l_{0i}, x_i \geq 0)$$

$$\xrightarrow{cool} \qquad\qquad\qquad\qquad \xrightarrow{cool_i}$$

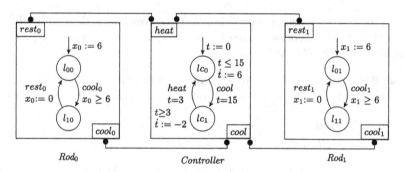

Fig. 1. Temperature controller system (Color figure online)

The executions of the system are longer. For illustration, we show the first three steps as obtained with the tool Hymitator [21]:

$$(lc_0, l_{00}, l_{01}, 15 \geq t \geq 0 \wedge t + 36 = 6x_0 \wedge t + 36 = 6x_1) \xrightarrow{cool | cool_0}$$
$$(lc_1, l_{10}, l_{01}, 15 \geq t \geq 3 \wedge t + 2x_0 = 32 \wedge t + 2x_1 = 32) \xrightarrow{heat | rest_0}$$
$$(lc_0, l_{00}, l_{01}, 15 \geq t \geq 3 \wedge t = 3 + 6x_0 \wedge t + 84 = 6x_1)$$

We note that within these steps the system is safe, and, in fact, it is never the case that the temperature reaches the value 15 with both x_i being less than 6.

3   Compositional Verification

At the heart of our method is the verification rule (VR) from [5]. Its beauty is in its simplicity and genericity. Assume that a system consists of n components B_i interacting by means of an interaction set γ, and that the property that the system should satisfy is Ψ. If components B_i and interactions γ can be locally characterised by means of invariants (here denoted $CI(B_i)$, resp. $II(\gamma)$), and if Ψ can be proved to be a logical consequence of the conjunction of the local invariants, then Ψ is a global invariant. In Fig. 2, the symbol $\vdash$ is used to underline that the logical implication can be effectively proved (for instance with an SMT solver) and the notation "$B \models \Box \Psi$" is to be read as "Ψ holds in every reachable state of B".

Thanks to its genericity, (VR) can be instantiated with respect to different modelling frameworks. In [2] we took timed systems as a case of study. Next, we make the move towards (parametric) hybrid systems.

$$\frac{\vdash \bigwedge_i CI(B_i) \wedge II(\gamma) \rightarrow \Psi}{\|_\gamma B_i \models \Box \Psi} \quad \text{(VR)}$$

Fig. 2. Compositional verification

3.1   Component Invariants

Component invariants characterise the reachable states of components when considered alone. More precisely, given that the set of the reachable symbolic states

(l_j, ζ_j) of an arbitrary component B is finite, its invariant is defined by the disjunction $\vee_j (l_j \wedge \zeta_j)$, where by abuse of notation l_j is used to denote the predicate that holds whenever B is at location l_j.

Example 2. As an illustration, after simplifications, the component invariants for the controller and for the rods from our running example are as follows:

$$CI(\textit{Controller}) = (lc_0 \wedge 15 \geq t \geq 0) \vee (lc_1 \wedge 15 \geq t \geq 3)$$
$$CI(\textit{Rod}_i) = (l_{0i} \wedge x_i \geq 0) \vee (l_{1i} \wedge x_i \geq 6) \tag{1}$$

We note the correspondence between these formulae and the local executions as shown in Sect. 2.

3.2 Interaction Invariants

Interaction invariants are over-approximations of the global state space allowing us to disregard certain tuples of local states as unreachable. Interaction invariants $II(\gamma)$ are induced by the synchronisations and have the form of global conditions involving control locations of components. Previous work considered boolean conditions [5] as well as linear constraints [33] as methods for generating $II(\gamma)$.

Example 3. For simplicity, we show the interaction invariant corresponding to the set of interactions between the controller and rod$_0$:

$$II(\{heat \mid rest_0, cool \mid cool_0\}) = (l_{00} \vee lc_1) \wedge (l_{10} \vee lc_0). \tag{2}$$

The invariant is given in conjunctive normal form to stick to the formalism in [5]. The disjunctions represent the so called "initially marked traps" in a Petri net which corresponds to the synchronisation skeleton of our model. Intuitively, a trap can be seen as a set of places which always contains tokens if they have tokens initially. To better "see" Formula (2), the reader can transform it in disjunctive normal form, and after eliminating conjunctions such as $l_{00} \wedge l_{10}$ (a component cannot be at two locations simultaneously), what remains is the disjunction $(l_{00} \wedge lc_0) \vee (l_{10} \wedge lc_1)$. In this particular case, the invariant is an exact characterisation of the global state space of the untimed (sub)system $Controller \| Rod_0$.

3.3 History Clocks and Auxiliary Constraints

As argued in [2], a direct application of the rule (VR) may be too weak in the sense that the component and the interaction invariants derived from the traps are usually not enough to prove global properties, especially when such properties involve relations between clocks in different components. For instance, in the temperature controller scenario, we cannot show that shutdown does not hold by only having at hand the invariants for components and interactions: any valuation such that $t = 15$ and $x_i < 6$ satisfies $CI(\textit{Controller}) \wedge_i CI(\textit{Rod}_i) \wedge \wedge$ $II(\gamma) \wedge shutdown$. History clocks allow to decouple the analysis for components and for their composition. They make it possible to derive new global constraints from the simultaneity of interactions and the synchrony of time progress.

Adding History Clocks. History clocks are associated with actions and inter-actions. For a component B we use B^h to denote its extension with history clocks. The extension of the system is obtained from the extensions of the components alone together with the history clocks for interactions. As an illustration, Fig. 3 shows the extension of the system in Fig. 1.

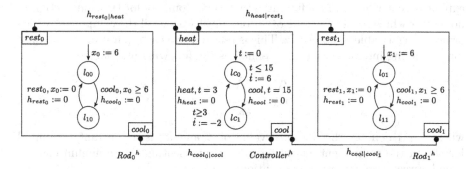

Fig. 3. Illustrating components with history clocks for (Inter)actions

The mechanism of history clocks can be understood as follows. When an interaction α takes place, the history clocks h_α and h_a associated to α and to any action $a \in \alpha$ are reset. Thus they measure the time passed from the last occurrence of α, respectively of a. We note that, since there is no timing constraint involving history clocks, the behaviour of the components is not changed by the addition of history clocks.

Generating Interaction Equalities from History Clocks. The starting point is the following basic fact: a history clock h_a for an action a from a last executed interaction α is necessarily *less* than any h_β with β another interaction containing a. This is because the clocks of the actions in α are the last ones being reset. Consequently, given a common action a of $\alpha_1, \alpha_2, \ldots, \alpha_p$, h_a is the minimum of h_{α_i}, $h_a = \min_{i \in [p]} h_{\alpha_i}$. The resulting invariant for a given interaction set γ is denoted as $\mathcal{E}(\gamma)$ and defined as follows:

$$\mathcal{E}(\gamma) = \bigwedge_{a \in Act(\gamma)} h_a = \min_{\alpha \in \gamma, a \in \alpha} h_\alpha.$$

Example 4. For our running example, $\mathcal{E}(\gamma)$ is given by the conjunction:

$$h_{heat} = \min_{i \in \{0,1\}} h_{rest_i} \wedge h_{cool} = \min_{i \in \{0,1\}} h_{cool_i}. \tag{3}$$

Generating Inequalities from Conflicting Interactions. The (in)equality constraints shown previously allow to relate local constraints obtained separately from the component invariants. Without conflicts, that is, when interactions do not share any action, the generated invariants are quite tight in the sense that $\mathcal{E}(\gamma)$ is essentially a conjunction of equalities. However, $\mathcal{E}(\gamma)$ is weaker in the presence of conflicts because any action in conflict can be used in different interactions. The disjunctions (implicit in the definition of min) in $\mathcal{E}(\gamma)$ reflect precisely this uncertainty. History clocks on interactions are introduced to capture the time lapses between conflicting interactions. The basic information we can exploit is that when two conflicting interactions compete for the same action a, no matter which one is first, the other one must wait until the component which owns a is again able to execute a. This is referred to as a "separation constraint" for conflicting interactions and is defined as the following invariant:

$$\mathcal{S}(\gamma) = \bigwedge_{a \in Act(\gamma)} \bigwedge_{\substack{\alpha \neq \beta \in \gamma \\ a \in \alpha \cap \beta}} | h_\alpha - h_\beta | \geq k_a$$

where $| x |$ denotes the absolute value of x and k_a is a constant computed locally on the component executing a, and representing the minimum elapsed time between two consecutive executions of a.

Remark 3. If in the case of timed automata exact methods to compute k_a exist[5], in the case of hybrid systems, we are not aware of such approaches. However, a simple but incomplete heuristics to determine a correct value for k_a is to guess and do a local model-check.

Example 5. For our running example, we have that $\mathcal{S}(\gamma)$ is given by:

$$| h_{heat|rest_0} - h_{heat|rest_1} | \geq k_{heat} \wedge | h_{cool|cool_0} - h_{cool|cool_1} | \geq k_{cool}. \tag{4}$$

By inspecting the model, one can note that the constants k_{cool} and k_{heat} are both equal to the sum of the time lapses at lc_0 and lc_1 which reduces to 8.

3.4 Revisiting (VR)

With the new the clock constraints $\mathcal{E}$ and $\mathcal{S}$, the generalisation of the rule (VR) from Sect. 2 boils down to checking the validity of the following formula:

$$\underbrace{\wedge_i CI(B_i^h) \wedge II(\gamma) \wedge \mathcal{E}(\gamma) \wedge \mathcal{S}(\gamma)}_{GI} \rightarrow \Psi \tag{5}$$

or equally the unsatisfiability of $GI \wedge \neg\Psi$.

The soundness of (VR) follows from the basic fact that the conjunction of invariants is in turn an invariant and from the observation that each of the constituting elements of GI is an invariant.

---

[5] We refer to [13] for an approach which reduces the computation to finding a shortest path in a weighted graph built from the zone graph associated of a timed automaton.

Example 6. As an illustration, we work through our running example from head to tail. We recall that we take, as a safety state property, $\Psi := \neg shutdown$ with $shutdown$ being $t = 15 \wedge_i x_i < 6$. We first reproduce the component invariants for the rods and the controller extended with history clocks as provided by Hymitator.

$$CI(Rod_i^h) = (l_{0i} \wedge x_i \geq 6)$$
$$\vee (l_{1i} \wedge x_i \geq 6 + h_{cool_i})$$
$$\vee (l_{0i} \wedge h_{cool_i} \geq h_{rest_i} \wedge h_{rest_i} \geq 0 \wedge x_i = h_{rest_i})$$
$$\vee (l_{1i} \wedge x_i = h_{rest_i} \geq h_{cool_i} \wedge h_{rest_i} \geq 6 + h_{cool_i})$$

$$CI(Controller^h) = 15 \geq t \wedge$$
$$\vee ((lc_0 \wedge t \geq 0)$$
$$\vee (lc_1 \wedge t \geq 3 \wedge 15 = t + 2h_{cool})$$
$$\vee (lc_0 \wedge t \geq 3 \wedge 12 + 6h_{cool} = 45 + t \wedge 3 + 6h_{heat} = t)$$
$$\vee (lc_1 \wedge t \geq 3 \wedge 15 = t + 2h_{cool} \wedge 3t + 6h_{heat} = 57))$$

These local invariants together with the interaction invariant, the (in)equality and the separation constraints represented by Formulae (3), (4) are an instantiation of GI. We feed this instantiation together with $shutdown$ to Z3 and ask for a solution. The result "no solution" allows us to conclude that the system is safe. To give an intuition why this is indeed the case, we take a closer look at the formulae at hand. The only problematic case is when both rods are at the initial locations (at the other location we already knew from Formula (1) that $x_i \geq 6$). The relevant equations are $x_i = h_{rest_i}$. Let us assume that the controller is at lc_0 (the other location is dismissed by the interaction invariant). To have a shutdown, t is 15. Consequently, h_{cool} is 8 and h_{heat} is 2. Assume that the minimum between h_{rest_i} is h_{rest_0}, that is, $x_0 = 2$. By the separation constraint, h_{rest_1} is at least 10 and implicitly x_1 can be used for cooling, consequently, the system is so far safe.

4 Bringing Parameters into Play

In this section we present some ongoing research about parameters and their roles within our framework. We distinguish two levels where parameters can enter the scene: (1) at component level, and this leads to systems of *parametric* LHAs, and (2) at system level, and this leads to *parameterised* hybrid systems.

4.1 Parametric LHAs

At component level, parameters may represent for instance physical constants dependent of the environment or values that the designer should set such as timing constraints which are to be known only at deployment. Working with parameters in early stages of development has the direct benefit that it makes it possible to explore different design choices and evaluate their robustness.

To handle parameters at the level of components, it suffices to split $\mathcal{X}$ into 2 disjoint sets $\mathcal{V}$ and $\mathcal{P}$, where $\mathcal{V}$ plays the role of $\mathcal{X}$ as in Definition 1 while $\mathcal{P}$ stores parameters. Parameters can be seen as a particular type of variables whose values do not change over time.

Returning to the temperature controller example, we recall that the constants used in the system are values for minimum and maximum bounds, recovering times for rods, temperature increase and decrease rates. If we see all these as parameters, the corresponding system is the one illustrated in Fig. 4.

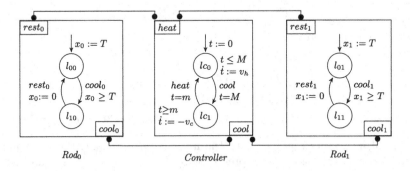

Fig. 4. Parametric temperature controller system

To apply (VR) on systems with components as parametric LHAs, all the methods for computing local invariants, as described in Sect. 3, except one, remain unchanged. The computation of interaction invariants and equality constraints only depends on the set of interactions. Neither does the computation of component invariants, however the output reflects parameters instead of constants. As an illustration, the component invariant for the controller computed with Hymitator is as follows:

$$
\begin{aligned}
CI(\mathit{Controller}^h) = &M \geq t \wedge M \geq 0 \\
&\wedge \big((lc_0 \wedge t \geq 0) \\
&\vee (lc_1 \wedge t \geq m \wedge M = t + 2h_{cool}) \\
&\vee (lc_0 \wedge t \geq m \wedge 4m + 6h_{cool} = 3M + t \wedge m + 6h_{heat} = t) \\
&\vee (lc_1 \wedge t \geq m \wedge M = t + 2h_{cool} \wedge m + 3t + 6h_{heat} = 4M) \big)
\end{aligned}
$$

The exception is the computation of separation constraints. The exact parametric value could be manually computed. In the case of the running example, one can show that k_{cool} and k_{heat} are both equal to $(M - m)(1/v_c + 1/v_h)$. Generalising such computations may seem hopeless. We note that not being able to compute separation constraints does not mean that (VR) is no longer applicable, but that it is less stronger. Also, in the case when the component where one needs to compute separation constraints does not have parameters, then (VR) preserves its strength. In our running example, this boils down to T being the only parameter. For the sake of reaching a conclusion, let us continue our thought experiment irrespective of being able to automatically compute separation constraints. We do so by asking the question: "knowing that by default variables are understood as universally quantified, does it make sense to input (VR) as is to Z3?" If we look at our running example, it is apparent that the system would not be safe for any value of T. In fact, by a closer analysis, for the system to be safe it is sufficient that the sum of the time lapse for the controller to raise the temperature and twice the time lapse for the two rods to refrigerate, i.e., $(M - m)(1/v_h + 2/v_r)$, is greater than T. From this, we reach a more general remark that verification of parametric (hybrid) systems boils down to a synthesis problem. Basically, what we would like to ask (VR) is to synthesise concrete values such that the constraints we have just derived manually are satisfied.

As a side remark and as a justification of our thought experiment, we note that parameter synthesis for hybrid systems has already been addressed first in [25] and later refined in [11,20,21]. However, doing it compositionally is new.

To effectively tackle the new synthesis problem, a first approach is to quantify the parameters in (VR) existentially. However, as argued in [11], this would give us just one set of "good" parameters. In this sense, it would be of interest to follow the approach from [11] which basically computes all the good parameters by finding the bad ones: the good parameters are simply the domains from which the bad parameters are eliminated. Regarding this direction, our experiments with tactics for eliminating quantifiers and simplifying formulae in Z3 did not lead to concrete results. Experimenting along the first direction is more on the positive side. For instance, if we ask Z3 to solve $\exists T. GI[M \leftarrow 15, m \leftarrow 3] \wedge \Psi$ it yields a solution where T is 1. This is, indeed, a valid value but we would be interested in finding the maximal T for which a rod is allowed to recover without leading to a shutdown. We could find such a value in an iteratively manner, by means of a binary search, for instance, to advance at a faster pace. How useful would recent max-SMT techniques [7] be for finding optimal solutions and at what extent this approach can be automated and generalised to handle multiple parameters needs still to be investigated.

4.2   Parameterised Hybrid Systems

Taking parameters at system level is more inline with our previous work in [3]. There, we have made use of a small model result to verify parameterised timed systems, that is, timed systems with arbitrary many replicated components. The verification of parameterised systems is usually refered to as "uniform verification". As an illustration, we use our running example: the controller together with an arbitrary number of rods forms a parameterised hybrid system.

Concretely, in [3], we have shown how (VR) can be extended to tackle uniform verification of a restricted[6] class of $\forall^*\exists^*$ properties for parameterised timed systems. The underlying technicality was to "massage" the formula corresponding to (VR), that is, $GI \rightarrow \Psi$ into a restricted $\forall^*\exists^*$ property. Thanks to this,

---

[6] The restriction consists in only allowing linear constraints on variables and comparisons between indices while disallowing comparisons between variables and indices.

we were able to apply a small model result which allowed us to reduce uniform verification to the verification of a small number of replicas. The bound is mostly related to the number of universal quantifiers behind (VR). The methodology in [3] naturally extends to parameterised hybrid systems. The only difference is in computing local invariants, as shown in Sect. 3.

Remark 4. So far, the setup from [3] only allows replicas as *identical* copies. Consequently, as is, the framework cannot handle parametric components. This would be a wanted feature as it is not infrequent that guards in components are parametric in the number of components. It is even the case of our running example: the parameterised temperature controller system cannot be safe for an arbitrary number n of rods unless the guard in the replicated rod depends on n. However, technically, such a guard does not fit our $\forall^*\exists^*$ properties. It would be of interest to see if we could borrow ideas from [22] to relax our restrictions.

5 Conclusions

We presented a compositional approach to the verification of hybrid systems. On the positive side, thanks to compositionality itself and to the speed of SMT solvers such as Z3, the approach scales quite well. On the negative side, while working with abstractions we run into false positives. In principle, false positives could be eliminated by means of a CEGAR approach but further experiments are needed to evaluate the real strength of the method.

Besides clarifying the points raised in Sect. 4, we would be interested in a few more experiments. One is about using tools such as Hycomp [12] or flow* [8]. Hycomp has the advantage that it uses IC3 [40] for a property driven computation of the set of reachable states. In principle, this would allow us to have smaller component invariants. flow* handles non-linear hybrid automata, thus it would make it possible to effectively experiment with (VR) and non-linear hybrid systems. Ideally, we would like to have a (VR)-based platform where different tools for computing sets of reachable states of hybrid automata could be plugged in. Some effort in this direction is already visible [4] at the level of input formats. It would be helpful to have a similar result at the level of output.

Another direction we intend to look into is moving towards hybrid I/O automata [34] as a more suitable model for PLCs.

Regarding modelling aspects, we also note that many of the hybrid systems we came across in the literature have global variables and in general they are described in a "monolithic" manner. This latter observation brings us to the issue of decomposing hybrid systems into components. As we have mentioned, in the temperature controller example, we did the decomposition by hand. To automate such a decomposition, a possible approach we could look into is the one from [38] which is based on strongly connected components. In a different direction, it would be of interest at what extent would results from algebraic geometry be useful.

Acknowledgements. We would like to thank Chih-Hong Cheng for his friendly feedback and for sharing some ideas about possible ways to tackle decomposition.

References

1. Alur, R., Courcoubetis, C., Halbwachs, N., Henzinger, T.A., Ho, P.-H., Nicollin, X., Olivero, A., Sifakis, J., Yovine, S.: The algorithmic analysis of hybrid systems. Theor. Comput. Sci. **138**, 3–34 (1995)
2. Aştefănoaei, L., Rayana, S.B., Bensalem, S., Bozga, M., Combaz, J.: Compositional invariant generation for timed systems. In: Ábrahám, E., Havelund, K. (eds.) TACAS 2014 (ETAPS). LNCS, vol. 8413, pp. 263–278. Springer, Heidelberg (2014)
3. Aştefănoaei, L., Rayana, S.B., Bensalem, S., Bozga, M., Combaz, J.: Compositional verification of parameterised timed systems. In: Havelund, K., Holzmann, G., Joshi, R. (eds.) NFM 2015. LNCS, vol. 9058, pp. 66–81. Springer, Heidelberg (2015)
4. Bak, S., Bogomolov, S., Johnson, T.T.: HYST: a source transformation and translation tool for hybrid automaton models. In: HSCC (2015)
5. Bensalem, S., Bozga, M., Sifakis, J., Nguyen, T.-H.: Compositional verification for component-based systems and application. In: Cha, S.S., Choi, J.-Y., Kim, M., Lee, I., Viswanathan, M. (eds.) ATVA 2008. LNCS, vol. 5311, pp. 64–79. Springer, Heidelberg (2008)
6. Bogomolov, S., Donzé, A., Frehse, G., Grosu, R., Johnson, T.T., Ladan, H., Podelski, A., Wehrle, M.: Abstraction-based guided search for hybrid systems. In: Bartocci, E., Ramakrishnan, C.R. (eds.) SPIN 2013. LNCS, vol. 7976, pp. 117–134. Springer, Heidelberg (2013)
7. Brockschmidt, M., Larraz, D., Oliveras, A., Carbonell, E.R., Rubio, A.: Compositional safety verification with max-smt. In: FMCAD (2015)
8. Chen, X., Ábrahám, E., Sankaranarayanan, S.: Flow*: An analyzer for non-linear hybrid systems. In: Sharygina, N., Veith, H. (eds.) CAV 2013. LNCS, vol. 8044, pp. 258–263. Springer, Heidelberg (2013)
9. Chen, X., Schupp, S., Makhlouf, I.B., Ábrahám, E., Frehse, G., Kowalewski, S.: A benchmark suite for hybrid systems reachability analysis. In: Havelund, K., Holzmann, G., Joshi, R. (eds.) NFM 2015. LNCS, vol. 9058, pp. 408–414. Springer, Heidelberg (2015)
10. Cimatti, A.: Application of SMT solvers to hybrid system verification. In: FMCAD (2012)
11. Cimatti, A., Griggio, A., Mover, S., Tonetta, S.: Parameter synthesis with IC3. In: FMCAD (2013)
12. Cimatti, A., Griggio, A., Mover, S., Tonetta, S.: HyComp: An SMT-based model checker for hybrid systems. In: Baier, C., Tinelli, C. (eds.) TACAS 2015. LNCS, vol. 9035, pp. 52–67. Springer, Heidelberg (2015)
13. Courcoubetis, C., Yannakakis, M.: Minimum and maximum delay problems in real-time systems. Formal Methods Syst. Des. **1**, 385–415 (1992)
14. Damm, W., Möhlmann, E., Rakow, A.: Component based design of hybrid systems: a case study on concurrency and coupling. In: HSCC (2014)
15. David, A., Larsen, K.G., Legay, A., Poulsen, D.B.: Statistical model checking of dynamic networks of stochastic hybrid automata. ECEASST **66** (2013)
16. Donzé, A.: Breach, A toolbox for verification and parameter synthesis of hybrid systems. In: Touili, T., Cook, B., Jackson, P. (eds.) CAV 2010. LNCS, vol. 6174, pp. 167–170. Springer, Heidelberg (2010)

17. Eggers, A., Ramdani, N., Nedialkov, N., Fränzle, M.: Improving SAT modulo ODE for hybrid systems analysis by combining different enclosure methods. In: Barthe, G., Pardo, A., Schneider, G. (eds.) SEFM 2011. LNCS, vol. 7041, pp. 172–187. Springer, Heidelberg (2011)

18. Frehse, G.: Compositional Verification of Hybrid Systems using Simulation Relations. Ph.D. thesis, Radboud Universiteit Nijmegen (2005)

19. Frehse, G., Le Guernic, C., Donzé, A., Cotton, S., Ray, R., Lebeltel, O., Ripado, R., Girard, A., Dang, T., Maler, O.: SpaceEx: Scalable verification of hybrid systems. In: Gopalakrishnan, G., Qadeer, S. (eds.) CAV 2011. LNCS, vol. 6806, pp. 379–395. Springer, Heidelberg (2011)

20. Frehse, G., Jha, S.K., Krogh, B.H.: A counterexample-guided approach to parameter synthesis for linear hybrid automata. In: Egerstedt, M., Mishra, B. (eds.) HSCC 2008. LNCS, vol. 4981, pp. 187–200. Springer, Heidelberg (2008)

21. Fribourg, L., Kühne, U.: Parametric verification and test coverage for hybrid automata using the inverse method. Int. J. Found. Comput. Sci. 24, 233–249 (2013)

22. Habermehl, P., Iosif, R., Vojnar, T.: What else is decidable about integer arrays? In: Amadio, R.M. (ed.) FOSSACS 2008. LNCS, vol. 4962, pp. 474–489. Springer, Heidelberg (2008)

23. Henzinger, T.A.: The theory of hybrid automata. In: LICS (1996)

24. Henzinger, T.A., Minea, M., Prabhu, V.S.: Assume-guarantee reasoning for hierarchical hybrid systems. In: Benedetto, M.D., Sangiovanni-Vincentelli, A.L. (eds.) HSCC 2001. LNCS, vol. 2034, pp. 275–290. Springer, Heidelberg (2001)

25. Henzinger, T.A., Wong-Toi, H.: Using HyTech to synthesize control parameters for a steam boiler. In: Abrial, J.-R., Börger, E., Langmaack, H. (eds.) FMIA 1996. LNCS, vol. 1165. Springer, Heidelberg (1996)

26. Hermanns, H., Krčál, J., Křetínský, J.: Compositional verification and optimization of interactive markov chains. In: D'Argenio, P.R., Melgratti, H. (eds.) CONCUR 2013 – Concurrency Theory. LNCS, vol. 8052, pp. 364–379. Springer, Heidelberg (2013)

27. Ho, P.-H.: Automatic Analysis of Hybrid Systems. Ph.D. thesis, Cornell University (1995)

28. Jaffe, M.S., Leveson, N.G., Heimdahl, M.P.E., Melhart, B.E.: Software requirements analysis for real-time process-control systems. IEEE Trans. Softw. Eng. 17, 241–258 (1991)

29. Jeannin, J., Platzer, A.: dtl2: Differential temporal dynamic logic with nested temporalities for hybrid systems. In: IJCAR (2014)

30. Johnson, T.T., Mitra, S.: A small model theorem for rectangular hybrid automata networks. In: Giese, H., Rosu, G. (eds.) FORTE 2012 and FMOODS 2012. LNCS, vol. 7273, pp. 18–34. Springer, Heidelberg (2012)

31. Johnson, T.T., Mitra, S.: Anonymized reachability of hybrid automata networks. In: Legay, A., Bozga, M. (eds.) FORMATS 2014. LNCS, vol. 8711, pp. 130–145. Springer, Heidelberg (2014)

32. Kong, S., Gao, S., Chen, W., Clarke, E.: dReach: δ-reachability analysis for hybrid systems. In: Baier, C., Tinelli, C. (eds.) TACAS 2015. LNCS, vol. 9035, pp. 200–205. Springer, Heidelberg (2015)

33. Legay, A., Bensalem, S., Boyer, B., Bozga, M.: Incremental generation of linear invariants for component-based systems. In: ACSD (2013)

34. Lynch, N.A., Segala, R., Vaandrager, F.W.: Hybrid I/O automata. Inf. Comput. 185, 105–157 (2003)

35. de Moura, L., Bjørner, N.S.: Efficient e-matching for SMT solvers. In: Pfenning, F. (ed.) CADE 2007. LNCS (LNAI), vol. 4603, pp. 183–198. Springer, Heidelberg (2007)

36. Mover, S.: Verification of Hybrid Systems using Satisfiability Modulo Theories. Ph.D. thesis, FBK-IRST/DIT (2014)

37. Mover, S., Cimatti, A., Tiwari, A., Tonetta, S.: Time-aware relational abstractions for hybrid systems. In: EMSOFT (2013)

38. Oehlerking, J.: Decomposition of Stability Proofs for Hybrid Systems. Ph.D. thesis, Carl von Ossietzky Universität, Oldenburg (2011)

39. Quesel, J.-D., Platzer, A.: Playing hybrid games with KeYmaera. In: Gramlich, B., Miller, D., Sattler, U. (eds.) IJCAR 2012. LNCS, vol. 7364, pp. 439–453. Springer, Heidelberg (2012)

40. Somenzi, F., Bradley, A.R.: IC3: where monolithic and incremental meet. In: FMCAD (2011)

41. Testylier, R., Dang, T.: NLTOOLBOX: A library for reachability computation of nonlinear dynamical systems. In: Van Hung, D., Ogawa, M. (eds.) ATVA 2013. LNCS, vol. 8172, pp. 469–473. Springer, Heidelberg (2013)

42. Zhang, L., She, Z., Ratschan, S., Hermanns, H., Hahn, E.M.: Safety verification for probabilistic hybrid systems. Eur. J. Control **18**, 588–590 (2012)

Array Abstraction with Symbolic Pivots

Reiner Hähnle$^{(\boxtimes)}$, Nathan Wasser, and Richard Bubel

Department of Computer Science, Technische Universität Darmstadt,
Darmstadt, Germany
{haehnle,wasser,bubel}@cs.tu-darmstadt.de

Abstract. We present a novel approach to automatically generate invariants for loops manipulating arrays. The intention is to achieve formal verification of programs over arrays without the need for user-specified loop invariants. Many loops iterate and manipulate collections. Finding useful, i.e., sufficiently precise invariants for those loops is a challenging task, in particular, if the iteration order is complex. Our approach partitions an array and provides an abstraction for each of these partitions. Symbolic pivot elements are used to compute the partitions. In addition we integrate a faithful and precise program logic for sequential (Java) programs with abstract interpretation using an extensible multi-layered framework to compute array invariants. The presented approach has been implemented. Results of experiments are reported.

Keywords: Loop invariant generation · Program verification · Abstract interpretation · Array abstraction

1 Introduction

This paper is dedicated to Frank S. de Boer on the occasion of his 60th birthday. I met Frank in ca. 2006 during a phase in my research where I had become unhappy with the progress in formal verification of concurrent software. I was looking for partners who would be willing to co-develop a formal concurrent modeling language amenable to scalable formal specification and verification. At that time Frank and Einar B. Johnsen had been working on the distributed modeling framework CREOL and we decided to team up. From this contact eventually the EU project HATS evolved where we developed the cloud-aware, concurrent OO modeling language ABS as well as the ongoing EU project ENVISAGE where we look at SLAs. Looking back on ten years of intense collaboration, joint publications, and countless bottles of good wine enjoyed together, I can say: it was a great ride and I am looking forward to continue it! I learned a lot from Frank: he is a true generalist with a vast and deep knowledge in formal methods, his energy and creativity are contagious (and, occasionally, exasperating) and, most importantly, there is always fun to be had! Thank you, Frank, for these years together and let's have a toast to many more to come! — RH.

The work has been funded by the DFG priority program 1496 *Reliably Secure Software Systems*.

© Springer International Publishing Switzerland 2016
E. Ábrahám et al. (Eds.): de Boer Festschrift, LNCS 9660, pp. 104–121, 2016.
DOI: 10.1007/978-3-319-30734-3_9

Deductive program analysis and verification must determine a trade-off between the complexity of the properties they ascertain, the precision of the analysis, i.e., the percentage of issued false warnings, and the degree of automation.

Improving automation for medium to complex properties by maintaining an acceptable degree of precision requires addressing one of the sources for interaction (or otherwise loss of precision). One kind of interaction derives from the elimination of quantifiers, another one is the provision of program annotations such as method contracts, loop invariants or assertions that serve as hints for the underlying theorem prover. Providing useful annotations, in particular, loop invariants is a time-consuming and difficult task, which requires experience in writing formal specifications on the part of the user. This hinders wide-spread adoption of formal verification in industry.

Here we focus on the automatic generation of loop invariants. We improve upon previous work [1] of some of the co-authors in which a theoretical framework was developed that integrates deductive reasoning and abstract interpretation. We extend this by a novel approach for automatic generation of invariants for loops that manipulate arrays. This loop invariant generation works by partitioning arrays automatically using a new concept to which we refer as *symbolic pivots*. A symbolic pivot expresses the symbolic value of a term (in particular an array index) at the end of every loop iteration. When these symbolic pivots have certain properties we can generate highly precise partitions. The content of array partitions is represented as an abstract value which describes the value of the partition's elements. An important feature is that the degree of abstraction, that is, the precision is adaptive.

Further, we integrate a faithful and precise program logic for sequential (Java) programs with abstract interpretation using an extensible multi-layered framework to compute array invariants. The presented approach has also been implemented as a proof of concept based on the KeY verification system [2].

2   Background

2.1   Program Logic

We introduce our program logic and calculus, and explain our integration of value-based abstraction based on previous work [1] by some of the authors.

We stress that our implementation works for nearly full sequential Java [2], but for readability we restrict ourselves here to a fragment with integer arrays as the only kind of objects. The program logic presented below extends the logic in [1] by an explicit heap model and array types.

Syntax. We work with a first order dynamic logic which is closely related to Java Card DL [2]. Its signature is a collection of the symbols that can be used to construct formulas:

Definition 1 (Signature). *A signature Σ is a tuple $((\mathcal{T}, \preceq), \mathcal{P}, \mathcal{F}, \mathcal{PV}, \mathcal{V})$ consisting of a set of types $\mathcal{T}$ together with a type hierarchy $\preceq$, predicates $\mathcal{P}$, functions $\mathcal{F}$, program variables $\mathcal{PV}$ and logical variables $\mathcal{V}$. Types contain at least $\top$,*

Heap, LocSet, int *and* int[] *with* ⊤ *being the top element and the other types ordered directly below* ⊤.

Our logic consists of terms Trm (write Trm_T for terms of type T), formulas For, programs $Prog$ and updates Upd. Besides some extensions we elaborate on below, terms and formulas are defined as in standard first-order logic. Importantly, there is a difference between logical variables and program variables: both are terms, but logical variables must not occur in programs and can be bound by a quantifier. On the other hand, program variables can occur in programs, but cannot be bound by a quantifier. Syntactically, program variables are flexible function constants, whose value can be changed by executing a program.

Updates are discussed in [2] and can be viewed as generalized explicit substitutions. The grammar of updates is: $\mathcal{U} ::= (\mathcal{U} \,\|\, \mathcal{U}) \mid x := t$ where $x \in \mathcal{PV}$ and t is a term of the same type or subtype as x. Updates can be applied to terms and formulas: given a term t then $\{\mathcal{U}\}t$ is also a term (analogous for formulas). The only other non-standard operator for terms and formulas in our logic is the conditional term: let φ be a formula and ξ_1, ξ_2 are both terms of compatible type or are both formulas, then if (φ) $then$ (ξ_1) $else$ (ξ_2) is also a term or formula.

There is a modality called box $[\cdot]\cdot$ which takes a program as first parameter and a formula as second parameter. Intuitively the meaning of $[p]\phi$ is that if program p terminates without throwing an exception then in its final state the formula ϕ holds (our programs are deterministic). Thus the box modality expresses partial correctness. The formula $\phi \rightarrow [p]\psi$ has the exact same meaning as the Hoare triple $\{\phi\}$ p $\{\psi\}$. In contrast to Hoare logic, dynamic logic allows nested modalities. The grammar for programs is:

$$p ::= x = t \mid x[t] = t \mid p; p \mid \texttt{skip} \mid \texttt{if}\,(\phi)\,\{p\}\,\texttt{else}\,\{p\} \mid \texttt{while}\,(\phi)\,\{p\}$$

where $x \in \mathcal{PV}$, t, φ are terms/formulas. Syntactically valid programs are well-typed and do not contain logic variables, quantifiers or modalities.

The program skip should have no effect. We write if (φ) {p} as an abbreviation for if (φ) {p} else { skip }.

Semantics. Terms, formulas and programs are evaluated with respect to a first order structure.

Definition 2 (First Order Structure, Variable Assignment). *Let D be a non-empty domain of elements. A first order structure $M = (D, I, s)$ consists of*

1. *an interpretation I which assigns each*
   - $T \in \mathcal{T}$ *a non-empty domain $D^T \subseteq D$ s.t. $\forall S \in \mathcal{T}.\ S \preceq T \rightarrow D^S \subseteq D^T$*
   - $f : T_1 \times \ldots \times T_n \rightarrow T \in \mathcal{F}$ *a function $I(f) : D^{T_1} \times \ldots \times D^{T_n} \rightarrow D^T$*
   - $p : T_1 \times \ldots \times T_n \in \mathcal{P}$ *a relation $I(p) \subseteq D^{T_1} \times \ldots \times D^{T_n}$*
2. *a state $s : \mathcal{PV} \rightarrow D$ assigning each program variable $v \in \mathcal{PV}$ of type T a value $s(v) \in D^T$. We denote the set of all states by States.*

We fix the interpretation of some types and symbols: $I(\texttt{int}) = \mathbb{Z}$, $I(\top) = D$ *and the arithmetic operations* $+, -, /, \%, \ldots$ *as well as the comparators* $<, >, \leq, \geq, \doteq$ *are interpreted according to their standard semantics.*

In addition we need the notion of a variable assignment $\beta : \mathcal{V} \to D$ *which assigns each logical variable to an element of its domain.*

Definition 3 (Evaluation). *Given a first order structure* (D, I, s) *and a variable assignment* β, *we evaluate terms* t *(of type* T*) to a value* $val_{D,I,s,\beta}(t) \in D^T$, *formulas* φ *to a truth value* $val_{D,I,s,\beta}(\varphi) \in \{tt, ff\}$, *updates* $\mathcal{U}$ *to a function* $val_{D,I,s,\beta}(\mathcal{U}) : S \to S$, *and programs* $\mathbf{p}$ *to a set of states* $val_{D,I,s,\beta}(\mathbf{p}) \in 2^S$ *with* $val_{D,I,s,\beta}(\mathbf{p})$ *being either empty or a singleton set.*

A formula φ *is called* valid *iff* $val_{D,I,s,\beta}(\varphi) = tt$ *for all* non-empty *domains* D, *all* interpretations I, *all* states s *and all* variable assignments β.

The evaluation of terms and formulas without programs and updates is almost identical to standard first-order logic and omitted for brevity. The evaluation of an elementary *update* with respect to a first order structure (D, I, s) and variable assignment β is defined as follows:

$$val_{D,I,s,\beta}(\mathbf{x} := t)(s') = \begin{cases} s'(\mathbf{y}), & \mathbf{y} \neq \mathbf{x} \\ val_{D,I,s,\beta}(t), & otherwise \end{cases}$$

The evaluation of a parallel update $val_{D,I,s,\beta}(\mathbf{x}_1 := t_1 \parallel \mathbf{x}_2 := t_2)$ maps a state s' to a state s'' such that s'' coincides with s' except for the program variables $\mathbf{x}_1, \mathbf{x}_2$ which are assigned the values of the terms t_i in parallel. In case of a clash between two sub-updates (i.e., when $\mathbf{x}_i = \mathbf{x}_j$ for $i \neq j$), the rightmost update "wins" and overwrites the effect of the other. The meaning of a term $\{\mathcal{U}\}t$ and of a formula $\{\mathcal{U}\}\varphi$ is that the result state of the update $\mathcal{U}$ should be used for evaluating t and φ, respectively.

A *program* is evaluated to the set of states that it may terminate in when started in s. We only consider deterministic programs, so this set is always either empty (if the program does not terminate) or it consists of exactly one state.[1] The semantics of a program formula $[\mathbf{p}]\varphi$ is that φ should hold in all result states of the program $\mathbf{p}$, which corresponds to partial correctness of $\mathbf{p}$ relative to φ.

Heap Model. The only heap objects we support in our programs (for this paper— implemented are all Java reference types) are integer typed arrays. We use an explicit heap model similar to [3]. Heaps are modelled as elements of type `Heap`, with two functions *store* : `Heap` $\times$ `int[]` $\times$ `int` $\times$ `int` $\to$ `Heap` to store values on the heap and *select* : `Heap` $\times$ `int[]` $\times$ `int` $\to$ `int` to retrieve values from the heap.

For instance, *store*$(h, \mathbf{a}, \mathbf{i}, 3)$ returns a new heap which is identical to heap h except for the i-th element of array $\mathbf{a}$ which is assigned the value 3. To retrieve the value of an array element $\mathbf{b[j]}$ we write *select*$(h, \mathbf{b}, \mathbf{j})$. There is a special

---

[1] While programs themselves are deterministic, we can introduce at least some non-determinism through the symbolic input values, which while having a single value in each model leave open which model is under consideration.

program variable **heap** which refers to the heap accessed by programs. We abbreviate $select(\textbf{heap}, a, i)$ with $a[i]$. To ease quantification over array indices, we use $\forall x \in [l..r).\phi$ as abbreviation for $\forall x.((l \leq x \wedge x < r) \rightarrow \phi))$. Further, we write $\forall x \in arr.\phi$ for $\forall x \in [0..arr.\texttt{length}).\phi$, where $arr.\texttt{length}$ denotes how many elements the array arr contains.

Closely related to heaps are location sets which are defined as terms of type **LocSet**. Semantically, an element of **LocSet** describes a set of program locations. A program location is a pair (a, i) with $val_{D,I,s,\beta}(a) \in D^{\texttt{int}[]}$, $val_{D,I,s,\beta}(i) \in \mathbb{Z}$ which represents the memory location of the array element $a[i]$. Syntactically, location sets can be constructed by functions over the usual set operations. We use some convenience functions and write $a[l..r]$ to represent syntactically the locations of the array elements $a[l]$ (inclusive) to $a[r]$ (exclusive). Further, we write $a[*]$ for $a[0..a.\texttt{length}]$.

Calculus. We use a *sequent calculus* to prove that a formula is valid. *Sequents* are tuples $\Gamma \Rightarrow \Delta$ with Γ (the *antecedent*) and Δ (the *succedent*) being finite sets of formulas. The meaning $val_{D,I,s,\beta}(\Gamma \Rightarrow \Delta)$ of a sequent is the same as that of the formula $val_{D,I,s,\beta}(\bigwedge \Gamma \rightarrow \bigvee \Delta)$. A sequent calculus *rule* is given by the rule schema,

$$\frac{seq_1 \ \cdots \ seq_n}{seq}$$

where $seq_1, \ldots, seq_n$ (the *premisses* of the rule) and seq (the *conclusion* of the rule) are sequents. A rule is *sound* iff the conclusion's validity follows from the validity of all premisses.

A sequent proof is a tree where each node is annotated with a sequent. The root node is annotated with the sequent to be proven valid. A rule is applied by matching its conclusion with a sequent of a leaf node and attaching the premisses as its children. If a branch of the tree ends in a leaf that is trivially true, the branch is called closed. A proof is closed if all its leaves are closed.

All first-order calculus rules are standard, so we explain only selected sequent calculus rules which deal with formulas involving programs. Given a suitable strategy for rule selection, the sequent calculus implements a symbolic interpreter. For example, the assignment rule for a program variable is as follows:

assignment
$$\frac{\Gamma \Rightarrow \{\mathcal{U}\}\{\texttt{x} := t\}[\texttt{r}]\varphi, \Delta}{\Gamma \Rightarrow \{\mathcal{U}\}[\texttt{x = } t\texttt{; r}]\varphi, \Delta}$$

The assignment rule for an array location adds constraints to the value the index can have, as if this value were not within the valid range for the array, an **ArrayIndexOutOfBoundsException** would be thrown, in which case we have nothing more to prove, as φ need only be shown for programs terminating without throwing exceptions.

assignment$_{array}$
$$\frac{\Gamma, i \geq 0, i < \texttt{a.length} \Rightarrow \{\mathcal{U}\}\{\texttt{heap} := store(\texttt{heap}, \texttt{a}, i, t)\}[\texttt{r}]\varphi, \Delta}{\Gamma \Rightarrow \{\mathcal{U}\}[\texttt{a}[i] \texttt{ = } t\texttt{; r}]\varphi, \Delta}$$

The assignment rules move an assignment into an update. Updates accumulate in front of modalities during symbolic execution of the program. Once the program has been symbolically executed, the update is applied to the formula behind the modality, thereby computing its weakest precondition. Symbolic execution of *conditional statements* split the proof into two branches:

$$\text{ifElse} \quad \frac{\Gamma, \{\mathcal{U}\}g \Rightarrow \{\mathcal{U}\}[\texttt{p1; r}]\varphi, \Delta \qquad \Gamma, \{\mathcal{U}\}!\,g \Rightarrow \{\mathcal{U}\}[\texttt{p2; r}]\varphi, \Delta}{\Gamma \Rightarrow \{\mathcal{U}\}[\texttt{if } (g) \texttt{ \{p1\} else \{p2\}; r}]\varphi, \Delta}$$

For a *loop*, the simplest approach is to *unwind* it. However, loop unwinding works only if the number of loop iterations has a concrete bound.

$$\text{loopUnwind} \quad \frac{\Gamma, \{\mathcal{U}\}g \Rightarrow \{\mathcal{U}\}[\texttt{p; while } (g) \texttt{ \{p\}; r}]\varphi, \Delta \qquad \Gamma, \{\mathcal{U}\}!\,g \Rightarrow \{\mathcal{U}\}[\texttt{r}]\varphi, \Delta}{\Gamma \Rightarrow \{\mathcal{U}\}[\texttt{while } (g) \texttt{ \{p\}; r}]\varphi, \Delta}$$

For unbounded loops we can use, for example, a *loop invariant* rule. To apply the loop invariant rule a loop specification consisting of a formula (the loop invariant) *Inv* and an assignable (modifies) clause *mod* is needed. The first premiss (initial case) ensures that the loop invariant *Inv* is valid before entering the loop. The second premiss (preserves case) ensures that *Inv* is preserved by an arbitrary loop iteration, while for the third premiss (use case), we have to show that after executing the remaining program, the desired postcondition φ holds.

$$\text{loopInvariant} \quad \frac{\begin{array}{ll} \Gamma \Rightarrow \{\mathcal{U}\}Inv, \Delta & \text{initial} \\ \Gamma, \{\mathcal{U}\}\{\mathcal{V}_{mod}\}(g \wedge Inv) \Rightarrow \{\mathcal{U}\}\{\mathcal{V}_{mod}\}[\texttt{p}]Inv, \Delta & \text{preserves} \\ \Gamma, \{\mathcal{U}\}\{\mathcal{V}_{mod}\}(\neg g \wedge Inv) \Rightarrow \{\mathcal{U}\}\{\mathcal{V}_{mod}\}[\texttt{r}]\varphi, \Delta & \text{use case} \end{array}}{\Gamma \Rightarrow \{\mathcal{U}\}[\texttt{while } (g) \texttt{ \{p\}; r}]\varphi, \Delta}$$

In contrast to standard loop invariants, we keep the context (Γ, Δ) in the second and third premiss, following [2]. This is sound, because we use an *anonymizing update* $\mathcal{V}_{mod} = (\mathcal{V}_{mod}^{vars} \parallel \mathcal{V}_{mod}^{heap})$ which is constructed as follows: Let $x_1, \ldots, x_m$ be the program variables and $a_1[t_1], \ldots, a_n[t_n]$ be the array locations occurring on the left-hand sides of assignments in the loop body p. For each $i \in \{1..n\}$ let $l_i, r_i : \texttt{int}$ be chosen such that $val_{D,I,s,\beta}(t_i)$ at the program point $a_i[t_i] = t$; is always between $val_{D,I,s,\beta}(l_i)$ (inclusive) and $val_{D,I,s,\beta}(r_i)$ (exclusive). Then $a_i[l_i..r_i]$ are terms of type LocSet describing all array locations of a_i which might be changed by the loop. The anonymizing updates are:

$$\mathcal{V}_{mod}^{vars} := \{x_1 := c_1 \parallel \ldots \parallel x_m := c_m\}$$
$$\mathcal{V}_{mod}^{heap} := \{\texttt{heap} := anon(\ldots anon(\texttt{heap}, a_1[l_1..r_1], anonH_1), \ldots, a_n[l_n..r_n], anonH_n)\}$$

where the c_i are fresh constants of the same type as x_i and $anonH_i$ are fresh constants of type Heap. The function $anon(h1, locset, h2)$ takes two heaps $h1, h2$ and a location set *locset* and returns a heap that is equal to $h1$ except for the locations mentioned in *locset* whose values are set to the values of these locations in $h2$. Informally, the anonymizing updates assign all program variables that might be changed by p and all locations enumerated in *mod* an unknown value about which only the information provided by the invariant *Inv* is available.

Updates can be simplified and applied to terms and formulas using the set of (schematic) rewrite rules given in [2,4].

2.2   Integrating Abstraction

We summarize from [1] how to integrate abstraction into our program logic. This integration provides the technical foundation for generating loop invariants.

Definition 4 (Abstract Domain). *Let D be a* concrete domain *(e.g., of a first-order structure). An* abstract domain A *is a countable lattice with partial order $\sqsubseteq$ and join operator $\sqcup$ and without infinite ascending chains.[2] It is connected to D with an* abstraction function $\alpha : 2^D \rightarrow A$ *and a* concretization function $\gamma : A \rightarrow 2^D$ *which form a Galois connection* [5].

Instead of extending our program logic by abstract elements, we use a different approach to refer to the element of an abstract domain:

Definition 5 ($\gamma_{\alpha,\mathbb{N}}$-symbols). *Given an abstract domain $A = \{\alpha_1, \alpha_2, \ldots\}$. For each abstract element $\alpha_i \in A$ there are infinitely many constant symbols $\gamma_{\alpha_i,j} \in \mathcal{F}$, $j \in \mathbb{N}$ with $I(\gamma_{\alpha_i,j}) \in \gamma(\alpha_i)$, as well as a unary predicate χ_{α_i} where $I(\chi_{\alpha_i})$ is the characteristic predicate of set $\gamma(\alpha_i)$.*

In the definition above the interpretation I of a symbol $\gamma_{\alpha_i,j}$ is restricted to one of the concrete domain elements represented by α_i, but it is not fixed. This is important for the following notion of weakening: with respect to the symbols occurring in a given (partial) proof P and a set of formulas C, we call an update $\mathcal{U}'$ (P,C)-weaker than an update $\mathcal{U}$ if $\mathcal{U}'$ describes at least all state transitions that are also allowed by $\mathcal{U}$. Formally, given a fixed D, then $\mathcal{U}$ is weaker than $\mathcal{U}'$ iff for any first order structure $M = (D, I, s, \beta)$ there is a first order structure $M' = (D, I', s, \beta)$ with I and I' being two interpretations coinciding on all symbols used so far in P and in C and if for both structures $val_M(C) = tt$ and $val_{M'}(C) = tt$ holds, then for all program variables v the equation $val_M(\{\mathcal{U}\}v) = val_{M'}(\{\mathcal{U}'\}v)$ must hold.

Example 1. Consider the abstract sign domain for integers:

$$\gamma(\top) = \mathbb{Z} \qquad \gamma(\leq) = \{i \in \mathbb{Z} \mid i \leq 0\}$$
$$\gamma(\geq) = \{i \in \mathbb{Z} \mid i \geq 0\} \qquad \gamma(\text{neg}) = \{i \in \mathbb{Z} \mid i < 0\}$$
$$\gamma(\text{pos}) = \{i \in \mathbb{Z} \mid i > 0\} \qquad \gamma(0) = \{0\}$$
$$\gamma(\emptyset) = \{\}$$

---

[2] The limitation to only finite ascending chains ensures termination of our approach without the need to introduce widening operators. An extension to infinite chains with widening would be easily realizable, but so far was unnecessary.

Let P be a partial sequent proof with $\gamma_{\leq,3}$ not occurring in P. Then update $\mathtt{i} := \gamma_{\leq,3}$ is $(P, \emptyset)$-weaker than update $\mathtt{i} := -5$ or update $\mathtt{i} := c$ with a constant c (occurring in P) provided $\chi_{\leq}(c)$ holds.

The weakenUpdate rule from [1] integrates abstraction into our calculus:

$$\text{weakenUpdate} \quad \frac{\Gamma, \{\mathcal{U}\}(\bar{\mathbf{x}} \doteq \bar{c}) \Rightarrow \exists \bar{\gamma}.\{\mathcal{U}'\}(\bar{\mathbf{x}} \doteq \bar{c}), \Delta \quad \Gamma \Rightarrow \{\mathcal{U}'\}\varphi, \Delta}{\Gamma \Rightarrow \{\mathcal{U}\}\varphi, \Delta}$$

where $\bar{\mathbf{x}}$ are all program variables occurring as left-hand sides in $\mathcal{U}$ and $\bar{c}$ are fresh skolem constants. The formula $\exists \bar{\gamma}.\psi$ is a shortcut for $\exists \bar{y}.(\chi_{\bar{a}}(\bar{y}) \wedge \psi[\bar{\gamma}/\bar{y}])$, where $\bar{y} = (y_1, \ldots, y_m)$ is a list of fresh first order variables of the same length as $\bar{\gamma}$, and where $\psi[\bar{\gamma}/\bar{y}]$ stands for the formula obtained from ψ by replacing all occurrences of a symbol in $\bar{\gamma}$ with its counterpart in $\bar{y}$. Performing value-based abstraction thus becomes replacement of an update by a weaker update. In particular, we do not perform abstraction on the program, but on the *symbolic state*.

3   Loop Invariant Generation for Arrays

We refine the value-based abstraction approach from the previous section for dealing with arrays. Rather than introducing a dedicated abstract domain for arrays (e.g., abstracting an array to its length), we extend the abstract domain of the array elements to a range within the array. Given an index set (range) R, an abstract domain A for array elements can be extended to an abstract domain A_R for arrays by copying the structure of A and renaming each α_i to $\alpha_{R,i}$. The $\alpha_{R,i}$ are such that $\gamma_{\alpha_{R,i,j}} \in \{arr \in \mathcal{D}^{\mathtt{int}\,[]} \mid \forall k \in R.\chi_{\alpha_i}(arr[k])\}$.

Example 2. Extending the sign domain for integers gives for each range $R \subseteq \mathbb{N}$:

$$\gamma(\top_R) = \mathcal{D}^{\mathtt{int}\,[]}$$
$$\gamma(\leq_R) = \{arr \in \mathcal{D}^{\mathtt{int}\,[]} \mid \forall k \in R.\, arr[k] \leq 0\}$$
$$\gamma(\geq_R) = \{arr \in \mathcal{D}^{\mathtt{int}\,[]} \mid \forall k \in R.\, arr[k] \geq 0\}$$
$$\gamma(\mathrm{neg}_R) = \{arr \in \mathcal{D}^{\mathtt{int}\,[]} \mid \forall k \in R.\, arr[k] < 0\}$$
$$\gamma(\mathrm{pos}_R) = \{arr \in \mathcal{D}^{\mathtt{int}\,[]} \mid \forall k \in R.\, arr[k] > 0\}$$
$$\gamma(0_R) = \{arr \in \mathcal{D}^{\mathtt{int}\,[]} \mid \forall k \in R.\, arr[k] \doteq 0\}$$
$$\gamma(\emptyset_R) = \{\}$$

Fixing $R = \{0, 2\}$, we have $\gamma(\geq_{\{0,2\}}) = \{arr \in \mathcal{D}^{\mathtt{int}\,[]} \mid arr[0] \geq 0 \wedge arr[2] \geq 0\}$. Importantly, the array length itself is irrelevant, provided $arr[0]$ and $arr[2]$ have the required values. Therefore the arrays (we deviate from Java's array literal syntax for clarity) $[0, 3, 6, 9]$ and $[5, -5, 0]$ are both elements of $\gamma(\geq_{\{0,2\}})$.

Of particular interest are the ranges containing (at least) all elements modified within a loop. One such range is $[0..arr.\mathtt{length})$. This range can always be taken as a fallback option if no more precise range can be found.

3.1   Loop Invariant Rule with Value and Array Abstraction

We present the rule invariantUpdate, which splits the loop invariant of the rule loopInvariant into an abstract update $\mathcal{U}'$ and an invariant Inv. While $\mathcal{U}'$ abstracts only the non-heap values, Inv can contain invariants about arrays on the heap.

invariantUpdate

$$\frac{\begin{array}{l} \Gamma, \{\mathcal{U}\}(\bar{\mathtt{x}} \doteq \bar{c}) \Rightarrow \exists \bar{\gamma}.\{\mathcal{U}'\}(\bar{\mathtt{x}} \doteq \bar{c}), \Delta \\ \Gamma, \mathtt{old} \doteq \{\mathcal{U}\}\mathtt{heap} \Rightarrow \{\mathcal{U}\}Inv, \Delta \\ \Gamma, \mathtt{old} \doteq \{\mathcal{U}\}\mathtt{heap}, \{\mathcal{U}'_{mod}\}(g \wedge Inv), \{\mathcal{U}'_{mod}\}[\mathtt{p}](\bar{\mathtt{x}} \doteq \bar{c}) \Rightarrow \exists \bar{\gamma}.\{\mathcal{U}'_{mod}\}(\bar{\mathtt{x}} \doteq \bar{c}), \Delta \\ \Gamma, \mathtt{old} \doteq \{\mathcal{U}\}\mathtt{heap}, \{\mathcal{U}'_{mod}\}(g \wedge Inv) \Rightarrow \{\mathcal{U}'_{mod}\}[\mathtt{p}]Inv, \Delta \\ \Gamma, \mathtt{old} \doteq \{\mathcal{U}\}\mathtt{heap}, \{\mathcal{U}'_{mod}\}(\neg g \wedge Inv) \Rightarrow \{\mathcal{U}'_{mod}\}[r]\varphi, \Delta \end{array}}{\Gamma \Rightarrow \{\mathcal{U}\}[\mathtt{while} \ (g) \ \{\mathtt{p}\}; \ r]\varphi, \Delta}$$

The first premiss is identical to the left premiss of weakenUpdate, introducing a suitable abstraction $\mathcal{U}'$ of $\mathcal{U}$. The symbols $\bar{\mathtt{x}}, \bar{c}, \bar{\gamma}$ and $\exists \bar{\gamma}\varphi$ are also defined as in the weakenUpdate rule. From $\mathcal{U}'$ we obtain $\mathcal{U}'_{mod} := (\mathcal{U}' \parallel \mathcal{V}^{heap}_{mod})$ by anonymizing the heap locations that might be changed in the loop body as explained in Sect. 2.1. Anonymization of local variables $\mathcal{V}^{vars}_{mod}$ is not required, as it is already part of $\mathcal{U}'$. More precisely, $\mathcal{U}'$ can contain updates $\mathtt{x} := \gamma_{\alpha_i,j}$ which combine the anonymization of $\mathcal{V}^{vars}_{mod}$ with an invariant based on the abstract domain.

The identifier $\mathtt{old}$ is a fresh constant and used in the invariant Inv to refer to the heap before loop execution. Inv contains invariants related to the heap. Intuitively $\mathcal{U}'_{mod}$ and Inv together express all states in which the program could be before or after any iteration of the loop. The first two premisses together ensure that the abstract update $\mathcal{U}'_{mod}$ and the invariant Inv are a valid weakening of the original update $\mathcal{U}$. The following two premisses ensure that $\mathcal{U}'_{mod}$ and Inv actually constitute a loop invariant: for any given interpretation of $\mathcal{U}'_{mod}$ satisfying Inv executing the loop body results in an abstract state no weaker than $\mathcal{U}'_{mod}$ in which Inv remains valid. The last premiss is the use case, where the desired postcondition φ must be established based on the state after exiting the loop and after execution of the remaining program.

Given the program $\mathtt{p}$ in Listing 1.1, we can apply the assignment rule twice to $\Gamma \Rightarrow \{\mathcal{U}\}[\mathtt{p}]\varphi, \Delta$ which leads to $\Gamma \Rightarrow \{\mathcal{U} \parallel \mathtt{i} := 0 \parallel \mathtt{j} := 0\}[\mathtt{while}\ldots]\varphi, \Delta$. Now invariantUpdate can be applied with the values in Fig. 1: the update $\mathcal{U}'$ is equal to the original update $\mathcal{U}$ except for the values of $\mathtt{i}$ and $\mathtt{j}$ which can both be any non-negative number. The arrays $\mathtt{b}$ and $\mathtt{c}$ have (partial) ranges anonymized, while $\mathtt{a}$ is not anonymized as

Listing 1.1. Example

```
i = 0; j = 0;
while(i < a.length) {
    if (a[j] > 0) j++;
    b[i] = j;
    c[2*i] = 0;
    i++;
}
```

it is not changed by the loop. The invariants in Inv express that (a) $\mathtt{a}$ contains positive values at all positions prior to the current value of $\mathtt{j}$, (b) the anonymized values[3] in $\mathtt{b}$ are all non-negative, and (c) the anonymized values in $\mathtt{c}$ are equal to 0 or to their original values, if the loop has not (yet) modified them.

---

[3] Note choosing the range $[0..\mathtt{i})$ for the array $\mathtt{b}$ is sound even when $\mathtt{i} \geq \mathtt{b.length}$, as an uncaught $\mathtt{ArrayIndexOutOfBoundsException}$ is treated as non-termination.

$$\mathcal{U}' = (\mathcal{U} \parallel \mathtt{i} := \gamma_{\geq,1} \parallel \mathtt{j} := \gamma_{\geq,2})$$

$$\mathcal{V}^{heap}_{mod} = \mathbf{heap} := anon(anon(\mathbf{heap}, \mathtt{b}[0..i], anonHeap_1), \mathtt{c}[*], anonHeap_2)$$

$$Inv = (\forall k \in [0..\mathtt{j}]. \; \chi_>(\mathtt{a}[k]))$$

$$\land \; (\forall k \in [0..\mathtt{i}]. \; \chi_\geq(\mathtt{b}[k]))$$

$$\land \; (\forall m \in c. \; (m < 2 * i \land m\%2 \doteq 0) \rightarrow \chi_0(\mathtt{c}[2 * m]))$$

$$\land \; (\forall m \in c. \; \neg(m < 2 * i \land m\%2 \doteq 0) \rightarrow (\mathtt{c}[m] \doteq select(\mathbf{old}, \mathtt{c}, m)))$$

Fig. 1. Values for invariantUpdate

Algorithm 1. Generating an abstract update and invariant fixpoint

---

input : the sequent *seq*
output: the fixpoint $\mathcal{U}'$ with valid $\mathcal{V}^{heap}_{mod}$ and *Inv*, as $(\mathcal{U}'_m, Inv)$

1 $\mathcal{U}'_m \leftarrow \mathcal{U}$;
2 **while** *true* **do**
3 $\quad$ /* seq is of the form: $\Gamma \Rightarrow \{\mathcal{U}'_m\}[\mathtt{while}\ (g)\ \{p\};\ r]\varphi, \Delta$ $\qquad$ */
4 $\quad$ $\mathcal{U}^* \leftarrow \mathcal{U}'_m$; $Inv \leftarrow \Gamma \cup !\Delta$;
5 $\quad$ $seq \leftarrow (\Gamma, \{\mathcal{U}'_m\}g \Rightarrow \{\mathcal{U}'_m\}[p; \mathtt{while}(g)\{p\}; r]\varphi, \Delta)$;
6 $\quad$ perform symbolic execution on *seq*;
7 $\quad$ /* all branches either closed or loop entry reached again $\qquad$ */
8 $\quad$ **foreach** *open branch with* $\Gamma_i \Rightarrow \{\mathcal{U}_i\}[\mathtt{while}\ (g)\ \{p\};\ r]\varphi, \Delta_i$ **do**
9 $\quad\quad$ $(Inv, \mathcal{U}^*) \leftarrow (Inv, \mathcal{U}^*) \sqcup (\Gamma_i \cup !\Delta_i, \mathcal{U}_i)$; $\quad$ // see Definition 6 for $\sqcup$
10 $\quad$ **end**
11 $\quad$ **if** $\mathcal{U}'_m$ *is (P,Inv)-weaker than* $\mathcal{U}^*$ **then**
12 $\quad\quad$ **return** $(\mathcal{U}'_m, Inv)$;
13 $\quad$ **end**
14 $\quad$ $\mathcal{U}'_m \leftarrow \mathcal{U}^*$; $\Gamma \leftarrow \Gamma \cup \{\mathcal{U}'_m\}Inv$;
15 $\quad$ $seq \leftarrow (\Gamma \Rightarrow \{\mathcal{U}'_m\}[\mathtt{while}\ (g)\ \{p\};\ r]\varphi, \Delta)$;
16 **end**

3.2 Computation of the Abstract Update and Invariants

We generate the values of $\mathcal{U}'$, $\mathcal{V}^{heap}_{mod}$ and *Inv* as required by invariantUpdate *automatically* in a side proof, by symbolic execution of single loop iterations until a fixpoint is found. For each value change of a variable during the execution of a loop iteration the abstract update $\mathcal{U}'$ will set this variable to a value at least as weak as its value both before and after loop execution. We generate $\mathcal{V}^{heap}_{mod}$ and *Inv* by examining each array modification[4] and anonymizing the entire range within the array (expressed in $\mathcal{V}^{heap}_{mod}$) while adding a partial invariant to the set *Inv*. Once a fixpoint for $\mathcal{U}'$ is reached, we can refine $\mathcal{V}^{heap}_{mod}$ and *Inv* by performing in essence a second fixpoint iteration, this time anonymizing possibly smaller ranges and potentially adding more invariants. We explain this now step by step.

---

[4] Later we also examine each array access (read or write) in if-conditions to gain invariants such as $\forall k \in [0..\mathtt{j}]. \; \chi_>(select(\mathbf{heap}, \mathtt{a}, k))$ in the example above.

Algorithm 2. Concrete update join $\sqcup_{upd}$

---
input : $((C_1, \mathcal{U}_1), (C_2, \mathcal{U}_2))$
output: the weaker constraint/update pair $(C_{res}, \mathcal{U}_{res})$

1 $(\mathcal{U}_{res} \parallel \mathbf{heap} := h') \leftarrow (C_1, \mathcal{U}_1) \sqcup_{abs} (C_2, \mathcal{U}_2)$;   // heap update h' ignored
2 $(C_{res}, h) \leftarrow (C_1, \{\mathcal{U}_1\}\mathbf{heap}) \,\hat{\sqcup}\, (C_2, \{\mathcal{U}_2\}\mathbf{heap})$;   // see Definition 7 for $\hat{\sqcup}$
3 $\mathcal{U}_{res} \leftarrow (\mathcal{U}_{res} \parallel \mathbf{heap} := h)$;
4 **return** $(C_{res}, \mathcal{U}_{res})$

The first step is to generate $\mathcal{U}'$ (with valid but imprecise $\mathcal{V}_{mod}^{heap}$ and Inv). For this we use Algorithm 1 with input $seq = (\Gamma \Rightarrow \{\mathcal{U}\}[\mathtt{while}\ (g)\ \{p\};\ r]\varphi, \Delta)$, the conclusion of invariantUpdate.

The algorithm requires to compute the join $\sqcup$ of pairs of invariants and updates. In [1] a concrete implementation for joining updates $(C_1, \mathcal{U}_1) \sqcup_{abs} (C_2, \mathcal{U}_2)$ with

$$\sqcup_{abs} : (2^{For} \times Upd) \times (2^{For} \times Upd) \rightarrow Upd$$

was computed as follows: For each update $\mathbf{x} := v$ in $\mathcal{U}_1$ or $\mathcal{U}_2$ the generated update is $\mathbf{x} := v$, if $\{\mathcal{U}_1\}x \doteq \{\mathcal{U}_2\}x$ under C_1, C_2 respectively. Otherwise it is $\mathbf{x} := \gamma_{\alpha_i, j}$ for some α_i where $C_1 \Rightarrow \chi_{\alpha_i}(\{\mathcal{U}_1\}x)$ and $C_2 \Rightarrow \chi_{\alpha_i}(\{\mathcal{U}_2\}x)$ are valid. For a simple heap abstraction this returns (for some $n \in \mathbb{N}$) $\mathbf{heap} := \gamma_{\top, n}$ for any non-identical heaps. As we wish to join the heaps meaningfully, which leads to the generation of constraints, our update join operation has the signature

$$\sqcup : (2^{For} \times Upd) \times (2^{For} \times Upd) \rightarrow (2^{For} \times Upd).$$

Definition 6 (Joining Updates). *Any operation $\sqcup$ satisfying the following properties is an* update join operation: *Let $\mathcal{U}_1$, $\mathcal{U}_2$ be arbitrary updates in a proof P and let C_1, C_2 be formula sets representing constraints on the update values. Then for $(C, \mathcal{U}) = (C_1, \mathcal{U}_1) \sqcup (C_2, \mathcal{U}_2)$ the following holds for $i \in \{1, 2\}$: (a) $\mathcal{U}$ is (P, C_i)-weaker than $\mathcal{U}_i$, (b) $C_i \Rightarrow \{\mathcal{U}_i\} \bigwedge C$, and (c) $\sqcup$ is associative and commutative up to first-order reasoning.*

Let $C_1, \mathcal{U}_1$ and $C_2, \mathcal{U}_2$ be constraint/update pairs. $(C_1, \mathcal{U}_1) \sqcup_{upd} (C_2, \mathcal{U}_2)$ computes the update $\mathcal{U}_{res}$ and the set of heap restrictions C_{res} as shown in Algorithm 2. Intuitively, if all the restrictions in C_{res} are satisfied by the heap under update $\mathcal{U}_{res}$ then $\mathcal{U}_{res}$ is the lattice join of $\mathcal{U}_1$ and $\mathcal{U}_2$.

Lemma 1. $\sqcup_{upd}$ *is an update join operator.*
    The proof is in the appendix of the extended technical report [6].

Definition 7 (Joining Heaps). *Any operator with the signature*

$$\hat{\sqcup} : (2^{For} \times Trm_{\mathsf{Heap}}) \times (2^{For} \times Trm_{\mathsf{Heap}}) \rightarrow (2^{For} \times Trm_{\mathsf{Heap}})$$

is a heap join operator *if it satisfies the properties: Let h_1, h_2 be arbitrary heaps in a proof P, C_1, C_2 be formula sets representing constraints on the heaps* *(and possibly also on other update values) and let $\mathcal{U}$ be an arbitrary update. Then for $(C, h) = (C_1, h_1) \mathbin{\hat{\sqcup}} (C_2, h_2)$ the following holds for $i \in \{1, 2\}$: (a) $(\mathcal{U} \parallel \mathtt{heap} := h)$ is (P, C_i)-weaker than $(\mathcal{U} \parallel \mathtt{heap} := h_i)$, (b) $C_i \Rightarrow \{\mathcal{U} \parallel \mathtt{heap} := h_i\} \wedge C$, and (c) $\hat{\sqcup}$ is associative and commutative up to first-order reasoning.*

We define the set of *normal form heaps* $\mathcal{H}_{NF} \subset Trm_{\mathtt{Heap}}$ to be those heap terms that extend $\mathtt{heap}$ with an arbitrary number of preceding stores or anonymizations. For a heap term $h \in \mathcal{H}_{NF}$ we define

$$
writes(h) := \begin{cases} \emptyset & \text{if } h = \mathtt{heap} \\ \{h\} \cup writes(h') & \text{if } h = store(h', a, idx, v) \text{ or } h = anon(h', a[l..r], h'') \end{cases}
$$

A concrete implementation $\hat{\sqcup}_{heap}$ of $\hat{\sqcup}$ is given as follows: We reduce the signature to $\hat{\sqcup}_{heap} : (2^{For} \times \mathcal{H}_{NF}) \times (2^{For} \times \mathcal{H}_{NF}) \rightarrow (2^{For} \times \mathcal{H}_{NF})$. This ensures that all heaps we examine are based on $\mathtt{heap}$ and is a valid assumption when taking the program rules into account, as these maintain this normal form. As both heaps are in normal form, they must share a common subheap (at least $\mathtt{heap}$). The largest common subheap of h_1, h_2 is defined as $lcs(h_1, h_2)$ and all writes performed on this subheap can be given as $writes_{lcs}(h_1, h_2) := writes(h_1) \cup writes(h_2) \setminus (writes(h_1) \cap writes(h_2))$. Algorithm 3 shows how the join of heaps $(C_1, h_1) \mathbin{\hat{\sqcup}_{heap}} (C_2, h_2)$ is calculated.

Lemma 2. *The concrete implementation $\hat{\sqcup}_{heap}$ is a heap join operator on the reduced signature $(2^{For} \times \mathcal{H}_{NF}) \times (2^{For} \times \mathcal{H}_{NF}) \rightarrow (2^{For} \times \mathcal{H}_{NF})$.*

The proof is in the appendix of the extended technical report [6].

Example 3. With the precondition $P = \forall n \in \mathtt{b}.\ select(\mathtt{heap}, \mathtt{b}, n) \doteq -1$ and the program in Listing 1.1, we demonstrate the first steps of Algorithm 1 with $seq = P \Rightarrow \{\mathtt{i} := 0 \parallel \mathtt{j} := 0\}[\mathtt{while}\ldots]\varphi$: After initialization $Inv = \{P\}$ and $\mathcal{U}^* = (\mathtt{i} := 0 \parallel \mathtt{j} := 0)$. At line 8 of Algorithm 1 we have two open branches:

$$P, \{\mathcal{U}^*\}g, \neg(select(\mathtt{heap}, \mathtt{a}, 0) > 0) \Rightarrow$$
$$\{\mathtt{i} := 1 \parallel \mathtt{j} := 0 \parallel \mathtt{heap} := store(store(\mathtt{heap}, \mathtt{b}, 0, 0), \mathtt{c}, 0, 0)\}[\mathtt{while}\ldots]\varphi \quad (1)$$

$$P, \{\mathcal{U}^*\}g, select(\mathtt{heap}, \mathtt{a}, 0) > 0 \Rightarrow$$
$$\{\mathtt{i} := 1 \parallel \mathtt{j} := 1 \parallel \mathtt{heap} := store(store(\mathtt{heap}, \mathtt{b}, 0, 1), \mathtt{c}, 0, 0)\}[\mathtt{while}\ldots]\varphi \quad (2)$$

Algorithm 3. Concrete heap join $\hat{\sqcup}_{heap}$

---

    input : $((C_1, h_1), (C_2, h_2))$
    output: the weaker constraint/heap pair (C_{res}, h_{res})

1 $h_{res} \leftarrow lcs(h_1, h_2)$; $C_{res} \leftarrow \emptyset$; $W \leftarrow writes_{lcs}(h_1, h_2)$;
2 **foreach** $anon(h, a[l..r], anonHeap)$ or $store(h, a, idx, v) \in W$ **do**
3      $h_{res} \leftarrow anon(h_{res}, a[*], anonHeap')$;
4      $i_1, i_2 \leftarrow$ the indices of the smallest α_{i_j} such that
          $C_j \Rightarrow \forall k \in a.\ \chi_{\alpha_{i_j}}(select(h_j, a, k))$;
5      $C_{res} \leftarrow C_{res} \cup \{\forall k \in a.\ \chi_{\alpha_{i_1} \sqcup \alpha_{i_2}}(select(\mathtt{heap}, a, k))\}$
6 **end**

We can use Algorithm 2 to compute the update join of the original $(\{P\}, \mathcal{U}^*)$ with $(\{P, \{\mathcal{U}^*\}g, \neg(select(\mathsf{heap}, \mathsf{a}, 0) > 0)\}, \mathtt{i} := 1 \parallel \mathtt{j} := 0 \parallel \mathsf{heap} := h_1)$ provided by (1), where $h_1 = store(store(\mathsf{heap}, \mathsf{b}, 0, 0), \mathsf{c}, 0, 0)$. This produces $(C_{res}, \mathtt{i} := \gamma_{\geq,1} \parallel \mathtt{j} := 0 \parallel \mathsf{heap} := h_{res})$, where (C_{res}, h_{res}) is a heap join of $(\{P\}, \mathsf{heap})$ and $(\{P, \{\mathcal{U}^*\}g, \neg(select(\mathsf{heap}, \mathsf{a}, 0) > 0)\}, h_1)$. Algorithm 3 can compute the latter as follows: the largest common subheap is $h' = \mathsf{heap}$, so we have $W = \{store(store(\mathsf{heap}, \mathsf{b}, 0, 0), \mathsf{c}, 0, 0), store(\mathsf{heap}, \mathsf{b}, 0, 0)\}$, therefore:

$$C_{res} = \{\forall m \in \mathsf{b}. \; \chi_{\leq}(select(\mathsf{heap}, \mathsf{b}, m)), \; \forall n \in \mathsf{c}. \; \chi_{\top}(select(\mathsf{heap}, \mathsf{c}, n))\}$$
$$h_{res} = anon(anon(\mathsf{heap}, \mathsf{b}[*], anonH_1), \mathsf{c}[*], anonH_2)$$

At line 9 of Algorithm 1 we have $\mathcal{U}^* = (\mathtt{i} := \gamma_{\geq,1} \parallel \mathtt{j} := 0 \parallel \mathsf{heap} := h_{res})$ and $Inv = C_{res}$. Now the algorithm joins updates with the second open branch, checks if a fixpoint has been found (it has not) and enters the next iteration.

4   Symbolic Pivots

Algorithm 1 computes an abstract update $\mathcal{U}'$ expressing the state of all non-heap program variables before and after each loop iteration and, in particular, before entering the loop. It also computes $\mathcal{V}^{heap}_{mod}$ and Inv, which give information about the state of the heap before and after each loop iteration. However, as a consequence of the definition of heap joins in Algorithm 3, this information is rather weak as it assumes any update to an array element could cause a change at any index. To remedy this situation we refine $\mathcal{U}'$. The main idea is to keep track of the ranges within a given array where a modification has been made and where it has not been modified. The boundary indices of such ranges are often called *pivot* in array algorithms. To obtain invariants that are valid in any state before and after a loop iteration, obviously, these pivots must be symbolic.

We start with an example that illustrates the difficulties of computing *symbolic pivots*. Consider Listing 1.2. A naïve approach to recording pivots would be to consider just the array modification statement, here "d[i] = j;", and infer that the modifications to d occur at the index given by the value of i. But this is completely wrong here. Variable i has the constant value 0 at the beginning of each iteration, while the array modifications occur at indices based on the value of j. This is problematic to detect for

Listing 1.2. Inferring Modified Array Elements

```
int i = 0;
int j = 5;
while (j < a.length) {
    i = j + 1;
    d[i] = j;
    j = i + 1;
    i = 0;
}
```

analyses based on control flow graphs, but easy for our value-sensitive approach. The reason is that the update created during a loop iteration of the example immediately shows that the value of i is unchanged.

The problem remains that while we know, for example, that in the first iteration of the loop the array element d[6] is set to 5, we cannot infer *why* that particular index was chosen. But we need to know this to generate valid invariants. McMillan [7] points out this problem while analyzing multiple, successive iterations of a loop and then attempts to infer why array elements at specific indices were modified. Our approach allows a more uniform analysis: first we calculate an over-approximation of the modified ranges, resulting in γ-terms which are integer abstractions that constitute correct boundaries of array ranges. Based on these γ-terms we then execute symbolically one iteration of the loop whereby we keep track of modifications to array elements.

Example 4. Running Algorithm 1 on the loop in Listing 1.2 results in the following updates for non-heap variables: ($i := 0 \parallel j := \gamma_{>,1}$) Symbolic execution of a loop iteration started with $\gamma_{>,1}$ as the value of j leads to the following update:

$$i := 0 \parallel j := \gamma_{>,1} + 2 \parallel \text{heap} := store(\text{heap}, d, \gamma_{>,1} + 1, \gamma_{>,1})$$

Value $\gamma_{>,1}$ was the initial value of j, so we can conclude that the array elements are modified at the value of $j + 1$ in each iteration.

Now we describe how this can be made to work in the general case. Consider the sequent $\Gamma \Rightarrow \{\mathcal{U}\}[\text{while}(g)\{p\};\ r]\varphi, \Delta$ and the update $\mathcal{U}'$ computed by Algorithm 1. Then an update $\mathcal{U}''$ which maps all variables but heap just as $\mathcal{U}'$ does and maps heap as the original $\mathcal{U}$ did remains weaker than $\mathcal{U}$, as $\mathcal{U}'$ is weaker than $\mathcal{U}$. Applying Algorithm 1 to sequent $\Gamma \Rightarrow \mathcal{U}''[\text{while}(g)\{p\};\ r]\varphi, \Delta$ we obtain open subgoals of the form $\Gamma_i \Rightarrow \{\mathcal{U}_i\}[\text{while}\ (g)\ \{p\};\ r]\varphi, \Delta_i$. Aside from the values for heap, $\mathcal{U}'$ is weaker than $\mathcal{U}_i$, as $\mathcal{U}'$ is a fixpoint. We therefore do not have to join any non-heap variables when computing $(\mathcal{U}^*, Inv)$, as fixpoints for those are already calculated and will not change.

When joining constraint/heap pairs we distinguish between three types of writes (see Sect. 3.2): (a) anonymizations, which are kept, as well as any invariants generated for them occurring in the constraints, (b) stores to concrete indices, for which we create a store to the index either of the explicit value (if equal in both heaps) or of a fresh $\gamma_{i,j}$ of appropriate type, and (c) stores to variable indices, which we turn into symbolic pivots (and, hence, stronger invariants) as follows. Given a $store(h, a, idx, v)$ to a variable index, idx is expressible as a function $index(\gamma_{i_0,j_0}, \ldots, \gamma_{i_n,j_n})$. These γ_{i_x,j_x} can be linked to program variables in the update $\mathcal{U}'$, which contains updates $\text{pv}_x := \gamma_{i_x,j_x}$. We can therefore represent idx as a function $sp(\ldots \text{pv}_x \ldots)$ and call it a *symbolic pivot*.

Example 5. Continuing Example 4, d is modified at index $index(\gamma_{>,1}) = \gamma_{>,1}+1$. As $\gamma_{>,1}$ was the value of j, the symbolic pivot is $sp(j) = j + 1$.

The final step is to exploit the shape of symbolic pivots to derive certain kinds of inductive invariants. For this we need two abbreviations. Formula $P(\mathcal{W})$ is defined for a fixed update $\mathcal{U}$, array a, and symbolic pivot sp as: $P(\mathcal{W}) := \forall k \in [\{\mathcal{U}\}sp..\{\mathcal{W}\}sp).\ \{\mathcal{W}\}\chi_{\alpha_j}(select(\text{heap}, a, k))$. Then $P(\mathcal{U})$ is trivially valid, as we are quantifying over an empty set. Likewise, it is easy to show that the instance $Q(\mathcal{U})$ of the following formula $Q(\mathcal{W})$ is valid:

$$\forall k \notin [\{\mathcal{U}\}sp..\{\mathcal{W}\}sp).\ select(\{\mathcal{W}\}\text{heap}, \{\mathcal{W}\}a, k) \doteq select(\{\mathcal{U}\}\text{heap}, \{\mathcal{W}\}a, k)$$

Therefore, anonymizing an array a with $anon(h, a[*], anonHeap)$ and adding invariants $P(\mathcal{U}^*)$ and $Q(\mathcal{U}^*)$ for the contiguous range $[\{\mathcal{U}\}sp..\{\mathcal{U}^*\}sp)$ is inductively sound if $P(\mathcal{U}') \Rightarrow P(\mathcal{U}_i)$ and $Q(\mathcal{U}') \Rightarrow Q(\mathcal{U}_i)$ hold. The same is true for the range $[\{\mathcal{U}^*\}sp..\{\mathcal{U}\}sp)$, hence w.l.o.g. in the sequel $\{\mathcal{U}^*\}sp \geq \{\mathcal{U}\}sp$.

Definition 8 (Iteration Affine). *Given a sequent* $\Gamma \Rightarrow \{\mathcal{U}\}[p]\varphi, \Delta$ *where* p *starts with* $\mathtt{while}$, *a term* t *is called* iteration affine, *if there exists step* $\in \mathbb{Z}$ *such that for any* $n \in \mathbb{N}$, *if we unwind and symbolically execute the loop* n *times, for each subgoal with sequent* $\Gamma_i \Rightarrow \{\mathcal{U}_i\}[p]\varphi, \Delta_i$ *there is some* v, *such that* $\Gamma_i \cup !\Delta_i \Rightarrow \{\mathcal{U}_i\}t \doteq v$ *and* $\Gamma \cup !\Delta \Rightarrow \{\mathcal{U}\}t + n * step \doteq v$.

From iteration affine symbolic pivots we can directly construct inductive invariants over array ranges as follows. First, after unwinding a loop body once we posit a symbolic pivot sp as iteration affine using $step := (\{\mathcal{U}'\}sp) - (\{\mathcal{U}\}sp)$, where $\mathcal{U}'$ is the program state after executing the loop body. Then simply add the constraint $n \geq 0 \wedge (\{\mathcal{U}\}sp) + n * step \doteq v$ for a fresh n in further fixpoint iterations and ensure that $(\{\mathcal{U}'\}sp) \doteq v + step$ holds. If this is not the case, then sp is not iteration affine and we remove the constraint in following fixpoint iterations. Otherwise, once a fixpoint is found we know the exact array elements that may be modified, as sp is iteration affine. To express an affine range as a location set is difficult. To avoid it, we anonymize the entire array and create the following invariants for the modified and unmodified partitions (using the symbols of Definition 8) where $M := (k \geq \{\mathcal{U}\}sp \wedge k < sp \wedge (k - \{\mathcal{U}\}sp)\%step \doteq 0)$:

$$\forall k \in arr. \; M \rightarrow \chi(arr[k]) \tag{3}$$

$$\forall k \in arr. \; \neg M \rightarrow arr[k] \doteq select(\{\mathcal{U}\}\mathtt{heap}, arr, k) \tag{4}$$

Example 6. This symbolic pivot $j+1$ from Example 5 is iteration affine, expressible as $6 + it * 2$ for the it-th iteration, based on the initial value of $j + 1$ being 6 and each successive value for $j + 1$ being two more than the last value. We therefore store in variable $\mathtt{old}$ the value of $\mathtt{heap}$ before the loop, anonymize all elements of $\mathtt{d}$ and add the invariants:

$$\forall k \in \mathtt{d}. \; (k \geq 6 \wedge k < j + 1 \wedge (k - 6)\%2 \doteq 0) \rightarrow \chi_{>}(\mathtt{d}[k])$$

$$\forall k \in \mathtt{d}. \; (k < 6 \vee k \geq j + 1 \vee (k - 6)\%2 \neq 0) \rightarrow \mathtt{d}[k] \doteq select(\mathtt{old}, \mathtt{d}, k)$$

Besides array modifications, our approach can also add invariants based on read-only array accesses that influence control flow. The steps involved are similar: *(i)* calculate the symbolic pivot, *(ii)* determine whether it is iteration affine, and *(iii)* generate an invariant with a contiguous or affine range. However, as no anonymization takes place for an unmodified array, no invariant of the form (4) is generated.

Our approach automatically produces all invariants in Fig. 1: affine invariants for array $\mathtt{c}$ and contiguous invariants for array $\mathtt{b}$ and the unmodified array $\mathtt{a}$.

5   Implementation

The presented approach has been implemented as a proof-of-concept (available at http://www.key-project.org/symbolic-pivots/) and integrated into a variant

Table 1. Experimental results.

Method	LocSets modified	Automatically generated array invariants
`arrayInit`	$a[0..i]$	$\forall j_1 \in [0..i).\ \mathtt{a}[j_1] \doteq 0)$
`arrayMax`	-	$\forall j_7 \in [0..i).\ \mathtt{a}[j_7] \leq \mathtt{max}^{\mathrm{a}}$
`arraySplit`	$b[0..j]$, $c[0..k]$	$\forall j_5 \in [0..j).\ \mathtt{b}[j_5] > 0),\ \forall j_6 \in [0..k).\ \mathtt{c}[j_6] \leq 0)$
`firstNotNull`	-	$\forall j_0 \in [0..i).\ \mathtt{a}[j_0] \doteq 0$
`sentinel`	-	$\forall j_{11} \in [0..i).\ \mathtt{a}[j_{11}] \neq \mathtt{x}$

[a] Relational abstract domains are not directly possible in our approach, but
we can generate invariants containing terms such as $\chi_{\leq}(\mathtt{a}[j_7] - \mathtt{max})$, which is
equivalent to the relational invariant $\mathtt{a}[j_7] \leq \mathtt{max}$.

of the KeY verification system for Java, which focuses on checking programs
for secure information flow. In this context less strong invariants than for functional verification are sufficient and the precision of the automatically generated
invariants is, therefore, good enough in many cases.

In addition to the array example in Listing 1.1 we created a small test suite
based on benchmarks given in related work [8,9] and display the resulting array
invariants produced by our approach in Table 1. The generation time is still quite
high, ranging from a few seconds to ten minutes. The relatively long runtime is
due to the current status of the implementation, which does not perform any
caching and is instrumented with debug statements. In addition, the implementation currently uses solely the internal proof producing theorem prover for the
invariant computation. Switching to an SMT solver for pure first-order steps
should increase speed significantly. One additional reason for long runtimes is
that in addition to the invariants generated for the array elements themselves,
we also generate some useful invariants only semi-related to the array elements,
such as the following for the `arraySplit` example (using Java notation for conditional terms):

$$\mathtt{i} \leq \mathtt{a.length} \quad \wedge \quad \mathtt{j} = \sum_{q=0}^{i-1}(\mathtt{a}[q] > 0\ ?\ 1:0) \quad \wedge \quad \mathtt{k} = \sum_{q=0}^{i-1}(\mathtt{a}[q] > 0\ ?\ 0:1).$$

6   Related Work

To find a fixpoint for non-heap variables we perform something akin to *array
smashing* [10] for any array modification in a loop. Our refinements based on
symbolic pivots later remedy much of the lost precision. In [11] invariants based
on linear loop-dependent scalars (i.e. variables which can be modified by a loop)
are computed. In [12] variables within a loop are specified according to a number of properties: increasing, dense, etc. There are similarities between iteration
affine variables and linear loop-dependent scalars as well as the variables determined in [12]. Our approach uses symbolic execution to determine iteration affine
terms, in particular in array indices, which do not have to coincide with iteration

affine variables. *Range predicates* are used in [13] to express knowledge about all elements of an array within a given range. These could be used to express our affine range invariants about modified elements, however they are not strong enough to express the affine range invariants about unmodified elements. In [14] abstract domains need to be explicitly supplied for the array indices, offering more possibilities than our approach. However, our notion of iteration affine indices offers the equivalent of an infinite number of abstract domains for array indices which do not need to be explicitly supplied. Their approach also does not allow for additional information to be added about array elements without overwriting old information. In contrast to CEGAR [15] which starts abstract and refines the abstraction stepwise, we start with a fully precise modeling and perform abstraction only on demand and confined to a part of the state. In [16] arrays are modeled as (many) contiguous partitions, while we allow both contiguous partitions as well as affine ranges. In [8] templates are used to introduce quantified formulas from quantifier-free elements, while we allow the underlying abstract domain to function as a "template." In [9] modification of array elements is modeled by abstracting the program: the array is replaced by multiple array slices containing abstract values. The text of the program is used to influence which slices are generated. By abstracting only program states, we can keep much higher precision. Further, our use of symbolic execution lets us view the *result* of the loop body, rather than just the text, allowing two equivalent loop bodies to be treated the same with our approach. In [17] *foot-prints* are introduced which track what part of the program state can be changed by a statement. Using these they can reason about recursive programs containing unbounded arrays (modelled as total functions).

7   Conclusion and Future Work

We presented a novel approach to generate loop invariants for loops that perform operations on arrays. It integrates smoothly into a framework which combines deduction and abstract interpretation. As future work we intend to improve the flexibility of the partitioning by supporting more shapes than affine ranges and on improvements needed for the treatment of nested loops. We will also extend our approach to the diamond modality $\langle \cdot \rangle \cdot$, which expresses total correctness. We investigate several speed ups including avoidance of repeated symbolic execution by reusing the symbolic execution tree of one general run, cache strategies for joins and use of an SMT solver for pure first-order reasoning steps. We intend to integrate our approach into the framework presented in [18] to avoid their need for user specified loop invariants.

References

1. Bubel, R., Hähnle, R., Weiß, B.: Abstract interpretation of symbolic execution with explicit state updates. In: de Boer, F.S., Bonsangue, M.M., Madelaine, E. (eds.) FMCO 2008. LNCS, vol. 5751, pp. 247–277. Springer, Heidelberg (2009)

2. Beckert, B., Hähnle, R., Schmitt, P.H. (eds.): Verification of Object-Oriented Software. LNCS (LNAI), vol. 4334. Springer, Heidelberg (2007)

3. Weiß, B.: Deductive Verification of Object-Oriented Software – Dynamic Frames, Dynamic Logic and Predicate Abstraction. Ph.D. thesis, KIT., January 2011

4. Rümmer, P.: Sequential, parallel, and quantified updates of first-order structures. In: Hermann, M., Voronkov, A. (eds.) LPAR 2006. LNCS (LNAI), vol. 4246, pp. 422–436. Springer, Heidelberg (2006)

5. Cousot, P., Cousot, R.: Abstract interpretation: a unified lattice model for static analysis of programs by construction or approximation of fixpoints. In: 4th Symposium on Principles of Programming Languages (POPL), pp. 238–252. ACM (1977)

6. Wasser, N., Bubel, R., Hähnle, R.: TR: array abstraction with symbolic pivots. Technical report, Department of Computer Science, Technische Universität Darmstadt, Germany, August 2015

7. McMillan, K.L.: Quantified invariant generation using an interpolating saturation prover. In: Ramakrishnan, C.R., Rehof, J. (eds.) TACAS 2008. LNCS, vol. 4963, pp. 413–427. Springer, Heidelberg (2008)

8. Gulwani, S., McCloskey, B., Tiwari, A.: Lifting abstract interpreters to quantified logical domains. SIGPLAN Not. 43(1), 235–246 (2008)

9. Halbwachs, N., Péron, M.: Discovering properties about arrays in simple programs. SIGPLAN Not. 43(6), 339–348 (2008)

10. Blanchet, B., Cousot, P., Cousot, R., Feret, J., Mauborgne, L., Miné, A., Monniaux, D., Rival, X.: Design and implementation of a special-purpose static program analyzer for safety-critical real-time embedded software. In: Mogensen, T.Æ., Schmidt, D.A., Sudborough, I.H. (eds.) The Essence of Computation. LNCS, vol. 2566, pp. 85–108. Springer, Heidelberg (2002)

11. Dillig, I., Dillig, T., Aiken, A.: Fluid updates: beyond strong vs. weak updates. In: Gordon, A.D. (ed.) ESOP 2010. LNCS, vol. 6012, pp. 246–266. Springer, Heidelberg (2010)

12. Kovács, L., Voronkov, A.: Finding loop invariants for programs over arrays using a theorem prover. In: Chechik, M., Wirsing, M. (eds.) FASE 2009. LNCS, vol. 5503, pp. 470–485. Springer, Heidelberg (2009)

13. Jhala, R., McMillan, K.L.: Array abstractions from proofs. In: Damm, W., Hermanns, H. (eds.) CAV 2007. LNCS, vol. 4590, pp. 193–206. Springer, Heidelberg (2007)

14. Cousot, P., Cousot, R., Logozzo, F.: A parametric segmentation functor for fully automatic and scalable array content analysis. In: Proceedings of the 38th Symposium on Principles of Programming Languages, POPL 2011, pp. 105–118. ACM (2011)

15. Clarke, E., Grumberg, O., Jha, S., Lu, Y., Veith, H.: Counterexample-guided abstraction refinement. In: Emerson, E.A., Sistla, A.P. (eds.) CAV 2000. LNCS, vol. 1855. Springer, Heidelberg (2000)

16. Gopan, D., Reps, T., Sagiv, M.: A framework for numeric analysis of array operations. SIGPLAN Not. 40(1), 338–350 (2005)

17. de Boer, F.S., de Gouw, S.: Being and change: reasoning about invariance. In: Meyer, R., Platzer, A., Wehrheim, H. (eds.) Olderog-Festschrift. LNCS, vol. 9360, pp. 191–204. Springer, Heidelberg (2015). doi:10.1007/978-3-319-23506-6_13

18. Hentschel, M., Käsdorf, S., Hähnle, R., Bubel, R.: An interactive verification tool meets an IDE. In: Proceedings of the 11th International Conference on Integrated Formal Methods, pp. 55–70 (2014)

Modeling Role-Based Systems
with Exogenous Coordination

Philipp Chrszon[(⊠)], Clemens Dubslaff, Christel Baier, Joachim Klein,
and Sascha Klüppelholz

Faculty of Computer Science, Technische Universität Dresden, Dresden, Germany
{chrszon,dubslaff,baier,klein,klueppel}@tcs.inf.tu-dresden.de

Abstract. The concept of roles is a promising approach to cope with
context dependency and adaptivity of modern software systems. While
roles have been investigated in conceptual modeling, programming languages and multi-agent systems, they have been given little consideration
within component-based systems.

In this paper, we propose a hierarchical role-based approach for modeling relationships and collaborations between components. In particular, we consider the channel-based, exogenous coordination language Reo
and discuss possible realizations of roles and related concepts. The static
requirements on the binding of roles are modeled by rule sets expressed
in many-sorted second-order logic and annotations on the Reo networks
for role binding, context and collaborations, while Reo connectors are
used to model the coordination of runtime role playing. The ideas presented in this paper may serve as a basis for the formalization and formal
analysis of role-based software systems.

1 Introduction

Separation of concerns [19] is a well-established and accepted principle which
appears in many modeling languages for computer systems. For instance, exogenous coordination languages such as Reo [2] aim at a clear separation of computational aspects and coordination (for a survey on coordination languages,
cf. [38]). Within Reo, components encapsulate the operational behavior at the
interface level and capture the computational aspects. For coordinating the components exogenously, a network of channels is used, which allows for any kind of
synchronous and asynchronous communication. A further prominent example for
separation of concerns is the distinction between entities and their relationships
that is used, e.g., within the entity-relationship model for modeling relational
databases. Entities and relationships are naturally complemented by the concept of roles [43]. Roles are often considered as placeholders in relationships and

The authors are supported by the DFG through the collaborative research cen-
tre HAEC (SFB 912), the Excellence Initiative by the German Federal and State
Governments (cluster of excellence cfAED and Institutional Strategy), the Research
Training Groups QuantLA (GRK 1763) and RoSI (GRK 1907), and the DFG/NWO-
project ROCKS, and Deutsche Telekom Stiftung.

E. Ábrahám et al. (Eds.): de Boer Festschrift, LNCS 9660, pp. 122–139, 2016.
DOI: 10.1007/978-3-319-30734-3_10

collaborations that are filled, i.e., played, by entities [41]. In this sense, roles are an abstraction of the expected behavior of the role player. They can be dynamically acquired and dropped by the role player, depending on the context and the relationships between their respective role players. Consider the example of a soccer player who participates in a local team and has the fortune to be also a player of the national team. In one team, he may play as a defender, while in the other team he plays as a midfielder. The respective role he acquires thus depends on the team he currently plays in, i.e., its local or national context. The team describes a collaboration by the roles of the team's players and additionally defines the relationships between the players through their roles as well. This justifies viewing roles as intermediaries between entities and relationships. Moreover, it promotes a further separation of concerns: roles encapsulate the varying aspects and behaviors of role players in different contexts. Therefore, roles improve the maintainability and extensibility of context-dependent systems with dynamically emerging collaborations between entities.

Although roles are intuitive and commonly understood, there is no generally accepted definition of roles [45]. Guarino and Welty stated in [23] that roles are such entities for which the ontological characterizations of *anti-rigidity* and *dependence* hold. Rigidity denotes that a property holds for an entity at all times and independently from the context, e.g., the property of being a person is rigid as it holds until the entity ceases to exist. The dual term anti-rigidity denotes properties that can cease to hold. For instance, a person can be a customer, but can also stop being a customer without ceasing to be a person. The second ontological notion of dependence describes entities whose existence depends on another entity, e.g., a customer is dependent on a vendor. Additionally, both customer and vendor depend on context, i.e., the exchange of money and goods. In the area of multi-agent systems and agent coordination, roles are widely regarded as an abstraction of behavior and are associated with a set of *requirements*, *capabilities* and *obligations* [13]. An agent must satisfy requirements in order to play a certain role and engages in collaborations with other agents according to its obligations. In object-oriented modeling and programming languages, the only commonly accepted trait of roles is that they can be played by unrelated objects [36,43]. For surveys about how roles can be further characterized, we refer to [36,43,45].

Towards modeling and designing role-based systems, several approaches have been proposed in the literature. In the Agent-Group-Role (AGR) meta-model for organizations in multi-agent systems [21,22], related agents play roles in groups. The group manager, which is a special role, coordinates role acquisition and removal of other actors. The role-oriented programming environment ROPE [11] uses a coordination language derived from Petri nets. The BRAIN proposal supports the analysis, design and implementation of role-based agent systems [14]. Within this approach, the notion of agent evolution as a central concept is introduced [12]. In the Actor-Role-Coordinator (ARC) approach, an agent system is divided in three distinct layers consisting of agents, roles and coordinators [42]. Roles are used as an abstraction of agent behavior and coordinate a group of agents by means of message manipulation. Fasli presented a multi-modal logic framework based on the BDI paradigm (beliefs, desires, intentions) [20]. For a survey of role-based agent interaction models, see [13]. An operational model for role-based systems following the so-called *Helena approach* was presented in [24], where components play roles in groups to collaborate towards a goal. Their formal model combines relational and context-dependent roles and allows the application of model-checking techniques to reason about, e.g., reachability of the collaboration goal.

In this paper, we adopt the notion of roles that is commonly found in conceptual modeling (cf., e.g., [43]). Particularly, we rely on the meta-model for roles by Kühn et al. [35]. There, the concept of *compartments* is introduced, which captures both the collaborative and context-dependent nature of roles. Many role-based approaches consider either the collaborative or context-dependent aspect of roles, but not their combination [36,43]. As roles constitute intermediaries between entities and their relationships, and can be played by their assigned role players depending on their contexts, the coordination of roles is a central point when modeling role-based systems. Thus, it is rather natural to employ specialized coordination languages to describe role playing. However, coordination languages with roles and contexts have been given little consideration in the literature. For instance, [44] compared Reo with the ARC model and the Russian Reflective Dolls (RRD) approaches but focuses mainly on the expressivity of coordination languages, rather than on role-based systems.

The major goal of this paper is to provide first steps towards a theory of role-based exogenous coordination principles. For this, we rely on the channel-based coordination language Reo and show how to embed role-specific concepts. While previous work on role-based coordination mainly deals with monolithic approaches annotating role-playing agents, our framework is compositional and introduces *roles components* that might have their own behavior and are linked to their players via networks of channels that orchestrate the role-playing mechanisms. Role components can be bound to *atomic components* and *compartments*. Atomic components are standing for basic objects without incorporating role-based behaviors. Compartments are formalized by sets of role components, capable to formalize relationships or collaborations. By a set of rules expressed with logical formulas, we define static constraints on possible role bindings. We show that (as compartments describe *sets* of roles) many-sorted second-order logic provides an appropriate formalism with useful applications. Based on the logical characterization of role binding, the actual binding is modeled using coordination glue code in the form of Reo connectors to connect role players with role components and perform exogenous coordination to guarantee correct role playing. By annotating the modeled Reo network with compartments and role bindings, an organizational view of the system is induced.

The embedding of our formalism in Reo allows the application of the full machinery that has been developed for Reo also in the scope of role-based systems. In particular, the formal semantics for Reo [4,10,15,26] facilitate formal analysis and verification. Izadi et al. [25] introduced model checking techniques for Reo networks using compositional reduction and abstraction techniques. In [16], Clarke presented a temporal logic and model-checking techniques for Reo networks with dynamic reconfigurations. The tool Vereofy [7,8] enables the verification of Reo connectors by means of model checking. Pourvatan et al. [39] provided an analysis technique based on symbolic executions of Reo networks. Kokash et al. [32,33] developed mappings from semantic formalisms for Reo to the process algebraic specification language of mCRL2 to enable data flow analysis in Reo networks. Proença and Clarke [40] presented data abstraction techniques for Reo networks. To reason about quantitative properties, Reo networks have been extended with timing constraints [5] and stochastic annotations [6,37]. These existing formalisms and tools for formal analysis and verification provide a well-grounded foundation that allow reasoning about role-based properties.

Outline: After a short primer on the exogenous coordination language Reo in Sects. 2 and 3 presents our framework for modeling role-based systems in Reo. There, we start with the building blocks to model roles, then illustrate role playing of atomic components and compartments and end with the formal framework on role binding. In Sect. 4, we discuss the application of formal analysis techniques and further research raised by our new framework.

2   A Short Primer on Reo Networks

We provide here a brief, high-level overview of the main concepts of Reo as well as the graphical representations we use in this paper for depicting Reo networks. For further details we refer to [2,10]. A Reo network, also called Reo circuit, is built from *components*, *channels* and *nodes*. In general, components serve to encapsulate operational behavior and can interact with the rest of the network via one or more interface ports (depicted as ○). Keeping to the spirit of exogenous coordination, with the coordination glue code between the components being formed by the Reo network, components generally do not know and need not be concerned about the environment in which they are used. Various semantics for Reo networks have been considered in the literature (see, e.g., [4,10,15,26]). On an intuitive level, it makes sense to think in terms of tokens that can be created, propagated, duplicated and consumed by the various parts of the network and that might optionally carry additional information (data). Channels in Reo have two channel ends and provide a rich variety of ways in which the activity at their incoming and outgoing ends can be related. Numerous channel types are predefined and the user may additionally provide customized channel semantics as needed. One of the most basic channels is the *synchronous channel* ⟶, which atomically propagates a token from its incoming end to its outgoing end. In contrast, the *FIFO1* channel ⟶▢⟶ can consume a token at its incoming end, store it in a single buffer cell, and can then propagate the token (and its data) later on via its outgoing end. Channels do not have to be unidirectional. For example, the *synchronous drain* channel ⟶⟵ has two incoming ends and may only consume tokens at both ends simultaneously. In contrast, the *asynchronous drain* ⟶‖⟵ can only consume a token at exactly one of its ends at the same time. Another important channel is, e.g., the filter channel, whose behavior depends on the concrete data attached to a token. In case that the data matches the corresponding filter condition, the filter channel behaves as a synchronous channel and blocks otherwise. All these channels can serve as the basic building blocks for ensuring synchronicity and asynchronicity between different parts of the Reo network. The channel ends can connect to the interface ports of components as well as to Reo nodes, which serve to coordinate the flow of tokens between the connected channel ends. The standard Reo node (depicted as •) exhibits a *merger-replicator* semantics for passing tokens from the connected channel ends: Simultaneously, on the input side, it will nondeterministically choose exactly one of the available tokens (merge semantics). On the output side, it will propagate the token to all connected channel ends (replication semantics), duplicating as necessary. Crucially, a token can only be passed on if all the channel ends connected on the output side of the node are willing to consume the token simultaneously. This behavior allows for the elegant synchronization of an arbitrary number of connected channel ends. A variant of the standard node is the *router node* (depicted as ⊗), which retains the merger semantics on the input side but, in each step, propagates the token to exactly one of the connected channel ends on the output side.

From these basic ingredients, Reo networks representing a wide variety of interaction and coordination patterns can be built. A Reo network that provides such coordination is called a connector. This clear separation of computation inside components and coordination between components allows the construction of systems from reusable and easily exchangeable components and connectors. However, as the number of components of the system grows, Reo networks become increasingly complex. The ability to hierarchically encapsulate Reo networks into new components that can be used as building blocks on higher levels enables convenient separation of concerns and eases the design process of Reo networks. For this, the internal behavior of the Reo network is hidden from a higher-level Reo network perspective and interface ports are defined to allow for coordination of the new constructed component using a hiding mechanism.

Constraint automata [10] provide a compositional operational semantics for Reo, which enables standard verification techniques developed for labeled transition systems (see, e.g., [7,8,30,31,33]). This includes verification both of the coordination patterns in a network and – whenever automata-based specifications of the components' behavior are available – of the whole system.

3   Modeling Roles and Relationships in Reo

We introduce the concept of roles in the exogenous coordination language Reo to provide a methodology for constructing component-based systems. The Reo components we consider can be arbitrary Reo networks with interface ports arising, e.g., from hiding internal behaviors. On top of the Reo components used in the Reo network to model the system, also the role-based view on the network is organized in a hierarchical fashion. However, in contrast to the hiding operator applied to Reo networks to constitute components, we annotate role-specific information to the components itself, providing a role-based modeling hierarchy orthogonal to the component-based modeling hierarchy of the Reo coordination language. The basic building blocks of this hierarchy are *atomic components*, *role components* and *compartments*. Atomic components stand for basic entities or agents which do not contain any role-specific behaviors, e.g., a person, a computer participating in a network, or a daemon run by an operating system. Role components encapsulate role-specific behaviors which enhance capabilities of entities, e.g., a soccer player role which can be played by a person, a server role which can be played by a computer within a network, or a scheduling role enhancing a daemon functionality. Compartments are built by collections of roles, i.e., by annotating sets of role components. They model relationships, collaborations and contexts of entities playing certain roles. For instance, following the examples mentioned above for atomic components and role components, a soccer team defines the context some soccer players are playing in, a file transfer compartment models the protocol to exchange data between servers and clients, or a desktop compartment coordinates the execution of daemons on desktop computers (which differs from the daemon coordination on server platforms). Compartments itself may serve as entities which also can play roles. Thus, the annotation of Reo components as atomic or the annotation of sets of role components as compartments, which both can be bound to roles, forms a role-based hierarchy of the Reo network. Obviously, the binding process of roles goes along with the modeling of the role-based system and should follow certain rules. For instance, a male person would in general not be bound to a daughter or mother role. We express such constraints within logical formulas in many-sorted second-order logic over possible annotations to the role-based Reo network.

In the following, we describe our approach for modeling role-based Reo networks in detail. For this, we follow the steps usually undertaken while modeling a role-based system within our framework. First, we introduce the building blocks of role components and how they are bound to (atomic) components. Then, we describe the role hierarchy established through compartments and their roles. Although the logical formulas for the rules of role binding on atomic components and compartments are usually fixed at the beginning of the modeling process (and possibly refined slightly during the construction of the Reo network), we introduce the formal framework for these rules at the end of this section. The reason for choosing this order is twofold. On the one hand, we would like to stepwise introduce the ingredients required to model role-based Reo networks in the order which forms the modeling hierarchy. For the formal framework of constraints on role bindings, however, all these ingredients have to be assumed as given. On the other hand, the formal framework for role-binding constraints does not require a Reo network with role-based annotations and can be used for more general purposes, not relying on Reo as coordination language. Thus, we describe the role-binding constraints separately from the Reo network modeling.

3.1   Representation of Roles

Components differ conceptually from both agents and objects. We consider the notion of components as an abstraction of behavior with a well defined interface [1]. Indeed, a component can represent both an agent or an object or even sets thereof. Adopting the notion of roles as sets of requirements and obligations, roles could be modeled directly in the component-based framework of Reo by incorporating all role behaviors in Reo components. However, this approach leads to monolithic components that combine both their own and their roles' behavior. Hence, following this approach, there is no direct separation of concerns between behaviors of agents and objects and their capabilities enacted by the specific roles they play. Thus, modeling agents requires the knowledge of all roles and their behavior beforehand, which is in contrast to a compositional modeling approach. We thus propose a different approach where roles are considered as first-class entities that are represented and implemented by components. This approach has several important implications. Since a role instance is effectively a component, it can have its own state and behavior. Therefore, the role-specific behavior is encapsulated and not distributed over numerous components. Furthermore, this means a role can be played by several unrelated components. In our framework, a role adapts a component to a specific context, enabling the component to collaborate with other components in the same context. For example, a role component can implement a special communication protocol. The idea of adapting components by role-playing fits into the exogenous coordination model of Reo, because a component does not need to "know" the roles it plays. Furthermore, this approach eases reasoning about role-based systems as basic behaviors from agents and behaviors arising by role playing are separated and can be distinguished already during the modeling process.

3.2   Role Binding and Role Playing

To describe the concept of role binding and role playing incorporated into our framework, we first consider the basic case where both the role player and the role itself are modeled by Reo components. Before an atomic component can play certain roles, the roles must be bound to the component. The binding is realized by creating a Reo connector between the role components and the atomic component. This binding connector serves two tasks: It enables the atomic component to play the bound roles, and it realizes the coordination between the role components and the atomic component.

Every role comes with a set of capabilities and requirements. The capabilities gained by playing a role are encapsulated in the role component. A role component may provide additional ports, which equips the atomic component with additional means for communication. Obviously, a role component can only be bound to certain atomic components. These requirements are reflected in the set of ports the atomic component must provide and the set of rules specified in second-order logic over role names which we define in the last part of this section.

For the construction of the role binding connector, the full Reo framework can be employed. Thus, the binding connector may be arbitrarily complex and can implement various means of interaction and coordination between the atomic component and its role components. In the following illustrations, we depict atomic components as standard Reo components and role components with rounded corners. Role binding is indicated by a dotted area around one atomic component and its bound roles.

Depending on how a role adapts an atomic component, different connectors may be appropriate. If a role component only adds additional behaviors, a connection realized by a standard Reo node is sufficient, as shown in Fig. 1 (a). Here, the output of the component C and role component R is merged, but R can neither modify nor block the output of C (assuming fairness). In the opposite case, the role binding removes or suppresses certain behavior of the atomic component. Here, the role component acts as a filter that only lets pass certain output data. This functionality can be realized by the connector shown in (b). The synchronous drain channel forces the synchronization between C and R for every outgoing message. Thus, if R refuses to synchronize, C cannot complete its send operation. Since the synchronous drain consumes both incoming messages, R the role component cannot add behavior by forging additional output data. In the most general case, a bound role component may suppress or modify any output of the atomic component and can create output data on its own as well. This is realized by the connector shown in (c), where all output data of C flows through R.

Obviously, the binding pattern shown in (c) subsumes both (a) and (b), making them to seem redundant. However, the fact that the role component in (a) cannot modify or suppress output data is apparent in the binding connector, while in (c) one would have to examine the implementation of the role component to establish the same guarantee. Thus, by using behavior-restricting binding connectors, certain guarantees can be established without taking the components' concrete implementations into account. This also illustrates the compositional modeling approach for role-based systems where the coordination between roles is visible from the glue code between the role components and the playing atomic component.

While in Fig. 1(a) to (c) only one role is bound, a binding connector may also bind more than one role component to an atomic component, as exemplified in Fig. 1(d). Furthermore, the binding can introduce additional interface ports. The Reo networks N_1 and N_2 between the atomic component and the role components coordinate the role playing. Depending on the desired behavior, different connectors may be used in place of N_1 and N_2. For example, placing a router node ($\otimes$) between C and $R_1, R_2, \cdots, R_n$ ensures that only exactly one role can be played at any given time. Contrarily, by using a standard Reo node ($\bullet$) for N_1 all bound roles must be played at the same time. The network N_2 determines the output behavior. For instance, if a standard Reo node is used, the output of exactly one role component is selected nondeterministically and sent to all output ports. Certainly, more complex connectors may be used for N_2, such as a connector that merges the output data of the role components by creating tuples.

To illustrate the binding of role components to an atomic component in more detail, we turn to our first running example that shows a concrete implementation of the pattern presented in Fig. 1(d).

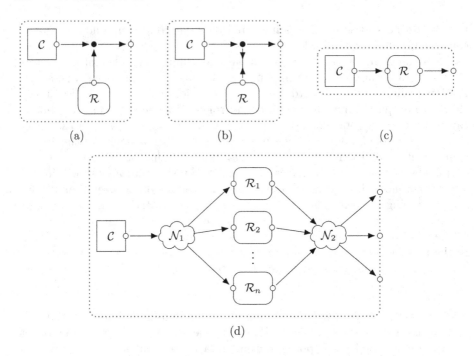

Fig. 1. Patterns for binding role components to an atomic component

Example 1. Figure 2 depicts a wine vending machine. The role components "white" and "red" add the capability to serve white wine and red wine, respectively. This is modeled by a pattern similar to Fig. 1(d) with two roles. For a formal semantics of the depicted Reo network, a compatible formalism to describe its components is required. In Fig. 3 we show two constraint automata [10], one capturing the operational behavior of the vending machine (without wine serving capabilities) and one for each wine role component. These constraint automata combined with the depicted Reo network directly yield the formal semantics for the vending machine, i.e., a constraint automaton modeling the whole behavior of the wine vending machine. Without any role playing, the wine vending machine dispenses drinks directly when it received the payment. After binding the white and red-wine role, the respective wine is only dispensed after the selection port is activated through exogenous coordination.

Until now, we only considered role binding which is a prerequisite for role playing. In our approach, a role is actively played if the behavior of its role component is observable, i.e., whenever one or more of its ports are active. Clearly, not all possible combinations of active roles are useful or valid. In our example of a wine vending machine, which is able to serve both red and white wine, it should not occur that both roles are played at the same time, i.e., eventually serving ros? wine. Thus, a binding connector not only connects an atomic components and its role components, but also coordinates role playing.

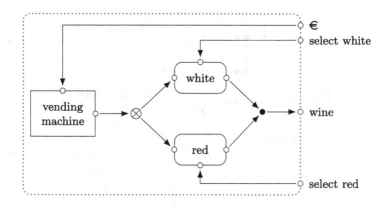

Fig. 2. Role binding connector of a wine vending machine

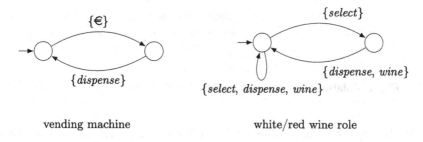

Fig. 3. Constraint automata for the vending machine and one wine role

In our wine vending machine, the merger semantics of the Reo node (on the right) ensures that only one role component can be active at the same time.

3.3 Role Relationships and Compartments

Roles often depend on one or more counter-roles [23]. Consider again Example 1 of a wine vending machine. Surely, a vending machine is only useful if there are customers that buy the goods it offers. Thus, both the *white* and *red* roles are dependent on a *white wine customer* and a *red wine customer*, respectively. While the previous section dealt with the relationship of role components and their role player, this section focuses on the relationships between role components.

Similar to role binding, role relationships are realized by Reo connectors between role components. The purpose of a role relationship connector is the coordination of role components, i.e., it influences and controls role playing. For instance, the connector depicted in Fig. 4 ensures that the vending machine plays the *white* role whenever the person plays the *white wine customer* role. As for role binding connectors, the coordination realized by the relationship connector can be arbitrarily complex. In our example, the connector has two purposes. First, it serves as a sequencer that allows for selecting wine only after money has been paid, modeled by the upper *FIFO1* channels (—▢▸ depicts a filled

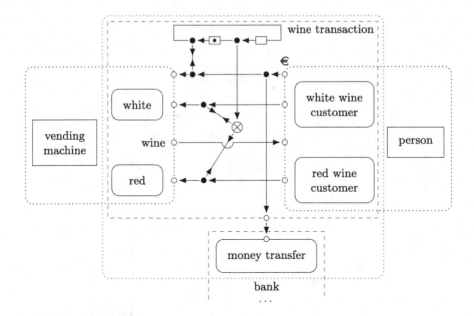

Fig. 4. Relationship connector in the wine transaction compartment

FIFO1 channel). Second, it disallows simultaneous selection of white and red wine, ensured by the *router node* in the center (depicted as ⊗).

Roles not only depend on relationships with other roles, but also on a context. Clearly, a person playing the *white wine customer* role cannot buy wine from a soda vending machine. Only in connection with a *white* wine role in a *wine transaction* context the *white wine customer* role can be played. We adopt the notion of *compartments* [36] as a representation of context and the collaboration of its roles. Compartments contain sets of role components and their role relationship connectors, depicted by a dashed rectangle surrounding their contained role components (see Fig. 4).

An important aspect of the wine *transaction* compartment is the payment. The customer may choose to pay using a credit card or paying cash. But then, the transaction itself plays the role of a *money transfer* in a *bank* compartment. Thus, not only atomic components, but also compartments themselves can play roles. Since compartments are sub-networks that may have external ports, the role binding approach presented in Sect. 3.2 can be applied to compartments as well.

As every role component is part of a compartment and every compartment can play roles itself, our modeling approach is hierarchical. Starting from atomic components as basic building blocks, role binding can be nested arbitrarily deep. Returning to our running example, the *bank* compartment itself may play the role of a *borrower* of another bank. Again, this bank can also play the role of a *borrower* of yet another bank, and so on.

3.4   Role-Based Reo Networks and Role-Binding Constraints

To formalize Reo networks modeling role-based systems, we use the concept of *types*. Types abstract away actual operational behavior and coordination to encapsulate the role-based view on parts of the Reo network. Every role component, atomic component or compartment as they appear during the modeling process illustrated in the last sections will be assigned a type. For what follows, let $\mathfrak{A}$ be the set of *atomic component types*, $\mathfrak{R}$ the set of *role component types*, and $\mathfrak{C}$ the set of *compartment types*. During the modeling process of role-based Reo networks, the types are usually known beforehand.

Definition 1. *A* role-based Reo network *is a tuple* $(\mathcal{N}, C_{atom}, C_{role}, \Delta, \beta,$ $type_{atom}, type_{role}, type_{cprt})$ *where*

- $\mathcal{N}$ *is a Reo network over a set C of components,*
- *the set C_{atom} of atomic components and the set C_{role} of role components are disjoint subsets of C,*
- $\Delta \subseteq 2^{C_{role}}$ *is the set of compartments,*
- $\beta\colon C_{role} \to C_{atom} \cup \Delta$ *is a total function binding roles to atomic components or compartments,*
- $type_{atom}\colon C_{atom} \to \mathfrak{A}$, $type_{role}\colon C_{role} \to \mathfrak{R}$ *and* $type_{cprt}\colon \Delta \to \mathfrak{C}$ *annotate atomic components, role components and compartments with their type, respectively.*

In Example 1 we did not distinguish between types and their instances resulting in the role-based Reo network. Thus, the types can be assumed to agree with the instance names in this case. To illustrate how types are incorporated in role-based Reo networks, we chose an example from the soccer domain, which will serve as the running example for the rest of this section.

Example 2. Let $\mathfrak{A} = \{\mathsf{person}\}$, $\mathfrak{R} = \{\mathsf{keeper}, \mathsf{defender}, \mathsf{midfielder}, \mathsf{attacker}\}$, and $\mathfrak{C} = \{\mathsf{SoccerTeam}, \mathsf{Tournament}\}$ be types. Figure 5 depicts a part of a role-based Reo network, where the type assignment to some instance is done by captions of the form "instance : type". Frank as a person is capable of playing the role of a defender in both, his local and the national team. Whereas in the local team he plays with number 16 (as an instance of a player in the team), he has the role of number 7 in the national team. Edwin, as the second person we consider, can play the role of the keeper in the national team. Besides other players not depicted in Fig. 5, Frank and Edwin can take part in a world cup competition within the national team, modeled by a competitor role of the team instantiated as the second team in group B. We omitted the actual coordination networks as they concern only the role playing and do not appear within the annotations for role-based Reo networks. For instance, it can be assumed that the coordination network between Frank and its two defender roles models that he cannot play both roles simultaneously. Furthermore, the cloud in the national team compartment depicted in Fig. 5 stands for a coordination network and could also include state, e.g., that the color of the national team is orange.

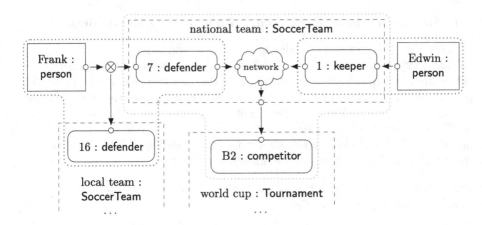

Fig. 5. Role-based Reo network of a soccer tournament

It is clear that a role-based Reo network should follow rules which guarantee consistency of the model according to the domain described. In the soccer domain for instance, it is nonsensical that a team attempts to play the role "keeper" in a competition. We express such rules which have to be obeyed for role-based Reo networks with formulas in many-sorted second-order logics (SOL). The sorts we distinguish here are the ones of role players (denoted *RolePlayer*) and role instances (denoted *RoleInst*). Atomic components and compartments are of sort *RolePlayer*, whereas role components are of the sort *RoleInst*. Role instances are assigned to role players by β of sort *RoleInst* $\rightarrow$ *RolePlayer*. First-order variables range over atomic components and role components. For each atomic component type and role component type we identify its name with a predicate of arity one, evaluating to true if it is interpreted over an instance of that type. Similarly, a predicate for each compartment type is true if interpreted over a second-order variable containing all the role components of a compartment of that type. Set predicates (such as $\in$ and $\subseteq$) evaluate to false when applied on atomic components as role player instance. We call a set of sentences $\mathfrak{F}$ over the described SOL a *role rule set* and say that a role-based Reo network is *valid* if the network is a model for all sentences in $\mathfrak{F}$.

A common restriction on role binding (see, e.g., [24,35]) is the requirement that every role instance is part of at most one compartment. We do not enforce this restriction in our framework, e.g., to allow for modeling a father-son relation as a compartment contained in a family-relation compartment. However, this rule can be included into our role rule set as an SOL sentence

$$\forall RoleInst\ x, RolePlayer\ Y, Z.\ x \in Y \cap Z \ \Rightarrow\ Y = Z$$

Turning to our running example from the soccer domain, the rule that at least one keeper has to play in every soccer team can be expressed by the SOL sentence

$$\forall RolePlayer\ T.\ \mathsf{SoccerTeam}(T) \Rightarrow \exists RoleInst\ k.\ \mathsf{keeper}(k) \wedge k \in T$$

The restriction that every keeper role has to be played by a person is also useful:

$$\forall RoleInst\ k.\ \mathsf{keeper}(k) \Rightarrow \mathsf{person}(\beta(k))$$

It is easy to see that the role-based Reo network depicted in Fig. 5 is valid when the role rule set contains exactly the rules above. Usually, one fixes a role rule set according to the chosen domain and then models a valid role-based Reo network as described in the last two sections.

4   Conclusions and Future Work

We presented an approach on how the exogenous coordination language Reo can be used to model role-based systems. For this, we introduced a formal framework to express static requirements on the binding of roles to their role players, based on atomic component types, role component types and compartment types over which rules in many-sorted SOL are stated. In role-based Reo networks, instances of atomic component types and role component types correspond to concrete Reo components, whereas instances of compartment types include role components and a coordination network between them. Within our approach, the purpose of Reo is to model the coordination between roles and their players (e.g., to guarantee operational requirements on role playing) and between the roles in compartments. The latter also allows the coordination of the collaboration of roles taking place in compartments, an important feature of compartments not apparent within the "contexts" a role appears in. Obviously, modeling the coordination of roles remains a highly sophisticated task within our framework, where several conformance requirements are only given implicitly. For instance, although a soccer player can have a role in the local as well as the national team, he should not play both roles simultaneously. Thus, formal analysis of the operational behavior and the role playing over time is desirable to guarantee correctness of the role-base system model.

Formal Semantics and Analysis for Role-Based Reo Networks. There has been extensive research on formal semantics for Reo [26]. When the components as the building blocks of role-based Reo networks (e.g., atomic components or role components) are modeled using Reo compatible formalisms, we directly obtain a formal operational semantics, e.g., in terms of a constraint automaton. Such operational semantics captures all the modeled role-based behaviors and fulfills the static constraints on role binding provided by our framework. By introducing, e.g., additional port labels for ports which define whether a role is active or not, we can rely on standard analysis techniques to check conformance of role playing requirements. For instance, model-checking tools such as Vereofy [8] or mCRL2 [32,33] can then be used to check run-time requirements on role-based Reo networks. Such tools would allow for checking invariants on simultaneous role playing, e.g., whether roles are only played together with their counter-roles or whether in a soccer team at least seven but at most eleven players are acting.

Future Work. Several directions on how our approach can be extended are left for further work. On the modeling side, our framework currently supports only static role models without dynamic binding and unbinding. For this, research on rewriting operations already applied to Reo networks in [34] could be used in combination with methods ensuring that the role-based Reo network remains valid according to role rule sets. Concerning constraints on temporal aspects, the notion of role rule sets could be extended with temporal logic formulas, for which, however, a semantics on an operational model of Reo networks has to be developed in more detail. Also, an extension of role rule sets containing (contextualized) description logics [27] could be imagined. On the formal analysis side, algorithms to check many-sorted SOL requirements on role binding for role-based Reo networks could be investigated. Reasoning about the role rule sets itself, e.g., checking whether some rules are contradictory, requires specialized algorithms, possibly only applicable onto fragments of the logics we presented. An open field is also to incorporate annotations into the operational semantics of role-based Reo networks to reason about compatibility [17,18], e.g., whether the behavior of a player matches the roles' requirements and vice versa. In this spirit, also the formalization of collaboration goals [24] expressed for each compartment and their reachability during runtime could be investigated. Another aspect within our framework is controller synthesis [28–31] with respect to temporal requirements, e.g., as stated above. As usual, the coordination between components in component-based system modeling is the most difficult part. Thus, the modeling process of role-based Reo networks could heavily benefit from synthesized controllers serving as coordinating connectors between players and their bound roles, e.g., by synthesizing the Reo glue code [3,9].

References

1. Arbab, F.: Abstract behavior types: a foundation model for components and their composition. In: de Boer, F.S., Bonsangue, M.M., Graf, S., de Roever, W.-P. (eds.) FMCO 2002. LNCS, vol. 2852, pp. 33–70. Springer, Heidelberg (2003)
2. Arbab, F.: Reo: a channel-based coordination model for component composition. Math. Struct. Comput. Sci. **14**, 329–366 (2004)
3. Arbab, F., Baier, C., de Boer, F.S., Rutten, J., Sirjani, M.: Synthesis of Reo circuits for implementation of component-connector automata specifications. In: Jacquet, J.-M., Picco, G.P. (eds.) COORDINATION 2005. LNCS, vol. 3454, pp. 236–251. Springer, Heidelberg (2005)
4. Arbab, F., Rutten, J.J.M.M.: A coinductive calculus of component connectors. In: Wirsing, M., Pattinson, D., Hennicker, R. (eds.) WADT 2003. LNCS, vol. 2755, pp. 34–55. Springer, Heidelberg (2003)
5. Arbab, F., Baier, C., de Boer, F.S., Rutten, J.M.M., Sirjani, M.: Models and temporal logical specifications for timed component connectors. Softw. Syst. Model. **6**(1), 59–82 (2007)
6. Arbab, F., Meng, S., Moon, Y.-J., Kwiatkowska, M.Z., Hongyang, Q.: Reo2MC: a tool chain for performance analysis of coordination models. In: 7th Joint Meeting of the European Software Engineering Conference and the ACM SIGSOFT International Symposium on Foundations of Software Engineering, pp. 287–288. ACM (2009)

7. Baier, C., Blechmann, T., Klein, J., Klüppelholz, S.: Formal verification for components and connectors. In: de Boer, F.S., Bonsangue, M.M., Madelaine, E. (eds.) FMCO 2008. LNCS, vol. 5751, pp. 82–101. Springer, Heidelberg (2009)
8. Baier, C., Blechmann, T., Klein, J., Klüppelholz, S.: A uniform framework for modeling and verifying components and connectors. In: Field, J., Vasconcelos, V.T. (eds.) COORDINATION 2009. LNCS, vol. 5521, pp. 247–267. Springer, Heidelberg (2009)
9. Baier, C., Klein, J., Klüppelholz, S.: Synthesis of Reo connectors for strategies and controllers. Fundamenta Informaticae **130**(1), 1–20 (2014)
10. Baier, C., Sirjani, M., Arbab, F., Rutten, J.J.M.M.: Modeling component connectors in Reo by constraint automata. Sci. Comput. Program. **61**(2), 75–113 (2006)
11. Becht, M., Gurzki, T., Klarmann, J., Muscholl, M.: ROPE: role oriented programming environment for multiagent systems. In: Cooperative Information Systems (CoopIS 1999), pp. 325–333 (1999)
12. Cabri, G., Ferrari, L., Leonardo, L.: Rethinking agent roles: extending the role definition in the brain framework. In: Systems, Man and Cybernetics (SMC 2004), vol. 6, pp. 5455–5460. IEEE (2004)
13. Cabri, G., Leonardi, L., Ferrari, L., Zambonelli, F.: Role-based software agent interaction models: a survey. Knowl. Eng. Rev. **25**(04), 397–419 (2010)
14. Cabri, G., Leonardi, L., Zambonelli, F.: BRAIN: a framework for flexible role-based interactions in multiagent systems. In: Meersman, R., Schmidt, D.C. (eds.) CoopIS 2003, DOA 2003, and ODBASE 2003. LNCS, vol. 2888, pp. 145–161. Springer, Heidelberg (2003)
15. Clarke, D., Costa, D., Arbab, F.: Connector colouring I: synchronisation and context dependency. Sci. Comput. Program. **66**(3), 205–225 (2007)
16. Clarke, D.: A basic logic for reasoning about connector reconfiguration. Fundamenta Informaticae **82**(4), 361–390 (2008)
17. de Alfaro, L., da Silva, L.D., Faella, M., Legay, A., Roy, P., Sorea, M.: Sociable interfaces. In: Gramlich, B. (ed.) FroCos 2005. LNCS (LNAI), vol. 3717, pp. 81–105. Springer, Heidelberg (2005)
18. de Alfaro, L., Henzinger, T.A.: Interface theories for component-based design. In: Henzinger, T.A., Kirsch, C.M. (eds.) EMSOFT 2001. LNCS, vol. 2211, pp. 148–165. Springer, Heidelberg (2001)
19. Dijkstra, E.W.: On the role of scientific thought. In: Selected Writings on Computing: A Personal Perspective, pp. 60–66. Springer, New York (1982). Transcribed 1974
20. Fasli, M.: Social interactions in multi-agent systems: a formal approach. In: Intelligent Agent Technology (IAT 2003), pp. 240–246. IEEE (2003)
21. Ferber, J., Gutknecht, O.: A meta-model for the analysis and design of organizations in multi-agent systems. In: Multi Agent Systems (ICMAS 1998), pp. 128–135. IEEE (1998)
22. Ferber, J., Gutknecht, O., Michel, F.: From agents to organizations: an organizational view of multi-agent systems. In: Giorgini, P., Müller, J.P., Odell, J.J. (eds.) AOSE 2003. LNCS, vol. 2935, pp. 214–230. Springer, Heidelberg (2004)
23. Guarino, N., Welty, C.A.: A formal ontology of properties. In: Dieng, R., Corby, O. (eds.) EKAW 2000. LNCS (LNAI), vol. 1937, pp. 97–112. Springer, Heidelberg (2000)
24. Hennicker, R., Klarl, A.: Foundations for ensemble modeling – the Helena approach. In: Iida, S., Meseguer, J., Ogata, K. (eds.) Specification, Algebra, and Software. LNCS, vol. 8373, pp. 359–381. Springer, Heidelberg (2014)

25. Izadi, M., Movaghar, A., Arbab, F.: Model checking of component connectors. In: 31st Annual International Computer Software and Applications Conference, (COMPSAC), pp. 673–675. IEEE Computer Society (2007)
26. Jongmans, S.-S.T.Q., Arbab, F.: Overview of thirty semantic formalisms for Reo. Sci. Ann. Comput. Sci. **22**(1), 201–251 (2012)
27. Klarman, S., Gutiérrez-Basulto, V.: Two-dimensional description logics of context. In: Description Logics (DL 2011), vol. 745. CEUR Workshop Proceedings (2011)
28. Klein, J.: Compositional synthesis and most general controllers. Ph.D. thesis, Technische Universität Dresden (2013)
29. Klein, J., Baier, C., Klüppelholz, S.: Compositional construction of most general controllers. Acta Informatica, Spec. Issue: Combining Compositionality Concurrency: Part 2 **52**(4–5), 443–482 (2015)
30. Klüppelholz, S.: Verification of branching-time and alternating-time properties for exogenous coordination models. Ph.D. thesis, Technische Universität Dresden (2012)
31. Klüppelholz, S., Baier, C.: Alternating-time stream logic for multi-agent systems. Sci. Comput. Program. **75**(6), 398–425 (2010)
32. Kokash, N., Krause, C., de Vink, E.P.: Data-aware design and verification of service compositions with Reo and mCRL2. In: Symposium on Applied Computing (SAC 2010), pp. 2406–2413. ACM (2010)
33. Kokash, N., Krause, C., de Vink, E.P.: Reo + mCRL2: a framework for model-checking dataflow in service compositions. Formal Aspects Comput. **24**(2), 187–216 (2012)
34. Krause, C., Maraikar, Z., Lazovik, A., Arbab, F.: Modeling dynamic reconfigurations in Reo using high-level replacement systems. Sci. Comput. Program. **76**(1), 23–36 (2011)
35. Kühn, T., Böhme, S., Götz, S., Aßmann, U.: A combined formal model for relational context-dependent roles. In: Software Language Engineering (SLE 2015) (2015, to appear)
36. Kühn, T., Leuthäuser, M., Götz, S., Seidl, C., Aßmann, U.: A metamodel family for role-based modeling and programming languages. In: Combemale, B., Pearce, D.J., Barais, O., Vinju, J.J. (eds.) SLE 2014. LNCS, vol. 8706, pp. 141–160. Springer, Heidelberg (2014)
37. Moon, Y.-J., Silva, A., Krause, C., Arbab, F.: A compositional model to reason about end-to-end QoS in stochastic Reo connectors. Sci. Comput. Program. **80**, 3–24 (2014)
38. Papadopoulos, G.A., Arbab, F.: Coordination models and languages. Adv. Comput. **46**, 329–400 (1998)
39. Pourvatan, B., Sirjani, M., Hojjat, H., Arbab, F.: Symbolic execution of Reo circuits using constraint automata. Sci. Comput. Program. **77**(7–8), 848–869 (2012)
40. Proença, J., Clarke, D.: Data abstraction in coordination constraints. In: Canal, C., Villari, M. (eds.) ESOCC 2013. CCIS, vol. 393, pp. 159–173. Springer, Heidelberg (2013)
41. Reenskaug, T., Wold, P., Lehne, O.A.: Working with Objects: The Ooram Software Engineering Method. Manning, Greenwich (1996)
42. Ren, S., Yu, Y., Chen, N., Marth, K., Poirot, P.-E., Shen, L.: Actors, roles and coordinators — a coordination model for open distributed and embedded systems. In: Ciancarini, P., Wiklicky, H. (eds.) COORDINATION 2006. LNCS, vol. 4038, pp. 247–265. Springer, Heidelberg (2006)
43. Steimann, F.: On the representation of roles in object-oriented and conceptual modelling. Data Knowl. Eng. **35**(1), 83–106 (2000)

44. Talcott, C., Sirjani, M., Ren, S.: Comparing three coordination models: Reo, ARC, and RRD. In: Foundations of Coordination Languages and Software Architectures (FOCLASA 2007). Electronic Notes in Theoretical Computer Science, vol. 194, no. 4, pp. 39–55. Elsevier (2008)
45. Zhu, H., Zhou, M.: Roles in information systems: a survey. IEEE Trans. Syst. Man Cybern. Part C **38**(3), 377–396 (2008)

Vats: A Safe, Reactive Storage Abstraction

Dave Clarke$^{(\boxtimes)}$ and Tobias Wrigstad

Department of Information Technology, Uppsala University, Uppsala, Sweden
dave.clarke@it.uu.se

Abstract. The rise of multicore computers has hastened the advent of multifarious abstractions to facilitate the construction of parallel programs. This paper presents another: the *vat*. A vat is like a variable, but it has various actions attached to it that can block, transform and react to changes to the vat. Vats can be combined together in various ways, linking the behaviours of the vats together, resulting in various synchronisation mechanisms. Vats are powerful enough to encode (part of) many existing mechanisms including promises, condition variables, LVars and reactive programming.

1 Introduction

Parallel processors, and the problems they pose, have found their way onto our desktops and into our pockets — virtually every modern computer has a parallel processor. Due to the inefficiency of increasing single processor speeds, the future (and indeed the last decade), is increasingly parallel. Programming increasingly parallel computers to effectively utilise the available resources is an open problem. In particular, implementations of algorithms that cannot be trivially partitioned into essentially unrelated computations suffer the pain of coordinating operations that share data. As efficient parallel programs lack a notion of global time, novel programming abstractions are needed to express and enforce invariants over multiple values and dependencies between computations without unnecessary serialisation of computation.

In this paper we explore one such abstraction, a programming language construct called the *vat*. Vats share a lot in common with futures, promises, atomic sets, and event-based and reactive programming. Vats are single or multi-valued records with actions that fire under certain conditions. These actions allow consistency checking, notification and decoration of vat contents to be triggered transparently. Vats can be configured with different access and action semantics. Several configurations correspond to complicated patterns of concurrent programming, such as multi-object atomicity. Vats are accessed using safe asynchronous reads and writes returning futures. This allows non-blocking reads in the presence of contention, such as reads that overlap with consistency checks, or reads that are issued prior to proper initialisation.

Partly funded by the EU project FP7-612985 UpScale: From Inherent Concurrency to Massive Parallelism through Type-based Optimisations.

E. Ábrahám et al. (Eds.): de Boer Festschrift, LNCS 9660, pp. 140–154, 2016.
DOI: 10.1007/978-3-319-30734-3_11

Vats naturally support event-based programming where actions fire as side-effects of writes. Combined with multi-valued or linked vats, this extends naturally to (albeit crude) reactive programming, for example, allowing the definition of a certain field to be the sum of two other fields.

The contributions of the paper are as follows: the notion of vat (Sects. 2 and 3), which is essentially a memory cell with triggerable actions that modify its behaviour; a formal static and dynamics semantics of a core calculus of vats (Sect. 4); extensions to the vat concept (Sect. 5); and the application of vats to some programming problems (Sect. 6). The paper concludes with a discussion of related work (Sect. 7) and conclusion (Sect. 8).

2   Introduction by Example: Monotonic Integer Variable

The code below describes a vat containing a single integer. Writes to the vat can only increase the contents of the field, and the value stored in the vat is rounded to the nearest multiple of 10. Non-increasing writes are rejected.

```
vat int {
  pre (Undefined, new) = Quo True
  pre ((Defined old, new) = Quo (new >= old)
  trans (_, new) = Quo (((new + 5) / 10) * 10)
  post (_, new) = if new > threshold
               then Deregister (do_action ())
               else Quo ()
  fail _ = Quo (notify "Number was not large enough")
} x;
```

The pre action prevents assignments of values less than the stored value. The transform action rounds the new value to the nearest multiple of 10. The post action waits for the first value assigned value over a certain threshold before firing the corresponding action. If the pre action results in false, the fail action is triggered, which notifies that the number is not large enough. In all cases, the return value is wrapped with either `Deregister` or `Quo` to indicate whether the function should be deregistered after being triggered or not, allowing one-shot call-backs in a simple manner.

3   Vanilla Vats

A vat can be thought of as a single field which can be asynchronously read and written. The field is initially uninitialised. A number of actions of different kinds can be attached to the field to adapt and react to attempted writes to the field:

Pre Actions (1). Actions that trigger on writing to the vat, before the write is published, *i.e.*, available to those reading the vat. Pre actions block an assignment whenever they are false.

Transformation Actions (2.a). Actions that trigger as part of an assignment to a vat, whenever the pre action evaluates to true. Transformation actions operate on the value to be assigned and the old value and produce a new value to be assigned. This value can be published.

Post Actions (3). Actions that are triggered after the assignment has been published. These run asynchronously and possibly in parallel.

Fail Actions (2.b). Actions that are triggered if the pre action fails. These run asynchronously and possibly in parallel.

Actions are triggered by writing to a vat's field. The order in which actions proceed is indicated by the numbers above, where (2.a) and (2.b) depend on the result of (1). An actual state change is not published (observable outside the vat) until after the transformation has been performed.

Through pre actions, vats support consistency checking. Through transformation actions, vats support decoration [10], for example, allowing the interface type to differ from the storage type, or even replacing bad values with default values in the spirit of defensive programming. Through post actions, vats naturally support event-based programming where actions fire as side-effects of writes. This is conceptually similar to the observer pattern [10] and Java listeners. Finally, through fail actions, vats support safe clean up.

3.1 Reading and Writing Vats

Vats can be read and written, just like variables, but unlike reads and writes on variables, these operations on vats are asynchronous. Asynchronous reads and writes are always safe—these serialise writes against all other accesses.

Asynchronous reads and writes of a vat have the following types:

– read :: Vat $\tau \to$ Fut τ
– write :: Vat $\tau \to \tau \to$ Fut Bool

These return immediately, and the respective results becomes available via the future when the read/write succeeds. A read will not produce a result until the vat is initialised. The Boolean returned by write indicates whether or not the write succeeded.[1]

3.2 Action Types

Pre, post, transformation and fail actions are given to the vat. These functions can depend on the initial value (which may be undefined) in the vat and the to-be-assigned value, and actions may also deregister themselves from the vat after running, for instance, to allow run-once actions. To capture this information, the following data types are used (borrowing Haskell's notation).

---

[1] For performance, non-blocking synchronous reads and write can be allowed. If used in a multi-threaded setting, these are subject to data races and may observe inconsistent or uninitialised states of vats. Synchronous reads and writes have the following types:

– sread :: Vat $\tau \to \tau$
– swrite :: Vat $\tau \to \tau \to$ Bool — result indicates whether write succeeded.

The first data type captures whether a value is defined or not, and the second captures the old and new values involved in a transformation:

$$\texttt{data Partial } \tau = \texttt{Undefined} \mid \texttt{Defined } \tau$$
$$\texttt{type Update } \tau = (\texttt{Partial } \tau, \tau)$$

The third datatype supplements the return value of an action with a status that indicates whether or not the action should remain registered:

$$\texttt{data Status } \tau = \texttt{Quo } \tau \mid \texttt{Deregister } \tau$$

Quo v indicates that the action should remain registered, and Deregister v indicates that it should be deregistered. In both cases, the return value is v.

For a vat of type Vat τ, the actions that are given to the vat are as follows. In each case, the action gets the old and new values via the Update datatype, and the detachment status is indicated using the Status datatype.

- A pre action has type Update $\tau \rightarrow$ Status Bool — for the given input and old value, the pre action indicates whether the input is an acceptable value to store in the vat — true indicates that it is.
- A transformer has type Update $\tau \rightarrow$ Status τ — for the given input and old value, the transformer returns a new value to store in the vat.
- A post action has type Update $\tau \rightarrow$ Status Void — for the given input and old value, a post action asynchronously performs some action.
- A fail action has type Update $\tau \rightarrow$ Status Void — for the given input and previous value, a fail action asynchronously performs some action.

These core actions can be used to define more specialised actions. The following classes of actions are envisioned: *permanent actions* will be triggered on all subsequent writes to a vat, and return the Quo element of the Status datatype to indicate their permanence; *ephemeral actions* will fire only once, at the next write of a field, and will return the Deregister element of the Status datatype to indicate their impermanence; and *fugacious actions* may deregister themselves after firing and are in this sense conditionally permanent, and will return the appropriate element of the Status datatype.

Ephemeral actions are useful for notifications of state changes that are irreversible, for example, when a value is first initialised, or when a client is interested in just the next update. Fugacious actions are useful for example to monitor monotonic changes, such as when a counter hits a certain threshold (to avoid triggering the alarm repeatedly as the counter continues to rise), or simply to get the next n updates.

3.3   Action Composition: Chains

A single vat may have multiple actions of every kind. These can conceptually be combined into a single action of each kind. Multiple pre actions can be combined by taking the conjunction of their results. The order in which they are run is undefined, so shared mutable state should be avoided.

Multiple transformation actions are combined by chaining them so that the least recently added transformation is applied first and the most recent is applied last. The composition operation is

$$(\text{\o}) :: (\text{Update } \tau \rightarrow \tau) \rightarrow (\text{Update } \tau \rightarrow \tau) \rightarrow (\text{Update } \tau \rightarrow \tau)$$
$$f \text{ \o } g = \lambda(old, new) \rightarrow f \ (\text{Defined } new, g \ (old, new))$$

Function g is applied first then f. The old value for function f is original new value, and new value is the result of applying function g. Multiple post actions are combined by firing them all asynchronously. Multiple fail actions are combined like post actions.

3.4   Varieties of Vats

Vats themselves are a very generic data structure, but they can be used in many different ways. Asynchronous reads and writes are the default, but direct synchronous reads and writes may also be possible. Vats may be uninitialised or initialised, write-once or write-many. The interface of a vat, which consists essentially of a read and write operation, can be split into two, allowing vats that cannot be written by whosoever does not have access to the write operations. Such vats can be used purely as observers, perhaps of actions performed on other vats. The pre, post, transformation and fail actions of a vat may be specified at construction time, or may be specified subsequently.

3.5   Extending the Vat Interface

On top of the core actions of a vat, more convenient functions can be built, using futures and streams to carry the values written to the vat:

- all :: Vat $\tau \rightarrow$ Stream τ — converts a vat into a stream, starting from the element available at the point which all is applied.
- allST :: Vat $\tau \rightarrow (\tau \rightarrow$ Bool$) \rightarrow$ Stream τ — converts a vat into a stream, keeping only the elements satisfying a predicate passed in, starting from the element at the point which allST is applied.
- next :: Vat $\tau \rightarrow$ Fut τ — returns a future which will contain the next value written to the vat.
- nextST :: Vat $\tau \rightarrow (\tau \rightarrow$ Bool$) \rightarrow$ Fut τ — returns a future which will contain the next value written to the vat satisfying a predicate.
- feed :: Stream $\tau \rightarrow$ Vat $\tau \rightarrow$ Void — takes a stream and a vat and writes each element from the stream into the vat.
- chain :: Vat $\tau \rightarrow (\tau \rightarrow \tau') \rightarrow$ Vat τ' — takes a vat and a function and returns a new vat into which all of the values of the first vat are written, after first being pumped through the function.[2]

---

[2] A better result type for this function would be ReadVat τ, corresponding to just the read interface of a vat.

These functions can readily be implemented on top of vats, assuming sufficiently expressive future and stream libraries.

4   Semantics

This section gives the semantics of a vanilla variety vat. A number of simplifications are made to keep the semantics tractable. Each vat has a single pre, transformation and post action, which cannot be changed, and no fail action. Furthermore, these actions depend only on the new value. Consequently, the types of the actions are simplified also. This core semantics can be readily built upon to model the extensions described in this paper.

The core vat language includes the lambda calculus extended with constructs for spawning tasks (async), working on futures (get and $\leadsto$), for reading, writing and creating vats, and locks. Expressions highlighted with a grey box are used only under-the-hood. The language is concurrent, and different tasks communicate via vats.

$$v ::= v_t \mid f \mid F \qquad v_\perp ::= v \mid \perp$$

$$e ::= v \mid x \mid \lambda x.e \mid e\,e \mid \texttt{if } e \texttt{ then } e \texttt{ else } e \mid \texttt{async } e \mid \texttt{get } e \mid e \leadsto e \mid \texttt{read } e \mid \boxed{\texttt{read! } e} \mid$$

$$\texttt{write } e\,e \mid \boxed{\texttt{write! } e\,e} \mid \texttt{new Vat}(e,e,e) \mid \boxed{\texttt{lock}(e)\{e\}} \mid \boxed{\texttt{unlock}(e)\{e\}}$$

v denotes values, $v_\perp$ denotes possibly undefined values, e are expressions. f ranges over future ids. F ranges over vat ids.[3] Expressions such as let $\texttt{let } x = e \texttt{ in } e$ and sequencing $e; e$ can be encoded in the standard fashion.

async e spawns a new task. The get operation has type $\texttt{Fut } \tau \to \tau$. It blocks until the value in the future becomes available (aka *fulfilled*) and returns that value. Future chaining $\leadsto$ sets up a function to be run as a new task when a future is fulfilled. read reads a vat safely and asynchronously, returning a future that will contain the vat's current value. read! reads a vat synchronously, subverting the lock. write writes a vat safely and asynchronously, triggering the actions associated with the vat. Its result is a future containing a Boolean which eventually indicates whether or not the write was successful. write! performs a synchronous write on a vat, subverting the lock, without triggering any of the actions. new Vat(e_1, e_2, e_3) creates a new vat: e_1 is the pre action, e_2 is the transformation, and e_3 is the post action. For simplicity, only one of each function is given and these functions cannot be changed after the creation of vat. lock$(e)\{e\}$ and unlock$(e)\{e\}$ are terms introduced during expressing evaluation to lock and unlock vats.

4.1   Dynamic Semantics

The dynamics semantics is based on an evolving configuration consisting of runtime representations of vats, futures, tasks, and chains:

$$\texttt{config} ::= \epsilon \mid (\texttt{vat}_F^\pi \; v_\perp \; pr \; tr \; po) \mid (\texttt{fut}_g \; v) \mid (\texttt{task}_g \; e) \mid (\texttt{chain}_g \; h \; \lambda x.e) \mid \texttt{config config}$$

$$\pi ::= \texttt{U} \mid \texttt{L}$$

---

[3] Vats were originally called Franks.

ϵ is an empty configuration and complex configurations are formed by concatenation of configurations config config. Configurations concatenation is associative and commutative with ϵ as its unit. The other configuration types are as follows:

- $(\text{vat}_F^\pi \ v_\perp \ pr \ tr \ po)$ — a vat with id F, lock status π, current value v (or undefined), pre action pr, transformation tr and post action po.
- $(\text{task}_g \ e)$ — task running expression e whose result will be stored in future g.
- $(\text{fut}_g \ v)$ — a fulfilled future with id g holding value v.
- $(\text{chain}_g \ h \ \lambda x.e)$ — a function $\lambda x.e$ chained on future h, whose result will be stored in future g.

The dynamic semantics is presented in a style combining elements of rewriting logic [15] and evaluation context-based reduction semantics [8]. Evaluation contexts are expressions with a single hole that indicates where evaluation will occur next:

$$E ::= [] \mid E\,e \mid v\,E \mid \text{if } E \text{ then } e \text{ else } e \mid \text{get } E \mid E \rightsquigarrow e \mid v \rightsquigarrow E \mid \text{read } E \mid \text{read! } E \mid$$
$$\text{write } E\,e \mid \text{write } v\,E \mid \text{write! } E\,e \mid \text{write! } v\,E \mid \text{newVat}(E, e, e) \mid$$
$$\text{newVat}(v, E, e) \mid \text{newVat}(v, v, E) \mid \text{lock}(E)\{e\} \mid \text{unlock}(E)\{e\} \mid \text{unlock}(v)\{E\}$$

The reduction rules are grouped together in Fig. 1. The first three rules demonstrate basic operations on futures. The fourth rule shows async spawning a new task. The fifth rule shows a completed task converted into a fulfilled future. The sixth rule shows an asynchronous read converted into a task performing a synchronous read, after first grabbing a lock. The seventh rule shows the actual read. The next two rules give the same story for writes. The asynchronous write involves a lock, testing the pre action, performing the transformation action, and firing post actions, where appropriate. The third last rule shows vat creation and the last two deal with locking and unlocking vats.

4.2   Static Semantics

We assume that some basic set of types $\mathcal{T}$ are provided and a collection of values $\mathcal{V}$, which for convenience may be annotated with their type v_τ, where $\tau \in \mathcal{T}$. We have, for instance, $()_{\text{Void}}, \text{true}_{\text{Bool}}, \text{false}_{\text{Bool}} \in \mathcal{V}$.

Types have the syntax $\tau ::= t \mid \text{Bool} \mid \text{Void} \mid \tau \to \tau \mid \text{Vat } \tau \mid \text{Fut } \tau$, where $t \in \mathcal{T}$. Typing environments have the syntax $\Gamma ::= \epsilon \mid \Gamma, f : \tau \mid \Gamma, F : \tau \mid \Gamma, x : \tau$. The typing judgements are:

- $\Gamma \vdash \text{ok}$ — environment Γ is a-okay
- $\Gamma \vdash e : \tau$ — expression e has type τ in environment Γ
- $\Gamma \vdash \text{config ok}$ — configuration config is a-okay in environment Γ

The rules for expression (Fig. 2) and configuration typing (Fig. 3) are mostly unsurprising. The function defs(config) extracts the set of future and vat names defined in configuration config.

(1) $(\mathsf{fut}_g\ v)\ (\mathsf{task}_h\ E[\mathsf{get}\ g]) \to (\mathsf{fut}_g\ v)\ (\mathsf{task}_h\ E[v])$

(2) $(\mathsf{task}_h\ E[g \rightsquigarrow \lambda x.e]) \to (\mathsf{task}_h\ E[f])\ (\mathsf{chain}_f\ g\ (\lambda x.e))$ f is fresh

(3) $(\mathsf{fut}_g\ v)\ (\mathsf{chain}_f\ g\ (\lambda x.e)) \to (\mathsf{fut}_g\ v)\ (\mathsf{task}_f\ ((\lambda x.e)\ v))$

(4) $(\mathsf{task}_g\ E[\mathsf{async}\ e]) \to (\mathsf{task}_g\ E[h])\ (\mathsf{task}_h\ e)$ h is fresh

(5) $(\mathsf{task}_f\ v) \to (\mathsf{fut}_f\ v)$

(6)
$$
\begin{aligned}
&(\mathsf{vat}_F^\pi\ v\ pr\ t\ po)\ (\mathsf{task}_g\ E[\mathsf{read}\ F]) \to \\
&\quad (\mathsf{vat}_F^\pi\ v\ pr\ t\ po)\ (\mathsf{task}_g\ E[h])\ (\mathsf{task}_h\ (\mathsf{lock}(F)\{\mathsf{read!}\ F\})) \\
&\quad\quad f\ \text{is fresh}
\end{aligned}
$$

(7) $(\mathsf{vat}_F^\pi\ v\ pr\ t\ po)\ (\mathsf{task}_g\ E[\mathsf{read!}\ F]) \to (\mathsf{vat}_F^\pi\ v\ pr\ t\ po)\ (\mathsf{task}_g\ E[v])$

(8)
$$
\dfrac{e = \mathsf{lock}(F)\{\mathbf{if}\ pr\ v'\mathbf{then\ let}\ r = t\ v'\ \mathbf{in\ write!}\ F\ r;\mathsf{async}\ (po\ r);\mathbf{true\ else\ false}\}}{(\mathsf{vat}_F^\pi\ v\ pr\ t\ po)\ (\mathsf{task}_g\ E[\mathsf{write}\ F\ v']) \to (\mathsf{vat}_F^\pi\ v\ pr\ t\ po)\ (\mathsf{task}_g\ E[h])\ (\mathsf{task}_h\ e)}
$$
h is fresh

(9) $(\mathsf{vat}_F^\pi\ v\ pr\ t\ po)\ (\mathsf{task}_g\ E[\mathsf{write!}\ F\ v']) \to (\mathsf{vat}_F^\pi\ v'\ pr\ t\ po)\ (\mathsf{task}_g\ E[()])$

(10) $(\mathsf{task}_g\ E[\mathsf{new\ Vat}(v,v',v'')]) \to (\mathsf{vat}_F^U\ \bot\ v\ v'\ v'')\ (\mathsf{task}_g\ E[F])$ F is fresh

(11) $(\mathsf{vat}_F^U\ v\ pr\ t\ po)\ (\mathsf{task}_g\ E[\mathsf{lock}(F)\{e\}]) \to (\mathsf{vat}_F^L\ v\ pr\ t\ po)\ (\mathsf{task}_g\ E[\mathsf{unlock}(F)\{e\}])$

(12) $(\mathsf{vat}_F^L\ v\ pr\ t\ po)\ (\mathsf{task}_g\ E[\mathsf{unlock}(F)\{v\}]) \to (\mathsf{vat}_F^U\ v\ pr\ t\ po)\ (\mathsf{task}_g\ E[v])$

Fig. 1. Reduction rules (obvious ones omitted)

$$\dfrac{}{\epsilon \vdash \mathsf{ok}} \qquad \dfrac{\Gamma \vdash \mathsf{ok} \quad x \notin \mathrm{dom}(\Gamma)}{\Gamma, x : \tau \vdash \mathsf{ok}} \qquad \dfrac{\Gamma \vdash \mathsf{ok} \quad f \notin \mathrm{dom}(\Gamma)}{\Gamma, f : \mathsf{Fut}\ \tau \vdash \mathsf{ok}} \qquad \dfrac{\Gamma \vdash \mathsf{ok} \quad F \notin \mathrm{dom}(\Gamma)}{\Gamma, F : \mathsf{Vat}\ \tau \vdash \mathsf{ok}}$$

$$\dfrac{\Gamma \vdash \mathsf{ok} \quad v_t \in \mathcal{V}}{\Gamma \vdash v_t : t} \qquad \dfrac{\Gamma \vdash \mathsf{ok} \quad \alpha : \tau \in \Gamma \quad \alpha \in \{f, F, x\}}{\Gamma \vdash \alpha : \tau}$$

$$\dfrac{\Gamma \vdash \mathsf{ok}}{\Gamma \vdash \bot : \tau} \qquad \dfrac{\Gamma, x : \tau \vdash e : \tau'}{\Gamma \vdash \lambda x.e : \tau \to \tau'} \qquad \dfrac{\Gamma \vdash e : \mathsf{Bool} \quad \Gamma \vdash e' : \tau' \quad \Gamma \vdash e'' : \tau'}{\Gamma \vdash \mathbf{if}\ e\ \mathbf{then}\ e'\ \mathbf{else}\ e'' : \tau'}$$

$$\dfrac{\Gamma \vdash e : \tau}{\Gamma \vdash \mathsf{async}\ e : \mathsf{Fut}\ \tau} \qquad \dfrac{\Gamma \vdash e : \mathsf{Fut}\ \tau}{\Gamma \vdash \mathsf{get}\ e : \tau} \qquad \dfrac{\Gamma \vdash e : \mathsf{Fut}\ \tau \quad \Gamma \vdash e' : \tau \to \tau'}{\Gamma \vdash e \rightsquigarrow e' : \mathsf{Fut}\ \tau'}$$

$$\dfrac{\Gamma \vdash e : \mathsf{Vat}\ \tau}{\Gamma \vdash \mathsf{read}\ e : \mathsf{Fut}\ \tau} \qquad \dfrac{\Gamma \vdash e : \mathsf{Vat}\ \tau}{\Gamma \vdash \mathsf{read!}\ e : \tau} \qquad \dfrac{\Gamma \vdash e : \mathsf{Vat}\ \tau \quad \Gamma \vdash e' : \tau}{\Gamma \vdash \mathsf{write}\ e\ e' : \mathsf{Fut}\ \mathsf{Bool}}$$

$$\dfrac{\Gamma \vdash e : \mathsf{Vat}\ \tau \quad \Gamma \vdash e' : \tau}{\Gamma \vdash \mathsf{write!}\ e\ e' : \mathsf{Void}} \qquad \dfrac{\Gamma \vdash e : \tau \to \mathsf{Bool} \quad \Gamma \vdash e' : \tau \to \tau \quad \Gamma \vdash e'' : \tau \to \mathsf{Void}}{\Gamma \vdash \mathsf{new\ Vat}(e,e',e'') : \mathsf{Vat}\ \tau}$$

$$\dfrac{\Gamma \vdash e : \mathsf{Vat}\ \tau \quad \Gamma \vdash e' : \tau'}{\Gamma \vdash \mathsf{lock}(e)\{e'\} : \tau'} \qquad \dfrac{\Gamma \vdash e : \mathsf{Vat}\ \tau \quad \Gamma \vdash e' : \tau'}{\Gamma \vdash \mathsf{unlock}(e)\{e'\} : \tau'}$$

Fig. 2. Type rules

$$\frac{\Gamma \vdash \mathsf{ok}}{\Gamma \vdash \epsilon \ \mathsf{ok}} \qquad \frac{g : \mathsf{Fut}\ \tau \in \Gamma \quad \Gamma \vdash v : \tau}{\Gamma \vdash (\mathsf{fut}_g\ v)\ \mathsf{ok}} \qquad \frac{g : \mathsf{Fut}\ \tau \in \Gamma \quad \Gamma \vdash e : \tau}{\Gamma \vdash (\mathsf{task}_g\ e)\ \mathsf{ok}}$$

$$\frac{F : \mathsf{Vat}\ \tau \in \Gamma \quad \Gamma \vdash v_\perp : \tau \quad \Gamma \vdash pr : \tau \to \mathsf{Bool}}{\Gamma \vdash tr : \tau \to \tau \quad \Gamma \vdash po : \tau \to \mathsf{Void}}$$
$$\frac{}{\Gamma \vdash (\mathsf{vat}_F^\tau\ v_\perp\ pr\ tr\ po)\ \mathsf{ok}}$$

$$\frac{\Gamma, x : \tau \vdash e : \tau' \quad f : \mathsf{Fut}\ \tau', g : \mathsf{Fut}\ \tau \in \Gamma}{\Gamma \vdash (\mathsf{chain}_f\ g\ \lambda x.e)\ \mathsf{ok}} \qquad \frac{\Gamma \vdash \mathsf{config}_0\ \mathsf{ok} \quad \Gamma \vdash \mathsf{config}_1\ \mathsf{ok}}{\mathsf{defs}(\mathsf{config}_0) \cap \mathsf{defs}(\mathsf{config}_1) = \emptyset}$$
$$\frac{}{\Gamma \vdash \mathsf{config}_0\ \mathsf{config}_1\ \mathsf{ok}}$$

Fig. 3. Configuration typing

5 Chocolate Vats

A number of extensions to the vanilla vat concept are now considered: *multi-value vats*, which contain two or more fields, *linked vats*, which connects two independent vats together, *nested vats*, which are vats within vats, and *type-changing vats*, which permit type-changing transformations to the values written to a vat.

5.1 Multi-value Vats

Multi-value vats contain two or more fields. The fields may be updated separately or together. Multi-value vats may have *and-* or *or*-trigger semantics, which control when actions trigger:

or-vat. Actions are triggered on every field assignment. Assignments to individual fields are published as in vanilla vats.

and-vat. Actions are triggered only after all fields in the vat have been assigned. Assignments to individual fields are not published until an assignment to each field has been made and after the pre action succeeds and the transformation has been performed. Writes to individual fields are blocked until all fields are written. Subsequent writes to fields written but not published are also blocked.

For multi-value vats, pre actions and transformations work together to protect and preserve multi-object invariants, because these operate at the vat level, not on the level of the fields in the vat.

The informal semantics of multi-value and- and or-vats and their actions are now given in terms of a multi-vat containing two fields of types τ and τ'.

And-Vats. And-vats are synchronisers. Pairs of writes to the two fields are synchronised together. Unmatched write attempts to one field are blocked until a matching write attempt to the other field is made.

– Pre actions, type `Update` $(\tau, \tau') \to$ `Status Bool`, run when attempts have been made to assign both fields.

- Transformer, type Update $(\tau, \tau') \to$ Status (τ, τ'), fires when both arguments are available.
- Post actions, type Update $(\tau, \tau') \to$ Status Void, fire when the pre actions succeed.
- Fail actions, Update $(\tau, \tau') \to$ Status Void fire when the pre actions fail.

The types of these functions are the same as for a vat containing a pair, namely Vat (τ, τ'), but the semantics differ. In the multi-value vat case, both fields of the vat can be updated independently, but they are synchronised, whereas in the vat containing a pair case, the pair would be updated atomically.

Example 1. Consider a vat with fields f, g and h, keeping track of a number of tasks to process, how many are currently being processed, and the number of tasks processed, respectively. The sum $f + g + h$ should be invariant. An and-vat naturally allows this by requiring that f, g and h all be updated before the updates can be read. One can imagine transform actions trigger updates of f and h on writes to g, and similar, or pre actions checking the internal consistency.

Or-vats. Or-vats are a bit like mergers in that the (successful) writes to either of the fields triggers the actions. The information that only one of the two fields is updated with each call to the vat's actions is encoded in the datatype wrapped values passed to the actions. The following Update type is used to indicate which of the two values was updated, along with the status of the field:

$$\text{data Presence } \tau = \text{Absent} \mid \text{Present } \tau$$
$$\text{type Update } \tau = (\text{Defined } \tau, \text{Present } \tau)$$

The types of the actions are as follows, using the new type:

- Pre action: Update $\tau \to$ Update $\tau' \to$ Status Bool.
- Transformer: Update $\tau \to$ Update $\tau' \to$ Status (Partial τ, Partial τ').
- Post action: Update $\tau \to$ Update $\tau' \to$ Status Void
- Fail action: Update $\tau \to$ Update $\tau' \to$ Status Void

The pre action, transformer, post action and fail fire for each update to the two fields, according to their usual semantics. The transformer action has a more complicated type to account for the fact that it may apply to fields that are undefined and may therefore need to preserve the undefined state.

Example 2. Consider a vat with two linked fields f and g, such that when one field is updated, the value stored in the other field is 100 minus the value stored in the first field.

```
or-vat (f : int, g : int) {
  trans (_, newf) (_, Absent) = Quo (Defined newf, Defined (100 - newf))
  trans (_, Absent) (_, newg) = Quo (Defined (100 - newg), newg)
} x;
```

5.2   Linked Vats

Links connect two or more vats and synchronise the publishing of values to those vats. That means that publishing a write to one vat will be delayed until all other writes are ready to be published. In this sense, vats are like Ada's rendezvous mechanism [6].

Example 3. Consider bidirectional relationships. These are often tricky to encode, especially in a concurrent program if the values that must be kept in sync are not co-located. A vat with a field spouse could require spouse.spouse == this, which would be satisfied by two writes performed in separate steps, after which triggers fire.

Links do not offer any way of checking or amending the values written. Nested vats offer this functionality.

5.3   Nested Vats

Vats are nested when the inner fields of a multi-vat are also vats. Nested vats extend the notion of links by empowering the link with the capabilities of a vat. In this situation the actions on the inner vats and outer vats interact to produce more complex behaviours. Again, two main semantics are possible: and-semantics on the outer vat synchronises writes to the inner vats; or-semantics on the outer vat results in the outer vat's actions being run for every successful write to some inner vat. In both cases, the inner vat actions are run first, then the outer vats. Publication of a write attempt requires that both inner and outer vat pre actions succeed.

The semantics are as follows: when a field of an inner vat is assigned, the inner vat pre action is tested. If it fails, the fail action is run and we are done. If it succeeds, the transformation is run, producing a candidate value for the inner vat—this value is *not* published. (If or-semantics is used, the result of the transformation plus the current value of the other field is used in the next step. If and-semantics is used, the result of separately transforming both fields is used in the next step.) After the transformation, candidate values for the one or more inner vats have been produced, the outer vat's pre action is run. If that fails, no value is published and the outer fail actions are triggered. (Inner fail actions do not fire.) If the pre action succeeds, the outer transformation is run, the result is assigned into the fields. Then the post actions, both inner and outer, can be run on the final published values.

Note the transactional nature of this description—no result is published unless all pre actions succeed and after both inner and outer transformations are applied.

Example 4. Consider the or-vat example in Sect. 5.1. Instead of using integer fields f and g, the following vats containing integers are used. This vat performs validation on the integer to ensure that it is within 0 and 100.

```
vat int {
  pre (_, new) = Quo (new >= 0 && new <= 100)
};
```

Here we assume that the default transform action is essentially the identity function, it results in the written value being published.

When used in the context of the or-vat, this means that whenever a field is written, the inner vat validates the value written before the outer vat can do its work. Collectively, this will ensure that the values assigned to the fields both remain between 0 and 100.

5.4   Type-Changing Vats

A type-changing vat is a vat where the type written, the type stored, and the type read possibly differ.

The most general type-changing vat, type TCVat τ τ' τ'', accepts elements of some type τ but stores them as another type τ' after performing some transformation, effectively of type $\tau \to \tau'$, and producing values of type τ'' for reads. One can think of τ as an input type, and τ' as a kind of state type, and the transformation as a state transformer, and τ'' as some kind of observation type.

The types of the component functions of a type-changing vat are a little different; the type to encode the input to various actions is now:

$$\text{type Update } \sigma \ \tau = (\text{Partial } \tau, \sigma)$$

Reads and writes of type changing vats have the following types:

- read :: TCVat τ τ' τ'' $\to$ Fut τ''
- write :: TCVat τ τ' τ'' $\to$ τ $\to$ Fut Bool

The types of the pre, post and fail actions are more or less the same as before, except they now take as input an element of the Update datatype. For instance, a transformation on a vat of type TCVat τ τ' τ'' has type Update τ τ' $\to$ Status τ'.

Two variations of the idea are as follows. By letting $\tau'' = \tau'$, one writes a value of a given type, which is transformed into another type, the type that is read. Alternatively, if $\tau'' = \tau$, the types of read and write become TCVat τ τ' τ $\to$ Fut τ' and TCVat τ τ' τ $\to$ τ $\to$ Fut Bool, respectively, which correspond approximately, after unravelling the details, to the types of the get and put operations of a bidirectional lens [9].

Example 5. A simple example of a type-changing vat is one which takes as input a pair of number, and produces as output a single number—their sum.

6   Applied Vats

Example 6 (Condition Variable). A vat can model a *condition variable*. To do so, a post action is set up that tests the condition on each value published in the field. If the condition holds, the corresponding action associated with the condition variable is executed and the post action is deregistered.

```
post (_, new) = if cond new then Deregister (do_action ()) else Quo ()
```

Example 7 (Promise). A *promise* [13] is similar to a future, but makes the fulfilment responsibility explicitly available to the programmer. A promise can be modelled as follows. Create an uninitialised vat and perform a read on it to get a future that will be fulfilled when the vat is assigned. Pass the future to whoever wants the result, pass the vat to whoever will produce a result. Writing to the vat fulfils the future.

Example 8 (Reactive Program). A simple example *reactive program* stores the continual sum of two vats into another vat. Create two vats which will contain the integers being assigned. Nest these two vats within a type-changing vat that has and-semantics to synchronise and converts the pair of values into a single value (Example 5). An alternative is to use three vats and the post action of the link (of the first two vats) writes the sum into a third vat.

Example 9 (LVars). LVars [12], or lattice-values variables, can be modelled by combining monotonicity, a transform action implementing a lattice-valued vat (combining the old and new values appropriately) and post actions that fire after a threshold is reached, as in the example in Sect. 2.

Example 10 (Preferential Attachment). A more involved example is the preferential attachment algorithm for computing random, scale-free graphs [3]. Without going into too much detail, the graph is constructed by adding each new node to the graph by connecting it to k distinct, randomly-chosen, existing nodes. The data structure used in the algorithm is an array a containing the nodes of each edge in consecutive elements. Adding a new edge for node j involves randomly selecting an index i in the array for the nodes left of j, and writing the values j and $a[i]$ in the next two positions in the array, that is, $a[2j] = j$ and $a[2j + 1] = a[i]$ (after checking that $a[i]$ is unique for j). The indices, $i_{0,...n-1}$ can all be computed in parallel, but $a[2j + 1]$ cannot be computed until $a[i]$ is known, which again may depend upon some earlier part of the array. Where $a[i]$ is not computed, a fire-once post trigger can be installed that forwards its result to $a[2j + 1]$.

Rather than storing an integer in the array a, a's elements can be vats. Each vat contains the array for the connections of a single node. Each assignment $a[2j + 1] = a[i]$ becomes a read of an element in the array in the vat whose result is written to the target location (the equivalent of $a[2j + 1]$). Before the write can succeed, disjointness is tested in the pre action; the fail action can retry with a different index value. After the write succeeds, vats depending on $a[2j + 1]$ will fire.

7   Related Work

Vats share commonalities with various other programming constructs. We review some here—others were covered in Sect. 6.

Futures [2,5] and promises [13] act as placeholders for asynchronously computed values, allowing asynchronous programs to avoid blocking until the values are actually needed and be expressed in a direct style instead of continuation passing style. Future chaining and promise pipelining allow callbacks to be registered that trigger when a value is computed, similar to vats' post actions.

Multi-value and-vats are reminiscent of atomic sets in AJ [7,14]. In AJ, programmers declare atomic sets and map variables (and their containing objects) into these sets. Variables inside a set must be updated atomically, and synchronisation is inserted automatically by the compiler. Atomic sets may span several objects. Multi-value and-vats group variables that must all be updated before the updates become visible through reads. This allows the preservation of invariants that span multiple locations without requiring updates to come from a single modifying thread. The downside of this design is the possibility of concurrent, conflicting updates of a vat, preventing it from reaching a consistent state.

The post actions of a vat are essentially observers (listeners in Java's parlance) [10]. In Java, observers are tied to a specific protocol, whereas post actions can be any closure expression, and registration, de-registration and notification is handled manually. Vats' actions were inspired by before, around and after advice of aspects [11]. Before advice are typically able to block the progression to the following join point (in our case, always an assignment), *e.g.,* by throwing an exception. Aspects are more general by nature.

The fact that a vat is read asynchronously and that the read will succeed only after the vat is initialised makes that aspect of vats similar to IVars [1].

8   Conclusion

This paper presented the vat, a data structure for parallel programming. The vat is like an asynchronous container with various actions attached to it to block or modify its behaviour. Clients can attach actions that respond to changes in a vat, enabling the creation of reactive programming structures. Work is underway to incorporate vats into the Encore programming language [4]. Future work will include gaining experience programming with vats and refining their interface and semantics.

References

1. Arvind, Nikhil, R.S., Pingali, K.: I-structures: data structures for parallel computing. ACM Trans. Program. Lang. Syst. **11**(4), 598–632 (1989)
2. Baker Jr., H.G., Hewitt, C.: The incremental garbage collection of processes. In: Proceedings of the 1977 Symposium on Artificial Intelligence and Programming Languages, pp. 55–59. ACM, New York (1977)
3. Barabási, A.-L., Albert, R.: Emergence of scaling in random networks. Science **286**(5439), 509–512 (1999)
4. Brandauer, S., et al.: Parallel objects for multicores: a glimpse at the parallel language encore. In: Bernardo, M., Johnsen, E.B. (eds.) SFM 2015. LNCS, vol. 9104, pp. 1–56. Springer, Heidelberg (2015)

5. de Boer, F.S., Clarke, D., Johnsen, E.B.: A complete guide to the future. In: De Nicola, R. (ed.) ESOP 2007. LNCS, vol. 4421, pp. 316–330. Springer, Heidelberg (2007)
6. Department of Defense. Reference Manual for the Ada Programming Language, ANSI/MIL-STD-1815A (1983)
7. Dolby, J., Hammer, C., Marino, D., Tip, F., Vaziri, M., Vitek, J.: A data-centric approach to synchronization. ACM Trans. Program. Lang. Syst. **34**(1), 4:1–4:48 (2012)
8. Felleisen, M., Hieb, R.: The revised report on the syntactic theories of sequential control and state. Theor. Comput. Sci. **103**(2), 235–271 (1992)
9. Nathan Foster, J., Greenwald, M.B., Moore, J.T., Pierce, B.C., Schmitt, A.: Combinators for bidirectional tree transformations: a linguistic approach to the view-update problem. ACM Trans. Program. Lang. Syst. **29**(3), 17 (2007)
10. Gamma, E., Helm, R., Johnson, R., Vlissides, J.: Design Patterns: Elements of Reusable Object-oriented Software. Addison-Wesley Longman Publishing Co. Inc., Boston (1995)
11. Kiczales, G., Lamping, J., Mendhekar, A., Maeda, C., Lopes, C., Loingtier, J.-M., Irwin, J.: Aspect-oriented programming. In: Akşit, M., Matsuoka, S. (eds.) ECOOP 1997. LNCS, vol. 1241, pp. 220–242. Springer, Heidelberg (1997)
12. Kuper, L., Turon, A., Krishnaswami, N.R., Newton, R.R.: Freeze after writing: quasi-deterministic parallel programming with lvars. In: Jagannathan, S., Sewell, P. (eds.) The 41st Annual ACM SIGPLAN-SIGACT Symposium on Principles of Programming Languages, POPL 2014, San Diego, CA, USA, 20–21 January 2014, pp. 257–270. ACM (2014)
13. Liskov, B.H., Shrira, L.: Promises: linguistic support for efficient asynchronous procedure calls in distributed systems. In: Wise, D.S. (ed.) Proceedings of the SIGPLAN Conference on Programming Lanugage Design and Implementation (PLDI 1988), Atlanta, GE, USA, pp. 260–267. ACM, June 1988
14. Marino, D., Hammer, C., Dolby, J., Vaziri, M., Tip, F., Vitek, J.: Detecting deadlock in programs with data-centric synchronization. In: Proceedings of the 2013 International Conference on Software Engineering, ICSE 2013, Piscataway, NJ, USA, pp. 322–331. IEEE Press (2013)
15. Meseguer, J.: Rewriting logic as a semantic framework for concurrency: a progress report. In: Sassone, V., Montanari, U. (eds.) CONCUR 1996. LNCS, vol. 1119, pp. 331–372. Springer, Heidelberg (1996)

Denotational and Operational Preciseness of Subtyping: A Roadmap

Dedicated to Frank de Boer on the Occasion of His 60th Birthday

Mariangiola Dezani-Ciancaglini[1], Silvia Ghilezan[2], Svetlana Jakšić[2], Jovanka Pantović[2], and Nobuko Yoshida[3]([⊠])

[1] Università di Torino, Turin, Italy
[2] Univerzitet u Novom Sadu, Novi Sad, Serbia
[3] Imperial College London, London, UK
n.yoshida@imperial.ac.uk

Abstract. The notion of subtyping has gained an important role both in theoretical and applicative domains: in lambda and concurrent calculi as well as in object-oriented programming languages. The soundness and the completeness, together referred to as the preciseness of subtyping, can be considered from two different points of view: denotational and operational. The former preciseness is based on the denotation of a type, which is a mathematical object describing the meaning of the type in accordance with the denotations of other expressions from the language. The latter preciseness has been recently developed with respect to type safety, i.e. the safe replacement of a term of a smaller type when a term of a bigger type is expected.

The present paper shows that standard proofs of operational preciseness imply denotational preciseness and gives an overview on this subject.

1 Introduction

A subtyping relation is a pre-order (reflexive and transitive relation) on types that validates the principle: if σ is a subtype of τ (notation $\sigma \leq \tau$), then a term of type σ may be provided whenever a term of type τ is needed; see Pierce [35] (Chap. 15) and Harper [20] (Chap. 23).

Partly supported by COST IC1201 BETTY and DART bilateral project between Italy and Serbia.

M. Dezani-Ciancaglini—Partly supported by EU H2020-644235 Rephrase project, EU H2020-644298 HyVar project, ICT COST Actions IC1402 ARVI and Ateneo/CSP project RunVar.

S. Ghilezan et al.—Partly supported by ON 174026 and III 44006 projects of the Ministry of Education, Science and Technological Development, Republic of Serbia.

N. Yoshida—Partly supported by EPSRC EP/K011715/1, EP/K034413/1, and EP/L00058X/1, and EU Project FP7-612985 UpScale.

© Springer International Publishing Switzerland 2016
E. Ábrahám et al. (Eds.): de Boer Festschrift, LNCS 9660, pp. 155–172, 2016.
DOI: 10.1007/978-3-319-30734-3_12

In this paper we will discuss key properties of subtyping, i.e. denotational and operational preciseness. We will introduce these notions in the next two paragraphs.

Denotational Preciseness. A usual approach to preciseness of subtyping for a calculus is to consider the interpretation of a type σ (notation $[\![\sigma]\!]$) to be a set that describes the meaning of the type in accordance with the denotations of the terms of the calculus, in general a subset of the domain of a model of the calculus.

> A subtyping relation is denotationally sound when $\sigma \leq \tau$ implies $[\![\sigma]\!] \subseteq [\![\tau]\!]$ and denotationally complete when $[\![\sigma]\!] \subseteq [\![\tau]\!]$ implies $\sigma \leq \tau$.
> A subtyping relation is denotationally precise if it is both denotationally sound and denotationally complete.

This well-established powerful technique is applied to the pure λ-calculus with arrow and intersection types by Barendregt et al. [4], to a call-by-value λ-calculus with arrow, intersection and union types by van Bakel et al. [2] and by Ishihara and Kurata [25], to a wide class of calculi with arrow, union and pair types by Vouillon [38], and to a concurrent λ-calculus by Dezani and Ghilezan [15]. More recently denotational preciseness was studied for binary sessions [11] and synchronous multiparty sessions [16].

Operational Preciseness. Operational soundness is just the key principle mentioned at the beginning of this section: if $\sigma \leq \tau$, then a term of type σ may be provided whenever a term of type τ is needed. As a simple example nat $\leq$ real and a natural number can always play the role of a real number. Operational completeness requires that, if $\sigma \nleq \tau$, then there are

- a context expecting a term of type τ and
- a term of type σ

such that this context filled with this term behaves badly. As a simple example nat $\nleq$ bool, the negation $\neg$ requires a boolean argument and the term $\neg 5$ is stuck.

To define formally operational soundness and completeness we need a boolean predicate bad on terms, standard typing judgements $\Gamma \vdash M : \sigma$ (where Γ is a mapping from variables to types and M is a term) and evaluation contexts C.

> A subtyping relation is operationally sound when $\sigma \leq \tau$ implies that if (for some ρ) $x : \tau \vdash C[x] : \rho$ and $\vdash M : \sigma$, then bad($C[M]$) is false, for all C and M.
> A subtyping relation is operationally complete when $\sigma \nleq \tau$ implies that $x : \tau \vdash C[x] : \rho$ and $\vdash M : \sigma$ and bad($C[M]$), for some ρ, C and M.
> A subtyping relation is operationally precise if it is both operationally sound and operationally complete.

Operational soundness immediately follows from the subject reduction theorem, when the subtyping is used in a subsumption rule. A general methodology to prove operational completeness is the following one:

- [**Step 1**] Characterise the negation of the subtyping relation by inductive rules.
- [**Step 2**] For each type σ define a *characteristic context* C_σ, which behaves well when filled with terms of type σ.
- [**Step 3**] For each type σ define a *characteristic term* M_σ, which has only the types greater than or equal to σ.
- [**Step 4**] Show that if $\sigma \nleq \tau$, then $\mathsf{bad}(C_\tau[M_\sigma])$.

These four steps are the guideline of the proofs in the literature, as we will illustrate in this paper.

Background and Related Work. Ligatti et al. [27] first define operational preciseness of subtyping and apply it to subtyping iso-recursive types. They consider a typed λ-calculus enriched with naturals, reals, pair and case constructors/destructors, and roll/unroll. The predicate $\mathsf{bad}(M)$ holds when M reduces to a stuck term, i.e. to an irreducible term which is not a value. They propose new algorithmic rules for subtyping iso-recursive types and show that they are operationally precise.

Dezani and Ghilezan [15] adapt the ideas of Ligatti et al. [27] to the setting of the concurrent λ-calculus with intersection and union types of [14]. For the operational preciseness they take the view that evaluation of well-typed terms always terminates. This means that the predicate **bad** coincides with non termination. In this calculus applicative contexts are enough. Notably, soundness and completeness are made more operational by asking that some applications converge instead of being typable. To sum up, the definition of operational preciseness becomes:

A subtyping $\leq$ is operationally precise when $\sigma \leq \tau$ if and only if there are no closed terms M, N such that ML converges for all closed terms L of type τ and N has type σ and MN diverges.

The main result of this paper is the operational preciseness of the subtyping induced by the standard set theoretic interpretation of arrow, intersection and union types.

Chen et al. [11] first give a general formulation of preciseness for session calculi, where processes are typed by sets of pairs (channels, session types) [22]. The session types prescribe how the channels can be used for communications. The calculus of processes includes an **error** process and $\mathsf{bad}(P)$ holds when process P reduces to **error**. The typing judgements for closed processes are of the form $\vdash P \triangleright \{a : T\}$, assuring that the process P has a single free channel a whose type is T. The judgement $\vdash C[a : T] \triangleright \emptyset$ means that filling the hole of C with any process P typed by $a : T$ produces a well-typed closed process. We get: A subtyping $\leq$ is precise when, for all session types T and S:

$$T \leqslant S \iff \left(\begin{array}{l} \text{there do not exist } C \text{ and } P \text{ such that:} \\ \vdash C[a : S] \triangleright \emptyset \text{ and } \vdash P \triangleright \{a : T\} \text{ and } C[P] \longrightarrow^* \text{error} \end{array} \right)$$

When the only-if direction ($\Rightarrow$) of this formula holds, we say that the subtyping is sound; when the if direction ($\Leftarrow$) holds, we say that the subtyping is complete. The first result of [11] is that the well-known session subtyping, the branching-selection subtyping [13], is sound and complete for the synchronous dyadic calculus. Next, the authors show that in the asynchronous calculus, this subtyping is incomplete for type-safety: that is, there exist session types T and S such that T can safely be considered as a subtype of S, but $T \leq S$ is not derivable by the subtyping. They propose an asynchronous subtyping system (inspired by [32]) which is sound and complete for the asynchronous dyadic calculus. The method gives a general guidance to design rigorous channel-based subtypings respecting desired safety properties.

Dezani et al. [16] consider the synchronous version [26] of the multiparty session calculus in [12,23]. For the operational preciseness they take the view that well-typed sessions never get stuck. Therefore the predicate bad is true for processes which cannot reduce, but contain pending communications. The preciseness of the branching-selection subtyping [13] is shown using a novel notion of characteristic global type.

A framework which is closely related to the above described works is semantic subtyping. In semantic subtyping, each type is interpreted as the set of values having that type and subtyping is subset inclusion between type interpretations [10]. This gives a precise subtyping as soon as the calculus allows to distinguish operationally values of different types.

Semantic subtyping was first proposed by Castagna and Benzaken through the development of the $\mathbb{C}$Duce project [17]. $\mathbb{C}$Duce is a modern XML-oriented functional language. Distinctive features of $\mathbb{C}$Duce are a powerful pattern matching, first class functions, over-loaded functions, a very rich type system (with arrow, sequence, pair, record, intersection, union, difference type constructs), precise type inference for patterns and error localisation, and a natural interpretation of types as sets of values. It is enriched also with some important implementation aspects: in particular, a dispatch algorithm that demonstrates how static type information can be used to obtain very efficient compilation schemas.

Semantic subtyping has been also studied in [8] for a π-calculus with a patterned input and in [9] for a session calculus with internal and external choices and typed input. Types are built using a rich set of type constructors including union, intersection and negation: they extend IO-types in [8] and session types in [9]. Semantic subtyping is precise for the calculi of [8,9,17], thanks to the type case constructor in [17], and to the blocking of inputs for values of "wrong" types in [8,9].

Bonsangue et al. [6] recently have developed an elegant coalgebraic foundation for coinductive types, which gives a sound and complete characterisation of semantic subtyping in terms of inclusion of maximal traces.

Outline. Sections 2 and 3 deal with typed extensions of λ-calculus, and discuss preciseness of iso-recursive and intersection/union types, respectively. Session calculi are considered in Sects. 4 and 5. Section 4 is devoted to synchronous and asynchronous binary types, Sect. 5 instead to synchronous multiparty types. Section 6 shows how the existence of characteristic terms as defined in [**Step 3**] implies denotational preciseness. Section 7 concludes with some directions for further work.

2   Iso-Recursive Types

In [27] the authors consider a typed λ-calculus enriched with naturals, reals, pair and case constructors/destructors, and roll/unroll. The syntax of types, terms and values of this calculus (dubbed $L_{+\times}^{\to\mu}$) is given in Fig. 1.

$$\sigma ::= \mathsf{nat} \mid \mathsf{real} \mid \sigma \to \tau \mid \sigma \times \tau \mid \sigma + \tau \mid \mu t.\sigma \mid t$$

$$M ::= \mathsf{n} \mid \mathsf{r} \mid \mathsf{succ}(M) \mid \mathsf{neg}(M) \mid \mathsf{fun}\ f(x:\sigma):\tau\ =\ M \mid MM \mid x \mid (M,M) \mid M.\mathsf{fst} \mid M.\mathsf{snd} \mid$$
$$\mathsf{inl}_\sigma(M) \mid \mathsf{inr}_\sigma(M) \mid \mathsf{case}\ M\ \mathsf{of}\ \mathsf{inl}\ x \Rightarrow M_1\ \mathsf{else}\ \mathsf{inr}\ y \Rightarrow M_2 \mid \mathsf{roll}(M) \mid \mathsf{unroll}(M)$$

$$V ::= \mathsf{n} \mid \mathsf{r} \mid \mathsf{fun}\ f(x:\sigma):\tau\ =\ M \mid (V,V) \mid \mathsf{inl}_\sigma(V) \mid \mathsf{inr}_\sigma(V) \mid \mathsf{roll}(V)$$

Fig. 1. Types, terms and values of $L_{+\times}^{\to\mu}$.

The operational semantics of $L_{+\times}^{\to\mu}$ is call-by-value. The operator succ reduces only when the argument is a natural and unroll is the left inverse of roll. The remaining reduction rules are standard.

The most interesting subtyping rule tells that $\mu t.\sigma$ is a subtype of $\mu t.\tau$ if we can derive from $\mu t.\sigma \leq \mu t.\tau$ that their unfolded versions are in the subtype relation. More precisely:

$$\frac{\Sigma, \mu t.\sigma \leq \mu t.\tau \vdash \sigma[\mu t.\sigma/t] \leq \tau[\mu t.\tau/t]}{\Sigma \vdash \mu t.\sigma \leq \mu t.\tau}$$

where Σ is a set of subtyping judgments. The type system is as expected, in particular roll and unroll correspond to fold and unfold of recursive types.

The core of the completeness proof is the construction of characteristic contexts and terms for closed types, as discussed in the Introduction. This construction is delicate since some types (for example $\mu t.t$) are not inhabited. The type inhabitation is decidable and every non inhabited type is subtype of all types. Figure 2 shows some of the characteristic contexts and terms for the types of [27]. Notice that in that paper they are used in the proof without grouping them in a unique definition. We omit the case of the sum type being similar to that of the product type. Also, the characteristic contexts and terms for recursive types are missing, since they are quite tricky depending on the external constructor obtained by unfolding the types.

For example $\mathsf{nat} \to \mathsf{nat} \not\leq \mathsf{real} \to \mathsf{nat}$. The characteristic context of $\mathsf{real} \to \mathsf{nat}$ is $C_{\mathsf{nat}}[[\ ]M_{\mathsf{real}}] = \mathsf{succ}([\ ]2.5)$. The characteristic term of $\mathsf{nat} \to \mathsf{nat}$ is

$$\mathsf{fun}\ f(x:\mathsf{nat}):\mathsf{nat}\ =\ (\mathsf{fun}\ g(y:\mathsf{nat}):\mathsf{nat}\ =\ M_{\mathsf{nat}})(C_{\mathsf{nat}}[x]),$$

type σ	characteristic context C_σ	characteristic term M_σ
nat	succ[ ]	5
real	neg[ ]	2.5
$\tau_1 \to \tau_2$	$C_{\tau_2}[[\ ]M_{\tau_1}]$	fun $f(x : \tau_1) : \tau_2 = M$
$\tau_1 \times \tau_2$	$(C_{\tau_1}[[\ ].\mathsf{fst}], C_{\tau_2}[[\ ].\mathsf{snd}])$	(M_{τ_1}, M_{τ_2})

Fig. 2. Characteristic contexts and terms, where $M = (\mathsf{fun}\ g(y : \tau) : \tau_2 = M_{\tau_2})(C_{\tau_1}[x])$ and τ is the type of $C_{\tau_1}[x]$ when x has type τ_1.

i.e.
$$\mathsf{fun}\ f(x : \mathsf{nat}) : \mathsf{nat} = (\mathsf{fun}\ g(y : \mathsf{nat}) : \mathsf{nat} = 5)(\mathsf{succ}\ x).$$

The term $C_{\mathsf{real}\to\mathsf{nat}}[M_{\mathsf{nat}\to\mathsf{nat}}]$ is then

$$\mathsf{succ}((\mathsf{fun}\ f(x : \mathsf{nat}) : \mathsf{nat} = (\mathsf{fun}\ g(y : \mathsf{nat}) : \mathsf{nat} = 5)(\mathsf{succ}\ x))2.5).$$

This term reduces to

$$\mathsf{succ}((\mathsf{fun}\ g(y : \mathsf{nat}) : \mathsf{nat} = 5)(\mathsf{succ}\ 2.5))$$

which is stuck, since succ 2.5 is stuck.

The main result of [27] is:

Theorem 1. *The subtyping of $L_{+\times}^{\to\mu}$ is operationally precise.*

3   Intersection and Union Types

In this section, we present and discuss the results from [15] on denotational and operational preciseness of the subtyping relation in the setting of the concurrent λ-calculus with intersection and union types (dubbed $\lambda_{\oplus\|}$) introduced in [14]. The syntax of types, terms, values, and total values of this calculus is given in Fig. 3. The only atomic type is the universal type ω. There are both call-by-name variables (ranged over by x) and call-by-value variables (ranged over by v). The constructor $\oplus$ is the non-deterministic choice and the constructor $\|$ is the parallel operator.

$$\sigma ::= \omega \mid \sigma \to \sigma \mid \sigma \wedge \sigma \mid \sigma \vee \sigma$$
$$M ::= x \mid v \mid (\lambda x.M) \mid (\lambda v.M) \mid (MM) \mid (M \oplus M) \mid (M\|M)$$
$$V ::= v \mid \lambda x.M \mid \lambda v.M \mid V\|M \mid M\|V$$
$$W ::= v \mid \lambda x.M \mid \lambda v.M \mid W\|W$$

Fig. 3. Types, terms, values, and total values of $\lambda_{\oplus\|}$.

The reduction relation formalises the behaviour of a machine which evaluates in a synchronous way parallel compositions, until a value is produced. Partial values, i.e. values which are not total, can be further evaluated, and this is essential for applications of a call-by-value abstraction (rule $(\beta_v \|)$). The reduction rules which enable this behaviour are the following

$$(\mu_v) \quad \frac{N \longrightarrow N' \quad N \notin \mathsf{Val}}{(\lambda v.M)N \longrightarrow (\lambda v.M)N'} \quad (\beta_v \|) \quad \frac{V \longrightarrow V' \quad V \in \mathsf{Val}}{(\lambda v.M)V \longrightarrow M[V/v]\|(\lambda v.M)V'}$$

According to [14] a term is *convergent* if all reduction paths reach values.

The type system with intersection and union types is dually reflecting the conjunctive and disjunctive operational semantics of $\|$ and $\oplus$. The subtyping relation on *Type*, the set of all types, is the smallest pre-order such that

1. $\langle Type, \leq \rangle$ is a distributive lattice, where $\wedge$ is the meet, $\vee$ is the join, ω is the top;
2. the arrow satisfies
   (a) $\sigma \to \omega \leq \omega \to \omega$;
   (b) $(\sigma \to \rho) \wedge (\sigma \to \tau) \leq \sigma \to \rho \wedge \tau$;
   (c) $\sigma \geq \sigma', \tau \leq \tau' \Rightarrow \sigma \to \tau \leq \sigma' \to \tau'$.

Notice that the standard axiom $(\sigma \to \rho) \wedge (\tau \to \rho) \leq \sigma \vee \tau \to \rho$ [2,25] is unsound for $\lambda_{\oplus\|}$, as proven in [14].

Regarding operational preciseness, divergent terms are the ones that are not convergent and the predicate bad coincides with divergence. Closed convergent and divergent terms are completely characterised by the types $\omega \to \omega$ and ω, respectively [14].

As said in the Introduction, it is enough to consider applicative context, that we call *test tems*. Figure 4 gives test and characteristic terms, where $\mathbf{I} = \lambda x.x$ and $\Omega = (\lambda x.xx)(\lambda x.xx)$. For example $M_{\omega \to \omega} = \lambda x.\Omega$ and $N_{\omega \to \omega} = \lambda v.\mathbf{I}$. More interestingly $M_{(\omega \to \omega) \to \omega \to \omega} = \lambda x.((\lambda v.\mathbf{I})x)(\lambda y.\Omega)$ applied to a term returns $\lambda y.\Omega$ only if the term reduces to a value. Similarly $N_{(\omega \to \omega) \to \omega \to \omega} = \lambda v.(\lambda v'.\mathbf{I})(v(\lambda x.\Omega))$ applied to a term which reduces to a value, first applies this term to $\lambda x.\Omega$, and then reduces to $\mathbf{I}$ only if the result of this application reduces to a value too.

The key property of test terms is:

if M is a closed term, then $N_\sigma M$ converges if and only if M has type σ.

As a consequence $\sigma \not\leq \tau$ implies the divergence of $N_\tau M_\sigma$, i.e. $\mathsf{bad}(N_\tau M_\sigma)$.

The denotational preciseness of this subtyping is obtained for the standard set-theoretic interpretation of arrow, intersection and union types. The key tool is the existence of characteristic terms, as shown in Sect. 6.

To sum up, the main result in [15] is:

Theorem 2 (Denotational and Operational Preciseness).

1. *The subtyping of the $\lambda_{\oplus\|}$-calculus is operationally precise.*
2. *The subtyping of the $\lambda_{\oplus\|}$-calculus is denotationally precise.*

type σ	test term N_σ	characteristic term M_σ
ω	$\lambda x.\mathbf{I}$	Ω
$\tau_1 \to \tau_2$	$\lambda v.N_{\tau_2}(v M_{\tau_1})$	$\lambda x.(N_{\tau_1} x) M_{\tau_2}$
$\tau_1 \wedge \tau_2$	$\lambda x.(N_{\tau_1} x \oplus N_{\tau_2} x)$	$M_{\tau_1} \| M_{\tau_2}$
$\tau_1 \vee \tau_2$	$\lambda v.(N_{\tau_1} v \| N_{\tau_2} v)$ where $\tau_1 \vee \tau_2 \neq \omega$	$M_{\tau_1} \oplus M_{\tau_2}$

Fig. 4. Test and characteristic terms.

4 Binary Session Types

This section presents results from [11] stating that the well-known branching-selection subtyping (defined in Fig. 7) is precise for the synchronous session calculus. As it happens that this subtyping is incomplete for type-safety for the asynchronous session calculus, the authors propose an asynchronous subtyping relation and prove that it is precise for the asynchronous session calculus.

4.1 Synchronous Session Calculus

A *binary session* is a series of interactions between two parties, possibly with branching and recursion, and serves as a unit of abstraction for describing communication protocols. The syntax of the synchronous session calculus is given in Fig. 5. The input process $\sum_{i \in I} u?l_i(x_i).P_i$ waits on channel u for a label l_i and a channel to replace x_i inside P_i $(i \in I)$. The output process sends on channel u the label l and the channel u'. The process $\mathtt{def}\ D\ \mathtt{in}\ P$ is a recursive agent and $X\langle \tilde{u} \rangle$ is a recursive variable. The process $(\nu ab)P$ is a restriction which binds two channels, a and b in P, making them co-channels, i.e. allowing them to communicate.

$$P ::= \mathbf{0} \mid X\langle \tilde{u} \rangle \mid \sum_{i \in I} u?l_i(x_i).P_i \mid u!l\langle u' \rangle.P \mid P \oplus P \mid P|P \mid \mathtt{def}\ D\ \mathtt{in}\ P \mid (\nu ab)P \mid \mathtt{error}$$

$$u ::= a \mid x \qquad D ::= \quad X(\tilde{x}) = P$$

Fig. 5. Syntax of synchronous processes.

Operational semantics is given by a reduction relation between the synchronous processes. The main rule is

[R-COM-SYNC]

$$\frac{k \in I}{(\nu ab)(a!l_k\langle c \rangle.P \mid \sum_{i \in I} b?l_i(x_i).Q_i) \longrightarrow (\nu ab)(P \mid Q_k\{c/x_k\})}.$$

sessiontype T	characteristic process $\mathbf{P}(u,T)$
end	0
t	$X_\mathbf{t}\langle u\rangle$
$\&_{i\in I}?l_i(S_i).T_i$	$\Sigma_{i\in I}\, u?l_i(x).(\mathbf{P}(u,T_i)\mid \mathbf{P}(x,S_i))$
$\oplus_{i\in I}\,!l_i\langle S_i\rangle.T_i$	$\oplus_{i\in I}(\nu ab)(u!l_i\langle a\rangle.\mathbf{P}(u,T_i)\mid \mathbf{P}(b,\overline{S}_i))$
$\mu t.S$	$\text{def } X_\mathbf{t}(x) = \mathbf{P}(x,S) \text{ in } X_\mathbf{t}\langle u\rangle$

Fig. 6. Types and characteristic synchronous processes.

$$[\text{SUB-END}]\quad \frac{}{\text{end}\leqslant \text{end}}$$

$$[\text{SUB-BRA}]\quad \frac{\forall i\in I: S_i\leqslant S_i'\quad T_i\leqslant T_i'}{\&_{i\in I\cup J}?l_i(S_i).T_i \leqslant \&_{i\in I}?l_i(S_i').T_i'}$$

$$[\text{SUB-SEL}]\quad \frac{\forall i\in I: S_i'\leqslant S_i\quad T_i\leqslant T_i'}{\bigoplus_{i\in I}!l_i\langle S_i\rangle.T_i \leqslant \bigoplus_{i\in I\cup J}!l_i\langle S_i'\rangle.T_i'}$$

Fig. 7. Synchronous subtyping.

It describes the communication between an output $(a!l_k\langle c\rangle.P)$ and an input $(\sum_{i\in I} b?l_i(x_i).Q_i)$ at two co-channels a and b, where the label l_k is selected and channel c replaces x_k into the k-th input branch (Q_k). Other rules are standard.

The synchronous session calculus includes an error process and bad(P) holds when process P reduces to error. There are four kinds of processes which generate error: a session with mismatch between corresponding output and input labels, a session where one of two co-channels is missing, a session where two co-channels are both subjects of outputs, and a session where two co-channels are both subjects of inputs.

The syntax of *synchronous session types* is given in Fig. 6. As usual *session duality* [22] plays an important rôle for session types. The function $\overline{T}$, defined below, yields the dual of the session type T.

$$\overline{\&_{i\in I}?l_i(S_i).T_i} = \bigoplus_{i\in I}!l_i\langle S_i\rangle.\overline{T_i} \quad \overline{\bigoplus_{i\in I}!l_i\langle S_i\rangle.T_i} = \&_{i\in I}?l_i(S_i).\overline{T_i}$$
$$\overline{\mathbf{t}} = \mathbf{t} \quad \overline{\mu t.T} = \mu t.\overline{T} \quad \overline{\text{end}} = \text{end}$$

The type system is the standard one for session calculi, see e.g. [13]. The subtyping relation is given in Fig. 7, where the double line in rules indicates that the rules are interpreted *coinductively* [35] (Chap. 21). The type system enjoys the property of subject reduction, which implies operational soundness of the synchronous subtyping.

It can be verified that the relation $\not\leqslant$, presented in Fig. 8, is the negation of the synchronous subtyping.

The characteristic process offering communication T on identifier u for the synchronous calculus, denoted by $\mathsf{P}(u,T)$, is given in Fig. 6.

For type S and channel b, the characteristic context is defined as

$$C_{S,b} = [\,]\mid \mathbf{P}(b,\overline{S}).$$

[N-END R]   [N-END L]   [N-BRASEL]   [N-SELBRA-SYNC]

$$\frac{T \neq \text{end}}{\text{end} \not\trianglelefteq T} \qquad \frac{T \neq \text{end}}{T \not\trianglelefteq \text{end}} \qquad \underset{i \in I}{\&} ?l_i(S_i).T_i \not\trianglelefteq \underset{j \in J}{\bigoplus} !l'_j\langle S'_j\rangle.T'_j \qquad \underset{j \in J}{\bigoplus} !l'_j\langle S'_j\rangle.T'_j \not\trianglelefteq \underset{i \in I}{\&} ?l_i(S_i).T_i$$

[N-LABEL BRA]   [N-LABEL SEL]   [N-EXCH BRA]

$$\frac{\exists j \in J \,\forall i \in I : l_i \neq l'_j}{\underset{i \in I}{\&} ?l_i(S_i).T_i \not\trianglelefteq \underset{j \in J}{\&} ?l'_j(S'_j).T'_j} \qquad \frac{\exists i \in I \,\forall j \in J : l_i \neq l'_j}{\underset{i \in I}{\bigoplus} !l_i\langle S_i\rangle.T_i \not\trianglelefteq \underset{j \in J}{\bigoplus} !l'_j\langle S'_j\rangle.T'_j} \qquad \frac{\exists i \in I \,\exists j \in J : l_i = l'_j \quad S_i \not\trianglelefteq S'_j}{\underset{i \in I}{\&} ?l_i(S_i).T_i \not\trianglelefteq \underset{j \in J}{\&} ?l'_j(S'_j).T'_j}$$

[N-EXCH SEL]   [N-CONT BRA]   [N-CONT SEL]

$$\frac{\exists i \in I \,\exists j \in J : l_i = l'_j \quad S'_j \not\trianglelefteq S_i}{\underset{i \in I}{\bigoplus} !l_i\langle S_i\rangle.T_i \not\trianglelefteq \underset{j \in J}{\bigoplus} !l'_j\langle S'_j\rangle.T'_j} \qquad \frac{\exists i \in I \,\exists j \in J : l_i = l'_j \quad T_i \not\trianglelefteq T'_j}{\underset{i \in I}{\&} ?l_i(S_i).T_i \not\trianglelefteq \underset{j \in J}{\&} ?l'_j(S'_j).T'_j} \qquad \frac{\exists i \in I \,\exists j \in J : l_i = l'_j \quad T_i \not\trianglelefteq T'_j}{\underset{i \in I}{\bigoplus} !l_i\langle S_i\rangle.T_i \not\trianglelefteq \underset{j \in J}{\bigoplus} !l'_j\langle S'_j\rangle.T'_j}$$

Fig. 8. Negation of synchronous subtyping.

Finally, it can be proven that $T \not\leqslant S$ implies

$$\text{bad}((\nu ab)C_{S,b}[\mathbf{P}(a,T)]) = \text{bad}((\nu ab)(\mathbf{P}(a,T) \mid \mathbf{P}(b,\overline{S}))).$$

For example (omitting $\mathbf{0}$ and final end) let $T = !l_1(\text{end}).?l_2(\text{end})$ and $S = ?l_2(\text{end}).!l_1(\text{end})$, then $T \not\leqslant S$. By definition

$$\begin{aligned}\mathbf{P}(a,T) &= (\nu c_1 d_1)(a!l_1\langle c_1\rangle.\mathbf{P}(a,?l_2(\text{end})) \mid \mathbf{P}(d_1,\text{end}))\\ &= (\nu c_1 d_1)(a!l_1\langle c_1\rangle.a?l_2(x).(\mathbf{P}(a,\text{end}) \mid \mathbf{P}(x,\text{end})))\\ &= (\nu c_1 d_1)(a!l_1\langle c_1\rangle.a?l_2(x))\end{aligned}$$

We get $\overline{S} = !l_2(\text{end}).?l_1(\text{end})$ and

$$\begin{aligned}\mathbf{P}(b,\overline{S}) &= (\nu c_2 d_2)(b!l_2\langle c_2\rangle.\mathbf{P}(b,?l_1(\text{end})) \mid \mathbf{P}(d_2,\text{end}))\\ &= (\nu c_2 d_2)(b!l_2\langle c_2\rangle.b?l_1(y).(\mathbf{P}(b,\text{end}) \mid \mathbf{P}(y,\text{end})))\\ &= (\nu c_2 d_2)(b!l_2\langle c_2\rangle.b?l_1(y))\end{aligned}$$

Then

$$\begin{aligned}(\nu ab)C_{S,b}[\mathbf{P}(a,T)] &= (\nu ab)(\mathbf{P}(a,T) \mid \mathbf{P}(b,\overline{S}))\\ &= (\nu ab)((\nu c_1 d_1)(a!l_1\langle c_1\rangle.a?l_2(x)) \mid (\nu c_2 d_2)(b!l_2\langle c_2\rangle.b?l_1(y)))\end{aligned}$$

and this last process reduces to error, since the two co-channels are both subjects of outputs.

In [11], the main result for synchronous subtyping is:

Theorem 3 (Preciseness for Synchronous Session Calculus). *The synchronous subtyping relation is operationally precise for the synchronous session calculus.*

4.2 Asynchronous Session Calculus

The asynchronous session calculus is obtained from the rules for the synchronous ones by extending the synchronous calculus of Fig. 5 with queues:

[N-LABEL-ASYNC]
$$\frac{\exists i_0 \in I \; \exists n_0 \in N \; \forall j \in J_{n_0} : l_j^{n_0} \neq l_{i_0}}{\bigoplus_{i \in I} !l_i \langle S_i \rangle.T_i \not\leqslant \mathscr{A}[\bigoplus_{j \in J_n} !l_j^n \langle S_j^n \rangle.T_j^n]^{n \in N}}$$

[N-EXCH-ASYNC]
$$\frac{\exists i_0 \in I \; \exists n_0 \in N \; \exists j_0 \in J_{n_0} : l_{j_0}^{n_0} = l_{i_0} \;\; S_{j_0}^{n_0} \not\leqslant S_{i_0}}{\bigoplus_{i \in I} !l_i \langle S_i \rangle.T_i \not\leqslant \mathscr{A}[\bigoplus_{j \in J_n} !l_j^n \langle S_j^n \rangle.T_j^n]^{n \in N}}$$

[N-CONT-ASYNC]
$$\frac{\exists i_0 \in I \; \exists n_0 \in N \; \exists j_0 \in J_{n_0} : l_{j_0}^{n_0} = l_{i_0} \;\; T_{i_0} \not\leqslant \mathscr{A}[T_{j_0}^n]^{n \in N}}{\bigoplus_{i \in I} !l_i \langle S_i \rangle.T_i \not\leqslant \mathscr{A}[\bigoplus_{j \in J_n} !l_j^n \langle S_j^n \rangle.T_j^n]^{n \in N}}$$

[N-BRA-ASYNC]
$$\frac{\& \notin T}{T \not\leqslant \&_{i \in I} ?l_i(S_i).T_i}$$

[N-SEL-ASYNC]
$$\frac{\oplus \notin T}{\bigoplus_{i \in I} !l_i \langle S_i \rangle.T_i}$$

Fig. 9. Negation of asynchronous subtyping.

$$P ::= \ldots \mid ab \blacktriangleright h \qquad h ::= \varnothing \mid l \langle a \rangle \mid h \cdot h.$$

A queue $ab \blacktriangleright h$ is used by channel a to enqueue messages in h and by channel b to dequeue messages from h.

Reduction rules for asynchronous processes are obtained from the rules for the synchronous processes by replacing [R-COM-SYNC] with the following two rules:

[R-SEND-ASYNC]
$$ab \blacktriangleright h \mid a!l \langle c \rangle.P \longrightarrow ab \blacktriangleright h \cdot l \langle c \rangle \mid P$$

[R-RECEIVE-ASYNC]
$$\frac{k \in I}{ab \blacktriangleright l_k \langle c \rangle \cdot h \mid \sum_{i \in I} b?l_i(x_i).P_i \longrightarrow ab \blacktriangleright h \mid P_k \{c/x_k\}}$$

In presence of queues, reduction to error includes deadlocks, that are sessions with inputs waiting to dequeue messages from queues that will stay empty, and orphan messages, that are messages in queues that will never be received.

To define asynchronous subtyping, the notion of asynchronous context is introduced, that is a sequence of branchings containing indexed holes:

$$\mathscr{A} ::= [\;]^n \mid \&_{i \in I} ?l_i(S_i).\mathscr{A}_i.$$

The asynchronous subtyping relation is obtained by extending synchronous subtyping relation by the rule:

[SUB-PERM-ASYNC]
$$\frac{\forall i \in I \; \forall n \in N : \quad S_i^n \leqslant S_i \quad T_i \leqslant \mathscr{A}[T_i^n]^{n \in N} \quad \& \in \mathscr{A} \quad \& \in T_i}{\bigoplus_{i \in I} !l_i \langle S_i \rangle.T_i \leqslant \mathscr{A}[\bigoplus_{i \in I \cup J_n} !l_i \langle S_i^n \rangle.T_i^n]^{n \in N}}.$$

Using this rule we get for example $!l_1(\mathbf{end}).?l_2(\mathbf{end}) \leq ?l_2(\mathbf{end}).!l_1(\mathbf{end})$, which does not hold in the synchronous subtyping, as shown in previous subsection.

The negation rules of asynchronous subtyping are the rules of Fig. 8 excluding rule [N-SELBRA-SYNC], extended by the rules of Fig. 9.

The characteristic process offering communication T on identifier u for the asynchronous calculus, denoted by $\mathbf{P}(u,T)$, is defined as in Fig. 6, but for the case of T being $\bigoplus_{i \in I} !l_i \langle S_i \rangle.T_i$, which becomes:

$$\bigoplus_{i \in I} (\nu ab)(u!l_i \langle a \rangle.\mathbf{P}(u,T_i) \mid \mathbf{P}(b, \overline{S}_i) \mid ba \blacktriangleright \varnothing \mid ab \blacktriangleright \varnothing).$$

For type S and channel b, the characteristic context is defined as

$$C_{S,b} = [\,] \mid \mathbf{P}(b, \overline{S}) \mid ba \blacktriangleright \varnothing \mid ab \blacktriangleright \varnothing.$$

For $T \not\leqslant S$, we can prove that there are $T' \leqslant T$ and $S' \geq S$ such that

$$\mathsf{bad}((\nu ab)(C_{S',b}[\mathbf{P}(a, T')]) = \mathsf{bad}((\nu ab)(\mathbf{P}(a, T') \mid \mathbf{P}(b, \overline{S'}) \mid ba \blacktriangleright \varnothing \mid ab \blacktriangleright \varnothing)).$$

Notice that $S' \geq S$ if and only if $\overline{S'} \leqslant \overline{S}$.

For example let $T = !l_1(\mathsf{end}) \oplus !l_2(\mathsf{end})$ and $S = !l_1(\mathsf{end})$, then $T \not\leqslant S$. By definition

$$
\begin{aligned}
\mathbf{P}(a, T) &= (\nu c_1 d_1)(a!l_1\langle c_1 \rangle . \mathbf{P}(a, \mathsf{end}) \mid \mathbf{P}(d_1, \mathsf{end}) \mid d_1 c_1 \blacktriangleright \varnothing \mid c_1 d_1 \blacktriangleright \varnothing) \oplus \\
&\quad (\nu c_2 d_2)(a!l_2\langle c_2 \rangle . \mathbf{P}(a, \mathsf{end}) \mid \mathbf{P}(d_2, \mathsf{end}) \mid d_2 c_2 \blacktriangleright \varnothing \mid c_2 d_2 \blacktriangleright \varnothing) \\
&= (\nu c_1 d_1)(a!l_1\langle c_1 \rangle \mid d_1 c_1 \blacktriangleright \varnothing \mid c_1 d_1 \blacktriangleright \varnothing) \oplus \\
&\quad (\nu c_2 d_2)(a!l_2\langle c_2 \rangle \mid d_2 c_2 \blacktriangleright \varnothing \mid c_2 d_2 \blacktriangleright \varnothing).
\end{aligned}
$$

We also get $\overline{S} = ?l_1(\mathsf{end})$ and

$$\mathbf{P}(b, \overline{S}) = b?l_1(y).(\mathbf{P}(b, \mathsf{end}) \mid \mathbf{P}(y, \mathsf{end})) = b?l_1(y).$$

Then

$$
\begin{aligned}
(\nu ab)C_{S,b}[\mathbf{P}(a, T)] =\ & (\nu ab)(\mathbf{P}(a, T) \mid \mathbf{P}(b, \overline{S}) \mid ba \blacktriangleright \varnothing \mid ab \blacktriangleright \varnothing) \\
=\ & (\nu ab)((\nu c_1 d_1)(a!l_1\langle c_1 \rangle \mid d_1 c_1 \blacktriangleright \varnothing \mid c_1 d_1 \blacktriangleright \varnothing) \oplus \\
& (\nu c_2 d_2)(a!l_2\langle c_2 \rangle \mid d_2 c_2 \blacktriangleright \varnothing \mid c_2 d_2 \blacktriangleright \varnothing) \mid \\
& b?l_1(y) \mid ba \blacktriangleright \varnothing \mid ab \blacktriangleright \varnothing) \\
\longrightarrow\ & (\nu ab)((\nu c_2 d_2)(a!l_2\langle c_2 \rangle \mid d_2 c_2 \blacktriangleright \varnothing \mid c_2 d_2 \blacktriangleright \varnothing) \mid \\
& b?l_1(y) \mid ba \blacktriangleright \varnothing \mid ab \blacktriangleright \varnothing) \\
\longrightarrow\ & (\nu ab)(\nu c_2 d_2)(d_2 c_2 \blacktriangleright \varnothing \mid c_2 d_2 \blacktriangleright \varnothing \mid \\
& b?l_1(y) \mid ba \blacktriangleright \varnothing \mid ab \blacktriangleright l_2\langle c_2 \rangle) \\
\longrightarrow\ & \mathsf{error}
\end{aligned}
$$

where the reduction to error is due to the mismatch between the input label l_1 and the label l_2 of the message.

In [11], the main result for asynchronous subtyping is:

Theorem 4 (Preciseness for Asynchronous Subtyping). *The asynchronous subtyping relation is operationally precise for the asynchronous session calculus.*

5   Multiparty Session Types

In [16] the authors show operational and denotational preciseness of the subtyping introduced in [13] for a simplification of the synchronous multiparty session calculus in [26]. The calculus is obtained by eliminating both shared channels for session initiations and session channels for communications inside sessions.

$$P ::= 0 \mid X \mid \mathsf{p}?\ell(x).P \mid \mathsf{p}!\ell(e).P \mid P+P \mid \text{if } e \text{ then } P \text{ else } P \mid \mu X.P$$
$$\mathcal{M} ::= \mathsf{p} \triangleleft P \mid \mathcal{M} \mid \mathcal{M}$$

Fig. 10. Processes and multiparty sessions.

$$S ::= \mathsf{nat} \mid \mathsf{int} \mid \mathsf{bool}$$
$$G ::= \mathsf{p} \to \mathsf{q} : \{\ell_i(S_i).G_i\}_{i \in I} \mid \mu \mathsf{t}.G \mid \mathsf{t} \mid \mathsf{end}$$
$$T ::= \bigwedge_{i \in I} \mathsf{p}?\ell_i(S_i).T_i \mid \bigvee_{i \in I} \mathsf{q}!\ell_i(S_i).T_i \mid \mu \mathsf{t}.T \mid \mathsf{t} \mid \mathsf{end}$$

Fig. 11. Sorts, global types and multiparty session types.

A multiparty session is a series of interactions between a fixed number of participants, possibly with branching and recursion, and serves as a unit of abstraction for describing communication protocols. The syntax of processes and multiparty sessions is given in Fig. 10. The values are natural numbers n, integers i, and boolean values true and false. The expressions e are variables or values or expressions built from expressions by applying the operators $\mathsf{succ}, \mathsf{neg}, \neg, \oplus$, or the relation $>$. The input process $\mathsf{p}?\ell(x).P$ waits for an expression with label ℓ from participant p and the output process $\mathsf{q}!\ell(e).Q$ sends the value of expression e with label ℓ to participant q. The external choice $P + Q$ offers to choose either P or Q. The process $\mu X.P$ is a recursive process. An equi-recursive view is taken, not distinguishing between a process $\mu X.P$ and its unfolding $P\{\mu X.P/X\}$. If $\mathsf{p} \triangleleft P$ is well typed (see typing rules in [16]), then participant p does not occur in process P, since we do not allow self-communications.

The computational rules of multiparty sessions are closed with respect to the structural congruence (defined as expected) and reduction contexts (empty and parallel composition). Here we recall only the main rule [R-COMM] which states that participant q sends the value v choosing label ℓ_j to participant p which offers inputs on all labels ℓ_i with $i \in I$.

[R-COMM]
$$\frac{j \in I \qquad e \downarrow v}{\mathsf{p} \triangleleft \sum_{i \in I} \mathsf{q}?\ell_i(x).P_i \mid \mathsf{q} \triangleleft \mathsf{p}!\ell_j(e).Q \longrightarrow \mathsf{p} \triangleleft P_j\{v/x\} \mid \mathsf{q} \triangleleft Q}$$

The value v of expression e (notation $e \downarrow v$) is as expected, see [16]. The successor operation succ is defined only on natural numbers, the negation neg is defined on integers (and then also on natural numbers), and $\neg$ is defined only on boolean values. The internal choice $e_1 \oplus e_2$ evaluates either to the value of e_1 or to the value of e_2.

In order to define the operational preciseness of subtyping it is crucial to formalise when a multiparty session contains communications that will never be executed.

$$[\text{SUB-END}] \atop \text{end} \leqslant \text{end}$$

$$[\text{SUB-IN}] \quad \frac{\forall i \in I: \quad S_i' \leq : S_i \quad T_i \leqslant T_i'}{\bigwedge_{i \in I \cup J} \mathsf{p}?\ell_i(S_i).T_i \leqslant \bigwedge_{i \in I} \mathsf{p}?\ell_i(S_i').T_i'}$$

$$[\text{SUB-OUT}] \quad \frac{\forall i \in I: \quad S_i \leq : S_i' \quad T_i \leqslant T_i'}{\bigvee_{i \in I} \mathsf{p}!\ell_i(S_i).T_i \leqslant \bigvee_{i \in I \cup J} \mathsf{p}!\ell_i(S_i').T_i'}$$

Fig. 12. Subtyping of multiparty session types.

$$[\text{NSUB-ENDL}] \quad \frac{T \neq \text{end}}{T \not\leqslant \text{end}}$$

$$[\text{NSUB-ENDR}] \quad \frac{T \neq \text{end}}{\text{end} \not\leqslant T}$$

$$[\text{NSUB-DIFF-PART}] \quad \frac{\mathsf{p} \neq \mathsf{q} \quad \dagger, \ddagger \in \{?, !\}}{\mathsf{p}\dagger\ell_1(S_1).T_1 \not\leqslant \mathsf{q}\ddagger\ell_2(S_2).T_2}$$

$$[\text{NSUB-OUT-IN}] \atop \mathsf{p}!\ell_1(S_1).T_1 \not\leqslant \mathsf{p}?\ell_2(S_2).T_2$$

$$[\text{NSUB-IN-OUT}] \atop \mathsf{p}?\ell_1(S_1).T_1 \not\leqslant \mathsf{p}!\ell_2(S_2).T_2$$

$$[\text{NSUB-IN-IN}] \quad \frac{\ell_1 \neq \ell_2 \text{ or } S_2 \not\leq : S_1 \text{ or } T_1 \not\leqslant T_2}{\mathsf{p}?\ell_1(S_1).T_1 \not\leqslant \mathsf{p}?\ell_2(S_2).T_2}$$

$$[\text{NSUB-OUT-OUT}] \quad \frac{\ell_1 \neq \ell_2 \text{ or } S_1 \not\leq : S_2 \text{ or } T_1 \not\leqslant T_2}{\mathsf{p}!\ell_1(S_1).T_1 \not\leqslant \mathsf{p}!\ell_2(S_2).T_2}$$

$$[\text{NSUB-INTR}] \quad \frac{T \not\leqslant T_1 \text{ or } T \not\leqslant T_2}{T \not\leqslant T_1 \wedge T_2}$$

$$[\text{NSUB-UNIL}] \quad \frac{T_1 \not\leqslant T \text{ or } T_2 \not\leqslant T}{T_1 \vee T_2 \not\leqslant T}$$

$$[\text{NSUB-INTL-UNIR}] \quad \frac{\forall i \in I \, \forall j \in J \, T_i \not\leqslant T_j'}{\bigwedge_{i \in I} T_i \not\leqslant \bigvee_{j \in J} T_j'}$$

Fig. 13. Negation of subtyping of multiparty session types.

Definition 1. *A multiparty session $\mathscr{M}$ is stuck if $\mathscr{M} \not\equiv \mathsf{p} \triangleleft \mathbf{0}$ and there is no multiparty session $\mathscr{M}'$ such that $\mathscr{M} \longrightarrow \mathscr{M}'$. A multiparty session $\mathscr{M}$ gets stuck, notation $\mathtt{stuck}(\mathscr{M})$, if it reduces to a stuck multiparty session.*

A stuck multiparty session is a bad multiparty session, i.e. $\mathsf{bad}(\mathscr{M}) = \mathtt{stuck}(\mathscr{M})$.

The type system is the simplification of that in [26] due to the new formulation of the calculus. Figure 11 contains syntax of sorts, global types and session types.

Global types describe the whole conversation scenarios of multiparty sessions. Session types correspond to projections of global types on the individual participants.

Subsorting $\leq$: on sorts is the minimal reflexive and transitive closure of the relation induced by the rule: $\mathtt{nat} \leq : \mathtt{int}$. Subtyping $\leqslant$ on session types takes into account the contra-variance of inputs, the covariance of outputs, and the standard rules for intersection and union. Figure 12 gives the coinductive subtyping rules.

The proof of operational soundness of subtyping follows from the subsumption rule and the safety theorem of the type system.

The proof of operational completeness comes in four steps as stated in Introduction.

The characterisation of the negation of the subtyping is given in Fig. 13.

session type T	characteristic process $\mathscr{P}(\mathsf{T})$
end	$\mathbf{0}$
t	$X_{\mathbf{t}}$
$\mathsf{p}?\ell(\mathtt{nat}).\mathsf{T}'$	$\mathsf{p}?\ell(x).\text{if } \mathtt{succ}(x) > 0 \text{ then } \mathscr{P}(\mathsf{T}') \text{ else } \mathscr{P}(\mathsf{T}')$
$\mathsf{p}?\ell(\mathtt{int}).\mathsf{T}'$	$\mathsf{p}?\ell(x).\text{if } \mathtt{neg}(x) > 0 \text{ then } \mathscr{P}(\mathsf{T}') \text{ else } \mathscr{P}(\mathsf{T}')$
$\mathsf{p}?\ell(\mathtt{bool}).\mathsf{T}'$	$\mathsf{p}?\ell(x).\text{if } \neg x \text{ then } \mathscr{P}(\mathsf{T}') \text{ else } \mathscr{P}(\mathsf{T}')$
$\mathsf{p}!\ell(\mathtt{nat}).\mathsf{T}$	$\mathsf{p}!\ell(5).\mathscr{P}(\mathsf{T}')$
$\mathsf{p}!\ell(\mathtt{int}).\mathsf{T}'$	$\mathsf{p}!\ell(-5).\mathscr{P}(\mathsf{T}')$
$\mathsf{p}!\ell(\mathtt{bool}).\mathsf{T}'$	$\mathsf{p}!\ell(\mathtt{true}).\mathscr{P}(\mathsf{T}')$
$\mathsf{T}_1 \wedge \mathsf{T}_2$	$\mathscr{P}(\mathsf{T}_1) + \mathscr{P}(\mathsf{T}_2)$
$\mathsf{T}_1 \vee \mathsf{T}_2$	if $\mathtt{true} \oplus \mathtt{false}$ then $\mathscr{P}(\mathsf{T}_1)$ else $\mathscr{P}(\mathsf{T}_2)$
$\mu\mathbf{t}.\mathsf{T}'$	$\mu X_{\mathbf{t}}.\mathscr{P}(\mathsf{T}')$

Fig. 14. Characteristic processes.

The characteristic process $\mathscr{P}(\mathsf{T})$ of type T is defined in Fig. 14 by using the operators $\mathtt{succ}$, $\mathtt{neg}$, and $\neg$ to check if the received values are of the right sort and exploiting the correspondence between external choices and intersections, conditionals and unions.

The authors define the characteristic global type $\mathscr{G}(\mathsf{T}, \mathsf{p})$ of type T for participant p, that describes the communications between p and all participants which occur in T (notation $\mathtt{pt}\{\mathsf{T}\}$). Moreover, after each communication involving p and some $\mathsf{q} \in \mathtt{pt}\{\mathsf{T}\}$, participant q starts a cyclic communication involving all participants in $\mathtt{pt}\{\mathsf{T}\}$ both as receivers and senders. The characteristic context for $\mathsf{p} \triangleleft \mathscr{P}(\mathsf{T})$ is built using the characteristic global type of type T for participant p.

We do not give here the definitions of characteristic global types and characteristic contexts, we only show an example. Let $\mathsf{T} = \mathsf{p}_1!\ell_1(\mathtt{nat}).\mathsf{p}_2!\ell_2(\mathtt{nat})$ and $\mathsf{T}' = \mathsf{p}_2!\ell_2(\mathtt{nat}).\mathsf{p}_1!\ell_1(\mathtt{nat})$. Clearly $\mathsf{T} \not\leqslant \mathsf{T}'$ and $\mathscr{P}(\mathsf{T}) = \mathsf{p}_1!\ell_1(5).\mathsf{p}_2!\ell_2(5)$. The characteristic context for $\mathsf{p} \triangleleft \mathscr{P}(\mathsf{T})$ is $[\,] \mid \mathsf{p}_1 \triangleleft \mathsf{p}_2?\ell_2(x)... \mid \mathsf{p}_2 \triangleleft \mathsf{p}?\ell_2(x)...$ and the process

$$\mathsf{p} \triangleleft \mathsf{p}_1!\ell_1(5).\mathsf{p}_2!\ell_2(5) \mid \mathsf{p}_1 \triangleleft \mathsf{p}_2?\ell_2(x)... \mid \mathsf{p}_2 \triangleleft \mathsf{p}?\ell_2(x)...$$

is stuck, since participant p wants to send a message to participant p_1, who instead is ready to receive a message from participant p_2, who in turn expects a message from participant p.

The main result of [16] is:

Theorem 5. *The synchronous multiparty session subtyping is operationally precise.*

6 Characteristic Terms for Denotational Preciseness

It is standard [11,15,16,21] to interpret a type σ as the set of closed terms typed by σ, i.e.

$$[\![\sigma]\!] = \{M \mid\ \vdash M : \sigma\}$$

In this case denotational soundness immediately follows from the subsumption rule. Moreover, the existence of characteristic terms as defined in [**Step 3**] at page 3 implies denotational completeness. By definition characteristic terms enjoy the following key property:

$$\vdash M_\sigma : \tau \text{ implies } \sigma \leqslant \tau.$$

We get denotational completeness, since if $\sigma \not\leqslant \tau$, then $M_\sigma \in [\![\sigma]\!]$, but $M_\sigma \notin [\![\tau]\!]$.

Theorem 6 (Denotational Preciseness). *The existence of characteristic terms for a subtyping relation implies its denotational preciseness.*

This theorem implies the denotational preciseness of the subtypings which are shown to be operationally precise in previous sections. In particular the denotational preciseness of $L_{+\times}^{\to\mu}$ is new, since Ligatti et al. [27] only consider operational preciseness.

7   Conclusion

The present paper discusses some recent results of preciseness for subtyping of typed functional and concurrent calculi.

Operational completeness requires that all empty (i.e. not inhabited) types are less than all inhabited types. This makes unfeasible an operationally complete subtyping for the pure λ-calculus, both in the case of polymorphic types [28] and of intersection and union types. In fact inhabitation is undecidable for polymorphic types being equivalent to derivability in second order logic, while [37] shows undecidability of inhabitation for intersection types, which implies undecidability of inhabitation for intersection and union types.

An interesting open problem we plan to study is an extension of λ-calculus enjoying operational preciseness for the decidable subtypings between polymorphic types discussed in [28,36].

The formulation of preciseness along with the proof methods and techniques described in this paper could be useful to examine other subtypings and calculi. Our future work includes the applications to higher-order processes [29–31], polymorphic types [7,18,19], fair subtypings [33,34] and contract subtyping [3]. We plan to use the characteristic processes in typecheckers for session types. More precisely, the error messages can show processes of given types when type checking fails. One interesting problem is to find the necessary and sufficient conditions to obtain completeness of the generic subtyping [24]. Such a characterisation would give preciseness for the many type systems which are instances of [24]. The notion of subtyping for session types is clearly connected with that of type duality. Various definitions of dualities are compared in [5], and we plan to investigate if completeness of subtyping can be used in finding the largest safe duality.

A last question we plan to investigate is whether preciseness of subtyping is meaningful for object-oriented calculi [1].

References

1. Abadi, M., Cardelli, L.: A Theory of Objects. Monographs in Computer Science. Springer, New York (1996)
2. van Bakel, S., Dezani-Ciancaglini, M., de' Liguoro, U., Motohama, Y.: The minimal relevant logic and the call-by-value lambda calculus. Technical Report TR-ARP-05-2000, The Australian National University (2000)
3. Barbanera, F., de Liguoro, U.: Two notions of sub-behaviour for session-based client/server systems. In: Kutsia, T., Schreiner, W., Fernández, M. (eds.) PPDP, pp. 155–164. ACM (2010)
4. Barendregt, H., Coppo, M., Dezani-Ciancaglini, M.: A filter lambda model and the completeness of type assignment. J. Symbolic Logic 48(4), 931–940 (1983)
5. Bernardi, G., Dardha, O., Gay, S.J., Kouzapas, D.: On duality relations for session types. In: Maffei, M., Tuosto, E. (eds.) TGC 2014. LNCS, vol. 8902, pp. 51–66. Springer, Heidelberg (2014)
6. Bonsangue, M.M., Rot, J., Ancona, D., de Boer, F.S., Rutten, J.J.M.M.: A coalgebraic foundation for coinductive union types. In: Esparza, J., Fraigniaud, P., Husfeldt, T., Koutsoupias, E. (eds.) ICALP 2014, Part II. LNCS, vol. 8573, pp. 62–73. Springer, Heidelberg (2014)
7. Caires, L., Pérez, J.A., Pfenning, F., Toninho, B.: Behavioral polymorphism and parametricity in session-based communication. In: Felleisen, M., Gardner, P. (eds.) ESOP 2013. LNCS, vol. 7792, pp. 330–349. Springer, Heidelberg (2013)
8. Castagna, G., De Nicola, R., Varacca, D.: Semantic subtyping for the pi-calculus. Theoret. Comput. Sci. 398(1–3), 217–242 (2008)
9. Castagna, G., Dezani-Ciancaglini, M., Giachino, E., Padovani, L.: Foundations of session types. In: PPDP, pp. 219–230. ACM (2009)
10. Castagna, G., Frisch, A.: A gentle introduction to semantic subtyping. In: Caires, L., Italiano, G.F., Monteiro, L., Palamidessi, C., Yung, M. (eds.) ICALP 2005. LNCS, vol. 3580, pp. 30–34. Springer, Heidelberg (2005)
11. Chen, T.-C., Dezani-Ciancaglini, M., Yoshida, N.: On the preciseness of subtyping in session types. In: Chitil, O., King, A., Danvy, O. (eds.) PPDP, pp. 135–146. ACM Press (2014)
12. Coppo, M., Dezani-Ciancaglini, M., Padovani, L., Yoshida, N.: A gentle introduction to multiparty asynchronous session types. In: Bernardo, M., Johnsen, E.B. (eds.) SFM 2015. LNCS, vol. 9104, pp. 146–178. Springer, Switzerland (2015)
13. Demangeon, R., Honda, K.: Full abstraction in a subtyped pi-calculus with linear types. In: Katoen, J.-P., König, B. (eds.) CONCUR 2011. LNCS, vol. 6901, pp. 280–296. Springer, Heidelberg (2011)
14. Dezani-Ciancaglini, M., de 'Liguoro, U., Piperno, A.: A filter model for concurrent lambda-calculus. SIAM J. Comput. 27(5), 1376–1419 (1998)
15. Dezani-Ciancaglini, M., Ghilezan, S.: Preciseness of subtyping on intersection and union types. In: Dowek, G. (ed.) RTA-TLCA 2014. LNCS, vol. 8560, pp. 194–207. Springer, Heidelberg (2014)
16. Dezani-Ciancaglini, M., Ghilezan, S., Jaksic, S., Pantovic, J., Yoshida, N.: Precise subtyping for synchronous multiparty sessions. In: PLACES, EPTCS 203, pp. 29–44 (2016)
17. Frisch, A., Castagna, G., Benzaken, V.: Semantic subtyping: dealing set-theoretically with function, union, intersection, and negation types. J. ACM 55(4), 1–64 (2008)

18. Gay, S.J.: Bounded polymorphism in session types. Math. Struct. Comput. Sci. **18**(5), 895–930 (2008)

19. Goto, M., Jagadeesan, R., Jeffrey, A., Pitcher, C., Riely, J.: An extensible approach to session polymorphism. Math. Struct. Comput. Sci. **26**(3), 465–509 (2016)

20. Harper, R.: Practical Foundations for Programming Languages. Cambridge University Press, Cambridge (2013)

21. Hindley, J.R.: The completeness theorem for typing lambda-terms. Theoret. Comput. Sci. **22**, 1–17 (1983)

22. Honda, K., Vasconcelos, V.T., Kubo, M.: Language primitives and type discipline for structured communication-based programming. In: Hankin, C. (ed.) ESOP 1998. LNCS, vol. 1381, pp. 122–138. Springer, Heidelberg (1998)

23. Honda, K., Yoshida, N., Carbone, M.: Multiparty asynchronous session types. In POPL, pp. 273–284. ACM (2008). A full version will appear in Journal of the Association for Computing Machinery

24. Igarashi, A., Kobayashi, N.: A generic type system for the pi-calculus. Theoret. Comput. Sci. **311**(1–3), 121–163 (2004)

25. Ishihara, H., Kurata, T.: Completeness of intersection and union type assignment systems for call-by-value lambda-models. Theoret. Comput. Sci. **272**(1–2), 197–221 (2002)

26. Kouzapas, D., Yoshida, N.: Globally governed session semantics. In: D'Argenio, P.R., Melgratti, H. (eds.) CONCUR 2013. LNCS, vol. 8052, pp. 395–409. Springer, Heidelberg (2013)

27. Ligatti, J., Blackburn, J., Nachtigal, M.: On subtyping-relation completeness, with an application to iso-recursive types. Technical report, University of South Florida (2014)

28. Mitchell, J.C.: Polymorphic type inference and containment. Inf. Comput. **76**(2/3), 211–249 (1988)

29. Mostrous, D.: Session Types in Concurrent Calculi: Higher-Order Processes and Objects. PhD thesis, Imperial College London (2009)

30. Mostrous, D., Yoshida, N.: Session-based communication optimisation for higher-order mobile processes. In: Curien, P.-L. (ed.) TLCA 2009. LNCS, vol. 5608, pp. 203–218. Springer, Heidelberg (2009)

31. Mostrous, D., Yoshida, N.: Session typing and asynchronous subtyping for the higher-order π-calculus. Inf. Comput. **241**, 227–263 (2015)

32. Mostrous, D., Yoshida, N., Honda, K.: Global principal typing in partially commutative asynchronous sessions. In: Castagna, G. (ed.) ESOP 2009. LNCS, vol. 5502, pp. 316–332. Springer, Heidelberg (2009)

33. Padovani, L.: Fair subtyping for multi-party session types. In: De Meuter, W., Roman, G.-C. (eds.) COORDINATION 2011. LNCS, vol. 6721, pp. 127–141. Springer, Heidelberg (2011)

34. Padovani, L.: Fair subtyping for open session types. In: Fomin, F.V., Freivalds, R., Kwiatkowska, M., Peleg, D. (eds.) ICALP 2013, Part II. LNCS, vol. 7966, pp. 373–384. Springer, Heidelberg (2013)

35. Pierce, B.C.: Types and Programming Languages. MIT Press, Cambridge (2002)

36. Tiuryn, J., Urzyczyn, P.: The subtyping problem for second-order types is undecidable. Inf. Comput. **179**(1), 1–18 (2002)

37. Urzyczyn, P.: The emptiness problem for intersection types. J. Symbolic Logic **64**(3), 1195–1215 (1999)

38. Vouillon, J.: Subtyping union types. In: Marcinkowski, J., Tarlecki, A. (eds.) CSL 2004. LNCS, vol. 3210, pp. 415–429. Springer, Heidelberg (2004)

A Sound and Complete Hoare Logic for Dynamically-Typed, Object-Oriented Programs

Björn Engelmann[✉] and Ernst-Rüdiger Olderog

Department of Computing Science, University of Oldenburg, Oldenburg, Germany
{bjoern.engelmann,ernst.ruediger.olderog}@informatik.uni-oldenburg.de

Abstract. A simple dynamically-typed, (purely) object-oriented language is defined. A structural operational semantics as well as a Hoare-style program logic for reasoning about programs in the language in multiple notions of correctness are given. The Hoare logic is proved to be both sound and (relative) complete and is – to the best of our knowledge – the first such logic presented for a dynamically-typed language.

Keywords: Tagged Hoare Logic · Dynamic typing · Pure object-orientation · Program verification · Axiomatic semantics · Soundness · Relative completeness · Multiple notions of correctness · Completeness for total correctness

1 Introduction and Related Work

While dynamic typing itself was introduced with the advent of LISP decades ago and more and more dynamically-typed programs are written as languages like JavaScript, Ruby and Python are gaining popularity, to the current day, no sound and complete program logic has been published for any such language.

In an attempt to bridge this Gap between static- and dynamically-typed languages, we focus our inquiry on completeness (for closed programs) and on studying the proof-theoretic implications of dynamic typing. This differentiates our work from other axiomatic semantics published mainly for JavaScript [9,15] as their focus lies more on soundness and direct applicability to real-world programming languages.

Hence, to avoid getting tangled in the details of any real-world programming language, we introduce a small dynamically-typed object-oriented (OO) language called **dyn**[1].

This work is supported by the German Research Foundation through the Research Training Group (DFG GRK 1765) SCARE (www.scare.uni-oldenburg.de).

[1] One may ask whether it is at all possible to obtain a sound and relatively complete Hoare logic for **dyn** in light of Clarke's incompleteness result [5]. However, Clarke's argument is not applicable to **dyn** for various reasons elaborated in [7, Appendix C].

E. Ábrahám et al. (Eds.): de Boer Festschrift, LNCS 9660, pp. 173–193, 2016.
DOI: 10.1007/978-3-319-30734-3_13

Additionally, in previous work [8] the authors developed a technique for reducing the effort of verifying a dynamically-typed program to the level of verifying an equivalent statically-typed one. This technique, however, assumed the existence of a sound and complete program logic for the dynamically-typed language. The current work hence substantiates this assumption.

Besides presenting the Hoare logic, there are further technical contributions:

(1) Tagged Hoare Logic, a novel notation for Hoare triples making the notion of correctness explicit and thereby allowing the (previously separated) Hoare logics for partial correctness, strong (= failsafe) partial correctness, typesafe partial correctness and total correctness to be merged into a single proof system and to concisely express the rules of this system.

(2) A novel technique to specify loop variants circumventing a common incompleteness issue in Hoare logics for total correctness (see proof of Theorem 5).

As detailed in [7, Sect. 7], we consider our results as a stepping stone towards similar proof systems for real-world languages.

Our paper is organized as follows. In Sect. 2, we introduce the language **dyn**. In Sect. 3, its operational semantics is defined. In Sect. 4, its axiomatic semantics (Hoare logic) is introduced. In Sect. 5, we briefly touch upon soundness of this Hoare logic, and in Sect. 6, we prove its (relative) completeness for closed programs.

Notation: $\mathbb{N}_m^n \equiv \{n, ..., m\}$, $\mathbb{N}_m \equiv \mathbb{N}_m^0$, $S_1 S_2$ denotes concatenation of the sequences S_1 and S_2, $\{S\}$ is the set of all elements of the sequence S.

2   Dynamically-Typed Programs

We will study a language called **dyn**, whose syntax is depicted in Fig. 1. Like its popular real-world siblings JavaScript, Ruby and Python, **dyn** is a dynamically-typed purely OO-programming language. However, to focus our inquiry on dynamic typing, we chose not to model other features commonly found in these languages like method update, closures or eval().

As customary in such languages, **dyn** desugars operations to method calls. Consequently, the only built-in operation in **dyn** is object equality. Everything else is defined in **dyn** itself. However, a syntactic distinction between built-in operations and method calls is necessary for the convenient distinction between (side-effect-free) expressions and (side-effecting) statements. In order to make **dyn** programs resemble their real-world counterparts, we had to allow method calls as well as assignments in expressions. For example, a := b := 5 is a valid **dyn** expression with the side-effect of assigning 5 to both a and b.

Since types in **dyn** are a property of values rather than variables, there is no need to declare the latter. Following its real-world counterparts, both local- and instance variables in **dyn** are created upon their first assignment. Accessing a variable that has not been assigned before results in a (runtime) type error.

Other reasons for type errors are non-boolean conditions in conditionals or while-loops and method call receivers whose class does not support a method matching name and arity of the call (MethodNotFound).

3   Operational Semantics

In Fig. 2, we define an operational semantics of **dyn** in the style of Hennessy and Plotkin [11,14]. It is based on a set *Conf* of *configurations*, which are pairs $C = \langle s, \sigma \rangle$ consisting of a statement s of **dyn** and a state σ, assigning values to variables. By syntax-directed rules, the operational semantics defines which *transitions* $\langle s, \sigma \rangle \rightarrow \langle s', \sigma' \rangle$ are possible between configurations.

As **dyn** is a purely OO-language, the value domain is the set $\mathbb{O}$ of *objects*, including the special objects *null* (the usual OO-null value) and $\boxtimes$ (marking non-existing variables). The definition of states and state updates is standard and therefor omitted (see e.g. [2]).

For a given program, we denote the set of all variables as $\mathfrak{V} = \mathfrak{V}_L \uplus \mathfrak{V}_I \uplus \mathfrak{V}_S$ where $\mathfrak{V}_L$ is the set of local variables, $\mathfrak{V}_I$ the set of instance variables and $\mathfrak{V}_S = \{\text{self}, \mathbf{r}\}$ the set of special variables. self is special because it cannot be assigned to in programs and $\mathbf{r}$ will be explained below. We also use the set of all classes $\mathfrak{C}$ with each class $C \in \mathfrak{C}$ having a set of methods $\mathfrak{M}_C$ and $\mathfrak{M} = \bigcup_{C \in \mathfrak{C}} \mathfrak{M}_C$.

Usually, in a structural operational semantics, expressions are assumed to be side-effect-free and the effect of assignments can hence be expressed as an axiom $\langle v := e, \sigma \rangle \rightarrow \langle \emptyset, \sigma[v := \sigma(e)] \rangle$. In **dyn**, however, expressions are side-effecting. We hence need to evaluate the assignment $v := e$ in two steps: first evaluating the expression e and then assigning its resulting value to the variable v. Furthermore, we need an interface between these two steps: A way by which the assignment can determine the result of the previously evaluated expression e. For this purpose, we introduce a special variable $\mathbf{r}$ of type $\mathbb{O}$ as well as the convention that every expression or statement will store its result in $\mathbf{r}$. Note that this construction works only due to dynamic typing: In a statically-typed programming language, expressions would evaluate to values of different types which could not well be assigned to a single variable. The choice of object as the unifying supertype of all values is common in pure OO-languages: When everything is an object, clearly every expression will evaluate to one. Furthermore, as $\mathbf{r}$ is the only statement that does not change anything (not even $\mathbf{r}$), we define the empty program as $\mathbf{r}$, stipulate $(\mathbf{r}; s) \equiv (s; \mathbf{r}) \equiv s$ for all statements s and call the configurations $\langle \mathbf{r}, \sigma \rangle$ for some state σ final.

For **dyn**, we use class-based OO and model object creation as activation[2]. We introduce a "representative" object θ_C for each class C as well as a special instance variable @c not allowed to occur in programs for maintaining both the instance-class relation and the activation state of each object.

We call an object o with $o.@\mathbf{c} = null$ *inactive*, meaning it is "not yet created". Initially, all objects (except *null* and the representatives θ_C for each class C) are inactive. We suppose an infinite enumeration of objects $o_1, o_2, \ldots$ containing every object (both active and inactive) exactly once and introduce a function $\gamma : \Sigma \mapsto \mathbb{O}$ mapping every state $\sigma \in \Sigma$ to the object o_k with the least index k that is inactive in σ.

---

[2] Assuming an infinite sequence of already existing, but deactivated objects, object creation boils down to picking the next one and marking it as "activated".

Upon its creation, an object o is assigned a class C and is henceforth regarded an instance of C. Technically, this is achieved by resetting the value of $o.@\mathbf{c}$ to θ_C (see the rule for object creation). We use $init_C$ to denote the initial (internal) state of an object of class C: $init_C.@\mathbf{c} = \theta_C$ and $init_C.@v = \boxtimes$ for all $@v \in \mathfrak{V}_I \setminus \{@\mathbf{c}\}$.

We can then formally define the predicates $bool(o)$ and $bool(o, b)$ used in Fig. 2 to check for boolean values as

$bool(o) \equiv o.@\mathbf{c} = \theta_{bool}$ for all $o \in \mathbb{O}$ and

$bool(o, b) \equiv bool(o) \wedge b \leftrightarrow o.@to\_ref \neq null^3$ for all $o \in \mathbb{O}, b \in \mathbb{B}$.

Note how the rule for assignment uses the two-step idea to handle side-effecting expressions. The rules for conditionals and while loops also use it to evaluate the condition first and then branch on its result. Since no type system guarantees this result to be boolean, further distinguished behaviors for failures and type errors are necessary. The same holds for receivers of method calls.

Additionally, the rules for method call (or better: **begin local**-blocks) and object creation instantiate all local- and instance variables to $\boxtimes$, which marks them as "not yet created" and causes **typeerror** in the rule of variable access.

Note also the handling of special variables in method calls: on entry, self is set to the receiver of the method call while on exit **r** intentionally remains unmodified to pass the return value back to the caller.

4   Axiomatic Semantics

4.1   Tagged Hoare Logic

The original paper of Hoare [12] considers partial correctness. Other "notions of correctness" like strong partial correctness and total correctness were added later as separate proof systems. While termination as a liveness property might justify this special handling, there seem to be little reason to grant this special place also to properties like failsafety and typesafety. They do, however, affect the proof rules (mostly by adding additional preconditions) and hence triggered the creation of new proof systems for new "notions of correctness". Additionally, the term "total correctness" was interpreted as "the absence of any kind of fault" and hence strongly depends on what other faults the authors are considering. Furthermore, in this abundance of available proof systems, tool designers are forced to choose which one to implement, depriving their users of the choice which properties they actually want to verify. From a tool-design perspective, it would be much better to make all properties part of the specification, have a single proof system dealing with them and allowing the users to choose which guarantees to derive for which part of the program. We hence propose the formalism of *tagged Hoare logic*, a uniform framework for all these properties featuring a single proof system to treat them.

A (big step) program semantics maps programs and initial states to sets of final states. Traditionally, each notion of correctness needs its own program semantics

---

^{3} Other methods to distinguish the values true and false are conceivable.

Syntax of **dyn**:

$Prog \ni \pi ::= \overrightarrow{class} \; s$

$Class \ni class ::= \textbf{class } C < C \; \{\overrightarrow{meth}\}$

$Meth \ni meth ::= \textbf{method } m(\overrightarrow{u})\{s\}$

$\quad | \; \textbf{rename } m \; m$

$Stmt \ni s ::= s; s \; | \; e$

$Expr \ni e ::= null \; | \; u \; | \; @v \; | \; self \; | \; e == e$

$\quad | \; e \; is\_a? \; C \; | \; e.m(\overrightarrow{e}) \; | \; \textbf{new } C(\overrightarrow{e})$

$\quad | \; u := e \; | \; \textbf{if } e \textbf{ then } s \textbf{ else } s \textbf{ end}$

$\quad | \; @v := e \; | \; \textbf{while } e \textbf{ do } s \textbf{ done}$

$(u \in \mathfrak{V}_L, @v \in \mathfrak{V}_I, C \in \mathfrak{C}, m \in \mathfrak{M})$

Syntactic sugar:

$e_1 \oplus e_2 \equiv e_1.m_\oplus(e_2)$

if e **then** s **end** $\equiv$

if e **then** s **else** null **end**

$false \equiv \textbf{new } bool(null) \qquad [] \equiv \textbf{new } list()$

$true \equiv false.not() \qquad [..., o] \equiv [...].add(o)$

$0 \equiv \textbf{new } num(null)$

$n \equiv (n-1).succ()$ for $n \in \mathbb{N}$

$"" \equiv \textbf{new } string(null, null),$

$"...a" \equiv "...".addchar(n_a)$ where $n_a \in \mathbb{N}$ is the ASCII-code of character a.

Fig. 1. Syntax of **dyn**

1. $\langle null, \sigma \rangle \; \rightarrow \; \langle \mathbf{r}, \sigma[\mathbf{r} := null] \rangle$

2. $\langle v, \sigma \rangle \; \rightarrow \; \langle \mathbf{r}, \sigma[\mathbf{r} := \sigma(v)] \rangle$ where $v \in \mathfrak{V}$ and $\sigma(v) \neq \boxtimes$

3. $\langle v, \sigma \rangle \; \rightarrow \; \langle \mathbf{r}, \textbf{typeerror} \rangle$ where $v \in \mathfrak{V}$ and $\sigma(v) = \boxtimes$

4. $\dfrac{\langle e, \sigma \rangle \; \overset{*}{\rightarrow} \; \langle \mathbf{r}, \tau \rangle}{\langle v := e, \sigma \rangle \; \rightarrow \; \langle \mathbf{r}, \tau[v := \tau(\mathbf{r})] \rangle}$ where $v \in \mathfrak{V}$

5. $\dfrac{\langle s_1, \sigma \rangle \; \rightarrow \; \langle s_2, \tau \rangle}{\langle s_1; s, \sigma \rangle \; \rightarrow \; \langle s_2; s, \tau \rangle}$

6. $\dfrac{\langle e, \sigma \rangle \; \overset{*}{\rightarrow} \; \langle \mathbf{r}, \tau \rangle \qquad bool(\tau(\mathbf{r}), true)}{\langle \textbf{if } e \textbf{ then } s_1 \textbf{ else } s_2 \textbf{ end}, \sigma \rangle \; \rightarrow \; \langle s_1, \tau \rangle} \qquad \dfrac{\langle e, \sigma \rangle \; \overset{*}{\rightarrow} \; \langle \mathbf{r}, \tau \rangle \qquad bool(\tau(\mathbf{r}), false)}{\langle \textbf{if } e \textbf{ then } s_1 \textbf{ else } s_2 \textbf{ end}, \sigma \rangle \; \rightarrow \; \langle s_2, \tau \rangle}$

7. $\dfrac{\langle e, \sigma \rangle \; \overset{*}{\rightarrow} \; \langle \mathbf{r}, \tau \rangle \qquad \tau(\mathbf{r}) = null}{\langle \textbf{if } e \textbf{ then } s_1 \textbf{ else } s_2 \textbf{ end}, \sigma \rangle \; \rightarrow \; \langle \mathbf{r}, \textbf{fail} \rangle}$

8. $\dfrac{\langle e, \sigma \rangle \; \overset{*}{\rightarrow} \; \langle \mathbf{r}, \tau \rangle \qquad \neg bool(\tau(\mathbf{r}))}{\langle \textbf{if } e \textbf{ then } s_1 \textbf{ else } s_2 \textbf{ end}, \sigma \rangle \; \rightarrow \; \langle \mathbf{r}, \textbf{typeerror} \rangle}$

9. $\langle \textbf{while } e \textbf{ do } s \textbf{ done}, \sigma \rangle \; \rightarrow \; \langle \textbf{if } e \textbf{ then } s; \textbf{while } e \textbf{ do } s \textbf{ done else } null \textbf{ end}, \sigma \rangle$

10. $\langle \overrightarrow{u} := \overrightarrow{v}, \sigma \rangle \; \rightarrow \; \langle \mathbf{r}, \sigma[\overrightarrow{u} := \sigma(\overrightarrow{v})] \rangle$ where $\overrightarrow{u}, \overrightarrow{v} \in \mathfrak{V}_L^+$

11. $\langle \textbf{begin local } \overrightarrow{u} := \overrightarrow{v}; s \textbf{ end}, \sigma \rangle \; \rightarrow \; \langle \overrightarrow{u'u} := \overrightarrow{v}\overrightarrow{\boxtimes}; s; \overrightarrow{u'u} := \sigma(\overrightarrow{u'u}), \sigma \rangle$

    where $\{\overrightarrow{u'u}\} = \mathfrak{V}_L \setminus (\{\overrightarrow{u}\} \cup \mathfrak{V}_S)$ and $\overrightarrow{\boxtimes}$ is a fitting sequence of $\boxtimes$ values.

12. $\dfrac{\langle e_i, \sigma_i \rangle \; \overset{*}{\rightarrow} \; \langle \mathbf{r}, \sigma_{i+1} \rangle \text{ for all } i \in \mathbb{N}_n}{\langle e_0.m(e_1, ..., e_n), \sigma_0 \rangle \; \rightarrow \; \langle \textbf{begin local } self, \overrightarrow{u} := \sigma_1(\mathbf{r}), ..., \sigma_{n+1}(\mathbf{r}); s \textbf{ end}, \sigma_{n+1} \rangle}$

    where $\sigma_1(\mathbf{r}) \neq null$, $\textbf{method } m(u_1, ..., u_n)\{s\} \in \mathfrak{M}_C$ and $\sigma_1(\mathbf{r}.@c) = \theta_C$.

13. $\dfrac{\langle e_0, \sigma_0 \rangle \; \overset{*}{\rightarrow} \; \langle \mathbf{r}, \sigma_1 \rangle \qquad \sigma_1(\mathbf{r}) = null}{\langle e_0.m(e_1, ..., e_n), \sigma_0 \rangle \; \rightarrow \; \langle \mathbf{r}, \textbf{fail} \rangle} \qquad \dfrac{\langle e_0, \sigma_0 \rangle \; \overset{*}{\rightarrow} \; \langle \mathbf{r}, \sigma_1 \rangle \qquad \sigma_1(\mathbf{r}) \neq null}{\langle e_0.m(e_1, ..., e_n), \sigma_0 \rangle \; \rightarrow \; \langle \mathbf{r}, \textbf{typeerror} \rangle}$

    where $\sigma_1(\mathbf{r}.@c) = \theta_C$ and $\not\exists \textbf{method } m(u_1, ..., u_n)\{s\} \in \mathfrak{M}_C$

14. $\langle \textbf{new } C(e_1, ..., e_n), \sigma \rangle \; \rightarrow \; \langle \textbf{new}_C.init(e_1, ..., e_n), \sigma \rangle$

15. $\langle \textbf{new}_C, \sigma \rangle \; \rightarrow \; \langle \mathbf{r}, \sigma[o := init_C][\mathbf{r} := o] \rangle$ where $o = \gamma(\sigma)$

16. $\dfrac{\langle e_i, \sigma_i \rangle \; \overset{*}{\rightarrow} \; \langle \mathbf{r}, \sigma_{i+1} \rangle \text{ for all } i \in \{0, 1\}}{\exists b : \mathbb{B} \bullet b \leftrightarrow \sigma_1(\mathbf{r}) = \sigma_2(\mathbf{r}) \wedge (s_r \equiv true \wedge b \vee s_r \equiv false \wedge \neg b)} \\ \dfrac{}{\langle e_0 == e_1, \sigma_0 \rangle \; \rightarrow \; \langle s_r, \sigma_2 \rangle}$

17. $\dfrac{\langle e, \sigma \rangle \; \overset{*}{\rightarrow} \; \langle \mathbf{r}, \sigma_1 \rangle, \exists b : \mathbb{B} \bullet b \leftrightarrow \sigma_1(\mathbf{r}.@c) = \theta_C \wedge (s_r \equiv true \wedge b \vee s_r \equiv false \wedge \neg b)}{\langle e \; is\_a? \; C, \sigma \rangle \; \rightarrow \; \langle s_r, \sigma_1 \rangle}$

Fig. 2. dyn's structural operational semantics.

as they differ in what characteristics of a computation they guarantee. We define the (infinite) set of (finite or infinite) computations as $Comp = Conf^* \cup Conf^\omega$ and those of a program s starting in an initial state σ as

$$Comp(s, \sigma) = \{C_0, C_1, ... \mid C_0 = \langle s, \sigma \rangle \wedge \forall i \bullet C_i \to C_{i+1}\} \subset Comp .$$

Let the symbol ρ denote a typical element of $Comp$. We now introduce the following tags along with their respective error states:

$$Tags = \{\text{terminates}, \text{typesafe}, \text{failsafe}\}.$$

Each tag stands for a notion of correctness that in addition to partial correctness avoids one type of error: **terminates** avoids divergence (infinite computations), **typesafe** avoids type errors (e.g., non-boolean expressions as loop conditions), and **failsafe** avoids runtime failures (e.g.; method not found). The tagged program semantics $\mathcal{M}_{\text{tags}}$ defined below will record any occurring error by a special error state of the set $\Sigma_\perp = \{\perp, \text{typeerror}, \text{fail}\}$. The mapping from tags to error states is $\hbar: Tags \mapsto \Sigma_\perp$ with $\hbar\,(\text{terminates}) = \perp$, $\hbar\,(\text{typesafe}) = \text{typeerror}$, and $\hbar\,(\text{failsafe}) = \text{fail}$.

Let $\Sigma_+ = \Sigma \uplus \Sigma_\perp$, where Σ is the set of proper states. To define the tagged program semantics $\mathcal{M}_{\text{tags}}$, we need appropriate selectors:

$$\mathcal{S} : Tags \cup \{\emptyset\} \mapsto Comp \mapsto \mathcal{P}(\Sigma_+)$$

with

$$\mathcal{S}_\emptyset(\rho) = \begin{cases} \{\tau\} & \text{if } \rho = C_0, ..., C_n \wedge C_n = \langle \mathbf{r}, \tau \rangle \wedge \tau \in \Sigma \\ \{\} & \text{otherwise} \end{cases}$$

$$\mathcal{S}_{\text{terminates}}(\rho) = \begin{cases} \{\perp\} & \text{if } \rho \text{ is infinite} \\ \{\} & \text{otherwise} \end{cases}$$

$$\mathcal{S}_{\text{tag}}(\rho) = \begin{cases} \{\hbar\,(\text{tag})\} & \text{if } \rho = C_0, ..., C_n \wedge C_n = \langle \mathbf{r}, \hbar\,(\text{tag}) \rangle \\ \{\} & \text{otherwise} \end{cases}$$

for all other tags. Finally, we are able to define tagged program semantics

$$\mathcal{M} : \mathcal{P}(Tags) \mapsto Prog \mapsto \Sigma \mapsto \mathcal{P}(\Sigma_+)$$

allowing arbitrary combinations of correctness notions. Let $\textbf{tags} \subseteq Tags$, then

$$\mathcal{M}_{\textbf{tags}}[\![s]\!](\sigma) = \bigcup\{\mathcal{S}_{\textbf{tag}}(\rho) \mid \rho \in Comp(s, \sigma), \textbf{tag} \in \textbf{tags} \cup \{\emptyset\}\}$$

which is certainly the most central ingredient of a Tagged Hoare Logic. However, we first need to extend the semantics of our assertions (see Fig. 3) to also include tags

$$[\![p]\!]_{\textbf{tags}} = \{\sigma \mid \sigma \in \Sigma \wedge \sigma, \textbf{tags} \models p\}$$

before we can properly define the meaning of our Tagged Triples:

Definition 1 (Tagged Hoare Triples). $\models \{p\}s\{\textbf{tags} \wedge q\}$ iff $\mathcal{M}_{\textbf{tags}}[\![s]\!]([\![p]\!]_{\textbf{tags}}) \subseteq [\![q]\!]_{\textbf{tags}}$ where $\models$ denotes semantic truth of *Tagged Hoare Triples*.

Note that the semantics $\mathcal{M}_{\mathbf{tags}}[\![s]\!]$ of a program s can produce error states, but the semantics $[\![p]\!]_{\mathbf{tags}}$ and $[\![q]\!]_{\mathbf{tags}}$ of the assertions p and q do not tolerate any error states. Thus $\models \{p\}s\{\mathbf{tags} \wedge q\}$ formalizes program correctness in the sense of the tags $\mathbf{tags}$ as desired.

4.2   Assertion Language

Before going into details of the program logic, we introduce the assertion language **AL**. Its syntax is depicted in Fig. 3. Essentially, it is predicate logic with quantification over finite sequences of typed elements – weak second order logic. We extend the logic with constants c_ε and operations $op(\overrightarrow{l})$ corresponding to **dyn**'s syntactic sugar for boolean values, natural numbers, strings and lists (which includes the usual arithmetic operations on both booleans and natural numbers). Also, c_ε contains constants θ_C denoting the representative objects of all classes $C \in \mathfrak{C}$. Note that our assertion language is statically typed, as usual. Its type system however is simplistic: basic types $\mathbb{T} = \{\mathbb{N}, \mathbb{O}, \mathbb{B}, \mathbb{S}\}$ form a flat lattice with $\top$ and $\bot$ and a type constructor τ^* for finite sequences of elements of type τ.

Assertions contain typed logical expressions (l). Such expressions consist of accesses to logical variables (of some type $t \in \mathbb{T}$), local program variables (of type $\mathbb{O}$) including the self-reference self, instance variables ($l.@x$ where both l and the result are of type $\mathbb{O}$), typed constants and typed operations. Note that contrary to programming expressions, logical expressions are able to access instance variables of objects other than self.

Assertions are then constructed from equations between logical expressions of identical type, boolean connectives and quantification over finite sequences.

Following [4], undefined operations like dereferencing a *null* value or accessing a sequence with an index that is out of bounds ($l[n]$ with $n \geq |l|$) yield a *null* value and equality is non-strict with respect to such values (*null* = *null* is *true*) in order to keep assertions two-valued. Also, for logical expressions $l \in LExp$, we extend the state-access to $\sigma(l)$ in the canonical way.

To link programming language-objects with assertion-values, we define

Definition 2 (Mapping Predicates).[4,5] ($\forall o : \mathbb{O},\, n : \mathbb{N},\, b : \mathbb{B}$)

$\mathbb{N}(o) \equiv o \neq null \wedge o.@\mathbf{c} = \theta_{num}$

$\mathbb{N}(o, n) \equiv \mathbb{N}(o) \wedge n = 0 \rightarrow o.@\mathrm{pred} = null \wedge n > 0 \rightarrow \mathbb{N}(o.@\mathrm{pred}, n - 1)$

$\mathbb{B}(o) \equiv o \neq null \wedge o.@\mathbf{c} = \theta_{bool}$ $\mathbb{B}(o, b) \equiv \mathbb{B}(o) \wedge b \leftrightarrow o.@\mathrm{to\_ref} \neq null$

To see that mapping predicates are necessary for completeness, consider the intermediate assertion p in the following program

$P \equiv \mathbf{if}\, b\, \mathbf{then}\, x := 5\, \mathbf{else}\, x := true\, \mathbf{end}\{p\};$

$\qquad \mathbf{if}\, x\, \text{is\_a?}\, bool\, \mathbf{then}\, \mathbf{if}\, x\, \mathbf{then}\, x := 10\, \mathbf{end}\, \mathbf{else}\, x := x * 2\ \ \mathbf{end}$

---

[4] The predicate $\mathbb{N}(o, n)$ is recursive. However, the technique used for proving the case for primitive recursion in [7, Lemma 5], allows expressing it in **AL**.

[5] @pred and @to_ref are instance variables of the classes num and bool, respectively.

$Asrt \ni a ::= l = l \mid [\![l]\!] \in \{Cl\} \mid \neg a \mid a \wedge a \mid \exists v : t^* \bullet a \mid \textbf{tag}$ $t \in \mathbb{T}, \textbf{tag} \in \mathcal{T}ags$

$LExp \ni l ::= v \mid \mathfrak{u} \mid l.@\mathfrak{x} \mid null \mid \boxtimes \mid \textbf{self} \mid \textbf{if } l \textbf{ then } l \textbf{ else } l \textbf{ end} \mid c_\varepsilon \mid op(\overrightarrow{l})$

$\{+, -, *, div, mod, <, =, \wedge, \neg, |\cdot|, \cdot[n]\} \subseteq op$ (brackets are used for disambiguation)

$Cl ::= \epsilon \mid CL$ $CL ::= C \mid C, CL$ $C \in \mathfrak{C}$

with the usual abbreviations: $a_1 \vee a_2 \equiv \neg(\neg a_1 \wedge \neg a_2)$, $a_1 \rightarrow a_2 \equiv \neg a_1 \vee a_2$, $a_1 \leftrightarrow a_2 \equiv a_1 \rightarrow a_2 \wedge a_2 \rightarrow a_1$, $\forall v : t^* \bullet a \equiv \neg \exists v : t^* \bullet \neg a$, $true \equiv (null = null)$, $false \equiv \neg true$, $Qv : t \bullet a \equiv Qv : t^* \bullet |v| = 1 \wedge a[v[0]/v]$ for $Q \in \{\forall, \exists\}$, $l \equiv l = true$ if l is of type $\mathbb{B}$.

Fig. 3. Syntax of the assertion language **AL**

Since **AL** is statically typed, we must also give a type to the program variable x. Now, giving it the type $\mathbb{N}$ would allow us to express $x = 5$, but not $x = true$ while giving it the type $\mathbb{B}$ raises the converse problem. However, using mapping predicates, it is possible to accurately describe the set of intermediate states as $\mathbb{N}(x, 5) \vee \mathbb{B}(x, true)$. From this observation it is not hard to see that $\{true\}P\{x = 10\}$ (or $\{true\}P\{\mathbb{N}(x, 10)\}$) is not derivable without mapping predicates.

In assertions, tags may appear, e.g., **typesafe** $\rightarrow v \neq \boxtimes$. We use the notation $\sigma, \textbf{tags} \models a$ to denote the fact that the assertion a is true in the state σ under the tags **tags**. The definition of $\models$ is standard except for the case

$$\sigma, \textbf{tags} \models \textbf{tag} \text{ iff } \textbf{tag} \in \textbf{tags}.$$

4.3 (Tagged) Hoare Logic for Dynamically Typed Programs

Our exposition of the proof rules of $\mathcal{H}$ will use three substitutions on assertions. Proper definitions for all three can be found in [7, Appendix B].

The special variable **r** may appear in both pre- and postconditions. In preconditions it references some initial value, in postconditions the return value of the last executed expression. Note that it is important that **r** can appear in preconditions. Otherwise the weakest precondition $WP(\mathbf{r}, \mathbf{r} = null)$ would not be expressible which would induce incompleteness.

For a **dyn** statement s let $var(s)$ ($change(s)$) denote the set of variables accessed in s (appearing on the left of an assignment in s). For an assertion p let $free(p)$ denote the set of free variables of p and $p[v := t]$ the result of substituting t for v in p.

AXIOM: VAR   VAR-TAG

$\{p[\mathbf{r} := v]\}v\{p\}$ $\{\textbf{typesafe} \rightarrow v \neq \boxtimes\}v\{\textbf{tags}\}$

Note: includes the case of $v \equiv \textbf{self}$.

AXIOM: IVAR   IVAR-TAG

$\{p[\mathbf{r} := \textbf{self}.@v]\}@v\{p\}$ $\{\textbf{typesafe} \rightarrow \textbf{self}.@v \neq \boxtimes\}@v\{\textbf{tags}\}$

RULE: ASGN (both normal and instance variables)   AXIOM: CONST

$$\frac{\{p\}e\{\mathbf{tags} \wedge q[v := \mathbf{r}]\}}{\{p\}v := e\{\mathbf{tags} \wedge q\}} \text{ where } v \in \mathfrak{V} \qquad \{p[\mathbf{r} := null]\}null\{\mathbf{tags} \wedge p\}$$

RULE: SEQ

$$\frac{\{p\}s_1\{\mathbf{tags} \wedge r\} \qquad \{r\}s_2\{\mathbf{tags} \wedge q\}}{\{p\}s_1; s_2\{\mathbf{tags} \wedge q\}}$$

RULE: COND

$$\frac{\begin{array}{c}\{p\}e\{\mathbf{tags} \wedge r \wedge \mathbf{failsafe} \to \mathbf{r} \neq null \wedge \mathbf{typesafe} \to (\mathbf{r} \neq null \to \mathbb{B}(\mathbf{r}))\} \\ \{r \wedge \mathbb{B}(\mathbf{r}, true)\}s_1\{\mathbf{tags} \wedge q\} \\ \{r \wedge \mathbb{B}(\mathbf{r}, false)\}s_2\{\mathbf{tags} \wedge q\}\end{array}}{\{p\} \text{ if } e \text{ then } s_1 \text{ else } s_2 \text{ end } \{\mathbf{tags} \wedge q\}}$$

RULE: LOOP

$$\frac{\begin{array}{c}\{p\}e\{\mathbf{tags} \wedge p' \wedge \mathbf{failsafe} \to \mathbf{r} \neq null \wedge \mathbf{typesafe} \to (\mathbf{r} \neq null \to \mathbb{B}(\mathbf{r}))\} \\ \{p' \wedge \mathbb{B}(\mathbf{r}, true)\}s\{\mathbf{tags} \wedge p\} \\ \{p' \wedge \mathbb{B}(\mathbf{r}, true) \wedge r(z)\}s; e\{p' \wedge \mathbf{terminates} \to \forall z' : \mathbb{N} \bullet r(z') \to z' < z\}\end{array}}{\{p\} \text{ while } e \text{ do } s \text{ done } \{\mathbf{tags} \wedge p'[\mathbf{r} := b] \wedge \mathbb{B}(b, false) \wedge \mathbf{r} = null\}}$$

where b is a logical variable of type $\mathbb{B}$, z is a logical variable of type $\mathbb{N}$ that does not appear in p, p', e or s, $r(z)$ is a predicate with z among its free variables such that $\forall \sigma \bullet \sigma \models p' \to \exists z' : \mathbb{N} \bullet r(z')$ and $r(z')$ is the result of substituting z' for z in $r(z)$.

RULE: CONS

$$\frac{p \to p_1, \{p_1\}s\{\mathbf{tags'} \wedge q_1\}, q_1 \to q, \mathbf{tags'} \supseteq \mathbf{tags}}{\{p\}s\{\mathbf{tags} \wedge q\}}$$

RULE: BLCK   AXIOM: PASGN

$$\frac{\{p\}\overrightarrow{u}\,\overrightarrow{u} := \overrightarrow{t}\,\overrightarrow{\boxtimes}; s\{\mathbf{tags} \wedge q\}}{\{p\} \text{ begin local } \overrightarrow{u} := \overrightarrow{t}; s \text{ end}\{\mathbf{tags} \wedge q\}} \qquad \{p[\overrightarrow{u} := \overrightarrow{t}]\}\overrightarrow{u} := \overrightarrow{t}\{\mathbf{tags} \wedge p\}$$

where $\mathfrak{V}_L \cap \mathit{free}(q) = \emptyset$, $\{\overrightarrow{u}\} \subseteq \mathfrak{V}_L$ and $\{\overrightarrow{t}\} \subseteq \mathfrak{V}_L \cup \{null\}$, $\{\overrightarrow{\overline{u}}\} = \mathfrak{V}_L \setminus \{\overrightarrow{u}\}$ and $\overrightarrow{\boxtimes}$ is a fitting sequence of $\boxtimes$ constants.

RULE: METH

$$\frac{\begin{array}{c}\{p_i\}e_i\{\mathbf{tags} \wedge p_{i+1}[v_i := \mathbf{r}]\} \text{ for } i \in \mathbb{N}_n \\ \{p_{n+1}\}v_0.m(v_1, ..., v_n)\{\mathbf{tags} \wedge q\}\end{array}}{\{p_0\}e_0.m(e_1, ..., e_n)\{\mathbf{tags} \wedge q\}}$$

where the v_i are fresh local variables that do not occur in any e_j for all $i, j \in \mathbb{N}_n$.

RULE: REC

$$A \vdash \{p\}s\{\textbf{tags} \wedge q\},$$
$$A' \vdash \{p_i \wedge r_i(z)\}\textbf{begin local self}, \overrightarrow{u_i} := l_i, \overrightarrow{v_i}; s_i \textbf{ end}\{\textbf{tags}_i \wedge q_i\}, i \in \mathbb{N}_n^1$$
$$p_i \rightarrow (\textbf{failsafe} \rightarrow l_i \neq null \wedge \textbf{typesafe} \rightarrow l_i \neq null \rightarrow l_i.@\textbf{c} = \theta_{C_i}), i \in \mathbb{N}_n^1$$
$$\overline{\{p\}s\{\textbf{tags} \wedge q\}}$$

where $\textbf{method } m_i(\overrightarrow{u_i})\{s_i\} \in \mathfrak{M}_{C_i}$, $A = \{\{p_i\}l_i.m_i(\overrightarrow{v_i})\{\textbf{tags}_i \wedge q_i\} \mid i \in \mathbb{N}_n^1\}$, $A' = \{\{p_i \wedge (\textbf{terminates} \rightarrow \forall z' : \mathbb{N} \bullet r_i(z') \rightarrow z' < z)\}l_i.m_i(\overrightarrow{v_i})\{\textbf{tags}_i \wedge q_i\} \mid i \in \mathbb{N}_n^1\}$, z is a logical variable of type $\mathbb{N}$ that does not occur in p_i, q_i and s_i for $i \in \mathbb{N}_n^1$ and is treated in the proofs as a constant, $r_i(z)$ for $i \in \mathbb{N}_n^1$ are predicates with z among their free variables such that $\forall \sigma \bullet \sigma \models p_i \rightarrow \exists z' : \mathbb{N} \bullet r_i(z')$ for all $i \in \mathbb{N}_n^1$ and $r_i(z')$ denotes the result of substituting z' for z in $r_i(z)$.

AXIOM: EQUAL

$$\{true\}\textbf{u}_0 == \textbf{u}_1\{\textbf{tags} \wedge \mathbb{B}(\textbf{r}, \textbf{u}_0 = \textbf{u}_1)\}$$

RULE: CNST

$$\frac{\{p\}\textbf{new}_C.init(\overrightarrow{e})\{\textbf{tags} \wedge q\}}{\{p\}\textbf{new } C(\overrightarrow{e})\{\textbf{tags} \wedge q\}}$$

AXIOM: IS_A

$$\{true\}\textbf{u}_0 \ is\_a? \ C\{\textbf{tags} \wedge \mathbb{B}(\textbf{r}, \llbracket \textbf{u}_0 \rrbracket \in \{C\})\}$$

AXIOM: NEW

$$\{p[\textbf{r} := \textbf{new}_C]\}\textbf{new}_C\{\textbf{tags} \wedge p\}$$

The auxiliary rules as well as some others are mostly standard and hence omitted. Their tagged versions are given in [7], however.

The fact that dyn-expressions have side effects is mirrored in several rules: Like their corresponding rules in the operational semantics, the usual axiom for assignment is turned into a rule and the COND and LOOP rules both evaluate the condition before branching on its result in an intermediate state.

The rules PASGN, BLCK, METH and REC are needed to handle method calls. After handling side effecting expressions in arguments beforehand (METH) and ensuring that methods are only called on receivers supporting them (last premise of REC), method calls are assumed to satisfy the same properties as a block executing the body of the called method in an environment with local variables suitably initialized by parallel assignment (BLCK,PASGN).

The rules CNST and NEW handle object creation using the respective substitution defined in [7, Appendix B].

The LOOP and REC rules feature a novel form of loop variants / recursion bound. The basic idea is to use a predicate $r(z)$ instead of the usual integer expression t in order to allow quantification within loop variants / recursion bounds. While this was primarily introduced to circumvent a common incompleteness issue in Hoare logics for total correctness (see proof of Theorem 5 for details), note that it also allows using mapping predicates directly in loop variants / recursion bounds, i.e. proving

$$\{\mathbb{N}(i)\} \textbf{ while } i > 0 \textbf{ do } i := i - 1 \textbf{ done } \{\textbf{terminates}\}$$

with $r(z) \equiv \mathbb{N}(i, z)$.

5   Soundness

Soundness follows from a standard inductive argument. The extended version [7] further elaborates the case of the LOOP rule.

6   Completeness

In this Section, we will prove the axiomatic semantics of **dyn** (relative) complete [6] with respect to its operational semantics following the seminal completeness proof of Cook and Gorelick [6,10] as well as its extension to OO-programs due to de Boer and Pierik [4]. That is, given a closed program π with a finite set of class definitions, we prove that $\vDash \{p\}\pi\{q\}$ implies $\vdash_{\mathcal{H},\mathcal{T}} \{p\}\pi\{q\}$ assuming a complete proof system $\mathcal{T}$ for the assertion language **AL**.

Traditionally, completeness proofs are structured into 3 steps. First, the assertion language is shown to be expressive, then the system is proven complete for all statements of the programming language and finally, it is shown to be complete for recursive methods using the concept of most general correctness formulas. Since both the first and the last step rely on techniques for "freezing" program states and for evaluating assertions on such frozen states, we follow [4] in prepending a step for developing adequate freezing techniques for **dyn**.

Completeness proofs for Hoare Logics have been extended and refined for several decades now. Unfortunately, due to space restrictions we will not be able to give a proper account to the numerous ideas and intriguing details in the works of our predecessors, but must assume a certain familiarity with such proofs on the side of the reader. For the same reason, we will not be able to present the proof as a whole, but will concentrate on those parts we had to adapt.

6.1   Freezing the Initial State

As noticed by Gorelick [10], achieving completeness requires that the assertion language is able to capture every aspect of a program state in logical variables, in order to "freeze" this information during program execution and allow the postcondition to compare the initial- to the final state. Pierik and de Boer [4] pointed out that in OO-contexts this additionally requires freezing the internal states of all objects existing in the state, necessitating a more sophisticated freezing-strategy.

While their approach stores objects and the values of their instance variables class-wise, which is difficult in a dynamically-typed language like **dyn**, the basic idea is fortunately still applicable. We use a logical variable obj of type $\mathbb{O}^*$ to store a (finite) sequence of all existing objects:

$$all(obj) \equiv \forall o : \mathbb{O} \bullet \exists i : \mathbb{N} \bullet i < |obj| \wedge obj[i] = o$$

Since *obj* establishes a bijection from natural numbers to objects, its allows encoding states as sequences of natural numbers. For convenience, we introduce a polymorphic[6] *pos* function satisfying $\forall \tau : \mathbb{T} \bullet \forall e : \tau, s : \tau^* \bullet s[pos(s, e)] = e$

We introduce an enumeration $ivar : \mathfrak{V}_I^*$ of all instance variables and define the following predicate for freezing states:

$$code(\overline{x}, obj, \varsigma) \equiv |\varsigma| = |ivar| + 1 \wedge |\varsigma[0]| = |\overline{x}| \wedge obj[0] = \boxtimes \wedge$$
$$\forall i : \mathbb{N} \bullet i < |\overline{x}| \rightarrow \varsigma[0][i] = pos(obj, x_i) \wedge$$
$$\forall i, j : \mathbb{N} \bullet (i < |ivar| \wedge j < |obj|) \rightarrow ivar[i] = @v \wedge obj[j] = o \rightarrow \varsigma[i+1][j] = pos(obj, o.@v)$$

where $\overline{x} = x_1, ..., x_n$ is a sequence of local variables. The predicate $code(\overline{x}, obj, \varsigma)$ uses the sequence *obj* to capture the state of all local variables in $\overline{x}$ as well as all objects in *obj* in the frozen state ς of type $(\mathbb{N}^*)^*$. Note that ς can capture the internal states of all existing objects without referencing any of them.

Also note that this is indeed satisfiable for all states as $\boxtimes \in \mathbb{O}$ and $\boxtimes \in obj$. Furthermore, we say that ς encodes σ and write

$$\sigma \sim \varsigma \text{ iff } \sigma \models \exists obj : \mathbb{O}^* \bullet all(obj) \wedge code(\overline{x}, obj, \varsigma)$$

with $\{\overline{x}\} = \mathfrak{V}_L \cup \mathfrak{V}_S$.

Lemma 1 (Left-Totality of $\sim$). $\forall \sigma : \Sigma \bullet \exists \varsigma : (\mathbb{N}^*)^* \bullet \sigma \sim \varsigma$.

Finally, we are ready to define a predicate transformer Θ (called the "freezing function" in [4]). However, while in their work, Θ also bounds all quantification and replaces instance variable dereferencing by lookups in sequences, we additionally translate all object expressions into expressions of type $\mathbb{N}$ to allow simulating computations directly on the frozen states.

We hence have the following main cases for our predicate transformer $\Theta_{obj}^{\overline{x}}(\varsigma)$:

- $(l.@v)\Theta_{obj}^{\overline{x}}(\varsigma) \equiv \varsigma[pos(ivar, @v) + 1][l\Theta_{obj}^{\overline{x}}(\varsigma)]$
- $u\Theta_{obj}^{\overline{x}}(\varsigma) \equiv \varsigma[0][pos(\overline{x}, u)]$ where u is a program variable in $\overline{x}$
- $u\Theta_{obj}^{\overline{x}}(\varsigma) \equiv u'$ where u is a logical variable of type $\mathbb{O}$ and u' is a fresh logical variable of type $\mathbb{N}$
- $(l_1 = l_2)\Theta_{obj}^{\overline{x}}(\varsigma) \equiv l_1\Theta_{obj}^{\overline{x}}(\varsigma) = l_2\Theta_{obj}^{\overline{x}}(\varsigma)$ where l_1 and l_2 are of type $\mathbb{O}$.
- $(\exists o : \mathbb{O} \bullet p)\Theta_{obj}^{\overline{x}}(\varsigma) \equiv (\exists o' : \mathbb{N} \bullet 0 \leq o' < |obj| \rightarrow p\Theta_{obj}^{\overline{x}}(\varsigma))$

$\Theta_{obj}^{\overline{x}}(\varsigma)$ transforms any assertion p in such a way that it operates on the frozen state ς instead of the real program variables. Like the Θ in [4], our $\Theta_{obj}^{\overline{x}}(\varsigma)$ hence satisfies the following property

Theorem 1 (Invariance). $\vdash \{p\Theta_{obj}^{\overline{x}}(\varsigma)\} s \{p\Theta_{obj}^{\overline{x}}(\varsigma)\}$ *for all statements s and assertions p as long as $\overline{x}$ contains all program variables used and obj contains all objects accessed in p.*

---

[6] We use the polymorphic version for the sake of readability although the type system of **AL** does not allow polymorphism. However, polymorphic functions can be emulated using one version for each element type.

It can hence replace Θ in the remaining argument. Note that $p\Theta_{obj}^{\overline{x}}(\varsigma)$ is a property of ς as its truth value is independent of any particular state. We hence write $\models p\Theta_{obj}^{\overline{x}}(\varsigma)$ if its truth value is true. Also observe

Lemma 2 (Freezing). $\sigma \models q \quad iff \quad \sigma \sim \varsigma \land \models q\Theta_{obj}^{\overline{x}}(\varsigma)$

6.2   Expressivity

Cook [6] first discussed the importance of an expressive assertion language for the completeness of a Hoare logic. In essence, the assertion language must be able to express the strongest postcondition $SP(s, p)$ for all statements s and preconditions p.

In the last Section, we already established that it is possible to capture all information about a state in a structure consisting of finite sequences of natural numbers. Using Gödelization, one can take this a step further and encode these sequences themselves as a single natural number. Then, we consider a predicate $comp_s$ of type $\mathbb{N} \times \mathbb{N} \mapsto \mathbb{N}$ simulating **dyn** computations on such frozen states and note that, since such computations are by definition computable, it can be defined as a μ-recursive function.

By [7, Theorem 6], it is hence expressible in our assertion language and we can use it within our assertions without any loss of generality. For convenience, we will omit the Gödelization step and instead use a version of $comp_s$ operating on frozen states as defined above. To formalize the idea that $comp_s$ simulates **dyn** computations on frozen states, we stipulate

Lemma 3. $comp_s = \{(\varsigma, \varsigma') \mid \forall \sigma, \sigma' \bullet (\sigma \sim \varsigma \land \sigma' \sim \varsigma') \to \sigma' \in \mathcal{M}[\![s]\!](\sigma)\}$

Using $comp_s$ we can show the following:

Theorem 2 (Definability of Weakest Preconditions). *For all postconditions q and statements s, the precondition*
$$p \equiv \forall \varsigma, \varsigma' \bullet (all(obj) \land code(\overline{x}, obj, \varsigma') \land comp_s(\varsigma', \varsigma)) \to q\Theta_{obj}^{\overline{x}}(\varsigma)$$
satisfies $[\![p]\!] = \{\sigma \mid \mathcal{M}[\![s]\!](\sigma) \subseteq [\![q]\!]\}$.

The proof can be found in [7]. Since definability of weakest preconditions is equivalent to the definability of strongest postconditions [13], we have

Theorem 3 (Expressiveness). *The assertion language $\boldsymbol{AL}$ is expressive with respect to its standard interpretation and the programming language $\boldsymbol{dyn}$.*

6.3   Completeness for Statements

As usual [6,10], the core of our completeness proof consists of an induction over the structure of a statement s. Since several of our rules deviate from theirs, we need to exchange these cases in argument. We will concentrate on the most interesting cases.

Induction Basis:

- $s \equiv$ u: Assume $\models \{p\}u\{q\}$. Then, by the operational semantics, $p \to q[\mathbf{r} := u]$ must also be true. It is hence derivable in $\mathcal{T}$ and the desired result follows from the VAR axiom followed by applying the rule of consequence (CONS). *Typesafety:* Assume $\models \{p\}u\{\mathbf{typesafe} \wedge q\}$. Then $\{p\}u\{q\}$ and $\{p\}u\{\mathbf{typesafe}\}$ must also be true. The former can thus be derived using above argumentation and the latter implies $p \to u \neq \boxtimes$, which is hence derivable in $\mathcal{T}$ and the axiom VAR-TAG followed by an applying the rule of consequence (CONS) derives $\{p\}u\{\mathbf{typesafe}\}$. Now the rule of conjunction (CONJ) followed by the rule of consequence (CONS) derives the desired result. **failsafe** and **terminates** can be derived using the axiom VAR-TAG without any preconditions.
- $s \equiv$ @v: Just like the case for u, applying IVAR instead of VAR and IVAR-TAG instead of VAR-TAG.

Induction Hypothesis: $\models \{p\}s\{q\} \to \vdash_{\mathcal{H},\mathcal{T}} \{p\}s\{q\}$ for all assertions p, q and all statements s of a program π containing no recursive method calls.

Induction Step:

- u := e: Assume $\models \{p\}u := e\{\mathbf{tags} \wedge q\}$. Then according to the operational semantics, $\{p\}e\{\mathbf{tags} \wedge q[u := \mathbf{r}]\}$ must also be. By the induction hypothesis, it is hence derivable. An application of the rule ASGN derives the desired result.
- $s \equiv$ **if** e **then** s_1 **else** s_2 **end**: Assume $\{p\}$ **if** e **then** s_1 **else** s_2 **end** $\{\mathbf{tags} \wedge q\}$ is true. Then, by the expressiveness of the assertion language and the operational semantics, there is an intermediate assertion r such that $\{p\}e\{\mathbf{tags} \wedge r\}$, $\{r \wedge \mathbb{B}(\mathbf{r}, true)\}s_1\{\mathbf{tags} \wedge q\}$ and $\{r \wedge \mathbb{B}(\mathbf{r}, false)\}s_2\{\mathbf{tags} \wedge q\}$ are also true and hence derivable by the induction hypothesis. Now an application of the rule COND derives the desired result. *Failsafety:* Since above argumentation already ensured that e, s_1 and s_2 are all failsafe, the only additional requirement is $\{p\}e\{\mathbf{r} \neq null\}$. However, since the case $\mathbf{r} = null$ leads to failure in the operational semantics, this must hold for any execution of s in order to be failsafe and hence must be derivable by the induction hypothesis.

  Typesafety: The same argumentation as for failsafety applies here, only the additional requirement is $\{p\}e\{\mathbf{r} \neq null \to \mathbb{B}(\mathbf{r})\}$. Note that the case of $\mathbf{r} = null$ can be deliberately allowed, since it leads to a failure in the operational semantics and thus does not affect typesafety.

- $s \equiv$ **while** e **do** s_1 **done**: Assume $\{p\}$ **while** e **do** s_1 **done** $\{\mathbf{tags} \wedge q\}$ is true. Then, by the standard argument for while loops due to Cook [6] (and explained particularly well by Apt [1]), the expressiveness of the assertion language and the operational semantics, there are two assertions i and i' such that $p \to i$, $\{i\}e\{\mathbf{tags} \wedge i'\}$, $\{i' \wedge \mathbb{B}(\mathbf{r}, true)\}s_1\{\mathbf{tags} \wedge i\}$ and $i'[b/\mathbf{r}] \wedge \mathbb{B}(b, false) \wedge \mathbf{r} = null \to q$ are true and hence derivable by the induction hypothesis and the completeness of $\mathcal{T}$. While i is the loop invariant of s, i' is an intermediate state neccessary because in **dyn**, e could have side-effects. Now, an application of the LOOP rule followed by the rule of consequence derives the desired result. *Termination:* see [7]

Failsafety & Typesafety: the exact same argument as for conditionals applies here as well.

6.4   Completeness for Recursive Methods

The methodology for proving a Hoare logic complete for recursive procedures by using most general correctness formulas is due to Gorelick [10]. It was extended to OO-programs by De Boer and Pierik [4].

A curious implication of dynamic dispatch under dynamic typing is that the lack of type information prohibits pinpointing the exact target of a method call. For instance, the weakest precondition of the call x.size() with respect to the postcondition $\mathbb{N}(\mathbf{r}, 5)$ must include all possibilities like the case of the variable x referring to a string of length 5 as well as x referring to a list of size 5. In general, the weakest precondition of a method call $l.m(v_1, ..., v_n)$ is the disjunction of all weakest preconditions derivable as described in the proof of Theorem 4 from the most general correctness formulas of all methods C.m of arity n of all classes $C \in \mathfrak{C}$, each conjoined with the corresponding type assumption $[\![l]\!] \in \{C\}$. Note that this methodology introduces an implicit closed world assumption as it fails when using a method with a different set of classes. However, we regard this problem as one of modularity rather than completeness and thus out of scope.

As our tagged Hoare logic incorporates different notions of correctness, we generalize Gorelick's idea to a set of most general correctness formulas. The most general correctness formulas for a statement s are

$$MGF(s) = \{\{WP(s, init)\}s\{init\}\} \cup \{\{WP_{\mathbf{tag}}(s, true)\}s\{\mathbf{tag}\} \mid \mathbf{tag} \in \mathcal{T}ags\}$$

with $init \equiv all(obj) \wedge code(\overline{x}, obj, \varsigma)$. The reason for this is obvious: From $MGF(s)$, we can deduce $\{WP_{\mathbf{tags}}(s, q)\}s\{\mathbf{tags} \wedge q\}$ with $\mathbf{tags} \subseteq \mathcal{T}ags$ using the conjunction rule. The converse is not in all cases possible.

The results from Sect. 6.3 imply that above set can be derived for any **dyn** statement s given that they are true. Should, e.g., s raise a type error on all inputs then $WP_{\mathbf{typesafe}}(s, true) \equiv false$ and $\{false\}s\{\mathbf{typesafe}\}$ is derivable.

Theorem 4 (MGFs). $\models \{p\}s\{\mathbf{tags} \wedge q\} \rightarrow MGF(s) \vdash_{\mathcal{H}, \mathcal{T}} \{p\}s\{\mathbf{tags} \wedge q\}$

Proof. Assume $\models \{p\}s\{\mathbf{tags} \wedge q\}$. Then $\{p\}s\{q\}$ and $\{p\}s\{\mathbf{tag}\}$ for all $\mathbf{tag} \in \mathbf{tags}$ are also all true.

(1) $\vdash \{p\}s\{q\}$: For technical convenience only we assume that p and q do not contain free occurrences of the logical variables used to freeze states. If they do, these need to be renamed using the substitution rule. By Theorem 1 we have $\{q\Theta_{obj}^{\overline{x}}\}s\{q\Theta_{obj}^{\overline{x}}\}$. An application of the conjunction rule yields

$$\{q\Theta_{obj}^{\overline{x}} \wedge WP(s, init)\}s\{q\Theta_{obj}^{\overline{x}} \wedge init\}$$

Next, we have to prove $p \rightarrow q\Theta_{obj}^{\overline{x}} \wedge WP(s, init)$. Assume $\sigma \models p$. Then by $\models \{p\}s\{q\}$, for all $\sigma' \in \mathcal{M}[\![s]\!](\sigma)$, we have $\sigma' \models q$. By Lemma 2, we have $\sigma' \models q\Theta_{obj}^{\overline{x}} \wedge init$. Now, by Theorem 1, we have $\vdash \{q\Theta_{obj}^{\overline{x}}\}s\{q\Theta_{obj}^{\overline{x}}\}$, and by soundness of our proof system $\models \{q\Theta_{obj}^{\overline{x}}\}s\{q\Theta_{obj}^{\overline{x}}\}$. Hence, $\sigma \models q\Theta_{obj}^{\overline{x}}$ and by the definition of WP, $\sigma \models WP(s, init)$. Therefore, $p \rightarrow q\Theta_{obj}^{\overline{x}} \wedge WP(s, init)$ holds and since $q\Theta_{obj}^{\overline{x}} \wedge init \rightarrow q$ follows directly from Lemma 2, an application of the rule of consequence derives $\{p\}s\{q\}$.

(2) $\vdash \{p\}s\{\mathbf{tag}\}$: if true, then $p \rightarrow WP_{\mathbf{tag}}(s, true)$ must also be and is hence derivable by the completeness of $\mathcal{T}$. Since $\{WP_{\mathbf{tag}}(s, true)\}s\{\mathbf{tag}\} \in MGF(s)$, an application of the consequence rule derives the desired result.

(3) $\vdash \{p\}s\{\mathbf{tags} \wedge q\}$: One application of the conjunction rule per tag in $\mathbf{tags}$ completes the proof. $\qquad\square$

Finally, since our recursion rule is identical to the one devised by Gorelick [10] for this purpose, we are now able to apply the same inductive argument used by Gorelick for proving our Hoare logic complete for recursive methods.

Lemma 4. *Let* $M_i \equiv l_i.m_i(\overrightarrow{v_i})$ *denote the ith (possibly recursive) method call occurring in a closed program* π *and let* $A = \bigcup_{i=1}^n MGF(M_i)$ *be the set of most general correctness formulas about these method calls then for all statements* s *of* π *and all assertions* p *and* q: $\models \{p\}s\{q\} \rightarrow A \vdash_{\mathcal{H},\mathcal{T}} \{p\}s\{q\}$

Proof. By induction over the structure of s. Most cases are as in the proof for the non-recursive case. Most interesting is the new case for method calls: $s \equiv l_i.m_i(\overrightarrow{v_i})$: Assuming $\models \{p\}s\{q\}$ and s is the ith method call M_i in our program, then $MGF(s) \subseteq A$ and hence $A \vdash \{p\}s\{q\}$ by Theorem 4. As Gorelick [10] pointed out, this also holds for recursive method calls.

Theorem 5 (Completeness for Recursive Methods)
$\models \{p\}s\{\mathbf{tags} \wedge q\} \qquad \rightarrow \qquad \vdash_{\mathcal{H},\mathcal{T}} \{p\}s\{\mathbf{tags} \wedge q\}$
for any statement s *of a closed program* π *containing possibly recursive method calls and all assertions* p *and* q.

Proof. Expressiveness of **AL** guarantees the expressibility of $WP_{\mathbf{tags}}(s, q)$ for any statement s and postcondition q. Hence by setting $q \equiv init$ and $s \equiv M_i$ for any $i \in \mathbb{N}_n^1$ we can see that the set A of most general correctness formulas of all method calls is expressible in our logic. Now, since by definition of $WP_{\mathbf{tags}}$, these formulas are true, we have by Lemma 4

$A \vdash_{\mathcal{H},\mathcal{T}} \{p_i\} \mathbf{begin\,local}\,self, \overrightarrow{u_i} := l_i, \overrightarrow{v_i}; s_i \,\mathbf{end}\{q_i\}$ as well as

$A \vdash_{\mathcal{H},\mathcal{T}} \{p_{\mathbf{tag},i}\} \mathbf{begin\,local}\,self, \overrightarrow{u_i} := l_i, \overrightarrow{v_i}; s_i \,\mathbf{end}\{\mathbf{tag}\}$ for all $\mathbf{tag} \in \mathcal{T}ags$

with $p_i \equiv WP(M_i, init)$, $q_i \equiv init$, $p_{\mathbf{tag},i} \equiv WP_{\mathbf{tag}}(M_i, true)$ and s_i denoting the method body of the method called in M_i for all $i \in \mathbb{N}_n^1$. Note that above statements establish the assumptions in the set A and together allow deriving the assumptions for the REC rule of the form

$A \vdash_{\mathcal{H},\mathcal{T}} \{p_i \wedge r_i(z)\} \mathbf{begin\,local}\,self, \overrightarrow{u_i} := l_i, \overrightarrow{v_i}; s_i \,\mathbf{end}\{\mathbf{tags}_i \wedge q_i\}$

for all $i \in \mathbb{N}_n^1$. As for the case not concerned with termination, we can simply set $r_i(z) \equiv z = z$. Furthermore, assuming $\models \{p\}s\{q\}$, by Lemma 4 we have

$A \vdash \{p\}s\{\mathbf{tags} \wedge q\}$

Now these are just the premises of the REC rule. Note that in the case not concerned with termination, the set of assumptions A is derivable from A' by applying the consequence rule to each element. Hence, an application of the REC rule derives the desired result and completes the proof.

Termination: for proving termination of **dyn** programs, the rules LOOP and REC must be altered to support so-called loop-variants or recursion bounds. Usually, these take the form of an integer expression t whose value a) must be > 0 whenever the loop / recursive method is entered (thus forcing termination when reaching zero) and b) must decrease on every iteration / recursive call. Note that this methodology syntactically restricts the loop variant / recursion bound to be an integer expression of the assertion language. Now, as observed by Apt, De Boer and Olderog in [2], this method introduces incompleteness in the case of total correctness, since it assumes the integer expressions of the assertion language to be able to express any necessary loop-variant / recursion bound. However, while-loops and recursive methods allow **dyn**-programs to calculate any μ-recursive function and hence obviously also to bound the number of loop iterations by any μ-recursive function, while the set of integer operations available in the assertion language might be quite limited (e.g. in our case lacking exponentiation). We circumvent this problem by introducing a new form of loop-variants and recursion bounds, which allow the use of quantifiers. The old form used a logical variable z of type $\mathbb{N}$ to store the value of t before a loop iteration ($t = z$ in the precondition) and compare it to the new value in the postcondition ($t < z$). Our new form uses a predicate $r(z)$ with z among its free variables instead of $t = z$ and the logical expression $\forall z' : \mathbb{N} \bullet r(z') \rightarrow z' < z$ where $r(z')$ denotes the result of substituting z' for z in r instead of $t < z$. Firstly, observe that this is a conservative extension as one may set $r \equiv t = z$ for some integer expression t. Secondly, note that by [7, Lemma 5], r may compute any μ-recursive function and is thus contrary to integer expressions able to express any function computable by **dyn**-programs including exponentiation. $\square$

7   Example

Since we already proved the Hoare Logic relative complete, the program depicted in Fig. 4 was chosen to be a simple but instructive example of how the rules for assignments and method calls are applied rather than a demonstration of the Logic's expressive power. While the program's type safety problem boils down to path sensitivity and could thus be solved also by advanced type inference algorithms, most statically-typed languages do not use a path sensitive algorithm for reasons of scalability. Hence it can be considered typical for dynamically-typed languages.

Although it does not look like it, there are plenty of method calls hidden in this example. Remember that the operations $+$ on lines 11 and 14 is desugared to a call to a method m_+ on their first operand (x in both cases) and that constants like 5 are desugared to quite a few constructor- and method calls (see Fig. 1). To make type safety non-obvious, we give the following assumptions about our environment:

$$\{\mathbb{N}(v_0, n_0) \wedge \mathbb{N}(v_1, n_1)\}v_0.m_+(v_1)\{\textbf{typesafe} \wedge \mathbb{N}(\mathbf{r}, n_0 + n_1)\}$$

```
01 method num_or_bool(b)
02 requires 𝔹(b)
03 ensures typesafe ∧ (𝔹(b, true) ∧ ℕ(r, 12)∨
04                      𝔹(b, false) ∧ 𝕊(r, "foobar"))
05 {
06   if b then
07     x := y := 5; z := 2
08   else
09     x := "foo"; y := "bar"
10   end;
11   if x is_a? num then x := x + z end;
12   assert typesafe ∧ (𝔹(b, true) ∧ ℕ(x, 7) ∧ ℕ(y, 5)∨
13                      𝔹(b, false) ∧ 𝕊(x, "foo") ∧ 𝕊(y, "bar"));
14   x + y
15 }
```

Fig. 4. A simple dynamically-typed program

$\{\mathbb{S}(v_0, s_0) \wedge \mathbb{S}(v_1, s_1)\} v_0.m_+(v_1) \{\textbf{typesafe} \wedge \mathbb{S}(r, s_0 s_1)\}$

So $+$ is a typesafe operation when applied to numerics (where is denotes addition) and strings (where is denotes concatenation), but we do not know anything about applications to mixed operands (adding a string to a numeric or the other way around). Also note that the variable z only exists in the case that b is $true$. If that is not the case, accessing it in line 11 would result in a type error.

In order to reason about the desugared constants, we also need to assume

$\{[\![v0]\!] \in \{num\} \wedge v_1 = null\} v_0.init(v_1) \{\textbf{typesafe} \wedge \mathbb{N}(r, 0)\}$

$\{\mathbb{N}(v_0, n)\} v_0.succ() \{\textbf{typesafe} \wedge \mathbb{N}(r, n + 1)\}$

$\{[\![v_0]\!] \in \{string\} \wedge v_1 = null\} v_0.init(v_1) \{\textbf{typesafe} \wedge \mathbb{S}(r, "")\}$

$\{\mathbb{S}(v_0, s) \wedge \mathbb{N}(v_1, n)\} v_0.addchar(v_1) \{\textbf{typesafe} \wedge \exists c : \mathbb{S} \bullet ascii(c, n) \wedge \mathbb{S}(r, sc)\}$

where $ascii(c, n)$ iff c is a single-character string and the ASCII-code of this character is n.

Using these assumptions, it is possible to derive

$\{true\}$

$\textbf{new } num(null).succ().succ().succ().succ().succ()$

$\{\textbf{typesafe} \wedge \mathbb{N}(r, 0 + 1 + 1 + 1 + 1)\}$

which, by syntactic sugaring and an application of the CONS rule turns into $\{true\}5\{\textbf{typesafe} \wedge \mathbb{N}(r, 5)\}$ as well as

$\{true\}2\{\textbf{typesafe} \wedge \mathbb{N}(r, 2)\}$,

$\{true\} "foo" \{\textbf{typesafe} \wedge \mathbb{S}(r, "foo")\}$ and $\{true\} "bar" \{\textbf{typesafe} \wedge \mathbb{S}(r, "bar")\}$ which we will not show in desugared form.

Now, using the ASGN rule, we can derive the following statements about the assignments in line 7 and 9:

$\{true\}z := 2\{\textbf{typesafe} \wedge \mathbb{N}(z, 2)\}$

$\{true\}x := y := 5\{\textbf{typesafe} \wedge \mathbb{N}(x, 5) \wedge \mathbb{N}(y, 5)\}$

$\{true\}x := "foo"\{\textbf{typesafe} \wedge \mathbb{S}(x, "foo")\}$

$\{true\}y := \text{``}bar\text{''}\{\textbf{typesafe} \wedge \mathbb{S}(y, \text{``}bar\text{''})\}$

Note how the two applications of the ASGN rule neccessary to derive the case for x := y := 5 interact by passing the result of y := 5 in the variable **r**. Using the rules INV and SEQ, these can be combined into

$\{true\}\text{x} := \text{y} := 5; \text{z} := 2\{\textbf{typesafe} \wedge \mathbb{N}(\text{x}, 5) \wedge \mathbb{N}(\text{y}, 5) \wedge \mathbb{N}(\text{z}, 2)\}$

$\{true\}\text{x} := \text{``}foo\text{''}; \text{y} := \text{``}bar\text{''}\{\textbf{typesafe} \wedge \mathbb{S}(\text{x}, \text{``}foo\text{''}) \wedge \mathbb{S}(\text{y}, \text{``}bar\text{''})\}$

using the INV rule, we can thus derive

$\{\mathbb{B}(b, true)\}\text{x} := \text{y} := 5; \text{z} := 2$

$\{\textbf{typesafe} \wedge \mathbb{B}(b, true) \wedge \mathbb{N}(\text{x}, 5) \wedge \mathbb{N}(\text{y}, 5) \wedge \mathbb{N}(\text{z}, 2)\}$

$\{\mathbb{B}(b, false)\}\text{x} := \text{``}foo\text{''}; \text{y} := \text{``}bar\text{''}$

$\{\textbf{typesafe} \wedge \mathbb{B}(b, false) \wedge \mathbb{S}(\text{x}, \text{``}foo\text{''}) \wedge \mathbb{S}(\text{y}, \text{``}bar\text{''})\}$

an application of the CONS rule yields

$\{\mathbb{B}(b, true)\}\text{x} := \text{y} := 5; \text{z} := 2\{\textbf{typesafe} \wedge q\}$

$\{\mathbb{B}(b, false)\}\text{x} := \text{``}foo\text{''}; \text{y} := \text{``}bar\text{''}\{\textbf{typesafe} \wedge q\}$

where $q \equiv (\mathbb{B}(b, true) \wedge \mathbb{N}(\text{x}, 5) \wedge \mathbb{N}(\text{y}, 5) \wedge \mathbb{N}(\text{z}, 2) \vee$

$\mathbb{B}(b, false) \wedge \mathbb{S}(\text{x}, \text{``}foo\text{''}) \wedge \mathbb{S}(\text{y}, \text{``}bar\text{''}))$

Since the postconditions are identical, we can then apply the COND rule with

$\{\mathbb{B}(b)\}b\{\textbf{typesafe} \wedge (\exists b' : \mathbb{B} \bullet \mathbb{B}(\text{r}, b') \wedge \mathbb{B}(b, b')) \wedge \text{r} \neq null \rightarrow \mathbb{B}(\text{r})\}$

which can be derived using the VAR and CONS rules to yield

$\{\mathbb{B}(b)\}$

```
06    if  b  then
07        x := y := 5;  z := 2
08    else
09        x := ''foo'';  y := ''bar''
10    end;
```

$\{\textbf{typesafe} \wedge q\}$ (1)

Now we use the specification of the method m_+ (for numerics) and the VAR, VAR-TAG and CONS rules to derive

$\{\mathbb{N}(\text{x}, n_0) \wedge \mathbb{N}(\text{z}, n_1)\}\text{x} + \text{z}\{\textbf{typesafe} \wedge \mathbb{N}(\text{r}, n_0 + n_1)\}$

and then apply the ASGN rule to yield

$\{\mathbb{N}(\text{x}, n_0) \wedge \mathbb{N}(\text{z}, n_1)\}\text{x} := \text{x} + \text{z}\{\textbf{typesafe} \wedge \mathbb{N}(\text{x}, n_0 + n_1)\}$

after using the IS_A axiom and the CONS rule to derive

$\{true\}\text{x} \ is\_a? \ num\{\textbf{typesafe} \wedge \mathbb{B}(\text{r}, [\![\text{x}]\!] \in \{num\}) \wedge \text{r} \neq null \rightarrow \mathbb{B}(\text{r})\}$

we can apply the COND, INV and CONS rules to yield

$\{q\} \textbf{if} \ \text{x} \ is\_a? \ num \ \textbf{then} \ \text{x} := \text{x} + \text{z} \ \textbf{end}; \{q_1\}$ (2)

with $q_1 \equiv (\mathbb{B}(b, true) \wedge \mathbb{N}(\text{x}, 7) \wedge \mathbb{N}(\text{y}, 5) \vee$

$\mathbb{B}(b, false) \wedge \mathbb{S}(\text{x}, \text{``}foo\text{''}) \wedge \mathbb{S}(\text{y}, \text{``}bar\text{''}))$

Note that q_1 is just what was asserted in line 12 and 13. Finally, we employ the specification of the method m_+ both for numerics and strings and rules DISJ and CONS to derive

$\{q_1\}\text{x} + \text{y}\{\textbf{typesafe} \wedge (\mathbb{B}(b, true) \wedge \mathbb{N}(\text{r}, 12) \vee$ (3)

$\mathbb{B}(b, false) \wedge \mathbb{S}(\text{r}, \text{''}foobar\text{''}))\}$

which is just the postcondition of our method **num_or_bool**. Combining
(1), (2) and (3) with the SEQ rule, we reach

$$\{\mathbb{B}(b)\}s_{num\_or\_bool}\{q_1\}$$

where $s_{num\_or\_bool}$ is the body of the method **num_or_bool** which hence satisfies its specification.   □

Note that the proof system ensures that all variables are properly initialized before access. Would some variable u be accessed without prior assignment, we would get an additional $u \neq \boxtimes$ literal in the precondition.

8   Conclusions and Outlook

We presented a sound and (relative) complete Hoare logic for **dyn**. Open are the issues of modularity (applicability to open programs) and allowing tags carrying additional information (to incorporate extensions like De Boer's footprints [3]).

Acknowledgements. We thank Dennis Kregel for noticing that restricting **r** causes incompleteness and him, Nils-Erik Flick and the anonymous referees for many useful comments on prior versions of this paper.

References

1. Apt, K.R.: Ten years of hoare's logic: a survey - Part I. ACM Trans. Program. Lang. Syst. **3**(4), 431–483 (1981). http://www.cs.cornell.edu/Courses/cs6860/2010fa/Handouts/Apt10years.pdf
2. Apt, K.R., de Boer, F.S., Olderog, E.R.: Verification of Sequential and Concurrent Programs. Texts in Computer Science, 3rd edn., p. 502. Springer, New York (2009)
3. de Boer, F.S., de Gouw, S.: Being and change: reasoning about invariance. In: Meyer, R., Platzer, A., Wehrheim, H. (eds.) Correct System Design. LNCS, vol. 9360, pp. 191–204. Springer, Heidelberg (2015). doi:10.1007/978-3-319-23506-6_13
4. de Boer, F.S., Pierik, C.: How to cook a complete hoare logic for your pet OO language. In: de Boer, F.S., Bonsangue, M.M., Graf, S., de Roever, W.-P. (eds.) FMCO 2003. LNCS, vol. 3188, pp. 111–133. Springer, Heidelberg (2004)
5. Clarke Jr., E.M.: Programming language constructs for which it is impossible to obtain good hoare axiom systems. J. ACM **26**(1), 129–147 (1979). http://www.cs.cmu.edu/~emc/papers/Papers%20In%20Refereed%20Journals/79_impossible_hoareaxiom.pdf
6. Cook, S.A.: Soundness and completeness of an axiom system for program verification. SIAM J. Comput. **7**(1), 70–90 (1978). http://www.cs.toronto.edu/~sacook/homepage/soundness.pdf
7. Engelmann, B., Olderog, E.: A Sound and Complete Hoare Logic for Dynamically-Typed, Object-Oriented Programs - Extended Version. CoRR abs/1509.08605 (2015). http://arxiv.org/abs/1509.08605
8. Engelmann, B., Olderog, E., Flick, N.E.: Closing the Gap - Formally Verifying Dynamically Typed Programs like Statically Typed Ones Using Hoare Logic - Extended Version. CoRR abs/1501.02699 (2015). http://arxiv.org/abs/1501.02699

9. Gardner, P., Maffeis, S., Smith, G.D.: Towards a program logic for JavaScript. In: Field, J., Hicks, M. (eds.) POPL, pp. 31–44. ACM (2012). http://citeseer.ist.psu.edu/viewdoc/summary?doi=10.1.1.221.302

10. Gorelick, G.A.: A Complete Axiomatic System for Proving Assertions about Recursive and Non-Recursive Programs. Technical report 75, Department of Computer Science, University of Toronto, Canada (1975)

11. Hennessy, M.C.B., Plotkin, G.D.: Full abstraction for a simple programming language. Proceedings of Mathematical Foundations of Computer Science. LNCS, vol. 74, pp. 108–120. Springer, New York (1979)

12. Hoare, C.A.R.: An axiomatic basis for computer programming. Commun. ACM **12**, 576–580, 583 (1969). https://www.cs.cmu.edu/~crary/819-f09/Hoare69.pdf

13. Olderog, E.R.: On the notion of expressiveness and the rule of adaptation. Theoret. Comput. Sci. **24**(3), 337–347 (1983). http://www.sciencedirect.com/science/article/pii/0304397583900099

14. Plotkin, G.D.: A structural approach to operational semantics. J. Logic Algebraic Program. **60–61**, 17–139 (2004). http://homepages.inf.ed.ac.uk/gdp/publications/sos_jlap.pdf

15. Qin, S., Chawdhary, A., Xiong, W., Munro, M., Qiu, Z., Zhu, H.: Towards an Axiomatic Verification System for JavaScript. In: Proceedings of the TASE 2011, Washington, DC, pp. 133–141. IEEE (2011)

Self-Reconfiguring Microservices

Maurizio Gabbrielli[1,2(✉)], Saverio Giallorenzo[1], Claudio Guidi[3],
Jacopo Mauro[4], and Fabrizio Montesi[5]

[1] Department of Computer Science and Engineering,
University of Bologna, Bologna, Italy
gabbri@cs.unibo.it
[2] INRIA, Focus Team, Bologna, Italy
[3] italianaSoftware, Imola, Italy
[4] Department of Informatics, University of Oslo, Oslo, Norway
[5] Department of Mathematics and Computer Science,
University of Southern Denmark, Odense, Denmark

Abstract. Microservices is an emerging paradigm for the development
of distributed systems that, originating from Service-Oriented Architecture, focuses on the small dimension, the loose coupling, and the dynamic
topology of services. Microservices are particularly appropriate for the
development of distributed systems in the Cloud. However, their dynamic
nature calls for suitable techniques for their automatic deployment. In
this paper we address this problem and we propose JRO (Jolie Redeployment Optimiser), a tool for the automatic and optimised deployment of
microservices written in the Jolie language. The tool uses Zephyrus, a
state of the art tool that automatically generates a fully detailed Service-
Oriented Architecture configuration starting from a partial and abstract
description of the target application.

Keywords: Microservices · Service-Oriented Architecture · Automatic
deployment · Optimal component allocation

1 Introduction

Microservices [16] is an emerging paradigm for the development of distributed
systems that evolved from Service-Oriented Architecture [18] (SOA). The key
aspect of microservices is that the idea of using services as components is
pervasive.

In typical SOAs, services are used as an overlay meant to integrate and coordinate autonomous information systems. This coordination is obtained via communications, which operate using standard protocols. Such information systems
can be built following different methodologies; in practice, many of them are

Supported by the EU project FP7-644298 *HyVar: Scalable Hybrid Variability for
Distributed, Evolving Software Systems* and CRC (*Choreographies for Reliable and
efficient Communication software*), grant no. DFF–4005-00304 from the Danish
Council for Independent Research.

© Springer International Publishing Switzerland 2016
E. Ábrahám et al. (Eds.): de Boer Festschrift, LNCS 9660, pp. 194–210, 2016.
DOI: 10.1007/978-3-319-30734-3_14

legacy systems. Microservices explore a different direction, i.e., that of using services as the inner components of an information system. This allows to apply to microservices the same principles that apply to component-based software engineering. For example, since microservices should be small (or, better, "micro") it should be natural to follow principles towards cohesion, such as the Single Responsibility Principle[1].

Moreover, in this paradigm even the components of a single software application are all autonomous services that can interact only through message passing. This has the important benefit of obtaining a loosely-coupled implementation of the internals of an application, thus facilitating modularity and scalability. Due to the fact that microservices are already loosely-coupled, operate via message passing, and offer APIs to be invoked by external software it is easier to coordinate information systems based on microservices.

To understand how microservices support scalability, suppose that a service in a system is under heavy load. Since all the other components can interact with this service only through its message interface, we can replace it with a load balancer that offers the same API and forwards requests to a new subsystem running a set of replicated instances of the original service. From the loose coupling property of microservices we obtain that the rest of the system remains unchanged, independently from its implementation details. This feature makes the topology of a microservices architecture (i.e., the number of its components and their interactions) very dynamic.

Due to their properties, one of the main application contexts of microservices is the deployment of distributed systems in the Cloud [36]. Indeed, in the Cloud it is easy to scale the infrastructure of a system by adding or removing instances of virtual machines. However, allocating and deploying services on that machines while the system is running is a complex task. Usually the deployment of services is done either manually or it is handled programmatically with pre-configured deployment schemas that tools like Puppet [43] and Chef [40] automate. In either cases, the developers and DevOps[2] must carefully define where — in which virtual machine — services must be deployed and specify their connections. The planning of the deployment of a system must balance between the cost of its resources and its performances. Even in systems composed of few types of services, devising such a *deployment plan* quickly becomes a cumbersome and complex task due to dependencies between services and availability of different kinds of virtual machines, with different range of resources and costs. When looking for an *optimal plan* the task becomes extremely difficult, also from a theoretical perspective, since very easily one encounter NP-hard [26] and even undecidable problems [8].

In this paper, we address the problem of automatic optimal deployment planning of microservices. We assume the use of reconfigurable microservices, thus

---

[1] This is a well know example from the object oriented world, stating that there should never be more than one reason for a class to change.

[2] DevOps are professionals that collaborate in the development of programs by reporting their experiences with tests and deployments scenarios to developers [11].

abstracting from the preservation, partition, and consistency of their state and data between successive re-deployments. We present Jolie Redeployment Optimiser (JRO), a tool for the automatic and optimised deployment of microservices written in the Jolie language [21,30–32]. Jolie is an open-source programming language for developing distributed applications based on microservices which combines computation and composition primitives in an intuitive and concise syntax. In Jolie each component is a (micro)service that can communicate with other components by sending and receiving messages over a network. The behaviour and deployment of a Jolie service are orthogonal: they can be independently defined and recombined as long as they have compatible typing. In order to support concurrency, a service can run multiple instances of its behaviour, called processes. Processes can direct messages to each other by using arbitrary sets of data, a mechanism commonly called message correlation [38] and borrowed from Service-Oriented Architectures. The semantics of processes and correlation in Jolie is formally defined [29] and used in studies aiming at providing formal properties on service systems, such as those based on choreography languages [4,33]. Jolie also includes useful features for the programming of dynamic service systems such as embedding that allows the supervised execution of sub-services inside of other services [28]. Embedding can be used at runtime to enable service mobility and the runtime adaptation of parts of a running process [23].

The Jolie Redeployment Optimiser tool is based on the following three main components:

Zephyrus. [7] A tool that automatically generates, starting from a partial and abstract description of the target application, a fully detailed architecture, indicating which and how many components are needed to realize such application, how to distribute them on virtual machines, and how to bind them together. Zephyrus is also capable of producing *optimal* architectures, minimizing the amount of needed virtual machines while still guaranteeing that each service has its needed share of computing resources (CPU power, memory, bandwidth, etc.) on the machine where it gets deployed.

Jolie Enterprise (JE). A distributed framework for deploying and managing microservices written in the Jolie language. Jolie Enterprise exposes Application Program Interfaces (APIs) (*i*) to access all the data related to the platforms and services running in the managed system, (*ii*) to deploy, start, stop, and remove services, and (*iii*) to monitor their performances and resource consumption.

Jolie Reconfiguration Coordinator (JRC). A tool that, given a desired configuration and a context for the deployment (provided by Jolie Enterprise) interacts with Zephyrus to produce the optimised deployment planning.

We depict in Fig. 1 how JRC, JE, and Zephyrus interact in JRO, starting from a desired configuration and its actual deployment. The sequence of interactions in Fig. 1 can be described as follows.

1. The User defines the requirements of the deployment, e.g., how many instances of a service must be deployed or that some type of services cannot run in the same machine with others.

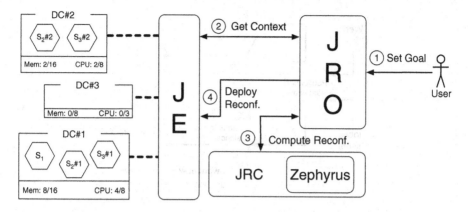

Fig. 1. JRO workflow

2. JRO retrieves from JE the context of the deployment, i.e., the available virtual machines in the system (in the figure $DC\#1$, $DC\#2$, and $DC\#3$).
3. JRO uses JRC which uses Zephyrus to find the optimal solution.
4. If the User agrees with the solution, JRO proceeds with the orchestration of the deployment, instructing JE on how services should be deployed, linked or removed.

To the best of our knowledge JRO is the first tool allowing to optimally deploy a microservice based application.

Structure of the Paper. Section 2 presents a comprehensive, real-world use-case to illustrate how JRO works from the user perspective. In Sect. 3 we describe the details of JRO and its features. Section 4 contains a discussion on related work and our closing remarks.

2   Example

In this section, we show how JRO can be used to deploy a realistic SOA using as a running example a blog microservices architecture [27]. As depicted in Fig. 2, the blog comprises 5 types of microservices for post publication and commenting:

- Auth enables the users of the blog to authenticate themselves;
- Posts allows an *author* to edit a post. Posts needs an instance of Auth to authenticate authors;
- Comments Balancer dispatches the submission of comments from the *readers* to an instance of the Comments service;
- Comments receives the submission of a comment and publishes it. Comments needs an instance of Comments Balancer to receive incoming submissions and an instance of Auth to authenticate the reader who sent the comment;
- Publication Gateway is the service accessed by clients to read the blog. Publication Gateway needs and instance of Auth to let *readers* access the contents of the blog.

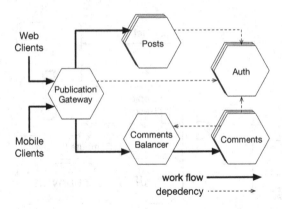

Fig. 2. Blog microservices architecture.

All these services come with some information related to the resources that they require to be installed. In particular, every service specifies how much RAM and processing power it needs, to how many services it can provide its functionalities (Provision) and the number and the type of services it requires to work (Dependencies)[3]. In the table below we summarize this information for the services of the blog.

Service	Mem	CPU	Dependencies	Provision
`Auth`	50	2	-	5
`Posts`	20	1	Auth: 1	1
`Comments Balancer`	50	4	-	∞
`Comments`	30	1	Auth: 1, Comments Balancer: 1	1
`Gateway`	50	4	Auth: 1	∞

Observe that the profiling of `Comments Balancer` and `Gateway` marks a theoretical infinite provision. This is because these services do no intensive computation and they just dispatch requests towards other services. The `Auth` instead can be used by 5 other services instances, whether they may be `Post`, `Comment`, or `Gateway` services.

The usual way of setting up an instance of the blog to satisfy some expected traffic load requires to reserve some virtual machines and deploy a certain number of `Post`, `Comment`, `Comment Balancer`, and `Gateway` services, which in turn need the deployment of several `Auth` services. Besides the deployment, it would be also necessary to connect all the deployed services — e.g., all `Post` services to their correspondent `Auth` services — in such a way that they can sustain the expected load and do not generate bottlenecks.

---

[3] We assume that this information, usually obtained through some profiling of the services, has to be initially entered by the service developer.

With JRO all these concerns are handled automatically and it is guaranteed that the obtained deployment respects the initial desiderata.

For example, let us consider that a DevOps wants to deploy two `Posts` services, two `Comments` services, and a `Gateway`. In JRO she does that by specifying the following string.

```
Post = 2 and Comments = 2 and Gateway = 1
```

These services are usually deployed on a cloud or some (private) cluster of machines. In the context of this work, we use the term of Deployment Containers (DC) to capture the notion of the basic unit where services can be deployed, whether they may be virtual machines, physical machines, or containers a la Docker [13]. A DC is characterised by a cost and some resources that it can provide. For this running example, let us consider the two DCs reported below and characterised by their *Cost*, expressed in dollar/month, *Memory* expressed in MB, and processing power, expressed in processor units (CPU).

DC	Cost	Memory	CPU
Small	4	60	2
Big	6	100	4

When the DevOps enters her desiderata, JRO automatically computes the optimal (i.e., the least expensive) configuration that satisfies her request. In our case, the computed configuration is the one reported in Fig. 3, where a `Gateway` service and a `Comments Balancer` service are deployed in two separated Big DC, two `Comments` services are in a Small DC and the remaining services (one `Auth` and two `Post`) are on another Big DC.

The DevOps obtained a correct configuration but she realises that it is not right for fault tolerance and load balancing reasons. Indeed, deploying on the

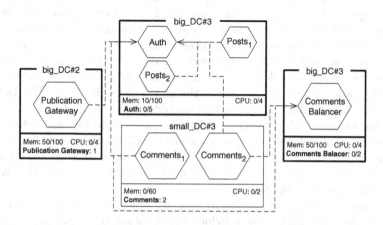

Fig. 3. First configuration.

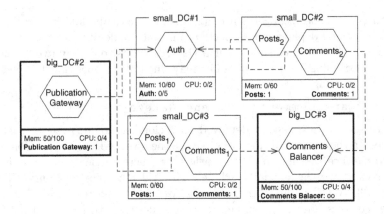

Fig. 4. Fault tolerant configuration.

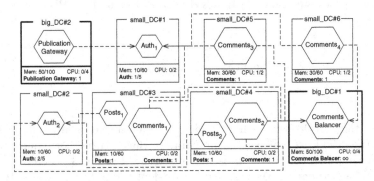

Fig. 5. Configuration with additional 2 Comment service.

same DC respectively two Post services and two Comments services can lead to outages in case of high load or crash of one of the DCs. Hence, the DevOps wants to specify that services of the same kind should be deployed on different machines. With JRO it is also possible to express constraints on the co-location and distribution of services. Let us suppose that DevOps requires that every DC contains at most one Post, one Comments, and one Auth service and that the Auth service cannot be co-located with a Post or Comments service. In this case, the configuration computed by JRO is the one depicted in Fig. 4. The DevOps finally accepts the solution and deploys the obtained configuration.

Let us now make the case that, after some usage, the DevOps notices that many users comment the same post, which overloads the Comments services and slows down the responsiveness of the blog. To cope with the high load on comments, the DevOps wants to re-deploy the architecture of the blog with a total of four Comments services.

JRO makes very easy to specify the re-deployment of an architecture. It is sufficient to modify the previous specification by requiring 4, instead of 2, Comments services. JRO produces the configuration depicted in Fig. 5.

Observe that the increase of 2 `Comments` requires the addition of an additional `Auth` service to handle the increase in authentication requests generated by all the `Comments` services. This is done automatically and the DevOps does not need to handle any dependency between services.

As a final example, let us consider that the profiling of the blog changes. This can be due to a wrong initial profiling or to the introduction of a new version of the services of the blog. In this case, some service of the blog can require more or less resources to work correctly. JRO covers also this case: the DevOps just needs to update the previous profiling and rerun the tool to redistribute the component in the optimal way.

3   JRO

In this section, we detail how JRO works. As previously mentioned, the execution phases of JRO are summarized in Fig. 1. The deployment of a new configuration or the reconfiguration of an existing one is triggered by the user that enters her desiderata. JRO queries the deployment platform (in our case it is JE) to retrieve the current deployed configuration and the list of the services that could be deployed with their resource needs and dependencies. These data are then encoded and submitted to Zephyrus to obtain a tentative final configuration. This configuration is presented to the user, which may accept it or refuse it by entering a different specification. If a configuration is accepted, it is deployed on the target deployment platform by issuing the commands to install and run the services. The user has only to enter her goals and, if desired, perform the optional step of deciding if accepting or not a given configuration.

JRO can be used in an interactive way to refine the configuration until an acceptable one is obtained. To make this process automatic, JRO requires the services to be annotated with their profiling, i.e., that each service is annotated with its resource consumption, its dependencies, and its capabilities. In JRO annotations are written in a JSON file that, by convention, has the same name and is stored on the same location of the Jolie service. For example, the JSON annotation associated to the `Post` service is the following:

```
1  {"cost":
2        { "Memory": 20, "CPU": 1 } ,
3     "dependencies":
4        { "Auth" : 1 }
5  }
```

At Line 2, we specify that the service requires the use of a 1 CPU and 20 MB of memory[4]. At Line 4, we specify that `Post` depends on the functionalities provided by the `Auth` service. Hence, to be properly installed, it needs the location of an existing `Auth` to invoke.

---

[4] This number is given just for illustrative purposes. The real service consumes indeed more resources.

In the annotation, it is also possible to quantify the number of other services that can exploit the functionalities provided be the annotated services. This can be done by means of the `provide` property. For example, the `Auth` service is annotated with {"provide" : 5}, which indicates that every instance of `Auth` can receive invocation from at most 5 different services.

JRO automatically retrieves the information related to the running SOA by exploiting the JE APIs. In particular, it finds what are the Deployment Components (DC) that are running, their resources (e.g., the number of CPUs and the RAM), and the services deployed on of them. Since the available DCs may not be enough to deploy the desired system, it is possible to specify additional resources to use that may be acquired from a cloud provider and their monetary cost.

The list of deployment components is given as a JSON object with two properties: `DC_description`, which describes the different types of deployment components, and `DC_availability`, which specifies the number of available instances for each of these types. A deployment component type is identified by a name, the list of the resources it provides, and a cost that the user has to pay in order to use it. For instance, the following JSON object defines the possibility of using 5 `c3.large` and 3 `c3.xlarge` Amazon AWS instances as deployment components.

```
1   { "DC_description": [
2     { "name" : "c3.large", "cost" : 105,
3       "provide_resources" : {"CPU" : 2, "Memory" : 375} },
4     { "name" : "c3.xlarge", "cost" : 210
5       "provide_resources" : {"CPU" : 4, "Memory" : 750} } ],
6     "DC_availability": {
7       "c3.large" : 5, "c3.xlarge" : 3 } }
```

The `c3.large` AWS machine is identified as a deployment component type that provides 2 CPUs and 3.75 GB of RAM. When used, this type of deployment component costs 105 dollars per month.

As previously mentioned, the DevOps triggers the execution of JRO by entering the specification of the target configuration. The DevOps does not need to design the final configuration and she rather declares some constraints (e.g., number of services she wants to deploy, co-installation or distribution requirements) of the final configuration. All these goals and desiderata are expressed in a domain specific language called *Service Desiderata Language* (SDA). In the remainder of this section, we first detail this language and then describe the integration of Zephyrus via JRC and how the final configuration, if accepted, is actually deployed in JE.

3.1   Service Desiderata Language (SDA)

The Service Desiderata Language (SDA) is an ad-hoc language created to succinctly state the constraints that the final configuration should entail. As shown in Fig. 6, which reports the SDA grammar defined using the ANTLR tool[5], a

---

[5] ANTLR (ANother Tool for Language Recognition) - http://www.antlr.org/.

```
1  spec
2    : expr comparisonOP expr | spec boolOP spec | 'true'
3    | 'not' spec | '(' spec ')' ;
4  expr
5    : 'DC[' resourceFilter '|' simpleExpr ']'
6    | 'DC[' simpleExpr ']'
7    | expr arithmeticOP expr | simpleExpr ;
8  resourceFilter
9    : STRING comparisonOP INT
10   | resourceFilter ';' resourceFilter ;
11 simpleExpr
12   : exprNoDC comparisonOP exprNoDC
13   | simpleExpr boolOP simpleExpr |
14   | 'true' | 'not' spec | '(' spec ')' ;
15 exprNoDC :
16   INT | STRING
17   | exprNoDC arithmeticOP exprNoDC ;
18 comparisonOP : '<=' | '<' | '=' | '>=' | '>' ;
19 arithmeticOP : '+' | '-' | '*' ;
20 boolOP : 'and' | 'or' | 'impl' | 'iff' ;
```

Fig. 6. SDA grammar.

constraint is a specification `spec` of basic constraints `expr comparisonOP expr` (Line 2) combined using the usual logical connectives. These basic constraints specify how many services the user desires to create. An expression `expr` could identify either an integer value or the number of services.

With this expressiveness, it is possible to add constraints that abstract away from the DC. For instance, one might require, as in the running example, the deployment of at least 2 `Post` and 2 `Comments` services as follows.

```
Post >= 2 and Comments >= 2
```

More complex constraints can be stated to restrict the applications installed on the DC. These constraints are expressed (Line 5) with the notation `DC[ resourceFilter | simpleExpr ]` where `resourceFilter` is an optional sequence of constraints on the resources provided by the DC and `simpleExpr` is an expression. `DC[ resourceFilter | simpleExpr ]` denotes the number of deployment components that satisfy the resource constraints of `resourceFilter` and that contain objects satisfying the expression `simpleExpr`. For instance, we can specify that no deployment component having less than 8 CPUs should contain more than one `Post` service as follows.

```
DC[ CPU <= 8 | Post > 1 ] = 0
```

It is also possible to express constraints on co-location or distribution. This is an important feature when dealing with performances — e.g., by co-locating services that frequently interact —, or with security or fault handling — e.g., by keeping some kinds of services separated. As an example, consider the case in Sect. 2 in which we forbid to co-locate the Post and the Comments services on the same DC. Such requirement is easily stated with the following constraint.

```
DC[ Post > 0 and Comments > 0 ] = 0
```

3.2   JRC

When the specification and the information on the running configuration are retrieved, they must be transformed and encoded in order to exploit the engine of the Zephyrus configurator. This task is performed by JRC, which processes the available information to generate the *universe file* of components required by Zephyrus [7]. Services have to be encoded into Aeolus components since Zephyrus requires as input a representation of the components following the Aeolus model specification [8]. In Aeolus, a component is a grey-box showing relevant internal states and the actions that can be acted on the component to change its state during the deployment process. Each state activates "provide" and "require" ports that represent functionalities that the component offers and needs, respectively.

In this context, a service S for JRO can be simply seen as an Aeolus component with two states: an initial state Init representing the fact that S is not yet deployed, and an On state meaning that the service has been deployed. If the service has some initialization parameters (e.g., Post requires a service Auth) these are seen as require ports.

In Aeolus, it is possible to associate numbers to ports to deal with capacity/replication constraints. The number associated to a *require* port indicates the minimal number of distinct components that should provide resources to satisfy the requirement. The number associated to the *provide* port stands instead for the maximal amount of distinct components that can use the provided functionality. In our setting, the number of service dependencies is therefore the number associated to the *require* port. Dually, the number of services that can use the functionalities of a given service is the number associated to the *provide* of its Aeolus representation.

Zephyrus requires as additional input also the specification file containing the encoding of the constraints that should be satisfied in the final configuration following an ad-hoc specification language, and the location file containing the list of the containers to be used to deploy the components. The generation of these files from the available information is quite straightforward since the Zephyrus specification language is more expressive than SDA because, thanks to the chosen encoding, the notion of component and ports in the Aeolus model collapses into the notion of services (i.e., components and ports share the same domain).

When all the input of Zephyrus is generated, JRC runs the configurator. This is the most computational intensive task of the entire process[6]. We use Zephyrus to compute the cheapest solution satisfying the user desiderata.

---

[6] As formalized in [6], the problem solved by Zephyrus is NP-hard.

3.3 Deployment of the Final Configuration

When the configuration is returned and it is accepted by the DevOps, JRO removes the services that are deployed but not present in the final configuration and then starts to deploy the new services on the virtual machines defined in the configuration computed by using Zephyrus.

In the final configuration the dependencies between the components are the connection between the services. Since the services are developed in Jolie, satisfying a dependency can be performed simply by changing the configuration of the output port of the dependent service with the appropriate location and the setting of the protocol needed to reach the required service. Services that do not have dependencies are deployed before those requiring these services. In case of a circular dependency (e.g., service A requires service B that requires A), first JRO deploys the services, then it retrieves their inbound connection data, and finally it dynamically rebinds their output ports.

It is important to notice here that, while in principle any suitable platform could be used for the deployment of service, the use of the Jolie Enterprise framework simplify considerably this task.

Jolie Enterprise is structured on two main nodes: the control panel and the cloud node. The Jolie microservices are deployed and run within cloud nodes, while the control panel offers a set of Web APIs for interacting with the cloud nodes by using operations such as setService, startService, stopService and getServiceList. Operation setService registers a service in the cloud node, startService executes it, stopService stops its current execution, and getServiceList returns the list of all the available services along with its execution status (running, disabled). In our implementation of JRO we have created a service, called ResourceManager, which can call Jolie Enterprise APIs in order to get the current configuration of the system, consisting of active services and inactive services. Such a configuration is then passed to JRC to obtain an output containing the new desired configuration for the system. At this stage, the ResourceManager calls again the Jolie Enterprise APIs in order to deploy and execute the new configuration.

The Jolie Enterprise is a proprietary solution and therefore is not freely available. Nevertheless, JRC, the core part of the JRO, is open-source and available at https://github.com/jolie/jrc. This tool can be used to support other deployment platforms providing the same functionalities of JE. JRC is provided along with the input and configurations for all the outputs of the running scenario in Sect. 2.

4   Related Work and Conclusion

Nowadays, developing applications for the cloud is usually accomplished by relying on the Infrastructure as a Service (IaaS) or the Platform as a Service (PaaS) levels. The IaaS level provides a set of low-level resources forming a "bare" computing environment. Developers pack the whole software stack into virtual machines containing the application and its dependencies and run them on physical machines of the provider's cloud. Exploiting the IaaS directly allows a great flexibility but requires also a great expertise and knowledge of both the cloud infrastructure and the application components involved in the process. The most common solutions for the deployment of a cloud application is still to rely on pre-configured virtual machines (e.g., Bento Boxes [15], Cloud Blueprints [5], and AWS CloudFormation [1]) or to exploit configuration management tools such as Puppet [43] or Chef [40] to better customize the application.

At the PaaS level (e.g., [3,19]) a full development environment is provided. Applications are directly written in a programming language supported by the framework offered by the provider, and then automatically deployed to the cloud. The high-level of automation comes however at the price of flexibility: the choice of the programming language to use is restricted to the ones supported by the PaaS provider, and the application code must conform to specific APIs. Application in PaaSes are usually scalable and can exploit the elasticity of the cloud to accommodate more requests. However, we are not aware of PaaSes that can guarantee the optimal automatic allocation of services allowing the minimization of the cost of the entire application.

In this work, we combine the flexibility typical of the IaaS level with the high-level automation typical of the PaaS level by allowing the DevOps to specify their SOAs and then automatically deploying the specified SOAs, optimising its costs, its performances, and its resource consumption.

The most similar approach to ours is Aeolus Blender [12] from which we draw inspiration. Blender is a software product for the automatic deployment and configuration of complex distributed software systems in the "cloud". It relies on a configuration optimiser (i.e., Zephyrus as also in our case) and an ad-hoc deployment planner [24] to deploy real-life applications on an OpenStack cloud. However, differently from our tool, Blender requires every service lifecycle to be described with the Armonic formalism [25] which essentially uses state machines to represent the different steps that need to be performed to deploy a service. Due to the fact that Jolie services can be easily deployed and do not need complex iteration patterns to be installed, we were able to simplify the entire deployment process requiring to the user to specify just the resource consumption of the services and thus avoiding the use of a planner to compute the sequence of deployment action to perform. Moreover, differently from Blender, JRO can also deal with configurations where services depend on each other.

Another related work is [10] that relies on Zephyrus to allocate objects to deployment containers starting from a program in modelling language ABS (Abstract Behavioural Specification) where classes are annotated to indicate the resource consumption of their objects.

JRO can be easily extended to handle other services or applications written in different languages. Indeed, we only require that the installation of such components does not involve an interaction with other components and that their dependencies could be configured after their installation. In particular, we can capture and deploy SOA relying on stateless services or application following the best practice of the "immutable server" approach [34,35]. In any case, our interest lies in how we can suitably change the configuration of a system. This depends on the property that the system supports reconfiguration, which can be achieved in different ways. In this work, we have used Jolie to support the writing and execution of services. As mentioned in Sect. 1, Jolie services support concurrency by running multiple instances of their behaviour, called processes. Processes in Jolie can be stateful or stateless. In the former case, a popular approach for supporting reconfiguration is using distributed agreement algorithms among the replicated processes [14,22,39]. There are other technologies that we could have combined with JRO, e.g., Erlang [2] or other frameworks based upon the actor model [20]. Both Jolie processes and actors are meant as executable instances of a behaviour, to be run inside of a service. The main differences between the two approaches are in what kind of behaviours can be written and in the primitives for communications, e.g., Jolie processes explicitly specify the data used to identify other processes, whereas actors usually leave this duty to another layer and assume that the other actors can be explicitly found via direct references. These differences are orthogonal w.r.t. our work, which focuses on how to change reconfigurations rather than the details of how processes (or actors) are implemented in services.

Apart from this immediate generalization, we see several other directions for future developments in order to obtain a more inclusive and enhanced tool for the automatic and optimised deployment of micro services. First, the human interface part did not receive the due attention so far. We are therefore planning to construct a suitable GUI which allows one to graphically define the desired specification and its modifications, as in the case of the Blender GUI[7].

On a different level, we plan to integrate in our system an existing monitoring functionality of Jolie Enterprise in order to be able to determine the current load of the system and therefore to be able to automatically balance the load, possibly modifying the configuration, in order to maintain some given service level agreements for the deployed services. Suitable extensions of such a monitoring tool could also be used to combine run time checking with static analysis (e.g., based on types) in order to ensure the correctness of the system, and more generally to verify service level agreements along the lines described in [9,37]. The same techniques can be also exploited to automatize the deployment of system developed by means of choreographic languages [17,41,42].

We would also like to address some of the current limitations of JRO due to the use of the Zephyrus configurator. In particular, we would like to extend Zephyrus in order to be able to find the best deployment configuration given a user-specified maximal cost and a maximal resource consumption. We also intend to add support for annotations with parametric costs that depend on service parameters. Finally, we would also like to tackle the computational aspects involved in the process of finding the optimal configuration allowing the users to exploit heuristics – such as local search techniques – in order to quickly get good but possibly sub-optimal solutions.

---

[7] For some example of GUIs we can adopt within JRO we invite the interested reader to see the screen cast at http://www.aeolus-project.org/.

4.1   A Note on Columbus' Egg

The idea of integrating Zephyrus with Jolie Enterprise to obtain a tool for the automatic and optimised deployment of microservices is a very simple one, yet it can be the basis of a very effective tool which can have a significant impact on real applications.

In this sense, this idea is in line with one of the most distinguishing features of Frank as a researcher: the strive for simplicity, also when working on very complicate subjects. Indeed Frank has often been looking for "Columbus' eggs", sometime he has found them, and once he actually made public this attitude in front of a distinguished audience. Before the anecdote, a note on these "eggs": "A Columbus egg refers to a brilliant idea or discovery that seems simple or easy after the fact. The expression refers to an apocryphal story in which Christopher Columbus, having been told that discovering the Americas was inevitable and no great accomplishment, challenges his critics to make an egg stand on its tip. After his challengers give up, Columbus does it himself by tapping the egg on the table to flatten its tip" (Wikipedia).

So here is the story. In 1997, at the Thirteenth Annual Conference on Mathematical Foundations of Programming Semantics, Frank was presenting a paper co-authored with one of the authors of this paper. That conference was celebrating also the 65th birthday of Dana Scott, so most of the experts on semantics of programming languages were there. While presenting his paper, Frank mentioned the fact that one of the adopted technical solutions was a kind of Columbus' egg. Having seen that some people in the audience had a strange reaction, Frank asked plainly whether they knew the story. Since many people answered "no", Frank spent almost the rest of his time telling the story of Columbus and his famous egg, rather than presenting the paper.

Thank you Frank, and our best wishes for finding many more Columbus' eggs.

References

1. Amazon. AWS CloudFormation. https://aws.amazon.com/cloudformation/. Accessed January 2016
2. Armstrong, J.: Programming Erlang. Pragmatic Bookshelf, Raleigh (2013)
3. Microsoft Azure. https://azure.microsoft.com. Accessed January 2016
4. Carbone, M., Montesi, F.: Deadlock-freedom-by-design: multiparty asynchronous global programming. In: POPL, pp. 263–274. ACM (2013)
5. CenturyLink. Cloud Blueprints. https://www.ctl.io/blueprints/. Accessed January 2016
6. Cosmo, R.D., Lienhardt, M., Mauro, J., Zacchiroli, S., Zavattaro, G., Zwolakowski, J.: Automatic application deployment in the cloud: from practice to theory and back. In: CONCUR. LIPIcs, vol. 42, pp. 1–16. Schloss Dagstuhl - Leibniz-Zentrum fuer Informatik (2015)
7. Cosmo, R.D., Lienhardt, M., Treinen, R., Zacchiroli, S., Zwolakowski, J., Eiche, A., Agahi, A.: Automated synthesis and deployment of cloud applications. In: ASE, pp. 211–222. ACM (2014)

8. Cosmo, R.D., Mauro, J., Zacchiroli, S., Zavattaro, G.: Aeolus: a component model for the cloud. Inf. Comput. **239**, 100–121 (2014)

9. de Boer, F.S., de Gouw, S.: Combining monitoring with run-time assertion checking. In: Bernardo, M., Damiani, F., Hähnle, R., Johnsen, E.B., Schaefer, I. (eds.) SFM 2014. LNCS, vol. 8483, pp. 217–262. Springer, Heidelberg (2014)

10. de Gouw, S., Lienhardt, M., Mauro, J., Nobakht, B., Zavattaro, G.: On the integration of automatic deployment into the ABS modeling language. In: Dustdar, S., Leymann, F., Villari, M. (eds.) ESOCC 2015. LNCS, vol. 9306, pp. 49–64. Springer, Heidelberg (2015)

11. DevOps. http://devops.com/. Accessed January 2016

12. Di Cosmo, R., Eiche, A., Mauro, J., Zavattaro, G., Zacchiroli, S., Zwolakowski, J.: Automatic deployment of services in the cloud with aeolus blender. In: Barros, A., Grigori, D., Narendra, N.C., Dam, H.K. (eds.) ICSOC 2015. LNCS, vol. 9435, pp. 397–411. Springer, Heidelberg (2015)

13. Docker Inc. Docker. https://www.docker.com/. Accessed January 2016

14. Fischer, M.J., Lynch, N.A., Paterson, M.S.: Impossibility of distributed consensus with one faulty process. J. ACM (JACM) **32**(2), 374–382 (1985)

15. Flexiant. Bento Boxes. https://www.flexiant.com/2012/12/03/application-pro visioning/. Accessed January 2016

16. Fowler, M., Lewis, J.: Microservices (2014). http://martinfowler.com/articles/microservices.html. Accessed January 2016

17. Gabbrielli, M., Giallorenzo, S., Montesi, F.: Applied choreographies (2015). CoRR, abs/1510.03637

18. Georgakopoulos, D., Papazoglou, M.P.: Service-Oriented Computing. The MIT Press, Cambridge (2008)

19. Google App Engine. https://cloud.google.com/appengine/docs. Accessed January 2016

20. Hewitt, C., Bishop, P., Steiger, R.: A universal modular ACTOR formalism for artificial intelligence. In: IJCAI, pp. 235–245. William Kaufmann (1973)

21. Jolie.: Programming Language. http://www.jolie-lang.org/. Accessed January 2016

22. Lamport, L.: Paxos made simple. ACM SIGACT News **32**(4), 18–25 (2001)

23. Lanese, I., Bucchiarone, A., Montesi, F.: A framework for rule-based dynamic adaptation. In: Wirsing, M., Hofmann, M., Rauschmayer, A. (eds.) TGC 2010, LNCS, vol. 6084, pp. 284–300. Springer, Heidelberg (2010)

24. Lascu, T.A., Mauro, J., Zavattaro, G.: A planning tool supporting the deployment of cloud applications. In: ICTAI, pp. 213–220. IEEE (2013)

25. Mandriva. Armonic. https://armonic.readthedocs.org/en/latest/index.html. Accessed January 2016

26. Mauro, J., Zavattaro, G.: On the complexity of reconfiguration in systems with legacy components. In: Italiano, G.F., Pighizzini, G., Sannella, D.T. (eds.) MFCS 2015. LNCS, vol. 9234, pp. 382–393. Springer, Heidelberg (2015)

27. Montesi, F.: Hack your way through the microservices revolution. http://www.infoworld.com/article/2903590/application-development/hack-your-way-through-the-microservices-revolution.html. Accessed January 2016

28. Montesi, F.: JOLIE: a Service-oriented Programming Language. Master's thesis, University of Bologna (2010)

29. Montesi, F., Carbone, M.: Programming services with correlation sets. In: Kappel, G., Maamar, Z., Motahari-Nezhad, H.R. (eds.) ICSOC 2011. LNCS, vol. 7084, pp. 125–141. Springer, Heidelberg (2011)

30. Montesi, F., Guidi, C., Lucchi, R., Zavattaro, G.: JOLIE: a java orchestration language interpreter engine. Electr. Notes Theor. Comput. Sci. **181**, 19–33 (2007)
31. Montesi, F., Guidi, C., Zavattaro, G.: Composing services with JOLIE. In: Proceedings of ECOWS, pp. 13–22 (2007)
32. Montesi, F., Guidi, C., Zavattaro, G.: Service-oriented programming with Jolie. In: Bouguettaya, A., Sheng, Q.Z., Daniel, F. (eds.) Web Services Foundations, pp. 81–107. Springer, New York (2014)
33. Montesi, F., Yoshida, N.: Compositional choreographies. In: D'Argenio, P.R., Melgratti, H. (eds.) CONCUR 2013 – Concurrency Theory. LNCS, vol. 8052, pp. 425–439. Springer, Heidelberg (2013)
34. Morris, K.: Immutableserver (2013). http://martinfowler.com/bliki/Immutable Server.html. Accessed January 2016
35. Netflix. Building with legos (2011). http://techblog.netflix.com/2011/08/building-with-legos.html. Accessed January 2016
36. Nginx. Adopting microservices at netflix: Lessons for architectural design (2015). https://www.nginx.com/blog/microservices-at-netflix-architectural-best-practices/. Accessed January 2016
37. Nobakht, B., de Gouw, S., de Boer, F.S.: Formal verification of service level agreements through distributed monitoring. In: Dustdar, S., Leymann, F., Villari, M. (eds.) ESOCC 2015. LNCS, vol. 9306, pp. 125–140. Springer, heidelberg (2015)
38. Oasis, B.: Web services business process execution language (2007). http://docs.oasis-open.org/wsbpel/2.0/wsbpel-v2.0.html
39. Ongaro, D., Ousterhout, J.: In search of an understandable consensus algorithm. In: USENIX, pp. 305–320 (2014)
40. Opscode. Chef. http://www.opscode.com/chef/. Accessed January 2016
41. Preda, M.D., Gabbrielli, M., Giallorenzo, S., Lanese, I., Mauro, J.: Dynamic choreographies - safe runtime updates of distributed applications. In: Holvoet, T., Viroli, M. (eds.) COORDINATION. LNCS, vol. 9037, pp. 67–82. Springer, Heidelberg (2015)
42. Preda, M.D., Giallorenzo, S., Lanese, I., Mauro, J., Gabbrielli, M.: AIOCJ: a choreographic framework for safe adaptive distributed applications. In: Combemale, B., Pearce, D.J., Barais, O., Vinju, J.J. (eds.) SLE 2014. LNCS, vol. 8706, pp. 161–170. Springer, Heidelberg (2014)
43. Puppetlabs. Puppet. http://puppetlabs.com/. Accessed January 2016

Statically and Dynamically
Verifiable SLA Metrics

Elena Giachino[1]([⊠]), Stijn de Gouw[2], Cosimo Laneve[1], and Behrooz Nobakht[2]

[1] Department of Computer Science and Engineering,
University of Bologna – INRIA Focus, Bologna, Italy
{elena.giachino,cosimo.laneve}@unibo.it
[2] SDL Fredhopper, Amsterdam, The Netherlands
{sgouw,bnobakht}@sdl.com

Abstract. There is a gap between run-time service behaviours and the contracted quality expectations with the customers that is due to the informal nature of service level agreements. We explain how to bridge the gap by formalizing service level agreements with metric functions. We therefore discuss an end-to-end analysis flow that can either *statically* verify if a service code complies with a metric function or use *run-time* monitoring systems to report possible misbehaviours. In both cases, our approach provides a feedback loop to fix and improve the metrics and eventually the resource configurations of the service itself.

1 Introduction

In Cloud Services and in Web Services, in general, resource provisioning is defined by means of legal contracts agreed upon by service providers and customers, called *service level agreements* – SLA. Legal contracts usually include measurement methods and scales that are used to set the boundaries and margins of errors that apply to the behaviour of the service, as well as the legal requirements under different jurisdictions. The SLA documents have no standardized format nor terminology, and do not abide by any precise definition, notwithstanding some recent attempts towards standardization – see [2] and the references therein.

Because of this informal nature, there is a significant gap between SLAs and the corresponding services whose quality levels they constrain. As a consequence, SLAs are currently not integrated in the software artefacts, and assessing whether a service complies with an SLA or not is always a point of concern. As a consequence, providers, in order to avoid legal disputes, very often over-provide resources to services with the result of wasting resources and making services more expensive.

This paper presents the approach taken in the EU Project Envisage [2] where the gap between (parts of) SLAs and services is bridged by (*i*) using simple

This paper is funded by the EU project FP7-610582 ENVISAGE: Engineering Virtualized Services, http://www.envisage-project.eu.

© Springer International Publishing Switzerland 2016
E. Ábrahám et al. (Eds.): de Boer Festschrift, LNCS 9660, pp. 211–225, 2016.
DOI: 10.1007/978-3-319-30734-3_15

formal descriptions of SLAs in terms of *metric functions* and by (*ii*) defining a mathematical framework that is able either to derive the SLA quality levels from the service programs and to verify possible violations or to monitor service behaviours and document SLA quality levels mismatches.

Among the properties whose qualities are constrained by SLA documents [11], we focus in Sect. 2 on *performance* by analyzing the objectives that set the boundaries and margins of errors of service's behaviours. In Sect. 3, these objectives are formalized in terms of metric functions. Having at hand these functions, we address the problem to verify whether a given service complies with them or not. Two techniques are discussed in this paper for verifying performance properties of services: the *static-time* techniques and the *run-time* ones.

In static-time techniques, the compliance of a service with respect to a metric function is shown by means of analysis tools that either directly verify the code (static analysis), or an underlying mathematical model (model checking, simulation, etc.). Whenever the service does not comply with the metric function, the designer triggers a sequence of code refinements that lead to compliance. As an example, consider *resource capacity* that measures how much a critical resource is used by a service. Section 4 reports a static analysis technique that uses so-called behavioural types. These behavioural types are abstract descriptions of programs that support compositional reasoning and that retain the necessary information to derive resource usage. By means of behavioral types, we use either a cost equation evaluator – the solver systems [1, 7] – or a theorem prover – the KeY system [3] – to prove compliance with the SLA. For instance, we demonstrate that the response time of a given method does not exceed a certain user-defined threshold.

In run-time techniques, the enforcement of properties is accomplished by using code that is external to the service and that continuously monitors it. In facts, there are (performance) metric functions that cannot be (even in principle) fully verified statically, due to factors under external control, such as the requests per minute by end users and failing machines in the underlying infrastructure. As an example, consider the percentage of successful requests, namely the number of requests processed by the service without a failure due to its infrastructure over the total number of received requests. In Sect. 5, we report a technique that uses an external monitoring system filtering service's replies, counts them, and records the erroneous ones. The correctness of the composite system consisting of the service and monitoring code is established by means of either static analysis techniques or model checking.

Figure 1 describes the flow of analysis techniques used in our approach. A *feedback loop* ensures corrections and improvements to the system. In particular, if the static analysis reports that a service does not match an SLA constraint, then, during the negotiation phase that constraint can be either relaxed or the resource configuration can be extended accordingly (with a possible charge for the client). Similarly, if a monitoring system verifies a run-time violation of an SLA constraint then, in order to avoid expensive penalties, the service providers trigger the resource configuration system to increase service's resources.

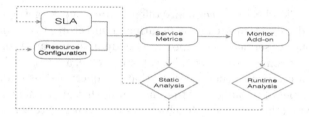

Fig. 1. Analysis Flow: *Resource Configuration* refers to the configuration of resource types that are used for the service; *Service Metrics* denotes the set of metrics that define the quality of the service. The *dashed* lines present a feedback loop to a previous phase of analysis.

In Sect. 6 we discuss the issue of SLA metrics that have conflicting requirements. In this case, it is necessary to determine an upper bound in time for reaching a stable resource configuration. We also discuss complex metrics that actually are compositions of basic metrics discussed in Sect. 3. We report our analysis of related works and conclude in Sect. 7.

2   SLAs and Performance Properties

In the "Cloud Service Level Agreement Standardisation Guidelines" document [11], the qualities of services are assessed with SLAs according to the properties they have, which range from performance to security and to data management. In this paper, we will focus on *performance*. We discuss how it can be formalized and evaluated on source code of services.

The article [11] distinguishes three kinds of performance properties: *availability, response time*, and *capacity*. Availability is the property of a service to be accessible and usable on demand. By detailing the notion of "usability", one gets different instances of availability and corresponding service metrics. For instance (*i*) *level of uptime*, is the time in a defined period the service is up, over the total possible available time; (*ii*) *percentage of successful requests*, is the number of requests processed without an error over the total number of submitted requests; (*iii*) *percentage of timely service provisioning requests*, is the number of service provisioning requests completed within a defined time period over the total number of service provisioning requests. Response time is the time period between a client request event and a service response event. The service metrics that are used to constrain response time may return either an *average time* or a *maximum time*, given a particular form of request. Capacity is the maximum amount of some resource used by a service. It also includes the service throughput metric, namely the minimum number of requests that can be processed by a service in a stated time period.

The example below discusses an industrial e-commerce use case and its corresponding SLA constraints about performance. The next section formalises the involved metrics and we show how to verify/enforce them in the rest of the paper.

Example 1. A Cloud Service company offers search and targeting facilities on large product databases over cloud computing architectures to e-commerce companies. The offered services are exposed at endpoints and are typically implemented to accept connections over HTTP. For example, a *query API* allows users to query over a product catalog. Assume that the query API is implemented by means of a number of resources (virtual machines) that are managed in a mutual exclusive way by a load balancer (each resource is launched to serve *exactly one* instance of the query API). When an e-commerce company signs the SLA contract with the Cloud Service company, the performance properties of the query API are constrained by the following metrics:

- *95 % of requests is completed within 1 min, 2 % within 3 min and 1 % within 5 min.* This is the "percentage of timely service provisioning requests" metric and it is used by the operations team of the Cloud Service company to set up an environment for the customer that includes the necessary resources to match the constraints. It is additionally used by the support team of the Cloud Service company to manage communications with the customer during the lifetime of the service for the customer.
- *the service completes 8 queries per minute from 9:00 to 18:00 and 4 queries per minute otherwise.* This is a service throughput metric and forms the basis of many decisions (technical or legal) thereafter, such as the definition of the necessary resources for the e-commerce company.
- *the service replies to a query request (with the result or with a failure) within 7 min.* This is a response time metric and may be determined by the size of database as well as by the size of the data managed by the query service (whenever the service accepts queries that are unbounded).

3   Metrics' Formalization

To determine the precise level of a metric, and verify whether the service matches the agreed levels, an indisputable formalisation is needed, rather than the informal descriptions in the previous section. There have been several attempts to formalize SLAs, using techniques ranging from semantic annotations [17], to rewriting logics [19] and to constraint programming [5]. In this paper, following [18], we use a very simple formalization based on *service metric functions*.

Service metric functions aggregate a set of basic measurements into a single number that indicates the quality of a certain service characteristic. For instance $\mu(\tau)$ and $\nu(\tau, \delta)$ are two functions that respectively take one and two inputs, where

- τ is an interval of the form $[\mathsf{d}.t, \mathsf{d}'.t']$, where d, d' are days ($\mathsf{d}, \mathsf{d}' \in \{1, \cdots, 366\}$) and t, t' are seconds in the day ($t, t' \in \{0, \cdots, 86399\}$);
- δ can be an upper bound to the size in bytes of client's requests, a time bound for getting a reply, or an upper bound to the number of resources used by the service.

To illustrate how performance metrics that are informally defined in SLA documents can be formalized, we further elaborate Example 1. In particular,

- the percentage of timely service provisioning requests of a service s can be formalized by the following function PTS_s:

$$\text{PTS}_s([1.0,\ 366.86399], x) = \begin{cases} 0,95 & \text{if } x = 60s \\ 0,97 & \text{if } x = 180s \\ 0,98 & \text{if } x = 300s \end{cases}$$

- the service throughput of a service s can be formalized by the function ST_s as follows:

$$\text{ST}_s([1.t,\ 366.t'], 60) = \begin{cases} 4 & \text{if } t = 0 \text{ and } t' = 32399 \\ 8 & \text{if } t = 32400 \text{ and } t' = 64800 \\ 4 & \text{if } t = 64801 \text{ and } t' = 86399 \end{cases}$$

- the response time of a service s can be defined by the following function RT_s:

$$\text{RT}_s([1.0,\ 366.86399]) = 420s$$

4 Static-Time Analysis

Several static-time analysis techniques are possible to verify service properties and, in particular, service metrics like response time. In this section we discuss two approaches we use in the Envisage Project and we apply them to the response time metric of Example 1. We refer to [8,10] for further details on the technique described in Sect. 4.1. We refer to [3,6] for details on the technique discussed in Sect. 4.3.

4.1 Behavioural Types

Behavioural types are abstract descriptions of programs that highlight the relevant informations to derive a particular property. This derivation usually consists of three steps:

1. an inference system parses the service program and returns a behavioural type;
2. the behavioural types are translated into low-level descriptions that are adequate for a solver;
3. the low-level descriptions are fed to a solver which produces the output.

It turns out that behavioural types support compositional reasoning and are therefore adequate for SLA compliance, while low-level descriptions are not compositional (and too intensional).

In the case of response time analysis, the behavioural types carry informations about costs of operations that are extracted directly from the source program. This means that the source program retains either resource-consumption annotations or resource-aware commands. The following code snippets use

```
String searchDB(String s) {          class DataBase {
  String u, v ;                          String query(String s) {
  u = DB.query(s) ;                        String z = this.elaborate(s);
  job(h) ;                                 String value = this.search(z);
  v = this.add_info(u) ;                   job(k) ;
  return v; }                              return value; }
                                       ... }
```

Fig. 2. The service `searchDB` performing a query on a database.

explicit primitives for expressing the consumption of resources; in particular, the statement `job(e)` specifies a requirement of `e` CPU resources and is instrumental for modeling the time: depending on the available resources its execution might take an observable amount of time proportional to its cost. For instance, the execution of `job(6)` when only 3 CPU resources are available will be executed within $6/3=2$ units of time.

We illustrate our technique with two examples derived from Example 1. We assume a simple setting where every instance runs in the same machine with a fixed *capacity* of c CPU resources.

Consider the service that performs a query on a database, in Fig. 2. The method `searchDB` sends a given query to the database and, when the result of the query is returned, it enhances the result with some information before returning it to the client. The `job(h)` statement specifies that the local operations of `searchDB` require h CPU resources. The `query` method, which is implemented in a different class `DataBase`, receives a query, evaluates it, searches the corresponding item in the database, and returns the result. The overall cost for these operations is k CPU resources, as specified by `job(k)`. In this example we assume the methods `elaborate` and `search` contain no `job` statements, thus they do not require any resources. Their resource requirements are part of the k resources declared for the `query` method.

An informal argument gives `(k+h)/c` as the total time required by `searchDB` to reply to a query, where c are the available CPU resources. This means that if we have a *ResponseTime* requirement of completing this method within a specific number of time units, then we are able to establish the minimum CPU resources of a configuration that complies with the SLA.

To formalise the above argument, we extract the program features that are relevant for the time analysis. The resulting descriptions are called *behavioral types* and primarily highlight cost annotations and method invocations. For example, the behavioural types of the above methods are

```
Service.searchDB(a[x], b[y]) { DataBase.query(b[y]) § h/x
} : _

Service.addinfo(a[x]) {0} : _

DataBase.query(a[x]) {
  DataBase.elaborate(a[x]) § DataBase.search(a[x])
  § k/x } : _

DataBase.elaborate(a[x]) {0} : _

DataBase.search(a[x]) {0} : _
```

where

- the parameter a[x] binds the this object identity to a and the available capacity to x; similarly, b[y] binds the object identity of the receiver of the query invocation to b and its allocated capacity to y;
- the cost h/x is due to the amount of CPU requested by job(h) and the available CPU resources x (similarly for k/x);
- the term _ is the time information corresponding to the returned value, which is in this case empty;
- the term 0 is the empty behaviour, meaning that no time units are consumed.

With the behavioural type specifications at hand, we use two techniques for deriving services' properties: one is completely automatic and uses solvers of cost equations, and another is semi-automatic (but more precise) and uses theorem provers. We discuss them in detail in the following two subsections.

4.2   The Cost Equation Solver

To evaluate behavioural types specifications, we translate them into so-called *cost equations*, which are suitable for solvers available in the literature [1,7]. These cost equations are terms

$$m(\overline{x}) = exp \quad [se]$$

where m is a (cost) function symbol, exp is an expression that may contain (cost) function symbols applications. In some cases, more than one equation may be defined for the same function symbol: for instance the if-then-else statement has one equation for each branch. In this case, se is an expression representing the conditions under which the corresponding cost must be taken into account.

Basically, we translate behavioural types of methods into cost equations, where (i) method invocations are translated into function applications, and (ii) cost expressions occurring in the types are left unmodified. For example, the translations of the foregoing methods are:

```
searchDB(x,y) = query(y) + h/x + addinfo(x)
query(x) = elaborate(x) + search(x) + k/x
addinfo(x) = elaborate(x) = search(x ) = 0
```

It is worth to observe that, in this case, being $x = y = $c, the solver returns (h+k)/c, as we anticipated previously.

Let us consider a variation of this example, where the service and the database run on different machines. In this case the configuration will include at least two different machines, let us call them m_s and m_d with respectively c_s and c_d allocated CPU resources. At the time of the creation of the service instance we can specify on which machine it will be deployed, by using a statement of the form:

```
Service service = new Service in ms;
```

Analogously, for the database we have

```
Database database = new Database in m_d ;
```

In this setting, all invocations on external machines are to be considered asynchronous, where the caller and the callee execute simultaneously, and the synchronization occurs when the caller attempt to access the result of the invocation. The snippet of the method searchDB is therefore refined into the following code where the asynchronous invocation is noted with "!" instead of "." and Fut<String> is the type of a future String value.

```
String searchDB(String s) {
    String u, v ; Fut<String> w ;
    w = DB!query(s) ;
    job(h) ;
    u = w.get ;
    v = this.add_info(u) ;
    return(v);
}
```

The operation w.get explicitly synchronizes the caller with the callee. In this case, the cost equations of the above methods are

$$searchDB(x,y) = max(query(y) \ , \ h/x) + addinfo(x)$$
$$query(x) = elaborate(x) + search(x) + k/x$$
$$addinfo(x) = elaborate(x) = search(x \ ) = 0$$

Being $x = c_s$ and $y = c_d$, the solver returns the total cost of $max(h/c_s, k/c_d)$.

4.3   The KeY System

There are cases where the cost equations solver either fails to deliver a result or the result is so over-approximated that it becomes unusable. In particular, the cost equations $m(\overline{x}) = exp \ [se]$ that the solver takes as inputs are constrained by the fact that se is a boolean expression in a decidable fragment of Peano arithmetic – *presburger arithmetic* which admits only addition and multiplication by integer constants. Therefore, whenever behavioural types use expressions that are not written in presburger arithmetics, we extend them by manually adding preconditions and in the postconditions specifying costs and metrics.

We use a semi-interactive theorem prover called KeY [6], which uses symbolic execution to analyze programs. Properties are specified in KeY using *dynamic logic* [20] and are demonstrated using the *sequent calculus* [9]. It turns out that most proof steps (usually more than 99 %) are automatically applied by the proof search strategies. Behavioral types plus KeY verification support a compositional analysis: each type can be analyzed in isolation, on the basis of its own definition and only the contracts of the other methods – without knowledge of the underlying definition of the other behavioral types. This is not the case of cost equations that, once produced, are a monolithic, global specification.

KeY can be leveraged by following the steps below:

1. replace the cost expression c in method bodies by an assignment time = time+c;;
2. add method contracts, specifying in the postcondition of each method the expected response time using the variable time and the capacities of machines;

3. prove the resulting instrumented program with KeY.

Applying these steps yields the following annotated behavioral types:

```
//@ ensures time == \old(time) + k/y + h/x;
Service.searchDB(a[x], b[y]) {
      DataBase.query(b[y]) ⸴ time = time + h/x
      } : _

//@ ensures time == \old(time);
Service.addinfo(a[x]) {0} : _

//@ ensures time == \old(time) + k/x;
DataBase.query(a[x]) {
      DataBase.elaborate(a[x]);
      DataBase.search(a[x]) ⸴ time = time + k/x
      } : _

//@ ensures time == \old(time);
DataBase.elaborate(a[x]) {0} : _

//@ ensures time == \old(time);
DataBase.search(a[x]) {0} : _
```

For parallel programs with asynchronously executing threads, the above instrumentation might overestimate the actual time and cost consumed: it always sums the cost of tasks. In these cases, the behavioural type is x.m() ||| y.n(), rather than x.m(); y.n() (the operation "|||" represents parallel composition). KeY derives the cost of x.m() ||| y.n() by taking the maximum of the costs of x.m() and of y.n().

A useful task that KeY supports is the formal proof that response times of a method are under a defined threshold. This is achieved by the same instrumentation discussed above. The only change needed is in the behavioural types of methods: one can adjust the postcondition with an assertion of the form time < d, where d is a symbolic threshold. This is shown in the contract below.

```
//@ ensures time time < d;
Service.searchDB(a[x], b[y]) {
      ...
      }
```

5   Run-Time Analysis

In order to enforce service metrics that cannot be verified statically (because of factors under external control, such as the underlying infrastructure) we use code external to the service that continuously monitors it. We discuss this technique using two service metrics of Example 1: the percentage of timely service provisioning requests and the service throughput.

A simple implementation of the function PTS_s defined in Sect. 3 uses a monitoring method that intercepts all the HTTP invocations to a service and their corresponding replies. This allows the monitor to record the time taken by every request to be completed. Consider the following pseudo-code for this method

```
void monitor_service_time() {
   (service,method,msg,client,m_id) = HttpRequest.intercept();
   time_start = time();
   reply = service.method(msg);
   time_end = time();
   HttpResponse.send(client,reply,m_id);
   log(m_id,time_start,time_end);
}
```

The method **percentage** takes as input a time window and returns **true** if the percentage of requests complies with the definition of PTS_s, is implemented by the monitor:

```
boolean percentage(Time t_begin, Time t_end){
   boolean v = true ;

   /* retrieve from the log the total number of messages
      served in the time window */
   nmb_msg = get_total_messages(t_begin, t_end) ;

   /* check whether the SLA percentages of served requests
      correspond to the observed ones */
   nmb_msg_completed = find(t_begin, t_end, 60) ;
   v = v && (nmb_msg_completed/nmb_msg <= 0.95) ;   //95% in 1 min
   nmb_msg_completed = find(t_begin, t_end, 180) ;
   v = v && (nmb_msg_completed/nmb_msg <= 0.97) ;   //97% in 3 mins
   nmb_msg_completed = find(t_begin, t_end, 300) ;
   v = v && (nmb_msg_completed/nmb_msg <= 0.98) ;   //98% in 5 mins

   return v;
}
```

Similarly, the monitor implementing the service metric ST_s in Sect. 3 is the method:

```
boolean throughput(Log_file d, Time t_begin, Time t_end){
   int daily = 0;
   int nightly = 0;

   /* collects the number of the served requests during the two
      specified time-frames */
   for each (m_id, time_init, time_end) in d {
      if ((time_init >= 32400) && (time_init <= 64800))  // 9:00-18:00
            daily = daily + 1 ;
      else nightly = nightly + 1 ;
   }
   /* return true if 8 queries per minute are completed in 9:00-18:00
      and 4 queries per minute in the remaining time */

   return ( ((daily/60*9)>8) && ((nightly/60*15)>4) );
}
```

The above straightforward development of monitoring systems allows service providers to report violations of the agreed SLA. However, the ultimate goal for a provider is to *maintain* the resource configuration in such a way that SLA violations remain under a given threshold while minimizing the cost of the system. The first objective can be achieved by adding resources to the service (for instance, adding more CPUs).

To this aim, the monitoring platform works in two cyclic phases: *observation* and *reaction*. The observation phase takes measurements on services – the foregoing methods **percentage** and **throughput**. Subsequently, if an SLA mismatch is observed, in the reaction phase, the number of allocated resources are increased. The monitoring platform developed in the Envisage Project also allows to *decrease* the number of resources if it is too costly/high [18]. The following `reaction` method verifies every 300 s whether the percentage of timely service provisioning requests is reached and, in case of failures, adds one more CPU:

```
void reaction(Service s) {
   Time t ; Bool v ;
   t = time() ;
   idle(300) ;
   v = percentage(d,t, t+300) ;
   if (!v) MonitoringPlatform ! allocate(s) ;
}
```

Correctness of the monitoring framework (i.e. that the monitors converge within a user-given time towards the service level objectives specified in an SLA) was investigated in [18]. The idea is to translate the code for the program *including the monitoring code* into timed automata for use with UPPAAL [4]. The service level constraints from SLAs are translated into deadlines for the automata. The translation can be done automatically, along the lines of [12]. It is then possible to prove that, if all timed automata are schedulable (no missed deadline), then the SLA of the service is satisfied in the given timeframe.

6 Further Aspects of Metrics' Definition and Verification

In the previous sections we have discussed basic service metrics used in SLA documents. In this section we address two additional issues: (i) metrics may be conflicting: one metric requires an increase of resources allocated to a service, while another one requires a decrease of the same resources, and (ii) particular services may require complex service metrics.

Conflicting Metrics. Consider the following SLA constraints for the first example of Sect. 4.1:

$$\text{ST}_{\text{searchDB}}([1.t, \ 366.t'], 60) \ = \ \begin{cases} 4 & \text{if } t = 0 \text{ and } t' = 32399 \\ 8 & \text{if } t = 32400 \text{ and } t' = 64800 \\ 4 & \text{if } t = 64801 \text{ and } t' = 86399 \end{cases}$$

$$\text{RT}_{\text{searchDB}}([1.0, \ 366.86399]) \ = \ 420s$$

The analysis of Sect. 4.2 gave an upper bound for `searchDB` response time of `(k+h)/c` time units. Letting the available amount of CPU resources be 2 and k=5 and h=15, then we have a response time of 10 s. This satisfies the RT_s metrics, since it is well below the maximum response time imposed by the SLA. Therefore the initial configuration of 2 CPU resources is found to be well suited for assuring the required QoS. Notice that, considering the time for executing a single request of `searchDB`, we can deduce that the $\text{ST}_{\text{searchDB}}$ value is indeed reasonable. In addition, assume that `monitor_service_time`, which observes the execution of the service, has not logged any entry where `time_end-time_begin` is greater then 420 s – i.e. the response time is still matched.

However, the launch of the **throughput** monitor reports that only 4 requests are served per minute, which violates the SLA (requiring to serve 8 requests per minute during the day) because of latency problems for scheduling the requests or for connecting to the database. Henceforth, the **reaction** method requests to the monitoring platform and obtains a machine with 2 additional CPU resources. The service is moved on the new machine and the **throughput** monitor doesn't find any violation anymore. However, during the night, half of the resources would have been sufficient for meeting the SLA requirement (which is only 4 requests per minute during the night). The customer is paying for unnecessary resources.

To overcome such issues, we consider an additional metric defining the *budget* for the service with respect to particular time windows:

$$\text{Budget}_{\texttt{searchDB}}([1.t,\ 366.t']) = \begin{cases} 40 & \text{if } t = 0 \text{ and } t' = 32399 \\ 80 & \text{if } t = 32400 \text{ and } t' = 64800 \\ 40 & \text{if } t = 64801 \text{ and } t' = 86399 \end{cases}$$

Namely, $\text{Budget}_{\texttt{searchDB}}$ specifies that, during the day, the customer is willing to pay up to 80, while only half for the night.

The techniques discussed in Sect. 4 may verify whether a service complies with $\text{Budget}_{\texttt{searchDB}}$ or not. In particular, an adequate budget is the cost of the minimum number of resources the program needs to execute, which is the cost of an upper bound of resources needed by the program. Taking CPUs as relevant resources and assuming that each CPU resource costs 10, then the analysis will approve $\text{Budget}_{\texttt{searchDB}}$, since the allocated money is enough to pay for 8 resources during the day and 4 during the night. However, a run-time CPU reallocation has been triggered by the **throughput** monitor. It turns out that the budget compliance is not met anymore because the expenses for the resource usage double the nightly budget. In this case, the **budget_monitor** reacts by requiring a deallocation of half of the CPU units during the night.

It is worth to notice that the allocations and deallocations required by a monitoring system may lead to a cyclic behaviour that does not reach any stable point. Therefore, in order to enforce stability, we also consider the notion of *service guarantee time*, namely the total amount of time from the start of the monitoring platform that a service is expected to meet its expectations of the SLA. In facts, we use the following refined version of **reaction** method of Sect. 5:

```
void reaction(Service s) {
    Time t ; Bool v ;
    t = time() ; idle(300) ;
    v = percentage(d, t, t+300) ;
    if (!v) {
            if (t > global_time_start + t_G) { // SLA is violated
                    notify(s, ''SLA violation'') ;
            } else MonitoringPlatform.allocate(s) ;
    }
}
```

Composite Metrics. SLA documents may contain (performance) metrics that are not directly defined in terms of those in Sect. 3 but are a composition of them. We discuss an example.

Example 2. A mobile search app provides mobile offline search by means of on-device search indices that are built and distributed by a cloud service. A primary motivations for mobile offline search, besides increasing search availability and strengthen user privacy, is to reduce search latency by using consistently fast on-device storage rather than accessing mobile and Wi-Fi network with highly variable latency. As a consequence, the most relevant aspect for evaluating the quality of the provided service is the *freshness of index data on the mobile device*. This property specifies time-related guarantees about the interval between the publication of a document in the cloud and its indexing and availability on the mobile device.

The metric freshness of index data on the mobile device, noted FID, actually is the sum of the response time RT_s and the delivery time DT_s, namely the time to transfer the data to the devices. This last metric DT_s depends on the data size of the response and the available bandwidth. While the data size δ is a parameter, the *bandwidth* metric $B(\tau)$ is another basic *capacity* metric (which has not been discussed in Sect. 3). $B(\tau)$ is expressed in Mb/s and defines the minimum amount of bandwidth required by the service in a particular time frame. It turns out that $DT_s(\tau, \delta) = \delta / B(\tau)$ and, therefore, we may define

$$FID(\tau, \delta) = DT_s(\tau, \delta) + RT_s(\tau, \delta).$$

7 Conclusions and Related Works

The methodology we have presented in this paper is being devised in the context of the EU Project Envisage [2]. The aim of the project is to develop a semantic foundation for virtualization and SLA that makes it possible to efficiently develop SLA-aware and scalable services, supported by highly automated analysis tools using formal methods. SLA-aware services are able to control their own resource management and renegotiate SLA across the heterogeneous virtualized computing landscape. The two examples we analyze in this contribution are taken from industrial case studies in the aforementioned project: the service described in Example 1 is an actual service provided by Fredhopper Cloud Services[1]. The mobile app presented in Example 2 is the Memkite app by Atbrox[2].

In the Envisage Project we also use other techniques for analyzing services, such as simulations and test generation covering critical scenarios. We intend to investigate if these additional techniques can be used for SLA compliance (and to what extent). For example, if they can provide augmented precision or more detailed descriptions of misbehaviours.

Related Work. Several proposals define a language or a framework to formalize SLAs. However, there is no study how such SLAs can be used to verify or monitor the service and upgrade it as necessary. In this respect, up-to our knowledge, our technique that uses both static time analysis and run-time analysis is original.

---

[1] http://www.sdl.com/products/fredhopper/.

[2] http://atbrox.com/.

As regards SLA formalizations, we recall few recent efforts. WSLA [14] introduces a framework that defines SLAs in a technical way and breaks down customer agreements in terms to be monitored. SLAng [15] introduces a language for defining metrics that deal with the *problems of networks* and studies a technique to ensure the corresponding service qualities. SLA* [13] introduces a generic language to specify SLAs with a fine-grained level of detail. In [16], a method is proposed to translate the SLA specification into an operational monitoring specification. This technique is being used by the EU Project SLA@SOI.

References

1. Albert, E., Arenas, P., Flores-Montoya, A., Genaim, S., Gómez-Zamalloa, M., Martin-Martin, E., Puebla, G., Román-Díez, G.: SACO: static analyzer for concurrent objects. In: Ábrahám, E., Havelund, K. (eds.) TACAS 2014 (ETAPS). LNCS, vol. 8413, pp. 562–567. Springer, Heidelberg (2014)
2. Albert, E., de Boer, F., Hähnle, R., Johnsen, E.B., Laneve, C.: Engineering virtualized services. In: Ali Babar, M., Dumas, M. (eds.) Proceedings of NordiCloud 2013, pp. 59–63. ACM Press (2013)
3. Beckert, B., Hähnle, R., Schmitt, P.H. (eds.): Verification of Object-Oriented Software. LNCS (LNAI), vol. 4334. Springer, Heidelberg (2007)
4. Behrmann, G., David, A., Larsen, K.G.: A tutorial on Uppaal. In: Bernardo, M., Corradini, F. (eds.) Formal Methods for the Design of Real-Time Systems, pp. 200–236. Springer, Heidelberg (2004)
5. Maria Grazia Buscemi and Ugo Montanari: Qos negotiation in service composition. J. Log. Algebr. Program. **80**(1), 13–24 (2011)
6. Din, C.C., Bubel, R., Hähnle, R.: A deductive verification tool for the concurrent modelling language ABS. In: Felty, A.P., Middeldorp, A. (eds.) Automated Deduction - CADE-25. LNCS, vol. 9195, pp. 517–526. Springer, Switzerland (2015)
7. Flores-Montoya, A., Hähnle, R.: Resource analysis of complex programs with cost equations. In: Garrigue, J. (ed.) APLAS 2014. LNCS, vol. 8858, pp. 275–295. Springer, Heidelberg (2014)
8. Garcia, A., Laneve, C., Lienhardt, M.: Static analysis of cloud elasticity. In: Proceedings of the 17th International Symposium on Principles and Practice of Declarative Programming, Siena, Italy, 14–16 July 2015, pp. 125–136. ACM (2015)
9. Gentzen, G.: Untersuchungen ber das logische schlieen. i. Math. Z. **39**(1), 176–210 (1935)
10. Giachino, E., Johnsen, E.B., Laneve, C., Pun, K.I.: Time complexity of concurrent programs. In: Proceedings of FACS 2015 (2015, to appear)
11. Cloud Select Industry Group: Cloud service level agreement standardisation guidelines. Developed as part of the Commissions European Cloud Strategy, June 2014. http://ec.europa.eu/information_society/newsroom/cf/dae/document. cfm?action=display&doc_id=6138
12. Jaghoori, M.M.: Composing real-time concurrent objects refinement, compatibility and schedulability. In: Arbab, F., Sirjani, M. (eds.) FSEN 2011. LNCS, vol. 7141, pp. 96–111. Springer, Heidelberg (2012)
13. Kearney, K.T., Torelli, F., Kotsokalis, C.: SLA*: an abstract syntax for Service Level Agreements. In: 2010 11th IEEE/ACM International Conference on Grid Computing (GRID), pp. 217–224. IEEE (2010)

14. Keller, A., Ludwig, H.: The WSLA framework: Specifying and monitoring service level agreements for web services. J. Netw. Syst. Manage. **11**(1), 57–81 (2003)
15. Davide Lamanna, D., Skene, J., Emmerich, W.: Slang: a language for defining service level agreements. In: Proceedings of (FTDCS 2003), p. 100. IEEE Computer Society (2003)
16. Mahbub, K., Spanoudakis, G., Tsigkritis, T.: Translation of SLAs into monitoring specifications. In: Wieder, P., Butler, J.M., Theilmann, W., Yahyapour, R. (eds.) Service Level Agreements for Cloud Computing, pp. 79–101. Springer, New York (2011)
17. Martin, D.L., Burstein, M.H., McDermott, D.V., McIlraith, S.A., Paolucci, M., Sycara, K.P., McGuinness, D.L., Sirin, E., Srinivasan, N.: Bringing semantics to web services with OWL-S. World Wide Web **10**(3), 243–277 (2007)
18. Nobakht, B., de Gouw, S., de Boer, F.S.: Formal verification of service level agreements through distributed monitoring. In: Dustdar, S., et al. (eds.) ESOCC 2015. LNCS, vol. 9306, pp. 125–140. Springer, Heidelberg (2015). doi:10.1007/978-3-319-24072-5_9
19. Okika, J.: Analysis and Verification of Service Contracts. Ph.D. thesis, Department of Computer Science, Aalborg University (2010)
20. Pratt, V.R.: Semantical considerations on floyd-hoare logic. In: 17th Annual Symposium on Foundations of Computer Science, 25–27 October 1976, Houston, Texas, USA, pp. 109–121 (1976)

Effectively Eliminating Auxiliaries

Stijn de Gouw[1,2] and Jurriaan Rot[3(✉)]

[1] CWI, Amsterdam, The Netherlands
[2] SDL, Amsterdam, The Netherlands
[3] LIP, Université de Lyon, CNRS, Ecole Normale Supérieure de Lyon, INRIA,
Université Claude-Bernard Lyon 1, Lyon, France
jurriaan.rot@ens-lyon.fr

Abstract. Auxiliary variables are used in the intermediate steps of a correctness proof to store additional information about the computation. We investigate for which classes of programs auxiliary variables can be avoided in the associated proof system, and give effective translations of proofs whenever this is the case.

1 Introduction

Auxiliary variables aid verification by storing additional information about the computation. Widely used instances include the recording of computation histories and the explicit access to control points via program counters. Auxiliary variables were first used by Clint [7] to prove properties about coroutines. Owicki [19] and Howard [13] used auxiliaries for reasoning about concurrent programs. Apt [1,3] used auxiliaries to obtain intermediate assertions that denote decidable sets, which is useful for runtime checking. Recent applications of auxiliary variables are found in the Java Modeling Language [5], where they are called ghost variables. The power of auxiliaries is further illustrated by the fact that Frank de Boer himself advocated their use [8].

Auxiliaries are used temporarily, in the intermediate steps of a correctness proof, by instrumenting the program with assignments. A rule by Owicki and Gries [20] removes auxiliaries in a later proof step. As argued by Clarke [6], this use of auxiliary variables breaks compositionality, since the program fragments in the premise of the rule are not strict subprograms of that in the conclusion. Compositionality is crucial for a modular, syntax-directed proof construction.

Naturally the question arises: can auxiliary variables be avoided? This is the case for while programs and for recursive programs, since they have relative complete proof systems that do not contain Owicki and Gries' rule. Clarke showed that auxiliaries can be avoided in correctness proofs of programs with so-called simple coroutines, and raised the question whether history variables are

J. Rot—The research of the second author was carried out at Leiden University and CWI. The second author is supported by the LABEX MILYON (ANR-10-LABX-0070) of Université de Lyon, within the program "Investissements d'Avenir" (ANR-11-IDEX-0007) operated by the French National Research Agency (ANR).

E. Ábrahám et al. (Eds.): de Boer Festschrift, LNCS 9660, pp. 226–241, 2016.
DOI: 10.1007/978-3-319-30734-3_16

necessary for concurrent programs with shared variables. Lamport [16] showed that the full power of histories is not needed, but that using auxiliary variables as program counters suffices. To the best of our knowledge, it remained open whether auxiliary variables can be eliminated entirely.

In this paper we investigate for which classes of programs auxiliary variables can be avoided, and aim to give effective translations of proofs whenever this is possible. Hoffmann and Pavlova [12] gave such a translation for while programs, and we previously announced (without proof) a similar result for recursive programs [9], where it was applied to a practical example. Here we give the full translation, relying on so-called adaptation rules.

We introduce a translation from proofs of disjoint parallel programs using auxiliary variables, to proofs that do not. Our proof system uses adaptation rules instead of Owicki/Gries' rule for auxiliary variables, and technically relies on existentially quantifying auxiliary variables in specifications. Thereby, we show that, contrary to what is suggested in [4], auxiliary variables are not needed for disjoint parallel programs in the presence of suitable adaptation rules.

For programs with shared variable concurrency, we show that auxiliary variables *are* essential, in the sense that the associated rule cannot be replaced by *any* set of adaptation rules. This answers the open question by Clarke [6] "whether there is a proof system similar to the one originally described by Owicki which does not require the use of history variables" and confirms Kleymann's intuition that this is not case [15].

2   Preliminaries

We first fix some notation. Throughout this paper, we consider the usual interpretation of Hoare triples $\{p\}\ S\ \{q\}$ with respect to *partial* correctness. We use a first-order assertion language. Given an assertion p, we denote its free variables by $free(p)$, substitution of a term t for a variable x in p by $p[x := t]$ and in a term t' by $t'[x := t]$. The variables in a term t are denoted by $var(t)$. For a statement S (statements will be defined in subsequent sections) we denote by $var(S)$ the variables occurring in S, and by $change(S)$ the variables that occur on the left-hand side of an assignment in S. Given a list of variables $\bar{z}$, the statement $(S)_{\bar{z}}$ is obtained from S by removing all assignments to variables in $\bar{z}$ (using **skip** if S becomes empty), and $\bar{z}|_S$ is the sublist of variables in $\bar{z}$ that occur in $change(S)$, i.e., $\bar{z}|_S = \bar{z} \cap change(S)$. We abuse notation by using set-theoretic operations on lists, as in the previous line.

2.1   Auxiliary Variables

Auxiliary variables store information about the computation. Formally, they are defined as follows.

Definition 1. *A closed list of auxiliary variables $\bar{z}$ for a given program is a sequence of program variables that appear only in assignments of the form $u := x$, where u is a variable in $\bar{z}$.*

The following rule, introduced by Owicki and Gries [20], allows to eliminate auxiliary variables in order to obtain the intended correctness triple:

$$\frac{\{p\}\ S\ \{q\}}{\{p\}\ (S)_{\bar{u}}\ \{q\}}\ \text{(OG)}$$

where $\bar{u}$ is a closed list of auxiliary variables for S, and $\bar{u} \cap \mathit{free}(q) = \emptyset$.

2.2 Adaptation Rules

Support for modular reasoning in Hoare logic requires *adaptation rules* to adapt the specifications of Hoare triples to a specific context. The simplest example of an adaptation rule is the usual consequence rule. Adaptation rules are furthermore essential for proof systems about recursive procedures [2]. We briefly recall several adaptation rules taken from [4] (Fig. 1) and [18] (Rule OLD).

$$\frac{\{p\}\ S\ \{q\}}{\{p \wedge r\}\ S\ \{q \wedge r\}}\ \text{(INV)} \qquad\qquad \frac{\{p\}\ S\ \{q\}}{\{\exists l.p\}\ S\ \{q\}}\ \text{(}\exists\text{-IN)}$$

where $\mathit{free}(r) \cap \mathit{change}(S) = \emptyset$ $\qquad$ where $l \notin \mathit{free}(q)$ and $l \notin \mathit{var}(S)$

$$\frac{\{p\}\ S\ \{q\}}{\{p[l := t]\}\ S\ \{l := t\}}\ \text{(SUBST)} \qquad \frac{p_0 \rightarrow p_1, \{p_1\}\ S\ \{q_1\}, q_1 \rightarrow q_0}{\{p_0\}\ S\ \{q_0\}}\ \text{(CONS)}$$

where $l \notin \mathit{var}(S)$ and $\mathit{var}(t) \cap \mathit{change}(S) = \emptyset$

Fig. 1. Adaptation rules

Rule INV provides a basic way to reason about assertions whose truth remains invariant under execution of S. Rule SUBST instantiates a logical variable. Rule $\exists$-IN allows weakening preconditions under certain conditions. Figure 2 shows an example derivation using some of these rules.

$$\frac{\dfrac{\{p\}\ S\ \{q\}\quad q \rightarrow \exists z.q}{\{p\}\ S\ \{\exists z.q\}}\ \text{(CONS)}}{\{\exists z.p\}\ S\ \{\exists z.q\}}\ \text{(}\exists\text{-IN)}$$

Fig. 2. Adding existential quantifiers

Definition 2 (Adaptation Completeness). *A proof system for a class of programs (ranged over by S) is* adaptation complete *if for all p, q, p', q': if*

$$\forall S.\ \models \{p\}\ S\ \{q\}\ \text{implies}\ \models \{p'\}\ S\ \{q'\}$$

then any derivation of $\{p\}\ S\ \{q\}$ can be extended to a derivation of $\{p'\}\ S\ \{q'\}$ (by only adding rule applications to the derivation).

Remark 1. In the definition of adaptation completeness, one usually restricts to satisfiable correctness triples. Partial correctness avoids this extra condition, since all correctness triples are satisfiable.

To obtain an adaptation complete proof system, we use an approach due to Olderog [18]. Given assertions p, q, r and a sequence of variables $\bar{x}$, consider the following assertion:

$$\forall \bar{y}(\forall \bar{z}(p \to q[\bar{x} := \bar{y}]) \to r[\bar{x} := \bar{y}]) \tag{1}$$

where $\bar{y}$ is a sequence of fresh variables (not occurring in p, q or r) of the same length as $\bar{x}$, and $\bar{z} = \mathit{free}(p, q) \backslash \{\bar{x}\}$. The crucial property of the assertion (1) is:

Lemma 1 (Olderog Adaptation Completeness). *The assertion* (1) *is the weakest assertion w such that* $\models \{w\}\ S\ \{r\}$ *for all finitely based state transformers[1] S with $var(S) = \bar{x}$ and* $\models \{p\}\ S\ \{q\}$.

Proof. See the text above Proposition 4.1 in [18]. □

We use assertion (1) to define an adaptation rule:

$$\frac{p' \to (\forall \bar{y}(\forall \bar{z}(p \to q[\bar{x} := \bar{y}]) \to q'[\bar{x} := \bar{y}])) \qquad \{p\}\ S\ \{q\}}{\{p'\}\ S\ \{q'\}} \text{ (OLD)}$$

with $\bar{z}$ and $\bar{y}$ defined as in (1), and $\bar{x} = var(S)$ the list of program variables.

By Lemma 1 it is straightforward to show that adding Rule OLD yields a proof system that is adaptation complete. In particular, Rule OLD satisfies the following two properties (not unexpectedly, given its adaptation completeness).

Lemma 2 (Other Adaptation Rules Redundant). *The adaptation rules given in Fig. 1 are derivable with Rule OLD.*

Lemma 3 (Collapsing Consecutive Applications of Rule OLD). *Multiple consecutive applications of Rule OLD can be replaced by a single application.*

3 While Programs

While programs form the basic building blocks for all the other classes of programs defined in the next sections. The syntax of while programs is as follows.

$$S ::= \textbf{skip} \mid u := t \mid S_1; S_2 \mid \textbf{if } b \textbf{ then } S_1 \textbf{ else } S_2 \textbf{ fi} \mid \textbf{while } b \textbf{ do } S \textbf{ od}$$

Figure 3 shows the standard proof system introduced by Hoare [10].

The next theorem shows that we can translate proofs of while-programs that use auxiliary variables to proofs without. Every rule application in the original proof is substituted, without having to consider the context of the enclosing proof, by at most three rule applications in the new proof. The translation is syntactic (no new loop invariants have to be invented) and fully automatic.

---

[1] Intuitively, a state transformer is finitely based if it reads and writes finitely many variables. See [18] for a precise definition.

$$\{p\} \text{ skip } \{p\} \text{ (SKIP)} \qquad \frac{\{p \wedge \neg B\} \ S_1 \ \{q\}, \{p \wedge B\} \ S_2 \ \{q\}}{\{p\} \text{ if } B \text{ then } S_1 \text{ else } S_2 \text{ fi } \{q\}} \text{ (COND)}$$

$$\{p[u := t]\} \ u := t \ \{p\} \text{ (ASGN)} \qquad \frac{\{p \wedge B\} \ S \ \{p\}}{\{p\} \text{ while } B \text{ do } S \text{ od } \{p \wedge \neg B\}} \text{ (LOOP)}$$

$$\frac{\{p\} \ S_1 \ \{r\}, \{r\} \ S_2 \ \{q\}}{\{p\} \ S_1; S_2 \ \{q\}} \text{ (SEQ)} \qquad \frac{p_0 \rightarrow p_1, \{p_1\} \ S \ \{q_1\}, q_1 \rightarrow q_0}{\{p_0\} \ S \ \{q_0\}} \text{ (CONS)}$$

Fig. 3. Proof system PW

Theorem 1 (Auxiliary Variables Redundant for While Programs). *Let $\bar{z}$ be a closed list of auxiliary variables for a statement S. There is an effective translation from any proof in* PW *+ Rule* OG *of $\{p\} \ S \ \{q\}$ into a proof of $\{\exists \bar{z}.p\} \ (S)_{\bar{z}} \ \{\exists \bar{z}.q\}$ in* PW.

Proof. The translation is defined by induction on the derivation. We proceed by a case distinction on the last proof rule applied in the derivation of $\{p\} \ S \ \{q\}$.

– Rule SKIP. The desired $\{\exists \bar{z}.p\} \ \text{skip} \ \{\exists \bar{z}.p\}$ follows by Rule SKIP.
– Rule ASGN. Then $\{p\} \ S \ \{q\}$ has the form $\{p[u := t]\} \ u := t \ \{p\}$. First note that for any assertion p and term t:

$$(\exists u.p[u := t]) \rightarrow (\exists u.p). \tag{2}$$

Next, we distinguish two cases:
1. u is an auxiliary variable, which implies $u \in \bar{z}$. Since $(u := t)_u$ is **skip**, we must find a derivation of $\{\exists \bar{z}.p[u := t]\} \ \text{skip} \ \{\exists \bar{z}.p\}$. By Rule SKIP we have $\{\exists \bar{z}.p[u := t]\} \ \text{skip} \ \{\exists \bar{z}.p[u := t]\}$. Thus the desired result follows from (2) by an application of Rule CONS.
2. u is a program variable, which entails $u \notin \bar{z}$ and $var(t) \cap \bar{z} = \emptyset$. Then $\{(\exists \bar{z}.p)[u := t]\} \ u := t \ \{\exists \bar{z}.p\}$, by Rule ASGN, and since u does not occur in $\bar{z}$, by Rule CONS: $\{\exists \bar{z}.p[u := t]\} \ u := t \ \{\exists \bar{z}.p\}$.
– Rule SEQ. Then $\{p\} \ S_1 \ \{r\}$ and $\{r\} \ S_2 \ \{q\}$ are derivable (for some intermediate assertion r). The induction hypothesis gives $\{\exists \bar{z}.p\} \ (S_1)_{\bar{z}} \ \{\exists \bar{z}.r\}$ and $\{\exists \bar{z}.r\} \ (S_2)_{\bar{z}} \ \{\exists \bar{z}.q\}$. If $(S_1)_{\bar{z}} = \text{skip}$ and $(S_1; S_2)_{\bar{z}} = (S_2)_{\bar{z}}$ (when S_1 consists of assignments to auxiliary variables) then the triple $\{\exists \bar{z}.p\} \ (S_1; S_2)_{\bar{z}} \ \{\exists \bar{z}.q\}$ follows by Rule CONS (similarly for the case $(S_2)_{\bar{z}} = \text{skip}$ and $(S_1; S_2)_{\bar{z}} = (S_1)_{\bar{z}}$). Otherwise $\{\exists \bar{z}.p\} \ (S_1; S_2)_{\bar{z}} \ \{\exists \bar{z}.q\}$ follows by Rule SEQ.
– Rule COND. Then $\{p \wedge B\} \ S_1 \ \{q\}$ and $\{p \wedge \neg B\} \ S_2 \ \{q\}$ are derivable, and $var(B) \cap \bar{z} = \emptyset$ (since auxiliaries do not occur in guards). By the induction hypothesis: $\{\exists \bar{z}.(p \wedge B)\} \ (S_1)_{\bar{z}} \ \{\exists \bar{z}.q\}$ and $\{\exists \bar{z}.(p \wedge \neg B)\} \ (S_2)_{\bar{z}} \ \{\exists \bar{z}.q\}$. Because $var(B) \cap \bar{z} = \emptyset$, applying Rule CONS yields $\{(\exists \bar{z}.p) \wedge B\} \ (S_1)_{\bar{z}} \ \{\exists \bar{z}.q\}$ and $\{(\exists \bar{z}.p) \wedge \neg B\} \ (S_2)_{\bar{z}} \ \{\exists \bar{z}.q\}$. Finally, by applying Rule COND we obtain $\{\exists \bar{z}.p\} \ (\text{if } B \text{ then } S_1 \text{ else } S_2 \text{ fi})_{\bar{z}} \ \{\exists \bar{z}.q\}$.
– Rule LOOP. Then $\{p \wedge B\} \ S \ \{p\}$ is derivable and $var(B) \cap \bar{z} = \emptyset$. By the induction hypothesis: $\{\exists \bar{z}.(p \wedge B)\} \ (S)_{\bar{z}} \ \{\exists \bar{z}.p\}$. Because $var(B) \cap \bar{z} = \emptyset$, applying Rule CONS yields $\{(\exists \bar{z}.p) \wedge B\} \ (S)_{\bar{z}} \ \{\exists \bar{z}.p\}$. Rule LOOP yields $\{\exists \bar{z}.p\} \ (\text{while } B \text{ do } S \text{ od})_{\bar{z}} \ \{(\exists \bar{z}.p) \wedge \neg B\}$.

- Rule CONS. Then $p_0 \rightarrow p_1$ and $q_1 \rightarrow q_0$ are valid, and $\{p_1\}\ S\ \{q_1\}$ is derivable. By the induction hypothesis: $\{\exists \bar{z}.p_1\}\ (S)_{\bar{z}}\ \{\exists \bar{z}.q_1\}$. Observe that for any assertion p and q, if $p \rightarrow q$ is valid, then so is $(\exists \bar{z}.p) \rightarrow (\exists \bar{z}.p)$. Hence from $p_0 \rightarrow p_1$ and $q_1 \rightarrow q_0$ we may deduce $(\exists \bar{z}.p_0) \rightarrow (\exists \bar{z}.p_1)$ and $(\exists \bar{z}.q_1) \rightarrow (\exists \bar{z}.q_0)$. Applying Rule CONS we obtain the desired $\{\exists \bar{z}.p_0\}\ (S)_{\bar{z}}\ \{\exists \bar{z}.q_0\}$
- Rule OG. Then $\{p\}\ S\ \{q\}$ is derivable, $\bar{u}$ is the list of auxiliaries used in the application of the rule, and q does not contain any variables from $\bar{u}$. Our goal is to prove $\{\exists \bar{z}.p\}\ ((S)_{\bar{u}})_{\bar{z}}\ \{\exists \bar{z}.q\}$. Applying the induction hypothesis with $\bar{u}, \bar{z}$ as the auxiliaries yields $\{\exists \bar{u}\bar{z}.p\}\ (S)_{\bar{u}\bar{z}}\ \{\exists \bar{u}\bar{z}.q\}$. Clearly $(\exists \bar{z}.p) \rightarrow (\exists \bar{u}\bar{z}.p)$, and since q does not contain $\bar{u}$ we also have $(\exists \bar{u}\bar{z}.q) \rightarrow (\exists \bar{z}.q)$, thus our goal follows from Rule CONS.   □

By instantiating Theorem 1 to the empty sequence of auxiliaries, we obtain:

Corollary 1 (Auxiliary Variables Redundant for While Programs). *There is an effective translation from any proof in* PW $+$ *Rule* OG *of* $\{p\}\ S\ \{q\}$ *into a proof of* $\{p\}\ S\ \{q\}$ *in* PW.

4   Recursive Programs

Programs with recursive procedures consist of a set of procedure declarations $D = \{P_i :: S_i \mid 1 \leq i \leq n\}$ and a main-statement S, where P_i is a procedure name and S_i and S are statements extending while-programs (Sect. 3) with:

$$S ::= P_i$$

which denotes a call to procedure P_i. The corresponding proof system requires a new ingredient: recursive procedures are proven correct *under a set of assumptions* about procedures. The assumptions are later discharged in a proof rule for procedure calls. Consequently, the statements that we derive with the proof system are not Hoare triples, but quadruples of the form $A \vdash \{p\}\ D|S\ \{q\}$ where A is a set of assumptions about the procedures $P_1, \ldots, P_n$ (i.e. Hoare triples $\{p_i\}\ P_i\ \{q_i\}$), and $D|S$ is a statement that can use the procedures declared in D (we omit D if it is clear from the context). Formally this requires adding sets of assumptions to all proof rules for while-programs given in Fig. 3, but since these changes are obvious (the rules are independent of the assumptions and do not manipulate them), we omit them. Two rules are introduced for reasoning about calls (Fig. 4). Rule ASMP shows how we can use the assumptions. Rule CALL discharges the assumptions, provided that we can prove the procedure body S_i and the main-statement S using them. Besides these two new rules, to obtain a complete proof system, it turns out that the adaptation rules introduced in Sect. 2 (with additionally a set of assumptions) are also needed [2]. This leads us to the following formal definition of the proof system.

Definition 3 (Proof System for Recursion). *Proof system* PR *consists of*

- *The rules in Fig. 4,*

$$A \vdash \{p\} \ D|S \ \{q\} \ \text{(ASMP)}$$
$$\text{if } (\{p\} \ D|S \ \{q\}) \in A$$

$$\frac{A\vdash\{p_i\} \ D|S_i \ \{q_i\} \ \text{for } i=1,\ldots,n \quad A\vdash\{p\} \ D|S \ \{q\}}{\vdash\{p\} \ D|S \ \{q\}} \ \text{(CALL)}$$
$$\text{where } D = \{P_i :: S_i \mid 1 \le i \le n\}$$

Fig. 4. New proof rules in proof system PR

- *The rules from* PW *(Fig. 3) under a set of assumptions,*
- *The adaptation rules (Fig. 1) under a set of assumptions.*

For recursive programs, the definition of $change(\ldots)$ is extended in the obvious way: $change(D|S)$ is the set of variables changed in S or any of the procedures called by S (declared in D). Along the same lines, $\bar{z}|_{(D|S)}$ is the sublist of variables from $\bar{z}$ changed by S or the procedures called by S. Furthermore, $(D|S)_{\bar{z}}$ is the program obtained from the statement S and procedure declarations D by removing all assignments to variables in $\bar{z}$ from S and the procedure bodies in D. The next definition uses these concepts to translate specifications.

Definition 4 (Translating Specifications). *Given a set of n Hoare triples $A = \{\{p_i\} \ S_i \ \{q_i\} \mid i = 1,\ldots,n\}$ and a closed list of auxiliary variables $\bar{z}$, we define the translation $TRANS(A,\bar{z})$ by $A = \{\{\exists\bar{z}|_{(D|S_i)}.p_i\} \ (D|S_i)_{\bar{z}} \ \{\exists\bar{z}|_{(D|S_i)}.q_i\} \mid i = 1,\ldots,n\}$.*

The above translation requires no creativity to find appropriate procedure specifications; it can be performed fully mechanically. Using the new specifications, the below theorem shows that auxiliary variables can be avoided in proofs, deleting the auxiliaries from the main statement and all procedure bodies.

Theorem 2 (Removing Auxiliaries). *Let $\bar{z}$ be a closed list of auxiliary variables for a recursive program $D|S$. There is an effective translation from any proof in PR + Rule OG of $A \vdash \{p\} \ D|S \ \{q\}$ into a proof of $TRANS(A,\bar{z}) \vdash \{\exists\bar{z}|_{(D|S)}.p\} \ (D|S)_{\bar{z}} \ \{\exists\bar{z}|_{(D|S)}.q\}$ in PR.*

Proof. The translation is defined by induction on the derivation, with a case analysis on the last proof rule applied in the derivation of $A \vdash \{p\} \ D|S \ \{q\}$. For readability we omit D if it is clear from the context.

- Rule SKIP. We need to prove $\{\exists\bar{z}|_{\textbf{skip}}.p\} \ \textbf{skip} \ \{\exists\bar{z}|_{\textbf{skip}}.p\}$ which is trivial, since $\bar{z}|_{\textbf{skip}}$ is empty.
- Rule ASGN. Then $\{p\} \ S \ \{q\}$ has the form $\{p[u := t]\} \ u := t \ \{p\}$, and we need to give a proof of $\{\exists\bar{z}|_{u:=t}.[u := t]\} \ u := t \ \{\exists\bar{z}|_{u:=t}.p\}$. If $u \in \bar{z}$ then $\bar{z}|_{u:=t} = u$ and $\{\exists u.p[u := t]\} \ \textbf{skip} \ \{\exists u.p\}$ is derived as in the proof of Theorem 1. If $u \notin \bar{z}$ then $\bar{z}|_{u:=t}$ is empty, so no translation is necessary.
- Rule SEQ. Then $\{p\} \ S_1 \ \{r\}$ and $\{r\} \ S_2 \ \{q\}$ are derivable. By the induction hypothesis, we get $\{\exists\bar{z}|_{S_1}.p\} \ (S_1)_{\bar{z}} \ \{\exists\bar{z}|_{S_1}.r\}$ and $\{\exists\bar{z}|_{S_2}.r\} \ (S_2)_{\bar{z}} \ \{\exists\bar{z}|_{S_2}.q\}$. Now since $change(S_i) \subseteq change(S_1; S_2)$ and $\bar{z} \cap (S_1; S_2)_{\bar{z}} = \emptyset$, by Fig. 2

we get $\{\exists \bar{z}|_{S_1;S_2}.p\}\ (S_1)_{\bar{z}}\ \{\exists \bar{z}|_{S_1;S_2}.r\}$ and $\{\exists \bar{z}|_{S_1;S_2}.r\}\ (S_2)_{\bar{z}}\ \{\exists \bar{z}|_{S_1;S_2}.q\}$. If $(S_1)_{\bar{z}} = \mathbf{skip}$ and $(S_1;S_2)_{\bar{z}} = (S_2)_{\bar{z}}$ (when S_1 consists of assignments to auxiliary variables) then $\{\exists \bar{z}|_{S_1;S_2}.p\}\ (S_1;S_2)_{\bar{z}}\ \{\exists \bar{z}|_{S_1;S_2}.q\}$ follows by Rule CONS (similarly for the case $(S_2)_{\bar{z}} = \mathbf{skip}$ and $(S_1;S_2)_{\bar{z}} = (S_1)_{\bar{z}}$). Otherwise, $\{\exists \bar{z}|_{S_1;S_2}.p\}\ (S_1;S_2)_{\bar{z}}\ \{\exists \bar{z}|_{S_1;S_2}.q\}$ follows by Rule SEQ.

- Rule COND, LOOP and CONS are treated similarly to the proof of Theorem 1. For COND we use Fig. 2 in the same way as in the above treatment of SEQ to extend the proofs of $\{\exists \bar{z}|_{S_i}.p_i\}\ (S_i)_{\bar{z}}\ \{\exists \bar{z}|_{S_i}.q_i\}$ for $i \in \{1,2\}$ that come from the induction hypothesis to proofs of $\{\exists \bar{z}|_S.p_i\}\ (S)_{\bar{z}}\ \{\exists \bar{z}|_S.p_i\}$ where $S = \mathbf{if}\ B\ \mathbf{then}\ S_1\ \mathbf{else}\ S_2\ \mathbf{fi}$.

- Rule INV. Then $\{p\}\ S\ \{q\}$ is derivable, and r is an assertion with $free(r) \cap change(S) = \emptyset$. By the induction hypothesis we infer $\{\exists \bar{z}|_S.p\}\ (S)_{\bar{z}}\ \{\exists \bar{z}|_S.q\}$. Applying the invariance rule gives $\{(\exists \bar{z}|_S.p) \wedge r\}\ (S)_{\bar{z}}\ \{(\exists \bar{z}|_S.q) \wedge r\}$. Since $\bar{z}|_S$ and $free(r)$ are disjoint, we have for any assertion p: $(\exists \bar{z}|_S.p \wedge r) \leftrightarrow ((\exists \bar{z}|_S.p) \wedge r)$, thus Rule CONS yields $\{\exists \bar{z}|_S.p \wedge r\}\ (S)_{\bar{z}}\ \{\exists \bar{z}|_S.q \wedge r\}$.

- Rule $\exists$-IN. Then $\{p\}\ D|S\ \{q\}$ is derivable and l does not occur in S, D and q. The induction hypothesis gives us $\{\exists \bar{z}|_S.p\}\ (D|S)_{\bar{z}}\ \{\exists \bar{z}|_S.q\}$. Since l also does not occur in $(D|S)_{\bar{z}}$ we apply Rule $\exists$-IN: $\{\exists l.\exists \bar{z}|_S.p\}\ (D|S)_{\bar{z}}\ \{\exists \bar{z}|_S.q\}$. Finally, the consequence rule gives $\{\exists \bar{z}|_S.\exists l.p\}\ (D|S)_{\bar{z}}\ \{\exists \bar{z}|_S.q\}$.

- Rule SUBST. Then $\{p\}\ D|S\ \{q\}$ is derivable, l does not occur in D or S and $var(t) \cap change(S) = \emptyset$. By the ind. hypothesis: $\{\exists \bar{z}|_S.p\}\ (D|S)_{\bar{z}}\ \{\exists \bar{z}|_S.q\}$. From Rule SUBST: $\{(\exists \bar{z}|_{(D|S)}.p)[l := t]\}\ (D|S)_{\bar{z}}\ \{(\exists \bar{z}|_{(D|S)}.q)[l := t]\}$. Since $\bar{z}|_{(D|S)}$ only contains variables that are changed, it is disjoint from l and $var(t)$, thus for any formula p we have the equivalence $(\exists \bar{z}|_{(D|S)}.p)[l := t] \leftrightarrow (\exists \bar{z}|_{(D|S)}.p[l := t])$. Hence, Rule CONS gives the desired correctness formula $\{\exists \bar{z}|_{(D|S)}.p[l := t]\}\ (D|S)_{\bar{z}}\ \{\exists \bar{z}|_{(D|S)}.q[l := t]\}$.

- Rule ASMP. Then $(\{p\}\ D|S\ \{q\}) \in A$. The definition of $TRANS(A, \bar{z})$ implies that $(\{\exists \bar{z}|_{(D|S)}.p\}\ (D|S)_{\bar{z}}\ \{\exists \bar{z}|_{(D|S)}.q\}) \in TRANS(A, \bar{z})$. Therefore $TRANS(A, \bar{z}) \vdash \{\exists \bar{z}|_{(D|S)}.p\}\ (D|S)_{\bar{z}}\ \{\exists \bar{z}|_{(D|S)}.q\}$ follows from Rule ASMP.

- Rule CALL. Then $A \vdash \{p_i\}\ D|S_i\ \{q_i\}$ for $i = 1,\ldots,n$ and $A \vdash \{p\}\ D|S\ \{q\}$ are derivable. The induction hypothesis gives us $TRANS(A, \bar{z}) \vdash \{\exists \bar{z}|_{(D|S)}.p_i\}\ (D|S_i)_{\bar{z}}\ \{\exists \bar{z}|_{(D|S)}.q_i\}$ for $i = 1,\ldots,n$, and $TRANS(A, \bar{z}) \vdash \{\exists \bar{z}|_{(D|S)}.p\}\ (D|S)_{\bar{z}}\ \{\exists \bar{z}|_{(D|S)}.q\}$. Thus we can apply Rule CALL to obtain the desired $\vdash \{\exists \bar{z}|_{(D|S)}.p\}\ (D|S)_{\bar{z}}\ \{\exists \bar{z}|_{(D|S)}.q\}$.

- Rule OG. Then $\{p\}\ S\ \{q\}$ is derivable, $\bar{u}$ is the list of auxiliaries used in the application of the rule, and q does not contain $\bar{u}$. Our goal is to prove

$$\{\exists \bar{z}|_{(S)_{\bar{u}}}.p\}\ ((S)_{\bar{u}})_{\bar{z}}\ \{\exists \bar{z}|_{(S)_{\bar{u}}}.q\}.$$

An application of the induction hypothesis with $\bar{u}, \bar{z}$ as the auxiliaries gives us $\{\exists \bar{u}\bar{z}|_S.p\}\ (S)_{\bar{u}\bar{z}}\ \{\exists \bar{u}\bar{z}|_S.q\}$. Since $change((S)_{\bar{u}}) \subseteq change(S)$ we have $(\exists \bar{z}|_{(S)_{\bar{u}}}.p) \rightarrow (\exists \bar{u}\bar{z}|_S.p)$. Since q does not contain $\bar{u}$ we also have $(\exists \bar{u}\bar{z}|_S.q) \rightarrow (\exists \bar{z}|_{(S)_{\bar{u}}}.q)$, thus our goal follows from Rule CONS. $\square$

Example 1. In [9], we proved the correctness of two sorting algorithms: Counting sort and Radix sort. Radix sort relies on an external sorting algorithm (Counting sort, for instance), and for its correctness it is crucial that the external sorting algorithm is *stable*, which means that equal elements in the input array appear in the same order in the output array. We formalized stability using an auxiliary array variable *idx* that keeps track of the original index in the input array of each element in the output array. This proves correctness with respect to an external (stable) sorting algorithm that updates *idx* appropriately. We would like to apply Theorem 2 (which appeared in a slightly different form in [9], without proof) to eliminate *idx* from the program, showing that Radix sort is correct whenever the external sorting algorithm is stable (without having to update *idx*). This is almost possible; the only small technical issue is that we assumed our assertion language to be first-order, while the translation of Theorem 2 relies on existentially quantifying the auxiliary (array) variable *idx*, thus we need second-order quantification. We leave a careful treatment of eliminating auxiliary array variables for future work.

From Theorem 2, we obtain an analogue of Corollary 1 for recursion.

Corollary 2 (Auxiliary Variables Redundant for Recursive Programs). *There is an effective translation from any proof in* PR + *Rule* OG *of* $A \vdash \{p\}\ D|S\ \{q\}$ *into a proof of* $A \vdash \{p\}\ D|S\ \{q\}$ *in* PR.

5 Disjoint Parallel Programs

The syntax of disjoint parallel programs extends the syntax of while programs with a parallel operator:

$$[S_1|| \ldots ||S_n]$$

for any $n \geq 2$, syntactically restricted to statements $S_1, \ldots, S_n$ that are *disjoint*, which means that $change(S_i) \cap var(S_j) = \emptyset$ for all $i, j \in \{1, \ldots, n\}$ with $i \neq j$.

The semantics of the parallel operator is modeled as usual by interleaving. The main proof rule for dealing with the parallel operator is as follows [4,11]:

$$\frac{\{p_i\}\ S_i\ \{q_i\}\ \text{for}\ i = 1 \ldots n}{\{\bigwedge_{i=1}^{n} p_i\}\ [S_1|| \ldots ||S_n]\ \{\bigwedge_{i=1}^{n} q_i\}}\ \text{(PDJ)}$$

where for all i, j with $i \neq j$: $free(p_i, q_i) \cap change(S_j) = \emptyset$.

Adding the above Rule PDJ to PW does not yield a satisfactory proof system, as shown by the next result (Exercise 7.9 in [4]).

Theorem 3 (Incompleteness of PW + Rule PDJ). *The triple*

$$\{x = y\}\ [x := x + 1||y := y + 1]\ \{x = y\}$$

is not provable in PW + *Rule* PDJ.

Proof. Suppose for a contradiction that $\{x = y\}\ [x := x + 1||y := y + 1]\ \{x = y\}$ has a proof. This proof must include an application of Rule PDJ:

$$\frac{\{p_1\}\ x := x + 1\ \{q_1\} \qquad \{p_2\}\ y := y + 1\ \{q_2\}}{\{p_1 \wedge p_2\}\ [x := x + 1||y := y + 1]\ \{q_1 \wedge q_2\}} \tag{3}$$

The only possible way that the proof can continue is by an application of Rule CONS, so the formulas below must be valid:

$$x = y \rightarrow p_1 \wedge p_2 \,, \tag{4}$$

$$q_1 \wedge q_2 \rightarrow x = y \,. \tag{5}$$

By the premise of the rule application (3), we have

$$p_i \rightarrow q_i[x := x + 1] \text{ for } i \in \{1, 2\} \,. \tag{6}$$

In particular, we have $p_1[x := y] \rightarrow q_1[x := y + 1]$. But $p_1[x := y]$ is valid by (4), and thus

$$q_1[x := y + 1]$$

is valid. Instantiating y to $x - 1$ then yields the validity of q_1.

In a similar way, we derive the validity of q_2. But this means that $q_1 \wedge q_2$ is equivalent to **true**, which contradicts (5). $\qquad\square$

The incompleteness result of Theorem 3 was introduced in [4] as a motivation for auxiliary variables.

Example 2. To see the use of auxiliary variables for disjoint parallel programs, we recall from [4] a proof of the triple $\{x = y\} \; [x := x + 1 \| y := y + 1] \; \{x = y\}$ that uses an auxiliary variable together with Rule OG. Given a fresh variable z (i.e., $x \neq z$ and $y \neq z$), the correctness triples

$$\{x = z\} \; x := x + 1 \; \{x = z + 1\} \qquad \text{and} \; \{y = z\} \; y := y + 1 \; \{y = z + 1\}$$

are proved by Rule ASGN. Using Rule PDJ we get

$$\{x = z \wedge y = z\} \; [x := x + 1 \| y := y + 1] \; \{x = z + 1 \wedge y = z + 1\}.$$

Now, consider the assignment $z := x$. Using Rule ASGN (and a simple application of Rule CONS) we get $\{x = y\} \; z := x \; \{x = z \wedge y = z\}$ and, using Rule SEQ:

$$\{x = y\} \; z := x; [x := x + 1 \| y := y + 1] \; \{x = z + 1 \wedge y = z + 1\}$$

from which we derive

$$\{x = y\} \; z := x; [x := x + 1 \| y := y + 1] \; \{x = y\}$$

by Rule CONS. Since z does not appear in the postcondition $x = y$, we may use Rule OG to obtain $\{x = y\} \; [x := x + 1 \| y := y + 1] \; \{x = y\}$.

It turns out that auxiliary variables are not necessary in the presence of suitable adaptation rules. This is shown by the next result, which generalizes the translation given in Theorem 1 to disjoint parallel programs.

Theorem 4 (Auxiliary Variables Redundant for Disjoint Parallelism).
Let $\bar{z}$ be a closed list of auxiliary variables occurring in a disjoint parallel program S. There is an effective translation from any proof in PW + Rules PDJ and OG of $\{p\} \; S \; \{q\}$ into a proof of $\{\exists \bar{z} |_S . p\} \; (S)_{\bar{z}} \; \{\exists \bar{z} |_S . q\}$ in PW + Rules PDJ, ∃-IN.

Proof. The proof is by induction on the derivation, similar to that of Theorem 2. The only remaining case (not treated in the proof of Theorem 2) is Rule PDJ.

– Rule PDJ. Then $\{p_i\}\ S_i\ \{q_i\}$ is derivable for $i \in \{1, \ldots, n\}$, and Rule PDJ is applied to get $\{\bigwedge_{i=1}^{n} p_i\}\ [S_1|| \ldots ||S_n]\ \{\bigwedge_{i=1}^{n} q_i\}$. By the induction hypothesis we have proofs of $\{\exists \bar{z}|_{S_i}.p_i\}\ (S_i)_{\bar{z}}\ \{\exists \bar{z}|_{S_i}.q_i\}$ for $i \in \{1, \ldots, n\}$. Let $S = [S_1|| \ldots ||S_n]$; by Fig. 2 we obtain proofs of $\{\exists \bar{z}|_S.p_i\}\ (S_i)_{\bar{z}}\ \{\exists \bar{z}|_S.q_i\}$ for $i \in \{1, \ldots, n\}$. Now applying Rule PDJ yields

$$\{\bigwedge_{i=1}^{n} (\exists \bar{z}|_S.p_i)\}\ (S)_{\bar{z}}\ \{\bigwedge_{i=1}^{n} (\exists \bar{z}|_S.q_i)\}. \tag{7}$$

For any $z \in \bar{z}|_S$, we have that z appears in exactly one of the S_i's, since the component programs are disjoint; say, in S_i. By the side-condition of the application of Rule PDJ in the original proof, we know that this means that z does not appear in any q_j with $j \neq i$. Therefore, we have the implication

$$(\bigwedge_{i=1}^{n} \exists \bar{z}|_S.q_i) \rightarrow \exists \bar{z}|_S. \bigwedge_{i=1}^{n} q_i.$$

Moreover, there is the easy implication $(\exists \bar{z}|_S. \bigwedge_{i=1}^{n} p_i) \rightarrow \bigwedge_{i=1}^{n}(\exists \bar{z}|_S.p_i)$. By (7), these two implications and Rule CONS, we conclude

$$\{\exists \bar{z}|_S. \bigwedge_{i=1}^{n} p_i\}\ (S)_{\bar{z}}\ \{\exists \bar{z}|_S. \bigwedge_{i=1}^{n} q_i\}$$

as desired.   □

Similar to the case of while and recursive programs, we obtain:

Corollary 3 (Auxiliary Variables Redundant for Disjoint Parallelism). *There is an effective translation from any proof in* PW *+ Rules* PDJ, OG *of* $\{p\}\ S\ \{q\}$ *into a proof of* $\{p\}\ S\ \{q\}$ *in* PW *+ Rules* PDJ, ∃-IN.

Example 3. We apply the translation of Theorem 4 to the proof of Example 2, choosing the empty sequence of auxiliaries (since there is no auxiliary to remove from the correctness triple we want to prove). The last rule application in that proof is Rule OG, which is translated to an application of Rule CONS:

$$\frac{\{\exists z(x = y)\}\ [x := x + 1||y := y + 1]\ \{\exists z(x = y)\}}{\{x = y\}\ [x := x + 1||y := y + 1]\ \{x = y\}} \text{(CONS)}$$

The proof of the correctness triple in the premise is a translation of the original proof of $\{x = y\}\ z := x; [x := x + 1||y := y + 1]\ \{x = y\}$ where the single variable z is chosen as the sequence of auxiliaries that are to be eliminated. It thus concludes with the translation of Rule CONS, with the premise (in the translated proof):

$$\{\exists z(x = y)\}\ [x := x + 1||y := y + 1]\ \{\exists z(x = z + 1 \land y = z + 1)\}.$$

This, in turn, arises from the translation of Rule SEQ, which concludes with an application of Rule CONS (since the assignment $z := x$ is eliminated), with premises:

$$\exists z(x = y) \rightarrow \exists z(x = z \land y = z) \text{ and} \qquad (8)$$

$$\{\exists z(x = z \land y = z)\} [x := x + 1 || y := y + 1] \{\exists z(x = z + 1 \land y = z + 1)\} \quad (9)$$

where (9) is derived from

$$\{x = z \land y = z\} [x := x + 1 || y := y + 1] \{x = z + 1 \land y = z + 1\}$$

using Fig. 2 (in the translation of Rule SEQ). The translated proof of the latter triple is the same as that of the original (see Example 2) since z does not appear in the statement.

6 Parallel Programs with Shared Variables

Parallel programs extend while-programs with a parallel operator $[S_1 || \ldots || S_n]$ for every $n > 1$ and an atomic region operator $\langle S \rangle$. Contrary to disjoint parallel programs considered in the previous section, here we make no assumptions on the statements appearing in $[S_1 || \ldots || S_n]$; in particular, this allows shared variables between different S_i's. For instance, in the current setting, we allow the program

$$[x := x + 2 || x := 0] \qquad (10)$$

but the arguments of the parallel operator are not disjoint.

For the atomic region, we have the following rule:

$$\frac{\{p\} \ S \ \{q\}}{\{p\} \ \langle S \rangle \ \{q\}} \ (\text{AT})$$

To reason about parallel composition, we use the notion of non-interference. Intuitively it expresses when an assertion is preserved by a given proof.

Definition 5 (Non-interfering Proofs). *A proof of $\{p\} \ S \ \{q\}$ does not interfere with a proof of $\{p'\} \ S' \ \{q'\}$ if for all assertions r occurring outside of an atomic region in $\{p'\} \ S' \ \{q'\}$ and any sub statement T of S occurring outside an atomic region, we have $\{pre(T) \land r\} \ T \ \{r\}$, for any assertion $pre(T)$ occurring as a precondition of T in the proof of $\{p\} \ S \ \{q\}$.*

The proof rule for the parallel operator is:

$$\frac{\text{Non-interfering proofs of } \{p_i\} \ S_i \ \{q_i\} \text{ for } i = 1 \ldots n}{\{\bigwedge_{i=1}^{n} p_i\} \ [S_1 || \ldots || S_n] \ \{\bigwedge_{i=1}^{n} q_i\}} \ (\text{PSV})$$

In [4] the premise of Rule PSV is formulated in terms of proof outlines. We refer to [4] for soundness and more details of these rules.

The proof system PW together with the above Rules PSV, AT is incomplete for the validity of correctness triples involving parallel programs with shared variables. Indeed, in [4, Lemma 8.6] it is shown that the triple

$$\{\mathbf{true}\} \ [x := x + 2 || x := 0] \ \{x = 0 \lor x = 2\}$$

is not provable using only PW + Rules PSV, AT. It is then shown that the above triple *is* provable using auxiliary variables together with Rule OG. In fact, the proof system PW + Rules PSV, AT, OG *is* complete [19].

One might expect that, similar to the treatment of disjoint parallelism in the previous section, we can again replace the rule for elimination of auxiliary variables by adaptation rules, while preserving completeness. However, as we show below in Theorem 5, that approach does not work: the proof system PW + Rules PSV, AT remains incomplete even with the addition of arbitrary adaptation rules. As explained in Sect. 2, the notion of "arbitrary adaptation rules" is captured precisely by adaptation completeness. Therefore, we use Rule OLD, which is adaptation complete for finitely based state transformers. (Whether it is adaptation complete for our parallel programs is open. Finitely based state transformers may be a larger class of programs than our parallel programs. Hence, for disjoint parallel programs there may be an adaptation rule which is stronger than Rule OLD.)

Theorem 5 (Auxiliaries Needed for Shared Variable Parallelism). *The triple*

$$\{\mathbf{true}\} \ [x := x + 2 || x := 0] \ \{x = 0 \lor x = 2\}$$

is not provable in PW + *Rules* AT, PSV, OLD.

Proof. Assume that $\{\mathbf{true}\} \ [x := x + 2 || x := 0] \ \{x = 0 \lor x = 2\}$ has a proof in PW + Rules AT, PSV, OLD. We show that this leads to a contradiction. The proof must include an application of Rule PSV:

$$\frac{\{p_1\} \ x := x + 2 \ \{q_1\} \qquad \{p_2\} \ x := 0 \ \{q_2\}}{\{p_1 \land p_2\} \ [x := x + 2 || x := 0] \ \{q_1 \land q_2\}} \ \text{(PSV)} \tag{11}$$

where the proofs of $\{p_1\} \ x := x + 2 \ \{q_1\}$ and $\{p_2\} \ x := 0 \ \{q_2\}$ are interference free. By Lemmas 2 and 3 we can assume without loss of generality that the proof then concludes immediately, with a single application of Rule OLD:

$$\frac{\mathbf{true} \rightarrow \forall y (\forall \bar{z}(p_1 \land p_2 \rightarrow (q_1 \land q_2)[x := y]) \rightarrow y = 0 \lor y = 2)}{\{p_1 \land p_2\} \ [x := x + 2 || x := 0] \ \{q_1 \land q_2\}} \ \text{(OLD)}$$

with $\bar{z} = \mathit{free}(p_1, p_2, q_1, q_2) \backslash \{x\}$. Instantiating the first premise with $x = 2, y = 4$ implies $\forall z ((p_1 \land p_2)[x := 2] \rightarrow (q_1 \land q_2)[x := 4]) \rightarrow \mathbf{false}$, which is equivalent to

$$\exists \bar{z}(p_1[x := 2] \land p_2[x := 2] \land \neg(q_1 \land q_2)[x := 4]). \tag{12}$$

As we will see below, this leads to a contradiction with the side conditions and premises of the application (11), which we list first. Validity of the premises implies

1. $p_1 \to q_1[x := x + 2]$ and
2. $p_2 \to q_2[x := 0]$.

and the interference freedom conditions amount to the validity of

3. $p_1 \wedge p_2 \to p_1[x := 0]$,
4. $p_1 \wedge p_2 \to p_2[x := x + 2]$,
5. $q_1 \wedge p_2 \to q_1[x := 0]$ and
6. $q_2 \wedge p_1 \to q_2[x := x + 2]$.

(Note that $\bar{z}$ may occur in p_1, p_2, q_1 or q_2 and is implicitly universally quantified.) By (12) we may choose a valuation for $\bar{z}$ under which the following formulas hold:

7. $p_1[x := 2]$,
8. $p_2[x := 2]$ and
9. $\neg(q_1 \wedge q_2)[x := 4]$.

Together with the above validities, we derive (under the same valuation):

10. $q_1[x := 4]$ (by 1, 7),
11. $q_2[x := 0]$ (by 2, 8),
12. $p_1[x := 0]$ (by 3, 7, 8),
13. $q_2[x := 2]$ (by 6, 11, 12),
14. $q_2[x := 4]$ (by 6, 7, 13) and
15. $(q_1 \wedge q_2)[x := 4]$ (by 10, 14).

But 9 is in contradiction with 15 (note that we do not use 4 and 5).   □

Remark 2. Theorem 5 strengthens [4, Lemma 8.6]: the latter is an incompleteness result for PW + Rules AT, PSV, CONS, but Rule CONS is subsumed by Rule OLD (see Sect. 2.2). For the proof system that includes OLD, the proof of [4, Lemma 8.6] immediately breaks, since it relies on the assumption that, in the proof assumed for a contradiction, the last applied rule is Rule CONS. In the presence of Rule OLD this assumption no longer holds, requiring a new proof.

Remark 3. Kleymann considers adaptation-complete proof systems for partial and total correctness of parallel programs in [14,15]. In fact, the technical report [14] contains a proof of the program in Theorem 5, directly contradicting the theorem; however, the proof in [14] is invalid, neglecting crucial noninterference conditions in the application of Rule PSV. It does not appear in [15].

Table 1. Main results

Class of programs	Proof system with auxiliaries	Proof system without auxiliaries
While	PW + Rule OG	PW
Recursion	PR + Rule OG	PR
Disjoint parallel	PW + Rules PDJ, OG	PW + Rules PDJ, ∃-IN
Parallel (shared var.)	PW + Rules AT, PSV, OG	*auxiliaries needed*

7   Conclusion and Future Work

We have shown that for while programs, recursive programs and disjoint parallel programs, auxiliary variables are not needed and can be avoided using adaptation rules. We presented concrete translations of proofs, which means that no new method contracts and invariants need to be invented. The size of the produced proofs is linear in terms of the original proofs. For parallel programs with shared variables, auxiliary variables are essential. Table 1 summarizes the main results.

It would be interesting to investigate the rôle of auxiliary variables for other classes of programs. One such class is programs that combine disjoint parallelism with recursion (cf. [17]). Of particular interest are object-oriented programs. A technical challenge there is that a naive translation of proofs that use fields as auxiliary variables introduces second-order quantification (over functions).

As Frank de Boer has experienced, *separation logic* [21] has emerged as the prime formalism for program correctness. We invite Frank to join us in our effort to extend our results to separation logic.

References

1. Apt, K.R.: Recursive assertions and parallel programs. Acta Inf. **15**, 219–232 (1981)
2. Apt, K.R.: Ten years of Hoare's logic: a survey - part 1. ACM Trans. Program. Lang. Syst. **3**(4), 431–483 (1981)
3. Apt, K.R., Bergstra, J.A., Meertens, L.G.L.T.: Recursive assertions are not enough - or are they? Theor. Comput. Sci. **8**, 73–87 (1979)
4. Apt, K.R., de Boer, F.S., Olderog, E.-R.: Verification of Sequential and Concurrent Programs. Texts in Computer Science. Springer, London (2009)
5. Burdy, L., Cheon, Y., Cok, D.R., Ernst, M.D., Kiniry, J.R., Leavens, G.T., Rustan, K., Leino, M., Poll, E.: An overview of JML tools and applications. STTT **7**(3), 212–232 (2005)
6. Clarke, E.M.: Proving correctness of coroutines without history variables. Acta Inf. **13**, 169–188 (1980)
7. Clint, M.: Program proving: coroutines. Acta Inf. **2**, 50–63 (1973)
8. de Gouw, S., de Boer, F., Ahrendt, W., Bubel, R.: Weak arithmetic completeness of object-oriented first-order assertion networks. In: van Emde Boas, P., Groen, F.C.A., Italiano, G.F., Nawrocki, J., Sack, H. (eds.) SOFSEM 2013. LNCS, vol. 7741, pp. 207–219. Springer, Heidelberg (2013)
9. de Gouw, S., de Boer, F.S., Rot, J.: Proof pearl: the KeY to correct and stable sorting. J. Autom. Reasoning **53**(2), 129–139 (2014)
10. Hoare, C.A.R.: An axiomatic basis for computer programming. Commun. ACM **12**(10), 576–580 (1969)
11. Hoare, C.A.R.: Towards a theory of parallel programming. In: Hoare, C.A.R., Perrott, R.H. (eds.) Operating System Techniques, pp. 61–71. Academic Press, New York (1972)
12. Hofmann, M., Pavlova, M.: Elimination of ghost variables in program logics. In: Barthe, G., Fournet, C. (eds.) TGC 2007. LNCS, vol. 4912, pp. 1–20. Springer, Heidelberg (2008)
13. Howard, J.H.: Proving monitors. Commun. ACM **19**(5), 273–279 (1976)

14. Kleymann, T.: Hoare logic and auxiliary variables. Technical report ECS-LFCS-98-399, Laboratory for Foundations of Computer Science, University of Edinburgh (1998)
15. Kleymann, T.: Hoare logic and auxiliary variables. Formal Aspects Comput. 11(5), 541–566 (1999)
16. Lamport, L.: Proving the correctness of multiprocess programs. IEEE Trans. Softw. Eng. 3(2), 125–143 (1977)
17. Nipkow, T.: Hoare logics for recursive procedures and unbounded nondeterminism. In: Bradfield, J.C. (ed.) CSL 2002. LNCS, vol. 2471, pp. 103–119. Springer, Heidelberg (2002)
18. Olderog, E.-R.: On the notion of expressiveness and the rule of adaption. Theor. Comput. Sci. 24, 337–347 (1983)
19. Owicki, S.S.: Axiomatic Proof Techniques for Parallel Programs. Outstanding Dissertations in the Computer Sciences. Garland Publishing, New York (1975)
20. Owicki, S.S., Gries, D.: An axiomatic proof technique for parallel programs I. Acta Inf. 6, 319–340 (1976)
21. Reynolds, J.C.: Separation logic: a logic for shared mutable data structures. In: 17th IEEE Symposium on Logic in Computer Science (LICS 2002), Proceedings, pp. 55–74 (2002)

Towards a Proof Method for Paradigm

L.P.J. Groenewegen[1], R. Kuiper[2], and E.P. de Vink[2,3](✉)

[1] Leiden Institute of Advanced Computer Science,
Leiden University, Leiden, The Netherlands
[2] Department of Mathematics and Computer Science,
Eindhoven University of Technology, Eindhoven, The Netherlands
[3] Centrum Wiskunde en Informatica, Amsterdam, The Netherlands
evink@win.tue.nl

Abstract. The paper describes two perspectives on a verification approach for Paradigm, a coordination modeling language specifying an architecture in terms of components and their collaborations. One perspective concentrates on a single collaboration: per collaboration, properties can be derived through a small set of proof rules. The other perspective concentrates on dynamic dependencies between collaborations: guided by the architecture and driven by shared components behavioral properties of the complete model can be established. Two Paradigm models, a parallel assignment and a linear pipeline of workers and buffers, illustrate the approach.

1 Introduction

Investigation of all kinds of parallel phenomena, such as communication, interaction, concurrency, collaboration and cooperation, arising inside as well as around ICT, has led to the development of the coordination language Paradigm. Most characteristic for Paradigm are its two notions of *phase* and *trap*: phase for a dynamic temporary constraint on currently possible process behavior; trap, within a phase, for a further dynamic constraint on the behavior for as long as the phase constraint remains imposed.

Phases and traps are the key ingredients to specify the coordination of components. Paradigm is organized such that consistency between group behavior of elaborating components described at their coordination level and separate component behavior decribed at the lower level is guaranteed. Based on phases and traps, mutual behaviour can be understood, specified and organized and their coordination can be designed and analyzed, see e.g. [3].

In the 90's Paradigm has been used for modeling software processes resulting in a combination of object-orientation and Paradigm, see e.g. [7,11]. Later Paradigm was gradually tuned to model self-adaptation as well, see e.g. [4,6]. The way we do this is by treating self-adaptation as a special form of normal on-the-fly coordination, be it originally unforeseen, which comes down to just-in-time foreseen coordination.

So far, formal analysis of Paradigm models has been done via model checking, in particular using mCRL2 and Prism, see [1–4]. But we have the strong

© Springer International Publishing Switzerland 2016
E. Ábrahám et al. (Eds.): de Boer Festschrift, LNCS 9660, pp. 242–260, 2016.
DOI: 10.1007/978-3-319-30734-3_17

impression, that it is possible to take advantage of Paradigm's modeling focus on collaboration of components rather more substantially. Here we put first steps into this direction and investigate a verification approach to Paradigm which on the one hand considers 'correctness formulas' capturing the interaction of a small group of components, and on the other hand distills behavioral properties of the total architecture from such formulas, thus exploiting the way the overall system is actually composed.

Compositional proof systems reduce the verification of a system to simpler, independent verification of its constituents. There are many choices of what constitutes a system: parallel components are an obvious one [12], but also concepts from object-orientation like class or subclass qualify [10]. We consider parallelism. As described in [13], a compositional proof system can be devised by including interference information in the specification of the components. The next step is then to split specifications in two parts, pertaining to the environment respectively to the component, conform rely-guarantee approaches as initiated in [9]. For Paradigm, the rules that govern a collaboration join the 'rely' and 'guarantee': a component engaged guarantees to restrict to the behavior that is committed to while relying on other components to behave accordingly.

In this paper we present a formalism to express properties of components and also of subsystems in a compositional manner. Moreover, the approach uses Rely/Guarantee ideas. In Paradigm a component consists of an STD, with its possible collaborations denoted at the level of and in terms of phases and traps: collaboration intentions. A system is constructed out of components and consistency rules. Consistency rules are specified in terms of the collaboration intentions denoting the allowed collaborations. Note, composition in Paradigm is not provided in a fixed manner, by combinators like sequential of parallel composition, but more flexibly: it is determined by the consistency rules. An execution trace then starts in a certain configuration and, by applying a sequence of consistency rules, it leads to another configuration. Our formalism exploits this by expressing properties as triples of a description of starting configurations, a sequence of consistency rules, and a description of end configurations.

We firstly consider properties of one component that may be involved in several collaborations simultaneously. For this case we provide compositional derivation rules to compose properties, enabling to combine properties for separate components as well as for shuffling sequences. Secondly, we extend the description to combinations of subsystems, each consisting of several components. The format to express properties remains essentially the same, but is used in a more general manner: both the configurations and the consistency rules may now pertain to different subsystems. We do not yet have proof rules to formally derive that such a combination of subsystems satisfies a specification, but we do propose a method to argue the satisfaction of a specification of a complete system by the combination of properties of the constituting component groups. The approach can, in the component case, be viewed as being of Rely/Guarantee nature in the sense that the consistency rules both determine what the component will rely on and what it will provide, but also what the environment will rely on and what it will provide. In the case of the subsystems, a Rely/Guarantee relation between components (now from different subsystems) can additionally be expressed in the description of the configurations.

In order to highlight the mainstay underlying our approach, on the one hand a formalism and proof rules to express and derive properties of the collaboration within a subsystem, and on the other hand the combination of such properties to prove global system properties, the paper is structured as follows: Sect. 2 provides an introduction to Paradigm and discusses a small model for the parallel assignment example. Section 3 introduces triples $\varphi\,[\,\Omega\,]\,\psi$ to express collaboration properties and gives basic proof rules to fuse triples concerning a group of components. A larger Paradigm model, concerning a linear pipeline of workers and buffers, is described in Sect. 4. Finally, in Sect. 5, we prove a property for the complete pipeline based on the analysis of smaller collaborations.

Acknowledgment. The authors, all present and former colleagues of Frank de Boer at TU/e, VU Amsterdam, Leiden University, and CWI, acknowledge inspiring discussions with Frank on semantics, proof theory, object-orientation, and many other topics in computer science and beyond.

2   A Paradigm Primer

The coordination modeling language Paradigm addresses coordination of interacting components. At the component level, detailed state transition diagrams specify the local, independent behavior of each individual component. At the coordination level, global roles specify the potential activity of a single component within a collaboration, while consistency rules describe the synchronization of the actual interaction of a group of collaborating components as a whole. In more detail, component interaction in Paradigm is specified through eight coherent definitions, see also [4]. Interaction is between sequentially defined component behaviour specified through state transition diagrams.

1. An *STD Z (state-transition diagram)* is a triple $Z = \langle \mathsf{ST}, \mathsf{AC}, \mathsf{TR} \rangle$ with ST the set of *states*, AC the set of *actions* and $\mathsf{TR} \subseteq \mathsf{ST} \times \mathsf{AC} \times \mathsf{ST}$ the set of *transitions* of Z; notation $x \xrightarrow{a} x'$ is used for a transition $(x, a, x') \in \mathsf{TR}$.

To keep track of an STD's actual running, we define

2. A *computation* κ of an STD $Z = \langle \mathsf{ST}, \mathsf{AC}, \mathsf{TR} \rangle$ is a finite or infinite string $\kappa = x_0 \xrightarrow{a_1} x_1 \xrightarrow{a_2} x_2 \xrightarrow{a_3} \ldots$ with $x_{i-1} \xrightarrow{a_i} x_i \in \mathsf{TR}$ for all indices $i \geqslant 1$ from κ. State x_0 is called the *starting state* of computation κ. In case of a finite computation κ, the string ends with a state: $x_0 \xrightarrow{a_1} x_1 \xrightarrow{a_2} \ldots \xrightarrow{a_n} x_n$ and such a state x_n is called the *final state* of κ.

Although time will remain implicit, it is assumed any transition is zero-time consuming. In addition we call a state x_i occurring in a computation κ the *current state* at the moment transition $x_{i-1} \xrightarrow{a_i} x_i$ occurs as well as at all later moments until (but not including) the next transition $x_i \xrightarrow{a_{i+1}} x_{i+1}$ occurs.

Built on the notion of STDs, Paradigm has four key notions: (i) *phase*, (ii) *trap*, (iii) *role*, and (iv) *consistency rule*. See items 3, 4, 6, and 7 below.

During collaboration a component gets influenced through a temporary constraint imposed on it from "elsewhere": a *phase*, which restricts a component to a sub-STD of the ongoing STD for a while. Similarly, during collaboration an ongoing STD contributes information towards the same "elsewhere" about progress within the phase: a *trap*, being a non-empty subset of the states of a phase which, as a subset, cannot be left as long as the phase remains imposed. As will get clear below, the "elsewhere" is the protocol regulating phase transfers on the basis of traps entered. Formally we have

3. A *phase* S of an STD $Z = \langle \mathsf{ST}, \mathsf{AC}, \mathsf{TR} \rangle$ is an STD $S = \langle \mathsf{st}, \mathsf{ac}, \mathsf{tr} \rangle$ such that $\mathsf{st} \subseteq \mathsf{ST}$, $\mathsf{ac} \subseteq \mathsf{AC}$ and $\mathsf{tr} \subseteq \{(x, a, x') \in \mathsf{TR} \mid x, x' \in \mathsf{st}, a \in \mathsf{ac}\}$.

4. A *trap* t of a phase $S = \langle \mathsf{st}, \mathsf{ac}, \mathsf{tr} \rangle$ of STD Z is a non-empty set of states $t \subseteq \mathsf{st}$ such that $x \in t$ and $x \xrightarrow{a} x' \in \mathsf{tr}$ imply $x' \in t$. If $t = \mathsf{st}$, the trap is called *trivial*. A trap t of phase S of STD Z *connects* phase S to a phase $S' = \langle \mathsf{st}', \mathsf{ac}', \mathsf{tr}' \rangle$ of Z if $t \subseteq \mathsf{st}'$. Such trap-based connectivity between two phases of Z is called a *phase transfer* and is denoted as $S \xrightarrow{t} S'$.

Thus a trap (of a phase) entered can be seen as a further constraint, where the STD commits to stay within that phase, allowing 'synchronization' at the coordination level to occur safely. Here 'committing' actually results from the behaviour-restricting effect of that phase: within the context of the phase, entering this trap of it means that a certain amount of progress has been established within the phase, a kind of final stage within the phase. Quite specifically, as long as the phase continues to be imposed, that progress cannot be undone since within the phase it is a trap of, the trap cannot be left.

Figure 1 visualizes three STDs, to be discussed in more detail later. Please note, starting and final states are indicated in UML 2.0 style: parts (a,b) have their starting states at the top and they have their final states at the bottom; part (c) has "$x = 0$" as its starting state and doesn't have a final state indicated.

Figure 2 parts (a,c,e) visualize three sets (so-called partitions) of phases and traps, one such set per STD from Fig. 1. One should observe, each phase from part (a) is a (carefully) shrunken fragment from STD P_1; per phase, one trap is indicated by a red rectangle (a red polygon in general); part (c) has phase PhX_0 containing many disjoint traps; it also has phase PhX_1 with one trap ξ_1 containing all states, so trap ξ_1 is trivial. In this figure every smallest possible trap, containing one state, corresponds to maximal progress; in general, a trivial trap corresponds to no particular progress yet, but within concrete phase PhX_1 this doesn't mean anything special, as there cannot be any progress at all. Contrarily (and this is common for most Paradigm models), Fig. 4 to be discussed in Sect. 4 presents examples of nontrivial traps which are relatively large and expressing progress in between "no progress yet" and "maximal progress": traps *doneT*, *doneG*, *notFull*, *nonEmpty*, *readyC* and *readyP*. It is the intuitive idea of measuring "sufficient progress" within a phase through keeping track of entering a particular trap, that paves the way to connecting traps, to phase transfers and from there to role dynamics as global STDs.

If a trap of a phase is moreover connecting to another phase, meaning that all states of the trap are states of the other phase too (but not necessarily a trap of it), the other phase is a possible candidate for being imposed next. This applies only after sufficient progress within the previous phase has occurred, i.e. after that connecting trap has indeed been entered. The trap being connecting, such a phase transfer from the old phase to the new phase will be sufficiently 'smooth': The restrictions of the old phase are being withdrawn, the restrictions of the new phase are being imposed, without an immediate need to change the current state. Thus, when changing the old phase to the new, the current state doesn't have to change before a transition (in accordance with the new phase imposed) can occur: Whatever that current state may be, it must as yet belong to the particular connecting trap used for the phase transfer. So from then on, steps are being taken according to the new phase imposed. In particular this means that any two subsequent phases of the same STD, must have a non-empty set of states in common, because a connecting trap is non-empty by definition.

A *role*, yet another STD, specifies the dynamics of phases and of connecting traps which can be used for a phase transfer. Thus, a role STD of an ordinary STD has phases of the ordinary STD as states and has connecting traps between these phases as transition labels. A *partition* is the set of phases and their traps underlying a role.

5. A *partition* $\pi = \{(S_i, T_i) \mid i \in I\}$ of an STD $Z = \langle \mathsf{ST}, \mathsf{AC}, \mathsf{TR} \rangle$, I a non-empty index set, is a set of pairs (S_i, T_i) consisting of a phase S_i of Z and of a set T_i of traps of S_i.
6. A *role* $Z(\pi)$ at the level of a partition $\pi = \{(S_i, T_i) \mid i \in I\}$ of an STD $Z = \langle \mathsf{ST}, \mathsf{AC}, \mathsf{TR} \rangle$ is an STD $Z(\pi) = \langle \widehat{\mathsf{ST}}, \widehat{\mathsf{AC}}, \widehat{\mathsf{TR}} \rangle$ with $\widehat{\mathsf{ST}} \subseteq \{S_i \mid i \in I\}$, $\widehat{\mathsf{AC}} \subseteq \bigcup_{i \in I} T_i$ and $\widehat{\mathsf{TR}} \subseteq \{S_i \xrightarrow{t} S_j \mid i, j \in I, \, t \in \widehat{\mathsf{AC}}\}$ a set of phase transfers. Z is called the *detailed* STD underlying *global* STD $Z(\pi)$, being role $Z(\pi)$.

Loosely speaking, coordination of component activity takes place at the level of the global or role STDs, while component computation takes place in the component's detailed STD itself. Such coordination exerts a combined and varying constraining effect on ongoing component computations, but always on the basis of relevant progress information provided by these components. A local computation step is allowed only if permitted by all current phases imposed; a 'coordination' step is enabled only if all collaborators have entered the relevant trap. By requiring traps to be connecting between phases, Paradigm syntactically guarantees vertical dynamic consistency between an ongoing STD and any of its likewise ongoing roles, see [3].

With respect to the three roles in parts (b,d,f) of Fig. 2, it is relevant to note that traps labeling a phase transfer are indeed connecting "from the previous phase to the next phase", i.e. from the old constraint imposed to the new constraint imposed via the connecting trap, thus guaranteeing smoothness of phase transfer in case of specific progress within the old phase.

Finally, a *consistency rule* synchronizes role steps from different roles in the collaboration. Such a rule can be seen as a *protocol step*, a coordination step belonging to the collaboration. All such protocol steps together then constitute the full protocol for the collaboration, and the dynamics of such a protocol consist of its subsequent protocol steps taken, i.e. of consistency rules being applied. More precisely: a group of consistency rules constitutes a *protocol* if all roles mentioned in the consistency rules from that group are not mentioned in consistency rules not from that group. In this way we can structurally and behaviorally separate collaborations from each other, as each collaboration has its own protocol, i.e. refers to a specific set of roles and of consistency rules.

7. A *consistency rule* ϱ for an ensemble of roles $Z_1(\pi_1), \ldots, Z_k(\pi_k)$ is a synchronization of one or more phase transfers from roles in the ensemble. A consistency rule ϱ is denoted as a nonempty '$\|$'-separated list of phase transfers taken from different roles from the ensemble.
8. A Paradigm *model* is an ensemble of STDs, roles thereof and consistency rules for these. A *protocol* P of a Paradigm model M is a subset of the set R of consistency rules belonging to M such that for any role $Z_i(\pi_i)$ occurring in a rule $\varrho \in P$ role $Z_i(\pi_i)$ does not occur in whatever consistency rule $\varrho' \in (R \backslash P)$. Any consistency rule ϱ belonging to a protocol P is called a *protocol step* of P.

Within the scope of this paper, we omit other types of consistency rules than described above. In [3] we distinghuish between consistency rules modelling orchestration and choreography.

Somewhat below Fig. 2, two groups of consistency rules are given: $CR_1^i(j)$, $CR_2^i(j,k)$, $CR_3^i(k)$ for $i = 1$ and $CR_1^i(j)$, $CR_2^i(j,k)$, $CR_3^i(k)$ for $i = 2$, actually together constituting one protocol as they all have role $X(FS)$ in common. Even without going into the specific details of phases and traps mentioned, one can understand such rules as follows; e.g. take rule $CR_1^1(j)$ for a fixed j

$$P_1(Asg): Ph_0^1 \xrightarrow{\theta_0} Ph_1^1(j) \parallel X(FS): PhX_0 \xrightarrow{\xi_0(j)} PhX_1$$

After sufficient progress both within (1) phase Ph_0^1 of role Asg of STD P_1, which means trap θ_0 has been entered, and within (2) phase PhX_0 of role FS of STD X, which means trap $\xi_0(j)$ has been entered, the two phase transfers

$$Ph_0^1 \xrightarrow{\theta_0} Ph_1^1(j) \quad \text{and} \quad PhX_0 \xrightarrow{\xi_0(j)} PhX_1$$

occur simultaneously. This immediately leads to new behavioral freedom for the two detailed STDs mentioned: As no other constraining effects from other roles can be taken into account (there are none), P_1 now is to proceed in accordance with phase $Ph_1^1(j)$, and X now is to proceed in accordance with phase PhX_1.

Next, we illustrate Paradigm for a relatively small and simple problem situation: the parallel program $(x := x + 1) \parallel (x := x + 2)$, consisting of two parallel assignments concerning a shared variable x. For the presentation below we distinguish sequential components P_1 and P_2, where $P_1 \triangleq x := x+1$ and $P_2 \triangleq x := x+2$. In view of modeling program $P_1 \parallel P_2$ as a Paradigm model we describe P_1 and P_2 by a separate STD. Figure 1(a), (b) visualizes these.

Because Paradigm does not address shared data and their usage in its models, we cannot so easily incorporate variable x, being shared by P_1 and P_2, into a Paradigm model. But in this case we must, as using variable x by one sequential

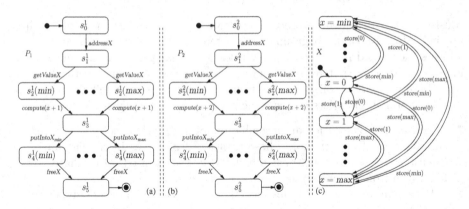

Fig. 1. STDs of (a) P_1, (b) P_2 and (c) X.

program, P_1 say, might influence the usage of variable x by the other. In view thereof we model variable x, and its particular usage by P_1 and P_2, by means of a separate STD, referred to as X in Fig. 1c.

As one can see from Fig. 1(a), (b), for one assignment both P_i execute a sequence of five steps: (1) addressing STD X by asking for its current value (fetch request), (2) getting X's current value through fetching (any value between $min, \ldots, max$ is possible), (3) computing a certain expression depending on that value (for simplicity we assume a single-valued outcome, without errors occurring), (4) informing STD X about the computation result as the new value to be stored (store request), (5) releasing STD X.

Contrarily, STD X lacks such step sequencing, as it is a complete graph: each state of it is reachable from any other state in one step. A state of X reflects the current value of variable x modeled by X. In each of its states $x = p$ where $p = min, \ldots, max$ it can either answer a fetch request or a store request. In case of a fetch it just stays in state $x = p$. In case of a store it goes directly to another state $x = r$ where $r = min, \ldots, max$ by taking the transition from $x = p$ to $x = r$ labelled by action $store(r)$, or it just stays in state $x = p$ in case r equals p. As specified, X starts from having value 0. At its detailed level X executes no steps at all (6) whenever it is to send its current value: instead, fetching and sending a value is done by a role step (one out of many from PhX_0 to PhX_1 in Fig. 2f). In addition, X executes one step (7) whenever it receives a value to be stored: storing that value by overwriting the previous value through changing its current state – but only if needed.

Given the result of computing $x+1$ by P_1 in state s_3^1 (right after its third step labelled $compute(x+1)$), P_1 should select action $putIntoX_{j+1}$ (whose index $j+1$ corresponds to the value computed) dependent on which of its second steps $getValueX$ it has taken. This in turn fully depends on the current state of X at the moment step $getValueX$ has been selected. (For P_2 similar observations can be made.) As can be seen below, the latter dependence is assured by consistency rule $CR_1^1(j)$, whereas the former dependence follows from phase $Ph_1^1(j)$ and its trap $\theta_1(j+1)$ as defined in Fig. 2a.

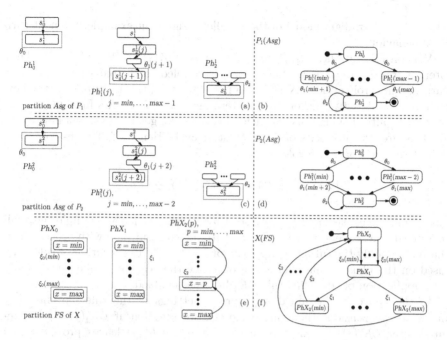

Fig. 2. *Asg* partition and role of P_1 (a,b) and P_2 (c,d), *FS* partition and role of X (e,f).

The coordination we want to model, i.e. the mutual interaction between the three STDs, assumes an atomic fetch-store cycle for variable x. Thus we model the details concerning both fetching and storing via one role of each STD of P_1 and P_2 for both requests as well as via one role of STD X for handling such requests, always in pairs. Roles are called $P_i(Asg)$, for $i = 1, 2$, and $X(FS)$, respectively, and visualized in the right part of Fig. 2. The partitions of the phases and traps comprising the roles *Asg* and *FS* are displayed on the left.

For P_i, index j of phase $Ph_1^i(j)$ is meant to reflect the state of X at the time of fetching. By our assumption errors do not occur, phase $Ph_1^i(max)$ of P_1 and the two phases $Ph_1^i(max-1), Ph_1^i(max)$ of P_2 are not present. During any phase $Ph_1^i(j)$ the actual computation is being carried out. Within such a phase $Ph_1^i(j)$ of P_i the value resulting from computing $j + i$, for $i = 1, 2$, is indicated via the parameter of trap $\theta_1(j+i)$, which will be entered certainly.

The consistency rules based on these roles, are as follows:

$$P_i(Asg)\colon Ph_0^i \xrightarrow{\theta_0} Ph_1^i(j) \ \| \ X(FS)\colon PhX_0 \xrightarrow{\xi_0(j)} PhX_1 \qquad (CR_1^i(j))$$

$$P_i(Asg)\colon Ph_1^i(j) \xrightarrow{\theta_1(k)} Ph_2^i \ \| \ X(FS)\colon PhX_1 \xrightarrow{\xi_1} PhX_2(k) \qquad (CR_2^i(j,k))$$

$$P_i(Asg)\colon Ph_2^i \xrightarrow{\theta_2} Ph_2^i \ \| \ X(FS)\colon PhX_2(k) \xrightarrow{\xi_2} PhX_0 \qquad (CR_3^i(k))$$

where rule $CR_1^i(j)$ is for fetching value j, rule $CR_2^i(j,k)$ for initiating storing value k and rule $CR_3^i(k)$ for finishing storing value k. This completes the specifi-

cation of the Paradigm model of the parallel assignment example. We next turn
to its behavior.

Via consistency rule $CR_1^i(j)$, imposing phase $Ph_1^i(j)$ on P_i (and thereby later
entering trap $\theta_1(j+i)$, as we have seen), is coupled to the old value of x, thus
starting a new role cycle of $X(FS)$. Via rule $CR_2^i(j,k)$, this is coupled to the new
value of x. Rule $CR_3^i(k)$ then couples termination of P_i to X's finishing its full
cycle. Only after having finished such a cycle, X can get involved in a new cycle,
which assures the atomicity of the fetch-store cycle. Hence a full fetch-store cycle
of X at the level of its FS role is

$$PhX_0 \xrightarrow{\xi_0(j)} PhX_1 \xrightarrow{\xi_1} PhX_2(k) \xrightarrow{\xi_2} PhX_0$$

Examining the consistency rules we see that in this particular example they will
be applied in a sequential order. Starting from a configuration with process X in
phase PhX_0 only the rules CR_1^i applies, for $i = 1, 2$. After execution of rule CR_1^i,
based on the phases, rule CR_2^i is the only one that can be applied next. Only
after application of rule CR_2^i, rule CR_3^i becomes enabled.

In the above, we assumed appropriate settings of the rule parameters j
and k. If we consider them more closely, we see that if $CR_2^i(j',k')$ is executed after $CR_1^i(j)$, we must have $j' = j$. For $CR_1^i(j)$ leaves process P_i in
phase $Ph_1^i(j)$, while $CR_2^i(j',k')$ assumes P_i to be in phase $Ph_1^i(j')$. Application of rule $CR_2^i(j',k')$ requires $\theta_1(k')$ to be a trap of phase $Ph_1^i(j')$. From Fig. 2
we see that $Ph_1^i(j')$ only has one trap, viz. trap $\theta_i(j' + i)$, for $i = 1, 2$. Thus,
we must have $k' = j' + i$. Finally, similar as for parameters j and j' in $CR_1^i(j)$
and $CR_2^i(j',k')$, we have that application of rule $CR_3^i(k'')$ following an application of rule $CR_2^i(j',k')$ is only possible when $k'' = k'$: regarding the process X,
the target phase $Ph_2^i(k')$ of $CR_2^i(j',k')$ must be the same as the source phase
$Ph_2^i(k'')$ of $CR_3^i(k'')$.

Taking the range of the parameters into account, we conclude that in the
respective collaborations, i.e. between P_1 and X, and between P_2 and X, the only
complete sequences of rule actions are of the form $CR_1^1(j)CR_2^1(j,j+1)CR_3^1(j+1)$,
for $min \leqslant j \leqslant max-1$, and $CR_1^2(k)CR_2^2(k,k+2)CR_3^2(k+2)$, for $min \leqslant k \leqslant$
$max-2$. For brevity we will use $CR_*^1(j)$ and $CR_*^2(k)$ for these sequences below.

So far we have relied on ad hoc reasoning in the context of the semantics
of the Paradigm model for the two parallel assignments. In the next section we
describe how sequences of rule actions are verified more systematically.

3   Proving Collaboration Properties

Let us refer by $\mathcal{PA}$ to the Paradigm model of the parallel assignments. We will
explain the operational semantics of Paradigm for the model $\mathcal{PA}$. As usual,
the operational semantics is based on configurations and transitions between
them [5,8]. Configurations for $\mathcal{PA}$ are of the form $\langle s, Ph; s', Ph'; x=h, PhX \rangle$ were
s, s' and $x=h$ are states of Ph, Ph' and PhX, which are in turn phases of P_1,
P_2 and X, respectively. A transition for $\mathcal{PA}$ can be

(i) a *local transition* based on a transition of one of the STDs, or

(ii) a *global transfer* based on one of the consistency rules.

A local transition only changes state for one of the components, i.e. P_1, P_2 or X. Reflecting the constraints put by the phases, a transition is allowed if present in all current phase(s) of the component. For example, because $s_0^1 \to s_1^1$ for action $addressX$ is in Ph_0^1 we have

$$\langle s_0^1, Ph_0^1; s_0^2, Ph_0^2; x=0, PhX_0 \rangle \longrightarrow \langle s_1^1, Ph_0^1; s_0^2, Ph_0^2; x=0, PhX_0 \rangle$$

but, since $s_1^1 \to s_2^1(0)$ is not in Ph_0^1,

$$\langle s_1^1, Ph_0^1; s_0^2, Ph_0^2; x=0, PhX_0 \rangle \not\longrightarrow \langle s_2^1(0), Ph_0^1; s_0^2, Ph_0^2; x=0, PhX_0 \rangle$$

Note, for a local transition, the state may change but not the phases.

A global transfer effects the phases of one or more components of a configuration. The transfer is determined by the selected consistency rule. The consistency rule can be applied if the components involved are in the phase as required by the rule and have moreover reached the specified traps within the phases. If multiple consistency rules are enabled, one is selected non-deterministically. It is a design obligation to see to it that the collaboration and coordination proceeds as desired, in particular that deadlock is avoided. As an example of a global transfer, the transfer

$$\langle s_1^1, Ph_0^1; s_5^2, Ph_2^2; x=2, PhX_0 \rangle \xrightarrow{CR_1^1(2)} \langle s_1^1, Ph_1^1(2); s_5^2, Ph_2^2; x=2, PhX_0 \rangle$$

is driven by consistency rule $CR_1^1(2)$, which requires P_1 to be in phase Ph_0^1 and in trap $\theta_0 = \{s_1^1\}$, and requires X to be in phase PhX_0 in trap $\xi_0(2) = \{x=2\}$. The rule $CR_1^1(2)$ labels the transfer and is in such a situation referred to as a rule action. For the Paradigm model $\mathcal{PA}$, the sets of tags or rule actions in $\{CR_1^1(j), CR_2^1(j,k), CR_3^1(k) \mid min \leqslant j \leqslant max-1\}$ and $\{CR_1^2(j), CR_2^2(j,k), CR_3^2(k) \mid min \leqslant j \leqslant max-2\}$ are called the collaboration alphabets Σ_1 and Σ_2 of $\mathcal{PA}$, respectively. We put $\Sigma = \Sigma_1 \cup \Sigma_2$.

Let $\mathcal{L}$ be a logic in which one can express properties of configurations. In particular, $\mathcal{L}$ includes characteristic formulas for sets of configurations. For example, in the context of the previous section, the formula $\varphi_{\langle x=0, PhX_0 \rangle}$ is satisfied precisely by all configurations $\langle s, Ph; s', Ph'; x=0, PhX_0 \rangle$ with s a state of Ph, Ph a phase of P_1, s' a state of Ph', Ph' a phase of P_2. We write $\gamma \models \varphi$, for a configuration γ and a formula φ, if γ satisfies φ. Thus $\langle s_0^1, Ph_0^1; s_0^2, Ph_0^2; x=0, PhX_0 \rangle \models \varphi_{\langle x=0, PhX_0 \rangle}$. For clarity we often write $\langle x=0, PhX_0 \rangle$ in place of $\varphi_{\langle x=0, PhX_0 \rangle}$.

Definition 1. *A triple* $\varphi [\Omega] \psi$ *with* $\varphi, \psi \in \mathcal{L}$, $\Omega \subseteq \Sigma^*$ *is valid, if for every configuration* γ *of a Paradigm model such that* $\gamma \models \varphi$, *and every computation* $\gamma \xrightarrow{w}{}^* \gamma'$ *such that* $w \in \Omega$ *it holds that* $\gamma' \models \psi$.

The set Ω is a set of sequences of rule actions, reflecting the behaviour at the coordination level. We provide non-trivial examples of valid triples below. However, in general, we have

- $\varphi\,[\,\Omega\,]\,$ **true** always holds
- $\varphi\,[\,\Omega\,]\,$ **false** holds if for no configuration γ such that $\gamma \models \varphi$ there is a computation $\gamma \xrightarrow{w}{}^* \gamma'$ with $w \in \Omega$

Typically, we obtain a triple of the form $\langle s, Ph_1, \ldots, Ph_n \rangle\,[\,\sigma\,]\,\psi$ for a component having n roles and a sequence σ from one or two collaboration alphabets, by inspection of the changes of the component when executing the transfers based on the rules mentioned in σ, possibly interspersed with local transitions. Recall, a local transition between two configurations does not carry a label, while a global transfer between to configurations is labelled by a rule action.

By application of the compositional rules discussed next, we obtain more complicated triples.

Conjunctive Rule. If $\varphi_1\,[\,\Omega\,]\,\psi_1$ and $\varphi_2\,[\,\Omega\,]\,\psi_2$, then also $(\varphi_1 \wedge \varphi_2)\,[\,\Omega\,]\,(\psi_1 \wedge \psi_2)$.

The soundness of the conjunctive rule is direct from the definition. If $\gamma \models \varphi_1 \wedge \varphi_2$ and $\gamma \xrightarrow{w}{}^* \gamma'$ for a string of rule actions $w \in \Omega$, then $\gamma' \models \psi_1$ because $\gamma \models \varphi_1$, and $\gamma' \models \psi_2$ because $\gamma \models \varphi_2$. The rule is typically used to combine triples for separate components. We shall see below that the triple $\langle s_0^1, Ph_0^1 \rangle\,[\,CR_1^1(0)CR_2^1(0,1)CR_3^1(1)\,]\,\langle s_5^1, Ph_2^1 \rangle$ for process P_1, and the triple $\langle x{=}0, PhX_0 \rangle\,[\,CR_1^1(0)CR_2^1(0,1)CR_3^1(1)\,]\,\langle x{=}1, PhX_0 \rangle$ for process X can be combined into the triple

$$\langle s_0^1, Ph_0^1; x{=}0, PhX_0 \rangle\,[\,CR_1^1(0)CR_2^1(0,1)CR_3^1(1)\,]\,\langle s_5^1, Ph_2^1; x{=}1, PhX_0 \rangle$$

for the two processes together.

Sequential Rule. Let σ, ϱ be two arbitrary rule sequences and φ and ψ two formulas. If $\varphi\,[\,\sigma\,]\,\chi$ and $\chi\,[\,\varrho\,]\,\psi$ hold for some formula χ then $\varphi\,[\,\sigma\varrho\,]\,\psi$ also holds.

Regarding the soundness, if $\gamma \models \varphi$ and $\gamma \xrightarrow{\sigma\varrho}{}^* \gamma''$, we can split the computation into $\gamma \xrightarrow{\sigma}{}^* \gamma' \xrightarrow{\varrho}{}^* \gamma''$. From $\varphi\,[\,\sigma\,]\,\chi$ we obtain $\gamma' \models \chi$, and from $\chi\,[\,\varrho\,]\,\psi$ we obtain $\gamma'' \models \psi$. The reverse of the rule only applies if we are able to characterize in the logic the set of configurations that can be reached from any γ such that $\gamma \models \varphi$ by a computation labeled σ. This can then serve as the intermediate formula χ. In the elaborated example below we will have that the triple

$$\langle x{=}0, PhX_0 \rangle\,[\,CR_1^1(0)CR_2^1(0,1)CR_3^1(1)\,]\,\langle x{=}1, PhX_0 \rangle$$

and the triple

$$\langle x{=}1, PhX_0 \rangle\,[\,CR_1^2(1)CR_2^2(1,3)CR_3^2(3)\,]\,\langle x{=}3, PhX_0 \rangle$$

yield the triple

$$\langle x{=}0, PhX_0 \rangle\,[\,CR_1^1(0)CR_2^1(0,1)CR_3^1(1)CR_1^2(1)CR_2^2(1,3)CR_3^2(3)\,]\,\langle x{=}3, PhX_0 \rangle$$

by the sequential rule.

Interleaving Rule. There exist formulas ψ_w for all $w \in \Omega$ such that $\varphi\,[\,w\,]\,\psi_w$ iff $\varphi\,[\,\Omega\,]\,\psi$ holds for $\psi = \bigvee\{\psi_w \mid w \in \Omega\}$.

The rule is referred to as the interleaving rule, since when applied the set of sequences of rule actions Ω is typically a set of the form $\sigma_1 \| \cdots \| \sigma_n$, a shuffle of sequences $\sigma_1, \ldots, \sigma_n$ stemming from different collaborations. The implication from left to right is direct from the definition. If $\gamma \models \varphi$ and $\gamma \xrightarrow{w}^* \gamma'$ for $w \in \Omega$ then $\gamma' \models \psi_w$, and, by the form of ψ, $\gamma' \models \psi$. For the implication from right to left, we can take $\psi_w = \psi$ for all w. In the example below we will encounter an enumeration of all the interleavings of two sequences σ and ϱ in a situation where we know that strict interleavings of σ and ϱ are not possible, thus $\psi_w = \textbf{false}$, in that case. For the combinations $\sigma\varrho$ and $\varrho\sigma$ we will have $\psi_{\sigma\varrho} = \psi_{\varrho\sigma} = \psi$ in the example. Since **false** vanishes in the disjunction we obtain from the interleaving rule a triple for ψ.

As a further illustration of the use of the above proof rules we consider the example of the two parallel assignments of the previous section. We claim that the Paradigm model $\mathcal{PA}$ satisfies

$$\langle s_0^1, Ph_0^1; s_0^2, Ph_0^2; x{=}0, PhX_0 \rangle \, [\, CR_*^1(j) \| CR_*^2(k) \,] \, \langle s_5^1, Ph_2^1; s_5^2, Ph_2^2; x{=}3, PhX_0 \rangle$$

for suitable parameters j and k and with $CR_*^1(j) = CR_1^1(j)CR_2^1(j, j{+}1)CR_3^1(j{+}1)$ and $CR_*^2(k) = CR_1^2(k)CR_2^2(k, k{+}2)CR_3^2(k{+}2)$. Thus, any computation started in configuration $\langle s_0^1, Ph_0^1; s_0^2, Ph_0^2; x{=}0, PhX_0 \rangle$ that executes the rules $CR_1^1(j)$, $CR_2^1(j, j{+}1)$, and $CR_3^1(j{+}1)$ consecutively in the collaboration of P_1 and X, and the rules $CR_1^2(k)$, $CR_2^2(k, k{+}2)$, and $CR_3^2(k{+}2)$, in that order, in the collaboration of P_2 and X, for suitable values of j and k, end in configuration $\langle s_5^1, Ph_2^1; s_5^2, Ph_2^2; x{=}3, PhX_0 \rangle$.

Computations starting from configuration $\langle s_0^1, Ph_0^1; s_0^2, Ph_0^2; x{=}0, PhX_0 \rangle$ do not exhibit arbitrary interleavings of sequences $CR_*^1(j)$ and $CR_*^2(k)$. Once CR_1^i has been executed by P_i, the other process P_{3-i} remains in its phase Ph_0^{3-i} and has to wait till X has returned in phase PhX_0 before any of the rules it is involved in can be executed. Therefore, there are no computations showing a sequence $w \in CR_*^1(j) \| CR_*^2(k)$ of a shape different from $CR_*^1(j)CR_*^2(k)$ or $CR_*^2(k)CR_*^1(j)$. Thus, it holds that

$$\langle s_0^1, Ph_0^1; s_0^2, Ph_0^1; x{=}0, PhX_0 \rangle \, [\, w \,] \, \textbf{false}$$

for $w \neq CR_*^1(j)CR_*^2(k), CR_*^2(k)CR_*^1(j)$.

Next, we determine the possible values for j and k. In configurations where $x{=}h$ and $j{\neq}h$ we have that X isn't in trap $\xi_0(j)$ and cannot reach it either. Also, no local transition is possible from state $x{=}h$ in phase PhX_0. Thus, it holds that $\langle x{=}h, PhX_0 \rangle [\, CR_1^i(j) \,] \textbf{false}$. However, if $j{=}h$, relying on cooperation from process P_i such that the sequence $CR_*^i(h)$ is executed, we obtain that x has been increased by i and has obtained value $h + i$. Therefore, on the one hand,

$$\langle x{=}h, PhX_0 \rangle [\, CR_*^i(j) \,] \, \textbf{false} \tag{1}$$

for $j{\neq}h$, while on the other hand

$$\langle x{=}h, PhX_0 \rangle [\, CR_*^i(h) \,] \langle x{=}h{+}i, PhX_0 \rangle \tag{2}$$

From triple (1) we obtain $\langle x{=}0, PhX_0 \rangle [\, CR_*^1(j)CR_*^2(k) \,]$ **false** for $j \neq 0$. Since by triple (2) $\langle x{=}0, PhX_0 \rangle [\, CR_*^1(0) \,] \langle x{=}1, PhX_0 \rangle$, and $\langle x{=}1, PhX_0 \rangle [\, CR_*^2(k) \,]$ **false** by (1) for $k \neq 1$, we get $\langle x{=}0, PhX_0 \rangle [\, CR_*^1(0)CR_*^2(k) \,]$ **false**, for $k \neq 1$, by the sequential rule. This combines into $\langle x{=}0, PhX_0 \rangle [\, CR_*^1(j)CR_*^2(k) \,]$ **false** for $j \neq 0$ or $k \neq 1$. Using $\langle s_0^1, Ph_0^1; s_0^2, Ph_0^2 \rangle [\, CR_*^1(j)CR_*^2(k) \,]$ **true** and the conjunctive rule, we arrive at

$$\langle s_0^1, Ph_0^1; s_0^2, Ph_0^2; x{=}0, PhX_0 \rangle [\, CR_*^1(j)CR_*^2(k) \,] \text{ \textbf{false}} \tag{3}$$

for $j \neq 0$ or $k \neq 1$. Similarly, interchanging $CR_*^1(j)$ and $CR_*^2(k)$, we have

$$\langle s_0^1, Ph_0^1; s_0^2, Ph_0^2; x{=}0, PhX_0 \rangle [\, CR_*^2(k)CR_*^1(j) \,] \text{ \textbf{false}} \tag{4}$$

for $k \neq 0$ or $j \neq 2$.

We next aim to derive a triple for the sequence $CR_*^1(0)CR_*^2(1)$. Analysis of the behavior of P_1 and X with respect to the rules in $CR_*^1(0)$ yields, respectively, the triples $\langle s_0^1, Ph_0^1 \rangle [\, CR_*^1(0) \,] \langle s_5^1, Ph_2^1 \rangle$ and $\langle x{=}0, PhX_0 \rangle [\, CR_*^1(0) \,] \langle x{=}1, PhX_0 \rangle$. Thus, $\langle s_0^1, Ph_0^1; x{=}0, PhX_0 \rangle [\, CR_*^1(0) \,] \langle s_5^1, Ph_2^1; x{=}1, PhX_0 \rangle$ by the conjunctive rule. Since P_2 is not involved in any of the rules of $CR_*^1(0)$, it holds that $\langle s_0^2, Ph_0^1 \rangle [\, CR_*^1(0) \,] \langle s_0^2, Ph_0^2 \rangle$, which can be used with the above for the conjunctive rule to deduce

$$\langle s_0^1, Ph_0^1; s_0^2, Ph_0^1; x{=}0, PhX_0 \rangle [\, CR_*^1(0) \,] \langle s_5^1, Ph_2^1; s_0^2, Ph_0^1; x{=}1, PhX_0 \rangle \tag{5}$$

Likewise we can derive

$$\langle s_5^1, Ph_2^1; s_0^2, Ph_0^1; x{=}1, PhX_0 \rangle [\, CR_*^2(1) \,] \langle s_5^1, Ph_2^1; s_5^2, Ph_2^1; x{=}3, PhX_0 \rangle \tag{6}$$

Therefore, by the sequential rule, we obtain from (5) and (6) that

$$\langle s_0^1, Ph_0^1; s_0^2, Ph_0^1; x{=}0, PhX_0 \rangle [\, CR_*^1(0)CR_*^2(1) \,] \langle s_5^1, Ph_2^1; s_5^2, Ph_2^1; x{=}3, PhX_0 \rangle \tag{7}$$

By symmetry, we conclude the formula

$$\langle s_0^1, Ph_0^1; s_0^2, Ph_0^1; x{=}0, PhX_0 \rangle [\, CR_*^2(0)CR_*^1(2) \,] \langle s_5^1, Ph_2^1; s_5^2, Ph_0^1; x{=}3, PhX_0 \rangle \tag{8}$$

to hold as well, settling the case for the sequence $CR_*^2(0)CR_*^1(2)$.

Finally, we combine the cases gathered so far using the interleaving rule. Put

$$\psi_w = \text{\textbf{false}} \qquad \text{for } w \neq CR_*^1(0)CR_*^2(1),\ CR_*^2(0)CR_*^1(2)$$
$$\psi_w = \langle s_5^1, Ph_2^1; s_5^2, Ph_0^1; x{=}3, PhX_0 \rangle \qquad \text{for } w = CR_*^1(0)CR_*^2(1),\ CR_*^2(0)CR_*^1(2)$$

Then we have from (3), (4), (5), and (8) that

$$\langle s_0^1, Ph_0^1; s_0^2, Ph_0^1; x{=}0, PhX_0 \rangle [\, w \,] \psi_w$$

for all $w \in CR_*^1(j) \parallel CR_*^2(k)$ and suitable parameters j and k. Hence, by the interleaving rule

$$\langle s_0^1, Ph_0^1; s_0^2, Ph_0^1; x{=}0, PhX_0 \rangle [\, CR_*^1(j) \parallel CR_*^2(k) \,] \langle s_5^1, Ph_2^1; s_5^2, Ph_0^1; x{=}3, PhX_0 \rangle \tag{9}$$

since $\bigvee \{\psi_w \mid w \in CR_*^1(j) \parallel CR_*^2(k)\} = \langle s_5^1, Ph_2^1; s_5^2, Ph_0^1; x{=}3, PhX_0 \rangle$. The triple of Eq. (9) captures the property that we aimed to prove.

4   A Paradigm Model of a Pipeline

As a larger Paradigm model we consider a linear pipeline with three workers Wrk_1, Wrk_2, Wrk_3, two buffers Buf_1, Buf_2, an input Buf_0, and an output Buf_3. They cooperate as follows, Wrk_i consuming one item from Buf_{i-1} (from input, if $i = 1$), working on it and producing it towards Buf_i (to output, if $i = 3$). All buffers have a fixed capacity, n say. When empty, no item can be taken from a buffer; when full, no item can be put into it. Contrarily, input and output are never restrictive. See Figs. 3 and 6(a,c) for STDs of workers and buffers.

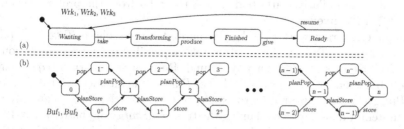

Fig. 3. (a) Three STDs Wrk_1, Wrk_2, Wrk_3, (b) two STDs Buf_1, Buf_2.

A worker visits four states sequentially, starting from state *Wanting*. A buffer precedes an actual *store* action or *pop* action by a preparatory step, *planStore* and *planPop*, respectively. Initially the buffers are empty.

The *Cons* and *Prod* partitions of the workers and the *Src* and *Snk* partitions of the buffers are drawn in Fig. 4. Roles at the level of theses partitions are given

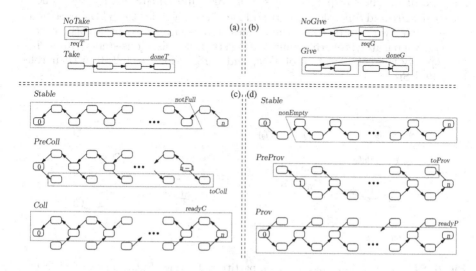

Fig. 4. Partitions (a) *Prod* (b) *Cons* for workers, (c) *Snk* and (d) *Src* for buffers.

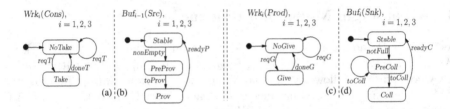

Fig. 5. Roles (a) *Cons*, (c) *Prod* for workers, (b) *Src* and (d) *Snk* for buffers.

in Fig. 5; parts (a,b) group the roles from the protocol given by rules CR_1^i–CR_4^i, fixed i, below; similarly, parts (c,d) group the roles from the protocol given by rules PR_1^i–PR_4^i, fixed i.

In its *Cons* role worker Wrk_i alternates between phase *Take* and phase *NoTake*. In phase *Take* the local action *take* is possible but no *resume* action. In phase *NoTake* this is the other way around. Reaching of the trap *reqT* triggers the collaboration with the providing buffer Buf_{i-1}, the interaction of $Wrk_i(Cons)$ and $Buf_{i-1}(Src)$ as captured by rules CR_1^i to CR_4^i. Clearly, Buf_{i-1} can only provide an item if non-empty, explaining the trap *nonEmpty* of phase *Stable*. Phase *PreProv* characterizes that the buffer is able to provide the item, but is actually doing so in phase *Prov*. Once trap *readyP* is reached in phase *Prov* the buffer can return –in its *Cons* role– to the stable situation.

A buffer also has a *Snk* partition and role, like a worker also has a *Prod* partition and role. These partitions and roles are very similar to the *Src* and *Cons* ones, although we treat the collaboration of $Wrk_i(Prod)$ and $Buf_i(Sink)$ slightly differently, see rules PR_1^i to PR_4^i below.

Two additional components Buf_0 and Buf_3 represent input and output located at beginning and end of the pipeline. Both have no counting behaviour specified. Their respective roles, $Buf_0(Src)$ and $Buf_3(Snk)$, are the same as the earlier *Src* and *Snk* roles of Buf_1 and Buf_2, see Fig. 6 for the STDs' partitions.

We have two sets of consistency rules, representing two protocols for each $i = 1, 2, 3$ separately, together constituting six protocols. Consistency rules CR_1^i–CR_4^i specify the collaboration of Wrk_i and Buf_{i-1}, for $i = 1, 2, 3$, in their roles *Cons* and *Src*.

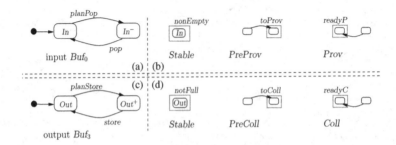

Fig. 6. STDs for (a) Buf_0 and (c) Buf_3, partitions for roles $Buf_0(Src)$ and $Buf_3(Snk)$.

$Wrk_i(Cons)$: $NoTake \xrightarrow{reqT} NoTake \parallel Buf_{i-1}(Src)$: $Stable \xrightarrow{nonEmp} PreProv$ (CR_1^i)

$Buf_{i-1}(Src)$: $PreProv \xrightarrow{toProv} Prov$ (CR_2^i)

$Wrk_i(Cons)$: $NoTake \xrightarrow{reqT} Take \parallel Buf_{i-1}(Src)$: $Prov \xrightarrow{readyP} Stable$ (CR_3^i)

$Wrk_i(Cons)$: $Take \xrightarrow{doneT} NoTake$ (CR_4^i)

When the worker, in need of an item, is in state $Wanting$ that coincides with trap $reqT$ of phase $NoTake$, and the providing buffer is stable and non-empty, i.e. is in the corresponding phase and trap, the buffer proceeds the provisioning (CR_1^i). Once this has been accomplished, via phase $PreProv$ and subsequently via phase $Prov$ (CR_2^i), then by reaching trap $readyP$ of the buffer's phase $Prov$, the worker is allowed to take it, while the buffer returns to its stable phase (CR_3^i). Once the worker has actually taken the item, being in trap $doneT$ of phase $Take$, it returns to phase $NoTake$ again (CR_4^i).

Consistency rules PR_1^i–PR_4^i specify the collaboration of worker Wrk_i and Buf_i, for $i = 1, 2, 3$, in their roles $Prod$ and Snk.

$Wrk_i(Prod)$: $NoGive \xrightarrow{reqG} NoGive \parallel Buf_i(Snk)$: $Stable \xrightarrow{notFull} PreColl$ (PR_1^i)

$Wrk_i(Prod)$: $NoGive \xrightarrow{reqG} Give \parallel Buf_i(Snk)$: $PreColl \xrightarrow{toColl} PreColl$ (PR_2^i)

$Wrk_i(Prod)$: $Give \xrightarrow{doneG} NoGive \parallel Buf_i(Snk)$: $PreColl \xrightarrow{toColl} Coll$ (PR_3^i)

$Buf_i(Snk)$: $Coll \xrightarrow{readyColl} Stable$ (PR_4^i)

The worker can dispense an item when in phase $NoGive$ trap $reqG$ has been reached, while the collecting buffer or output is stable, but not full, i.e. in phase $Stable$ and trap $notFull$ (PR_1^i). The worker proceeds to delivering the item by moving to phase $Give$, while the buffer remains stand-by in phase $PreColl$ (PR_2^i). The worker signals that the item has been dispensed off, via trap $doneG$, for the buffer to collect it in phase $Coll$ (PR_3^i). Once the item is collected by the buffer, witnessed by trap $readyC$, the buffer returns to its $Stable$ phase (PR_4^i).

5   Proving Model Properties

In this section we show how triples for specific collaborations can be glued together to verify a property for the complete system. Initially we focus on small subsystems, and we combine the local properties obtained to yield a property of the system as a whole. In this paper, we will consider a data flow property of the pipeline example.

For the Paradigm model of the pipeline, we shall verify that the number of $store$ actions by the output Buf_3 doesn't exceed the number of pop actions by the input Buf_0. More precisely, we will show

$$\#pop_0 - b_1 - b_2 - 4 \leqslant \#store_3 \leqslant \#pop_0 - b_1 - b_2 \tag{10}$$

where the *pops* and *stores* are executed by Buf_0 and Buf_3, respectively, and b_1, b_2 are the number of items in Buf_1 and Buf_2 at the moment of inspection. For simplicity, we assume the buffers Buf_1 and Buf_2 to be of capacity 3 rather than of arbitrary capacity n. Verification of this property by means of model checking, e.g. with the mCRL2 toolset, may be a chancy undertaking. However, application of the collaboration-driven approach as sketched in the previous section shows to be quite feasible.

The general idea is to first consider the situation for a worker, examining its simultaneous interaction with a providing buffer and a collecting buffer, to conclude a causality among the two rule sets involved. Next, we consider the situation for a buffer, establishing a relationship among the rule sets of the collaboration in which it has a role. Since *store* and *pop* actions correspond to specific phases, and phases correspond to specific rules, we are able to relate *pops* of the input all the way through the pipeline to *stores* of the output.

To be able to use patterns in observed behavior of consistency rules to prove a property in terms of local actions, we need to couple the actions to the rules: A *pop* of Buf_0 is only possible in its phase *Prov*. However, in this phase the action can only be executed once. Therefore, every *pop* implies that consistency rule CR_1^0 has again taken place. Similarly, action *store* by Buf_3 is only allowed in phase *Coll*. Only when trap *readyC* of this phase has been reached we are sure that the action has indeed been executed. Such is confirmed by consistency rule PR_4^3. So, for the analysis of the property we need to relate occurrences of CR_1^0 to those of PR_4^3.

When looking closer at the collaborations of Buf_{i-1}, Wrk_i, and Buf_i, for $i = 1, 2, 3$, these are governed by the groups of rules $CR_1^i, \ldots, CR_4^i$ vs. $PR_1^i, \ldots, PR_4^i$. Inspection of the operational semantics reveals that one can find characteristic formula φ_X and φ_Y, representing finite sets of configurations, such that

$$\varphi_X \left[\{ CR_1^i CR_2^i CR_3^i \} \cup (CR_1^i CR_2^i CR_3^i \parallel PR_4^i) \right] \varphi_Y \quad \text{and}$$

$$\varphi_Y \left[\{ PR_1^i PR_2^i PR_3^i \} \cup (PR_1^i PR_2^i PR_3^i \parallel CR_4^i) \right] \varphi_X \tag{11}$$

It follows that for the subsystem of Buf_{i-1}, Wrk_i, and Buf_i, for given index i, application of rules $CR_1^i CR_2^i CR_3^i$ *precedes* application of rules $PR_1^i PR_2^i PR_3^i$. Reversely, all but the first occurrence of the subsequence $CR_1^i CR_2^i CR_3^i$, and possibly the last, are enclosed by two subsequences $PR_1^i PR_2^i PR_3^i$. Moreover, considering the phases we readily see that the two rule sets are applied cyclically. Rules CR_1^i to CR_4^i can only be applied in that order. The same holds for PR_1^i to PR_4^i.

Next we shift to subsystems involving Wrk_i, Buf_i, and Wrk_{i+1}, for $i = 1, 2$. Because of the assumed buffer capacity of 3, we distinguish characteristic formula ψ_j^i, $j = 0, 1, 2, 3$, for which it holds that

$$\psi_{j-1}^i \left[CR_2^{i+1} \parallel (\varepsilon + PR_4^i) \right] \psi_j^i \quad \text{and}$$

$$\psi_j^i \left[PR_2^i PR_3^i \parallel (\varepsilon + CR_3^{i+1} + CR_3^{i+1} CR_4^{i+1}) \right] \psi_{j-1}^i \tag{12}$$

for $i = 1, 2$, $j = 1, 2, 3$ and were ε denotes the empty sequence of rule actions. For configurations satisfying formula ψ_j^i we have that Buf_i holds j elements. Thus, the buffer moves up from $j-1$ to j elements when rule CR_2^i is executed. Reversely, the buffer moves down from j to $j-1$ elements when rules PR_2^i and PR_3^i are executed.

Now let $\gamma_0 \xrightarrow{w}{}^* \gamma'$ be any computation of the full pipeline system running from its start configuration γ_0, where all buffers are in state In, 0, or Out and in stable phases for each partition, and where all workers are in state $Wanting$ and in phases $NoTake$ and $NoGive$. Suppose the number of $pops$ performed by Buf_0, denoted by $\#pop_0$, equals p. Then, as argued above, we have $\#CR_2^0 = p$, with $\#CR_2^0$ denoting the number of occurrences of rule action CR_2^0 in w. Since CR_2^0 is part of a subsequence $CR_1^0 CR_2^0 CR_3^0$, and the subsequences $CR_1^0 CR_2^0 CR_3^0$ and $PR_1^1 PR_2^1 PR_3^1$ of w alternate, as concluded from property (11), it follows that $p-1 \leqslant \#PR_2^1 \leqslant p$. Because of the relationship of PR_2^1, CR_2^2 and the content b_1 of Buf_1 of property (12), we obtain $p-b_1-1 \leqslant \#CR_2^2 \leqslant p-b_1$. Continuing along the pipeline we similarly obtain $p-b_1-2 \leqslant \#PR_2^3 \leqslant p-b_1$, and $p-b_1-b_2-3 \leqslant \#PR_3^3 \leqslant p-b_1-b_2$. Therefore, $p-b_1-b_2-4 \leqslant \#PR_4^3 \leqslant p-b_1-b_2$. Thus, for $\#store_3$, the number of $stores$ performed by Buf_3, we have $p-4-b_1-b_2 \leqslant \#store_3 \leqslant p-b_1-b_2$. Substituting $\#pop_0$ for p we obtain Eq. (10), as was to be shown.

Although only a sketch of a proof for the pipeline property has been given, the presentation aims to stress the component-driven nature of the approach guided by the form of the underlying architecture of the system. The split required by Paradigm, distinguishing local behaviour vs. global interaction, is rather useful for the modularity. Vertical reasoning focuses on the consequences of local transitions for consistency rules to become enabled, at least partially, when a transition makes the component to enter a trap of a phase, as well as on the restriction of the locus of control by phases and traps, being in a phase or trap implies being in a specific subset of states. Horizontal reasoning concerns the order in which consistency rules can be applied, thus it considers the synchronicity among phases and traps of multiple collaborating components. Clearly, more examples need to be examined and more case studies need to be performed to underpin the proposed method of (i) deriving triples for interacting component groups, and (ii) combining theses triples to verify the complete architecture. However, we argued that by reasoning about specific collaborations and by combining the emerging patterns we are able to deal with properties of larger systems modeled than a straightforward model checking approach of a Paradigm model, that is deemed to face state space explosion, would allow. The separation of global collaboration and local computation underlying Paradigm is expected to be helpful in pursuing this approach.

References

1. Andova, S., Groenewegen, L.P.J., Stafleu, J., de Vink, E.P.: Formalizing adaptation on-the-fly. In: Salaün, G., Sirjani, M. (eds.) Proceedings of FOCLASA. ENTCS, vol. 255, pp. 23–44 (2009)

2. Andova, S., Groenewegen, L.P.J., de Vink, E.P.: Towards dynamic adaptation of probabilistic systems. In: Margaria, T., Steffen, B. (eds.) ISoLA 2010, Part II. LNCS, vol. 6416, pp. 143–159. Springer, Heidelberg (2010)
3. Andova, S., Groenewegen, L.P.J., de Vink, E.P.: Dynamic consistency in process algebra: from paradigm to ACP. Sci. Comput. Program. **76**(8), 711–735 (2011)
4. Andova, S., Groenewegen, L.P.J., de Vink, E.P.: Dynamic adaptation with distributed control in Paradigm. Sci. Comput. Program. **94**, 333–361 (2014)
5. de Bakker, J.W., de Vink, E.P.: Control Flow Semantics. Foundations of Computing Series. The MIT Press, Cambridge (1996)
6. Cheng, B.H.C., de Lemos, R., Giese, H., Inverardi, P., Magee, J. (eds.): Software Engineering for Self-Adaptive Systems. LNCS, vol. 5525. Springer, Heidelberg (2009)
7. Engels, G., Groenewegen, L.: Specification of coordinated behaviour by SOCCA. In: Warboys, B.C. (ed.) EWSPT 1994. LNCS, vol. 772, pp. 128–151. Springer, Heidelberg (1994)
8. Groenewegen, L., de Vink, E.P.: Operational semantics for coordination in paradigm. In: Arbab, F., Talcott, C. (eds.) COORDINATION 2002. LNCS, vol. 2315, pp. 191–206. Springer, Heidelberg (2002)
9. Jones, C.B.: Development methods for computer programs including a notion of interference. Ph.D. thesis, Oxford University (1981)
10. Pierik, C., de Boer, F.S.: A proof outline logic for object-oriented programming. Theor. Comput. Sci. **343**, 413–442 (2005)
11. Reimer, W., Schäfer, W., Schmal, T.: Towards a dedicated object-oriented software process modeling language. In: Dannenberg, R.B., Mitchell, S. (eds.) ECOOP 1997 Workshops. LNCS, vol. 1357, pp. 299–302. Springer, Heidelberg (1998)
12. de Roever, W.-P., de Boer, F., Hannemann, U., Hooman, J., Lakhnech, Y., Poel, M., Zwiers, J.: Concurrency Verification: Introduction to Compositional and Noncompositional Methods. Cambridge University Press, New York (2001)
13. Xu, Q., de Roever, W.P., He, J.: The rely-guarantee method for verifying shared variable concurrent programs. Formal Aspects Comput. **9**(2), 149–174 (1997)

Toward a Formal Foundation for Time Travel in Stories and Games

Michiel Helvensteijn[1,2(✉)] and Farhad Arbab[1,3]

[1] Universiteit Leiden, Leiden, The Netherlands
[2] University College London, London, UK
`m.helvensteijn@ucl.ac.uk`
[3] Centrum voor Wiskunde En Informatica, Amsterdam, The Netherlands
`farhad.arbab@cwi.nl`

Abstract. Time-travel is a popular topic not only in science fiction, but in physics as well, especially when it concerns the notion of "changing the past". It turns out that if time-travel exists, it will follow certain logical rules. In this paper we apply the tools of discrete mathematics to two such sets of rules from theoretical physics: the Novikov Self Consistency Principle and the Many Worlds Interpretation of quantum mechanics. Using temporal logic, we can encode the dynamics of a time-travel story or game, and model-check them for adherence to the rules. We also present the first ever game-engine following these rules, allowing the development of technically accurate time-travel games.

1 Introduction

Time travel has long been a popular topic in science fiction and fantasy. Stories about backward time travel were written at least as far back as the 1700s [9,10]. Even though we do not know whether time travel is possible in the real world, general consensus among philosophers and theoretical physicists is that *if* it is possible, it will follow certain logical rules. This is especially relevant when it comes to the prospect of "changing the past". Many works of fiction play it rather fast and loose with these rules, if they follow a consistent set of rules at all. This is not to say that those stories are necessarily bad. However, we do feel that logical consistency is a worthy goal to strive for.

Take, for example, the movie "Back to the Future" [13]. While it is an excellent movie, it is also a good example of a story that heavily features time travel, but does not follow the rules. It takes place in California, 1985, and the only aberration is a car that can travel into the past. Marty McFly travels back 30 years and accidentally prevents his parents from getting together. We claim that even with a time-traveling DeLorean, there is still no mechanism by which Marty could then 'slowly fade out of existence'. As it turns out, there is no mechanism by which he could 'stop existing' at all. After all, if Marty was never born, he could not go back in time to prevent his parents from getting together in the first place. Generally, this situation is known as a *temporal paradox*. This specific version is a variation on the *grandfather paradox* [13, 285–294].

© Springer International Publishing Switzerland 2016
E. Ábrahám et al. (Eds.): de Boer Festschrift, LNCS 9660, pp. 261–276, 2016.
DOI: 10.1007/978-3-319-30734-3_18

In this paper, we look at time travel from a discrete mathematics point of view. We describe a way to model space-time as a *Kripke structure*, and a way to specify and model-check specific stories within that framework using *temporal logic*. We are not concerned about the physical mechanism through which time travel may be achieved (e.g., whether it is by magic, wormholes or flux capacitors). We just allow for models in which effect precedes cause, and explore the implications. We also present a JavaScript implementation of a game with time-travel mechanics following the rules described in this paper.

There are two main theories regarding temporal paradox that are generally accepted as sensible. These are the Novikov Self-consistency Principle and the Many-Worlds Interpretation of quantum mechanics. Both principles have one rule in common: "one cannot change recorded history". But they differ in how they handle attempts to do so.

Under *Novikov Self-consistency Principle (NSP)*, there is one fixed timeline, and any actions taken by a time traveler were 'part of history all along' [2]. Any space-time which would lead to paradox cannot exist, in the same way that a proposition which is simultaneously true and not true cannot exist. So under this principle, Marty McFly could never travel back in time and act the way he did in the movie. That time-line is impossible. *Circular causation* is still allowed, however, i.e., an event that (indirectly) causes itself. NSP can be captured with a *linear graph*, and described with the *temporal logic LTL_p*.

The *Many-Worlds Interpretation (MWI)* is more permissive than NSP. It does not restrict the occurrence of paradoxes, but rather provides a mechanism to channel them. Under this interpretation, time is not a line, but a tree, and where a paradox would otherwise occur, a branch exists to accommodate the contradictory state. With this theory, Marty McFly could prevent his parents from getting together and be none the worse for wear. From that moment, he would exist in an alternate branch of the timeline, merely having separated his 'alternate parents', and prevented 'alternate Marty' from being born. All models under NSP are also possible under MWI. The remaining models have to be *directed trees*, and described with the *temporal logic CTL_{lp}^**.

In Sect. 2, we examine both theories in relation to non-interactive storytelling, e.g., books and movies. Then, in Sect. 3, we look at how the situation changes when dealing with time-travel mechanics in *video games*. A human player complicates matters, because a developer has only limited control over their actions in the game. We describe a number of ways in which single-player games could nonetheless be developed. We then show why multiplayer games are a different story, not feasible under either theory, unless the rules of the game are prohibitively limited. Section 4 describes our implementation of a single player game engine that can work with both theories. To our knowledge, this is the first attempt to develop a game following these rules of time-travel. Finally, Sect. 5 concludes the paper and discusses future work.

Where relevant, we relate the concepts described in this paper to related concepts in quantum mechanics.[1]

---

[1] The authors are fairly confident in drawing these parallels, but it has to be noted that neither has a background in theoretical physics.

2   Time Travel in Non-interactive Storytelling

This section introduces a formal framework for talking about causation and time travel under the Novikov Self-consistency Principle (NSP) and the Many-Worlds Interpretation of quantum mechanics (MWI). It lays out the rules of these theories using Kripke structures and temporal logic, in such a way that a time travel story may be model-checked, assuming the relevant states and events of that story can be encoded into a formal structure.

We do not really expect science fiction writers to go through this process, but the rigor of a formal model does give valuable insight into what can and cannot happen when it comes to time travel. And the foundation provided in this section will be invaluable when we talk about game development in Sects. 3 and 4.

2.1   Modeling Space-Time

First, we represent models of space-time to encompass both NSP and MWI.

Definition 1. *Let $\mathfrak{S}$ represent the set of all possible spatial configurations or states for a given type of story. A space-time model is a tuple $m = (S, \rightarrow)$, where $S \subseteq \mathfrak{S}$ is a set of states and $\rightarrow \subseteq S \times S$ is an injective relation representing a time-step.[2] We write $\mathfrak{M}$ to denote the set of all such models. We write $\mathfrak{M}_L \subset \mathfrak{M}$ for the set of all such models where $\rightarrow$ is a partial function.[3]*

This allows possibly branching timelines with shapes like these:

To encode states for a typical time-travel scenario, we will often need some kind of spatial coordinate system which can be occupied by different types of interacting entities, especially when talking about games:

Definition 2. *In cases where we need to work with a spatial coordinate system, we can define $\mathfrak{S}$ as 2-dimensional $\mathfrak{D}$ space, describing two dimensions of discrete cells in space, occupied by elements of some set $\mathfrak{D}$:*

$$\mathfrak{S} = \mathbb{Z}^2 \rightarrow \mathfrak{D}$$

The definition of the set $\mathfrak{D}$ heavily depends on what types of entities and behaviors should play a role in our stories. It may contain any number of configurations for characters, accomodating for their inventory and equipment, even the memories of their past observations. There would also be configurations for relevant landscape features and artifacts that these characters can interact with.

Note that both space and time are divided into discrete steps, and constitute independent dimensions in this model. This means we cannot model special or general relativity. Indeed, we do not intend to.

---

[2] *injective*: each state has at most one predecessor, i.e., timelines do not merge.

[3] *(partial) function*: each state has at most one successor, i.e., timelines do not branch.

2.2 Immutable Timelines

To discuss NSP, which speaks of immutable timelines, we restrict our models to the set $\mathfrak{M}_L$ of non-branching timelines, or linear sequences of states (Definition 1).

We can see space-time models as Kripke structures [1]. As such, to encode the rules and events of a story under NSP, we can use the temporal logic LTL_p:

Definition 3. *The syntax of LTL_p is specified with the following grammar:*

$$
\begin{array}{lll}
\phi & ::= & p(s) \mid \top \mid \bot \mid \neg\phi \mid \phi \wedge \phi \mid \phi \vee \phi \mid & \textit{propositional operators} \\
& & \mathtt{X}\phi \mid \mathtt{G}\phi \mid \mathtt{F}\phi \mid \phi\mathtt{U}\phi \mid \phi\mathtt{R}\phi \mid & \textit{forward temporal modalities} \\
& & \mathtt{Y}\phi \mid \mathtt{H}\phi \mid \mathtt{O}\phi \mid \phi\mathtt{S}\phi \mid \phi\mathtt{T}\phi & \textit{backward temporal modalities}
\end{array}
$$

where ϕ is an LTL_p formula, and $p(s)$ is a truth statement about the 'current' space configuration $s \in S$. The formula $\mathtt{X}\phi$ indicates that ϕ holds in the next *state, $\mathtt{G}\phi$ indicates that ϕ holds in* all *future states, $\mathtt{F}\phi$ indicates that ϕ holds in* some *future state, $\phi_1\mathtt{U}\phi_2$ indicates that ϕ_2 holds in some future state and ϕ_1 holds in* all *future states until then, and $\phi_1\mathtt{R}\phi_2$ indicates that ϕ_2 holds in* all *future states until one where ϕ_1 holds. Their counterparts $\mathtt{Y}$, $\mathtt{H}$, $\mathtt{O}$, $\mathtt{S}$ and $\mathtt{T}$ have the same meanings, only taking the $\rightarrow$ operator backward instead of forward.*

Semantics for $m, s \models \phi$, with $m \in \mathfrak{M}_L$ and $s \in m$ are defined in the expected way [4, 7, 8]. We also write $m \models \phi$ and say that ϕ is globally *true in m iff for all states $s \in S$, we have $m, s \models \phi$.*

Chains of $\mathtt{X}$ or $\mathtt{Y}$ modalities will be common in the examples to follow, so we introduce the following shorthand notation:

Notation 4. *Given an integer $i \in \mathbb{Z}$ and LTL_p formula ϕ, define the following notation:*

$$
\mathtt{X}^i\phi = \left\{ \begin{array}{ll} \overbrace{\mathtt{X}\ldots\mathtt{X}}^{|i|}\phi & \text{if } i \geq 0 \\ \underbrace{\mathtt{Y}\ldots\mathtt{Y}}_{|i|}\phi & \text{if } i < 0 \end{array} \right.
$$

LTL_p is an extension of the better known temporal logic LTL, and adds backward modalities to it [7]. The two are equivalent with regard to expressiveness [4], but it has been proved that LTL_p is exponentially more succinct [8]. And clearly, LTL_p formulas will also be more intuitive than their pure LTL counterparts for specifying the behavior of time-travel.

2.3 Causality and the Observer Effect

A set of LTL_p formulas Φ can be used to describe a set of models $M \subset \mathfrak{M}_L$ by requiring that for all formulas $\phi \in \Phi$ and all models $m \in M$ we have $m \models \phi$. If M is the empty set, the specified behavior is paradoxical or otherwise logically inconsistent. If not, Φ satisfies NSP.

It is not always easy to intuit the meaning of arbitrary LTL_p formulas, so we will impose some structure on them and group them into sets that we will call *causality chains* or *observers*, depending on the situation:

Definition 5. *In the setting of NSP, define a* causality chain *or* observer *as a set of LTL_p formulas, each of one of two shapes. One shape represents causality, or observation triggering action. It is the following shape:*

$$\langle cause \rangle \implies \mathsf{X}^i \langle effect \rangle \qquad \text{causality } (NSP)$$

$\langle cause \rangle$ *and* $\langle effect \rangle$ *may not contain any temporal modalities. For specifying the 'mundane' type of causality, where cause directly precedes effect, we take $i = 1$. To have an effect precede or coincide with a cause, we can have $i < 1$, indicating 'backward time-travel' by $|i|$ steps.*

Initial conditions may be specified as follows:

$$\mathsf{OF} \langle conditions \rangle \qquad \text{initial conditions}$$

This indicates that there exists some state in the model that satisfies $\langle conditions \rangle$ (which, again, should contain no modalities).

A causality chain may or may not satisfy NSP, but it is easier to reason about than an arbitrary set of LTL_p formulas. It opens up a new type of visualization to help make sense of the dynamics of a set of models. The *causality diagram* in Fig. 1 shows a single causality chain following the normal flow of time in a linear space-time model. It starts with one or more initial condition rules, and propagates through space-time with one or more causality rules. Figure 2 (page 7) illustrates a causality chain going back in time.

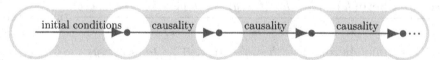

Fig. 1. A *causality diagram*. The large gray circles connected in the background represent the model $(S, \rightarrow)$, with time flowing from left to right. The smaller circles connected by arrows overlaid on top represent a single causality chain which, in this case, follows the normal flow of time.

Coupling the concepts of observation and causality chains corresponds to certain notions in quantum mechanics. Causality can be non-deterministic because of underspecification in the rules (with or without backward causality). We would expect to see multiple models satisfying such rules. But equivalently, we could say that the model, or certain states of the model, are in a *quantum superposition*. Narrowing the set of models through the application of a rule would then correspond to a *wavefunction collapse*. In essence, reality is formed by the act of observation. This is called the *observer effect*. The famous thought experiment known as Schrödinger's cat is a great example of this [11].

2.4 An Example: The Hero of Time

We now look at a concrete example that involves time-travel, and see how Novikov's principle might be violated in a concrete setting.

Example 1. We look at a 2-dimensional $\mathfrak{D}$ space so that we can model an 'overhead view' video-game (though we postpone discussion of interactivity until Sect. 3). Define the set $\mathfrak{D}$ of possible cell-occupants as follows, with $\langle data \rangle$ being some arbitrary data associated with the hero:

$$\mathfrak{D} \quad \ni \quad d \quad ::= \quad \textbf{nothing} \qquad \qquad \text{no occupant}$$
$$| \quad \textbf{hero}(\,\langle data \rangle\,) \qquad \text{a hero (with data)}$$

In the set of causality rules to follow, we use $\langle data \rangle$ to track the *history* of our hero as a sequence of triples (t, x, y) unambiguously specifying space-time coordinates. This allows us to distinguish multiple versions of him coexisting at the same time (as a consequence of time-travel) and to trace their lineage.

We'll present two sets of causality rules: C_L, in which the hero walks left, and C_R, in which he walks right. In both cases, he travels back in time by 2 steps if his age is divisible by 3. However, before taking any action, he looks at all the cells to his right. If he observes an older version of himself, he freezes in place.

We start with the rules that both sets have in common. Because these rules can be lengthy, we use a proof rule notation that can be straightforwardly translated to the corresponding LTL$_p$ formula. For all histories $h, h' \in (\mathbb{N} \times \mathbb{Z} \times \mathbb{Z})^*$ and coordinates $x, y \in \mathbb{Z}$, the set C contains:

$$\frac{}{\text{OF } s(0,0) = \textbf{hero}(\,(0,0,0)\,)} \text{ initial state}$$

$$\frac{s(x,y) = \textbf{hero}(\,h\,) \qquad h = h' {\frown} (t,x,y) \qquad \#h \mid 3 \qquad \neg\,{\ominus}\!\!\!{\rightarrow}(s,h,x,y)}{\text{X}^{-2}\, s(x,y) = \textbf{hero}(\,h \frown (t{-}2,x,y)\,)} \text{ time-travel}$$

$$\frac{s(x,y) = \textbf{hero}(\,h\,) \qquad h = h' \frown (t,x,y) \qquad {\ominus}\!\!\!{\rightarrow}(s,h,x,y)}{\text{X}\, s(x,y) = \textbf{hero}(\,h \frown (t{+}1,x,y)\,)} \text{ surprise}$$

$$\frac{s(x,y) = \textbf{hero}(\,h\,) \qquad h = h' \frown (t{-}1,x,y) \frown (t,x,y)}{\text{X}\, s(x,y) = \textbf{hero}(\,h \frown (t{+}1,x,y)\,)} \text{ frozen}$$

where $h \frown x$ is the concatenation of sequence h and element x, $\#h \mid 3$ indicates that the length of h is divisible by 3 and ${\ominus}\!\!\!{\rightarrow}(s,h,x,y)$ indicates that an older version of the hero is present somewhere to the right of the given coordinates:

$$\begin{aligned}{\ominus}\!\!\!{\rightarrow}(s,h,x,y) \quad = \quad &\exists x' > x\colon\ \exists h' \in (\mathbb{N} \times \mathbb{Z} \times \mathbb{Z})^*\colon\\ &s(x',y) = \textbf{hero}(\,h {\frown} h'\,) \,\wedge\, \text{valid}(h {\frown} h')\end{aligned}$$

and valid(h) indicates that the history h has a valid lineage traceable through the available rules. Finally, define rulesets C_L and C_R as supersets of C, the former having the hero walking left (when his age is indivisible by 3 and he is not exhibiting surprised inaction), and the latter having him walking right. Here are the respective causality rules:

$$\frac{s(x,y) = \textbf{hero}(\,h\,) \qquad h = h' {\frown} (t,x,y) \qquad \#h \nmid 3 \qquad \neg\,{\ominus}\!\!\!{\rightarrow}(s,h,x,y)}{\text{X}\, s(x{-}1,y) = \textbf{hero}(\,h \frown (t{+}1,x{-}1,y)\,)} \text{ walking } (C_L)$$

$$\frac{s(x,y) = \textbf{hero}(\,h\,) \quad h = h' {\frown} (t,x,y) \quad \#h \nmid 3 \quad \neg \ominus\!\!\rightarrow\!(s,h,x,y)}{\textbf{X}\ s(x{+}1,y) = \textbf{hero}(\,h \frown (t{+}1,x{+}1,y)\,)}\ \text{walking } (C_R)$$

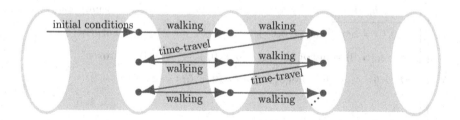

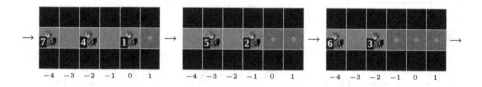

Fig. 2. Causality diagram for the 'walking left' observer C_L (Example 1). It goes back in time twice without causing any contradiction.

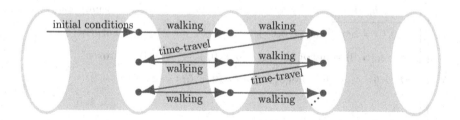

Fig. 3. Graphical representation of the 'walking left' observer C_L (Example 1). For each state, only a 3×6 area is shown. The instances of the hero also display their age (i.e., the length of their history). A black background indicates that a cell's content is unknown (cells on $y \neq 0$ are not specified by the causality rules). The cells observed by the hero ($\ominus\!\!\rightarrow$) at age 1, 2 and 3 are specially marked. This scenario corresponds with the causality diagram from Fig. 2. The graphical tiles come from our proof-of-concept implementation described in Sect. 4.

Lemma 1. *Walking left satisfies Novikov's self-consistency principle. Walking right leads to contradiction.*

Proof. To prove the former, we need only provide a model that satisfies the rules in C_L. Figure 3 shows a graphical representation of such a model, which corresponds with the causality chain of Fig. 2. Interpreting such a visualization may take some getting used to. The time-step relation $\rightarrow$ represents 'absolute' time. From the hero's reference point, he jumps back and forth between these states, so his history will be longer than the history of the world he inhabits.

To prove the second claim of the lemma, we take the rules of C_R and prove logical contradiction by natural deduction. We start with the state s_0 in the timeline $s_0 \rightarrow s_1 \rightarrow s_2 \rightarrow \cdots$ and with h_0, h_1 and h_2 defined as:

$$h_0 = (0,0,0) \qquad h_1 = h_0{\frown}(1,1,0) \qquad h_2 = h_1{\frown}(2,2,0).$$

The proof follows:

1	$s_0(0,0) = \mathbf{hero}(\,h_0\,)$	initial state
2	$\circlearrowright(s_0, h_0, 0, 0)$	assumption
3	$s_1(0,0) = \mathbf{hero}(\,h_0 \frown (1,0,0)\,)$	surprise, 1, 2
4	$\forall x': s_0(x',0) = \mathbf{hero}(\,h_0 \frown \ldots \frown (0,x',0)\,) \;\Rightarrow\; x' = 0$	frozen*, 3
5	$\exists x' > 0: s_0(x',0) = \mathbf{hero}(\,h_0 \frown \ldots \frown (0,x',0)\,)$	$\circlearrowright$, 2
6	$\bot$	$\bot$I, 4, 5
7	$\neg \circlearrowright(s_0, h_0, 0, 0)$	$\neg$I, 2–6
8	$s_1(1,0) = \mathbf{hero}(\,h_1\,)$	walking, 1, 7
9	$\circlearrowright(s_1, h_1, 1, 0)$	assumption
$\vdots$	*analogous to steps 3–5*	$\ldots^\star$
13	$\bot$	$\bot$I, 11, 12
14	$\neg \circlearrowright(s_1, h_1, 1, 0)$	$\neg$I, 9–13
15	$s_2(2,0) = \mathbf{hero}(\,h_2\,)$	walking, 8, 14
16	$\circlearrowright(s_2, h_2, 2, 0)$	assumption
$\vdots$	*analogous to steps 3–5*	$\ldots^\star$
20	$\bot$	$\bot$I, 18, 19
21	$\neg \circlearrowright(s_2, h_2, 2, 0)$	$\neg$I, 16–20
22	$s_0(2,0) = \mathbf{hero}(\,h_2 \frown (0,2,0)\,)$	time-travel, 15, 21
23	$\neg \exists x' > 0: s_0(x',0) = \mathbf{hero}(\,h_0 \frown \ldots \frown (0,x',0)\,)$	$\circlearrowright$, 7
24	$\bot$	$\bot$I, 22, 23

The steps marked * are by continuous application of the 'frozen' rule, and the fact that no other rule is applicable under the given conditions. The second and third analogous blocks of the proof are left out for brevity.

To put this proof in simpler terms: If the hero were to walk to the right twice, then travel back in time, he would make himself visible to his younger self, who is observing all the cells to his right. That means his younger self would be frozen, and could never travel back in time in the first place. This situation is comparable to the grandfather paradox in "Back to the Future". Figures 4 and 5 show the causality diagram and corresponding graphical illustration of this.

The causality rules of this example did not fully specify space-time. Although C_R could not be satisfied by any model, C_L could actually be satisfied by an infinite number of models, since the cells that were left black in the illustrations above were never fixed to any value. This allowed the time-travel steps in C_L.

Fig. 4. Causality diagram for the 'walking right' observer C_R (Example 1). It goes back in time, causing a paradox. This diagram illustrates why there is no linear model satisfying the ruleset C_R.

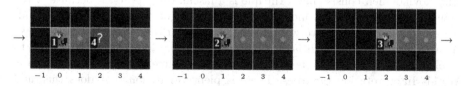

Fig. 5. A graphical representation of the 'walking right' observer C_R (Example 1). This scenario corresponds with the causality diagram from Fig. 4.

Because it was never *observed* that $s_1(-2, 0)$, $s_1(-4, 0)$, etc. actually contain **nothing**, they were still free to contain the hero.

This is why it makes sense to associate a set of causality rules to a specific observer of the system (Definition 5), be it an outside omniscient observer or a limited observer that is actually part of the system (as in Example 1). This also allows us to model multiple observers.

2.5   The Bootstrap Paradox

One last scenario of interest under NSP is the (possibly misnamed) *bootstrap paradox*. Imagine that the $\ominus\rightarrow$conditions for 'walking', 'time-travel' and 'surprise' in C_R were negated, i.e., that the hero would only act if he *did* see his older self in front of him, and would freeze in surprise otherwise. The word 'paradox' may be a misnomer, because far from causing contradiction, those rules are satisfied by two distinctly different types of model.

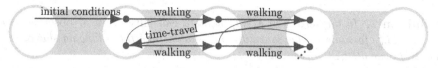

Fig. 6. One possible causality diagram for the 'walking right' observer C_R (Example 1), but with the $\ominus\rightarrow$ conditions negated. Note the three points where causality loops back on itself. The other possible causality diagram for this observer resembles Fig. 1 and has the hero frozen from the outset, never to thaw.

In the first type, the hero simply stands still in his initial spot, frozen in surprise from the outset. In the second type, the hero *does* see his older self in front of him, which allows him to walk, then travel back in time to *become* that older self. This second type of model is illustrated in Fig. 6. The phenomenon is also known as *circular causation*, or as a *causal loop*, but we find the 'bootstrap' metaphor quite apt. This term was popularized by the science fiction short story "By His Bootstraps", by Robert A. Heinlein [5].

2.6   Branching Timelines

The Novikov Self-consistency Principle is a fascinating approach because of the many interesting ways in which self-consistency might be enforced. But depending on the kind of story we want to tell, it may turn out to be too restrictive. A more forgiving approach is to allow seemingly paradoxical behavior, and to resolve it by introducing a new branch in the timeline. This is what the Many Worlds Interpretation proposes. There is plenty of fiction that does this, and examining it can also bring better insight into NSP.

To discuss MWI, we now expand our models to the full set $\mathfrak{M}$, which includes branching timelines (Definition 1). To encode rules on this sort of model, we need a more expressive language. The computational tree logic CTL_{lp}^{*} is a superset of LTL_p and introduces modalities for quantifying over paths:

Definition 6. *The syntax of CTL_{lp}^{*} is specified with the following grammar, which references the LTL_p grammar of Definition 3 and adds one rule to it:*

$$\psi \quad ::= \quad \neg\psi \mid \psi \wedge \psi \mid \psi \vee \psi \mid \mathsf{E}\phi \mid \mathsf{A}\phi$$
$$\phi \quad ::= \quad \psi \mid \langle \phi \text{ from definition 3} \rangle$$

where ψ is a CTL_{lp}^{*} formula, and ϕ is a formula in LTL_p with the added rule. The formula $\mathsf{E}\phi$ indicates that there exists a path inside the model that starts at the reference state and satisfies ϕ. The formula $\mathsf{A}\phi$ indicates that all paths inside the model that start at the reference state satisfy ϕ.

Semantics for $m, s \models \psi$, with $m \in \mathfrak{M}$ and $s \in m$ are defined in the expected way [6]. We also write $m \models \phi$ and say that ψ is globally true in m iff for all states $s \in S$, we have $m, s \models \psi$.

We alter the forms of our causality rules (Definition 5) correspondingly:

Definition 7. *In the setting of MWI, define a causality chain or observer as a set of CTL_{lp}^{*} formulas. The causality rule should take the following shape, and quantify over all LTL_p formulas ϕ:*

$$\langle cause \rangle \implies \underbrace{\mathsf{AX}^i}_{a} \big(\underbrace{\phi \Rightarrow}_{b} \underbrace{\mathsf{X}^{-1}\mathsf{EX}\,\phi \wedge \langle effect \rangle}_{c} \big) \qquad \textit{causality (MWI)}$$

This one is a bit more complicated than the one in Definition 5. Here is how the formula works: For having an effect i steps in the future (where i may be non-positive), we (a) go to all states that are at the specified depth, (b) remember the conditions that hold there as ϕ, and then (c) require that there exists some state at the same depth where the remembered conditions ϕ, as well as the specified effects, *hold. This state may turn out to be the original one where we remembered ϕ, or we may require the model to have a separate branch to accommodate the effect. Initial conditions may be specified as follows:*

AOF $\langle conditions \rangle$ *initial conditions*

Compared to Definition 5, we only added the A modality here.

This new causality rule is more complex so that it allows branching at paradoxical backward causality, as well as propagate forward causality in the proper way. When restricting ourselves to forward causality, we can simplify:

Lemma 2. *When $i \geq 1$, then for all LTL_p formulas ϕ we have:*

$$\left(\langle cause \rangle \Rightarrow \mathtt{AX}^i \left(\phi \Rightarrow \mathtt{X}^{-1}\mathtt{EX}\, \phi \wedge \langle effect \rangle \right) \right) \iff \left(\langle cause \rangle \Rightarrow \mathtt{AX}^i \langle effect \rangle \right)$$

Figure 7 shows a causality diagram for the 'walking right' scenario of Example 1, assuming the causality rules are encoded as per Definition 7, graphically depicted in Fig. 8. Besides the main timeline, the causality chain branches too, resulting in a *quantum clone*, i.e., a duplicate of the hero that can perpetually exist alongside the original.

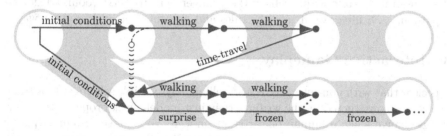

Fig. 7. Causality diagram for the 'walking right' observer C_R (Example 1) with causality rules encoded as per Definition 7. Under MWI, contradicting observed history causes a branch in the timeline. Note the hero's quantum clone, diverted from its intended path by the arrival of the original hero.

2.7 Temporal and Spatial Collision Detection

It should be noted that not all contradictions can be solved simply by branching the timeline. For instance: if, rather than twice walking right before time-traveling, the hero walks right once, then left once. Call this causality chain C_{RL}. After time-travel, he would materialize right onto his initial position $(0, 0)$, when a younger version of him is already standing there. In other words, the effect of the 'time-travel' rule would directly contradict the effect of the 'initial conditions' rule. The way we model 2D space, the two versions of the hero cannot simultaneously occupy the same cell. So there are no models satisfying C_{RL}, even under MWI.

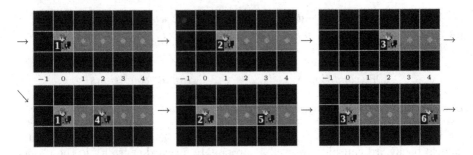

Fig. 8. A graphical representation of the 'walking right' observer C_R (Example 1) with causality rules encoded as per Definition 7. This scenario corresponds with the causality diagram from Fig. 7, the quantum clone now explicitly visible, frozen in place.

But this kind of contradiction is not inherently a *temporal* paradox. We would be in the same situation if two heroes were to simultaneously *walk* onto the same spot. Someone familiar with game development would tell us we have to implement *collision detection*, and build it into our rules to avoid the contradiction. The same can be said of the C_{RL} example. The designer of those rules would have to decide what should happen upon 'temporal collision' (e.g., block the time-travel attempt, push back the younger hero to make room, trigger an explosion, . . .), integrate it into the rules and prevent contradiction that way.

3   Interactive Gameplay

It is clear that with non-interactive storytelling, any possible self-consistent time-line can be constructed by the writer if they just model-check properly. However, things change when a human player is introduced. You can see a human player as an observer, but he is also an actor, and can decide to manipulate the world based on his observations. This creates some limitations in the real world, where actual time-travel (seemingly) does not exist.

3.1   Difficulties for Single-Player Games

The actions and memories of characters in a book are completely controlled by the author of the book. A game-designer can exert no such control over the real-world players of their game. Because the developer of a game has only limited control over the player's actions, unless the rules of the game are extremely restrictive, a player could choose to purposely cause paradox, violating Novikov's principle.

However, the authors feel that there is still a lot potential to a game like that if paradox is incorporated as a *lose condition* to be avoided. For example, he must resist the temptation to raid a treasure chest in the past that he has already raided in the present. It can also serve as a mechanism for in-game puzzles and a novel source of balance in gameplay. If the player avoids excessive observation during first playthrough of an area, he then gains more freedom to travel back to that time and place without causing paradox. He may on occasion be forced to literally 'look the other way' to allow his future self to pass by without being observed. Such a game could also employ the bootstrap paradox (Sect. 2.5) to great effect: put the player face-to-face with his future self, and then require him to reenact the scene later in order to maintain consistency.

Fig. 9. One human player taking the role of an observer. Under NSP, if he contradicts recorded history, it causes a paradox with no opportunity to branch: Game Over

The alternative of going by the Many Worlds Interpretation, allowing the player to continue in another branch, fixes the paradox problem, but introduces another. In the new branch, there will essentially be two versions of the player character: the older one who came from the previous branch, and the younger one native to the new branch. For the purpose of continuity, the player would naturally control the former, but how should the latter behave? Figure 10 illustrates this problem. Ideally, it should behave exactly how the human player would have done when faced with these alternate observations. Since we do seem to live in a world without actual time-travel, and it is not yet feasible to perform a brain-scan of the player in order to simulate his/her decision making process, the quantum clone will have to be controlled by a (relatively simplistic) AI.

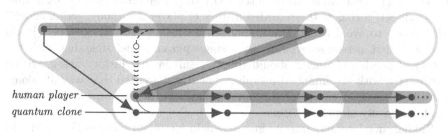

Fig. 10. One human player taking the role of an observer, starting out the same as the player in Fig. 9. Under MWI, if he contradicts recorded history, it causes a branch in the timeline. The question is: what should be the behavior of his quantum clone?

To our best knowledge, no game exists that properly follows either of the two time-travel principles discussed here. For example, in the game "The Legend of Zelda: Oracle of Ages" [3], the player can travel between two eras of the game world. In the past, he can move a boulder back and forth to control the flow of a small stream in the mountains, thereby choosing the course it will take when it becomes a mighty river in the present. The hero can go back and forth as often as he wishes to 'toggle' the direction of this river, and experience both versions of the present without experiencing paradox or quantum cloning. This is just an example; many other games use similar mechanics.

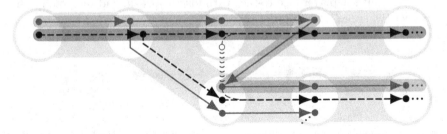

Fig. 11. Two players in the same game. One of them travels back in time, not violating his own recorded history, but violating that of the other player. Both players may individually satisfy Novikov's Self-consistency Principle, but the combined set of causality rules does not. This forces the two players into separate branches, devolving a two-player game into two single-player games. As an aside, note that there is not necessarily a need for quantum cloning in this scenario. So long as the player does not interfere, his past self can be programmed to perform the exact same actions the player did, and travel back in time also.

3.2 Additional Difficulties for Multi-player Games

While there are difficulties to overcome in designing a single-player time-travel game, the ones posed by the prospect of a multiplayer game are much harder to overcome. The problem stems from the fact that player 1 may travel back in time and (indirectly) change the recorded history of player 2 without having enough information to avoid this. Maintaining self-consistency for an observer should rely on a first person viewpoint. In a single-player game, tinkering with the history of another character should simply result in that history being written accordingly, with the intended meaning that it was written that way all along. But when the other character is a human player in the real world, that history was by necessity already written.

Taking such interaction to its logical conclusion in our framework would lead to an inexplicable Game Over for both players in the case of NSP, or to the players being forced into separate time-branches in the case of MWI. In the latter case, a two-player game would soon devolve into two single-player games (Fig. 11). To prevent this would be to either isolate the two players in space, which is not much better, or to severely restrict their freedom to time-travel.

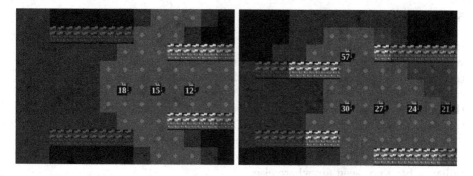

Fig. 12. A screenshot of the rudimentary time-travel game set up as a proof of concept. The graphical tiles used come from the open source game Nethack [12].

4   Implementation

We set out to implement a gameplay engine in JavaScript that supports both NSP and MWI. It is available as an open-source project on GitHub[4] and a rudimentary game is playable online as a proof of concept[5]. Figure 12 shows two screenshots of this game. We now briefly discuss our development techniques.

The `Observer` class takes front and center. It stores what is essentially a 4-dimensional array of recorded history, where the dimensions are 'time', 'x', 'y' and 'aspect'. The game has a top-down view on 2-dimensional space, and 'aspect' basically serves as the third spatial dimension. It can store the different types of knowledge that are to be had from each cell in space-time, such as `terrain` and `occupant`, where the former can (currently) indicate either a `wall` or a `floor`, and the latter can indicate either `nothing` or a `hero`, as in Example 1. Any aspect can also be `unknown`, indicating that it has not yet been observed. The division of aspects determines the granularity of what can be observed. The time dimension is not actually an array, but a tree, allowing the timeline to branch.

When observing a specific aspect of a specific cell, the observer appeals to an instance of the `Reality` class. This class generates parts of reality on-the-fly, not making any preassumptions about the occupation of cells until asked. The `Player` (which is also an `Observer`) can inject itself into specific points of reality by waiting, walking, or time-traveling. This is known as an *incursion*. If he ever injects himself in a place and time already known to be empty (or containing something else), this indicates a temporal paradox. Depending on the active game-mode, the game will either end, or the player will enter a new time-branch, and any quantum clones will be controlled by a randomizer.

Because multiple instances of the hero can be on-screen at the same time, there is not just a single `Player` object. Rather, each time the player 'moves around', he actually injects a copy of himself into the appropriate coordinates of space-time, and keyboard control is then transferred to the copy. The player will not notice the difference, but this makes it easier to keep the model complete.

---

[4] http://www.github.com/mhelvens/time-traveler.

[5] http://mhelvens.github.io/time-traveler.

5   Conclusion

In this paper we showed how to specify the dynamics of certain stories or universes with temporal logic, so that they can be model-checked for adherence to the rules of time-travel determined in the field of theoretical physics. Specifically, we looked at the rules under the *Novikov Self-consistency Principle*, and the rules under the *Many World Interpretation* of quantum mechanics. We did this both for non-interactive stories and for games.

Moreover, we have implemented a *game engine* in JavaScript following these rules, to allow the development of technically accurate time-travel games, something we have not seen anywhere else.

We learned a lot in working on this paper, and have identified a number of areas worth exploring further, and some choices we may want to reexamine in future work. For example, in this paper we specify time-travel dynamics directly in a *temporal logic*, and then create *causality diagrams* as a more or less informal visualization technique built on top of that. We now believe there may be much potential to causality diagrams as a primary notation.

Furthermore, it has been suggested that *quantum clones* might be controlled more realistically if we employ *machine learning* to approximate the decision making process of the human player. This certainly seems like an exciting idea.

References

1. Chellas, B.F.: Modal Logic: An Introduction, vol. 316. Cambridge University Press, Cambridge (1980)
2. Friedman, J., Morris, M.S., Novikov, I.D., Echeverria, F., Klinkhammer, G., Thorne, K.S., Yurtsever, U.: Cauchy problem in spacetimes with closed timelike curves. Phys. Rev. D **42**(6), 1915–1930 (1990)
3. Fujibayashi, H.: The Legend of Zelda: Oracle of Ages (2001). http://www.zelda.com/oracle
4. Gabbay, D., Pnueli, A., Shelah, S., Stavi, J.: On the temporal analysis of fairness. In: Proceedings of the 7th ACM SIGPLAN-SIGACT Symposium on Principles of Programming Languages, pp. 163–173. ACM (1980)
5. Heinlein, R.A.: By His Bootstraps, October 1941
6. Laroussinie, F., Schnoebelen, P.: Specification in CTL+ past for verification in CTL. Inf. Comput. **1**(156), 236–263 (2000)
7. Lichtenstein, O., Pnueli, A., Zuck, L.: The glory of the past. In: Kozen, D. (ed.) Logic of Programs 1981. LNCS, vol. 131, pp. 196–218. Springer, Heidelberg (1982)
8. Markey, N.: Temporal logic with past is exponentially more succinct. EATCS Bull. **79**, 122–128 (2003)
9. Nahin, P.: Time Travel: A Writer's Guide to the Real Science of Plausible Time Travel. Johns Hopkins University Press, Baltimore (2011)
10. Nahin, P.: Time Machines: Time Travel in Physics, Metaphysics, and Science Fiction, 2nd edn. Springer, New York (2014). Softcover reprint of the original, 2nd edn. 1999th edn
11. Schrödinger, E.: Die gegenwärtige situation in der quantenmechanik. Naturwissenschaften **23**(49), 823–828 (1935)
12. Stephenson, M.: NetHack (1987). http://www.nethack.org
13. Zemeckis, R.: Back to the Future, iMDB ID: tt0088763, July 1985

Industrial Application of Formal Models Generated from Domain Specific Languages

Jozef Hooman[1,2(✉)]

[1] Embedded Systems Innovation by TNO, Eindhoven, The Netherlands
jozef.hooman@tno.nl
[2] Radboud University, Nijmegen, The Netherlands

Abstract. Domain Specific Languages (DSLs) provide a lightweight approach to incorporate formal techniques into the industrial workflow. From DSL instances, formal models and other artefacts can be generated, such as simulation models and code. Having a single source for all artefacts improves maintenance and offers a high return on investment of the initial modelling effort. Since DSLs can be used to capture essential domain information at a high level of abstraction, this supports formal verification early in the development process. We discuss our experiences with this approach in a number of real industrial development projects.

1 Introduction

Many companies suffer from a long test and integration phase. The main reason is that a large number of problems are detected in this phase. Repairing these problems is often not easy and corrections might lead to new problems. Hence, it is difficult to manage this phase and to predict when it can be completed.

Our approach aims at detecting problems much earlier in the development process by means of various modelling techniques. Although it is well-known that it is very cost-effective to detect problems as early as possible (see, e.g., [31]), the main challenge is to realize this in an existing industrial development process with continuous pressure to meet deadlines. Therefore our approach tries to reduce the modelling effort by reusing models for multiple purposes, such as performance analysis and the generation of configuration files, tests or code.

In this paper we concentrate on the use of formal techniques to increase the confidence in the correctness of the models. In the industrial context, the use of lightweight formal methods has been advocated frequently [13,17]. These methods hide a lot of the mathematical details from the user and do not aim at generic modelling and analysis techniques. By specializing on a particular type of design pattern and a particular set of properties, more efficient and effective approaches can be developed.

As a starting point, we analyse the industrial use of the Analytical Software Design (ASD) approach [24] which is supported by commercial tooling. This approach combines a restricted tabular notation for component behaviour, formal

Supported by the Dutch national program COMMIT.

E. Ábrahám et al. (Eds.): de Boer Festschrift, LNCS 9660, pp. 277–293, 2016.
DOI: 10.1007/978-3-319-30734-3_19

verification of a limited number of properties, and code generation. The evaluation is based on a number of industrial development projects and a comparison with Uppaal [9].

Based on these experiences, we experiment with the use of Domain Specific Languages (DSLs). Recent DSL technology allows a fast definition of a dedicated language, the automatic generation of a powerful editor for this language, and a convenient mechanism to generate text (e.g., analysis models or code) from language instances. We report about experiences with DSLs in combination with various formal methods in a number of real industrial development projects.

Related Work. Related to ASD are commercial tools that combine formal methods and code generation. VDMTools[1] supports code generation from models specified using the VDM++ language [11]. The tool Atelier B[2] has been used to develop a number of safety-critical systems using the B-method [1]. The SCADE Suite[3] provides formal techniques for specification, verification and code generation. These techniques are quite generic and the correctness proofs for VDM and B models may require interactive theorem proving. ASD is much more restricted than the approaches mentioned above to achieve a high level of automation and to support compositional verification.

The use of DSLs has been proposed for more than a decade, see e.g. the overview in [30]. An early experiment to combine DSLs and formal methods has been described in [4]. In that paper, the correctness of instances of a DSL for process scheduling is verified using the B method. To increase the use of formal methods in industry, [10] proposes the encapsulation of formal methods within domain specific languages. A DSL of the railway domain is formalized by means of the algebraic specification language CASL [16]. Recent developments of the DSL technology make it feasible to apply this on a much larger industrial scale.

Industrial Context. Most of the work reported here was done at Philips Healthcare, with a focus on interventional X-Ray (iXR) systems, see Fig. 1. These systems are used for minimally invasive surgery, for instance, improving the throughput of a blood vessel by placing a stent via a catheter where the surgeon is guided by X-ray images. These techniques avoid, for instance, open heart surgery.

Overview. This paper is structured as follows. The ASD approach is evaluated in Sect. 2, which also includes a comparison to Uppaal. Based on our observations, Sect. 3 describes our approach to combine formal methods and DSLs in industry. Section 4 contains three industrial applications at Philips on components of iXR systems. Concluding remarks can be found in Sect. 5.

---

[1] http://www.vdmtools.jp/en/.

[2] http://www.atelierb.eu/en/.

[3] http://www.esterel-technologies.com/products/scade-suite/.

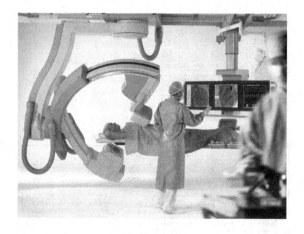

Fig. 1. Interventional X-ray system

2 Experiences with ASD

Section 2.1 contains a brief overview of the ASD method. More explanation, examples, and applications at Philips can be found in [15,21]. A summary of the experiences at Philips with ASD is given in Sect. 2.2. Section 2.3 compares ASD with Uppaal.

2.1 ASD Background

The Analytical Software Design (ASD) method [23,24] is a component-based technology that aims at enabling the application of formal methods into industrial practice. The approach has been supported by the commercial development tool ASD:Suite which embeds ASD into a software design environment. This tool was developed by the company Verum. After a re-start of this company, the approach was recently renamed to Dezyne, but our experiences concern the use of the original ASD method.

ASD Models. Models are represented in ASD by state-transition tables. The ASD approach distinguishes two types of models:

- An *interface model* specifies the external behaviour of a component without referring to any internal behaviour. This forms the formal contract of the interaction between the component and its clients.
- A *design model* implements a certain interface model and typically uses services of other components, the so-called *used components*, by referring to their interface models.

An example of ASD models is depicted in Fig. 2. It shows a part of a design model of a component (DComponent) with fragments of its interface model (IComponent) and two used interfaces (IUsedComp1 and IUsedComp2).

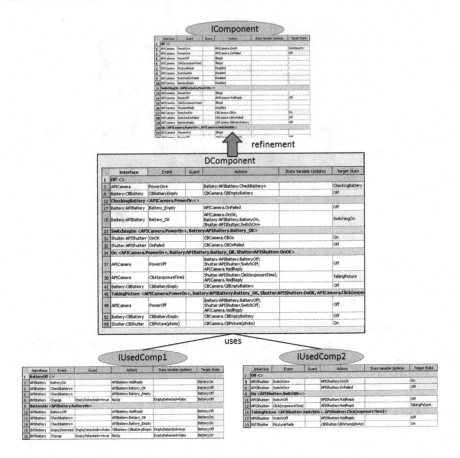

Fig. 2. Example of ASD models

Each model is a state machine, represented by a table. In every state the response to all possible input events has to be specified. It is possible to specify that an event is illegal in a certain state, i.e., that it should not occur in that state.

Design models should be deterministic; non-determinism is allowed in interface models. In ASD, communication between client and server components is asymmetric, using synchronous calls and asynchronous callbacks.

- Clients issue synchronous calls to server components, where the client is blocked until the server accepts the call and eventually returns it to the client.
- Servers can communicate with their clients by asynchronous callbacks. Callbacks are stored in a so-called callback queue (FIFO).

Another restriction is that an ASD component cannot make decisions based on the values of parameters in a received call. Only the names of calls or callbacks can influence the flow of control. Hence, ASD only supports data-independent control components. Other components have to be implemented in another way, e.g., by manual coding.

Formal Verification. The ASD:Suite automatically translates the ASD tabular specifications into CSP models and verifies them using the formal refinement checker FDR2 [26]. (FDR is an abbreviation of Failures-Divergence Refinement.) All CSP and FDR2 details are hidden from end-users. When a property does not hold, an error trace is represented as a sequence diagram.

Only a fixed set of properties can be verified. The main checks performed by the ASD:Suite are:

- *Consistency checks*: verify whether a design model is deterministic and correctly uses the interfaces of its used components.
- *Refinement checks*: verify whether the interface model of a component is correctly refined by the design model in combination with the interface models of the used components.

Observe that the ASD approach is compositional [8,14], since the refinement checks only use the interface models of the used components. This compositional way of verification avoids the well-known state space explosion problem and enables industrial scalability, because components can be checked in isolation. It requires, however, a careful design of the system such that the design pattern of ASD is used and the components themselves are kept small (to avoid state explosion at the component level).

Code Generation. ASD:Suite supports the generation of code from design models for a number of programming languages (C, C++, C#, Java), which is important for industrial acceptance. This avoids an error prone manual translation from models to code and is expected to improve productivity. Observe that the formal model and the code are both based on the same source, see Fig. 3.

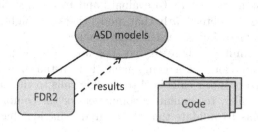

Fig. 3. The ASD approach

2.2 Industrial Application of ASD

The ASD approach has been used at Philips Healthcare in a number of different development projects. We summarize an extensive evaluation published before [22] concerning software quality and productivity:

- Since ASD only checks a limited set of properties, it may not always lead to defect-free software. However, compared to the industry standards, very few defects were found in the code generated by ASD. In general, most defects were easy to find and to fix.
- The data of the projects in which ASD was used indicate an improved productivity compared to industrial standards. This was partly due to the fact that after the modelling phase, verified code is generated automatically. It was also observed that less time was spent integrating and manually testing the generated code. Clearly, ASD prevented problems earlier in the development process. As an example, most developers were impressed by the fast detection of race conditions, because their experience is that these problems are difficult to detect by testing and usually show up very late in the development process with the conventional approach.

The limitations of the ASD method, however, might prevent large-scale introduction into the industrial workflow:

- The approach is limited to event-based control components. It is not suitable for low-level real-time controllers and data-intensive components. Designers find it difficult to decide what to do in ASD and what not.
- ASD assumes a hierarchical control architecture with synchronous method calls from top to bottom and asynchronous callbacks in the other direction. Although this gives a clear structure, it is not always easy to construct such a hierarchy, especially because the size of components and the number of callbacks should be small to allow fast model checking. Moreover, when software engineers are used to object-oriented designs this might require a paradigm shift.
- After a few changes, the state-transition tables might become large and difficult to maintain; there are hardly any structuring mechanisms, e.g., to indicate that a certain transition is common to a set of states.
- There is no systematic means to evaluate and to analyse the complexity of ASD models, e.g., to detect early that model checking might take too long or to decide that refactoring is needed after changes.
- Verification is limited; there is no possibility to express the desired input/output behaviour of a component. For instance, one would like to express that certain input calls lead to specific calls to the used components.
- There is no possibility to simulate a component or the combination of a number of components to validate that the desired behaviour has been modelled.

2.3 Comparison with Uppaal

Based on experiences with ASD, industrial users asked for other formal verification methods without the limitations of ASD. At FEI Company, where ASD is used to develop control software for electron microscopes, we experimented with additional support using Uppaal [9]. Uppaal is an integrated environment for modelling, validation and verification of systems modelled as networks of timed automata. The Uppaal tool was chosen because of its nice and understandable user interface and the simulation possibilities, which appeared to be attractive for industrial users. The most important reason was the possibility to verify other properties than the ASD checks, which increases the range of faults that can be detected early. The timing aspects of Uppaal have not been used, but might be relevant in later studies.

Uppaal Models. Uppaal uses timed automata with synchronous communication along channels, extended with data types (bounded integers, arrays, etc.). For more details about Uppaal we refer to [2].

Uppaal has been applied to a camera safety system. This system should guarantee that an expensive and very sensitive camera is protected against a too high dose of electrons. An important part of this system is the software that keeps track of the location of the camera, the blocking of the electron beam by other components and the intensity of the electron beam. This part of the software was generated using the ASD approach.

We translated the ASD models to Uppaal. Translating the tabular representation to the automata of Uppaal is rather straightforward. The main issue was that simulation and verification in Uppaal requires a closed set of models which includes the environment of the component(s) under study. We obtained a closed system by using the interface model of an ASD design model. This interface model was translated into an Uppaal model of a client of the component by reversing the direction of sending and receiving.

Formal Verification. Most important difference with ASD is that Uppaal allows the verification of user-defined properties which have to be expressed in a version of temporal logic. In general, we concentrated on properties that had not yet been verified by the standard checks of ASD:Suite. The properties to be verified have been defined in cooperation with the software architect and the system architect. By means of this verification, two major issues were found. These issues could not be found in the ASD approach since it does not allow this type of verification.

A disadvantage of above approach is that the temporal logic expressions are not easy to read by industrial users. As an alternative, we experimented with the use of observers, similar to [5]. An observer is an additional parallel automaton which observes the communication between the other automata and enters an error location when an incorrect trace is observed. This approach was more convenient for our industrial users.

Comparison from Industrial Perspective. We observed that ASD and Uppaal are complementary in many respects. The industrial engineers appreciate the possibilities to simulate the Uppaal models. This especially concerns the joint simulation of a number of components, which was clearly missing in ASD:Suite. A disadvantage, compared to the compositional approach of ASD, is that one more easily encounters the state explosion problem, so scalability of Uppaal is limited.

The larger range of verification possibilities of Uppaal is a clear advantage, although expressing properties in temporal logic is not very convenient for industrial users. The timing properties of Uppaal have not been used in our experiment, but the possibility to express timing is seen as a valuable asset. A strong point of ASD is the generation of code from a verified model. The fact that different programming languages are supported provides a kind of platform independence which is important to enable future technology changes.

3   Domain Specific Languages and Formal Methods

The experiences with ASD and Uppaal indicate that one would like to combine the strong points of different techniques. Making transformations between models of different formalisms, such as ASD and Uppaal, would be very time consuming. Typically, subtle semantic differences make it very hard to define a correct generic transformation. Given our experiences with the use of Domain Specific Languages (DSLs) to define the behaviour of frequently changing components at a high level of abstraction [19], we have combined this with the generation of formal models.

Our approach is based on Xtext[4], an Eclipse plugin on top of the Eclipse Modelling Framework. Based on the definition of a grammar, the Xtext plugin generates a meta-model, a parser and an Eclipse-based editor for the language defined by the grammar. Moreover, it generates convenient starting points to implement validation, scoping, and the generation of text (such as code and models) using the Xtend language[5] [3].

In addition to formal verifications tools, we also use simulations based on POOSL (Parallel Object Oriented Specification Language) [27]. POOSL is a formal modelling language for systems that include both software and digital hardware. The formal semantics of POOSL has been defined in [28] by means of a probabilistic structural operational semantics for the process layer and a probabilistic denotational semantics for the data layer. The operational semantics of POOSL has been implemented in a high-speed simulation engine called Rotalumis. Recently, by means of Xtext, a modern Eclipse IDE has been developed on top of an improved Rotalumis simulation engine[6].

For the (re)design of a component we proceed along the following steps:

1 Define a grammar in Xtext to capture the essential domain concepts.
2 Define an instances of the language defined in the previous step. Discuss this instance with domain experts to obtain a first definition of the required behaviour. When needed, the grammar is adapted.
3 Implement validation rules to check well-formedness properties of language instances.

---

[4] http://eclipse.org/Xtext/.
[5] http://eclipse.org/xtend/.
[6] http://poosl.esi.nl.

4 Implement a generator which yields a POOSL model that can be used to simulate the intended behaviour. Often we connect the simulated POOSL model by means of a socket to a visualization (e.g. in Java) of the externally visible behaviour. Adapt language instances after feedback of industrial stakeholders.

5 Implement a generator which yields a formal model that enables formal verification. We have used various formal techniques for this step. Clearly, language instances are adapted when errors are found.

6 Implement a generator which yields code, configuration files, or tests, depending on the industrial needs.

4 Applications of Combining DSLs with Formal Methods

The approach described in the previous section has been applied to three components of the iXR system introduced in Sect. 1. We have developed a DSL for collision prevention in combination with an SMT solver (Sect. 4.1), a DSL for power control, supported by SAL (Sect. 4.2) and a DSL for pedal handling with formal verification by means of mCRL2 (Sect. 4.3).

4.1 DSL Collision Prevention and SMT Solver

The first project is related to the moving parts of an iXR system. Such a system consists of one or two so-called C-arms, each carrying an X-ray generator and a detector. During the treatment of a patient, the C-arms, the detectors, and the patient table can be moved to obtain optimal projections for the images. Safety of an iXR system includes the avoidance of collisions between these heavy physical objects and with humans, such as patient and medical staff.

The goal of the project was to re-develop the collision prevention components in order to facilitate systematic reuse of safety-critical software across product configurations and medical applications. An overview is given in [20], details about the formal approach can be found in [18].

To stay close to the requirements formulation, we have developed a DSL which is targeted at the type of rules we want to express. These rules basically specify restrictions on the speed of the moving parts when the distances between these parts are below certain thresholds or when distance sensors detect an object (e.g., patient or medical staff). A part of a DSL instance is depicted in Fig. 4.

Basic validation checks have been implemented by means of the validation mechanism of Xtext. This includes, for instance, type checking and consistency checks on the hardware configuration. Clearly such checks are limited and there is a need for more analysis before generating code and performing time-consuming system tests. For the collision prevention component, the focus was on two types of analysis: performance evaluation of the required execution times and formal verification of correctness properties. This has been achieved by defining transformations to analysis models. Additionally, code has been generated, as shown in Fig. 5. We briefly discuss these three ingredients.

```
restriction ApproachingTableTopAndBeam
    activation
        Distance(TableTop, Beam) < 35 mm + 15 cm
    effects
        UserGuidance "TableTop and Beam approaching"
        relative limit TableTop*[Rotation, Translation],
                        Beam*[Rotation, Translation],
            at (Distance(TableTop, Beam) - 35 mm) / 15 cm

restriction VeryCloseTableTopAndBeam
    activation
        Distance(TableTop, Beam) < 20 mm
    effects
        UserGuidance "TableTop and Beam very close"
        relative limit TableTop*[Rotation, Translation],
                        Beam*[Rotation, Translation],
            at 0
    ...
```

Fig. 4. Part of a DSL instance for collision prevention

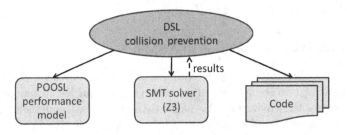

Fig. 5. DSL for collision prevention and transformations

Performance. The collision prevention component is part of a real-time control loop that executes with a certain frequency. Hence it is important that the collision prevention component can execute within the period of the real-time loop. The performance analysis of collision prevention concentrates on the computations needed to compute distances between objects [29]. It uses a generated POOSL model to perform simulations and to obtain statistics about expected execution times. The model uses performance profiles of the basic computation steps. Moreover, it has been calibrated using performance measurements on an existing component.

Formal Verification. To obtain fully automated and fast formal analysis, a generator has been written in Xtend which generates for every DSL instance an SMT (Satisfiability Modulo Theories) model. This model is analysed using the SMT-solver Z3 [7]. If the property does not hold, delta debugging is used to identify the rules in the DSL instance that contribute to the failure. This leads to warnings in the Eclipse-based editor for the DSL at appropriate places.

Formal verification addresses four types of correctness properties:

- Well-definedness of expressions; for instance, absence of division by zero.
- Speed limits are within the specified range.
- Safety of movement control; for instance, if two objects are close to each other and still approaching, then their speeds are restricted.
- Absence of deadlock; there is no position of the objects such that no further movements are possible.

To make formal verification feasible, several abstractions have been applied, e.g., concerning the acceleration characteristics of the physical objects and timing aspects. Using these abstractions, the experiments described in [18] show that fast analysis and user feedback is feasible for realistic instances of the DSL. For the correctness properties mentioned above, the applied abstractions may result in false positives. Moreover, for the deadlock check it may also result in false negatives. Nevertheless, also the deadlock check is useful as it can detect certain typical mistakes in the collision prevention rules.

Code Generation. For the generation of source code, a code generator has been developed that transforms the high-level concepts from our DSL into executable code. By means of some glue code, we have integrated the generated code within the existing system software. The result has been evaluated on the physical system, including all hardware components. This has been used to test whether a specific set of rules has been modelled correctly. Note that the analysis techniques help to find errors earlier, but they cannot detect everything. For instance, movement profiles might have some inaccuracy and heavy physical parts cannot be stopped immediately. After sufficient testing, the code generation can be used for generating production code and then it adds immediate value to the modelling efforts.

4.2   DSL Power Control and SAL

The second application concerns the power control component of an iXR system. This component is responsible for executing power control scenarios, such as start-up, shut down and power failure. During such a scenario the power control component is the master of the system and all other components follow the instructions of the power control component.

The power control component contains a generic part that needs to be configured for every release and every different hardware configuration. In the existing situation, the configuration files are difficult to maintain and to extend. Given the increasing system complexity of the product family, this will likely create problems in future releases. The business goal of the development project is to improve the maintainability and extendibility of the power control component. Additionally, there is a need to improve the existing test set which is very time consuming without having a large coverage.

As before, we define a DSL to express the essential information needed to generate the configuration files automatically from DSL instances. To increase the confidence in the correctness of DSL instances, we also generate a few analysis models such as a POOSL model, see Fig. 6. Formal verification has been done by means of SAL [12,25], because it also includes convenient support for test generation from a formal model. Instead of generating tests directly, we generate instances of a separate DSL to express test traces. This makes it possible to generate test for various test frameworks, but also test for the POOSL simulation and checks for the SAL models. This can be used to cross check the models and increase the confidence in the generators.

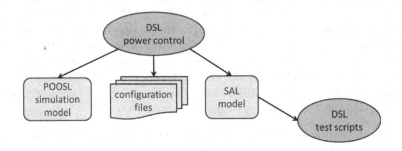

Fig. 6. DSL for power control and transformations

Simulation with POOSL. We implemented a generator which delivers a POOSL model for every DSL instance. By means of a socket, the simulation of a POOSL model is connected to a Java program which provides a Graphical User interface (GUI). This GUI contains buttons to simulate external input and to inject errors. It also shows the resulting power states of the connected devices. This simulation is very useful for a first validation of the model and to align with many parties (architects, designers, suppliers, service engineers, etc.) about the required system behaviour. In this way we detected a number of modelling mistakes and clarified a few issues concerning error handling in the power control component.

Checking Properties with SAL. To obtain exhaustive checks on DSL instances, a generator for SAL models has been implemented. A number of properties has been verified, e.g., expressing that certain groups of devices are in the same power state and that the preconditions for hardware components are fulfilled. By means of SAL, we detected a few additional errors, such as a situation where a device is not powered due to an error in the hardware precondition.

Generating Configuration Files and Tests. From the DSL we generated the configuration files. In addition we used SAL to generated a large number of test scripts. Note that these tests concern the overall system behaviour, including the generic software part, the configuration files and the hardware,

With the generated test cases, approximately twice as much transitions are covered compared to the manually written tests. These manually written tests were also were very time-dependent with many long waiting times. They could still fail due to a slow response of hardware, which typically resulted in a further increase of the waiting times. By having all concepts described in a clear and concise way using DSLs, we could make the test cases much more efficient. Instead of waiting all the time, the test tool now synchronizes with the power control component and immediately resumes the test case once the control component has reached the desired state.

4.3   DSL Pedal Handling and mCRL2

Our approach has also been applied to the pedal handling component of an iXR system. This component deals with the selection of types of X-ray (high dose or low dose, one or two X-ray sources) and starting and stopping X-ray by means of pedals. Since the current implementation is difficult to maintain, the aim is to refactor the component and partly re-implement it. Also an improvement of the user-perceived behaviour is foreseen. The work described here concentrates on obtaining an unambiguous description of the required behaviour and a good test environment which can be used to test whether new implementations conform to the required behaviour.

In this case, we have defined a DSL to capture the requirements concerning the externally visible behaviour of the component, including the error behaviour. The component has 25 possible input events (including 9 error events) and more than 50 possible output commands. The DSL describes for each input event the resulting output, i.e., the type of X-ray and the status of the user display (e.g., whether a live image is shown, a previously captured image, or a blank screen). A fragment of a DSL instance (changed and simplified for reasons of confidentiality) is shown in Fig. 7.

For each DSL instance we automatically generate a POOSL model to simulate the requirements, an mCRL2 model to verify properties of the model, and a test model suitable for model-based testing. Figure 8(a) contains an overview.

Simulation with POOSL. Similar to the previous section, the generated POOSL model has been coupled by means of a socket to a Java GUI which allows a simulation of pedal presses and the injection of errors. It shows the resulting X-ray and the display of images, as shown in Fig. 8(b). This visualization was very helpful to discuss unclear scenarios, especially in case of errors. It has been used extensively to discuss new behaviour with system architects and designers, resulting in significant changes of error handling behaviour. The simulation will be used as a reference for the implementation of the new behaviour.

Formal Verification with mCRL2. To obtain exhaustive checks on the requirements specification, we generate mCRL2 models. mCRL2 is a process algebra with extensions for data and time. The supporting toolset [6] includes the formal verification of processes with respect to properties expressed in a modal μ-calculus. To avoid that industrial users have to use this logic, we have extended the DSL with a simple language to express safety properties. This is sufficient to express important properties such as "no X-ray is generated if no pedal is pressed". A few errors in the requirements have been detected in this way.

```
trigger: LowOn guard: LowReq == false
  do: LowReq := true ;
      if NOT HighReq
      then if LowOK then OutputType := Fluo ;
                         Display := Live ;
           else OutputType := Standby ; Display := Blank ;
           fi
      fi
      ...
trigger: HighOff guard: HighReq == true
  do: HighReq := false ;
      if LowReq
      then if LowOK then OutputType := Fluo ;
                         Display := Live ;
           else OutputType := Standby ; Display := Blank ;
           fi
      else OutputType := Standby ; Display := Prev ;
      fi

trigger: LowError guard: LowOK == true do: LowOK := false ;
      ...
```

Fig. 7. Fragment of a DSL instance for pedal handling

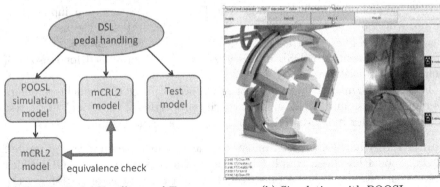

(a) DSL for Pedal Handling and Trans-   (b) Simulation with POOSL
formations

Fig. 8. Pedal handling

Observe that the translation to mCRL2 defines a formal semantics of our DSL. Discussions on the mCRL2 generator clarified a few points about the precise meaning of our DSL, e.g., concerning the level of atomicity. To increase our confidence in the generators we have used an existing translator for a subset of POOSL (covering the generated POOSL models) to mCRL2. We showed that, for a number of DSL instances, the mCRL2 model of the direct DSL to mCRL2 translation is bisimulation equivalent to the result of the combined DSL to

POOSL and POOSL to mCRL2 translations. These three transformations have been implemented by three different persons.

Model-Based Testing. Finally, we have defined a generator which translates DSL instances into a state machine represented in the Axini Modelling Language. The TestManager of the company Axini uses this model to perform model-based testing on an implementation. We have used this technique to validate our requirements model for the existing implementation. It led to a few adaptations of our DSL instance. When the new requirements model for the enhanced pedal handling behaviour has been fixed, we automatically obtain a test environment for the new implementation.

5 Concluding Remarks

Our experience in real industrial development projects indicates that the current DSL technology allows a fast and convenient introduction of formal methods. We observe two main categories of DSLs: (1) a DSL which expresses requirements and finally leads to tests; (2) a DSL which expresses the behaviour of a design, finally leading to code. In both cases, the generation of simulation models in combination with a visualization of externally visible behaviour is very important to align with many stakeholders such as users, marketing, system architects, and engineers. Next, the generation of formal models and exhaustive verification is useful to check consistency and important domain properties. Often it is convenient to include an easy-readable definition of properties in the DSL. An advantage of the DSL approach is that it leads to models that are already at a high level of abstraction. If needed, additional abstractions can be made in the generator.

Another advantage is that a DSL instance is the source of all generated artefacts. Any change in the DSL instance automatically leads to an update of all these artefacts. This avoids the usual maintenance problem to keep formal models consistent with the frequent changes in an industrial context. In this context it is important that there are a number of industrial benefits independent of formal techniques, such as easy changeable domain knowledge, platform independence, early simulation and validation of behaviour, and automatic generation of code or tests. Then the use of formal techniques is a small investment which fits easily in the overall approach and has additional benefits.

Acknowledgments. This paper summarizes results of earlier papers and collaborations with many people from Philips (including Mathijs Schuts, Robert Huis in 't Veld, and Rob Albers), the Eindhoven University of Technology (Ammar Osaiweran, Sarmen Keshishzadeh), and TNO-ESI colleagues (Arjan Mooij, Richard Doornbos). Many thanks goes to all of them for the very pleasant collaboration. The anonymous reviewers are acknowledged for several useful comments.

References

1. Abrial, J.-R.: The B-book: Assigning Programs to Meanings. Cambridge University Press, New York (1996)
2. Behrmann, G., David, A., Larsen, K.G.: A tutorial on UPPAAL. In: Bernardo, M., Corradini, F. (eds.) SFM-RT 2004. LNCS, vol. 3185, pp. 200–236. Springer, Heidelberg (2004)
3. Bettini, L.: Implementing Domain-Specific Languages with Xtext and Xtend. Packt Publishing Ltd., United Kingdom (2013)
4. Bodeveix, J.-P., Filali, M., Lawall, J., Muller, G.: Formal methods meet domain specific languages. In: Romijn, J.M.T., Smith, G.P., van de Pol, J. (eds.) IFM 2005. LNCS, vol. 3771, pp. 187–206. Springer, Heidelberg (2005)
5. Bozga, M., Graf, S., Ober, I., Ober, I., Sifakis, J.: The IF toolset. In: Bernardo, M., Corradini, F. (eds.) SFM-RT 2004. LNCS, vol. 3185, pp. 237–267. Springer, Heidelberg (2004)
6. Cranen, S., Groote, J.F., Keiren, J.J.A., Stappers, F.P.M., de Vink, E.P., Wesselink, W., Willemse, T.A.C.: An overview of the mCRL2 toolset and its recent advances. In: Piterman, N., Smolka, S.A. (eds.) TACAS 2013 (ETAPS 2013). LNCS, vol. 7795, pp. 199–213. Springer, Heidelberg (2013)
7. de Moura, L., Bjørner, N.S.: Z3: an efficient SMT solver. In: Ramakrishnan, C.R., Rehof, J. (eds.) TACAS 2008. LNCS, vol. 4963, pp. 337–340. Springer, Heidelberg (2008)
8. de Roever, W.-P., de Boer, F., Hanneman, U., Hooman, J., Lakhnech, Y., Poel, M., Zwiers, J.: Concurrency Verification: Introduction to Compositional and Non-compositional Methods. Cambridge University Press, New York (2001)
9. Doornbos, R., Hooman, J., van Vlimmeren, B.: Complementary verification of embedded software using ASD and Uppaal. In: Proceedings 8th International Conference on Innovations in Information Technology (IIT 2012), pp. 60–65 (2012)
10. Eakman, G., Reubenstein, H., Hawkins, T., Jain, M., Manolios, P.: Practical formal verification of domain-specific language applications. In: Havelund, K., Holzmann, G., Joshi, R. (eds.) NFM 2015. LNCS, vol. 9058, pp. 443–449. Springer, Heidelberg (2015)
11. Fitzgerald, J., Larsen, P.G., Mukherjee, P., Plat, N., Verhoef, M.: Validated Designs For Object-oriented Systems. Springer, London (2005)
12. Hamon, G., de Moura, L., Rushby, J.: Automated Test Generation with SAL. CSL Technical Note, SRI International, January 2005
13. Heitmeyer, C.L.: On the need for *practical* formal methods. In: Ravn, A.P., Rischel, H. (eds.) FTRTFT 1998. LNCS, vol. 1486, pp. 18–26. Springer, Heidelberg (1998)
14. Hooman, J.: Specification and Compositional Verification of Real-Time Systems. LNCS, vol. 558. Springer, Heidelberg (1991)
15. Hooman, J., Huis in 't Veld, R., Schuts, M.: Experiences with a compositional model checker in the healthcare domain. In: Liu, Z., Wassyng, A. (eds.) FHIES 2011. LNCS, vol. 7151, pp. 93–110. Springer, Heidelberg (2012)
16. James, P., Roggenbach, M.: Encapsulating formal methods within domain specific languages: A solution for verifying railway scheme plans. The Computing Research Repository, abs/1403.3034 (2014)
17. Jones, C.B., Jackson, D., Wing, J.: Formal methods light. Computer 29(4), 20–22 (1996)
18. Keshishzadeh, S., Mooij, A.J., Mousavi, M.R.: Early fault detection in DSLs using SMT solving and automated debugging. In: Hierons, R.M., Merayo, M.G., Bravetti, M. (eds.) SEFM 2013. LNCS, vol. 8137, pp. 182–196. Springer, Heidelberg (2013)

19. Mooij, A.J., Hooman, J., Albers, R.: Gaining industrial confidence for the introduction of domain-specific languages. In: Proceedings of IEESD 2013, pp. 662–667. IEEE Computer Society (2013)
20. Mooij, A.J., Hooman, J., Albers, R.: Early fault detection using design models for collision prevention in medical equipment. In: Gibbons, J., MacCaull, W. (eds.) FHIES 2013. LNCS, vol. 8315, pp. 170–187. Springer, Heidelberg (2014)
21. Osaiweran, A., Schuts, M., Hooman, J.: Experiences with incorporating formal techniques into industrial practice. Empirical Softw. Eng. 19(4), 1169–1194 (2014)
22. Osaiweran, A., Schuts, M., Hooman, J., Groote, J.F., van Rijnsoever, B.: Evaluating the effect of a lightweight formal technique in industry. STTT Int. J. Softw. Tools Technol. Transf. (STTT) 18(1), 93–108 (2016)
23. Broadfoot, G.H.: ASD case notes: costs and benefits of applying formal methods to industrial control software. In: Fitzgerald, J.S., Hayes, I.J., Tarlecki, A. (eds.) FM 2005. LNCS, vol. 3582, pp. 548–551. Springer, Heidelberg (2005)
24. Broadfoot, G.H., Broadfoot, P.J.: Academia and industry meet: some experiences of formal methods in practice. In: Proceedings of the Tenth Asia-Pacific Software Engineering Conference Software Engineering Conference, APSEC 2003, pp. 49–58. IEEE Computer Society (2003)
25. Shankar, N.: Combining theorem proving and model checking through symbolic analysis. In: Palamidessi, C. (ed.) CONCUR 2000. LNCS, vol. 1877, pp. 1–16. Springer, Heidelberg (2000)
26. Formal Systems. Failures-divergences refinement (FDR) (2014)
27. Theelen, B.D., Florescu, O., Geilen, M., Huang, J., van der Putten, P.H.A., Voeten, J.: Software/Hardware engineering with the parallel object-oriented specification language. In: Proceedings of MEMOCODE 2007, pp. 139–148. IEEE (2007)
28. van Bokhoven, L.J.: Constructive tool design for formal languages; from semantics to executing models. Phd thesis, Eindhoven University of Technology, The Netherlands (2004)
29. van den Berg, F., Remke, A., Mooij, A., Haverkort, B.: Performance evaluation for collision prevention based on a domain specific language. In: Balsamo, M.S., Knottenbelt, W.J., Marin, A. (eds.) Computer Performance Engineering. LNCS, vol. 8168, pp. 276–287. Springer, Heidelberg (2013)
30. van Deursen, A., Klint, P., Visser, J.: Domain-specific languages: an annotated bibliography. SIGPLAN Not. 35(6), 26–36 (2000)
31. Westland, J.C.: The cost of errors in software development: evidence from industry. J. Syst. Softw. 62, 1–9 (2002)

Formal Frameworks for Verifying Normative Multi-agent Systems

Max Knobbout, Mehdi Dastani, and John-Jules Ch. Meyer[✉]

Department of Information and Computing Sciences, Utrecht University,
P.O. Box: 80.089, 3508 TB Utrecht, The Netherlands
{M.Knobbout,J.J.C.Meyer}@uu.nl

Abstract. In this paper we concern ourselves with normative multi-agent systems, which are multi-agent systems governed by a set of norms. In these systems, the internals and architecture of the participating agents may be unknown to us, which disables us to make any strong assumption on the possible behaviour that these agents may exhibit. Thus, we cannot simply assume that the agents are aware of the norms, or that they are compliant with respect to the norms. In other words, a crucial problem that needs to be solved is how we can verify these systems if we have no idea whether the agents will be norm-obedient. This paper investigates two distinct formal frameworks which allow us to tackle this problem, namely in the first part of this paper we propose a logic-based framework which uses compliance types, and in the second part we propose a framework which tackles the problem from a mechanism-design perspective.

1 Introduction

A lot of work has contributed to the on-going field of (run-time and offline) verification of programs and systems, such as the verification of object-oriented programs [2] or the verification of agent programming with declarative goals [6]. The field we are interested in are normative multi-agent systems, which are multi-agent systems governed by a set of norms. In the spirit of this work, we are going to explore frameworks for the verification of normative multi-agent systems.

A multi-agent system is a computerized system that is composed of multiple interacting agents within an environment [16]. These systems are generally composed or designed with a specific goal in mind, and depending on the behaviour of the participating agents these goals may, or may not, be achieved. In order to regulate, coordinate and control these systems, norms have been proposed, leading to the field of research called normative multi-agent systems [5]. However, since the internals and architecture of the participating agents may be unknown to us, we cannot simply assume that the agents are aware of the norms, or that they are compliant with respect to the norms. In other words, a crucial problem that needs to be solved is how we can verify these systems if we have no idea whether the agents will be norm-obedient. This paper investigates two distinct

© Springer International Publishing Switzerland 2016
E. Ábrahám et al. (Eds.): de Boer Festschrift, LNCS 9660, pp. 294–308, 2016.
DOI: 10.1007/978-3-319-30734-3_20

formal frameworks which allow us to verify these systems. Formal verification is the act of rigorously proving (or disproving) that the system works as intended. Formal verification is of crucial importance if we are looking for a *guarantee* that the system is correct. Whenever the cost of defection is high, it is of importance that we know that a system is correct without actually having to run it.

In Sect. 2 we briefly introduce the model we use for normative multi-agent systems. In Sect. 3 we consider our first framework that uses compliance types. However, this framework does not take into account *why* the agents would behave norm-compliant, we just *assume* it is the case. In Sect. 4 we consider our second framework that does take these motives into account. Particularly, we assume the agents have some preferences (which are possibly unknown to us), and use solution concepts to predict what the agents will play. This approach tackles the problem from a mechanism design perspective. For a general overview of mechanism design we direct the reader to [13]. In Sect. 5 we discuss the paper.

2 Preliminaries

In this section we briefly introduce the model of execution we consider for multi-agent systems. We consider simple transition systems, consisting of states of the world, and a complete labelling of joint-actions over the transitions connecting these states. Moreover, we assume a set of atomic (negative or positive) sanctions, which represent certain fines and rewards we can give to the agents. They will play a role later, when we will introduce the notion of state-based norms.

Definition 1 (Multi-agent System). *A multi-agent system M is a tuple $(Q, q_0, S, Ags, act, \delta)$ such that:*

- *Q is a finite set of states.*
- *$q_0 \in Q$ the initial state.*
- *S is a finite set of atomic sanction propositions.*
- *$Ags = \{1, ..., n\}$ is a finite non-empty set of agents.*
- *$act : Ags \times Q \mapsto \mathbb{N}_{>0}$ is a function that assigns to each agent and each state the number of available actions. We identify the actions of agent $i \in Ags$ in state $q \in Q$ with the numbers $1 \ldots act(i, q)$. For each state $q \in Q$, a joint action is a vector $\boldsymbol{\alpha} = (\alpha_1, \ldots, \alpha_{|Ags|})$ such that $1 \leq \alpha_i \leq act(i, q)$ for every agent $i \in Ags$. Given a state $q \in Q$, we write $Act(q)$ for the set $\{1, \ldots, act(1, q)\} \times \cdots \times \{1, \ldots, act(|Ags|, q)\}$ of all possible joint actions.*
- *δ is a transition function which maps a state $q \in Q$ and joint action $\boldsymbol{\alpha} = (\alpha_1, \ldots, \alpha_{|Ags|}) \in Act(q)$ to the resulting next state $\delta(q, \boldsymbol{\alpha}) \in Q$.*

This model is thus concurrent, synchronous, decentralized, discrete and deterministic, and is similar to the notion of concurrent game structures found in [1]. Note that for the sake of simplicity, we only consider sanction propositions; in a more elaborate model states contain facts of the environment, which are assigned by a valuation function. A state-based norm can be modelled as a function that assigns sanctions to states. Note that a sanction can be a fine (e.g. pay x amount of money), but it can also be a reward. A state can then be considered 'desired' if the norm merely assigns positive sanctions (rewards) to this state and can be considered 'undesired' if the norm merely assigns negative sanctions (fines) to this state, but in general a norm can assign both positive and negative sanctions. Note This approach is closely related to the approach of [15], who defines 'red' and 'green' states as the desired/undesired states of a system. Formally, we define them as follows.

Definition 2 (State-Based Norm, Normative Multi-agent System). *Given a multi-agent system $M = (Q, q_0, S, Ags, act, \delta)$, a state-based norm γ is a function $\gamma : Q \mapsto \mathcal{P}(S)$ that maps a state of the multi-agent system to a set of sanction propositions. We write (M, γ) for the multi-agent system in which state-based norm γ is implemented and refer to such a tuple as a normative multi-agent system, and we write Γ_M for the set of all possible norms given M.*

As usual, a multi-agent system gives rise to a set of possible *runs* (alternatively computations) that can occur. A run, together with a state-based norm, gives rise to an infinite sequence of sanction-sets that occurs along such a run. We call such a sequence an *outcome* of a normative multi-agent system.

Definition 3 (Runs, Outcomes). *Given a multi-agent system $M = (Q, q_0, S, Ags, act, \delta)$, a run is defined as an infinite sequence $r = q_0 q_1 q_2 \cdots \in Q^\omega$ starting from initial state q_0 such that $\forall j \in \mathbb{N}_0$ there exists a joint action $\boldsymbol{\alpha} \in Act(q_j)$ such that $\delta(q_j, \boldsymbol{\alpha}) = q_{j+1}$. The set of all possible runs over M is denoted by $\mathcal{R}_M$. A run $r = q_0 q_1 q_2 \ldots$ and a state-based norm γ gives rise to an outcome $\gamma(r) = \gamma(q_0)\gamma(q_1)\gamma(q_2) \cdots \in \mathcal{P}(S)^\omega$. We write $\mathcal{O}_M = \{\gamma(r) \mid r \in \mathcal{R}_M \text{ and } \gamma \in \Gamma_M\}$ for the set of all possible outcomes given multi-agent system M.*

Thus, a run r and norm γ give rise to an outcome $\gamma(r)$. In this system agents can adopt strategies, which are mappings from finite sequences of states to an action of the respective agent. A strategy for each agent, referred to as a strategy profile, gives rise to a unique outcome of the normative multi-agent system.

Definition 4 (Strategies). *Given a multi-agent system $M = (Q, q_0, S, Ags, act, \delta)$, a strategy for an agent $i \in Ags$ is a mapping σ_i, mapping a finite sequence of states $q_0, ..., q_k \in Q^+$ to an element of $act(i, q_k)$. A strategy profile $\sigma = (\sigma_1, ..., \sigma_{|Ags|})$ is a tuple containing a strategy for each agent. A strategy profile σ, when executed in M, gives rise to a unique run from $\mathcal{R}_M$, and we write $run(\sigma)$ to denote this run.*

Thus, a multi-agent system M, a norm γ and a strategy profile σ give rise to a unique outcome $\gamma(run(\sigma)) \in \mathcal{O}_M$. Using these concepts, in the next section we provide a verification framework that allows us to verify normative multi-agent system using compliance types.

3   Verification Framework Using Compliance Types

Traditional offline verification of a multi-agent system typically takes on the following form. We are given a normative multi-agent system (M, γ) together with a set of desired outcomes $\mathcal{O}_{desired} \subseteq \mathcal{O}_M$, the latter depicting the set of outcomes that are desired by the designer of the system. The objective now is to verify whether the $\mathcal{O}_{desired}$ is *guaranteed*, i.e., whether it is the case that for all runs $r \in \mathcal{R}_M$ we have that $\gamma(r) \in \mathcal{O}_{desired}$. Such a set $\mathcal{O}_{desired}$ usually is specified by some temporal property of the system, for example "$\Box\neg$bad" stating that always nothing bad happens, or "$\Diamond$good" stating that somewhere in the future something good will happen. Linear Temporal Logic (LTL) as proposed in [14] is a logic that allows assertions of this form. An LTL formula φ can be evaluated along an outcome $o \in \mathcal{O}_M$ (remember that an outcome is an *infinite* sequence of sanction-sets). We will write $o \models \varphi$ whenever an outcome o satisfies an LTL formula φ, and assume the reader is familiar with the basics of LTL without explicitly defining the semantics. Verification then asks whether an LTL formula φ is valid in a normative multi-agent system (M, γ), i.e. whether for all runs $r \in \mathcal{R}_M$ we have that $\gamma(r) \models \varphi$.

Several refinements of LTL have been proposed to extend the possible verification questions one might ask. For example, Computation Tree Logic (CTL), as shown in [8], is a logic that allows explicit (universal and existential) quantification over the set of runs within a logical formula. Later, Alternating-time Temporal Logic (ATL), as introduced in [1], was introduced as an extension of CTL to reason about the possible runs that agents can *enforce*. This language allows even more refined assertions of the form $\langle\langle i \rangle\rangle \varphi$, where $i \in Ags$ is an agent and φ is a temporal formula (in actuality the language allows to reason about what *coalitions of agents* can enforce, but we do not need to go into such detail). Such a formula can be read as "agent i can enforce φ to be true", and such a formula can be evaluated along a normative multi-agent system. We say that $M, \gamma \models \langle\langle i \rangle\rangle \varphi$ is true if and only if there exists a strategy σ_i for agent i such that for all strategies σ_{-i} it is the case that $\gamma(run((\sigma_i, \sigma_{-i}))) \models \varphi$. Observe that we use notation σ_{-i} to denote the strategies of all the other agents apart from i, which together with σ_i gives rise to the strategy profile (σ_i, σ_{-i}).

Although these logics allow us to express complex temporal properties, in order to verify normative multi-agent systems an even more refined approach should arguably be taken. In this work, we do not assume that implementing a system of norms enforces every agent to be perfectly norm-obedient. However, a lot of strategy profiles the agents can adopt would be very implausible to occur. For example, in a smart road multi-agent system, it would be very implausible to consider a situation where all the agents would neglect all the norms (i.e. drive on the wrong side of the road). However, it might be plausible to consider that *some* of the agents are neglectful with respect to the norms, while the other agents are obedient. In other words, in order to verify these systems, it is important to consider more refined quantifications over the possible strategies that can occur. For example, is it the case that we are guaranteed that an outcome from $\mathcal{O}_{desired}$ is reached if all of the agents adopt a norm-obedient strategy? And, is this still the case if one of the agents adopts a strategy which breaks some of the norms? Related to the approach we have taken in [9], in order to express these kinds of properties, we introduce the notion of a *compliance type*.

Definition 5 (Compliance Types, Compliance Profile). *Given a multi-agent system M giving rise to a set of possible outcomes $\mathcal{O}_M$, we define a compliance type as a function $\tau : \mathcal{O}_M \mapsto \{0,1\}$ mapping outcomes to either 0 or 1. We say that an outcome $o \in \mathcal{O}_M$ is τ-compliant if and only if $\tau(o) = 1$. A compliance profile $\hat{\tau} = (\tau_1, \ldots, \tau_{|Ags|})$ is a tuple containing a compliance type τ_i for each agent i.*

In other words, different notions of compliance can be constructed, and a verifier of the system can choose these freely. A compliance type thus relates state-based norms with compliant behaviour. As an example, suppose we have a sanction atom v denoting some violation in the system. Then, we could define a compliance type $\tau_{\text{"never } v\text{"}}$ stating that v should never occur along an outcome as follows:

$$\tau_{\text{"never } v\text{"}}(o) = \begin{cases} 1 & \text{if } o \models \Box\neg v \\ 0 & \text{otherwise.} \end{cases}$$

Depending on our verification needs, more elaborate compliance types can also be defined, for example "sometimes v", or "at most n times v". We can lift the notion of compliant runs to compliant strategies as follows.

Definition 6 (Compliant Strategies). *Given a normative multi-agent system (M, γ) and compliance type τ, we say that a strategy σ_i for agent i is τ-compliant if and only if for all strategies σ_{-i} it is the case that $\gamma(run((\sigma_i, \sigma_{-i})))$ is τ-compliant.*

Intuitively, a strategy σ_i for agent i is τ-compliant if and only if all the outcomes that can occur if agent i would play this strategy are τ-compliant. Since we do not know what the actual compliance behaviour of the agents will be, we verify the system with respect to a set of possible compliance profiles. Using these concepts, we can state a version of the verification problem as follows.

Verification Problem 1. *The verification problem asks, given a normative system (M, γ) and a set of compliance profiles T, whether it is the case that for all $\hat{\tau} = (\tau_i, \tau_{-i}) \in T$ and for all agents $i \in Ags$ there exists a τ_i-compliant strategy σ_i for agent i such that for all τ_{-i}-compliant strategies σ_{-i} it is the case that:*

$$\gamma(run((\sigma_i, \sigma_{-i}))) \in \mathcal{O}_{\text{desired}}$$

In words, this verification problem asks to verify whether for each compliance type, each agent individually has a strategy aligned with this compliance type such that for all strategies of the other agents that are aligned with this compliance type, if the agents would adopt these strategies a desired outcome is reached. We can extend the language of ATL even further to give a logical characterization of the verification questions. Let φ be a formula characterizing $\mathcal{O}_{\text{desired}}$ and let $\hat{\tau} = (\tau_i, \tau_{-i})$ be a compliance profile. We say that

$$M, \gamma \models \langle\langle i \mid \hat{\tau} \rangle\rangle \varphi$$

is valid if and only if there exists a τ_i-compliant strategy σ_i for agent i such that for all τ_{-i}-compliant strategies σ_{-i} it is the case that $\gamma(run((\sigma_i, \sigma_{-i}))) \models \varphi$

(again, we do not concern ourselves with a formal definition of the underlying semantics). Such a logical language allows us to specify whether certain temporal properties (specified by φ) are true if the agents would behave according to certain compliant strategies (specified by $\hat{\tau}$). We can then logically characterize our verification task as follows. Given a normative system (M, γ), a set of compliance profiles T and a temporal formula φ representing the desired outcomes, verify whether:

$$\forall i \in Ags, \forall \hat{\tau} \in T : M, \gamma \models \langle\!\langle i \mid \hat{\tau} \rangle\!\rangle \varphi$$

This is related to the approach we take in [9]. In the next section we will look at an example to get some more intuition on how we can use these assertions to solve the verification problem.

3.1 Example

We consider the multi-agent system M and norm γ depicted in Fig. 1.

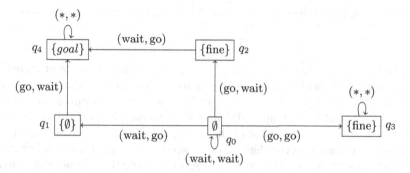

Fig. 1. Multi-agent system and norm consisting of two agents each controlling a train at opposite ends of a tunnel. The agents need to coordinate their actions to not perform action 'go' at the same time.

This system consists of two agents who, starting from initial state q_0 (middle bottom), can either perform a 'wait' or 'go' action. If they both wait, nothing happens, and if they both go, a dangerous situation occurs. If one of them goes and one of them waits, no dangerous situation occurs. The scenario corresponds to two agents controlling a train at opposite ends of the tunnels, and they must coordinate their actions to not end up in the tunnel at the same time. We have the state-based norm γ that assigns a positive sanction *goal* to state q_4, i.e. $\gamma(q_4) = \{goal\}$, a negative sanction fine to state q_2 and q_3, i.e. $\gamma(q_2) = \gamma(q_3) = \{\text{fine}\}$, and does not assign any (positive or negative) sanction to the remaining states. Note that these sanctions in some way reflect that we want the agents to choose the computation $q_0 q_1 (q_4)^\omega$, since this is the only computation for which positive sanction *goal* holds, while containing no negative sanction fine. It is our job to predict whether the agents will indeed, under reasonable assumptions, choose this computation, using our framework of compliance types. We define the following compliance types, τ_{obedient} and $\tau_{\text{neglectful}}$ using temporal logic:

$$\tau_{\text{obedient}}(o) = \begin{cases} 1 & \text{if } o \models \Box\neg\text{fine} \\ 0 & \text{otherwise.} \end{cases}$$

And:

$$\tau_{\text{neglectful}}(o) = 1$$

Thus, every possible outcome $o \in \mathcal{O}_M$ is $\tau_{\text{neglectful}}$-compliant, and this compliance type corresponds to a run in which the agents do not care about the norms. Moreover, given an outcome $o \in \mathcal{O}_M$, we have that o is τ_{obedient}-compliant if and only if $o \models \Box\neg\text{fine}$. In words, an outcome o is τ_{obedient}-compliant if it is never the case that sanction fine holds somewhere along o. For example, the outcome $\gamma(q_0(q_3)^\omega)$ is not τ_{obedient}-compliant, because:

$$\gamma(q_0(q_3)^\omega) \not\models \Box\neg\text{fine}$$

As another example, the outcome $\gamma((q_0)^\omega)$ is τ_{obedient}-compliant, because:

$$\gamma((q_0)^\omega) \models \Box\neg\text{fine}$$

We have for agent 1 that the strategy that always adopts action w at state q_0 is τ_{obedient}-compliant, while all the remaining strategies are not τ_{obedient}-compliant. To see why this is the case, observe that if agent 1 would adopt go at state q_0, then agent 2 could for example play action go to end up in state q_3, at which fine is the case. For agent 2, none of the strategies are τ_{obedient}-compliant. To see why this is the case, observe that for every strategy σ_2 agent 2 can select, there exists a strategy σ_1 for agent 1 such that $\gamma(run((\sigma_1, \sigma_2))) \models \Diamond\text{fine}$. Particularly, whatever agent 2 plays at initial state q_0, whenever agent 1 play go at this state, we either go to state q_2 or state q_3, both at which sanction fine is the case.

Now consider the following set $T = \{(\tau_{\text{obedient}}, \tau_{\text{neglectful}})\}$ containing a single compliance profile $(\tau_{\text{obedient}}, \tau_{\text{neglectful}})$. Let $\varphi = \Diamond goal$ be an LTL-formula that characterizes the set of desired runs of the system. Our verification problem now asks whether the following is the case:

$$\forall i \in \{1,2\} : M, \gamma \models \langle\!\langle i \mid (\tau_{\text{obedient}}, \tau_{\text{neglectful}})\rangle\!\rangle \Diamond goal$$

In order to show whether this is the case, observe that there exists a $\tau_{\text{neglectful}}$-strategy σ_2 for agent 2, particularly the strategy that plays action go at state q_0, such that for all τ_{obedient}-strategies σ_1 for agent 1, particularly the strategy mentioned earlier that always plays w at state q_0, such that $\Diamond goal$ is the case. In formula:

$$M, \gamma \models \langle\!\langle 2 \mid (\tau_{\text{obedient}}, \tau_{\text{neglectful}})\rangle\!\rangle \Diamond goal$$

However, we do not have that there exists a τ_{obedient}-strategy σ_1 for agent 1 such for all $\tau_{\text{neglectful}}$-strategies σ_2 for agent 2 it is the case that $\Diamond goal$. To see this, the only strategy for agent 1 we have to consider is again the one that always plays

w at state q_0. However, agent 2 can also play w forever in state q_0, resulting in outcome $\gamma((q_0)^\omega)$, for which we have that $\gamma((q_0)^\omega) \not\models \Diamond goal$. Thus, in formula, we have:

$$M, \gamma \not\models \langle\!\langle 1 \mid (\tau_{\text{obedient}}, \tau_{\text{neglectful}}) \rangle\!\rangle \Diamond goal$$

In other words, the norm γ does not pass our verification test. In particular, this example highlights that the strategic capabilities for the agents may differ given a particular compliance profile.

3.2 Framework Discussion

In this section we have given a basic logic-based framework in which normative multi-agent systems can be verified. The logic we briefly described allowed us to assert the verification question, but we have not yet discussed the complexity of such a logic (or the existence of a proof system). However, in [9] we used a similar approach of verifying normative systems by introducing an extension of ATL called an-ATL (abstract normative ATL), but instead of state-based norms we considered transition-based norms, and the compliance types we considered were related to the violation of such norms. We showed that verifying an-ATL formulas remains close to the complexity of ATL, and is thus a suitable candidate logic not only to express, but also to perform the verification task.

4 Verification Framework Using Mechanism Design

In the previous section, the verification problem we were concerned with was whether certain (compliant or non-compliant) behaviours of the agents can lead to desired outcomes of the normative multi-agent system. However, this approach does not take into account *why* the agents would behave in such a manner. The agents might have personal preferences that decide how they will behave, and our approach in the previous section does not take these motives into account. Moreover, these preferences might not be known to the designer of the system. Once we make the assumption that the agents have *some* preference, and we are interested in how the agents *will* behave, we enter the field of game theory. Game theory, in the broad sense, is the study of strategic decision making in the presence of (one or more) rational agents, which has its roots in [11]. For an elaborate introduction to the field of game theory, we direct the reader to [13].

Since we have state-based norms that, once implemented, can change the environment of the system, these norms can act as a *mechanism* that can change the underlying game. If we are interested in whether we can design a norm such that the *predicted* outcomes (using game theory) coincides with the *desired* outcomes, we enter the field of mechanism design. In mechanism design, *a mechanism* is, in the general sense, an institution, procedure, protocol or game for generating outcomes. For a general overview of mechanism design we direct the reader to [13], or for an overview that relates mechanism design to computer science, we direct the reader to [12]. In this paper, we consider that the state-based norms are the indirect mechanisms that can change the environment, and can thus lead to different outcomes. In order to predict the outcomes that will occur, we need to have some notion of what the agents *know* and what the agents *value*, which is referred to as an *agent type*. Note however, that a mechanism designer might not know the true types of the agents. In this paper we are not concerned with knowledge of the agents, i.e., we will just assume the agents have complete and perfect knowledge of the system and participating agents. Thus, an agent type is simply a preference over outcomes of the system, which we define as follows.

Definition 7 (Preference). *Given a multi-agent system M, a preference of an agent $i \in Ags$, denoted by $\succsim_i$, is a complete reflexive transitive binary relation over outcomes $\mathcal{O}_M$. If for two outcomes $o, o' \in \mathcal{O}_M$ it holds that $o \succsim_i o'$ and $o' \succsim_i o$, we write $o \sim_i o'$, and when $o \succsim_i o'$ and $o' \not\succsim_i o$, we write $o \succ_i o'$. A preference profile $\succsim = (\succsim_1, \ldots, \succsim_{|Ags|})$ consists of a preference of each agent.*

The reading of $o \succsim_i o'$ should be that agent i prefers outcome o at least as much as outcome o'. Thus, given a norm γ and two runs r and r' of the system, agent i prefers r at least as much as r' whenever $\gamma(r) \succsim_i \gamma(r')$. It is thus already apparent that norms can influence the runs that can occur by making some runs more attractive than other runs for an agent. We can use the preferences to predict the outcomes that will occur, and we can derive these by using concepts from game theory. Whenever we consider a certain type, in order to make a final prediction of the outcomes that will be achieved, we need certain rules that tell us which outcomes will be rationally optimal. In game theory, these formal rules are called the *solution concepts* that can be used for making these predictions. A multitude of these solution concepts exist, but the one we consider in this paper is that of a *Nash Equilibrium*, see e.g. [13].

Definition 8 (Nash Equilibrium). *Given a multi-agent system M, a norm γ, a preference profile $\succsim$ and a strategy profile $\sigma = (\sigma_1, \ldots, \sigma_{|Ags|})$, we say that σ constitutes a Nash Equilibrium in M if and only if for all $i \in Ags$ and strategies σ_i', it holds that $\gamma(run((\sigma_i, \sigma_{-i}))) \succsim_i \gamma(run((\sigma_i', \sigma_{-i})))$. We define $NE_\gamma(\succsim) = \{\gamma(run(\sigma)) \mid \sigma \text{ constitutes a Nash Equilibrium in } M\} \subseteq \mathcal{O}_M$ as the set of all NE outcomes given M, γ and $\succsim$.*

In words, a strategy profile constitutes a Nash Equilibrium if and only if no agent individually can gain something from deviating from their own respective strategy. Again, for a more detailed introduction to this concept, we refer the reader to [13]. The desired outcomes are the outcomes we want to have occur. In the context of normative systems, the desired outcomes are the ones that maintain order in society. For example, a typical criterion one may adopt in an utilitarian society is that wrong-doers should be punished. Because we do not know the true incentives of the agents (remember, the preferences of the agents might be unknown to us), we consider a set of possible preference profiles Θ. A *social choice rule* takes a possible preference profile, and combines these individual preference of the agents to give a set of desired outcomes of the system. In this paper, we assume that such a function is already specified to us, and are not concerned with whether such a rule can be specified given the criteria that we set on such a function (see for example Arrow's impossibility theorem [3]). This is the domain of social choice theory, which concerns itself with combining individual preference in order to reach social welfare [4].

Definition 9 (Social Choice Rule). *Given a multi-agent system M and a set of possible preference profiles Θ, a social choice rule $f : \Theta \mapsto \mathcal{P}(\mathcal{O}_M)$ is a function that maps a preference profile $\succsim \in \Theta$ to a set of outcomes $f(\succsim) \subseteq \mathcal{O}_M$.*

Thus, given a social-choice rule f and preference profile $\succsim$, we say that $f(\succsim)$ are the set of social optimal outcome, which are the outcomes we want to have occur. Because mechanism designers do not know which outcomes are optimal beforehand (the preferences are initially unknown to us), a more cautious approach has to be employed. This information must slowly be generated as the system is executed. The problem here is the fact that the agents in the system may have their own objectives, and may try to behave in a way that hides the truth. A typical goal of a mechanism designer is thus to develop mechanisms that are *incentive compatible*, meaning that the optimal strategy of the participants is to reveal the truth. An example of such a truth-revealing mechanism is Solomon's dilemma, which we will discuss in the next section. Formally, using such a social choice rule, mechanism design defines the following implementability relation.

Definition 10 (Nash Implementability). *Given a multi-agent system M and set of possible preference profiles Θ, we say that a norm γ NE-implements social choice rule f if and only if for all $\succsim \in \Theta$ it holds that $NE_\gamma(\succsim) \subseteq f(\succsim)$.*

Note that in actuality, the above relation defines that of *weak implementation*. Weak implementation demands that all the predicted outcomes $NE_\gamma(\succsim)$ are desired, i.e. are in the set $f(\succsim)$. In *full implementation*, we additionally demand that all desired outcomes are predicted, i.e. $NE_\gamma(\succsim) = f(\succsim)$ for all $\succsim \in \Theta$. However, when considering state-based norms, demanding full implementation might be too strong, since usually a single state-based norm can only generate a small subset of the possible outcomes. The verification problem we consider in this section can now be stated as follows.

Verification Problem 2. *The verification problem asks, given a normative system (M, γ), a set of possible preference profiles Θ and a social choice rule f, whether it is the case that γ NE-implements social choice rule f.*

Let us again look at an example to get some more intuition for the various complex notions introduced in this section.

4.1   Example

Solomon's dilemma is often used in literature to describe the idea of implementation theory and mechanism design. In this dilemma two women come before him, both claiming to be the mother of a child, and Solomon has to find out who is lying. In this paper we consider the version discussed in [10] where Solomon is able to give the mothers a fine. Let us first informally explain the problem and its relation to mechanism design. Solomon (the mechanism designer) initially does not know who the real mother is. Based on this he considers two preference profiles, one preference profile that represents the case in which mother 1 would be the real mother, and one preference profile that represents the case in which mother 2 is the real mother (how he constructs these possible preference profiles will be discussed below). But, as we already mentioned, Solomon does not know which of these preference profiles is the true one. Through a state-based norm, he can give the mothers fines in some states, and he can assign the child to one of the mothers in a state. It is clear that if mother 1 is the true mother, then the optimal outcome would be that mother 1 eventually gets the child forever, and that both mothers never receive any fine. If mother 2 is the true mother, then the optimal outcome would be that mother 2 eventually gets the child forever, and again that both mothers never receive any fine. This example makes it clear why a social choice rule is dependent on the preference profile: since we do not know who the real mother is, we cannot simply say that there exists one unique optimal outcome. It is Solomon's job to construct a norm such that the child is eventually given to the true mother forever without any fines given. We assume that Solomon can give a small fine to mother 1 (represented by sanction proposition $fine_1$) and a big fine to mother 2 (represented by sanction proposition $fine_2$). Note that $fine_2$ is tweaked precisely by Solomon such that this sanction is low enough that if mother 2 would be the real mother, she would care more about the child, while if mother 2 would *not* be the real mother, she would care more about the sanction. Of course this requires some accurate and knowledgeable estimations by Solomon, but we assume that he is wise enough to do this. Moreover, since the situation is symmetric, Solomon could have chosen $fine_1$ and $fine_2$ the other way around, but this is beyond the point of example. If $child_i$ represents that the child is given to mother i, and if $\succsim$ represents the preference profile in which mother 1 is the true mother and $\succsim'$ the preference profile in which mother 2 is the real mother, then it is Solomon's job to implement the following social choice rule f:

$$f(\succsim) = \{o \in \mathcal{O}_M \mid o \models \Diamond\Box(child_1 \wedge \neg child_2) \wedge \neg\Diamond(fine_1) \wedge \neg\Diamond(fine_2)\}$$
$$f(\succsim') = \{o \in \mathcal{O}_M \mid o \models \Diamond\Box(\neg child_1 \wedge child_2) \wedge \neg\Diamond(fine_1) \wedge \neg\Diamond(fine_2)\}$$

Solomon assumes that mother 1 always prefers any outcome over any other outcome if in that outcome she receives the child forever. However, if she does not receive the child forever, Solomon assumes that mother 1 prefers any outcome over any other outcome if this outcome does not contain fine $fine_1$. In order to represent such a preference, we can use the idea presented in [7] of using a preference order over LTL formulas. This preference can then formally be described as follows:

$$(\Diamond\Box child_1) \succ_1 (\Box\neg fine_1) \succ_1 \top$$

Such a list gives rise to a preference over outcomes in multi-agent system as follows. Given two arbitrary outcomes $o, o' \in \mathcal{O}_M$, we determine from left to right the *first* LTL formula that satisfies the outcome. Let us assume that for o this is the formula $\Box\neg\text{fine}_1$ (thus we have that $o \not\models \Diamond\Box\text{child}_1$) and o' this is the formula $\top$ (thus we have that $o' \not\models \Diamond\Box\text{child}_1$ and $o' \not\models \Box\neg\text{fine}_1$). Then, since $(\Box\neg\text{fine}_1) \succ_1 \top$, this would imply that $o \succ_1 o'$. If two outcomes o and o' satisfy the same formula, we say that $o \sim_1 o'$. If the last formula in such a list is $\top$, we know that such a list gives rise to a complete preference over all possible outcomes since this implies that for every possible outcome we can find at least one formula that is satisfied. This particular preference exactly states what we mentioned earlier: mother 1 always prefers any outcome over any other outcome if in that outcome she receives the child forever. However, if this is not the case, mother 1 prefers any outcome over any other outcome if this outcome does not contain fine fine_1.

For mother 2, king Solomon is in doubt about the following two preferences:

$$(\Diamond\Box(\text{child}_2 \wedge \neg\text{fine}_2)) \succ_2 (\Box\neg\text{fine}_2) \succ_2 \top$$
$$(\Diamond\Box\text{child}_2) \succ_2' (\Box\neg\text{fine}_2) \succ_2' \top$$

The first preference $\succsim_2$ states that mother 2 prefers an outcome over any other outcome if she is assigned the child without a fine given. If this is not the case, she would rather not receive a fine. Moreover, she does not care about the remaining outcomes. The second preference $\succsim_2'$ states that mother 2 prefers an outcome in which she is assigned the child, regardless of whether this outcome contains a fine or not, while the rest remains the same. In other words, he either considers that mother 2 cares more about the fine than the child, or more about the child than the fine; the first case represents the case in which mother 1 is the real mother, while the second case represents the case in which mother 2 is the real mother. Thus preference profile $\succsim = (\succsim_1, \succsim_2)$ represents the profile which mother 1 is the real mother, and preference profile $\succsim' = (\succsim_1, \succsim_2')$ represents the profile in which mother 2 is the real mother.

Now we are ready to give the solution to the problem, which is drawn in Fig. 2. Consider the multi-agent system M and norm γ depicted here. This system consists of two agents who, starting from initial state q_0 (below left), can claim to

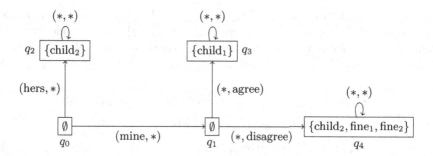

Fig. 2. Multi-agent system and norm consisting of two agents claiming whether they are the real mother.

be the real mother or not. Mother 1 can claim in q_0 that the child either belongs to her (action 'mine'), or that it belongs to the other mother (action 'hers'). If she performs action 'hers', mother 2 can either agree with this (action 'agree') or disagree with this (action 'disagree'). As can be seen in the figure, Solomon has implemented the state-based norm γ that assigns the child to mother 2 in q_2, i.e. $\gamma(q_2) = \{\text{child}_2\}$, assigns the child to mother 1 in q_3, i.e. $\gamma(q_3) = \{\text{child}_1\}$, and assigns the child to mother 2 while giving a small fine to mother 1 (sanction fine_1) and a big fine to mother 2 (sanction fine_2) in state q_4, i.e. $\gamma(q_4) = \{\text{child}_2, \text{fine}_1, \text{fine}_2\}$. But, is it indeed true that for $\Theta = \{\succsim, \succsim'\}$ we have that γ NE-implements social choice rule f? We will show that this is indeed the case in the remainder of this section.

Observe that in the normative multi-agent system, there exists only two possible strategies for each agent, which we refer to as σ_{hers} and σ_{mine} for mother 1, and σ_{agree} and σ_{disagree} for mother 2. The corresponding outcomes are the following:

γ	σ_{agree}	σ_{disagree}
σ_{hers}	$\gamma(q_0(q_2)^\omega)$	$\gamma(q_0(q_2)^\omega)$
σ_{mine}	$\gamma(q_0 q_1 (q_3)^\omega)$	$\gamma(q_0 q_1 (q_4)^\omega)$

Consider preference profile $(\succsim_1, \succsim_2)$. We have that $(\sigma_{\text{mine}}, \sigma_{\text{agree}})$ constitutes a Nash Equilibrium. To see why, observe that $\gamma(run((\sigma_{\text{mine}}, \sigma_{\text{agree}}))) \succ_1 \gamma(run((\sigma_{\text{hers}}, \sigma_{\text{agree}})))$ because:

$$\gamma(run((\sigma_{\text{mine}}, \sigma_{\text{agree}}))) \models \Diamond\Box\text{child}_1, \text{and,}$$
$$\gamma(run((\sigma_{\text{hers}}, \sigma_{\text{agree}}))) \models \neg\Diamond\Box\text{child}_1$$

Moreover, observe that $\gamma(run((\sigma_{\text{mine}}, \sigma_{\text{agree}}))) \succ_2 \gamma(run((\sigma_{\text{mine}}, \sigma_{\text{disagree}})))$ because:

$$\gamma(run((\sigma_{\text{mine}}, \sigma_{\text{agree}}))) \models \neg\Diamond\Box(\text{child}_2 \wedge \neg\text{fine}_2) \wedge \Box\neg\text{fine}_2, \text{and,}$$
$$\gamma(run((\sigma_{\text{mine}}, \sigma_{\text{disagree}}))) \models \neg\Diamond\Box(\text{child}_2 \wedge \neg\text{fine}_2) \wedge \neg\Box\neg\text{fine}_2$$

It is also not hard to verify that $(\sigma_{\text{mine}}, \sigma_{\text{agree}})$ is the only NE strategy profile, implying that $\text{NE}_\gamma((\succsim_1, \succsim_2)) = \{\gamma(run((\sigma_{\text{mine}}, \sigma_{\text{agree}})))\}$. Now consider strategy profile $(\succsim_1, \succsim'_2)$. We have that $(\sigma_{\text{hers}}, \sigma_{\text{disagree}})$ constitutes a Nash Equilibrium. To see why, observe that $\gamma(run((\sigma_{\text{hers}}, \sigma_{\text{disagree}}))) \succ_1 \gamma(run((\sigma_{\text{mine}}, \sigma_{\text{disagree}})))$ because:

$$\gamma(run((\sigma_{\text{hers}}, \sigma_{\text{disagree}}))) \models \neg\Diamond\Box\text{child}_1 \wedge \Box\neg\text{fine}_1, \text{and,}$$
$$\gamma(run((\sigma_{\text{mine}}, \sigma_{\text{disagree}}))) \models \neg\Diamond\Box\text{child}_1 \wedge \neg\Box\neg\text{fine}_1$$

Moreover, observe that $\gamma(run((\sigma_{\text{hers}}, \sigma_{\text{disagree}}))) \sim'_2 \gamma(run((\sigma_{\text{hers}}, \sigma_{\text{agree}})))$ because:

$$\gamma(run((\sigma_{\text{hers}}, \sigma_{\text{disagree}}))) \models \Diamond\Box(\text{child}_2 \wedge \neg\text{fine}_2), \text{and,}$$
$$\gamma(run((\sigma_{\text{hers}}, \sigma_{\text{agree}}))) \models \Diamond\Box(\text{child}_2 \wedge \neg\text{fine}_2)$$

It is again also not hard to verify that $(\sigma_{\text{hers}}, \sigma_{\text{disagree}})$ is the only NE strategy profile, implying that $\text{NE}_\gamma((\succsim_1, \succsim_2')) = \{\gamma(run((\sigma_{\text{hers}}, \sigma_{\text{disagree}})))\}$. Since we have that:

$$\gamma(run((\sigma_{\text{mine}}, \sigma_{\text{agree}}))) \models \Diamond\Box(\text{child}_1 \wedge \neg\text{child}_2) \wedge \neg\Diamond(\text{fine}_1) \wedge \neg\Diamond(\text{fine}_2), \text{and,}$$

$$\gamma(run((\sigma_{\text{hers}}, \sigma_{\text{disagree}}))) \models \Diamond\Box(\neg\text{child}_1 \wedge \text{child}_2) \wedge \neg\Diamond(\text{fine}_1) \wedge \neg\Diamond(\text{fine}_2)$$

We can conclude that $\text{NE}_\gamma(\succsim) \subseteq f(\succsim')$ and $\text{NE}_\gamma(\succsim') \subseteq f(\succsim')$ as needed. In other words, we have verified that it is indeed the case that, given possible preference profiles $\Theta = \{\succsim, \succsim'\}$, we have that γ NE-implements social choice rule f: the normative multi-agent system ensures that the child is eventually given to the real mother forever without any fines given.

4.2 Framework Discussion

In this section, we discussed how we can frame the verification problem of an multi-agent system using concepts from mechanism design. This idea is related to the work in [7], in which they call this "normative mechanism design". We believe that this field of research is an exciting new way in which normative systems can be studied: norms are viewed as a mechanism constituting a game, allowing us to state the verification problems (in the context of formal verification) as implementation problems (in the context of mechanism design).

5 Discussion

In this paper we have presented two distinct verification frameworks in which the correctness of normative multi-agent systems can be (dis)proven. In the first part we used compliance types, and showed how properties of a system can be expressed (and to marginal extent proven) using these types. In the second part we used mechanism design, and showed how implementability questions can be expressed (and to a marginal extend proven). Although both these approaches use norms as a mechanism to steer agents away (or towards) certain outcomes of the system, the main difference is the following:

- With compliance types, we assume certain compliance behaviour of the agents with respect to the norm. We do not know what the actual compliance behaviour of the agents will be, so we verify the system with respect to a set of possible compliance profiles.
- With mechanism design, we assume a certain preference relation over outcomes of the system. We do not know what the true preference of the agents are, so we verify the system with respect to a social choice rule, a solution concept and set of possible preference profiles.

These different approaches offer a generic starting point for which the verification task of normative multi-agent systems can be tackled. As we already mentioned in the introduction, normative systems are making their way into our everyday life. Formal verification is of crucial importance if we are looking for a *guarantee* that the system is correct. Whenever the cost of defection is high, it is of importance that we know that a system is correct without actually having to run it. Verification gives us this guarantee. Development of such methods and tools play an important role in the advancement of normative multi-agent systems and Artificial Intelligence in general.

References

1. Alur, R., Henzinger, T.A., Kupferman, O.: Alternating-time temporal logic. J. ACM **49**(5), 672–713 (2002)
2. Apt, K.R., de Boer, F.S., Olderog, E., de Gouw, S.: Verification of object-oriented programs: a transformational approach. J. Comput. Syst. Sci. **78**(3), 823–852 (2012)
3. Arrow, K.J.: A difficulty in the concept of social welfare. J. Polit. Econ. **58**(4), 328–346 (1950)
4. Arrow, K.J.: Social Choice and Individual Values. Yale University Press, New Haven (1951)
5. Boella, G., van der Torre, L., Verhagen, H.: Introduction to normative multiagent systems. Comput. Math. Organ. Theor. **12**(2–3), 71–79 (2006)
6. de Boer, F.S., Hindriks, K.V., van der Hoek, W., Meyer, J.J.C.: A verification framework for agent programming with declarative goals. J. Appl. Logic **5**(2), 277–302 (2007)
7. Bulling, N., Dastani, M.: Verifying normative behaviour via normative mechanism design. In: Proceedings of the Twenty-Second International Joint Conference on Artificial Intelligence (IJCAI 2011), pp. 103–108 (2011)
8. Clarke, E.M., Emerson, E.A.: Design and synthesis of synchronization skeletons using branching-time temporal logic. In: Logic of Programs Workshop, pp. 52–71 (1982)
9. Knobbout, M., Dastani, M.: Reasoning under compliance assumptions in normative multiagent systems. In: Proceedings of the 11th International Joint Conference on Autonomous Agents and Multiagent Systems (AAMAS 2012), pp. 331–340 (2012)
10. Moore, J.: Implementation, contracts and renegotiation in environments with complete information. Adv. Econ. Theor **1**, 182–282 (1992)
11. Neumann, J.V., Morgenstern, O.: Theory of Games and Economic Behavior. Princeton University Press, Princeton (1944)
12. Nisan, N.: Introduction to mechanism design (for computer scientists). In: Nisan, N., Roughgarden, T., Tardos, E., Vazirani, V. (eds.) Algorithmic Game Theory, pp. 209–242. Cambridge University Press, New York (2007)
13. Osborne, M., Rubinstein, A.: A Course in Game Theory. MIT Press, Cambridge (1994)
14. Pnueli, A.: The temporal logic of programs. In: Proceedings of the 18th Annual Symposium on Foundations of Computer Science, pp. 46–57 (1977)
15. Sergot, M.J.: Action and agency in norm-governed multi-agent systems. In: Artikis, A., O'Hare, G.M.P., Stathis, K., Vouros, G. (eds.) ESAW 2007. LNCS (LNAI), vol. 4995, pp. 1–54. Springer, Heidelberg (2008)
16. Wooldridge, M.: An Introduction to MultiAgent Systems, 2nd edn. Wiley Publishing, Chichester (2009)

Moessner's Theorem: An Exercise in Coinductive Reasoning in Coq

Robbert Krebbers[1](✉), Louis Parlant[2], and Alexandra Silva[3]

[1] Aarhus University, Aarhus, Denmark
mail@robbert.krebbers.nl
[2] École Normale Supérieure de Lyon, Lyon, France
[3] University College London, London, UK

Dedicated to Frank de Boer on the occasion of his 60th birthday.

Abstract. Moessner's Theorem describes a construction of the sequence of powers $(1^n, 2^n, 3^n, \ldots)$, by repeatedly dropping and summing elements from the sequence of positive natural numbers. The theorem was presented by Moessner in 1951 without a proof and later proved and generalized in several directions. More recently, a coinductive proof of the original theorem was given by Niqui and Rutten. We present a formalization of their proof in the Coq proof assistant. This formalization serves as a non-trivial illustration of the use of coinduction in Coq. During the formalization, we discovered that Long and Salié's generalizations could also be proved using (almost) the same bisimulation.

1 Introduction

Coinduction has grown in the last years as the prime principle to prove properties about dynamical and concurrent systems or, in general, structures that exhibit circularity. Formalizations of coinduction are becoming common in most proof assistants but the use thereof is not yet widespread, often due to the lack of good examples balancing expressivity and simplicity to be suitable tutorials for new users. This paper sets itself to provide such an example tutorial of formalized coinduction. Formal methods, concurrency, and verification have been central topics in Frank's research and in the last decade he was exposed (though not intentionally!) to coinduction frequently. We dedicate to Frank this paper on formalizing a result about Frank's favorite coinductive object – streams.

Streams constitute the most basic example of infinite objects and are often used to illustrate the use of coinduction to prove equivalence of algorithms producing infinite objects. A more elaborate example of the use of coinduction to prove the correctness of an algorithm that produces infinite objects is provided by Niqui and Rutten's proof of Moessner's Theorem [13].

Moessner's Theorem describes a procedure for constructing the stream of successive exponents $(1^n, 2^n, 3^n, \ldots)$, for every $n \geq 1$, with several steps of dropping

The work in this paper was developed when all authors were at the Radboud University, The Netherlands.

and summing elements of the stream of positive natural numbers. This procedure is quite simple: let us show the result for $n = 3$. Starting with the sequence of positive naturals $(1, 2, 3, 4, 5, 6, 7, 8, \ldots)$, one drops every *third* element to obtain the stream $(1, 2, 4, 5, 7, 8, \ldots)$. Then one computes the stream of the partial sums by adding to every element all the previous ones:

$$(1, 1 + 2, 1 + 2 + 4, 1 + 2 + 4 + 5, 1 + 2 + 4 + 5 + 7, \ldots) = (1, 3, 7, 12, 19, \ldots)$$

Then, one drops every *second* element of the latter sequence, giving rise to $(1, 7, 19, \ldots)$, and finally by taking partial sums, one gets: $(1, 8, 27, \ldots)$. The resulting stream contains indeed the expected elements: $(1^3, 2^3, 3^3, \ldots)$.

This result holds for any n: drop every n-th element of the sequence of positive naturals, then form partial sums, and then start again dropping every $(n-1)$-th element and summing, and proceed recursively. This process creates the stream of all positive naturals to the power of n: $(1^n, 2^n, 3^n, 4^n, 5^n, \ldots)$.

The above algorithm/procedure can easily be described as a functional program that takes n as a parameter. Moessner's Theorem now corresponds to the question of whether this program yields the stream $(1^n, 2^n, 3^n, 4^n, 5^n \ldots)$ for each $n \geq 1$. Since the stream $(1^n, 2^n, 3^n, 4^n, 5^n \ldots)$ is a functional program in itself, Moessner's Theorem can be proven by showing equivalence of these programs. Because these programs produce streams, the obvious technique to prove equivalence is to use *coinduction*. This was observed by Niqui and Rutten who provided a bisimulation witnessing the equivalence of these programs [13].

Related Work. Moessner's construction has attracted much attention over the years. The theorem was only conjectured by its discoverer [12]. The first proof was given shortly thereafter by Perron [17] (who, curiously, was the editor of the journal where the conjecture was submitted). The theorem was then the subject of several popular accounts and generalizations [4,8,11,14–16,20].

Paasche [14–16] generalized it by allowing the dropping intervals to increase at each step. This led to the construction of the stream containing the factorials and super-factorials. Long [10,11] and Salié [20] also generalized Moessner's result to apply to the situation in which the initial sequence is not the sequence of successive integers $(1, 2, 3, \ldots)$ but the arithmetic progression $(a, d+a, 2d+a, \ldots)$. They showed that the final sequence obtained by the Moessner construction is $(a \cdot 1^{n-1}, (d + a) \cdot 2^{n-1}, (2d + a) \cdot 3^{n-1}, \ldots)$.

Very recently, Hinze [7] and Niqui and Rutten [13] have given proofs involving concepts from functional programming, respectively calculational scans and the coalgebra of streams. The proof of Hinze covers Moessner's and Paasche's results whereas Niqui and Rutten's proof only covers the original Moessner's Theorem.

Kozen and the third author [9] have provided an algebraic proof that has the advantage of covering all the results mentioned above and opened the door to new generalizations of Moessner's original result. The foundations of this proof were formalized in NUPRL by Bickford *et al.* [2].

Clausen *et al.* [3] have also provided a formalization of Moessner's theorem in COQ, but their approach is very different from ours. Our result is more general and applies to $(1^n, 2^n, 3^n, \ldots)$ for any $n \geq 1$, whereas they provide a COQ tactic that *generates* a theorem for any given n by macro expansion. We furthermore also provide a proof of Long and Salié's generalization, that is both more general, and follows as a mere consequence of the original Moessner's Theorem.

Urbak [23] extended the results of Clausen *et al.* in his MSc thesis by exploring Moessner's theorem in a very general setting. Long and Salié's generalization is also a consequence of his work.

Contrary to the aforementioned Coq formalizations, we have setup our Coq development in such a way that it matches common mathematical practice in coinduction, as for example being used by Rutten [18]. We have abstracted from Coq's implementation of coinduction as much as possible by providing an abstraction on top of it to avoid for example guardedness issues in proofs. Also, we have made heavy use of Coq's notations machinery to obtain notations close to those on paper, and have automated parts of the proof that one would omit on paper too. As a result, we were able to formalize the proof of Niqui and Rutten in a very compact and concise way that is close to its original presentation. Our Coq development is 20 times shorter, in terms of lines of code, than Urbak's.

Contribution. We set ourselves to the quest of formalizing Niqui and Rutten's proof in the Coq proof assistant [5]. The interest in doing so is four-fold.

- On the one hand, as with every formalization, one is forced to go through all details of the *pen-and-paper* proof and potentially uncover flaws or omissions.
- On the other hand, and of more interest to us, coinduction in Coq is not widely used and good (tutorial) examples are lacking. Bisimulation proofs are very mechanical and particularly suited for automation/formalization in proof assistants. Hence, we hope that the present example can serve as non-trivial teaching/illustration material of a proof by coinduction in Coq.
- There is often just a shallow correspondence between formalizations and their original mathematical texts. We show that this is not necessarily the case by defining suitable abstractions. In particular, we abstract from Coq's internals for coinduction as much as possible. As a result, our formalization corresponds well to the paper by Niqui and Rutten, and is very compact.
- Lastly, in the process of formalizing Niqui and Rutten's proof, we uncovered a simple proof of Long [10,11] and Salié's [20] generalization. Though (once done) the generalization is not at all complicated, it was surprising to us that the extended version is just a corollary of the original Moessner's Theorem, and that the bisimulation did not have to be modified. The Coq formalization was achieved with a simple extra lemma.

Our Coq code is available at https://github.com/robbertkrebbers/moessner.

2   Streams and Coinduction

In the construction of Moessner's Theorem, streams and operations on them (in particular, drop and sum) play a central role. The set of *streams* A^ω with elements in A can be formally defined as $A^\omega = \{s \mid s\colon \mathbb{N} \to A\}$.

We denote the n-th element of the stream s by $s(n)$. Given a stream $s = (a_0, a_1, a_2, a_3, \ldots)$, we call $s(0) = a_0$ the *head* of the stream, and $(a_1, a_2, a_3, \ldots)$ the *tail* of the stream, which we denote by s'. The operations of head and tail define the following structure on the set of streams:

$$c \colon A^\omega \longrightarrow A \times A^\omega \qquad c(s) = (s(0), s'). \tag{1}$$

The functor F corresponding to the above structure is $F(X) = A \times X$. The set of streams A^ω is the greatest fixpoint of this functor. That is in essence why streams are *coinductive* type, in contrast with lists, which are the least fixpoint of the functor $G(X) = 1 + A \times X$.

In COQ we define streams using the latter view as a coinductive type instead of the functional view $\{s \mid s \colon \mathbb{N} \to A\}$. The coinductive view on streams allows for a simple and elegant definition of operations, as well as for proofs of properties on them. The coinductive approach to infinite datatypes enables a uniform extension to more complex types, such as infinite trees, λ-terms, automata, *etc.* [19].

Streams are the simplest examples of coalgebras and proofs of stream equality are prime illustrations of the power of the coinduction proof principle. Since in this paper we will only deal with streams, we will be introducing all general concepts concretely in this context. The proof of Moessner's Theorem is a beautiful example of *concrete coalgebra*.

Definition 1. *A relation $R \subseteq A^\omega \times A^\omega$ is a* bisimulation *if for every $(s, t) \in R$ it holds that $s(0) = t(0)$ and $(s', t') \in R$.*

The following theorem states the coinduction proof principle for streams, which enables one to prove equality of streams just by exhibiting a bisimulation relation containing the pair consisting of these two streams.

Theorem 1 (Coinduction Principle). *Let $R \subseteq A^\omega \times A^\omega$ be a bisimulation. For all $s, t \in A^\omega$ we have that $(s, t) \in R$ implies $s = t$.*

3   Basic Operations and Theorems on Streams in COQ

In this section we describe the COQ definitions of operations on streams that are needed to formalize Moessner's Theorem. Also, we describe the basic theorems and COQ infrastructure that we use for the formalization. In order to get started, we first define the type `Stream` A of streams A^ω with elements of type A.

```
CoInductive Stream (A : Type) : Type :=
  SCons : A →  Stream A →   Stream A.
Arguments SCons {_} _ _. (* Setup implicit arguments so Coq infers the
type [A] of [SCons : ∀  A : Type, A →  Stream A →   Stream A]. *)
Infix ":::" := SCons.
```

This definition resembles the well-known inductive definition of lists, but instead of the keyword `Inductive` we use the keyword `CoInductive`. Furthermore, note that ::: is the inverse map of the structure map on the set of streams given by head and tail, *cf.* (1) on page 4, and the keyword `CoInductive` is taking the greatest fixpoint of the functor $F(X) = A \times X$, as described in Sect. 2.

The `CoFixpoint` command is used to create corecursive definitions:

```
CoFixpoint repeat {A} (x : A) : Stream A := x ::: #x
where "# x" := (repeat x).
```

The stream #*x* represents the *constant stream* $(x, x, x, \ldots)$ that Niqui and Rutten denote by $\bar{x}$. Whereas recursive definitions in CoQ should be *terminating*, corecursive definitions should be *productive*. Intuitively this means that given a term of coinductive type (and in particular a `CoFixpoint`), it will always produce a constructor. The following is rejected by CoQ because this is not the case.

```
Fail CoFixpoint bad : Stream False := bad.
```

Since productivity is undecidable, corecursive definitions in CoQ should satisfy a decidable syntactical criterion (so as to enable decidable type checking) that guarantees productivity. This criterion is called the *guard condition*. Over simplified, this means that a `CoFixpoint` should have the following shape:

```
CoFixpoint f p⃗ : Stream A := x₀ ::: x₁ ::: ... ::: xₙ ::: f q⃗.
```

with $0 < n$. The definition of #x satisfies this condition, but bad does not.

Although the guard condition ensures that terms of coinductive type always produce a constructor, CoQ's computation rules do not allow `CoFixpoint` definitions to reduce. For example, # 10 does not reduce to 10 ::: #x. If it would, this process could be repeated infinitely many times, and would destroy the property that all computations in CoQ terminate. Instead, computation of coinductive types is performed lazily, and a `CoFixpoint` definition is only allowed to reduce whenever it is the operand of a pattern match construct.

Pattern matching can be used to decompose coinductive types. For streams, this mechanism allows us to define the common destructors `head` and `tail`.

```
Definition head {A} (s : Stream A) : A := match s with x ::: _ ⇒ x end.
Definition tail {A} (s : Stream A) : Stream A :=
  match s with _ ::: s ⇒ s end.
Notation "s '" := (tail s).
```

We use the notation s' for `tail` s so as to resemble the presentation of Niqui and Rutten. Of course, CoQ allows us to write expressions like s'' to denote the second tail of s. Notice that the term `head` (#10) indeed reduces to 10 because the `CoFixpoint` definition now becomes the operand of a pattern match construct.

We will not be using explicit pattern matching on streams anymore, and define everything in terms of `head` and `tail`. For example, see below the functions `map` and `zip_with` which lift functions on individual elements to whole streams.

```
CoFixpoint map {A B} (f : A → B) (s : Stream A) : Stream B :=
  f (head s) ::: map f (s').
CoFixpoint zip_with {A B C} (f : A → B → C)
    (s : Stream A) (t : Stream B) : Stream C :=
  f (head s) (head t) ::: zip_with f (s') (t').
```

3.1   Stream Equality, Bisimulation, and Coinduction

In order to support algebraic reasoning about streams, we need a notion that expresses that streams are element-wise equal. Since no finite expansion of the streams #f x and map f (#x) lead to equal terms, CoQ's notion of Leibniz equality = is too strong to accurately capture stream equality [1,6]. Therefore, we use the following coinductively defined relation of *bisimilarity*[1]:

```
CoInductive equal {A} (s t : Stream A) : Prop :=
  make_equal : head s = head t → s' ≡ t'→  s ≡ t
where "s ≡ t" := (@equal _ s t).
```

Since bisimilarity is defined as a coinductive type, proving that two streams are bisimilar corresponds to constructing a corecursive definition by the Curry-Howard correspondence (programs as proofs). For example, we can construct a proof of #f x ≡ map f (#x) by providing an explicit proof term as follows:

```
CoFixpoint repeat_map {A B} (f : A → B) x : #f x ≡ map f (#x) :=
  make_equal (#f x) (map f (#x)) eq_refl (repeat_map f x).
```

Here, eq_refl is a proof of f x = f x, and thus a proof of head (#f x)   = head (map f (#x)) by convertibility. Clearly, proving such properties by providing an explicit proof term is inconvenient, and should be avoided in practice.

CoQ's native support for coinductive proofs is not as good as its support for inductive proofs. There is just the primitive cofix tactic, which does not protect one from creating proofs that do not satisfy the guard condition. If a proof does not satisfy the guard condition, the proof will only be rejected when one closes the proof using Qed (that is when the proof is being checked by the kernel). This is different from the induction tactic, which cannot be used wrongly. Let us give a demonstration of the cofix tactic.

```
Lemma repeat_map x : #f x ≡ map f (#x).
Proof.
  cofix CH.
  (* We get a hypothesis [CH : #f x ≡ map f (#x)]. We should use it in
     such a way that the generated proof term is guarded. *)
  apply make_equal.
  * (* Prove that the heads are equal: [head (#f x) = head (map f (#x))]
    This holds by computation, so [reflexivity] will succeed. *)
    reflexivity.
  * (* Prove that the tails are equal: [(#f x)' ≡ (map f (#x))'] *)
    (* Unfold the definitions to obtain [#f x ≡ map f (#x)] *)
    (* NB: the exclamation mark ! performs a rewrite as many times as
       possible (but at least once) *)
    rewrite map_tail, !repeat_tail.
    (* Use the corecursive assumption [CH]. *)
    exact CH.
Qed.
```

---

[1] We use Leibniz equality for the heads because we only deal with streams of integers. In general, for example to consider streams of streams, this is still too restrictive.

In the above proof, it would be appealing to use the hypothesis CH straight-away. Of course, the generated proof term would not be guarded, and will therefore be rejected whenever we type Qed. Since we have to be extremely careful when to use the hypothesis generated by the cofix tactic, many tactics for automation cannot be used for coinductive proofs because they will use hypotheses eagerly and thus likely break the guard condition. Therefore we will look at two alternative approaches to proving stream equality.

The first approach is to define a *stream bisimulation* relation (see Definition 1), and then prove the coinduction proof principle (see Theorem 1). This is the core of the coinductive proof of Moessner's Theorem by Niqui and Rutten.

```
Definition bisimulation {A} (R : relation (Stream A)) : Prop :=
  ∀ s t, R s t →  head s = head t ∧  R (s') (t').
Lemma bisimulation_equal {A} (R : relation (Stream A)) s t :
  bisimulation R →  R s t →  s ≡ t.
```

Instead of having to produce a proof-term that satisfies the guard condition, one has to define a suitable bisimulation relation, and the problem of guardedness has moved once and for all to the proof of bisimulation_equal.

Another approach is to view streams Stream A as functions nat → A (as we have initially introduced streams in Sect. 2). The function s !! i gives the ith element $s(i)$ of the stream s. It is straightforward to prove that streams are bisimilar if and only if they are element-wise equal using the !! function.

```
Fixpoint elt {A} (s : Stream A) (i : nat) : A :=
  match i with 0 ⇒  head s | S i ⇒  s' !! i end
where "s !! i" := (elt s i).
Lemma equal_elt {A} (s t : stream A) : s ≡ t ↔  ∀ i, s !! i = t !! i.
```

For many streams !! enjoys nice properties. The lemma equal_elt is thus often useful to prove stream equality. For example, using the lemmas:

```
Lemma repeat_elt {A} (x : A) i : #x !! i = x.
Lemma map_elt {A B} (f : A →  B) s i : map f s !! i = f (s !! i).
```

we can give yet another proof of #f x ≡ map f (#x).

```
Lemma repeat_map x : #f x ≡ map f (#x).
Proof.
  apply equal_elt. intros i. rewrite map_elt, !repeat_elt. reflexivity.
Qed.
```

By using equal_elt, we have to prove that #f x !! i = map f (#x) !! i for any i. This trivially follows from the lemmas above.

3.2 Setoids

In order to enable algebraic reasoning about streams, we should be able to rewrite using bisimilarity. We thus prove that equal is an equivalence relation.

```
Instance equal_equivalence {A} : Equivalence (@equal A).
```

We use the `Instance` keyword instead of the `Lemma` keyword to register this fact with Coq's setoid machinery [21]. The setoid machinery uses Coq's type classes [22] under water, but we will not detail that here.

Of course, rewriting with bisimilarity gives rise to side-conditions: rewriting a subterm is allowed only if the subterm is an argument of a function that has been proven to *respect* bisimilarity. For the case of ::: this means that s ≡ t implies x ::: s ≡ x ::: t. In Coq this property can be expressed compactly by the following notation:

```
Instance SCons_proper {A} (x : A) : Proper (equal ⟹ equal) (SCons x).
```

This notation should be read as: if the arguments of `SCons x` are bisimilar, then so are the results. The arrow ⟹ should not be confused with the arrow → for function types. A property like the above must be proved for each function in whose arguments we wish to rewrite. For example:

```
Instance head_proper {A} : Proper (equal ⟹ eq) (@head A).
Instance tail_proper {A} : Proper (equal ⟹ equal) (@tail A).
Instance elt_proper {A} : Proper (equal ⟹ eq ⟹ eq) (@elt A).
```

3.3 Ring Structure

We define the operations for element-wise addition, multiplication, and subtraction, by lifting the operations on integers using `zip_with` and `map`.

```
Infix "⊕" := (zip_with Z.add). (* addition *)
Infix "⊖" := (zip_with Z.sub). (* subtraction *)
Infix "⊙" := (zip_with Z.mul). (* multiplication *)
Notation "⊖ s":= (map Z.opp s). (* additive inverse *)
```

Together with the constant streams #0 and #1, these operations introduce a ring structure on streams. To prove this result, we use the lemma `equal_elt` that relates bisimilarity to element-wise equality.

```
Lemma stream_ring_theory :
  ring_theory (#0) (#1) (zip_with Z.add) (zip_with Z.mul)
    (zip_with Z.sub) (map Z.opp) equal.
Add Ring stream : stream_ring_theory.
```

The command `Add Ring stream : stream_ring_theory` registers this fact, so that ring equations over streams can be solved automatically using the `ring` tactic. Automation for solving ring equations will be used heavily in Sect. 4.

```
Lemma Smult_plus_distr_r s t u : (t ⊕ u) ⊙ s ≡ (t ⊙ s) ⊕ (u ⊙ s).
Proof. ring. Qed.
```

The repeated multiplication defines the *stream power*, written $s^{\langle n \rangle}$:

```
Fixpoint Spow (s : Stream Z) (n : nat) : Stream Z :=
  match n with 0 ⇒ #1 | S n ⇒ s ⊙ s ^^ n end
where "s ^^ n" := (Spow s n).
```

3.4   Specific Stream Operations

In the last part of this section we define stream operations that are specifically used for Moessner's Theorem.

The stream of positive natural numbers **nats** is defined as the unique solution of the equations: $\texttt{nats}(0) = 1$ and $\texttt{nats}' = \overline{1} \oplus \texttt{nats}$. In order to define this stream in CoQ, we define a more general notion that makes use of an accumulator. The definition `Sfrom` i represents the stream $(i, 1 + i, 2 + i, \ldots)$.

```
CoFixpoint Sfrom (i : Z) : Stream Z := i ::: Sfrom (1 + i).
Notation nats := (Sfrom 1).
```

The equation of **nats** without an accumulator as given by Niqui and Rutten is not accepted by CoQ because the co-recursive call to **nats** is hidden behind the $\oplus$ operation. This is not allowed by the guard condition.

```
Fail CoFixpoint nats : Stream Z := 1 ::: #1 ⊕ nats. (* Not allowed *)
```

Although this definition is rejected by CoQ, we can still prove that the heads and tails of our definition satisfy the desired equations with respect to head and tail. This allows reasoning in the same way as on paper.

```
Lemma Sfrom_tail n : (Sfrom n)' ≡ #1 ⊕ Sfrom n.
```

Another operation that arises in the Moessner construction as described in the introduction is *partial sums* of a stream. This operation is informally defined by:

$$\Sigma\,(s_0, s_1, s_2, \ldots) = (s_0, s_0 + s_1, s_0 + s_1 + s_2, \ldots)$$

and formally by the equations $(\Sigma\,s)\,(0) = s(0)$ and $(\Sigma\,s)' = \overline{s} \oplus \Sigma\,s'$. In order to define the partial sums in CoQ we again need to make use of an accumulator, and prove that the definition satisfies the desired equation.

```
CoFixpoint Ssum (i : Z) (s : Stream Z) : Stream Z :=
   head s + i ::: Ssum (head s + i) (s').
Notation "'Σ' s" := (Ssum 0 s).
Lemma Ssum_tail s : (Σ s)' ≡ #head s ⊕ Σ s'.
```

The last operation we need to define the Moessner construction is *dropping*. We define a family of drop operators $D_k^i \colon A^\omega \to A^\omega$ as the solution of:

$$(D_k^{i+1}\,s)(0) = s(0) \quad (D_k^{i+1}\,s)' = D_k^i\,s' \quad (D_k^0\,s)(0) = s(1) \quad (D_k^0\,s)' = D_k^{k-2}\,s''.$$

The drop operator $D_k^i\,s$ repeatedly drops the i-th element of every block of k elements of s. For example, $D_3^1\,s = (s(0), s(2), s(3), s(5), s(6), s(8), \ldots)$. We use the notation $D@\{i,k\}\,s$ to denote this operation in CoQ.

```
CoFixpoint Sdrop {A} (i k : nat) (s : Stream A) : Stream A :=
   match i with
   | 0  ⇒  head (s') ::: D@{k-2,k} s''
   | S i ⇒  head s ::: D@{i,k} s'
   end
where"D@{ i , k } s" := (Sdrop i k s).
```

This definition is identical to the definition of Niqui and Rutten, but whereas they require $2 \le k$ and $0 \le i < k$, we allow any k and i (subtraction of naturals $i - j$ is a total COQ function that yields 0 in case $i < j$).

4   A Formalized Proof of Moessner's Theorem

We are now ready to formulate Moessner's Theorem using the stream operations that we have defined. For the case $n = 3$, as presented in the introduction, the theorem boils down to the stream equation $\Sigma \, \mathrm{D}_2^1 \, \Sigma \, \mathrm{D}_3^2 \, \mathsf{nats} = \mathsf{nats}^{\langle 3 \rangle}$.

The general case is slightly more involved (mainly due to the amount of indices), but still mirrors very well the informal construction:

$$\Sigma \, \mathrm{D}_2^1 \, \Sigma \, \mathrm{D}_3^2 \cdots \Sigma \, \mathrm{D}_n^{n-1} \, \mathsf{nats} = \mathsf{nats}^{\langle n \rangle}.$$

Niqui and Rutten start from the stream of ones, $\overline{1}$, and define an operator combining summing and dropping, namely $\Sigma_n^k = \Sigma \, \mathrm{D}_n^k$, which leads to a shorter formulation of the theorem: $\Sigma_2^1 \, \Sigma_3^2 \cdots \Sigma_{n+1}^n \overline{1} = \mathsf{nats}^{\langle n \rangle}$. The simplification by Niqui and Rutten of not starting from the stream nats of positive natural numbers but from the stream $\overline{1}$ of ones is justified by the equation $\mathsf{nats} = \Sigma \overline{1}$.

In order to state Moessner's Theorem formally we introduce the COQ definition $\Sigma \, @\{i,k,n\} \, s$ that recursively defines the sequence $\Sigma_k^i \cdots \Sigma_{n+k}^{n+i} \, s$.

```
Definition Ssigma (i k : nat) (s : Stream Z) : Stream Z := Σ D@{i,k} s.
Notation "Σ@{ i , k } s" := (Ssigma i k s).
Fixpoint Ssigmas (i k n : nat) (s : Stream Z) : Stream Z :=
  match n with
  | 0 ⇒ Σ@{i,k} s
  | S n ⇒ Σ@{i,k} Σ@{S i,S k,n} s
  end
where "Σ@{ i , k , n } s" := (Ssigmas i k n s).
```

Moessner's Theorem is then stated in COQ as:

```
Theorem Moessner n : Σ@{1,2,n} #1 ≡ nats ^^ S n.
```

4.1   The Bisimulation Relation

In order to prove Moessner's Theorem by coinduction, we define the bisimulation relation of Niqui and Rutten using an inductively defined relation.

```
Inductive Rn : relation (Stream Z) :=
  | Rn_sig1 n : Rn (Σ@{1,2,n} #1) (nats ^^ S n)
  | Rn_sig2 n : Rn (Σ@{0,2,n} #1) (nats ⊙ (#1 ⊕ nats) ^^ n)
  | Rn_refl s : Rn s s
  | Rn_plus s1 s2 t1 t2 : Rn s1 t1 → Rn s2 t2 → Rn (s1 ⊕ s2)(t1 ⊕ t2)
  | Rn_mult n s t : Rn s t → Rn (#n ⊙ s) (#n ⊙ t)
  | Rn_eq s1 s2 t1 t2 : s1 ≡ s2 → t1 ≡ t2 → Rn s1 t1 → Rn s2 t2.
```

The relation Rn is nearly a literate COQ translation of the bisimulation relation given by Niqui and Rutten. There are three small differences:

- Niqui and Rutten use indexes that count from 1 instead of 0. When working in a formal system, this is inconvenient, as it leads to many side-conditions.
- Since we consider streams of integers instead of streams of naturals (to make the generalizations in Sect. 5 possible), we had to explicitly close the bisimulation relation under scalar multiplication (using the constructor Rn_mult).
- Because we use bisimilarity to express stream equality, we had to close the bisimulation relation under it (using the constructor Rn_eq).

4.2 Proof Outline

In what follows we show that Rn is a bisimulation relation, from which Moessner's Theorem is a direct consequence.

```
Lemma bisimulation_Rn : bisimulation Rn.
Theorem Moessner n : Σ @{1,2,n} #1 ≡ nats ^^ S n.
Proof.
  eapply bisimulation_equal, Rn_sig1.
  apply bisimulation_Rn.
Qed.
```

In order to prove the lemma bisimulation_Rn, we have to prove that Rn s t implies head s = head t and Rn (s')(t'). This is proven by induction on the derivation of Rn. There are two interesting cases:

1. The case corresponding to the constructor Rn_sig1 for which we have to show that Rn (Σ @{1,2,n} #1) (nats ^^ S n) implies:

$$\text{head } (\Sigma \text{ @\{1,2,n\} \#1}) = (\text{nats ^^ S n})$$
$$\text{and}$$
$$\text{Rn } ((\Sigma \text{ @\{1,2,n\} \#1})') ((\text{nats ^^ S n})').$$

   This case is covered by [13, Propositions 5.1–5.2] and formalized in Sect. 4.3.
2. The case corresponding to Rn_sig2 involving (Σ @0,2,n #1) (nats ⊙ (#1 ⊕ nats) 'n). This case is covered by [13, Propositions 5.3–5.4] and formalized in Sect. 4.4.

The other cases follow from simple equational reasoning.

4.3 Case Rn (Σ@{1,2,n} #1)(nats ^^ S n)

In order to formalize the first case, we need to relate the heads and tails of the streams Σ @{1,2,n} #1 and nats ^^ S n. This case involves proving the equations below [13, Propositions 5.1–5.2]:

$$\text{head } (\Sigma\text{@\{1,2,n\} \#1}) = 1 = \text{head (nats ^^ S n)}$$
$$(\Sigma\text{@\{1,2,n\} \#1})' \equiv \text{sig\_seq 0 2 n}$$
$$\text{Rn nat\_seq n} \equiv (\text{nats ^^ S n})'$$

The auxiliary streams sig_seq and nat_seq are defined as:

```
Fixpoint sig_seq (i k n : nat) : Stream Z :=
  match n with
  | 0 ⇒ #1 ⊕ Σ@{i,k} #1
  | S n ⇒ Σ@{i,k,S n} #1 ⊕ sig_seq i k n
  end.
Fixpoint nat_seq (n : nat) : Stream Z :=
  match n with
  | 0 ⇒ #1 ⊕ nats
  | S n ⇒ nats ⊙ (#1 ⊕ nats) ^^ S n ⊕ nat_seq n
  end.
```

The lemmas involving the above equalities are proven by induction. Equational reasoning is supported by COQ's `ring` tactic for solving ring equations.

```
Lemma Ssigmas_head_S i k n : head (Σ@{S i,k,n} #1) = 1.
Lemma Ssigmas_S_tail i k n : (Σ@{S i,k,n} #1)' ≡ sig_seq i k n.
Lemma nats_pow_head n : head (nats ^^ n) = 1.
Lemma nats_pow_tail n : (nats ^^ S n)' ≡ nat_seq n.
Lemma Rn_sig_seq_nat_seq n : Rn (sig_seq 0 2 n) (nat_seq n).
```

4.4   Case Rn (Σ @{0,2,n} #1) (nats⊙ (#1⊕ nats) ^^ n)

In order to formalize the second case, we need to relate the heads and tails of Σ @{0,2,n} #1 and nats $\odot$ (#1 $\oplus$ nats)^^ n. This involves proving the equations below [13, Proposition 5.3-5.4]:

$$\text{head } (\Sigma @\{0,2,n\} \ \#1) = 2\ \hat{}\ n = \text{head } (\text{nats} \odot (\#1 \oplus \text{nats}) \ \hat{}\hat{}\ n)$$

$$(\Sigma @\{0,2,n\} \ \#1)' \equiv \text{bins\_sig\_seq } n\ 2\ n$$

$$\text{Rn }\ \text{bins\_seq } n\ n \equiv (\text{nats} \odot (\#1 \oplus \text{nats}) \ \hat{}\hat{}\ n)'$$

The auxiliary streams `bins_sig_seq` and `bins_seq` are defined as:

```
Fixpoint bins_seq (n j : nat) : Stream Z :=
  match j with
  | 0 ⇒ #bins n n ⊙ (#1 ⊕ nats)
  | S j ⇒ #bins n (n - S j) ⊙ nats ⊙ (#1 ⊕ nats) ^^ S j ⊕ bins_seq n j
  end.
Fixpoint bins_sig_seq (n k j : nat) : Stream Z :=
  match j with
  | 0 ⇒ #bins n n ⊙ (#1 ⊕ Σ@{k - 2,k} #1)
  | S j ⇒ #bins n (n - S j) ⊙ Σ@{k - 2,k,S j} #1 ⊕ bins_sig_seq n k j
  end.
Fixpoint bins (n i : nat) : Z :=
  match i with 0 ⇒ 1 | S i ⇒ bin n (S i) + bins n i end.
```

In this code, bin n i denotes the binomial coefficient $\binom{n}{i}$. The series bins n i of binomial coefficients, denoted a_i^n by Niqui and Rutten, looks like:

$$a_i^n = \binom{n}{i} + \cdots + \binom{n}{1} + \binom{n}{0} = \binom{n}{i} + \cdots + \binom{n}{1} + 1.$$

The formal proofs in this section are surprisingly tricky and involve intricate generalizations of the induction hypothesis. These results thus form a nice example that informal proofs often hide too many details under the carpet; Niqui and Rutten just write that the results are "straightforward" or "proven by induction". Let us take a look at an example [13, Proposition 5.3]:

```
Lemma nats_nats_pow_head n : head (nats ⊙ (#1 ⊕ nats) ^^ n) = 2 ^ n.
Lemma nats_nats_pow_tail n : (nats ⊙ (#1 ⊕ nats) ^^ n)' ≡ bins_seq n n.
```

The proof of the lemma nats_nats_pow_head is a trivial induction proof. We use basic properties about the heads of the operations for element-wise addition, multiplication and repeated multiplication. The lemma nats_nats_pow_tail cannot be proven by a mere induction on n. For the inductive step we were in need of the following auxiliary result:

```
Lemma bins_seq_SS n : bins_seq (S n) (S n) ≡ (#2 ⊕ nats) ⊙ bins_seq n n.
```

The formal proof of this auxiliary result is tricky, and requires a subtle generalization of the induction hypothesis. The subtlety arises from the fact that the lemma concerns bins_seq with the same value (namely S n) shared by both arguments. However, bins_seq is defined recursively on its second argument, whereas the first argument remains constant throughout the recursion. Therefore, we had to generalize the lemma bins_seq_SS such that both arguments are independent. The Coq statement of the generalized lemma is as follows.

```
Lemma bins_seq_SS_help n j :
  (j < n)%nat →
  bins_seq (S n) (S j) ≡ (nats ⊕ #2) ⊙ bins_seq n j ⊕
                         #bins n (n - S j) ⊙ nats ⊙ (#1 ⊕ nats) ^^ S j.
```

The above lemma is proven by induction on j. The main lemma bins_seq_SS is then proven by case analysis on n using the generalized lemma.

The other results from Niqui and Rutten, in particular [13, Proposition 5.4], also require a variety of helping lemmas whose proofs involve intricate generalizations of the induction hypothesis.

5   Long and Salié's Generalization

Long [10,11] and Salié [20] generalized Moessner's result to apply to the situation in which the initial sequence is not the sequence of successive integers $(1, 2, 3, \ldots)$ but the arithmetic progression $(a, d + a, 2d + a, \ldots)$. They showed that the final sequence obtained by the Moessner construction is $(a \cdot 1^{n-1}, (d+a) \cdot 2^{n-1}, (2d+a) \cdot 3^{n-1}, \ldots)$. We show that these results are a corollary of the version of Moessner's Theorem proven in Section 4. This is a new proof: Niqui and Rutten did not have it in their paper.

Similar to Section 4, where we started with the constant stream $(1, 1, 1, \ldots)$ instead of $(1, 2, 3, \ldots)$, we will here start with $(a, d, d, \ldots)$ instead of $(a, d + a, 2d + 2, \ldots)$. Clearly we have $\Sigma(a, d, d, \ldots) \equiv (a, a + d, a + 2d, \ldots)$, and hence $\Sigma_{n+1}^n(a, d, d, \ldots) \equiv (a, a + d, a + 2d, \ldots)$ for any $n \geq 1$. We can formulate Long and Salié's generalization of Moessner's Theorem thus as follows.

```
Corollary Moessner_ext a d n :
  Σ @{1,2,n} (a ::: #d) ≡ Σ (a ::: #d) ⊙ nats ^^ n.
```

The key observation to prove this generalization is the following lemma.

```
Lemma Moessner_ext_help a d : Σ (a ::: #d) ≡ #d ⊙ nats ⊕ #(a - d).
```

This lemma is straightforward to prove by showing that the heads and tails of both sides are equal. This involves just basic equational reasoning. It is essential that we consider streams of *integers* instead of *naturals*, since we want to allow the subtraction operation on the right hand side.

In order to prove the actual theorem, namely `Moessner_ext`, we perform case analysis on n. For the case 0, the result trivially holds, and for the case $1 + m$ we use the following derivation:

$$\Sigma_2^1 \cdots \Sigma_{(1+m)+2}^{(1+m)+1} (a ::: \overline{d}) \equiv \Sigma_2^1 \cdots \Sigma_{m+2}^{m+1} \Sigma (a ::: \overline{d})$$

$$\equiv \Sigma_2^1 \cdots \Sigma_{m+2}^{m+1} (\overline{d} \odot \mathbf{nats} \oplus \overline{a - d}) \tag{2}$$

$$\equiv \overline{d} \odot \Sigma_2^1 \cdots \Sigma_{m+2}^{m+1} \mathbf{nats} \oplus \overline{a - d} \odot \Sigma_2^1 \cdots \Sigma_{m+2}^{m+1} \overline{1} \tag{3}$$

$$\equiv \overline{d} \odot \mathbf{nats}^{\langle 2+m \rangle} \oplus \overline{a - d} \odot \mathbf{nats}^{\langle 1+m \rangle} \tag{4}$$

$$\equiv (\overline{d} \odot \mathbf{nats} \oplus \overline{a - d}) \odot \mathbf{nats}^{\langle 1+m \rangle}$$

$$\equiv \Sigma (a ::: \overline{d}) \odot \mathbf{nats}^{\langle 1+m \rangle} \tag{5}$$

Step 2 and 5 use the Lemma `Moessner_ext_help`, step 3 uses the fact that addition and scalar multiplication distribute through the partial sum and drop operations, and step 4 uses Moessner's Theorem twice.

6   Conclusions

We have presented a COQ formalization of Niqui and Rutten's proof of Moessner's Theorem [13], as well as a new proof for the generalization of Moessner's Theorem by Long and Salié. We will summarize the lessons learned from doing coinductive proofs in COQ.

Although COQ's syntactic guard condition for corecursive definitions is often believed to be too weak, it was strong enough to formalize this non-trivial coinductive proof without many complications. Most definitions of stream operations as given by Niqui and Rutten had a straightforward translation into a corresponding COQ definition. For some operations (*e.g.* nats and Σ), we had to modify the definition slightly, but we could easily prove that our alternative definition indeed satisfies the equations as given by Niqui and Rutten.

The guard condition was also hardly of any concern for proving properties. We only proved basic properties by guarded corecursion, and thereafter we typically proved stream equalities using the coinduction principle, element-wise equality, or equational reasoning using previously proved algebraic properties. Hence, in more involved proofs, there was never the issue of proofs being rejected because of COQ's guard condition.

A source of inconvenience is that CoQ's Leibniz equality is not extensional, and we thus had to resort to bisimilarity to capture stream equality. However, using the setoid machinery we could easily circumvent this source of inconvenience without noticeable overhead. We still had to prove that all stream operations respect bisimilarity, but those proofs were trivial. Hence, it would be useful if there was automation to do such proofs.

The proof of Moessner's Theorem involved some reasoning about ring equations over streams. CoQ's `ring` tactic turned out to be extremely valuable, because it could solve these equations fully automatically.

One thing worth remarking is that CoQ's notation system with unicode characters made it possible to type the proofs in a close notation to the one used by Niqui and Rutten. While formalizing their proof, we did not find any factual errors in the results. The challenge was that despite the good presentation of all definitions and auxiliary results, most proofs were hidden under the carpet. The proofs of the main propositions [13, Propositions 5.1–5.4] were claimed to be trivialities whereas they turned out to be more involved than expected.

In this paper we have moreover given a concise and original proof of Long and Salié's generalization. Although formalization did not directly help us discovering this proof, it was definitely of indirect use. Namely, formalization makes it very attractable to make as much parts of the proof development reusable. This was indeed the key to discovering our proof of this generalization.

We conclude that formalizing coinductive proofs as Moessner's Theorem in CoQ is feasible, and worth doing. Our CoQ formalization constitutes of a small library on general operations and theory on streams (348 lines), a proof of Moessner's Theorem for the case $n = 1$ (34 lines), for the case $n = 2$ (57 lines), and the general case (319 lines, including Long and Salié's generalization). This total of 758 lines of CoQ code (including white space), corresponds to approximately 7 and half pages of informal mathematical text, with many proofs omitted, and without Long and Salié's generalization.

Acknowledgments. The authors thank Dexter Kozen, Jan Rutten, Olivier Danvy, and the anonymous referees for useful comments and discussions. The last author learned from Frank many years ago that a good steak, a glass of excellent wine, and fantastic company can make the hardest of days seem distant and irrelevant in the grand scheme of things! Frank, we wish you the very best for the years to come!

References

1. Bertot, Y., Castéran, P.: Interactive theorem proving and program development. Coq'Art: the calculus of inductive constructions. In: Texts in TCS. Springer, Heidelberg (2004)
2. Bickford, M., Kozen, D., Silva, A.: Formalizing Moessner's theorem and generalizations in Nuprl (2013). http://www.nuprl.org/documents/Moessner/
3. Clausen, C., Danvy, O., Masuko, M.: A characterization of Moessner's sieve. Theor. Computut. Sci. **546**, 244–256 (2014)

4. Conway, J.H., Guy, R.K.: Moessner's magic. In: The Book of Numbers, pp. 63–65. Springer, New York (1996)
5. Coq Development Team: The Coq proof assistant reference manual. INRIA (2013)
6. Giménez, C.E.: Un Calcul de Constructions Infinies et son Application à la vérification de systèmes communicants. Ph.D. thesis, L'École Normale Supérieure de Lyon (1996)
7. Hinze, R.: Scans and convolutions— a calculational proof of Moessner's theorem. In: Scholz, S.-B., Chitil, O. (eds.) IFL 2008. LNCS, vol. 5836, pp. 1–24. Springer, Heidelberg (2011)
8. Honsberger, R.: More mathematical morsels. Dolciani Mathematical Expositions. Mathematical Association of America (1991)
9. Kozen, D., Silva, A.: On Moessner's theorem. Am. Math. Monthly **120**(2), 131–139 (2013)
10. Long, C.T.: On the Moessner theorem on integral powers. Am. Math. Monthly **73**(8), 846–851 (1966)
11. Long, C.T.: Strike it out-add it up. The Math. Gaz. **66**(438), 273–277 (1982)
12. Moessner, A.: Eine Bemerkung über die Potenzen der natürlichen Zahlen. Sitzungsberichte der Bayerischen Akademie der Wissenschaften, Mathematischnaturwissenschaftliche Klasse 1952, no. 29 (1951)
13. Niqui, M., Rutten, J.J.M.M.: A proof of Moessner's theorem by coinduction. High.-Ord. Symb. Comput. **24**(3), 191–206 (2011)
14. Paasche, I.: Ein neuer Beweis des moessnerischen Satzes. Sitzungsberichte der Bayerischen Akademie der Wissenschaften, Mathematischnaturwissenschaftliche Klasse 1952 **1**, 1–5 (1953)
15. Paasche, I.: Ein zahlentheoretische-logarithmischer Rechenstab. Math. Naturwiss. Unterr. **6**, 26–28 (1953,1954)
16. Paasche, I.: Eine Verallgemeinerung des moessnerschen Satzes. Compositio Mathematica **12**, 263–270 (1954)
17. Perron, O.: Beweis des Moessnerschen Satzes. Sitzungsberichten der Bayerischen Akademie der Wissenschaften, Mathematisch-naturwissenschaftliche Klasse 1951 **4**, 31–34 (1951)
18. Rutten, J.: A coinductive calculus of streams. Math. Struct. Comput. Sci. **15**, 93–147 (2005)
19. Rutten, J.: Universal coalgebra: a theory of systems. Theor. Comput. Sci. **249**(1), 3–80 (2000)
20. Salié, H.: Bemerkung zu einem Satz von Moessner. Sitzungsberichten der Bayerischen Akademie der Wissenschaften, Mathematisch-naturwissenschaftliche Klasse 1952 **2**, 7–11 (1952)
21. Sozeau, M.: A new look at generalized rewriting in type theory. J. Form. Reason. **2**(1), 41–62 (2009)
22. Sozeau, M., Oury, N.: First-class type classes. In: Mohamed, O.A., Muñoz, C., Tahar, S. (eds.) TPHOLs 2008. LNCS, vol. 5170, pp. 278–293. Springer, Heidelberg (2008)
23. Urbak, P.: A formal study of Moessner's sieve, M.Sc. thesis, Aarhus University (2015)

Towards a Kool Future

Dorel Lucanu[1]([✉]), Traian-Florin Şerbănuţă[2], and Grigore Roşu[3]

[1] Alexandru Ioan Cuza University, Iaşi, Romania
dlucanu@info.uaic.ro
[2] University of Bucharest, Bucharest, Romania
[3] University of Illinois at Urbana-Champaign, Urbana, USA

Abstract. The $\mathbb{K}$ framework was successfully used for defining formal semantics for several practical languages, e.g. C, Java, Java Script, but no language with distributed concurrent objects was defined in $\mathbb{K}$ up to now. In this paper we investigate how the model of asynchronous method calls, using the so-called *futures* for handling the return values, can be added to an existing $\mathbb{K}$ definition using the ideas from the Complete Guide to the Future paper. As the running example we use the $\mathbb{K}$ definition of KOOL, a pedagogical and research language that captures the essence of the object-oriented programming paradigm. This is a first step toward a generic methodology for modularly adding future-based mechanisms to allow asynchronous method calls.

1 Introduction

$\mathbb{K}$ (www.kframework.org) is a framework for formally defining the semantics of programming languages. The $\mathbb{K}$ definitions of the programming languages are executable, i.e. they can be used to execute programs written in the defined language, and can be used for program analysis and verification. The $\mathbb{K}$ Framework is scalable: several realistic languages, e.g. Java [4], C [9], Java Script [15], PHP [10], have already been defined in $\mathbb{K}$. The main ingredients of a $\mathbb{K}$ definition are configurations, computations and rules. *Configurations* organise the state in units called cells, which are labeled and can be nested. *Computations* are special nested list structures sequentialising computational tasks, such as fragments of program. $\mathbb{K}$ *(rewrite) rules* make it explicit which parts of the term they read-only, write-only, read-write, or do not care about. This makes $\mathbb{K}$ suitable for defining truly concurrent languages even in the presence of sharing. The only concurrency model described in some languages defined in $\mathbb{K}$ is that described by threads. No language including distributed concurrent objects is defined in $\mathbb{K}$ up to now.

Futures [14,25] are language constructs meant to represent awaited results for asynchronous calls. Roughly speaking, a future is a place holder for a result of an asynchronous concurrent computation. Once this computation is complete the computed result, called *future value*, fills the place holder. An access to an unresolved feature is a blocking operation.

The futures can be *transparent* or *explicit*. For the explicit case, the language includes specific constructs for creating futures and getting the results. On the

© Springer International Publishing Switzerland 2016
E. Ábrahám et al. (Eds.): de Boer Festschrift, LNCS 9660, pp. 325–343, 2016.
DOI: 10.1007/978-3-319-30734-3_22

other hand the implicit futures are handled by underlying middleware and the syntax of the language remains unchanged. Some languages allow futures to be passed as parameters to other processes; these are called *first class futures*. First class futures are useful for both object-oriented and procedural paradigms since they improve the concurrency patterns and offer more flexibility in design. Futures can be defined directly inside of a language [1,3,5,8,13] or as middleware using a component-based model [6,12,23].

In the *Complete Guide to the Future* [3], Frank de Boer et al. provide the semantics for an object-oriented language including explicit first class futures, defined as an extension of the Creol language [13]. The main features defined there include active multi-threaded objects, asynchronous method calls, and futures. A proof system for proving properties specific to concurrency is provided.

Inspired by [3], in this paper we investigate how the semantics of first class futures can be added, in a generic way, to languages that already have a formal semantics. We consider an object oriented language formally defined in the $\mathbb{K}$ Framework, namely KOOL, and we identify how the configuration is changed, which semantic rules have to be modified, in order to implement implicit futures, and which rules should be added to implement explicit futures. We rely on the modularity of the $\mathbb{K}$ framework and we claim that the number of changed rules is minimal (no rule unrelated to the extension was modified). Moreover, $\mathbb{K}$ definitions being executable, using the $\mathbb{K}$ tool, allow users to effectively test whether the semantics has the desired properties.

The underlying logics for $\mathbb{K}$ definitions are matching logic [16] and reachability logic [19,22]. Using the encoding of Hoare triples into reachability logic [18], we automatically have a translation of the proof system defined in the Complete Guide to the Future into reachability logic. This makes possible the use of provers like that reported in [21] for checking concurrency specific properties.

The paper is structured as follows. Section 2 includes a brief introduction to $\mathbb{K}$. The main ingredients of a $\mathbb{K}$ definition are exemplified using the KOOL programming language, which is a part of the $\mathbb{K}$ tutorial[1]. Section 3 presents KFUTURE, a version of KOOL with asynchronous methods calls modelled using futures. The main changes and new added constructs are briefly presented. Several experiments with the $\mathbb{K}$ tool are reported in Sect. 4. Finally, Sect. 5 concludes the paper and discusses future work opportunities.

2   A Kool Introduction to $\mathbb{K}$

In a nutshell, the $\mathbb{K}$ Framework [20] consists of computations, configurations, and rules. Computations are special sequences of tasks, where a task can be, e.g., a fragment of program that needs to be processed. Configurations are used to describe the program states and are organised as nested pools of cells holding syntactic and semantic information. $\mathbb{K}$ rules distinguish themselves by specifying only what is needed from a configuration, and by clearly identifying what

---

[1] http://www.kframework.org/index.php/K_Tutorial
  https://github.com/kframework/k/tree/master/k-distribution/tutorial.

changes, and thus, being more concise, more modular, and more concurrent than regular rewrite rules.

The running example is KOOL [17], a pedagogical and research language that captures the essence of the object-oriented programming paradigm. Among the object-oriented features included in KOOL we find the inheritance and the dynamic method dispatch mechanism. Moreover, KOOL is higher-order, allowing function abstractions to be treated like any other values in the language. The $\mathbb{K}$ definition of KOOL was the starting point for the $\mathbb{K}$ definition of Java [4].

Syntax and Computations. Computations extend syntax with an operation, "$\frown$", meaning to capture task sequentialization. The basic unit of computation is a *task*, which can either be a fragment of syntax, maybe with holes in it, or a semantic task, such as the recovery of an environment. The computation is abstracted away from the language designer via intuitive program languages syntax annotations like strictness constraints that specify the order of evaluation for its arguments. The decompositions of computations are similar to the use of stacks in abstract machines [11] and to the refocusing techniques for implementing reduction semantics with evaluation contexts [7].

$$Exp ::= Int \mid Id$$
$$\mid Exp + Exp \text{ [strict]}$$
$$\mid Exp \text{ (} Exps \text{) [strict]}$$
$$\dots$$

$$Decl ::= Type \; Exp$$
$$\mid Type \; Id \text{ (} Exp \text{) } Block$$
$$\mid Id \; Block$$
$$\mid Id \text{ extends } Id \; Block$$

$$Stmt ::= Decl$$
$$\mid Block$$
$$\mid Exp \text{ ;}$$
$$\mid \text{if (} Exp \text{) } Block \text{ else } Block \text{ [strict(1)]}$$
$$\dots$$

$$Block ::= \{ \; \}$$
$$\mid \{ \; Stmts \; \}$$
$$Exps ::= List(Exp,",")$$
$$Stmts ::= List(Stmt,"")$$

Fig. 1. A fragment of KOOL's syntax

Figure 1 includes a fragment of the syntax for KOOL, described using BNF notation. The strictness annotations add semantic information to the syntax by specifying the order of evaluation of arguments for the corresponding construct. This is achieved by the means of the heating/cooling rules, which are automatically generated from strictness annotations. The order of evaluation can be left unspecified (if using the "strict" attribute), or specified to happen in a given order using the "seqstrict" attribute. For instance, the "strict" attribute for the addition operator says that all arguments of addition are evaluated, but in an unspecified order, which is achieved by the following heating/cooling rules:

$$E_1 + E_2 \rightleftharpoons E_1 \frown \square + E_2 \qquad E_1 + E_2 \rightleftharpoons E_2 \frown E_1 + \square$$
$$I_1 \frown \square + E_2 \rightleftharpoons I_1 + E_2 \qquad I_2 \frown E_1 + \square \rightleftharpoons E_1 + I_2$$

When the strict attribute has parameters, only those parameters are evaluated. E.g., for the statement **if** only the first argument (the conditional expression) is evaluated. For seqstrict, no attributes specify the evaluation of all arguments in a left-to-right order, while a list of positions specifies that the given arguments are to be evaluated in the given order, allowing for different order of evaluation to be specified.

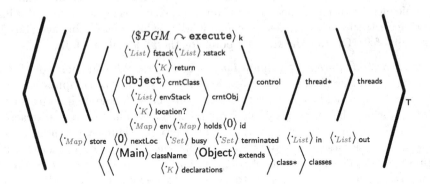

Fig. 2. KOOL configuration

Configurations. A configuration is a nested multiset of labeled cells, in which each elementary cell can contain either a list, a set, a bag, a map, or a computation. Figure 2 includes the configuration for the KOOL language. Here is a brief description of the cells (the tree-like structure of the list reflects the nesting structure of the cells):

T – top level cell;
    threads – holds a pool of thread cells;
        thread – holds the sub-configuration of a thread;
           k – holds the nested list of the computations for the thread;
           control – holds the local control state of the thread;
               fstack – holds the function stack;
               xstack – holds the stack of exceptions;
               return – holds the type of the value to be returned by the current method;
               crntObj – holds the description of the current object (this);
                  crntClass – holds the name of the current class which the current object belongs to;
                  envStack – holds the state of the object as a stack of environments (for each ancestor class an environment binding the fields of the class to their current locations);
                  location – holds the location where the object is stored;
           env – holds a map binding each name accessible by the thread to a store location;
           holds – include the locks held by the thread;
           id – holds a natural number that is the identity of the thread;

store – holds a global (shared by all threads) map binding the allocated
locations to some values; the fact that the environment is local but the
store is global allows for shared memory while preserving the visibility
domain of variables;

nextLoc – holds a natural number indicating the next free location;

busy – holds the locks which have been acquired but not yet released by
threads;

terminated – holds the unique identifiers of the threads which already terminated (needed for join);

in – holds the list of the input data (needed for reading statements);

out – holds the list of the output data (needed for writing statements);

classes – the pool of the classes of a KOOL program;

    class – holds the description of a class;

      classname – holds the name of the class;

      extends – holds the name of the parent class;

      declarations – holds the declarations for the class fields and methods.

The content specification for the elementary cells has a double role: (1) it
specifies the content of that cell in the initial configuration, and (2) it specifies
the type (sort) of the information stored in that cell. The dot notation is used
for the empty data structures: e.g., $\cdot_{List}$ denotes the empty list, $\cdot_{Set}$ denotes the
empty set, and so on. The special variable $\$PGM$ will be replaced in the initial
configuration with the program to be executed. The internal command **execute**
triggers the execution of the program after its preprocessing to fill the initial
configuration.

The star character following the name of a cell specifies the multiplicity of
that cell, i.e. a concrete configuration may include zero, one, or more cells of
that kind. For instance, a concrete configuration may include several **thread** cells
and/or several **class** cells.

𝕂 *Rules.* The transition relation defining the operational semantics of a language is described by 𝕂 rules. For instance, the rule giving the semantics for the
addition operator is

$$\frac{I_1 + I_2}{I_1 +_{Int} I_2}$$

where above the horizontal line is the pattern used for matching and below the
horizontal line is the pattern that defines the result term replacing the matched
term. This rule is applied only when the above pattern matches the top of the k
cell (we shall see later why). Since the syntax of this operator was defined with
the strict attribute, it follows that it is evaluated only after its arguments have
been evaluated to the integers I_1 and I_2. The operation $+_{Int}$ effectively adds
two integers. The semantics of the statement **if** is given by two rules:

$$\frac{\text{if } true \; B_1 \text{ else } \_}{B_1} \qquad \frac{\text{if } false \_ \text{ else } B_2}{B_2}$$

Recall that the syntax of if is strict only in the first argument, so only the condition expression is evaluated first to either *true* or *false*. The two rules corresponds to the two possible values returned by the evaluation of the condition expression.

Although $\mathbb{K}$ rules are in essence rewrite rules, there are several ways in which they differ from a regular rewrite rule. First, *in-place rewriting* (denoted by the horizontal bar) allows one to specify small changes into a bigger context, by underlining the part that needs to change and writing its replacement under the line, instead of repeating the context in both sides of a rewrite rule. For instance, the rule for addition will be applied only when the pattern $I_1 + I_2$ matches the top of the computation cell. This enables another optimisation, namely the ability of using anonymous variables (_) for the unused variables in the context (see, e.g., the rule for if).

Furthermore, $\mathbb{K}$ allows the use of *cell comprehension* for focusing only on the parts of the cells which are relevant, as in the rule for variable lookup:

$$\left\langle \underset{V}{X{:}Id} \; \cdots \right\rangle_k \; \langle \cdots X \mapsto L \cdots \rangle_{\text{env}} \; \langle \cdots L \mapsto V{:}Val \cdots \rangle_{\text{store}}$$

The lookup rule above rule specifies that when a variable X is the first computational task, and X is bound to some location L in the environment, and L is mapped to some value V in the store, then we rewrite X into V.

The ellipses at the left/right end of a cell are used to specify that there could be more items in that cell (in the corresponding side) in addition to what is explicitly specified. Note that the variable to be looked up is the first task in the k cell (the cell is closed to the left and open to the right), while the binding of X to L and the mapping of L to V can be anywhere in the env and store cells (these cells are open in both sides).

Finally, the process of *configuration abstraction* allows for mentioning only the relevant cells in a rule, by relying on the static structure of the declared configuration to infer the rest (*configuration concretization*). For instance, without $\mathbb{K}$'s configuration abstraction, the lookup rule above would have to also include the thread and threads cells. Configuration abstraction is crucial for modularity, because it gives the possibility to write definitions in a way that may not require to revisit existing rules when the configuration changes as new (orthogonal) language features are introduced.

Advanced Features of the KOOL Language Semantics. We conclude our brief introduction to $\mathbb{K}$ by showing the semantic rules defining the behavior of some important features of KOOL which would be affected by the introduction of futures in the next section.

The new Operator. The rule defining the operator new includes a more complex matching part and many local rewrites:

$$\left\langle \cfrac{\text{new } Class(Vs) \curvearrowright K}{(\texttt{create}(Class) \curvearrowright \texttt{storeObj} \curvearrowright Class(Vs)); \ \texttt{return this;}} \right\rangle_{\text{k}}$$

$$\left\langle \cfrac{Env}{\cdot_{Map}} \right\rangle_{\text{env}} \left\langle \cfrac{L}{L +_{Int} 1} \right\rangle_{\text{nextLoc}}$$

$$\left\langle \left\langle \cfrac{Obj}{\langle Class \rangle_{\text{crntClass}} \langle \texttt{ListItem}(\texttt{Object}, \langle \cdot_{Map} \rangle_{\text{env}}) \rangle_{\text{envStack}} \langle L \rangle_{\text{location}}} \right\rangle_{\text{crntObj}} \right.$$
$$\left. \left\langle \cfrac{\cdot_{List}}{\texttt{ListItem}(Env, K, C, \langle Obj \rangle_{\text{crntObj}} \langle T \rangle_{\text{return}})} \right\rangle_{\text{fstack}} \left\langle \cfrac{T}{Class} \right\rangle_{\text{return}} \ C \right\rangle_{\text{control}}$$

The semantics of **new** consists of two actions: memory allocation for the new object and execution of the corresponding constructor. Then the created object is returned as the result of the new operation. The rule matches a **new** expression on the top of the k cell, where the parameters Vs are already evaluated due to the strictness, and performs the following changes in the configuration:

- replaces the **new** expression with two actions, memory allocation for the new object (given by the auxiliary operations **create** and **storeObj**) and execution of the corresponding constructor, followed by the instruction returning the created object;
- stores the current environment, computation, control, object, and return type on the function stack;
- initializes the object creation process by emptying the local environment and the current object, and allocating a location in the store where the created object will be eventually stored;
- replaces the return type with the class of the newly created object.

Method Calls. The rule for method calls is somehow similar to that of the **new** operator:

$$\left\langle \cfrac{\texttt{methodClosure } (\_\text{->}T, Class, OL, Ps, S)(Vs) \curvearrowright K}{\texttt{mkDecls } (Ps, Vs) \ S \ \texttt{return } ;} \right\rangle_{\text{k}} \left\langle \cfrac{Env}{\cdot_{Map}} \right\rangle_{\text{env}}$$

$$\langle \cdots OL \mapsto \texttt{objecClosure } (\langle \_ \rangle_{\text{crntClass}}, Obj) \cdots \rangle_{\text{store}}$$

$$\left\langle \left\langle \cfrac{Obj'}{\langle Class \rangle_{\text{crntClass}} \ Obj} \right\rangle_{\text{crntObj}} \left\langle \cfrac{T'}{T} \right\rangle_{\text{return}} \right.$$
$$\left. \left\langle \cfrac{\cdot_{List}}{\texttt{ListItem } ((Env, K, C, \langle Obj' \rangle_{\text{crntObj}}, \langle T' \rangle_{\text{return}}))} \cdots \right\rangle_{\text{fstack}} \ C \right\rangle_{\text{control}}$$

Since the syntax for method calls is strict, the expression describing the method name is evaluated to the corresponding function value. Recall that KOOL is a higher-order language that allows the function abstractions to be treated like any other values. A function value is a closure that includes the method parameters, the body of the method, and the object value. The type held by a method closure is the entire type of the method in order to dynamically upcast values when passed to contexts where values of superclass types are expected. An *object value* consists of an `objectClosure`-wrapped bag containing the current class of the object and the environment stack of the object. The current class of an object will always be one of the classes mapped to an environment in the environment stack of the object. The rule matches a method call on top of the computation cell and performs the following changes in the configuration:

- replaces the method call with the method body followed by a `return;`;
- pushes the current environment, control data, current object and the return type onto the function stack;
- binds the actual arguments to formal parameters using the auxiliary operation `mkDecls`;
- updates the current object and the return type of the current method.

The arguments of the call are evaluated to a list of values *Vs* due to the strict attribute. The variable K matches the rest of the computation.

The `return` *statement* performs the dual operations:

- pops the environment, control data, current object and the return type from the function stack and stores them into the corresponding cells;
- checks the type of the returned value and passes it to the popped computation; note that its type is cast to that stored in the return cell.

$$\left\langle \frac{\texttt{return } V; \curvearrowright \_}{\texttt{subtype (typeOf } (V), \ T) \ \curvearrowright \texttt{true?} \curvearrowright \texttt{unsafeCast } (V, \ T) \curvearrowright K} \right\rangle_k$$

$$\left\langle \frac{\texttt{ListItem } ((Env, K, C))}{List} \cdots \right\rangle_{\text{fstack}} \left\langle \frac{T}{C} \right\rangle_{\text{return}} \left\langle \frac{\_}{Env} \right\rangle_{\text{env}}$$

3   KOOL with Futures

This section presents a language design exercise: adding support for futures to an existing object oriented language *executable* definition.

We chose KOOL as the reference object oriented language definition, because it is a relatively small but not trivial language designed for teaching students object oriented concepts and dynamic typing.

An important aspect of the exercise is given by the executability attribute of the definition: as expected, designing executable definitions requires more attention to details; on the other hand, these definitions are testable, making it easier to detect design glitches.

Although we took The Complete Guide to the Future [3] as a starting point for our definitional enterprise, we decided rather early on not supporting certain Creol-specific constructs such as nondeterministic choice and parallel composition, as futures themselves bring a high degree of nondeterminism and concurrency. The new language we obtained is called KFUTURE.

3.1 Syntax

The syntax of KOOL, excepting that for threads – which was removed –, remains unchanged and we only added the same constructs as in [3]:

$Exp ::= Exp \ ! \ Id(Exps)$ [strict(1)] $Guard ::= \ \texttt{wait}$
$\quad | \ Guard$ $\quad | \ Exp \ ? $ [strict]

$Type ::= \ ! \ Type$ $Id ::= \ \texttt{get}$ $Stmt ::= \ \texttt{await} \ Exp \ ;$

The expressions are enriched with asynchronous calls, a future reading operation `get`, and guards used to block/release the objects's tasks. The only added statement `await` is used for releasing tasks and $!T$ is the type of the futures returning values of type T.

3.2 Configuration

The configuration of the new language is represented in Fig. 3. KFUTURE objects are top-level independent agents [24], asynchronously communicating by means of futures.

Being an agent, each object carries its own state – holding fields and their values –, which can be altered only by the object's methods/tasks. Thus, the store cell is now object-local rather than global as in KOOL.

An object manages multiple tasks, each handling a specific future to which it is linked through the futureId cell. To ensure task atomicity, we follow the line in [3] and allow only one task being active at a time. Hence an object's tasks are split into the active-task and a pool of waiting-tasks.

Tasks are similar in essence to KOOL threads: the active-task cell includes almost all cells occurring in a thread cell. However, the location and environment stack envStack of an object are now at the top of the object cell, being shared by all tasks.

Futures (placed in the futures cell) serve as communication channels between objects. A future method invocation results in the creation of a new future cell containing data identifying the target object (oid), the method (closure) and its arguments. Each future has a state and will eventually produce a result.

To simplify the presentation, we have completely eliminated the threading constructs existing in the KOOL language. From a definitional point of view, this amounted to simply eliminating the extra syntax, cells in the configuration and specific threading rules in the definition. Section 4 shows how Java-like threads can be defined using futures.

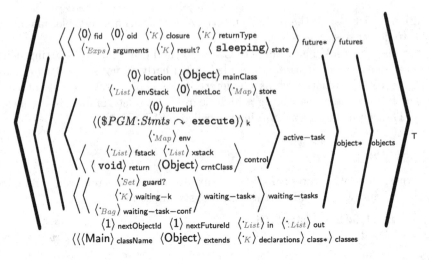

Fig. 3. The KFUTURE configuration

In the following, we first revisit the changes required to the KOOL semantics to reflect the new configuration architecture, then describe the semantics of futures as an addition to the existing semantics.

3.3 Objects and Methods

As objects are now full citizens of the configuration, several changes to the definition of KOOL are required to reflect that.

Object creation requires a redefinition of the semantics for **new**:

$$
\left\langle \frac{\mathbf{new}\ Class(Vs)}{\mathbf{object}\ (Id,\ Class,\ Class)\ .\ \$clinit(Vs)} \cdots \right\rangle_k \quad \left\langle \frac{Id}{Id +_{Int} 1} \right\rangle_{\mathsf{nextObjectId}}
$$

$$
\overline{}^{\ \dot{}Bag}
$$

$$
\langle \cdots \langle Id \rangle_{\mathsf{location}}\ \langle Class \rangle_{\mathsf{mainClass}}\ \langle \cdots \langle -1 \rangle_{\mathsf{futureId}}\ \langle \dot{}_K \rangle_k \cdots \rangle_{\mathsf{active-task}} \cdots \rangle_{\mathsf{object}}
$$

An instance of the class is created in the cell object and an unique identifier is assigned to it, while the new construct reduces to a method call to the special method $clinit on a reference to the newly created object, a method which: (1) performs basic object allocation and initialisation; (2) calls the constructor method; (3) returns a reference to the object. Hence, $clinit basically corresponds to the create(*Class*) ⤳ storeObj ⤳ (*Class*(*Vs*)); return this; sequence of tasks from the KOOL semantics for **new**, with the difference that now these tasks need to occur within the newly created object.

Object references replace KOOL's object closures. An object reference is a triple (*Id*, *MainClass*, *CurrentClass*), where *Id* corresponds to the contents of the object's location cell, *MainClass* corresponds to the contents of the mainClass cell, and *CurrentClass* corresponds to the current contents of the crntClass cell, as shown by the new semantics for this:

$$
\left\langle \frac{\texttt{this}}{\texttt{object }(Id, MClass, Class)} \cdots \right\rangle_{\mathsf{k}} \langle Id \rangle_{\mathsf{location}} \langle Class \rangle_{\mathsf{crntClass}} \langle MClass \rangle_{\mathsf{mainClass}}
$$

The replacement of object closures by object references, made mandatory by the KFUTURE extension, required redefining some of the other KOOL rules, mainly those related to method and field resolution. Note though that these changes are actually simplifications to the existing KOOL semantics, inspiring us to redesign future versions of KOOL to use references instead of closures as object values.

Method calls to foreign objects are desugared into (blocking) future invocations [3]:

$$
\left\langle \frac{\texttt{object }(Id, BClass, Class) \,.\, Method(Vs)}{(\,\texttt{object }(Id, BClass, Class)\,!\, Method(Vs))\,.\,\texttt{get}(`_{Exps})} \cdots \right\rangle_{\mathsf{k}} \langle Id' \rangle_{\mathsf{location}}
$$
$$
\textbf{requires } Id \neq_K Id'
$$

The condition expressed by the clause **requires** ensures that the called method belongs indeed to a foreign object.

Method calls for the current object remain basically the same as in KOOL. While convenient, this additionally is a proper way to treat self calls, avoiding deadlock (which would occur if handled as foreign object calls) while capturing the direct transfer of control which was a caveat of the workaround solution proposed in [3].

First, the method is looked up in the object's environment stack:

$$
\left\langle \frac{\texttt{object }(Id, BClass, \_) \,.\, Method(Vs)}{\texttt{lookupThis }(\langle ES \rangle_{\mathsf{envStack}}, BClass, Method)(Vs)} \cdots \right\rangle_{\mathsf{k}} \langle Id \rangle_{\mathsf{location}} \langle ES \rangle_{\mathsf{envStack}}
$$

Next, once a method is evaluated to a method closure, application saves the current context before binding the arguments and calling the method:

$$
\left\langle \frac{\texttt{methodClosure}(\_ \to T, Class, OL, Ps, S)(Vs) \curvearrowright K}{\texttt{mkDecls }(Ps, Vs)\ S \curvearrowright \texttt{return };} \right\rangle_{\mathsf{k}} \langle OL \rangle_{\mathsf{location}} \left\langle \frac{Env}{`_{Map}} \right\rangle_{\mathsf{env}}
$$

$$
\left\langle \left\langle \frac{`_{List}}{\texttt{ListItem }((Env, K, C\ \langle T' \rangle_{\mathsf{return}}\ \langle Class' \rangle_{\mathsf{crntClass}}))} \cdots \right\rangle_{\mathsf{fstack}} \left\langle \frac{Class'}{Class} \right\rangle_{\mathsf{crntClass}} \left\langle \frac{T'}{T} \right\rangle_{\mathsf{return}} C \right\rangle_{\mathsf{control}}
$$

The only changes from the corresponding KOOL rule are (1) the fact that we enforce that the method's object location is the same as the current object's location; and (2) since we are inside the same object, the only object-related which needs to be updated/saved/restored is the current class.

The KOOL rule for the **return** statement is preserved unchanged, although an additional rule will be added below to model returning from a future call.

3.4   Futures

Futures model asynchronous method calls as messages exchanged between objects. These exchanges are captured by the future cells in the configuration, which serve as communication channels between objects.

Future method invocations result in opening a channel (future) to the object owning the method, containing a request for executing the method:

$$\left\langle \frac{\text{object } (OId, Class, \_) \ ! \ Method(Vs) \ \cdots}{\text{preFuture } (F)} \right\rangle_{\mathsf{k}} \left\langle \frac{F}{F +_{Int} 1} \right\rangle_{\mathsf{nextFutureId}}$$

$$\overline{\langle \cdots \langle F \rangle_{\mathsf{fid}} \ \langle OId \rangle_{\mathsf{oid}} \ \langle \texttt{lookupMethod } (Class, Method) \rangle_{\mathsf{closure}} \ \langle Vs \rangle_{\mathsf{arguments}} \cdots \rangle}^{Bag}_{\mathsf{future}}$$

The future will initially be in the **sleeping** state, waiting to be activated by its corresponding object. The future invocation evaluates to a pre-future reference to the newly created future; this will become a full future reference once the return type of the method is known.

The activation of a **sleeping** *future* occurs when there are no active tasks running for the future's object, and consists in creating a task to initiate the method call, and changing the state of the future to **active** to prevent recurrent activations:

$$\left\langle \cdots \langle F \rangle_{\mathsf{fid}} \ \langle Id \rangle_{\mathsf{oid}} \ \langle Closure \rangle_{\mathsf{closure}} \ \langle Vs \rangle_{\mathsf{arguments}} \left\langle \frac{\texttt{sleeping}}{\texttt{active}} \right\rangle_{\mathsf{state}} \cdots \right\rangle_{\mathsf{future}}$$

$$\langle Id \rangle_{\mathsf{location}} \quad \frac{\langle \cdots \langle -1 \rangle_{\mathsf{futureId}} \ \langle \cdot K \rangle_{\mathsf{k}} \cdots \rangle_{\mathsf{active-task}}}{\langle \cdots \langle F \rangle_{\mathsf{futureId}} \ \langle \texttt{performCall } (Closure, Vs) \rangle_{\mathsf{k}} \cdots \rangle_{\mathsf{active-task}}}$$

The auxiliary operation **performCall** does the actual method invocation which is similar to the one in KOOL, only without saving a stack frame (because no context needs to be saved). The contents of the futureId cell links the task to its corresponding future. The value -1 in the futureId cell is used to signal that the object is idle.

Returning from a future call occurs when a **return** statement is encountered and there are no function frames on the function stack. When this happens, we need to set the returned value as the result of the corresponding future and to signal this to the caller by setting the state of the future to **complete**:

$$\frac{\langle\cdots \langle Id\rangle_{\text{futureId}} \ \langle \text{return } V \ ; \ \cdots\rangle_k \ \langle \ .List\rangle_{\text{fstack}} \cdots\rangle_{\text{active-task}}}{\langle\cdots \langle -1\rangle_{\text{futureId}} \ \langle \cdot_K\rangle_k \cdots\rangle_{\text{active-task}}}$$

$$\left\langle \ \cdots \langle Id\rangle_{\text{fid}} \ \left\langle \frac{\text{active}}{\text{completed}} \right\rangle_{\text{state}} \ \frac{\cdot Bag}{\langle V\rangle_{\text{result}}} \ \cdots \right\rangle_{\text{future}}$$

The active-task cell is resetted to indicate there is no current active task running.

Testing whether a future is resolved can be done using the ? operator:

$$\left\langle \frac{\text{future } (Id, \_) \ ?}{State =_K \text{ completed}} \ \cdots \right\rangle_k \ \langle Id\rangle_{\text{fid}} \ \langle State\rangle_{\text{state}}$$

The Semantics of **get**. Get can only be called on future references and blocks until the corresponding future contains a value, with the effect of "returning" that value to the caller:

$$\left\langle \frac{\text{future } (Id, T) \ . \ \text{get}(\cdot_{Exps})}{\text{subtype}(\ \text{typeOf}(V), T) \curvearrowright \text{true?} \curvearrowright \text{unsafeCast}(V, T)} \ \cdots \right\rangle_k \langle Id\rangle_{\text{fid}} \langle V\rangle_{\text{result}}$$

requires $isExceptionVal(V) \neq_K \text{true}$

The tasks associated to the "returning" value are the same to the ones from the KOOL rule for **return**, because we want to also extend the dynamic type checking aspect of the language over futures.

Another KOOL-related aspect is that of exception handling. Since KOOL gives semantics for exceptional behaviour, this has to be extended in the case of futures. Therefore, uncaught exceptions from a future call need to be propagated.

Exceptions and Futures. If there is no exception handler in the exception stack, the exception thrown by the **throw** statement is returned as an exceptional value:

$$\left\langle \frac{\text{throw } V \ ;}{\text{return exception } (V) \ ;} \ \cdots \right\rangle_k \ \langle \cdot List\rangle_{\text{xstack}}$$

When **get** is used on an exceptional value, the exception is thrown again:

$$\left\langle \frac{\text{future } (Id, \_) \ . \ \text{get}(\cdot_{Exps})}{\text{throw } V \ ;} \ \cdots \right\rangle_k \ \langle Id\rangle_{\text{fid}} \ \langle \text{ exception } (V)\rangle_{\text{result}}$$

3.5   Yielding Control and Rescheduling

As shown above, the semantics of **get** is blocking, which can be counter-productive when there are multiple concurrent asynchronous calls made to the same object.

The `await` *statement* allows one task to yield control until a condition is satisfied:

$$\frac{\texttt{await } (E \ ?) \ ;}{\texttt{waiting} (\langle\, \texttt{SetItem } (E \ ?)\rangle_{\texttt{guard}})} \qquad \frac{\texttt{await } (\texttt{wait}) \ ;}{\texttt{waiting} (\langle\, \texttt{SetItem } (\texttt{wait})\rangle_{\texttt{guard}})}$$

To avoid overcomplicating the semantics, we restrict conditions to conjunctions of disjunctions of elements of the *Guard* type (`wait` and *Exp* `?`). There are more rules like the above, handling conjunction and disjunction, and attempting to simplify guards; however, if the condition cannot be reduced to true, the active task will need to block and wait to be rescheduled.

Yielding Control. When `waiting` cannot be reduced, the active task is moved to the pool of waiting tasks and the object becomes idle:

$$\frac{\langle Task \ \langle\, \texttt{waiting} (\langle Guards\rangle_{\texttt{guard}}) \curvearrowright K \rangle_{\texttt{k}}\rangle_{\texttt{active−task}}}{\langle \cdots \langle -1\rangle_{\texttt{futureId}} \ \langle \dot{}_K\rangle_{\texttt{k}} \cdots \rangle_{\texttt{active−task}}}$$

$$\frac{}{\dot{}^{Bag} \quad \langle\langle Guards\rangle_{\texttt{guard}} \ \langle K\rangle_{\texttt{waiting−k}} \ \langle Task\rangle_{\texttt{waiting−task−conf}}\rangle_{\texttt{waiting−task}}}$$

Note that the `guard` cell argument of the `waiting` computation task, holding a disjunction of basic guards represented as a set, becomes the `guard` cell of the newly created `waiting-task`.

Departing from [3], we chose not to model tasks as a queue, but rather as a bag, to capture any possible scheduling policy.

Simplifying Guards. A waiting task's guard is removed if one of the futures it waits upon completes:

$$\frac{\langle \cdots \texttt{SetItem } (\texttt{future } (Id, \_) \ ?) \cdots \rangle_{\texttt{guard}}}{\dot{}^{Bag}} \ \langle Id\rangle_{\texttt{fid}} \ \langle\, \texttt{completed}\rangle_{\texttt{state}}$$

The `wait` guard is used to unconditionally yield control; therefore, once the task becomes a waiting task, we can dissolve the guard to allow its reactivation:

$$\left\langle \cdots \frac{\langle \cdots \texttt{SetItem } (\texttt{wait}) \cdots \rangle_{\texttt{guard}}}{\dot{}^{Bag}} \cdots \right\rangle_{\texttt{waiting−task}}$$

Regaining Control. If an object is idle and the guard of one of its waiting tasks has dissolved, then that waiting task can be reactivated:

$$\frac{\langle \cdots \langle -1\rangle_{\texttt{futureId}} \cdots \rangle_{\texttt{active−task}} \quad \langle\langle K\rangle_{\texttt{waiting−k}} \ \langle Task\rangle_{\texttt{waiting−task−conf}}\rangle_{\texttt{waiting−task}}}{\langle Task \ \langle K\rangle_{\texttt{k}}\rangle_{\texttt{active−task}} \qquad \dot{}^{Bag}}$$

3.6 Global and Local Future Invariants

In [3] a proof system for proving a set of monitor invariants that describe the release points is presented. A monitor invariant i is a local property of an object that must hold each time the `await` statement is scheduled. A monitor invariant is proved in the presence of global invariants I, which describe invariant properties of the future objects.

These invariants can be easily expressed as matching logic formulas [16], which can be thought as configuration terms with variables and constraints over these variables. We exhibit this by two simple examples. Let I be the global invariant: for any future z associated to the method m of the class C, if the state of z is completed then the return value is positive. I is formally expressed by the following matching logic formula, written using the abstraction mechanism:

$$\langle \texttt{C} \rangle_{\mathsf{mainClass}} \; \langle Oid \rangle_{\mathsf{oid}} \langle \cdots \; \texttt{ListItem}(\_, \langle \cdots \; \texttt{m} \; \mapsto L \; \cdots \rangle_{\mathsf{env}} \; \cdots \rangle_{\mathsf{envStack}}$$
$$\langle Oid \rangle_{\mathsf{location}} \langle \texttt{lookup}(L) \rangle_{\mathsf{closure}} \; \langle V \rangle_{\mathsf{result}} \; \langle \texttt{completed} \rangle_{\mathsf{state}} \quad \longrightarrow V > 0$$

In the left hand side of the implication we have (the abstraction of) a configuration term, which is a particular matching logic formula: the first line is a pattern matching objects of the class c having the method m stored at location L, and the second line is a pattern matching futures associated to the method m (via location L), and that are completed and have the return value V. The object reference Oid connects the future with its associated object. In the right hand side of the implication is the constraint on V.

Similarly, a monitor invariant saying that "for any instance of the class C, its field `fld` must have a nonzero value at any release point" is formally expressed as follows:

$$\langle \texttt{await} \; \cdots \rangle_{\mathsf{k}} \; \langle \cdots \; \texttt{fld} \; \mapsto X \; \cdots \rangle_{\mathsf{env}} \; \langle \texttt{C} \rangle_{\mathsf{crntClass}} \quad \longrightarrow X \neq 0$$

Writing the global and monitor invariants as matching logic formulas has the advantage that they are expressed in the same logic used to give semantics for the programming language. This allows the direct use of the semantics for proving the correctness of such properties. In particular, the correctness of invariants can be proved using the symbolic execution and the circular coinduction technique described in [2]. More precisely, that general technique can be combined with the proof system given in [3] to obtain a specialized prover parametric in the language definition. Since matching logic formulas are written at a lower level, by considering the configuration as particular formulas, a richer class of properties can be expressed. On the other hand, the abstraction level used in [3] can be preserved by developing tools that automatically translate higher-level formulas into matching logic formulas following the idea used in the MatchC prover [21].

4   Experiments

A main advantage of the formal semantics defined in $\mathbb{K}$ is that they are directly executable using the $\mathbb{K}$ tool. A first experiment we did was to test if the KOOL programs, used to test the KOOL definition, can be executed with the new semantics. All programs, excepting those including threads, were successfully executed and their executions produced the same outputs with those obtained with the definition of KOOL.

Multithreading Defined Through Futures. Even if the threads were removed from KOOL to define KFUTURE, the concept of threads can be somehow regained at the programming level. For example, one may define a base class **Thread** as follows:

```
class Thread {
  !void id;
  void run() { }  // to be overridden
  void start() {    id = this ! run();  }
  void join() {    await(id ?);  }
}
```

Then, specific threads can be defined by extending the class **Thread** with particular behaviour and overriding the method **run**.

The Thread class enables the concurrent execution of multiple threads. Note, however, that KOOL's globally shared memory is no longer directly available to the programmer, each object now carrying its own memory.

Nevertheless, the objects themselves are still globally shared and that suffices from a programming point of view. Programmers need only to assume a shared-memory model where all object data is hidden and thus only accessible through the interfaces provided by the objects, which is considered good object-oriented programming discipline.

Hence, KOOL with futures brings relative little change to the programming model, while providing certain important benefits at a semantics level: futures allow for all accesses to memory to be clearly sequentialized, enabling better abstraction and reasoning techniques for program analysis and verification.

Future-Induced Deadlocks. We tested the definition on various examples in order to see if there is a combination of method calls for foreign objects and those for the current object that leads to a deadlock. (Un)Fortunately we found such an example:

```
class A {
  B b;
  void A() { }
  void setB(B b) { this.b = b; }
  void callB() {    b.c ();  }
}

class B {
  A a;
  void B(A a) { this.a = a; a.setB(this); }
  void c() { print("It_works!"); }
  void callA() { a.callB (); }
}

class Main {
  void Main() {
    A a = new A();
    B b = new B(a);
    b.callA ();
  }
}
```

The A object a has a reference to the B object b, and the object b has a reference to a. The call of b.callA() triggers the call of a.callB(), which in turn triggers the call of b.c(). The execution blocked on a configuration with two active futures, the ones for b.callA() and a.callB(), and a sleeping future, that for b.c(). Although not present in Creol, this problem seems to originate in the identification between processes and objects proposed in [3].

5   Conclusion and Future Work

We presented an executable formal semantics, defined using the K Framework, for an object-oriented programming languages with asynchronous method calls modelled with futures. We used KOOL – an object oriented programming language already defined in K for teaching and research purposes – and we followed the line from [3] for the definition of the futures. However, there are some important points where the two approaches differ, e.g., the treatment of threads, method calls for the current object, the scheduling of the tasks inside of an object process. A main advantage of using K Framework is that the formal semantics of the language is directly executable by the K tool, hence no further encoding of the formal semantics to an executable framework is needed. The designed definition can be tested on programs, analysed, and adjusted according to the desired behaviour. In this way we found several more natural solutions for KFUTURE than those proposed in [3]. We also detected a case when the combination of the method calls for foreign objects with those of the current object can lead to a deadlock.

This exercise to define KFUTURE starting from that of KOOL was also a good test for the modularity of the K Framework. The configuration of KFUTURE is strongly different from that of KOOL: some cells were removed (e.g. those for threads), some cell have been added (e.g. for objects, futures, auxiliary constructs), and the nesting structure have been substantially changed. In this context, it is expected that the rules of KOOL to be changed in order to accommodate with the new configuration. This did not happen: from the 129 rules of KOOL, 8 have been removed because they give semantics for threads and 13 have been replaced with other 49 that give the semantics to both implicit and explicit futures. Besides the modular aspect of K, this numbers show also that the change is not trivial. Since the semantics is directly executable, all details have to be specifed.

The K definition of the new language, KFUTURE, can be found on the github repository, http://github.com/roKmania/KFuture, and it can be executed with the version 3.5.2 of the K tool, https://github.com/kframework/k/releases/tag/v3.5.2.

This exercise is a first step toward a methodology of how to add asynchronous methods/function calls with futures to an existing programming language defined in K. This methodology could allow to generalise the proof system proposed in [3], for verifying monitor invariant of the release points, to a generic proof system expressed in the terms of matching logic [16] and reachability logic [22].

Acknowledgements. This paper is written in honour of Frank de Boer on the occasion of his 60th birthday and celebrates his exceptional contribution to the object-oriented paradigm. The first author had the privilege to cooperate with Frank and he is deeply grateful to him for that fruitful experience.

The work presented here was partially supported by Romanian Contract 161/15.06.2010, SMIS-CSNR 602-12516 (DAK), which made possible the development of the main first versions of the $\mathbb{K}$ Framework.

References

1. Ábrahám, E., Grabe, I., Grüner, A., Steffen, M.: Behavioral interface description of an object-oriented language with futures and promises. J. Logic Algebraic Program. **78**(7), 491–518 (2009)
2. Arusoaie, A., Lucanu, D., Rusu, V.: A generic framework for symbolic execution: theory and applications. Research Report RR-8189, Inria, September 2015
3. de Boer, F.S., Clarke, D., Johnsen, E.B.: A complete guide to the future. In: De Nicola, R. (ed.) ESOP 2007. LNCS, vol. 4421, pp. 316–330. Springer, Heidelberg (2007)
4. Bogdănaş, D., Roşu, G.: K-Java: a complete semantics of Java. In: Proceedings of the 42nd Symposium on Principles of Programming Languages (POPL 2015), pp. 445–456. ACM, January 2015
5. Caromel, D., Henrio, L., Serpette, B.P.: Asynchronous and deterministic objects. In: Proceedings of the 31st ACM SIGPLAN-SIGACT Symposium on Principles of Programming Languages, POPL, 14–16 January 2004, Venice, Italy, pp. 123–134. ACM (2004)
6. Caromel, D., Henrio, L., Serpette, B.P.: Asynchronous sequential processes. Inf. Comput. **207**(4), 459–495 (2009)
7. Danvy, O., Nielsen, L.R.: Refocusing in reduction semantics. RS RS-04-26, BRICS, DAIMI, Department of Computer Science, University of Aarhus, Aarhus, Denmark, November 2004. This report supersedes BRICS report RS-02-04. A preliminary version appears in the informal proceedings of the Second International Workshop on Rule-Based Programming, RULE 2001, Electronic Notes in Theoretical Computer Science, vol. 59.4 (2001)
8. Din, C.C., Owe, O.: A sound and complete reasoning system for asynchronous communication with shared futures. J. Logical Algebraic Meth. Program. **83**(5–6), 360–383 (2014)
9. Ellison, C., Roşu, G.: An executable formal semantics of C with applications. In: Proceedings of the 39th Symposium on Principles of Programming Languages (POPL 2012), pp. 533–544. ACM (2012)
10. Filaretti, D., Maffeis, S.: An executable formal semantics of PHP. In: Jones, R. (ed.) ECOOP 2014. LNCS, vol. 8586, pp. 567–592. Springer, Heidelberg (2014)
11. Friedman, D.P., Wand, M., Haynes, C.T.: Essentials of Programming Languages, 2nd edn. MIT Press, Cambridge (2001)
12. Henrio, L., Khan, M.U.: Asynchronous components with futures: semantics and proofs in Isabelle/HOL. Electron. Notes Theor. Comput. Sci. **264**(1), 35–53 (2010)
13. Johnsen, E.B., Owe, O., Yu, I.C.: Creol: a type-safe object-oriented model for distributed concurrent systems. Theor. Comput. Sci. **365**(1–2), 23–66 (2006)
14. Halstead Jr., R.H.: MULTILISP: a language for concurrent symbolic computation. ACM Trans. Program. Lang. Syst. **7**(4), 501–538 (1985)
15. Park, D., Ştefănescu, A., Roşu, G.: KJS: a complete formal semantics of JavaScript. In: Proceedings of the 36th ACM SIGPLAN Conference on Programming Language Design and Implementation (PLDI 2015), pp. 346–356. ACM, June 2015

16. Roşu, G.: Matching logic – extended abstract. In: Proceedings of the 26th International Conference on Rewriting Techniques and Applications (RTA 2015). Leibniz International Proceedings in Informatics (LIPIcs), vol. 36, pp. 5–21. Dagstuhl, Germany, July 2015

17. Roşu, G., Şerbănuţă, T.: Kool - typed - dynamic. K Tutorial. http://www.kframework.org/index.php/K_Tutorial, https://github.com/kframework/k/tree/master/k-distribution/tutorial

18. Roşu, G., Ştefănescu, A.: From hoare logic to matching logic reachability. In: Giannakopoulou, D., Méry, D. (eds.) FM 2012. LNCS, vol. 7436, pp. 387–402. Springer, Heidelberg (2012)

19. Roşu, G., Ştefănescu, A., Ciobâcă, Ş., Moore, B.M.: One-path reachability logic. In: Proceedings of the 28th Symposium on Logic in Computer Science (LICS 2013), pp. 358–367. IEEE, June 2013

20. Roşu, G., Şerbănuţă, T.F.: An overview of the K semantic framework. J. Logic Algebraic Program. **79**(6), 397–434 (2010)

21. Roşu, G., Ştefănescu, A.: Checking reachability using matching logic. In: OOPSLA, pp. 555–574. ACM, Also available as technical report (2012). http://hdl.handle.net/2142/33771

22. Ştefănescu, A., Ciobâcă, Ş., Mereuta, R., Moore, B.M., Şerbănută, T.F., Roşu, G.: All-path reachability logic. In: Dowek, G. (ed.) RTA-TLCA 2014. LNCS, vol. 8560, pp. 425–440. Springer, Heidelberg (2014)

23. Welc, A., Jagannathan, S., Hosking, A.L.: Safe futures for Java. In: Proceedings of the 20th Annual ACM SIGPLAN Conference on Object-Oriented Programming, Systems, Languages, and Applications, OOPSLA, 16–20 October 2005, San Diego, CA, USA, pp. 439–453. ACM (2005)

24. Wooldridge, M.: An Introduction to MultiAgent Systems, 2nd edn. Wiley, New York (2009)

25. Yonezawa, A., Shibayama, E., Takada, T., Honda, Y.: Object-oriented concurrent programming-modelling and programming in an object-oriented concurrent language, ABCL/1. In: Object-oriented Concurrent Programming, pp. 55–89 (1987)

On the Expressiveness of Synchronization in Component Deployment

Jacopo Mauro[1] and Gianluigi Zavattaro[2]([✉])

[1] Department of Informatics, University of Oslo, Oslo, Norway
[2] Department of Computer Science and Engineering,
University of Bologna/INRIA FoCUS, Bologna, Italy
`gianluigi.zavattaro@unibo.it`

Abstract. The Aeolus component problem of automatic deployment of complex distributed component systems. In the general setting, the task of checking if a distributed application can be deployed is an undecidable problem. However, the current undecidability proof in Aeolus assumes the possibility to perform in a synchronized way atomic configuration actions on a set of interdependent components: this feature is usually not supported by deployment frameworks. In this paper we prove that even without synchronized configuration actions the Aeolus component model is still Turing complete. On the contrary, we show that other Aeolus features like capacity constraints and conflicts are necessary: if we remove the former the deployment problem becomes non-primitive recursive, while in the latter it becomes poly-time.

1 Introduction

Expressiveness of models for concurrent computation is one of those interest that accompanied Frank de Boer in his extremely productive and diversified research activity. For instance, in the early 90's he investigated the use of embedding as a tool for concurrent language comparison [6] and more recently he considered decidability/undecidability of termination problems to evaluate the expressiveness of basic features of the Actor concurrency model [5]. This paper falls in this line of research, by considering the Aeolus component model tailored to the analysis of automatic component deployment. The specific contribution of this paper is the study of the expressiveness of a specific mechanism for component configuration used to synchronously configure interdependent components. This is useful, for instance, when two components are mutually dependent and the easiest way to deploy them is to install them contemporaneously. Especially in a distributed component environment, such a synchronized installation is of difficult implementation. For this reason we have decided to investigate the impact of the elimination of this mechanism from the Aeolus model.

Supported by the EU projects FP7-610582 *Envisage: Engineering Virtualized Services* (http://www.envisage-project.eu) and FP7-644298 *HyVar: Scalable Hybrid Variability for Distributed, Evolving Software Systems* (http://www.hyvar-project.eu).

© Springer International Publishing Switzerland 2016
E. Ábrahám et al. (Eds.): de Boer Festschrift, LNCS 9660, pp. 344–359, 2016.
DOI: 10.1007/978-3-319-30734-3_23

The Aeolus component model has been proposed in [4,8] as a formal model to reason on the component deployment problem. Deployment and management of modern large scale component-based applications is a challenging task, and several tools and technologies are under development to support application architects and managers in these complex activities. According to the current mainstream approaches, such applications are either deployed by exploiting pre-configured virtual machines images, which already contain all the needed software components (see, e.g., Bento Boxes [9], Cloud Blueprints [3], or AWS CloudFormation [2]), or are designed by using drag-and-drop graphical tools like Juju [10] leaving the low-level component configuration to pre-programmed scripts or to automatic configuration tools like Puppet [16] or Chef [15].

Aeolus extends the classical notion of component, seen as a black-box that exposes *provide* and *require* ports, with a finite state automaton describing the component configuration life-cycle. The automaton states correspond to different configuration modalities, like *uninstalled, installed, running, stopped,* etc. and the transitions represent configuration actions like install, run, stop, etc. Depending on the internal state, the ports on the interface can be either active or inactive. For instance, an *uninstalled* component usually does not activate any require port, while it can activate require ports when it is in the *installed* state, and finally activate some provide port when it actually enters the *running* state. Another specific feature of the Aeolus model is that capacity constraints can be associated to the ports: a provide port could have a maximal number of connected require ports or a require port can ask for multiple providers offering a given functionality.[1] Additionally, in Aeolus it is also possible to express conflicts: components can activate special ports that forbids the activation of provide ports of a given type in the rest of the system.

In [4,8] we have investigated the expressiveness of the Aeolus component model, showing that it is Turing complete. From this expressiveness result we have, as a negative consequence, that in general the component deployment problem is not computable. More precisely, we proved the undecidability of the *achievability* problem. Given a finite universe of component types, a target component and a target state, the achievability problem consists of deciding if it possible to reach a final configuration containing at least one instance of the target component type in the target state by assuming the availability of an unbounded number of instances of the component types of the universe in their initial state.

The undecidability of achievability is proved by encoding counter machines, from which follows the Turing completeness of the Aeolus model. The proof relies on a specific feature of Aeolus called *multiple state change*: if there is a group of components that reciprocally depend one on another to advance in their internal configuration life-cycle, it is possible to synchronously and atomically change their state to allow all of them to progress. This specific feature of the model is clearly of non trivial implementation in distributed component systems

---

[1] This feature of the model is used to capture replication or fault tolerance requirements.

since it would require distributed synchronization and is usually not supported by deployment frameworks.

In this paper we investigate the impact of the removal of multiple state changes on the expressiveness of the Aeolus component model. The main result is that the model is still Turing complete, thus showing that the undecidability of achievability follows from its intrinsic complexity, and not from the expressive power of distributed synchronization.

As additional results, we show that this Turing completeness result relies on both capacity constraints and conflicts. In fact, if we remove at least one of these two features, achievability turns out to be decidable. In particular, if we remove conflicts it becomes poly-time, while if we remove capacity constraints (keeping conflicts), it turns out to be decidable but non-primitive recursive.

Comparison with Previous Work. The Aeolus component model was initially proposed in [8] where its Turing completeness was proved. In that paper, also the fragment of the Aeolus model without conflicts and capacity constraints was considered, showing that the achievability problem is poly-time for that fragment. In [7] the fragment without capacity constraints was studied, showing that the problem is decidable; its Ackerman-hardness was proved in [4]. A fragment of the Aeolus model without multiple state change (and without capacity constraints and conflicts) has been considered in [11,12] where a tool for automatic cloud application deployment was presented. In this paper we complete the analysis of the remaining relevant fragments without multiple state changes.

Structure of the Paper. In Sect. 2 we report the formal definition of the Aeolus component model following [4]. Turing completeness without multiple state change actions is proved in Sect. 3. In Sects. 4 and 5 we consider the two fragments obtained by removing, besides multiple state change actions, also capacity constraints or conflicts, respectively. Finally, in Sect. 6 we draw some concluding remarks.

2   The Aeolus Model

In this section we give a recap of the *Aeolus model* following [4].

We assume given the following disjoint sets: $\mathcal{I}$ for interfaces and $\mathcal{Z}$ for components. We use $\mathbb{N}$ to denote strictly positive natural numbers, $\mathbb{N}_\infty$ for $\mathbb{N} \cup \{\infty\}$, and $\mathbb{N}_0$ for $\mathbb{N} \cup \{0\}$.

We model component types as finite state automata indicating all possible component states and state transitions. When a component changes state, the sets of ports it requires from/provide to other components will also change: intuitively, the active ports changes depending on the internal state. A provide port represents the possibility of furnishing a functionality having a given interface. Similarly, a require port represents the need for a functionality with a given interface.

Definition 1 (Component Type). *The set Γ of component types of the Aeolus model, ranged over by $\mathcal{T}_1, \mathcal{T}_2, \ldots$ contains 5-ple $\langle Q, q_0, T, P, D \rangle$ where:*

- *Q is a finite set of states;*
- *$q_0 \in Q$ is the initial state and $T \subseteq Q \times Q$ is the set of transitions;*
- *$P = \langle \mathbf{P}, \mathbf{R} \rangle$, with $\mathbf{P}, \mathbf{R} \subseteq \mathcal{I}$, is a pair composed of the set of provide and the set of require ports, respectively;*
- *D is a function from Q to 2-ple in $(\mathbf{P} \nrightarrow \mathbb{N}_\infty) \times (\mathbf{R} \nrightarrow \mathbb{N}_0)$.*

Given a state $q \in Q$, $D(q)$ returns two partial functions $(\mathbf{P} \nrightarrow \mathbb{N}_\infty)$ and $(\mathbf{R} \nrightarrow \mathbb{N}_0)$ that indicate respectively the provide and require ports that q activates. The functions associate to the activate ports a numerical constraint indicating:

- for provide ports, the *maximum* number of bindings the port can satisfy,
- for require ports, the *minimum* number of required bindings to *distinct* components,
  - as a special case: if the number is 0 this indicates a conflict, meaning that there should be no other active port, in any other component, with the same interface.

When the numerical constraint is not explicitly indicated, we assume ∞ as default value for provide ports (i.e., they can satisfy an unlimited amount of requires) and 1 for require ports (i.e., one provide is enough to satisfy the requirement). We also assume that the initial state q_0 has no demands (i.e., the second function of $D(q_0)$ has an empty domain).

We now define configurations that describe systems composed by component instances and bindings that interconnect them. A configuration, ranged over by $\mathcal{C}_1, \mathcal{C}_2, \ldots$, is given by a set of component types, a set of deployed components with a type and an actual state, and a set of bindings. Formally:

Definition 2 (Configuration). *A configuration $\mathcal{C}$ is a 4-ple $\langle U, Z, S, B \rangle$ where:*

- *$U \subseteq \Gamma$ is the finite universe of all available component types;*
- *$Z \subseteq \mathcal{Z}$ is the set of the currently deployed components;*
- *S is the component state description, i.e., a function that associates to components in Z a pair $\langle \mathcal{T}, q \rangle$ where $\mathcal{T} \in U$ is a component type $\langle Q, q_0, T, P, D \rangle$, and $q \in Q$ is the current component state;*
- *$B \subseteq \mathcal{I} \times Z \times Z$ is the set of bindings, namely 3-ples composed by an interface, the component that requires that interface, and the component that provides it; we assume that the two components are distinct.*

In the following we will use a notion of configuration equivalence that relate configurations having the same instances up to renaming. This is used to abstract away from component identifiers and bindings.

Definition 3 (Configuration Equivalence). *Two configurations $\langle U, Z, S, B \rangle$ and $\langle U, Z', S', B' \rangle$ are equivalent, noted $\langle U, Z, S, B \rangle \equiv \langle U, Z', S', B' \rangle$, iff there exists a bijective function ρ from Z to Z' s.t.:*

1. $S(z) = S'(\rho(z))$ for every $z \in Z$; and
2. $\langle r, z_1, z_2 \rangle \in B$ iff $\langle r, \rho(z_1), \rho(z_2) \rangle \in B'$.

Notation: we write $\mathcal{C}[z]$ as a lookup operation that retrieves the pair $\langle \mathcal{T}, q \rangle = S(z)$, where $\mathcal{C} = \langle U, Z, S, B \rangle$. On such a pair we then use the postfix projection operators `.type` and `.state` to retrieve $\mathcal{T}$ and q, respectively. Similarly, given a component type $\langle Q, q_0, T, \langle \mathbf{P}, \mathbf{R} \rangle, D \rangle$, we use projections to (recursively) decompose it: `.states`, `.init`, and `.trans` return the first three elements; `.prov`, `.req` return $\mathbf{P}$ and $\mathbf{R}$; $.\mathbf{P}(q)$ and $.\mathbf{R}(q)$ return the two elements of the $D(q)$ tuple. When there is no ambiguity we take the liberty to apply the component type projections to $\langle \mathcal{T}, q \rangle$ pairs. For example, $\mathcal{C}[z].\mathbf{R}(q)$ stands for the partial function indicating the active require ports (and their arities) of component z in configuration $\mathcal{C}$ when it is in state q. We denote with $\mathcal{C}^{\#}_{\langle \mathcal{T}, q \rangle}$ the number of components of type $\mathcal{T}$ in state q in the configuration $\mathcal{C}$.

We are now ready to formalize the notion of configuration correctness:

Definition 4 (Configuration Correctness). *Let us consider the configuration* $\mathcal{C} = \langle U, Z, S, B \rangle$.

We write $\mathcal{C} \models_{req} (z, r, n)$ *to indicate that the require port of component* z, *with interface* r, *and associated number* n *is satisfied. Formally, if* $n = 0$ *all components other than* z *cannot have an active provide port with interface* r, *namely for each* $z' \in Z \setminus \{z\}$ *such that* $\mathcal{C}[z'] = \langle \mathcal{T}', q' \rangle$ *we have that* r *is not in the domain of* $\mathcal{T}'.\mathbf{P}(q')$. *If* $n > 0$ *then the port is bound to at least* n *active ports, i.e., there exist* n *distinct components* $z_1, \ldots, z_n \in Z \setminus \{z\}$ *such that for every* $1 \leq i \leq n$ *we have that* $\langle r, z, z_i \rangle \in B$, $\mathcal{C}[z_i] = \langle \mathcal{T}^i, q^i \rangle$ *and* r *is in the domain of* $\mathcal{T}^i.\mathbf{P}(q^i)$.

Similarly for provides, we write $\mathcal{C} \models_{prov} (z, p, n)$ *to indicate that the provide port of component* z, *with interface* p, *and associated number* n *is not bound to more than* n *active ports. Formally, there exist no* m *distinct components* $z_1, \ldots, z_m \in Z \setminus \{z\}$, *with* $m > n$, *such that for every* $1 \leq i \leq m$ *we have that* $\langle p, z_i, z \rangle \in B$, $S(z_i) = \langle \mathcal{T}^i, q^i \rangle$ *and* p *is in the domain of* $\mathcal{T}^i.\mathbf{R}(q^i)$.

The configuration $\mathcal{C}$ *is correct if for each component* $z \in Z$, *given* $S(z) = \langle \mathcal{T}, q \rangle$ *with* $\mathcal{T} = \langle Q, q_0, T, P, D \rangle$ *and* $D(q) = \langle \mathcal{P}, \mathcal{R} \rangle$, *we have that* $(p \mapsto n_p) \in \mathcal{P}$ *implies* $\mathcal{C} \models_{prov} (z, p, n_p)$, *and* $(r \mapsto n_r) \in \mathcal{R}$ *implies* $\mathcal{C} \models_{req} (z, r, n_r)$.

We now formalize how configurations evolve from one state to another one, by means of atomic actions:

Definition 5 (Actions). *The set* $\mathcal{A}$ *contains the following actions:*

- *stateChange*(z, q_1, q_2) *where* $z \in \mathcal{Z}$;
- *bind*(r, z_1, z_2) *where* $z_1, z_2 \in \mathcal{Z}$ *and* $r \in \mathcal{I}$;
- *unbind*(r, z_1, z_2) *where* $z_1, z_2 \in \mathcal{Z}$ *and* $r \in \mathcal{I}$;
- *new*$(z : \mathcal{T})$ *where* $z \in \mathcal{Z}$ *and* $\mathcal{T}$ *is a component type;*
- *del*(z) *where* $z \in \mathcal{Z}$.

The execution of actions can now be formalized using a labelled transition system on configurations, which uses actions as labels.

Definition 6 (Reconfigurations). *Reconfigurations are denoted by transitions* $\mathcal{C} \xrightarrow{\alpha} \mathcal{C}'$ *meaning that the execution of* $\alpha \in \mathcal{A}$ *on the configuration* $\mathcal{C}$ *produces a new configuration* $\mathcal{C}'$. *The transitions from a configuration* $\mathcal{C} = \langle U, Z, S, B \rangle$ *are defined as follows:*

$$\mathcal{C} \xrightarrow{stateChange(z,q_1,q_2)} \langle U, Z, S', B \rangle$$

$$if \; \mathcal{C}[z].\texttt{state} = q_1$$
$$and \; (q_1, q_2) \in \mathcal{C}[z].\texttt{trans}$$
$$and \; S'(z') = \begin{cases} \langle \mathcal{C}[z].\texttt{type}, q_2 \rangle \; if \, z' = z \\ \mathcal{C}[z'] \quad\quad\quad otherwise \end{cases}$$

$$\mathcal{C} \xrightarrow{bind(r,z_1,z_2)} \langle U, Z, S, B \cup \langle r, z_1, z_2 \rangle \rangle$$

$$if \; \langle r, z_1, z_2 \rangle \notin B$$
$$and \; r \in \mathcal{C}[z_1].\texttt{req} \cap \mathcal{C}[z_2].\texttt{prov}$$

$$\mathcal{C} \xrightarrow{unbind(r,z_1,z_2)} \langle U, Z, S, B \setminus \langle r, z_1, z_2 \rangle \rangle \quad if \; \langle r, z_1, z_2 \rangle \in B$$

$$\mathcal{C} \xrightarrow{new(z:\mathcal{T})} \langle U, Z \cup \{z\}, S', B \rangle$$

$$if \; z \notin Z, \mathcal{T} \in U$$
$$and \; S'(z') = \begin{cases} \langle \mathcal{T}, \mathcal{T}.\texttt{init} \rangle \; if \, z' = z \\ \mathcal{C}[z'] \quad\quad\quad otherwise \end{cases}$$

$$\mathcal{C} \xrightarrow{del(z)} \langle U, Z \setminus \{z\}, S', B' \rangle$$

$$if \; S'(z') = \begin{cases} \bot \quad\;\; if \, z' = z \\ \mathcal{C}[z'] \; otherwise \end{cases}$$
$$and \; B' = \{\langle r, z_1, z_2 \rangle \in B \mid z \notin \{z_1, z_2\}\}$$

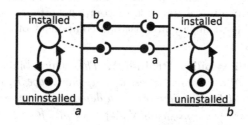

Fig. 1. On the need of a *multiple state change*: how to install a and b?

Notice that in the definition of the transitions there is no requirement on the reached configuration: the correctness of these configurations will be considered at the level of deployment runs as later detailed. Also, we observe that there are configurations that cannot be reached through sequences of the actions we have introduced. In Fig. 1, for instance, there is no way for package a and b to reach the installed state, as each package requires the other one to be installed *first*. In practice, when confronted with such situations—that can be found for example in FOSS distributions in the presence of loops of *Pre-Depends* that impose an order in the installation of two depending packages—current tools either perform all the state changes atomically, or, more often, they abort deployment.

The Aeolus model allows for simultaneous installations by introducing the notion of *multiple state change*.

Definition 7 (Multiple State Change). *A multiple state change action* $\mathcal{M} = \{stateChange(z^1, q_1^1, q_2^1), \cdots, stateChange(z^l, q_1^l, q_2^l)\}$ *is a set of actions of type state change on different components (i.e., $z^i \neq z^j$ for every $1 \leq i < j \leq l$). We use $\langle U, Z, S, B \rangle \xrightarrow{\mathcal{M}} \langle U, Z, S', B \rangle$ to denote the effect of the simultaneous execution of the state changes in $\mathcal{M}$: formally,*

$$\langle U, Z, S, B \rangle \xrightarrow{stateChange(z^1, q_1^1, q_2^1)} \cdots \xrightarrow{stateChange(z^l, q_1^l, q_2^l)} \langle U, Z, S', B \rangle$$

Notice that the order of execution of the state change actions does not matter as all the actions are executed on different components.

We can now define a *deployment run*, which is a sequence of actions that transform an initial configuration into a final correct one without violating correctness along the way. A deployment run is the output we expect from a planner, when it is asked how to reach a desired target configuration.

Definition 8 (Deployment Run). *A deployment run is a sequence $\alpha_1 \ldots \alpha_m$ of actions and multiple state changes such that there exist $\mathcal{C}_i$ such that $\mathcal{C} = \mathcal{C}_0$, $\mathcal{C}_{j-1} \xrightarrow{\alpha_j} \mathcal{C}_j$ for every $j \in \{1, \ldots, m\}$, and the following conditions hold:*

configuration correctness *for every $i \in \{0, \ldots, m\}$, $\mathcal{C}_i$ is correct;*
multiple state change minimality *if α_j is a multiple state change then there exists no proper subset $\mathcal{M} \subset \alpha_j$, or state change action $\alpha \in \alpha_j$, and correct configuration $\mathcal{C}'$ such that $\mathcal{C}_{j-1} \xrightarrow{\mathcal{M}} \mathcal{C}'$, or $\mathcal{C}_{j-1} \xrightarrow{\alpha} \mathcal{C}'$.*

We now have all the ingredients to define the notion of *achievability*, that is our main concern: given a universe of component types, we want to know whether it is possible to deploy at least one component of a given component type $\mathcal{T}$ in a given state q.

Definition 9 (Achievability Problem). *The achievability problem has as input a universe U of component types, a component type $\mathcal{T}$, and a target state q. It returns as output **true** if there exists a deployment run $\alpha_1 \ldots \alpha_m$ such that $\langle U, \emptyset, \emptyset, \emptyset \rangle \xrightarrow{\alpha_1} \mathcal{C}_1 \xrightarrow{\alpha_2} \cdots \xrightarrow{\alpha_m} \mathcal{C}_m$ and $\mathcal{C}_m[z] = \langle \mathcal{T}, q \rangle$, for some component z in $\mathcal{C}_m$. Otherwise, it returns **false**.*

Notice that the restriction in this decision problem to one component in a given state is not limiting. One can easily encode any given final configuration by adding a dummy provide port enabled only by the required final states and a dummy component with requirements on all such provides.

3   Turing Completeness Without Multiple State Changes

In [4,8] it is proved that the *Aeolus* component model is Turing complete. More precisely, we show how to reduce termination for 2 Counter Machines [14], a well-known Turing-complete computational model, in the achievability problem for the *Aeolus* component model. The presented reduction makes use of the multiple state change actions. In this section, we revisit that proof, showing that multiple state changes are not strictly necessary.

Before entering into the details, we observe that given a component type T it is always possible to modify it in such a way that its instances are persistent. To avoid the component deletion it is sufficient to impose a reciprocal dependence with a new auxiliary type of components. When this dependence is established the components cannot be deleted without violating configuration correctness. In [4] this reciprocal dependence was established via a multiple state change. However, multiple state changes are not the only way to enforce the persistence of an instance since the reciprocal dependence can be established by creating one binding at the time following a precise protocol.

In Fig. 2 we show an example of how a component type can be modified in order to reach our goal. Three new auxiliary states q_0', q_a', and q_b' are created, with q_0' becoming the new initial state. States q_a' and q_b' require and provide respectively ports a and b. Only one instance of T can be present at once in these two states. This is enforced by simultaneously providing and requiring the port e. The original states of T are modified to require the port a and provide the port b. Dually, the auxiliary component T_{aux} has an initial state q_0, a final one q_f, and two intermediate states q_a and q_b providing and requiring respectively ports a and b. Also in this case, at most one instance of T_{aux} can be in states q_a or q_b. We assume that the ports a, b, e and f are fresh, that is, they are not used by any other component type in the considered universe.

Given a component type T we denote this component type transformation with $\varphi(T)$. The φ transformation is defined to guarantee the establishment of

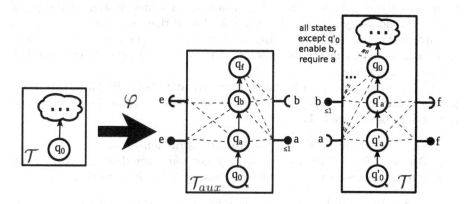

Fig. 2. Component type transformation φ.

two reciprocal bindings between pairs of $\mathcal{T}$ and $\mathcal{T}_{aux}$ instances that forbid their deletion. In particular, an instance of $\mathcal{T}$ cannot be deleted after the state q'_b was left while the instance of $\mathcal{T}_{aux}$ cannot be deleted after state q_a. This is due to the fact that after these states are left the instances are guaranteed to provide something required by the other instance. If we denote with $C^{\#}_{\langle p \rangle}$ the number of instances providing the port p, this property is captured as follows.

Property 1 (φ-persistence). A configuration $\mathcal{C}$ is φ-persistent if $C^{\#}_{\langle a \rangle} - C^{\#}_{\langle \mathcal{T}_{aux}, q_a \rangle} = C^{\#}_{\langle b \rangle} - C^{\#}_{\langle \mathcal{T}, q'_b \rangle}$.

The encoding φ preserves the φ-persistence.

Lemma 1. *If $\mathcal{C} \xrightarrow{\alpha} \mathcal{C}'$ and $\mathcal{C}$ is φ-persistent than also $\mathcal{C}'$ is φ-persistent.*

Proof. The proof can be done considering the type of α actions. Since φ-persistence considers just the amount of active ports of type a and b we can restrict to consider only actions that can alter these quantities.

If $\alpha = stateChange(z, q_0, q_a)$ a new port a is provided but at the same time an instance of type $\mathcal{T}_{aux}$ leaving the quantity $C^{\#}_{\langle a \rangle} - C^{\#}_{\langle \mathcal{T}_{aux}, q_a \rangle}$ unaltered. The same happens with $\alpha = stateChange(z, q_a, q_b)$ and for port b when $\alpha = stateChange(z, q'_a, q'_b)$ or $stateChange(z, q'_b, q_0)$.

When a and b are provided, by construction, the only way to reduce their amount is by deleting a component. A deletion of an instance of type $\mathcal{T}_{aux}$ in state q_0, q_a or the deletion of type $\mathcal{T}$ in states q'_0, q'_a, q'_b does not alter the amount of a or b ports provided. A deletion of an instance z of $\mathcal{T}$ or $\mathcal{T}_{aux}$ in a different state q' is not possible. In fact, if z is of type $\mathcal{T}$ than its deletion reduces $C^{\#}_{\langle b \rangle}$ by 1. But since there are exactly $C^{\#}_{\langle a \rangle} - C^{\#}_{\langle \mathcal{T}_{aux}, q_a \rangle} = C^{\#}_{\langle b \rangle} - C^{\#}_{\langle \mathcal{T}, q'_b \rangle}$ instances requiring a port b the deletion of z violates the configuration correctness. Similarly, the configuration correctness is violated also if z is of type $\mathcal{T}_{aux}$. $\square$

We can therefore consider, without loss of generality, components that can be deployed in a persistent way. This can lead to a modification of the proof of the undecidability of achievability for Aeolus [4] that does not assume to use multiple state changes. The original prove was by reduction from the termination problem in 2 Counter Machines (2CMs) [14], a well-known Turing-complete computational model.

A 2CM is a machine with *two registers* R_1 and R_2 holding arbitrary large natural numbers and a *program* P consisting of a finite sequence of numbered instructions of the two following types:

- $j : \mathsf{Inc}(R_i)$: increments R_i and goes to the instruction $j + 1$;
- $j : \mathsf{DecJump}(R_i, l)$: if the content of R_i is not zero, then decreases it by 1 and goes to the instruction $j + 1$, otherwise jumps to the l instruction.

A state of the machine is given by a tuple (i, v_1, v_2) where i indicates the next instruction to execute (the program counter) and v_1 and v_2 are the values contained in the two registers, respectively.

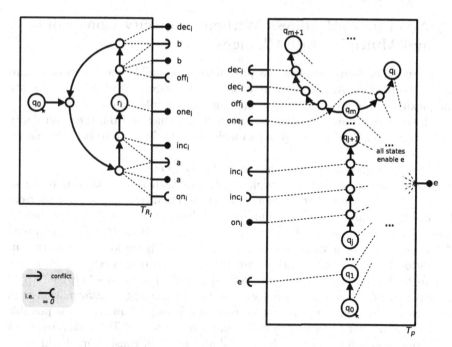

Fig. 3. Modeling 2 counter machines (2CMs) in the Aeolus model.

For modelling 2CMs a component to simulate the execution of the program instructions was used. The content v_i of the register R_i is modelled by v_i components in a particular state r_i. Increment instructions add one component in this state r_i, while decrement instructions move one component in state r_i to a different state. The state r_i activates a provide port one_i, so the simulation of a test for zero has simply to check the absence in the environment of active one_i ports. In particular, as depicted in Fig. 3, a component type T_P was used to simulate the execution of the program instructions while T_{R_1} and T_{R_2} were used for the two registers. All these components where made persistent by forcing the initial execution of multiple state changes creating reciprocal bindings with an additional component. However, the same can be obtained without the use of the multiple state change simply by applying the φ transformation.

We can therefore prove a stricter undecidability result.

Theorem 1. *The achievability problem is undecidable in the fragment of the Aeolus component model that does not support multiple state changes.*

Proof. The proof follows the same technique as the one used in [4] by considering the universe $U = \varphi(T_P) \cup \varphi(T_{R_1}) \cup \varphi(T_{R_2})$. □

4   Ackermann-Hardness Without Capacity Constraints and Multiple State Changes

In [4] the achievability problem was proven to be decidable but Ackermann-hard in the fragment of Aeolus without capacity constraints. Even in this case the complexity does not decrease if we also remove multiple state changes.

The complexity result in [4] was obtained by reduction from the coverability problem in reset Petri nets, a problem which is indeed known to be Ackermann-hard [17].

We start with some background on reset Petri nets.

A *reset Petri net RN* is a tuple $\langle P, T, m_0 \rangle$ such that P is a finite set of *places*, T is a finite set of *transitions*, and m_0 is a marking, i.e., a mapping from P to $\mathbb{N}$ that defines the initial number of tokens in each place of the net. A transition $t \in T$ is defined by a mapping $\bullet t$ (preset) from P to $\mathbb{N}$, a mapping $t \bullet$ (postset), and by a set of reset arcs $t \downarrow \subseteq P$. A configuration is a marking m. Transition t is enabled at marking m iff $\bullet t(p) \le m(p)$ for each $p \in P$. Firing t at m leads to a new marking m' defined as $m'(p) = m(p) -\bullet t(p) + t\bullet(p)$ if $p \notin t \downarrow$, and $m'(p) = 0$ otherwise; we denote this marking transformation with $m \mapsto m'$. A marking m is reachable from m_0 if $m_0 \mapsto^* m$, i.e., it is possible to produce m after firing finitely many times transitions in T. Given a reset net $\langle P, T, m_0 \rangle$ and a marking m, the coverability problem consists in checking for the existence of a reachable marking m' such that $m \le m'$, i.e. $m(p) \le m'(p)$ for every $p \in P$. In [17] it is proved that the coverability problem for reset nets is Ackermann-hard.

The encoding of reset Petri nets into Aeolus presented in [4] relied on three types of component types: $\mathcal{T}_p$ for modelling the tokens, $\mathcal{T}_t$ for the transitions, and $log(n)$ component types $\mathcal{T}_{C_i}$ (for $1 \le i \le log(n)$) for modeling the bits in a binary counter used to count the tokens to be produced or consumed during the simulation of a transition firing. Here n is the maximal number of tokens that one transition can produce or consume. The proof technique requires that the components for the transitions and the counter bits are unique and persistent. This was ensured via a transformation that exploited conflicts but also multiple state changes. This however, following the example of the φ transformation defined in the previous section, can be obtained also without the use of multiple state changes. The key idea to avoid a multiple state change is to create a mutual dependency between pairs of components in two phases and use the conflicts to ensure that only one component at a time can be present.

Figure 4 depicts the transformation η that guarantees persistence and forbids the presence of two distinct instances of the same component. This is obtained by requiring that all the states except the initial ones activate contemporaneously a require and a conflict port on the same interface (in the two component types in the Figure we use the fresh interfaces e and f, respectively). The interdependencies among the two component types are similar to those used in the φ transformation to guarantee persistency. The unique difference is that no capacity constraint is considered; indeed, this is no longer needed because, thanks to the simultaneous requirement and conflict on the interfaces e and f, and the

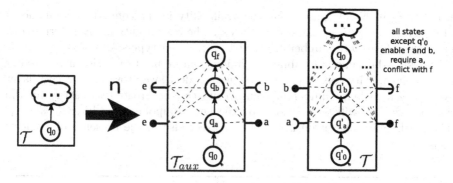

Fig. 4. Component type transformation η.

freshness of the ports a and b, a configuration has at most one a and one b provide port active.

Note that the size of $\eta(\mathcal{T})$ is polynomial w.r.t. the size of $\mathcal{T}$ because we are just introducing a new component type $\mathcal{T}_{aux}$ of constant size and we modify $\mathcal{T}$ by adding three new states and three ports.

We can now conclude the new version of the Ackermann-hardness result for the fragment of Aeolus without capacity constraints and multiple state changes.

Theorem 2. *The achievability problem is Ackermann-hard for the fragment of the Aeolus component model that does not support capacity constraints and multiple state changes.*

Proof. The proof follows the same technique as the one used in [4] with the difference that now the encoding of the Petri net $RN = (P, T, m_0)$ is $\Gamma_{RN} = \{\mathcal{T}_p \mid p \in P\} \cup \{\eta(\mathcal{T}_{C_i}) \mid i \in [1..\lceil \log(n)\rceil]\} \cup \{\eta(\mathcal{T}_T)\}$ where n is the largest number of tokens that can be consumed or produced by a transition in T and η is the transformation depicted in Fig. 4. □

5 Poly-time Without Conflicts and Multiple State Changes

In [12] it was proven that the achievability problem is poly-time considering the fragment of Aeolus where no capacity constraint, no multiple state changes, and no conflicts can be used.

This was done by means of an algorithm that builds a reachability graph used to check whether a given target component-state pair may be obtained. As detailed in Algorithm 1, the nodes of the reachability graph are organized in layers $Nodes_0$, $Nodes_1$, $\cdots$, $Nodes_n$ that are generated in subsequent phases. Initially, $Nodes_0$ contains all the pairs $\langle \mathcal{T}, \mathcal{T}.\texttt{init} \rangle$ corresponding to the initial states. Given $Nodes_j$, $Nodes_{j+1}$ is generated by copying the pairs already available in $Nodes_j$ and by adding those new pairs that can be reached by transitions from states in $Nodes_j$, assuming the availability in the context of components of type and state $\langle \mathcal{T}, q \rangle$ already in $Nodes_j$. The reachability analysis terminates since there is a finite number of possible component type-state pairs.

Luckily, the same reachability technique can be used to decide achievability also when capacity constraints can be used. Indeed, we prove that at each layer $Nodes_j$ a sufficient number of components can be created to satisfy all the constraints that will be activated by the new components at layer $Nodes_{j+1}$. The reachability algorithm is therefore correct also in the presence of capacity constraints.

Algorithm 1. REACHABILITYANALYSIS()

1: $Nodes_0 = \{\langle \mathcal{T}, \mathcal{T}.\text{init} \rangle \mid \mathcal{T} \in U\}$; $provPort = \bigcup_{\langle \mathcal{T}, q \rangle \in Nodes_0} \{\mathcal{T}.\mathbf{P}(q)\}$; $n = 0$
2: **repeat**
3:     $n = n + 1$
4:     $Arcs_n = \emptyset$; $Nodes_n = \emptyset$
5:     **for all** $\langle \mathcal{T}, q \rangle \in Nodes_{n-1}$ **do**
6:         **for all** $(q, q') \in \mathcal{T}.\text{trans}$ **do**
7:             **if** $\mathcal{T}.\mathbf{R}(q') \subseteq provPort$ **then**
8:                 $Nodes_n.\mathbf{add}(\langle \mathcal{T}, q' \rangle)$
9:     **for all** $\langle \mathcal{T}, q \rangle \in Nodes_n$ **do**
10:         $provPort.\mathbf{add}(\mathcal{T}.\mathbf{P}(q))$
11:     $Nodes_n = Nodes_{n-1} \cup Nodes_n$
12:     **for all** $\langle \mathcal{T}, q \rangle \in Nodes_{n-1}, \langle \mathcal{T}, q' \rangle \in Nodes_n$ **do**
13:         **if** $(q, q') \in \mathcal{T}.\text{trans}$ **then**
14:             $Arcs_n.\mathbf{add}(\langle \mathcal{T}, q' \rangle \longrightarrow \langle \mathcal{T}, q \rangle)$
15:         **if** $q == q'$ **then**
16:             $Arcs_n.\mathbf{add}(\langle \mathcal{T}, q' \rangle \cdots \langle \mathcal{T}, q \rangle)$
17: **until** $Nodes_{n-1} == Nodes_n$

Lemma 2. *Given a universe of components U, a component type $\mathcal{T}_{target}$, and a state q_{target}, we have that $\langle \mathcal{T}, q \rangle$ belongs to the reachability graph computed by Algorithm 1 if and only if there exists a deployment plan that deploys at least one component of type $\mathcal{T}$ in state q.*

Proof. We first consider the *only if* part. We prove that given $h_{\langle \mathcal{T}, q \rangle} > 0$ for every $\langle \mathcal{T}, q \rangle \in Nodes_n$, and given $h_p > 0$ for every provide port p activated by the component type-state pairs $\langle \mathcal{T}, q \rangle \in Nodes_n$, there exists a deployment plan from an empty configuration to a configuration containing at least $h_{\langle \mathcal{T}, q \rangle}$ components of type $\mathcal{T}$ state q, in which at least h_p provide ports with interface p have no incoming bindings (thus they are available to satisfy additional complementary require port with interface p). We proceed by induction on n.

The base case holds because $Nodes_0$ contains all the pairs with just initial states (Line 1) and components could always be created in their initial state because they have no requirements by definition.

In the inductive case we have that for every pair $\langle \mathcal{T}, q \rangle \in Nodes_{i+1} \setminus Nodes_i$ there exists a pair $\langle \mathcal{T}, q' \rangle \in Nodes_i$ where q' is a predecessor of q (Lines 5–8 of Algorithm 1). Moreover, for every require port r activated by the components of type-state $\langle \mathcal{T}, q \rangle \in Nodes_{i+1} \setminus Nodes_i$ there exists a pair $\langle \mathcal{T}'', q'' \rangle \in Nodes_i$ that activates a provide port r (Line 7).

By inductive hypothesis it is possible to obtain a configuration such that:

1. for every $\langle \mathcal{T}, q' \rangle \in Nodes_i$ it has at least

$$h_{\langle \mathcal{T}, q' \rangle} + \sum_{\langle \mathcal{T}, q \rangle \in Nodes_{i+1} \setminus Nodes_i} (h_{\langle \mathcal{T}, q \rangle} + max_p)$$

   components of type $\mathcal{T}$ in state q'. By max_p we mean the maximal value among all the h_p;

2. for every provide port p activated by a component type-state pair $\langle \mathcal{T}'', q'' \rangle \in Nodes_i$ in $Nodes_i$ there are at least

$$h_p + (maxRequire_p + 1) \times \sum_{\langle \mathcal{T}, q \rangle \in Nodes_{i+1} \setminus Nodes_i} (h_{\langle \mathcal{T}, q \rangle} + max_p)$$

   active provide port p that have no incoming binding. By $maxRequire_p$ we mean the maximal number of provide ports with interface p that are necessary to satisfy the requirements of one component instances of any possible type, in any possible state.

Thanks to point 1, starting from this configuration it is possible to perform for every pair $\langle \mathcal{T}, q \rangle$ of $Nodes_{i+1} \setminus Nodes_i$ exactly $h_{\langle \mathcal{T}, q \rangle} + max_p(h_p)$ state changes to obtain components of type $\mathcal{T}$ in state q. Indeed, point 2 guarantees there are enough free provide ports to satisfy the requirements of these components. Moreover, if the new state q activates new provide ports that were inactive in the previous state, we have the guarantee that it is possible to unbind these ports so that these components will have no incoming binding. Hence, for these interfaces p we will have at least h_p free provide ports.

Concerning pairs $\langle \mathcal{T}'', q'' \rangle \in Nodes_{i+1} \cap Nodes_i$, thanks to point 1 the reached configuration will contain at least $h_{\langle \mathcal{T}'', q'' \rangle}$ instances of type $\mathcal{T}''$ in state q''. By point 2, we also have the guarantee that for provide ports p activated by these pairs $\langle \mathcal{T}'', q'' \rangle$ at least h_p instances remain free in the new configuration. In fact, some of them (at most $maxRequire_p \times \sum_{\langle \mathcal{T}, q \rangle \in Nodes_{i+1} \setminus Nodes_i} (h_{\langle \mathcal{T}, q \rangle} + max_p)$) will be used to satisfy the requirements of the new component type-state pairs, and some other (at most $\sum_{\langle \mathcal{T}, q \rangle \in Nodes_{i+1} \setminus Nodes_i} (h_{\langle \mathcal{T}, q \rangle} + max_p)$) could become inactive due to a state change.

We now move to the *if* part. We proceed by contradiction. Let us suppose the existence of a deployment plan $\langle U, \emptyset, \emptyset, \emptyset \rangle \xrightarrow{\alpha_1} \mathcal{C}_1 \xrightarrow{\alpha_2} \ldots \xrightarrow{\alpha_m} \mathcal{C}_m$ such that $\mathcal{C}_m$ contains a component of type $\mathcal{T}$ in state q while $\langle \mathcal{T}, q \rangle$ is not present in the reachability graph. It is not restrictive to assume that $\mathcal{C}_m$ is the first configuration of the plan having such property (i.e., all the pairs $\langle \mathcal{T}', q' \rangle$ of the components in $\mathcal{C}_1, \cdots, \mathcal{C}_{m-1}$ are present in the reachability graph).

Obviously q cannot be an initial state of $\mathcal{T}$ since all the component types with their initial states are added in $Nodes_0$ (Line 1). Therefore we have that the last transition of the plan is $\mathcal{C}_{m-1} \xrightarrow{stateChange(i,s,q)} \mathcal{C}_m$. This action can be executed only if all the require ports activated by q are fulfilled by components in $\mathcal{C}_{m-1}$. For the previous assumption, we have that $\langle \mathcal{T}, s \rangle$, as well as all the pairs $\langle \mathcal{T}', q' \rangle$ of types and states of components in $\mathcal{C}_{m-1}$, are part of the computed reachability graph. Let $Nodes_j$ be the first layer containing all such pairs: by construction (Lines 5–8) we will have that $\langle \mathcal{T}, q \rangle \in Nodes_{j+1}$, thus contradicting the hypothesis.   □

As a consequence of Lemma 2 we have the following result.

Theorem 3. *The achievability problem is poly-time for the fragment of the Aeolus component model that does not support multiple state changes and conflicts.*

The proof immediately follows from Lemma 2 and the fact that Algorithm 1 is poly-time [12].

6   Conclusions

To the best of our knowledge Aeolus is the first formal model that is designed on purpose to address the specific problem of software component deployment in the cloud. It was first introduced in [8]. Differently from the definition of the language presented here, in [8] an additional kind of requirements—called *weak requirements*—was present. Differently from the requirements presented in this paper (formerly known as *strong requirements*) that needs to be enforced at every deployment step, weak requirements must be satisfied only at the end of a deployment run. The notion of weak requirement was removed from the model because we found out that their behavior could be simulated with normal requirements. In this paper we proved that also the notion of multiple state change can be removed because from the complexity point of view it does not have an impact. It is interesting to point out that this new foundational result reflects a recent technic adopted in the context of deployment tools for *package-based* software distributions [1] that replaces synchronous installation of circular dependent packages with multi-stage configuration protocol.

In this work we have considered the deployment of an application from scratch. If we assume the initial configuration is not empty, we move to a so-called *reconfiguration* problem. It is interesting to observe that this problem is harder than the achievability problem for the fragment without multiple state change and conflicts for which we prove in this paper that achievability is poly-time. In fact, in [13] we have recently proved that reconfiguration is PSpace complete already for the fragment without multiple state change, conflicts and capacity constraints.

References

1. Abate, P., Johannes, S.: Bootstrapping software distributions. In: CBSE 2013, pp. 131–142. ACM (2013)
2. Amazon. AWS CloudFormation. http://aws.amazon.com/cloudformation/
3. CenturyLink. Cloud Blueprints. http://www.centurylinkcloud.com/products/management/blueprints
4. Di Cosmo, R., Mauro, J., Zacchiroli, S., Zavattaro, G.: Aeolus: a component model for the cloud. Inf. Comput. **239**, 100–121 (2014)
5. de Boer, F.S., Jaghoori, M.M., Laneve, C., Zavattaro, G.: Decidability problems for actor systems. Logical Meth. Comput. Sci. **10**(4:5), 1–29 (2014)
6. de Boer, F.S., Palamidessi, C.: Embedding as a tool for language comparison. Inf. Comput. **108**(1), 128–157 (1994)
7. Di Cosmo, R., Mauro, J., Zacchiroli, S., Zavattaro, G.: Component reconfiguration in the presence of conflicts. In: Fomin, F.V., Kwiatkowska, M., Peleg, D. (eds.) ICALP 2013, Part II. LNCS, vol. 7966, pp. 187–198. Springer, Heidelberg (2013)
8. Di Cosmo, R., Zacchiroli, S., Zavattaro, G.: Towards a formal component model for the cloud. In: Eleftherakis, G., Hinchey, M., Holcombe, M. (eds.) SEFM 2012. LNCS, vol. 7504, pp. 156–171. Springer, Heidelberg (2012)
9. Flexiant. Bento Boxes. http://www.flexiant.com/2012/12/03/application-provisioning/
10. Juju, devops distilled. https://juju.ubuntu.com/
11. Lascu, T.A., Mauro, J., Zavattaro, G.: A planning tool supporting the deployment of cloud applications. In: ICTAI (2013)
12. Lascu, T.A., Mauro, J., Zavattaro, G.: Automatic component deployment in the presence of circular dependencies. In: Fiadeiro, J.L., Liu, Z., Xue, J. (eds.) FACS 2013. LNCS, vol. 8348, pp. 254–272. Springer, Heidelberg (2014)
13. Mauro, J., Zavattaro, G.: On the complexity of reconfiguration in systems with legacy components. In: Italiano, G.F., Pighizzini, G., Sannella, D.T. (eds.) MFCS 2015. LNCS, vol. 9234, pp. 382–393. Springer, Heidelberg (2015)
14. Minsky, M.: Computation: Finite and Infinite Machines. Prentice Hall, Englewood Cliffs (1967)
15. Opscode. Chef. http://www.opscode.com/chef/
16. Puppetlabs. Puppet. http://puppetlabs.com/
17. Schnoebelen, P.: Revisiting Ackermann-hardness for lossy counter machines and reset Petri nets. In: Hliněný, P., Kučera, A. (eds.) MFCS 2010. LNCS, vol. 6281, pp. 616–628. Springer, Heidelberg (2010)

Characterization of Simulation by Probabilistic Testing

Philipp Rümmer[✉] and Wang Yi

Department of Information Technology, Uppsala University, Uppsala, Sweden
philipp.ruemmer@it.uu.se

Abstract. Testing of systems naturally has a non-deterministic character: on the one hand, internal decisions of the system under test appear as non-determinism to an observer; on the other hand, the system under test inevitably receives inputs from the environment that are not controlled by the tester. To model both aspects, we investigate a probabilistic testing framework in which non-deterministic labelled transition systems are examined through execution of finite, probabilistic test-cases. We show that the simulation preorder on labelled transition systems can be tested probabilistically, elegantly recapturing the notion of conformance testing in this setting.

1 Introduction

For us, Frank is not only a great friend, but also a great scientist and a great leader. His contributions in many areas have been a source for inspiration in our work. His leadership has been a driving force in many large successful collaborating projects in Europe. Thank you Frank! Congratulations for the first successful 60 years; we look forward to working with you in the coming 60 years! The work presented in this paper was initiated many years ago when Frank was also a participant in a venue discussing research issues on concurrency and testing.

To study probabilistic phenomena such as randomisation and failure rates in distributed computing, significant research effort has been put into the extension of models and methods that have proven successful for non-probabilistic systems to the probabilistic setting. In the non-probabilistic setting, transition systems are well-established as a basic semantic model for sequential, concurrent, and distributed systems. This model has been extended in the literature to the probabilistic case by adding a mechanism for representing probabilistic choice.

In the work presented in this paper, we consider the specific combination of classical, *non-probabilistic* systems, examined with the help of *probabilistic* tests. More specifically, we consider tests as finite labelled transition systems that might contain both probabilistic and non-deterministic choice. As the main result, we show that the (non-probabilistic) simulation preorder can be tested by comparing the likelihood that probabilistic tests succeed. Probability, in this setting, is mainly used as a vehicle to examine the branching structure of processes, since probabilistic choice has the effect of copying and duplicating intermediate

E. Ábrahám et al. (Eds.): de Boer Festschrift, LNCS 9660, pp. 360–372, 2016.
DOI: 10.1007/978-3-319-30734-3_24

states of processes, in such a way that each copy can be examined separately. This concept has been exploited in a number of previous research results, including [1,2].

We outline how this theoretic result can practically be exploited in the context of *conformance testing,* where the relationship of a concrete implementation with an abstract behavioural specification is checked.

1.1 Related Work

Characterization of Bisimulation by Probabilistic Testing. Abramsky presented the first work in the 80s [1] to characterize bisimulation relations using probabilistic testing, which is the original motivation of this work. The essential idea of Abramsky is to utilize the "copying capability" in probability testing to characterize equivalence relations. In this work, we show that the copying feature can also be used to characterize simulation relation, which is a preorder. A relevant work along this line is [2], where we have shown that testing preorders can be characterized by simulation relations over probabilistic systems. The difference is that here we have probabilistic tests and the systems under test exhibit only non-deterministic behavior.

Statistical Model Checking. An area related to probabilistic testing is statistical model checking, which has been proposed as an alternative to exhaustive model checking for analyzing stochastic (e.g., timed or hybrid) systems [3,6]. In statistical model checking, the behavior of a system is *simulated,* thus obtaining a sample of possible system executions; afterwards, *hypothesis testing* is used to check whether the sample represents sufficient statistical evidence that some specification is satisfied or violated. In contrast to exhaustive methods, statistical model checking does not provide guarantees, but makes it possible to bound the likelihood of wrong answers. At the same time, runtime and memory consumption of statistical model checking can be drastically smaller than that of exhaustive techniques.

The results presented in this paper differ from statistical model checking methods in two important points: in our setting, it is the *tests* that are assumed to be probabilistic, whereas systems under test only exhibit non-deterministic behavior (in Sect. 3 and later); the situation in statistical model checking is the opposite. Second, we consider how testing is used to derive simulation relation between two systems, rather than checking that a system conforms to some independently defined property.

2 Preliminaries

We consider a model of probabilistic transition systems, containing probabilistic and non-deterministic choices as independent concepts. Processes, in most parts of the paper, are transition systems only containing non-deterministic choices, i.e., there is no probabilistic behaviour. In contrast, tests are defined as transition systems that can contain both non-deterministic and probabilistic behaviour, more precisely as finite trees in which certain states are "accepting." As we will see, in this setting it is possible to give an exceptionally simple and elegant characterisation of *simulation* in terms of *tests*.

Most of the definitions follow the lines of [2].

2.1   Basic Concepts

A *weighting* on a set S is a function $\sigma : S \to \mathcal{R}_{\geq 0}$ from S to nonnegative real numbers. For a set S, we use $\sigma(S)$ to denote $\sum_{s \in S} \sigma(s)$. A *probability distribution* on a finite set S is a weighting σ on S such that $\sigma(S) = 1$. A *sub-distribution* on a finite set S is a weighting σ on S such that $\sigma(S) \leq 1$. We use $s \in \sigma$ to denote that $\sigma(s) > 0$. The *support* $Supp(\sigma)$ of a weighting σ is the set of elements s with $s \in \sigma$. A distribution whose support is a singleton set is called a *deterministic distribution*. Let $Weight(S)$ and $Dist(S)$ denote the sets of weightings and probability distributions on S, respectively. We will sometimes identify a single state s with the deterministic distribution that assigns probability 1 to s.

If σ is a weighting on S and ρ is a weighting on R, then $\sigma \times \rho$ is a weighting on $S \times R$, defined by $(\sigma \times \rho)(\langle s, r \rangle) = \sigma(s) * \rho(r)$. If σ is a weighting on S and $h : S \to R$ is a function from S to R, then $h(\sigma)$ is a weighting on R, defined by $h(\sigma)(r) = \sum_{h(s)=r} \sigma(s)$. If σ and ρ are weightings on S, then $\sigma \leq \rho$ denotes that $\sigma(s) \leq \rho(s)$ for all $s \in S$.

2.2   Probabilistic Transition Systems

We assume a finite set $\mathcal{A}ct$ of atomic actions, ranged over by a and b.

Definition 1. *A (probabilistic) transition system is a pair $\langle S, \longrightarrow \rangle$, where*

- S *is a non-empty finite set of* states, *and*
- $\longrightarrow \subseteq S \times \mathcal{A}ct \times Dist(S)$ *is a finite transition relation.*

We use $s \xrightarrow{a} \sigma$ to denote that $\langle s, a, \sigma \rangle \in \longrightarrow$.

A (probabilistic) process is a tuple $\langle \langle S, \longrightarrow \rangle, \sigma_0 \rangle$, where $\langle S, \longrightarrow \rangle$ is a probabilistic transition system, and $\sigma_0 \in Dist(S)$ is an initial probability distribution on S.

We write $s \xrightarrow{a}$ to denote that there is a σ such that $s \xrightarrow{a} \sigma$, and say that a state s is *terminal* (written $s \not\xrightarrow{}$) if there is no a and σ such that $s \xrightarrow{a} \sigma$. By slight abuse of notation, we write $s \xrightarrow{a} s'$ if $s \xrightarrow{a} \sigma$ such that $s' \in \sigma$. A *finite tree* is a process $\langle \langle S, \longrightarrow \rangle, \sigma_0 \rangle$ such that every state $s' \in S$ can be reached by exactly one path $s_0 \xrightarrow{a_1} s_1 \xrightarrow{a_2} \cdots \xrightarrow{a_n} s_n = s'$ with $s_0 \in \sigma_0$.

Each state of a probabilistic transition system has a potential for future dynamic behavior. When an action is performed, the system makes a probabilistic "choice" of next state. Thus, at each point in time, a snapshot of the system state will be a distribution over possible states.

2.3   Probabilistic Testing

To study testing, we define a synchronous parallel composition operator for probabilistic transition systems, in which two processes $\mathcal{P}$ and $\mathcal{Q}$ execute in parallel while synchronizing on all actions in $\mathcal{Act}$.

Definition 2. *Let $\langle S, \longrightarrow \rangle$ and $\langle R, \longrightarrow \rangle$ be two transition systems. Their composition, denoted by the expression $\langle S, \longrightarrow \rangle \| \langle R, \longrightarrow \rangle$, is the transition system $\langle U, \longrightarrow \rangle$ where*

- *$U = S \times R$. A pair $(s,r) \in U$ is denoted $s\|r$.*
- *$\longrightarrow \subseteq U \times \mathcal{Act} \times Dist(U)$ is defined by*

$$s\|r \xrightarrow{a} \sigma \times \rho \qquad iff \qquad s \xrightarrow{a} \sigma \quad and \quad r \xrightarrow{a} \rho$$

The composition of two processes $\mathcal{P} = \langle \langle S, \longrightarrow \rangle, \sigma_0 \rangle$ and $\mathcal{Q} = \langle \langle R, \longrightarrow \rangle, \rho_0 \rangle$, denoted $\mathcal{P}\|\mathcal{Q}$, is the process $\langle \langle S, \longrightarrow \rangle \| \langle R, \longrightarrow \rangle, \sigma_0 \times \rho_0 \rangle$.

Following Wang and Larsen [5], we define tests as finite trees with a certain subset of the terminal states being "accepting states."

Definition 3. *A (probabilistic) test is a tuple $\langle \langle \langle T, \longrightarrow \rangle, \tau_0 \rangle, F \rangle$ in which the process $\langle \langle T, \longrightarrow \rangle, \tau_0 \rangle$ is a finite tree, and $F \subseteq T$ is a set of success states, each of which is terminal.*

A test $\mathcal{T}$ is applied to a process $\mathcal{P}$ by putting the process $\mathcal{P}$ in parallel with the test $\mathcal{T}$ and measuring the likelihood of reaching a success state.

We define a testing system as the parallel composition of a process and a test.

Definition 4. *Let $\mathcal{P} = \langle \langle S, \longrightarrow \rangle, \sigma_0 \rangle$ be a process and $\mathcal{T} = \langle \langle \langle T, \longrightarrow \rangle, \tau_0 \rangle, F \rangle$ be a test. The composition of $\mathcal{P}$ and $\mathcal{T}$, denoted $\mathcal{P}\|\mathcal{T}$, is called a testing system, defined as the process $\langle \langle S, \longrightarrow \rangle, \sigma_0 \rangle \| \langle \langle T, \longrightarrow \rangle, \tau_0 \rangle$ with success states $S \times F$.*

Our intention is that a testing system defines a probability of reaching a success state. However, since from each state there may be several outgoing transitions, such a probability is not uniquely defined. We will be interested in the maximal probabilities of success. These can be defined inductively on the structure of the testing system.

Definition 5. *Let $\mathcal{P}\|\mathcal{T}$ be a testing system, with a process $\mathcal{P} = \langle \langle S, \longrightarrow \rangle, \sigma_0 \rangle$ and test $\mathcal{T} = \langle \langle \langle T, \longrightarrow \rangle, \tau_0 \rangle, F \rangle$. For each state $s\|t$ of $\mathcal{P}\|\mathcal{T}$ we define its maximal probability of sucess, denoted $t\lceil s \rceil$ inductively by*

- *If $s\|t$ is terminal, then $t\lceil s \rceil = 1$ if t is a success state, else $t\lceil s \rceil = 0$.*
- *If $s\|t$ is not terminal, then*

$$t\lceil s \rceil = \max_{s\|t \xrightarrow{a} \sigma \times \tau} \left(\sum_{s'\|t'} (\sigma \times \tau)(s'\|t') * t'\lceil s' \rceil \right)$$

For a distribution σ on S and a distribution τ on T, we define

$$\tau\lceil\sigma\rceil = \sum_{s\|t}(\sigma \times \tau)(s\|t) * t\lceil s\rceil$$

We define $T\lceil P\rceil = \sigma_0\lceil\tau_0\rceil$.

We note that, using the definition of $\tau\lceil\sigma\rceil$, we simplify the definition of $t\lceil s\rceil$ to

$$t\lceil s\rceil = \max_{s\|t \xrightarrow{a} \sigma \times \tau} \tau\lceil\sigma\rceil$$

We now define a may-preorder of testing, which abstracts from the set of possible expected outcomes when testing a process P by a test T: *may*-testing considers the highest possible expected outcome of $P\|T$.

Definition 6. *Given two processes P and Q, define*

$$P \sqsubseteq_t Q \quad \text{iff} \quad \forall T : T\lceil P\rceil \leq T\lceil Q\rceil$$

The intention behind the definition of $\sqsubseteq_t$ is that intuitively, $P \sqsubseteq_t Q$ should mean that P refines Q with respect to "safety properties." The motivation is the following. We can regard the success states of a test as states defining when the tester has observed some "bad" or "unacceptable" behavior. A process then refines another one if it has a smaller potential for "bad behavior" with respect to any test. In the definition of $P \sqsubseteq_t Q$, this means that the maximal probability of observing bad behavior of P should not exceed the maximal probability of observing bad behavior of Q.

Example 7. Consider the following processes P and Q. The dashed arrows show the initial distribution of the processes, the straight arrows the (deterministic) transitions of the processes.

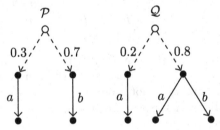

The probability that P may pass a test is always less or equal to the probability Q may pass the same test; therefore $P \sqsubseteq_t Q$. To see this, consider the sub-systems A_1, A_2, A_3:

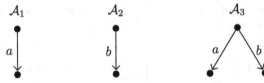

Clearly, for any test $\mathcal{T}$ it is the case that $\mathcal{T}\lceil\mathcal{A}_1\rceil \leq \mathcal{T}\lceil\mathcal{A}_3\rceil$ and $\mathcal{T}\lceil\mathcal{A}_2\rceil \leq \mathcal{T}\lceil\mathcal{A}_3\rceil$. This implies that

$$\mathcal{T}\lceil\mathcal{P}\rceil = 0.3 \cdot \mathcal{T}\lceil\mathcal{A}_1\rceil + 0.7 \cdot \mathcal{T}\lceil\mathcal{A}_2\rceil \leq 0.2 \cdot \mathcal{T}\lceil\mathcal{A}_1\rceil + 0.8 \cdot \mathcal{T}\lceil\mathcal{A}_3\rceil = \mathcal{T}\lceil\mathcal{Q}\rceil.$$

3   Characterization of Simulation by Probabilistic Testing

In the following, we restrict our attention to non-probabilistic processes, but consider the analysis of such processes with the help of probabilistic tests. We call a process $\langle\langle S, \longrightarrow\rangle, \sigma_0\rangle$ *non-probabilistic* if σ_0 is a deterministic distribution, and if, likewise, σ is deterministic for every $\langle s, a, \sigma\rangle \in \longrightarrow$. The main result of this section is the relationship between the may-preorder for non-probabilistic processes, established through execution of probabilistic tests, and the classical notion of *simulation* [4]:

Definition 8 (Simulation). *Let $\langle S, \longrightarrow\rangle$ and $\langle R, \longrightarrow\rangle$ be two non-probabilistic transition systems. A simulation relation between $\langle S, \longrightarrow\rangle$ and $\langle R, \longrightarrow\rangle$ is a binary relation $W \subseteq S \times R$ such that, whenever $(s, r) \in W$ and $s \xrightarrow{a} s'$, there is a state $r' \in R$ with $r \xrightarrow{a} r'$ and $(s', r') \in W$. We say that a process $\langle\langle S, \longrightarrow\rangle, s_0\rangle$ simulates a process $\langle\langle R, \longrightarrow\rangle, r_0\rangle$, denoted by $\langle\langle S, \longrightarrow\rangle, s_0\rangle \lhd \langle\langle R, \longrightarrow\rangle, r_0\rangle$, if there is a simulation relation W between $\langle S, \longrightarrow\rangle$ and $\langle R, \longrightarrow\rangle$ with $(s_0, r_0) \in W$.*

Lemma 9. *The relation $s \lhd r \equiv \langle\langle S, \longrightarrow\rangle, s\rangle \lhd \langle\langle R, \longrightarrow\rangle, r\rangle$ is the greatest simulation relation between the non-probabilistic transition systems $\langle S, \longrightarrow\rangle$ and $\langle R, \longrightarrow\rangle$.*

The simulation preorder is instrumental in various contexts, in particular (as discussed in the later sections of this paper) for checking the conformance of systems with behavioural specifications.

We are now able to give the main theorem of this section (and the paper), relating the may-preorder of testing with the classical simulation preorder. The result shows that the simulation preorder of non-probabilistic processes can be tested in a probabilistic setting, by considering tests possibly containing probabilistic choices.

Theorem 10 (Testability of simulation). *Suppose $\mathcal{P}, \mathcal{Q}$ are non-probabilistic processes. Then the following equivalence holds:*

$$\mathcal{P} \sqsubseteq_t \mathcal{Q} \quad \textit{iff} \quad \mathcal{P} \lhd \mathcal{Q}$$

For proving this theorem, we first need a number of intermediate results. We can first observe that every testing system gives rise to a finite set of *resolutions*, in which every state has an out-degree of at most one:

3.1   Linear Resolutions of Processes

Definition 11 (Linearity). *A finite tree $\langle\langle S, \longrightarrow\rangle, \sigma_0\rangle$ is called* linear *if $\sigma_0 = s_0$ is deterministic and every state has at most one outgoing transition:*

$$\text{for each } s \in S: \quad s \xrightarrow{a} \sigma \text{ and } s \xrightarrow{a'} \sigma' \quad \text{imply} \quad a = a' \text{ and } \sigma = \sigma'.$$

A linear resolution *of a finite tree $\mathcal{P} = \langle\langle S, \longrightarrow\rangle, \sigma_0\rangle$ is a maximum linear subtree $\langle\langle S', \longrightarrow'\rangle, \sigma_0\rangle$ of $\mathcal{P}$, i.e., a linear tree consisting of maximum subsets of states $S' \subseteq S$ and transitions $\longrightarrow' \subseteq \longrightarrow$ of $\mathcal{P}$. The set of resolutions of a tree $\mathcal{P}$ is denoted by $Res(\mathcal{P})$.*

The notion of linear resolutions naturally extends to finite *acyclic* processes, i.e., to processes in which the length of paths $s_0 \xrightarrow{a_1} s_1 \xrightarrow{a_2} \cdots \xrightarrow{a_n} s_n$ is bounded. Note that, by definition of a tree, the resolution $\langle\langle S', \longrightarrow'\rangle, \sigma_0\rangle$ is closed under transitions: $Supp(\sigma_0) \subseteq S'$ and $Supp(\sigma) \subseteq S$ for each $\langle s, a, \sigma\rangle \in \longrightarrow'$. Maximality implies that a resolution does not have more terminal states than the original tree, i.e., $s \not\longrightarrow'$ implies $s \not\longrightarrow$ for any $s \in S'$.

Intuitively, if a state of a process has two outgoing transitions $s \xrightarrow{a} \sigma$ and $s \xrightarrow{a'} \sigma'$, any linear resolution of the process will contain at most one of the transitions, and remove the other one; if s is a state that is kept in the resolution, exactly one of the transitions will be kept. In the case of a finite non-probabilistic tree, resolutions correspond to maximum paths starting in the root of the tree.

Example 12. The following diagrams illustrates a linear resolution of a finite tree $\mathcal{T}$. The resolution is drawn bold:

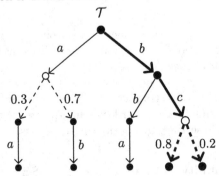

Note that probabilistic choices are kept in a resolution, so that linear resolutions do not necessarily form simple chains of transitions.

The notion of a resolution leads to a more explicit characterisation of the maximum success probability of running a test:

Lemma 13. *Let $\mathcal{P} \| \mathcal{T}$ be a testing system, composed of process $\mathcal{P} = \langle\langle S, \longrightarrow\rangle, \sigma_0\rangle$ and the test $\mathcal{T} = \langle\langle\langle T, \longrightarrow\rangle, \tau_0\rangle, F\rangle$. Then*

$$\mathcal{T}\lceil\mathcal{P}\rceil = \max_{R \in Res(\mathcal{P}\|\mathcal{T})} P(R)$$

where the success probability $P(R) = P_R(\sigma_0 \times \tau_0)$ *of a test system resolution* $R \in Res(\mathcal{P}\|\mathcal{T})$ *is recursively defined by:*

$$P_R(\sigma \times \tau) = \sum_{s\|t} (\sigma \times \tau)(s\|t) * P_R(s\|t)$$

$$P_R(s\|t) = \begin{cases} 1 & \textit{if } t \in F \textit{ is a success state} \\ 0 & \textit{if } s\|t \not\longrightarrow \textit{ is a terminal state with } t \notin F \\ P_R(\sigma \times \tau) & \textit{if } s\|t \xrightarrow{a} \sigma \times \tau \textit{ (in the resolution } R) \end{cases}$$

3.2 Necessary and Sufficient Conditions for the May-Preorder

It is unnecessary to consider the set of all tests for checking the may-preorder; rather, we can give necessary and sufficient conditions for the preorder by checking whether tests are guaranteed to succeed or not. These criteria will be helpful in proving the main Theorem 10 of the section:

Lemma 14. *For non-probabilistic processes* $\mathcal{P}, \mathcal{Q}$:

$$\mathcal{P} \sqsubseteq_t \mathcal{Q} \quad \textit{iff} \quad \forall \mathcal{T} : \left(\mathcal{T}\lceil\mathcal{P}\rceil = 1 \Longrightarrow \mathcal{T}\lceil\mathcal{Q}\rceil = 1 \right)$$

Proof. "$\Longrightarrow$" By definition, $\mathcal{P} \sqsubseteq_t \mathcal{Q}$ means $\forall \mathcal{T} : \mathcal{T}\lceil\mathcal{P}\rceil \leq \mathcal{T}\lceil\mathcal{Q}\rceil$, which implies the right-hand side of the equivalence.

"$\Longleftarrow$" Proving by contradiction, we assume $\forall \mathcal{T} : \left(\mathcal{T}\lceil\mathcal{P}\rceil = 1 \Longrightarrow \mathcal{T}\lceil\mathcal{Q}\rceil = 1 \right)$, but $\mathcal{P} \not\sqsubseteq_t \mathcal{Q}$, the latter of which implies that there is a test $\mathcal{T} = \langle\langle\langle T, \longrightarrow\rangle, \tau_0\rangle, F\rangle$ such that $\mathcal{T}\lceil\mathcal{P}\rceil > \mathcal{T}\lceil\mathcal{Q}\rceil$. According to Lemma 13, we can assume that $\mathcal{T}\lceil\mathcal{P}\rceil$ is realised by the resolution $R = \langle\langle S_R, \longrightarrow_R\rangle, \sigma_R\rangle \in Res(\mathcal{P}\|\mathcal{T})$, which means that the success probability of R is $P(R) = \mathcal{T}\lceil\mathcal{P}\rceil$.

We define a new test $\mathcal{T}' = \langle\langle\langle T', \longrightarrow'\rangle, \tau_0\rangle, F'\rangle$, in such a way that $\mathcal{T}'\lceil\mathcal{P}\rceil = 1$:

- $T' = \{t \in T \mid \exists s : s\|t \in S_R\}$ is the set of test states reachable in R;
- $\longrightarrow' = \{(t, a, \tau) \in \longrightarrow \mid \exists(s, a, \sigma) : (s\|t, a, \sigma \times \tau) \in \longrightarrow_R\}$ is the reduct of $\longrightarrow$ to transitions in R;
- $F' = \{t \in T' \mid \exists s : s\|t \not\longrightarrow_R\}$ are those test states that occur as final states in R.

To see that $\mathcal{T}'\lceil\mathcal{P}\rceil = 1$, observe that R also is a resolution of $\mathcal{P}\|\mathcal{T}'$; all terminal states of this resolution are success states.

Due to the assumption that $\forall \mathcal{T} : \left(\mathcal{T}\lceil\mathcal{P}\rceil = 1 \Longrightarrow \mathcal{T}\lceil\mathcal{Q}\rceil = 1 \right)$, this implies $\mathcal{T}'\lceil\mathcal{Q}\rceil = 1$; in other words, also $\mathcal{Q}\|\mathcal{T}'$ has a resolution R' in which all terminal states are success states. This means, in particular, that all success states of $\mathcal{T}$ reached in R are also reached in R', because otherwise R' would contain paths not leading to success. But then also the test system $\mathcal{Q}\|\mathcal{T}$ has a resolution R'' containing at least all success states reached in R, which implies $P(R'') \geq P(R)$ and contradicts the assumption $\mathcal{T}\lceil\mathcal{P}\rceil > \mathcal{T}\lceil\mathcal{Q}\rceil$. □

Similarly, it would be sufficient to consider tests with success probability 0 to characterise the may-preorder:

Lemma 15. *For non-probabilistic processes* $\mathcal{P}, \mathcal{Q}$:

$$\mathcal{P} \sqsubseteq_t \mathcal{Q} \quad \textit{iff} \quad \forall \mathcal{T} : \left(\mathcal{T}\lceil\mathcal{Q}\rceil = 0 \Longrightarrow \mathcal{T}\lceil\mathcal{P}\rceil = 0 \right)$$

3.3   The May-Preorder as Simulation

We prove the two directions of Theorem 10 separately. The more intricate proof concerns the observation that the may-preorder is a subset of the simulation preorder, which can be shown by induction over processes:

Lemma 16. *If $\mathcal{P} = \langle\langle S, \longrightarrow\rangle, s_0\rangle$ and $\mathcal{Q} = \langle\langle R, \longrightarrow\rangle, r_0\rangle$ are non-probabilistic processes, then:*

$$\mathcal{P} \sqsubseteq_t \mathcal{Q} \qquad implies \qquad \mathcal{P} \lhd \mathcal{Q}$$

Proof. We conduct a proof by contradiction, showing that $\mathcal{P} \not\lhd \mathcal{Q}$ implies $\mathcal{P} \not\sqsubseteq_t \mathcal{Q}$. Since $\lhd$ can be defined as a least fixed-point, we can prove the implication by means of induction over processes $\mathcal{P}, \mathcal{Q}$ not in simulation relation.

Assume $\mathcal{P} \not\lhd \mathcal{Q}$. Since $\lhd$ is the greatest simulation relation, this means that there is a transition $s_0 \xrightarrow{a} s'$, but for all a-transitions $r_0 \xrightarrow{a} r_1, \ldots, r_0 \xrightarrow{a} r_n$ of $\mathcal{Q}$ we have $\mathcal{P}' = \langle\langle S, \longrightarrow\rangle, s'\rangle \not\lhd \langle\langle R, \longrightarrow\rangle, r_i\rangle = \mathcal{Q}_i$ (for $i \in \{1, \ldots, n\}$). Together with the induction hypothesis and Lemma 14, this implies that there are tests $\mathcal{T}_1, \ldots, \mathcal{T}_n$ such that $\mathcal{T}_i\lceil\mathcal{P}'\rceil = 1$, but $\mathcal{T}_i\lceil\mathcal{Q}_i\rceil < 1$ for all $i \in \{1, \ldots, n\}$.

We construct a new test $\mathcal{T}$, in such a way that $\mathcal{T}\lceil\mathcal{P}\rceil = 1$, but $\mathcal{T}\lceil\mathcal{Q}\rceil < 1$. By Lemma 14, this implies $\mathcal{P} \not\sqsubseteq_t \mathcal{Q}$.

We assume $\mathcal{T}_i = \langle\langle\langle T_i, \longrightarrow_i\rangle, \tau_i\rangle, F_i\rangle$, and, without loss of generality, that the sets $(T_i)_{i=1}^n$ are pairwise disjoint. The test $\mathcal{T} = \langle\langle\langle T, \longrightarrow\rangle, t_0\rangle, F\rangle$ is defined by:

- $T = \{t_0\} \cup \bigcup_{i=1}^n T_i$, where t_0 is a fresh state not occurring in any of the sets T_i;
- $\longrightarrow = \{(t_0, a, \tau_a)\} \cup \left(\bigcup_{i=1}^n \longrightarrow_i\right)$, with τ_a being the distribution

$$\tau_a(t) = \begin{cases} \tau_i(t)/n & \text{if } t = t_i \\ 0 & \text{otherwise;} \end{cases}$$

- $F = \bigcup_{i=1}^n F_i$.

We then have $\mathcal{T}\lceil\mathcal{P}\rceil = 1$, since $\mathcal{T}_i\lceil\mathcal{P}'\rceil = 1$ for all $i \in \{1, \ldots, n\}$:

$$\mathcal{T}\lceil\mathcal{P}\rceil = t_0\lceil s_0\rceil = \max_{s_0\|t_0 \xrightarrow{b} \sigma \times \tau} \tau\lceil\sigma\rceil$$

$$\geq \tau_a\lceil s'\rceil = \sum_{i=1}^n \frac{\mathcal{T}_i\lceil s'\rceil}{n} = \sum_{i=1}^n \frac{\mathcal{T}_i\lceil\mathcal{P}'\rceil}{n} = \sum_{i=1}^n \frac{1}{n} = 1$$

Similarly, we can observe that $\mathcal{T}\lceil\mathcal{Q}\rceil < 1$:

$$\mathcal{T}\lceil\mathcal{Q}\rceil = t_0\lceil r_0\rceil = \max_{r_0\|t_0 \xrightarrow{b} \sigma \times \tau} \tau\lceil\sigma\rceil$$

$$= \max_{i\in\{1,\ldots,n\}} \tau_a\lceil r_i\rceil = \max_{i\in\{1,\ldots,n\}} \sum_{j=1}^n \frac{\tau_j\lceil r_i\rceil}{n} \overset{(*)}{<} 1$$

At $(*)$, we make use of the fact that $\tau_j\lceil r_i\rceil \leq 1$ for all $i, j \in \{1, \ldots, n\}$, but in particular $\tau_i\lceil r_i\rceil = \mathcal{T}_i\lceil\mathcal{Q}_i\rceil < 1$ for $i \in \{1, \ldots, n\}$. $\square$

The proof for the other direction of Theorem 10 proceeds by induction over tests:

Lemma 17. *If* $\mathcal{P} = \langle\langle S, \longrightarrow\rangle, s_0\rangle$ *and* $\mathcal{Q} = \langle\langle R, \longrightarrow\rangle, r_0\rangle$ *are non-probabilistic processes, then:*

$$\forall \mathcal{T} : \left(\mathcal{P} \lhd \mathcal{Q} \text{ implies } \mathcal{T}\lceil\mathcal{P}\rceil \leq \mathcal{T}\lceil\mathcal{Q}\rceil\right)$$

Proof. We prove the lemma by induction over tests $\mathcal{T} = \langle\langle\langle T, \longrightarrow\rangle, \tau_0\rangle, F\rangle$. Suppose $t_i \xrightarrow{a_i} \tau_i$ are all transitions outgoing from initial states $t_i \in \tau_0$, for $i \in \{1, \ldots, n\}$. For each $t \in T \setminus Supp(\tau_0)$, we can identify a sub-test $\mathcal{T}_t$ of $\mathcal{T}$ that has t as root.

Assuming $\mathcal{P} \lhd \mathcal{Q}$, the transitions outgoing from s_0 are $s_0 \xrightarrow{b_j} s_j$ (for $j \in \{1, \ldots, m\}$), and the transitions outgoing from r_0 are $r_0 \xrightarrow{c_l} r_l$ (for $l \in \{1, \ldots, k\}$). Due to $\mathcal{P} \lhd \mathcal{Q}$, we know that for every $j \in \{1, \ldots, m\}$ there is a $l_j \in \{1, \ldots, k\}$ such that $b_j = c_{l_j}$ and $\langle\langle S, \longrightarrow\rangle, s_j\rangle \lhd \langle\langle R, \longrightarrow\rangle, r_{l_j}\rangle$. By the induction hypothesis, it follows that $t\lceil s_j\rceil \leq t\lceil r_{l_j}\rceil$ for all $t \in T \setminus Supp(\tau_0)$. From this we can derive $\mathcal{T}\lceil\mathcal{P}\rceil \leq \mathcal{T}\lceil\mathcal{Q}\rceil$:

$$\mathcal{T}\lceil\mathcal{P}\rceil = \tau_0\lceil s_0\rceil = \sum_{t_0} \tau_0(t_0) \times t_0\lceil s_0\rceil \overset{(*)}{\leq} \sum_{t_0} \tau_0(t_0) \times t_0\lceil r_0\rceil = \mathcal{T}\lceil\mathcal{Q}\rceil$$

At $(*)$, we use the following sub-derivation, for a state $t_0 \in \tau_0$:

$$t_0\lceil s_0\rceil = \max_{s_0 \| t_0 \xrightarrow{a} \sigma \times \tau} \tau\lceil\sigma\rceil = \max_{\substack{i,j \\ t_i = t_0 \\ a_i = b_j}} \tau_i\lceil s_j\rceil = \max_{\substack{i,j \\ t_i = t_0 \\ a_i = b_j}} \sum_t \tau_i(t) * t\lceil s_j\rceil$$

$$\leq \max_{\substack{i,j \\ t_i = t_0 \\ a_i = b_j}} \sum_t \tau_i(t) * t\lceil r_{l_j}\rceil = \max_{\substack{i,j \\ t_i = t_0 \\ a_i = b_j}} \tau_i\lceil r_{l_j}\rceil \leq \max_{\substack{i,l \\ t_i = t_0 \\ a_i = c_l}} \tau_i\lceil r_l\rceil = t_0\lceil r_0\rceil$$

This concludes the proof.   □

Lemmas 16 and 17 together imply Theorem 10.

3.4   Linear Tests

Up to this point, we have considered tests as arbitrary finite trees that can, in particular, exhibit non-deterministic behaviour (transitions $t \xrightarrow{a} t_1$ and $t \xrightarrow{a} t_2$) or have states in which multiple actions are offered to the system under test (transitions $t \xrightarrow{a_1} t_1$ and $t \xrightarrow{a_2} t_2$). From the perspective of practical testing, both properties are somewhat unusual and can be difficult to implement. We show in this section that such a rich language of tests is in fact unnecessary, our main results (in particular Theorem 10) also hold if only *linear tests* (following Definition 11) are considered.

Definition 18. *Given two processes* $\mathcal{P}$ *and* $\mathcal{Q}$, *we define the* linear may-preorder *by:*

$$\mathcal{P} \sqsubseteq^l_t \mathcal{Q} \quad \text{iff} \quad \forall T : \left(T \text{ is linear} \Longrightarrow T\lceil\mathcal{P}\rceil \leq T\lceil\mathcal{Q}\rceil \right)$$

Lemma 19. *For non-probabilistic processes* $\mathcal{P}, \mathcal{Q}$, *the linear may-preorder coincides with the may-preorder:*

$$\mathcal{P} \sqsubseteq_t \mathcal{Q} \quad \text{iff} \quad \mathcal{P} \sqsubseteq^l_t \mathcal{Q}$$

Proof. "$\Longrightarrow$" Holds since every linear test is a test.

"$\Longleftarrow$" There are different ways to prove the implication; importantly, it can be observed that the proof of Lemma 16 only requires linear tests to be constructed, from which the implication follows.

We give an independent proof by contradiction as well. Assume $\mathcal{P} \sqsubseteq^l_t \mathcal{Q}$, but $\mathcal{P} \not\sqsubseteq_t \mathcal{Q}$. By Lemma 14, this means that there is a test T such that $T\lceil\mathcal{P}\rceil = 1$, but $T\lceil\mathcal{Q}\rceil < 1$. Since $T\lceil\mathcal{P}\rceil = 1$, by Lemma 13 there is a resolution $R \in Res(\mathcal{P}\|T)$ with $P(R) = 1$. In the same way as in the proof of Lemma 14, it is possible to derive a new, linear test T' from R with $T'\lceil\mathcal{P}\rceil = 1$; in fact, T' is a linear resolution of T.

From the assumption $\mathcal{P} \sqsubseteq^l_t \mathcal{Q}$, it follows that $T'\lceil\mathcal{Q}\rceil = 1$. However, $Res(\mathcal{Q}\|T') \subseteq Res(\mathcal{Q}\|T)$, which (by Lemma 13) implies $T\lceil\mathcal{Q}\rceil = 1$, contradicting the assumption $\mathcal{P} \not\sqsubseteq_t \mathcal{Q}$. $\quad\square$

Using Lemma 19 and Theorem 10, we can derive a stronger form of our main theorem:

Theorem 20 (Linear testability of simulation). *For non-probabilistic processes* $\mathcal{P}, \mathcal{Q}$, *the following equivalence holds:*

$$\mathcal{P} \sqsubseteq^l_t \mathcal{Q} \quad \text{iff} \quad \mathcal{P} \lhd \mathcal{Q}$$

4   Probabilistic Conformance Testing

Conformance testing is concerned with checking that a system (or a piece of software) behaves correctly with respect to a given specification or standard. Many well-known applications of testing, for instance the verification of partial functional properties, can be considered as a part of conformance testing. Since conformance can pertain to safety- and security-critical aspects, as well as to contractual commitments, it is of great practical importance when developing systems.

A common setup for conformance testing is that of *black-box testing,* which means that implementation details of the system under test (SUT) are not taken into account during the testing process. In this scenario, the SUT is executed for a finite (but large) set of concrete test inputs, observing the responses of the system, in order to answer (with high confidence) the question whether the SUT conforms with a given specification.

We discuss how probabilistic testing of simulation relations, developed in the last sections, can be used to formally capture this kind of testing. There are typically a number of sources of non-determinism that have to be considered:

- the SUT might appear to behave non-deterministically, due to internal mechanisms (like a scheduler) that are not visible to the environment;
- the specification can be non-deterministic, in order to describe a whole set of scenarios of system execution, and in order to allow some degree of freedom in the behavior of the SUT;
- the set of considered concrete tests can be generated randomly, according to some chosen distributions, and depending on the responses given by the SUT.

Example 21. We consider the following, simplistic model Q_1 of a server communicating with its environment using the messages *Msg* (sent to the server) and *Ack* (sent by the server). We adopt a discrete model of time and assume the presence of a further action *Tick*, expressing that one unit of time has passed. In the initial state Q_1, the server is expected to remain silent until it has received *Msg*; then, after at most two *Tick*s, the server is supposed to respond with an *Ack*, returning to the state Q_1:

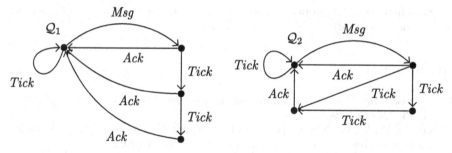

As a specification of an actual implementation P of such a server, it could be required that P *simulates* the model Q_1, i.e., $P \lhd Q_1$. Note that this kind of specification is able to capture very intricate behavioral properties related to the branching structure of a system. For instance, the model Q_2 mostly coincides with Q_1, but is stronger since it requires the server to decide about the delay before sending *Ack* at an earlier point ($Q_2 \lhd Q_1$, but $Q_1 \not\lhd Q_2$). Also, note that we disregard probabilistic aspects both of the implementation and the specification; while either might behave non-deterministically, we do not specify or check the distribution of behavior. □

4.1 Random Testing of Simulation Relations

A methodology for testing whether a SUT simulates a process (given as specification) can be as follows:

1. A number of linear, non-probabilistic tests is generated, and for each of the tests it is checked whether the SUT P passes the test (considering

the unique terminal state of the test as success state). This yields a multiset $O \subseteq Act^* \times \mathbb{B}$, recording both the sequences of input/output actions, and the test outcomes. The number of tests in O with positive outcome determines the overall success rate s_P of the SUT.

2. The set O is summarized as a single linear test T, using the distribution of tests in O to synthesize probabilities.

3. The measured success rate s_P is compared with the maximum success probability $T\lceil Q \rceil$ predicted by the specification. Since s_P can be considered as a lower bound of the precise maximum success probability $T\lceil P \rceil$ (for a sufficiently large number of tests), a result $s_P > T\lceil Q \rceil$ is an indication for $T\lceil P \rceil > T\lceil Q \rceil$, and by Theorem 10 for $P \not\lesssim Q$.

5   Conclusions

We have shown that the simulation relation between non-probabilistic processes can be characterised through probabilistic testing, and outlined how this result might be useful for the purpose of conformance testing on non-deterministic processes. It is planned to study this latter application on more detail, and evaluate how tools for property-based random testing can be used to implement the conformance testing approach in practice.

References

1. Abramsky, S.: Observation equivalence as a testing equivalence. Theor. Comput. Sci. **53**, 225–241 (1987)
2. Jonsson, B., Yi, W.: Testing preorders for probabilistic processes can be characterized by simulations. Theor. Comput. Sci. **282**(1), 33–51 (2002)
3. Legay, A., Delahaye, B., Bensalem, S.: Statistical model checking: an overview. In: Barringer, H., Falcone, Y., Finkbeiner, B., Havelund, K., Lee, I., Pace, G., Roşu, G., Sokolsky, O., Tillmann, N. (eds.) RV 2010. LNCS, vol. 6418, pp. 122–135. Springer, Heidelberg (2010)
4. Milner, R.: Communication and Concurrency. Prentice-Hall Inc., Upper Saddle River (1989)
5. Yi, W., Larsen, K.G.: Testing probabilistic and nondeterministic processes. In: Proceedings of the IFIP TC6/WG6.1 Twelth International Symposium on Protocol Specification, Testing and Verification XII, pp. 47–61. North-Holland Publishing Co., Amsterdam (1992)
6. Younes, H.L.S., Simmons, R.G.: Statistical probabilistic model checking with a focus on time-bounded properties. Inf. Comput. **204**(9), 1368–1409 (2006)

On Time Actors

Marjan Sirjani[1]([⊠]) and Ehsan Khamespanah[1,2]

[1] School of Computer Science, Reykjavik University, Reykjavik, Iceland
marjan@ru.is
[2] School of Electrical and Computer Engineering, University of Tehran, Tehran, Iran

Abstract. Actor model is a concurrent object-based computational model in which actors are the units of concurrency and communicate via asynchronous message passing. Timed Rebeca is an actor-based modeling language which is designed for modeling and analyzing of event-based and asynchronous systems with time constraints. Timed Rebeca is equipped with analysis techniques based on the standard semantics of timed systems, and also an innovative event-based semantics that is tailored for timed actor models. The developed techniques are applied on different applications using Afra toolset, the integrated development environment of Timed Rebeca. This paper is a survey on the published work on Timed Rebeca, its semantics, supporting tools, and applications.

Keywords: Actor model · Timed Rebeca · Verification · Reduction technique · Floating time transition system

Foreword

Frank is fun and frustration! This is what I told him 13 years ago and I still can hold to it. He is full of positive energy, and he works hard, although he has a rule: it's stupid to work on a sunny day! Frank is always full of great ideas, half of those I never understood! I listened to his Hoare logic presentation three times, without much success. He is a fantastic leader. He has the reasoning mind of a logician, and the wit of a philosopher, while he can understand Java like an experienced programmer.

We started working on timed actors in 2006, and we had our first paper on Timed Rebeca at the Nordic Workshop on Programming Theory in 2007. So, ten years have passed ... but if we look at our relative age, then nothing has changed. Congratulations Frank! For your 60th birthday! Wish you yet more success and happiness for the next 60 years to come!

1 Introduction

Modeling is crucial, both in science and engineering. We build models to be able to do analysis without having to deal with the details of a system's implementation. Edward Lee [1] emphasizes on the difference between engineers and

© Springer International Publishing Switzerland 2016
E. Ábrahám et al. (Eds.): de Boer Festschrift, LNCS 9660, pp. 373–392, 2016.
DOI: 10.1007/978-3-319-30734-3_25

scientists when they build and use a model. Engineers build a model to explore the design space and construct a system based on the model; and scientists build a model of an existing system to be able to analyze it. So, engineers do their best to build the system just like the model, and scientists do their best to build the model similar to the existing system. No matter we use a model as an engineer or a scientist, we need to have a faithful model in order to perform a valid analysis and/or design exploration.

We may hear the following question, mostly in more theoretical communities: "why yet another modeling language?" This question is usually asked if you mainly focus on the expressibility of the modeling languages. But usability and fidelity are also two crucial features of a modeling language, and their importance is very well acknowledged from a more practical point of view. Models need to be able to capture the characteristics of the system which affect the properties of our interest (fidelity), and we need to be able to understand and build a model with the least possible effort (usability). For example, object-oriented approaches were introduced with the philosophy of reducing the semantic gap between the real world problems and the models representing those problems; and their success is undeniable. With the growing need for various software applications, and fast changes in hardware and network infrastructures, the answer to the above question is simple: because we are not there yet! And with "change" being the only constant in our software world, we will possibly never be there!

The non-functional properties of different nature are becoming more crucial in correctness of a software system, demanding for new models and/or extensions of existing languages. Timing features are no more just performance concerns. In many software systems, nowadays, timing features are part of correctness properties. So, the so called non-functional properties are becoming first-class characteristics of a system like the functional ones.

The modeling language Rebeca (*Reactive Objects Language*) [2,3], is an operational interpretation of the actor model [4,5] provided with formal semantics and supported by model checking tools [6]. Rebeca is designed to be a usable and analyzable modeling language to bridge the gap between software engineers and formal method community. The application domain targeted by Rebeca is where we have event-driven systems, with asynchronous message passing. In Rebeca, we have non-blocking sends, no explicit receive, no shared variables, and non-preemptive method execution.

In this paper, we will provide a brief overview on Time Rebeca [7,8], the timed extension of Rebeca which is much praised by Frank de Boer. In the following sections, we will show how Floating Time Transition System is a natural semantics for event-based actor languages based on the work of [9]. Then we will have a short survey on state-based model checking of Timed Rebeca based on [10,11]. Finally, we will conclude by showing how Timed Rebeca is used for analysis and design exploration in real world case studies which were studied in [12,13].

2   Timed Rebeca

Timed Rebeca [7,8] is an extension of Rebeca [2,3] with time features for modeling and verification of time-critical systems. These primitives are added to Rebeca to address *computation time, message delivery time, message expiration,* and *period of occurrence of events.* In a Timed Rebeca model, each actor has its own local clock. The local clocks can be considered as synchronized distributed clocks. Methods are still executed atomically like in Rebeca, however passing of time while executing a method can be modeled. In addition, instead of having a queue for the messages, there is a bag of messages where messages are stored together with their time tags. The time tag of a message represents the time that the message arrived in the bag and can be taken to be served. The model is based on discrete events and discrete time.

$$
\begin{aligned}
Model ::= &\quad Class^*\ Main \\
Main ::= &\quad \textbf{main} \ \{ \ InstanceDcl^* \ \} \\
InstanceDcl ::= &\quad className\ rebecName(\langle rebecName\rangle^*) : (\langle literal\rangle^*); \\
Class ::= &\quad \textbf{reactiveclass}\ className\ \{\ KnownRebecs\ Vars\ MsgSrv^*\ \} \\
KnownRebecs ::= &\quad \textbf{knownrebecs}\ \{\ VarDcl^*\ \} \\
Vars ::= &\quad \textbf{statevars}\ \{\ VarDcl^*\ \} \\
VarDcl ::= &\quad type\ \langle v\rangle^+; \\
MsgSrv ::= &\quad \textbf{msgsrv}\ methodName(\langle type\ v\rangle^*)\ \{\ Stmt^*\ \} \\
Stmt ::= &\quad v = e;\ |\ v =?(e, \langle e\rangle^+);\ |\ Call;\ |\ if\ (e)\ \{\ Stmt^*\ \}[else\ \{\ Stmt^*\ \}]\ | \\
&\quad \textbf{delay}(t); \\
Call ::= &\quad rebecName.methodName(\langle e\rangle^*)\ [\textbf{after}(t)]\ [\textbf{deadline}(t)]
\end{aligned}
$$

Fig. 1. Abstract syntax of Timed Rebeca (from [9]). Angled brackets $\langle...\rangle$ are used as meta parenthesis, superscript + for repetition at least once, superscript $*$ for repetition zero or more times, whereas using $\langle...\rangle$ with repetition denotes a comma separated list. Brackets [...] indicates that the text within the brackets is optional. Identifiers *className, rebecName, methodName, v, literal,* and *type* denote class name, rebec name, method name, variable, literal, and type, respectively; and *e* denotes an (arithmetic, boolean or nondetermistic choice) expression.

Two major semantics are considered for Timed Rebeca: Floating Time Transition System (FTTS) [9] which is a natural event-based semantics for actors, and Timed Transition System (TTS) which is a standard state-based semantics for timed models. In the FTTS semantics, in each state, the local time of each actor can be different from the others, i.e., the execution of actors is not synchronized over their local times. In the TTS semantics the local time of all actors is the same. Note that when we talk about synchronized local clocks we are explaining the concept of time in the model, while TTS semantics respects this synchrony, in FTTS we relax the time synchronization constraint. Comparing to TTS, FTTS can be considered as a reduced state transition system where the event-based properties are preserved. A more detailed description is in Sect. 3. The syntax of Timed Rebeca is shown in Fig. 1 and we illustrate Timed Rebeca language constructs using a simple Network on Chip (NoC) example in Fig. 2 [12,14]. NoC is a promising architecture paradigm for many-core systems. As an example of a NoC, we modeled and analyzed ASPIN (Asynchronous Scalable Packet switching Integrated Network), which is a fully asynchronous two-dimensional NoC design with XY routing algorithm [15]. In the two-dimensional NoC design, each node has four adjacent nodes and four internal buffers for storing the incoming packets (one for each direction). Using XY routing algorithm, packets are moving along X direction first, then along Y direction, to reach their destination nodes. In ASPIN, packets are transferred through channels, using four-phase handshake communication protocol. The protocol uses two signals, namely *Req* and *Ack*, to implement four-phase handshaking protocol. This way, to transfer a packet, first the sender sends a request by raising *Req* signal, and waits for an acknowledgment which is the raising of *Ack* signal by the receiver. In the third phase, data is sent. Finally, after a successful communication all of the signals return to zero.

A Timed Rebeca model consists of a number of *reactive classes*, each describing the type of a certain number of *actors* (called *rebecs* in Timed Rebeca)[1]. As shown in Fig. 2, two different reactive classes, Manager and Router, are developed in the NoC model. Manager is the traffic generator of this model and Router is the model of a node in an ASPIN design. The local state of each actor is defined by the contents of its message bag and the values of its state variables. A composite id, using X-Y position (line 12), and buffer variables which show that the buffers are enable or busy (lines 13 and 14) are state variables of a Router, defined in a statevars block. Manager does not have any state variables in this model. The communication in Timed Rebeca takes place by asynchronous message passing among actors. Each actor has a set of *known rebecs* to which it can send messages. Manager, as the traffic generator of the model, may send message to any of the nodes; so, all the routers from r00 to r33 are its known rebecs. Contrarily, a router is only allowed to communicates with its neighbors, named North, East, South, and West (line 9). The actors instantiation and binding the known rebecs of actors are in the main block (lines 22–28). In this NoC model, a mesh of 16 Routers is created and known rebecs are set based on the topology of the mesh (e.g., as shown in line 25, router r13 is the north neighbor of r10, router r20 is the east neighbor of r10, router r11 is the south neighbor of r10, and router r00 is the west neighbor of r10).

The same as other actor models, reactive classes of Timed Rebeca declare the messages to which they can respond, defining *message servers*. As shown in Fig. 2, Manager has only generateTraffic message server and Router has four different message servers, init, getAck, reqSend, and giveAck (lines 17–20). The definition of a message server is the same as the definition of class methods

---

[1] In this paper we use rebec and actor interchangeably.

of Java except that it starts with msgsrv keyword and it does not have return value. To develop the Timed Rebeca model of ASPIN, four phase handshaking protocol is modeled using three message servers: reqSend, giveAck, and getAck. A router calls its reqSend message server to route a packet to its neighbors. A part of reqSend and giveAck message servers is shown in Fig. 3.

```
1 reactiveclass Manager {
2   knownrebecs {
3     Router r00, r10, ..., r33;
4   }
5   msgsrv generateTraffic() { ... }
6 }
7 reactiveclass Router {
8   knownrebecs {
9     Router North, East, South, West;
10  }
11  statevars {
12    byte Xid, Yid;
13    byte[4] bufNum;
14    boolean[4] full, enable, outMutex;
15  }
16  Router(byte X, byte Y) { ... }
17  msgsrv init() { ... }
18  msgsrv getAck() { ... }
19  msgsrv reqSend(byte Xtarget, byte Ytarget) { ... }
20  msgsrv giveAck(byte Xtarget, byte Ytarget) { ... }
21 }
22 main {
23   Manager m(r00,r10, ... ,r33): ();
24   Router r00(r03,r10,r01,r30): (0,0);
25   Router r10(r13,r20,r11,r00): (1,0);
26   ...
27   Router r33(r32,r03,r30,r23): (3,3);
28 }
```

Fig. 2. The Timed Rebeca model of ASPIN Network on Chip

As shown in Fig. 3, an actor can change its state variables through assignment statements (lines 6 and 7), make decisions through conditional statements (line 2), and communicate with other actor by sending messages (line 5). Recurrent and periodic behavior can be modeled by actors sending messages to themselves (line 9). Timed Rebeca adds three primitives to Rebeca to address timing issues: *delay, deadline* and *after*. A *delay* statement models the passing of time of an actor during the execution of a message server (line 12). Note that all other statements are assumed to execute instantaneously. The keywords *after* and *deadline* can be used in conjunction with a method call. The term **after** *n* indicates that it takes *n* units of time for the message to be delivered to its receiver (line 5). The ordering of messages in a message bag is based on the delivery times of messages. Each actor takes the first message from its message bag (the message with the earliest time tag), executes the corresponding message server, and then takes the next message (or waits for the next message to arrive), and so on. Messages are executed in a non-preemptive way (atomically). The term deadline n is used to show that if its related message is not taken in n units of time, it will be purged from the receiver's message bag automatically (line 21).

```
1 msgsrv reqSend(byte Xtarget, byte Ytarget) {
2   if(Xtarget > Xid) {
3     byte leavingDirection = ...;
4     if(outMutex[leavingDirection]) {
5       East.giveAck(Xtarget, Ytarget) after(50);
6       outMutex[leavingDirection] = false;
7       enable[leavingDirection] = false;
8     } else
9       self.reqSend(Xtarget, Ytarget) after(100);
10  } else if(Xtarget < Xid) { ... }
11  ...
12  delay(50);
13 }
14
15 msgsrv giveAck(byte Xtarget, byte Ytarget) {
16   if(Xtarget == Xid && Ytarget == Yid) {
17     //Consume the packet
18   } else if(!(Xtarget == Xid && Ytarget == Yid)) {
19     byte enteranceDirection = ...;
20     bufNum[enteranceDirection]++;
21     ((Router)sender).getAck() deadline (50);
22     self.reqSend(Xtarget, Ytarget) after(100);
23   }
24 }
```

Fig. 3. The body of two message servers of ASPIN model

The XY-routing algorithm is implemented inside reqSend (lines 1–13). lines 2 to 9 shows that how a packet is routed to its east neighbor. If the packet must be sent to the router's east neighbor (line 3) and its east outgoing buffer is free (line 4), message giveAck is sent to the east neighbor and the internal state of the sender router is changed to the condition after sending a message. Upon processing giveAck, first the destination address of the newly received packet is checked and the packet is consumed if its target address is set to that node. Otherwise, the packet is stored in the buffer of the receiver (line 20), acknowledgment is sent to the sender router by sending getAck message (line 21), and message reqSend is sent to itself to route the newly received packet toward its destination (line 22).

3 Event-Based Semantics: Floating Time Transition System

FTTS is defined in [16] as the natural semantics of Timed Rebeca. FTTS exploits the key features of actor models to generate very compact state transition systems. Having single threaded actors, with no shared variables, and no blocking send or receive, along with non-preemptive execution of each message server, ensures that the execution of a message server does not interfere with the execution of message servers of other actors. Therefore, all the statements of a given message server of an actor can be executed in isolation (even delay statements) during a single transition without considering the behavior of the other actors. This way, after performing a transition from one state to another state, different actors may be in different local times. The way the states of FTTS are generated handles the differences between the local times of actors. Such a semantics is reasonable when one is only interested in the order of the events of a model. FTTS may not be appropriate for reasoning about the synchronized global states of an actor model [9].

The operational semantics of a Timed Rebeca model $\mathcal{M}$ with the set of actors $\mathcal{I}$ is defined as Floating Time Transition System $FTTS = (S, s_0, Act, \hookrightarrow)$ where S is the set of states, s_0 is the initial state, Act is the set of actions, and $\hookrightarrow$ is the transition relation, as described below (from [17]).

States. A state $s \in S$ of the Timed Rebeca model $\mathcal{M}$ consists of the local states of actors plus their current time. The local state of an actor i in (the global) state s is the pair of the valuation of its state variables (shown by $V_{s,i}$) and the bag of its received messages (shown by $B_{s,i}$). The local time of the actor i is denoted as $now_{s,i}$. So, the state $s \in S$ is defined as $s = \prod_{i \in \mathcal{I}} (V_{s,i}, B_{s,i}, now_{s,i})$.

Initial State. In the initial state s_0 of the Timed Rebeca model $\mathcal{M}$, the state variables of the actors are set to their initial values (according to their types), the `initial` message is put in the bag of actors (their arrival times are set to zero), and the current times of all the actors are set to zero.

Actions. There is only one kind of action in FTTS, which is taking a message from the message bag and executing the corresponding message server entirely. The message $tmsg$ is denoted by a tuple $((sid, rid, mid), ar, dl)$ where sid is the id of its sender actor, rid is the id of the receiver actor, mid is the id of its corresponding message server, ar is its arrival time, and dl is its deadline. This way, the set of actions, Act, is defined as $Act = \bigcup_{i \in \mathcal{I}} ((\mathcal{I} \times \{i\} \times \mathcal{M}_i) \times \mathbb{N} \times \mathbb{N})$ where $\mathcal{M}_i$ is the set of message servers of actor i.

Transition Relations. We first define the notion of *release time* of a message. An actor a_i in a state $s \in S$ has a number of timed messages in its bag. The release time of the message $tmsg = ((sid, rid, mid), ar, dl) \in B_{s,i}$ is defined as $rt_{tmsg} = \max(now_{s,i}, ar)$ (Note that $ar < now_{s,i}$ means that $tmsg$ has arrived at some time when a_i has been busy executing another message server. Hence, $tmsg$ is ready to be processed at $now_{s,i}$). Consequently, the set of enabled messages of actor a_i in state s is $E_{s,i} = \{tmsg \in B_{s,i} \mid \forall tmsg' \in B_{s,i} \cdot rt_{tmsg} \leq rt_{tmsg'}\}$ which are the messages with the minimal release time. For a set of enabled messages $E_{s,i}$, enabling time $ET_{s,i}$ is defined as the release time of members of $E_{s,i}$.

Now we define the transition relation $\hookrightarrow \subset S \times Act \times S$ such that for every pair of states $s, t \in S$, we have $(s, tmsg, t) \in \hookrightarrow$ for every $tmsg \in E_{s,i} \wedge (\forall j \in \mathcal{I} \cdot ET_{s,i} \leq ET_{s,j})$. All the transitions of FTTS are called taking-event transitions and as a result of a taking-event transition labeled with $tmsg$, $tmsg$ is extracted from the bag of a_i, the local time of a_i is set to $ET_{s,i}$, and all the statements in the message server corresponding to $tmsg$ are executed sequentially. Here, a_i is called *enabled actor*. The effect of executing non-delay statements is changing the state variables of a_i and sending some messages to a_i or other actors. The effect of executing a delay statement with parameter $d \in \mathbb{N}$ is increasing the local time of a_i by d units of time.

```
1  reactiveclass Ping(3) {        12  reactiveclass Pong(3) {
2    knownrebecs { Pong po; }      13    knownrebecs { Ping pi; }
3    Ping() {                      14    msgsrv pong() {
4      self.ping();                15      pi.ping() after (1);
5    }                             16      delay(1);
6    msgsrv ping() {               17    }
7      po.pong() after(1);         18  }
8      delay(2);                   19  main {
9    }                             20    Ping ping(pong):();
10 }                               21    Pong pong(ping):();
11                                 22  }
```

Fig. 4. The Timed Rebeca model of ping pong example

To illustrate how FTTS is created for a Timed Rebeca model, we prepared a very simple model in Fig. 4, the *ping pong* example. In this example, there are two actors, Ping and Pong, which send messages to each other periodically. Without loss of generality, we assumed that the actors of this model do not have state variables. Figure 5 shows the beginning part of the FTTS of the ping pong example. The first enabled actor of the model is Ping (its constructor puts message ping in its bag, line 4), so the first executed message is ping. As shown in the detailed contents of the second state (the gray block), execution of the message ping, actor Ping is at time 2 (because of executing the delay statement in line 8); however, actor Pong is at time 0 as it does not execute any messages. Also, message pong is put in the bag of actor Pong which its release time is 1 (because of the value of after in line 7). The deadline of this message is ∞ as no specific value is set as the deadline of this message in line 7.

There is no explicit reset operator for the time in Timed Rebeca; so, progress of time results in an infinite number of states in FTTS. However, Timed Rebeca models are models of reactive systems which generally show periodic or recurrent behaviors. It means that, if the absolute time of the states are ignored, usually finite number of untimed traces are generated for Timed Rebeca models.

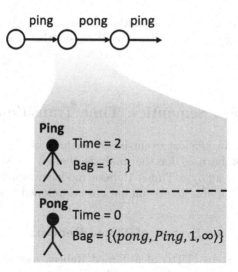

Fig. 5. The beginning part of the FTTS of ping pong example

Based on this fact, in [9] we presented a new notion for equivalence relation between two states to make FTTS finite, called *shift equivalence relation*. In the shift equivalence relation two states are equivalent if and only if they are the same except for the value of parts which are related to the time (i.e. the local times of actors, the arrival times of messages, and the deadlines of messages) and shifting the value of parts which are related to the time in one state makes it the same as the other one. This way, instead of preserving absolute value of time, only the relative difference of timing parts of states are preserved. As discussed in [9], for most systems of interest, shift equivalence relation succeeds to make their transition systems finite.

In FTTS, we have to make sure that the models are Zeno-free because a timed system with Zeno behavior does not exist in the real-world. As the model of time in Timed Rebeca is discrete, the execution of an infinite number of message servers in zero time is the only scenario resulting in Zeno behavior. So, the Zeno behavior happens if and only if there is a cycle of message server invocations among different actors without progress of time. This can be detected by static analysis of the Timed Rebeca model.

FTTS can be used for reasoning about event-based properties, i.e., the relations among actions of systems and the time where they are triggered (messages are taken from bags). The most expressive action-based logic which can be evaluated using FTTS is defined in [17]. As proved in [17], FTTS can be used for verification of properties in a form of the modal μ-calculus with weak modalities (a superset of event-based LTL properties). The weak modal μ-calculus has the same syntax as the modal μ-calculus, where we assume that the diamond ($\langle a \rangle \varphi$) and box ($[a]\varphi$) modalities are restricted to observable transitions, i.e., action a must be a taking-event transition. The semantics of this logic is identical to that of the μ-calculus, except for the semantics of the diamond and box operators — a state s satisfies $\langle a \rangle \varphi$ if there is an execution starting from state s to t, such that a is the only visible action, and t satisfies (inductively) φ. The semantics of box is defined dually.

4   The Standard Semantics: Time Transition System

FTTS can be used for efficient event-based analysis of Timed Rebeca models; however, it can not be used for the analysis against timed state-based properties. To be able to analyze Timed Rebeca models against timed state-based properties, a few mappings and techniques are developed based on TTS.

4.1   Time Transition System of Timed Rebeca

Time Transition System (TTS) of a Timed Rebeca model $\mathcal{M}$ is defined as a tuple $TTS = (S, s_0, Act, \rightarrow)$ where S is the set of states, s_0 is the initial state, Act is the set of actions, and $\rightarrow$ is the transition relation as described below (from [17]).

States. A state $s \in S$ of the Timed Rebeca model $\mathcal{M}$ consists of the local states of the actors, together with the current time of the state. The local state of actor a_i in (the global) state s is defined as the tuple $(V_{s,i}, B_{s,i}, pc_{s,i}, res_{s,i})$, where $V_{s,i}$ and $B_{s,i}$ are defined as the valuation of state variables and the bag of messages respectively (the same as in FTTS), $pc_{s,i} \in \{null\} \cup (\mathcal{M}_i \times \mathbb{N})$ is the program counter, and $res_{s,i} \in \mathbb{N}_0$ is the resuming time for actor a_i which executes a `delay` in s. The program counter tracks the execution of the current message server and is *null* if actor i is idle in s. So, state $s \in S$ can be defined as $\left(\prod_{i \in \mathcal{I}} (V_{s,i}, B_{s,i}, pc_{s,i}, res_{s,i}), now_s \right)$ where $now_s \in \mathbb{N}$ is the global current time of s.

Initial State. s_0 is the initial state of the Timed Rebeca model $\mathcal{M}$ where the state variables of the actors are set to their initial values (according to their types), the `initial` message is put in the bag of all actors having such a message server, the program counters of all actors are set to *null*, and the time of the state is set to zero.

Actions. There are three possible types of actions: taking a message $tmsg = ((sid, rid, mid), ar, dl)$, executing a statement by an actor (which we consider as an internal transition τ), and progress of $n \in \mathbb{N}$ units of time. Hence, the set of actions is $Act = \bigcup_{i \in \mathcal{I}} ((\mathcal{I} \times i \times \mathcal{M}_i) \times \mathbb{N} \times \mathbb{N}) \cup \{\tau\} \cup \mathbb{N}$.

Transition Relations. Before defining the transition relation, we introduce the notation $E_{s,i}$ which denotes the set of *enabled messages* of actor a_i in state s which contains the messages whose arrival time is less than or equal to now_s. The transition relation $\rightarrow \subset S \times Act \times S$ is defined such that $(s, act, t) \in \rightarrow$ if and only if one of the following conditions holds.

1. **(Taking a message for execution).** In state s, there exists actor a_i such that $pc_{s,i} = null$ and there exists $tmsg \in E_{s,i}$. Here, we have a transition of the form $s \xrightarrow{tmsg} t$. This transition results in extracting $tmsg$ from the message bag of r_i, setting $pc_{t,i}$ to the first statement of the message server corresponding to $tmsg$, and setting $res_{t,i}$ to now_t (which is the same as now_s). Note that $V_{t,i}$ remains the same as $V_{s,i}$. These transitions are called *taking-event transitions* and a_i is called *enabled actor*.

2. **(Internal action).** In state s, there exist a_i such that $pc_{s,i} \neq null$ and $res_{s,i} = now_s$. The statement of message server of a_i specified by $pc_{s,i}$ is executed and one of the following cases occurs based on the type of the statement. Here, we have a transition of the form $s \xrightarrow{\tau} t$.

   (a) Non-delay statements: the execution of such a statement may change the value of a state variable of actor a_i or send a message to another actor. Here, $pc_{t,i}$ is set to the next statement (or $null$ if there is no more statements). All other elements of t are the same as those of s.

   (b) The statement is a non-deterministic assignment: the execution of a non-deterministic assignment $a =?(e_1, ..., e_n)$ results in n different transitions from s to states $s_{v_1}, s_{v_2}, ..., s_{v_n}$, where $a = e_i$ in state s_{v_i}. The action is τ, and the execution of τ results in s_{v_i} $(1 \leq i \leq n)$.

   (c) Delay statement with parameter $d \in \mathbb{N}$: the execution of a delay statement sets $res_{t,i}$ to $now_s + d$. All other elements of the state remain unchanged. Particularly, $pc_{t,i} = pc_{s,i}$ because the execution of delay statement is not yet complete. The value of the program counter will be set to the next statement after completing the execution of delay (as will be shown in the third case).

   These transitions are called *internal transitions*.

3. **(Progress of time).** If in state s none of the conditions in cases 1 and 2 hold, meaning that $\nexists a_i \cdot ((pc_{s,i} = null \wedge E_{s,i} \neq \emptyset) \vee (pc_{s,i} \neq null \wedge res_{s,i} = now_s))$, the only possible transition is progress of time. In this case, now_t is set to $now_s + d$ where $d \in \mathbb{N}$ is the minimum value which makes one of the aforementioned conditions become true. The transition is of the form $s \xrightarrow{d} t$. For any actor a_i, if $pc_{s,i} \neq null$ and $res_{s,i} = now_t$ (the current value of $pc_{s,i}$ points to a delay statement), $pc_{t,i}$ is set to the next statement (or to $null$ if there are no more statements). These transitions are called *time transitions*. Note that when such a transition exists, there is no other outgoing transition from s.

We reuse ping pong example of Fig. 4 to illustrate how TTS is generated and be able to compare the FTTS and the TTS of this example. Figure 6 presents the beginning part of the TTS of the ping pong example. In this figure, the details of the fourth state is shown. As only one timed transition is in the path to the fourth state, the global time of the state is 1. Also, the execution of both Ping and Pong actors are suspended by delay statements until reaching time 2 (based on the value of the program counters and the resuming times). Executing the first statement of pong message server, a message is scheduled for Ping actor (line 15), shown as the only content of the bag of Ping.

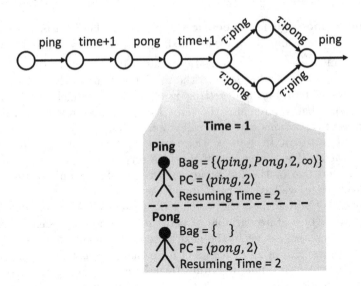

Fig. 6. The beginning part of the TTS of ping pong example

Based on TTS semantics, different mappings to existing languages and tools are created for Timed Rebeca. Recently a dedicated efficient tool is developed for TCTL model checking of Timed Rebeca.

4.2   Mapping Timed Rebeca to Timed Automata

We developed a mapping technique from Timed Rebeca models into timed automata [9,18] for generating the TTS of Timed Rebeca models and supporting state-based model checking. Timed automata [19] model is one of the most widely used modeling languages for modeling of realtime systems. UPPAAL toolset supports TCTL model checking of timed automata. In the proposed mapping, each actor is mapped into two timed automata, called *actor-behavior* automaton and *actor-bag* automaton. Additionally, one time automaton is defined to handle the behavior of *after* primitive for all actors, called *after-handler* automaton.

The actor-behavior automaton models the behavior of an actor according to the statements of its message servers and valuations of state variables. The state variables of each actor are mapped into variables of its corresponding actor-behavior automaton. The actor-behavior automaton, after receiving a message, moves to a state which represents the beginning of the corresponding message server. To model the behavior of a message server, its statements are mapped to the transitions of timed automata. The details of this mapping are presented in [9]. The actor-bag automaton handles the behavior of the message bag of each actor using an internal buffer called *messageQ*. The actor-bag accepts messages which are sent to its corresponding actor asynchronously, regardless of the state of the corresponding actor-behavior automaton. Then, actor-bag automaton delivers received messages upon the requests of its corresponding actor-behavior automaton. The after-handler automaton handles the messages which should be delivered to the actor-bag automata in the future (messages which are sent by the *after* primitive). The after-handler automaton accepts messages and put them into its buffer until the release time of the messages. When a message in the buffer of after-handler is released, it is sent to its corresponding actor-bag automaton.

The parallel composition of the resulting timed automata and the schedulability analysis of the model is done using UPPAAL [20]. Modeling of asynchronous message passing between actors using synchronous communication of timed automata increases the number of states dramatically [21]. We can apply some techniques, like using *committed states* and techniques that are presented in [22–24], to reduce the number of states of the resulting region transition system. However, as shown in [9], the technique stays inefficient for modeling asynchronous communication.

4.3   Mapping Timed Rebeca to Realtime Maude

Timed Rebeca is mapped into Realtime Maude [25,26] to support timed analysis of Timed Rebeca models with dynamic actor creation. Realtime Maude is a specification formalism and analysis tool for realtime systems based on rewriting logic [27]. Realtime Maude is highly expressive and is particularly suitable for formally specifying distributed realtime systems in an object-oriented way.

In the Realtime Maude model, a multiset of actor objects and messages represents the state of a Timed Rebeca model, where each actor object represents a rebec and each message in the multiset represents a message in the set of undelivered messages of the Timed Rebeca model. Communication between actors takes place by putting a message into the multiset of undelivered messages. This message is remained in the undelivered messages until its message delivery delay ends (i.e. the parameter specified by *after* keyword). The instantaneous actions of a rebec are formalized using rewrite rules, as shown in [10].

The "standard" object-oriented tick rule [25] is used to model time advance until the next time when something must "happen". The effect of time elapse on an actor is that the remaining time for a delay statement is decreased according to the elapsed time. For messages traveling between actors, their remaining delivery delays and deadline are decreased according to the elapsed time. In both cases, if the deadline expires before the message is served, the message is purged.

Using this mapping, we analyzed several Timed Rebeca models using the bounded-TCTL model checker engine of Realtime Maude. This mapping supports dynamic actor creation in the model, which is not supported by other approaches. Realtime Maude performs *bounded* model checking and needs high expertise to work with.

4.4   Direct TCTL Model Checking of Timed Rebeca Models

To overcome the inefficiencies of using back-end model checkers, we developed a dedicated TCTL model checking toolset for Timed Rebeca models. To this end, we directly generated the TTS of Timed Rebeca models and applied a modified version of the model checking algorithm of [28] for analysis against TCTL$_{\leq,\geq}$ properties. As shown in [11], the modified version of the algorithm analyzes a TTS with V states and E transitions against property Φ in $O((V \lg V + E)|\Phi|)$ which is the best possible TCTL$_{\leq,\geq}$ model checking algorithm for dense transition systems.

In [11] we also showed that for the majority of the timed actors, the proposed algorithm cover model checking against complete TCTL properties in pseudo polynomial time. However, UPPAAL only supports model checking for a fragment of TCTL and realtime Maude supports bounded-model checking of TCTL properties.

5   Timed Rebeca in Practice

Timed Rebeca is used in several applications such as modeling and analysis of routing algorithms for Network on Chips (NOCs) [12,14], and schedulability analysis of wireless sensor and actuator network applications (specifically, real-time continuous sensing application for structural health monitoring) [29]. Our NoC example is the basis and the reference model of the work of Din *et al.* in [30] which proposes a scalable verification technique for generic NoC models.

5.1   Analyzing NoCs

As mentioned in details in Sect. 2, Network on Chip (NoC) has emerged as a promising architecture paradigm for many-core systems. Asynchronous communication has become conspicuous in NoC design to overcome problems of clock skew and clock tree distribution of fully synchronous design. Thereby Globally Asynchronous Locally Synchronous (GALS) NoC has gained attention in design of such systems. In GALS NoCs, a sent packet might be delayed by a number of disrupting packets, which creates various end-to-end latencies. Thus, for analysis of such systems it is essential to consider all possible behaviors of the systems (at least for specific scenarios) and consider the whole state spaces. Simulation techniques cannot be applied to exhaustive search. As complexity grows in NoCs, functional verification and performance prediction in the early stages of the design process are suggested as ways to reduce the fabrication cost. Formal methods have gained more attention as alternative ways for analyzing NoC designs. Timed Rebeca is used in [12] to model two-dimensional mesh GALS NoCs with a four-phase handshake communication protocol, and functional and timing behaviors, the routing algorithm and communication protocol are captured in the model. Deadlock freedom, message arrival, and end-to-end packet latency are checked and the verification results are compared and matched to the simulation results of HSPICE[2] using 32 nm technology. This work is extended in [14] for comparing different routing algorithms in GALS NoCs.

---

[2] HSPICE provides the lowest level simulation for hardware designs. All the details of transistors and wires of hardware designs are considered in HSPICE simulator.

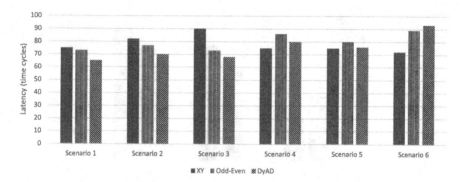

Fig. 7. Comparison among latencies of routing algorithms in six different scenarios

Comparing Routing Algorithms in NOC. In [14], Timed Rebeca models for the three following routing algorithms on GALS NoCs are developed: XY, Odd-Even, and Dynamic Adaptive Deterministic (DyAD). In XY routing algorithm, as the first step, packets move along the X direction until they reach the column of the destination. Then they move along the Y direction to reach their destinations. The Odd-Even routing algorithm works based on the Odd-Even turn model [31]; north-to-west and south-to-west turns are prohibited in routers located in an odd column, and east-to-south and east-to-north turns are prohibited in routers located in an even column. The odd-Even turn model restricts the turns in the packet path to ensure deadlock freedom. Finally, DyAD routing is a dynamic algorithm that uses a deterministic or adaptive routing based on different network congestion conditions. Each router monitors the occupation ratio of its input buffers; whenever one of the buffers passes the congestion threshold the corresponding neighboring routers are informed about the congestion. Routers priodically check their neighbors to change their routing algorithm into adaptive routing in case of congestion.

FTTS-based model checking of Timed Rebeca is used for comparing the performance of XY, Odd-Even, and DyAD algorithms. The NoC size in these comparisons is set to 4×4. The size of input buffers is set to 3 packets and congestion threshold is set to 33 %. To compare the three algorithms, six different scenarios describing different network traffics, are used. The selected scenarios are representers of widely occurring traffic patterns. As illustrated in Fig. 7 in the first three scenarios, DyAD and Odd-Even show less end-to-end packet latency as these algorithms are designed to avoid congestion. In the second three scenarios, there are disrupting packets in all possible directions. These scenarios investigate the impact of low latency of XY and Odd-Even algorithms which is the result of their simplicity in contrast to DyAD. As shown in Fig. 7, XY shows the best performance indicating that it works better in a fully chaotic situation.

Design Exploration for ASPIN Architecture on GALS NoC. ASPIN is a fully asynchronous two-dimensional mesh NoC with physically distributed

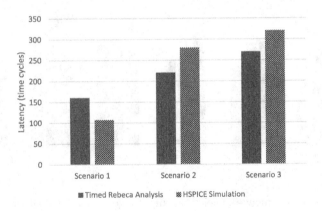

Fig. 8. Comparison among computed latencies for three different scenarios, using HSPICE simulation, and Timed Rebeca model checking

routers in each core. ASPIN uses the storage strategy of input buffering, and each input port is provided by an independent FIFO buffer. Packets arrived from different sides (from neighboring routers on four sides and the local core), are stored in the FIFO buffer of the input port. If there is more than one request for an output port, a round robin policy is used for the arbitration. ASPIN uses XY routing algorithm to route packets from output port of the source router to the input port of the destination router. Communications between routers are established using four-phase handshake protocol. The protocol uses two signals namely *Req* and *Ack*. To transfer a packet, first, the sender sends a request by rising the *Req* signal, and waits for an acknowledgment from the receiver. All signals must return to zero before the next packet could be sent.

Traditionally, simulating the ASPIN design using HSPICE is used for the analysis of these systems. HSPICE provides precise simulation results, and for that all the details of an ASPIN design must be specified prior to performing simulation. In addition, the time consumption of HSPICE simulation of ASPIN is very high. In [12], Timed Rebeca is used for modeling and Afra is used for the analysis of ASPIN designs. The comparison among the latencies which are measured using HSPICE simulation and Afra model checker is shown in Fig. 8. As shown in Fig. 8, three different packet generation scenarios (i.e., different traffics) are used in this comparison. As a result, having similar trends show that despite the fact that we captured much less details in Timed Rebeca comparing to HSPICE, Timed Rebeca analysis provides the same results in design exploration, and hence can be used for the required measurements. This comparison shows that using Timed Rebeca in the early stages of design helps designers in making suitable architectural decisions according to the desired performance of the systems.

To compare the new approaches with the simulation technique using HSPICE, the model of ASPIN for 32 nm CMOS technology was considered. Running each scenario in HSPICE for the analysis of one path took more than

24 h on a system with Core i7, 2.6 GHz processor and 24 GB of memory. In contrast running the scenarios and analyzing all the paths using the new approaches took less than 5 s.

5.2 Analyzing WSAN Applications

Distributed Wireless Sensor and Actuator Networks (WSANs) have become an attractive method of providing low-cost continuous monitoring in different applications. However, because of the complexity of concurrent and distributed programming, networking, and real-time and embedded requirements, building WSAN applications can be particularly challenging. In WSAN applications, coordination among distributed sensors must be well configured to achieve the optimum point which satisfies several constraints, including low power constraints, realtime deadlines of physical processes, and constraints on scheduling and resource utilization. Programmers often use informal worst-case analysis and debugging to ensure schedules that satisfy these requirements. Not only can this process be tedious and error-prone, it is inherently conservative and thus likely to lead to an inefficient use of resources. Moreover, the process fails to provide any safety guarantees for the resulting configuration.

Timed Rebeca is used to model a case study involving real-time continuous data acquisition for structural health monitoring and control (SHMC) of civil infrastructure [29]. This system has been implemented on the Imote2 wireless sensor platform, and has been deployed for long-term monitoring of several highway and railroad bridges [32]. Ensuring safe execution requires modeling the interactions between the CPU, sensor and radio within each node, as well as interactions between nodes. Moreover, the application tasks are not isolated from other aspects of the system: they execute alongside tasks belonging to other applications, middleware services, and operating system components. In this application, all periodic tasks (sample acquisition, data processing, and radio packet transmission) are required to complete before the next iteration starts. The results show that a safe configuration can be found which improves resource utilization compared to the previous informal schedulability analysis used in [32]. The sampling rate of the system can be increased by 7 % without encountering safety hazards.

6   Discussion and Related Work

Different approaches have been proposed for modeling and analysis of realtime systems. Timed automata [19], realtime Maude [25], and TCCS [33] are examples of modeling formalisms for design and analysis of realtime systems. For designing Timed Rebeca we looked into all the above languages and used the same basic ideas and concepts, we also have mappings to and extensive comparisons with timed automata [18] and realtime Maude [10].

Apart from these well-known and general purpose modeling formalisms, high level modeling languages are adopted for the realtime requirements. Actor model as an example of such languages is extended with timing features to address the functional behaviors of actors and the timing constraints on patterns of actor invocations. A realtime actor model, RT-synchronizer, is proposed in [34] as an example of actor model which enforces realtime relations between events. While RT-synchronizer is an abstraction mechanism for the declarative specification of timing constraints over groups of actors, Timed Rebeca allows us to work at a lower level of abstraction. Using Timed Rebeca, a modeler can easily capture the functional features of a system, together with the timing constraints for both computation and network latencies, and analyze the model from various points of view.

Creol [35] is a concurrent object based language which is designed in parallel with Rebeca. Concurrent objects of Creol can be checked for schedulability using the approach of [35], which is developed based on the same idea presented for Timed Rebeca in [36]. ABS [37] is an extension of Creol in multiple ways. While in Creol and its descendent, ABS, the focus has been on different modeling features, for Rebeca we kept the core of the language simple and avoided adding any complexity. Our focus has been on analysis and formal verification of Rebeca and its extension. Recently, Timed Rebeca is extended to capture probabilistic behaviour, the language is presented in [38].

References

1. Ptolemaeus, C.: System Design, Modeling, and Simulation using Ptolemy II. Ptolemy.org, Berkeley (2014)
2. Sirjani, M., Movaghar, A., Shali, A., de Boer, F.S.: Modeling and verification of reactive systems using Rebeca. Fundam. Inform. **63**(4), 385–410 (2004)
3. Sirjani, M., de Boer, F.S., Movaghar-Rahimabadi, A.: Modular verification of a component-based actor language. J. UCS **11**(10), 1695–1717 (2005)
4. Hewitt, C.: Description and Theoretical Analysis (Using Schemata) of PLANNER: A Language for Proving Theorems and Manipulating Models in a Robot. MIT Artificial Intelligence Technical Report 258, Department of Computer Science, MIT, April 1972
5. Agha, G.A.: ACTORS - A Model of Concurrent Computation in Distributed Systems. MIT Press series in artificial intelligence. MIT Press, Cambridge (1990)
6. Sirjani, M., Jaghoori, M.M.: Ten years of analyzing actors: Rebeca experience. In: Agha, G., Danvy, O., Meseguer, J. (eds.) Formal Modeling: Actors, Open Systems, Biological Systems. LNCS, vol. 7000, pp. 20–56. Springer, Heidelberg (2011)
7. Reynisson, A.H., Sirjani, M., Aceto, L., Cimini, M., Jafari, A., Ingólfsdóttir, A., Sigurdarson, S.H.: Modelling and simulation of asynchronous real-time systems using timed Rebeca. Sci. Comput. Program. **89**, 41–68 (2014)
8. Aceto, L., Cimini, M., Ingólfsdóttir, A., Reynisson, A.H., Sigurdarson, S.H., Sirjani, M.: Modelling and simulation of asynchronous real-time systems using timed Rebeca. In: Mousavi, M.R., Ravara, A. (eds.) FOCLASA. EPTCS, vol. 58, pp. 1–19 (2011)
9. Khamespanah, E., Sirjani, M., Sabahi-Kaviani, Z., Khosravi, R., Izadi, M.: Timed Rebeca schedulability and deadlock freedom analysis using bounded floating time transition system. Sci. Comput. Program. **98**, 184–204 (2015)

10. Sabahi-Kaviani, Z., Khosravi, R., Sirjani, M., Ölveczky, P.C., Khamespanah, E.: Formal semantics and analysis of timed Rebeca in real-time maude. In: Artho, C., Ölveczky, P.C. (eds.) FTSCS 2013. CCIS, vol. 419, pp. 178–194. Springer, Heidelberg (2014)
11. Khamespanah, E., Khosravi, R., Sirjani, M.: Efficient TCTL model checking algorithm for timed actors. In: Boix, E.G., Haller, P., Ricci, A., Varela, C. (eds.) Proceedings of the 4th International Workshop on Programming based on Actors Agents & Decentralized Control, AGERE! 2014, Portland, OR, USA, 20 October 2014, pp. 55–66. ACM (2014)
12. Sharifi, Z., Mosaffa, M., Mohammadi, S., Sirjani, M.: Functional and performance analysis of network-on-chips using actor-based modeling and formal verification. ECEASST **66** (2013)
13. Mechitov, K.A., Khamespanah, E., Sirjani, M., Agha, G.: A model checking approach for schedulability analysis of distributed real-time sensor network applications. In: Submitted for Publication (2015)
14. Sharifi, Z., Mohammadi, S., Sirjani, M.: Comparison of NoC routing algorithms using formal methods. In: Proceedings of PDPTA 2013 (2013)
15. Sheibanyrad, A., Greiner, A., Panades, I.M.: Multisynchronous and fully asynchronous nocs for GALS architectures. IEEE Des. Test Comput. **25**(6), 572–580 (2008)
16. Khamespanah, E., Sabahi-Kaviani, Z., Khosravi, R., Sirjani, M., Izadi, M.J.: Timed-Rebeca schedulability and deadlock-freedom analysis using floating-time transition system. In: Agha, G.A., Bordini, R.H., Marron, A., Ricci, A. (eds.) AGERE!@SPLASH, pp. 23–34. ACM (2012)
17. Khamespanah, E., Sirjani, M., Viswanathan, M., Khosravi, R.: Floating time transition system: more efficient analysis of timed actors. In: Braga, C., et al. (eds.) FACS 2015. LNCS, vol. 9539, pp. 237–255. Springer, Heidelberg (2016). doi:10.1007/978-3-319-28934-2_13
18. Izadi, M.J.: An Actor Based Model for Modeling and Verification of Real-Time Systems. Master's thesis, University of Tehran, School of Electrical and Computer Engineering, Iran (2010)
19. Alur, R., Dill, D.L.: A theory of timed automata. Theoret. Comput. Sci. **126**(2), 183–235 (1994)
20. Bengtsson, J., Larsen, K.G., Larsson, F., Pettersson, P., Yi, W.: UPPAAL - A tool suite for automatic verification of real-time systems. In: Alur, Rajeev, Sontag, Eduardo D., Henzinger, Thomas A. (eds.) HS 1995. LNCS, vol. 1066, pp. 232–243. Springer, Heidelberg (1996)
21. Lamport, L.: Real-time model checking is really simple. In: Borrione, D., Paul, W. (eds.) CHARME 2005. LNCS, vol. 3725, pp. 162–175. Springer, Heidelberg (2005)
22. Bengtsson, J.E., Jonsson, B., Lilius, J., Yi, W.: Partial order reductions for timed systems. In: Sangiorgi, D., de Simone, R. (eds.) CONCUR 1998. LNCS, vol. 1466, pp. 485–500. Springer, Heidelberg (1998)
23. Minea, M.: Partial Order reduction for model checking of timed automata. In: Baeten, J.C.M., Mauw, S. (eds.) CONCUR 1999. LNCS, vol. 1664, pp. 431–446. Springer, Heidelberg (1999)
24. Håkansson, J., Pettersson, P.: Partial order reduction for verification of real-time components. In: Raskin, J.-F., Thiagarajan, P.S. (eds.) FORMATS 2007. LNCS, vol. 4763, pp. 211–226. Springer, Heidelberg (2007)
25. Ölveczky, P.C., Meseguer, J.: Semantics and pragmatics of real-time maude. High. Order Symbolic Comput. **20**(1–2), 161–196 (2007)

26. Ölveczky, P.C., Meseguer, J.: The real-time maude tool. In: Ramakrishnan, C.R., Rehof, J. (eds.) TACAS 2008. LNCS, vol. 4963, pp. 332–336. Springer, Heidelberg (2008)

27. Meseguer, J.: Conditional rewriting logic as a unified model of concurrency. Theoret. Comput. Sci. **96**(1), 73–155 (1992)

28. Laroussinie, F., Markey, N., Schnoebelen, P.: Efficient timed model checking for discrete-time systems. Theoret. Comput. Sci. **353**(1–3), 249–271 (2006)

29. Mechitov, K., Khamespanah, E., Sirjani, M., Agha, G.: Schedulability Analysis of Distributed Real-Time Sensor Network Applications using Actor-Based Model Checking. Technical Report(2015)

30. Din, C.C., Tapia Tarifa, S.L., Hähnle, R., Johnsen, E.B.: History-based specification and verification of scalable concurrent and distributed systems. In: Butler, M., et al. (eds.) ICFEM 2015. LNCS, vol. 9407, pp. 217–233. Springer, Heidelberg (2015). doi:10.1007/978-3-319-25423-4_14

31. Chiu, G.: The odd-even turn model for adaptive routing. IEEE Trans. Parallel Distrib. Syst. **11**(7), 729–738 (2000)

32. Linderman, L., Mechitov, K., Spencer, B.F.: TinyOS-based real-time wireless data acquisition framework for structural health monitoring and control. Struct. Control Health Monit. **20**, 1007–1020 (2012)

33. Yi, W.: CCS + time = an interleaving model for real time systems. In: Albert, J.L., Monien, B., Rodríguez-Artalejo, M. (eds.) Automata, Languages and Programming. LNCS, vol. 510, pp. 217–228. Springer, Heidelberg (1991)

34. Ren, S., Agha, G.: RTsynchronizer: language support for real-time specifications in distributed systems. In: Gerber, R., Marlowe, T.J. (eds.) Workshop on Languages, Compilers, & Tools for Real-Time Systems, pp. 50–59. ACM (1995)

35. de Boer, F., Chothia, T., Jaghoori, M.M.: Modular schedulability analysis of concurrent objects in creol. In: Arbab, F., Sirjani, M. (eds.) FSEN 2009. LNCS, vol. 5961, pp. 212–227. Springer, Heidelberg (2010)

36. Jaghoori, M.M., de Boer, F.S., Sirjani, M.: Task scheduling in Rebeca. In: NWPT, pp. 16–18 (2007)

37. Albert, E., de Boer, F.S., Hähnle, R., Johnsen, E.B., Schlatte, R., Tarifa, S.L.T., Wong, P.Y.H.: Formal modeling and analysis of resource management for cloud architectures: an industrial case study using Real-Time ABS. Serv. Oriented Comput. Appl. **8**(4), 323–339 (2014)

38. Jafari, A., Khamespanah, E., Sirjani, M., Hermanns, H.: Performance analysis of distributed and asynchronous systems using probabilistic timed actors. ECEASST **70** (2014)

A Small-Step Semantics of a Concurrent Calculus with Goroutines and Deferred Functions

Martin Steffen[✉]

Department of Informatics, University of Oslo, Oslo, Norway
msteffen@ifi.uio.no

Abstract. In this paper, we present a small-step operational semantics for a small concurrent language supporting *deferred* function calls and related constructs in the style of the Go programming language. For lexical scoping, the presence of higher-order functions, but also the presence of the `defer`-command, requires the notion of *closures* in the semantics.

1 Introduction

New programming languages appear all the time, most as variations and evolutions of earlier languages or with new combinations of established features. Many new designs remain obscure or establish a niche existence, some enjoy their days in the sun, some new general purpose languages even rise to prominence to stay, sometimes accompanied by considerable hype. A recent promising newcomer is Go [13,18,19,36], a language "backed" by Google, which gained quite some momentum after its inception and after going public in 2009. Syntactically, Go's bloodline, tracing back to C, is noticeable in its surface syntax as well as in *simplicity* and conciseness as advertised design principles of the language.

At its core, Go is a lexically scoped, concurrent, imperative language with higher-order functions, supporting object-oriented design. How to most profitably and elegantly combine object-orientation with concurrency is a long-standing question. See for instance [2] for an early discussion of the issue, where the essential design decision is whether objects as units of data coincide with the units of concurrency (in which case the objects are "active") or objects and threads/processes etc. are different. In, e.g., his PhD thesis, Frank de Boer [10] proposed and studied the "parallel object-oriented language" POOL, whose design is firmly in the "active objects" camp, where objects basically are processes, exchanging messages over channels. Many popular concurrent object-oriented languages follow such a design, including actor languages, agent languages etc. The alternative is multi-threading as supported perhaps most prominently by Java and related languages.

The work was partially supported by the Norwegian-German bilateral PPP project GoRETech ("Go Runtime Enforcement Techniques").

© Springer International Publishing Switzerland 2016
E. Ábrahám et al. (Eds.): de Boer Festschrift, LNCS 9660, pp. 393–406, 2016.
DOI: 10.1007/978-3-319-30734-3_26

Go seems not to fit neatly into either camp. For a start, one may debate to which extent Go is object-oriented. Since the coinage of the term "object orientation" in Simula [9], being object-oriented has become a staple attribute of most modern languages in one way or the other, but unfortunately, there is not overly much consensus on what object-orientation exactly is. Whether or not Go is object-oriented is salomonically answered by the Go language FAQ as "yes and no". In general, the consensus opinion seems to be that Go is object-oriented but not entirely as you know it, and that at least that it supports object-oriented programming and design. Officially, there's no concept named "object" in the language, and classes and class inheritance as mechanisms of code reuse are missing. However, Go supports methods, which are functions with "receiver" as specific argument on which they are dynamically dispatched. The mechanism relies on interfaces, *structural* subtyping, there called "duck typing", as opposed to more conventional nominal subtyping disciplines (cf. [31]). In this paper, we ignore Go's static type system (and thereby its object-oriented features) concentrating on some aspects of non-local control flow and goroutines. For a very recent account of Go's type system and a formal calculus formalizing aspects of Go, see [30]. That work, however, does not capture deferred function calls, on which we concentrate in this paper.

Concerning concurrency, Go's primary feature is *asynchronous* function calls (resp. asynchronous method calls). The mechanism is baptized *goroutine* by the developers of the language (basically a lightweight form of threads with low overhead and lacking known thread synchronization mechanisms such as wait and signal). The second core concurrency construct is (typed) *channel* communication, in the tradition of languages like CSP [22,23] or Occam. Since (references to) channels can be sent over channels, Go allows "mobile channel" flexibility for communication as known from the π-calculus [32].

This paper concentrates on two aspects of Go, the structural, non-local control flow with Go's specific constructs of `defer`, `panic`, and `recover` and the notion of goroutines. Deferred function calls are to be executed when the surrounding function returns, and independently of whether that return is done following unexceptional control flow or while "panicking". The command `recover` can be used to exit panicking mode and return to normal execution. For lexical scoping, the small-step semantics uses a variant of closures, so-called capsules [25,26]. For the concurrent execution of multiple goroutines, we use simple *evaluation contexts* where the global configurations have to represent the parent-child relationship between goroutines.

2   A Calculus with Deferred Functions and Goroutines

After defining the abstract syntax of the calculus, we define a small-step semantics by structural, operational rules, where in a first step we concentrate on the behavior of one single goroutine (Sect. 2.2.1). Afterwards, Sect. 2.2.2 presents the global semantics, covering the concurrent execution of goroutines.

2.1   Abstract Syntax

The abstract syntax is given in Table 1. We elide types in this treatment, which will be covered in the technical report, so variable declarations and abstractions are untyped. The code is categorized into terms t and expressions e. A term t is either a value v, where values includes the truth values, the unit value, leaving further values such as integers etc. unspecified, as they are orthogonal to our semantics. A term var $x := e$ in t represents the sequential composition of first e followed by t, where the var-construct binds the local variable x in t, i.e., the construct is also used to represent local, lexical scopes. Furthermore, sometimes we write let $x = e$ in t, if the variable x is not *written to* in t, i.e., is used in a single-assignment fashion, and additionally use sequential composition $t_1; t_2$ as abbreviation for let $x = t_1$ in t_2, if x is not mentioned free in t_2 at all, i.e., if $x \notin fv(t_2)$. Expressions include function applications and conditionals. New goroutines are created with the expression go $((\lambda x.e_1)\ v)$. Values, which are evaluated expressions, are variables and function abstractions. We use () in this calculus also to represent the absence of a value.

The constructs defer, recover, and panic are used for structured, non-local control flow: panic and return work similar to throwing and catching exceptions and deferred code is executed when the surrounding function call returns, independent from whether a goroutine is panicking or not. Their semantics is discussed in more detail in Sect. 2.2.1. The construct return v is run-time syntax (hence underlined). Go itself has a "terminating statement" return, used to hand back results from callee to caller, if any. In our calculus, reducing a function application results in a value, which then is returned without a specific construct in the user-syntax. The return is inserted by the reduction rules to demarcate the boundaries of the function call's "stack-frames". This is necessary to appropriately capture the semantics of deferred code.

Table 1. Abstract syntax

$$
\begin{array}{lll}
t ::= v \mid \mathtt{var}\, x := e\, \mathtt{in}\, t & \text{terms} & (1)\\
e ::= t \mid v\, v \mid \mathtt{if}\, v\, \mathtt{then}\, e\, \mathtt{else}\, e \mid \mathtt{go}\, t & \text{expressions} &\\
\quad \mid\, \mathtt{defer}\, ((\lambda x.t)\, v) \mid \mathtt{recover} \mid \mathtt{panic}\, v \mid \underline{\mathtt{return}\, v} &&\\
v ::= x \mid () \mid \mathtt{true} \mid \mathtt{false} \mid \lambda x.t & \text{values} &
\end{array}
$$

2.2   Operational Semantics

Next we describe the small-step operational semantics of the calculus. The language offers higher-order functions and nested, lexical scopes. Thus function bodies can outlive their surrounding scope in which they are defined. As a consequence, lexical scoping for non-local variables requires a memory discipline more complex than a *stack*-based memory allocation and de-allocation. The phenomenon that a function definition can outlive its defining scope also occurs for deferred function calls, which are executed when the surrounding function returns and not at the place where the surrounding scope (which may be nested) ends. Similarly, goroutines, which are asynchronously executed function calls, have the same effect: when defined, variables refer lexically to a particular scope, but ultimate execution occurs "outside" that scope.

To represent such features, one conventionally uses *closures*. Closures [29] were first implemented in PAL [14,15] and first widely used in Scheme [34,35]. Go indeed supports closures to enable static scoping. Generally speaking, a closure is a function, i.e., an abstraction together with providing values for the abstraction's free variables.

The semantics in this section concentrates on the local semantics of one goroutine. For simplicity we also ignore reference values, concentrating on specifying the order of reduction in the presence of deferred functions. Instead of using full closures, which would typically require the introduction of references or locations, we make use of so called *capsules* in the formulation of the rules in this presentation. Capsules [25,26] have been recently introduced as a slightly simpler variant of closures to capture static binding in the presence of higher-order functions. We omit the treatment of references in this section; obviously, they are supported by Go, though. [25,26] prove that modeling local state with capsules resp. with closures is equivalent.

A capsule environment, or environment for short, is used to model local state, here for one sequential piece of code. An environment is a partial, finite function from variables to *values*. We use $\gamma, \gamma_1, \gamma', \dots$ for environments. By $dom(\gamma)$, we refer of the domain of γ. We use $\perp$ for the undefined value. Let's write $\bullet$ for the empty capsule environment. A binding from a variable x to a value v is written $[x \mapsto v]$, and in abuse of notation, we write $\gamma[x \mapsto v]$ if the mapping γ is updated by a new binding. That includes adding a new binding, resp., changing an already existing one for x. We also use the notation $[x_0 \mapsto v_1, \dots, x_n \mapsto v_n]$ or $[\vec{x} \mapsto \vec{v}]$ when referring to a concrete capsule.

Capsules then are tuples consisting of a term t and an environment γ. We write $\gamma \vdash t$ for a capsule. As a standard invariant, it's required (and maintained by the rules) that all free variables of t are covered by the environment, i.e., $dom(\gamma) \supseteq fv(t)$. To model panicking code, we assume one specific variable p not used otherwise. Note that the environment can contain bindings to abstractions which is reminiscent to the notion of *higher-order store* [33].

2.2.1   Defer, Panic, and Recover

Besides standard control-flow structures like loops and conditionals, Go supports various commands for *non-local* control flow. We concentrate on the following three ones, **defer**, **panic**, and **recover** (and ignore constructs like **goto** and **break**). Note that, resulting from a deliberate design decision, Go does *not* support exceptions, even if the behavior of **defer**, **panic**, and **recover** obviously represent some "exceptional" control flow.

The local steps are straightforward and are given as a small-step SOS between capsules. Rule R-VAR restructures a nested var-construct. As the construct generalizes sequential composition, the rule expresses associativity of that construct. Thus it corresponds to transforming $(e_1; t_1); t_2$ into $e_1; (t_1; t_2)$. Note that the grammar insists that, e.g., in an application, both the function and the arguments are values, analogously when acquiring a lock, etc. This form of representation is known as *a-normal form* [17]. Together with the rest of the rules, which perform a case distinction on the first non-var expression in a var-construct, a deterministic left-to-right evaluation is ensured.

Rule R-RED is the basic evaluation step, replacing in the continuation term t the local variable by the value v (where $[x \leftarrow v]$ is understood as capture-avoiding substitution). The var-construct introduces a new variable with an initial value v. To allow imperative update, a fresh variable y' is used to store the value in the environment, and y is replaced by y' in the continuation of the code. In case the variable is not updated in t, i.e., in a functional, single-assignment setting, the behavior can more simply but equivalently covered by a simple substitution:

$$\gamma \vdash \texttt{let } x{:}T = v \texttt{ in } t \rightarrow \gamma \vdash t[x \leftarrow v]$$

Table 2. Transition steps

$$\gamma \vdash \texttt{var } x_2 := (\texttt{var } x_1 := e_1 \texttt{ in } t_1) \texttt{ in } t_2 \ \rightarrow \ \gamma \vdash \texttt{var } x_1 := e_1 \texttt{ in } (\texttt{var } x_2 := t_1 \texttt{ in } t_2) \quad \text{R-VAR}$$

$$\frac{y' \text{ fresh}}{\gamma \vdash \texttt{var } y := v \texttt{ in } t \rightarrow \gamma[y' \mapsto v] \vdash t[y \leftarrow y']} \quad \text{R-RED}$$

$$\gamma \vdash x := v; t \ \rightarrow \ \gamma[x \mapsto v] \vdash t \quad \text{R-ASSIGN}$$

$$\gamma \vdash \texttt{var } x := \texttt{if true then } e_1 \texttt{ else } e_2 \texttt{ in } t \rightarrow \gamma \vdash \texttt{var } x := e_1 \texttt{ in } t \quad \text{R-IF}_1$$

$$\frac{x' \text{ fresh}}{\gamma \vdash \texttt{var } y := (\lambda x.e_1)v \texttt{ in } t \rightarrow \gamma[x' \mapsto v] \vdash \texttt{var } y := (\texttt{var } x_0 := e_1[x \leftarrow x'] \texttt{ in } \underline{\texttt{return}} \, x_0) \texttt{ in } t} \quad \text{R-APP}$$

$$\gamma \vdash \texttt{defer } e_1; (\texttt{var } x_0 := e_2 \texttt{ in } (\texttt{var } y := \underline{\texttt{return}} \, d \texttt{ in } t)) \rightarrow \quad \text{R-DEFER}$$
$$\gamma \vdash \texttt{var } x_0 := e_2 \texttt{ in } (\texttt{var } y := \underline{\texttt{return}} \, e_1; d \texttt{ in } t)$$

$$\gamma \vdash \texttt{panic } (v); (\texttt{var } x_0 := e_1 \texttt{ in } (\texttt{var } y := e_2 \texttt{ in } t)) \rightarrow \quad \text{R-PANIC}$$
$$\gamma[p \mapsto v] \vdash (\texttt{var } x_0 := () \texttt{ in } (\texttt{var } y := e_2 \texttt{ in } t))$$

$$\gamma \vdash \texttt{var } x := \texttt{recover } () \texttt{ in } t \rightarrow \gamma[p \mapsto \bot] \vdash \texttt{var } x := \gamma(p) \texttt{ in } t \quad \text{R-RECOVER}$$

$$\frac{\gamma(p) = \bot \qquad y' \text{ fresh}}{\gamma \vdash \texttt{var } y := \underline{\texttt{return}} \, v \texttt{ in } t \rightarrow \gamma[y' \mapsto v] \vdash t[z' \leftarrow v]} \quad \text{R-RETURN}_1$$

$$\frac{\gamma(p) = v \neq \bot \qquad y' \text{ fresh}}{\gamma \vdash \texttt{var } y := \underline{\texttt{return}} \, v \texttt{ in } t \rightarrow \gamma[p \mapsto \bot] \vdash \texttt{panic } (v); t[y' \leftarrow ()]} \quad \text{R-RETURN}_2$$

Sometimes, we will use the function let-construct and the simplified substitution rule when possible. In contrast to R-RED, the assignment treated in R-ASSIGN does not introduce a fresh variable but simply updates the value for an already existing one. Since the assignment does not return a (non-trivial) value, we use sequential composition as syntactic sugar for simplicity for the formulation of the rules. The treatment of conditionals is standard (the rule for `false`, symmetric to $R - If_1$, is omitted).

The next rule R-APP deals with function calls. Parameter passing is done call-by-value as given in R-APP, where the environment is updated to $\gamma[x' \mapsto v]$. The body of the function is treated by an appropriate substitution $e_1[x \leftarrow x']$. Besides that, the rule introduces a scope for a new variable x_0 used to store the result of the function body before passing it back to the caller. In a situation where x_0 is not mentioned in the function body e_1, the expression var $x_0 :=$ $e_1[x \leftarrow x']$ in x_0 corresponds to an (equivalent) η-expansion of the (instantiated) function body $e_1[x \leftarrow x']$. It should be noted that the run-time syntax <u>return</u> x_0 does *not* completely correspond to Go's terminating statement `return`. In our reduction semantics, the return syntax is used to demarcate the end of the top-level stack frame for the function instance currently being executed. The variable x_0 and the η-expanded form of the post-configuration in R-APP is introduced to capture the semantics of *deferred* code (see also R-DEFER).

Deferred code, more precisely, deferred function applications, is executed "when" the function in which the code is deferred, returns. In Go, the signature of a function can specify a named return parameter. For instance, a function taking an integer argument and returning an integer in a specified parameter x carries the signature `int (x int)`. The return parameter corresponds to the var-bound variable in rule R-APP. Deferred code, which is executed at the end of the function body, can access and change this return parameter. In the reduction rules, we omitted the type information; using a named return parameter introduces that variable with the function body as scope and is covered by the rule R-APP in that e_1 (and potential deferred code therein) can access and change x_0

The defer-statement is treated in R-DEFER. Defer allows code to be executed "later", exactly at the point where the surrounding function or method returns. An analogous `defer`-command has been introduced recently in Apple's Swift-language [24] as well. Concretely, only function applications, including partial applications, can be deferred in Go, but the rule abstractly mentions just an expression e_1. Note also that while deferred functions are allowed in Go to have a non-trivial return type, the value they eventually may return plays no role. The only way the deferred code can influence the outcome of the surrounding function (besides recovering from a panic) is by side-effects, which includes changing the surrounding function's return value, making use of named return parameters.

A further subtle point about deferred code is what happens if more than one piece of code is being deferred when executing a method body. The discipline adopted is that all of the deferred code will be executed upon return in a LIFO manner. In other words, each stack frame can be thought of being equipped with an "extra stack" of deferred code. Thus, deferred code follows a stack-discipline: within the stack-frame of the surrounding function, code deferred first will be executed last.

Once deferred, the deferred code is *"guaranteed"*[1] to be executed and thus a main purpose of the code is similar to code in the finally-clause of exception handling as in languages like Java: it can be used to "clean up" data structures, to close open connections or files, even in case something unexpected happens. There are some high-level differences between finally-clauses and deferred function calls. One is that try-catch-finally lexically indicates a block of code to which the finally-clause belongs to, and once entering the try-catch-finally statement, the final clause is (almost) guaranteed to be executed independent of how the try-block is exited. In contrast, a defer-statement may be defined inside a nested block inside a function body, but its execution is delayed until the surrounding function *body* is exited, not the immediately surrounding scope. As a result, the deferred code may typically outlive its immediately surrounding scope much in the same way that nested functions in a higher-order language may outlive their scope. As a consequence, to model or implement the mechanism adequately in a language with lexical scoping, *closures* (or here capsules) are needed.

In general, the mechanism of deferred calls offers greater flexibility compared to finally-clauses as in Java, as deferring code is done at run-time whereas try-catch-finally blocks are statically given. See for instance [3] for a calculus treating exceptions or [1] for a compositional Hoare-style proof system for a Java-like object-oriented language with *exceptions* à la Java.

Example 1. The code in Listing 1.1 illustrates lexical scoping and the need of closures for deferred functions: x in the body of the deferred function refers to the definition of x with value 7. However, this x is updated in the *same scope* later, the value being actually printed in the deferred way is 8. The closure therefore treats its non-local variables "by reference".[2] The increment x++ at the end of the function body refers clearly to the var-definition in the first line of the function body and hence has nothing to do with the variable being printed.

---

[1] There's an exception to this guarantee, though. Deferred code is executed independent from whether the goroutine panics or not, but it's executed only *if* the enclosing stack frame returns. Divergence may prevent that, and another reason for failing to return is that the goroutine containing the deferred code may be terminated due to the fact that its parent goroutine terminates. See Sect. 2.2.2.

[2] In other languages, an alternative semantics for closures exists as well, where, when building the closure, the non-local variables obtain their meaning passing them "by value" instead. Of course, a by-value treatment would make it impossible for deferred code to change the return value, after the main body has been exited, for instance due to a panic. Passing by value can be achieved here by handing over the value *explicitly* as an extra formal parameter, effectively using a "λ-lifted" version of the deferred code. Indeed, λ-lifting is a transformation used to give semantics to higher-order functions under lexical scoping [27] and an alternative to closures.

Listing 1.1. Defer, static scope, and mutable "non-local" variables

```
func main () {
    var x = 0
    {    var x = 7          // local, nested scope
        defer func () {
            fmt.Println(x)   // = 8
        } ()
        x = x+1
    }
    x++
}
```

□

The built-in function **panic** can be used to cause a "panic", which roughly corresponds to throwing an exception. Besides that, panics can occur due to a number of "natural causes" such as attempts to dereference null pointers, out-of-bounds access to arrays and slices, deadlocks, and many more situations. A panic causes the standard execution of a method or function to stop and the control flow to jump directly to the end of the function body. Before returning to the caller, any code previously deferred in the function body will be executed in LIFO fashion. In R-PANIC, x_0 is the designated callee-site variable to hand over the result of the function to the caller. Since no "non-exceptional" value is being returned in an (unrecovered) panicking call, x_0 is irrelevant and set to the corresponding types initial value. Omitting the type information, written summarily as () in R-PANIC. The value of the panic is remembered in γ using the "reserved variable" p. Note that executing deferred code at the end of a panicking function can execute a second panic, which will overwrite the previous one. At each point in time there is at most one panic active. To recover from a panic means to resume the standard mode of execution and a function body having recovered returns as value of the declared type to its caller (as opposed to propagating the panic). R-RECOVER simply retrieves the value of the previously caused panic from p and unsets it.

Example 2 (Defer Stack). The function f in the code from Listing 1.2 invokes two function calls in a deferred manner. Instead of deferring $(\lambda().z := z + 1)$ (), the derivation below just uses $z := z + 1$ for simplicity.

Listing 1.2. Stacked defers

```
func f () int {   // alternative: func f () (z int)
    var z = 1
    defer func () {
        z = z+1
    } ()
    defer func () {
        z = z+2
    } ()
    return z                    // 1
}
```

At the beginning of the reduction, in (2) below, we assume that the environment γ_1 contains the definition for the function f. The function in Listing 1.2

does not make use of named return parameters (the return type is just integers), hence the deferred abstraction cannot access it. Therefore, for illustration, the derivation treats x_0 via a let-binding and handing back the value is done via substitution in step from (12) to (13). Note in passing that if the updates to z were not done inside the deferred code, but the function would simply do $z := z + 1; z := z + 2; z$, then the returned value via z would be 4, not 1.

Similarly, if f would declare z as return parameter in its signature (in which case, z could not declared again via var in the same scope), the function would return 4. In the deviation below, the step from (4) to (5) would use variable z (and var) instead of the let-bound variable x_0 as shown below.

For reference, the environments in the reductions are, where the γ_1 at the start contains already the definition for the function named f, a binding which remains unchanged:

$$\gamma_2 = \gamma_1[z' \mapsto 1]$$
$$\gamma_3 = \gamma_1[z' \mapsto 3]$$
$$\gamma_4 = \gamma_1[z' \mapsto 4]$$

$$\gamma_1 \vdash \text{var } y := \underline{f} \text{ () in } t \rightarrow \quad (2)$$
$$\gamma_1 \vdash \text{var } y := (\lambda(). \text{ var } z := 1 \text{ in } ((\text{defer } z := z + 1); ((\text{defer } z{:=}z + 2); z)))) \text{ () in } t \rightarrow \quad (3)$$
$$\gamma_1 \vdash \text{var } y := (\text{let } x_0{=}(\text{var } z := 1 \text{ in } ((\text{defer } z{:=}z + 1); ((\text{defer } z{:=}z + 2); z))) \text{ in return } x_0) \text{ in } t \rightarrow \quad (4)$$
$$\gamma_1 \vdash \text{let } x_0{=}(\text{var } z := 1 \text{ in } ((\text{defer } z{:=}z + 1); ((\text{defer } z{:=}z + 2); z))) \text{ in } (\text{let } y{=}\text{return } x_0 \text{ in } t) \rightarrow \quad (5)$$
$$\gamma_1 \vdash \text{var } z{:=}1 \text{ in } (\text{let } x_0{=}(((\text{defer } z{:=}z + 1); ((\text{defer } z{:=}z + 2); z))) \text{ in } (\text{let } y{=}\text{return } x_0 \text{ in } t)) \rightarrow \quad (6)$$
$$\gamma_2 \vdash \text{let } x_0{=}(((\text{defer } z'{:=}z' + 1); ((\text{defer } z'{:=}z' + 2); z'))) \text{ in } (\text{let } y{=}\text{return } x_0 \text{ in } t) \rightarrow \quad (7)$$
$$\gamma_2 \vdash \text{defer } z'{:=}z' + 1; (\text{let } x_0{=}((\text{defer } z'{:=}z' + 2); z')) \text{ in } (\text{let } y{=}\text{return } x_0 \text{ in } t) \rightarrow \quad (8)$$
$$\gamma_2 \vdash \text{let } x_0{=}((\text{defer } z'{:=}z' + 2); z')) \text{ in } (\text{let } y{=}\text{return } (z'{:=}z' + 1); x_0 \text{ in } t \rightarrow \quad (9)$$
$$\gamma_2 \vdash \text{defer } z'{:=}z' + 2; (\text{let } x_0{=}z' \text{ in } (\text{let } y{=}\text{return } (z'{:=}z' + 1); x_0 \text{ in } t) \rightarrow \quad (10)$$
$$\gamma_2 \vdash \text{let } x_0{=}z' \text{ in } (\text{let } y{=}\text{return } z'{:=}z' + 2; (z'{:=}z' + 1; x_0) \text{ in } t \rightarrow \quad (11)$$
$$\gamma_2 \vdash \text{let } x_0{=}1 \text{ in } (\text{let } y{=}\text{return } z'{:=}z' + 2; (z'{:=}z' + 1; x_0) \text{ in } t) \rightarrow \quad (12)$$
$$\gamma_2 \vdash \text{let } y{=}\text{return } z'{:=}z' + 2; (z'{:=}z' + 1; 1) \text{ in } t \rightarrow \quad (13)$$
$$\gamma_2 \vdash z'{:=}z' + 2; (\text{let } y{=}\text{return } z'{:=}z' + 1; 1 \text{ in } t) \rightarrow \quad (14)$$
$$\gamma_3 \vdash \text{let } y{=}\text{return } z'{:=}z' + 1; 1 \text{ in } t \rightarrow \quad (15)$$
$$\gamma_3 \vdash z'{:=}z' + 1; (\text{let } y{=}\text{return } 1 \text{ in } t) \rightarrow \quad (16)$$
$$\gamma_4 \vdash \text{let } y{=}\text{return } 1 \text{ in } t \rightarrow \quad (17)$$
$$\gamma_4 \vdash t[y \leftarrow 1]. \quad (18)$$

□

2.2.2 Goroutines and Concurrent Execution

Concurrency is built into the core of Go, where the unit of concurrency is called *goroutine*, a pun on the notion of coroutines [8]. Coroutines are already a very old concept, originally introduced as a generalization of subroutines, namely roughly as a procedure that can repeatedly yield "intermediate" results, and for non-pre-emptive multitasking. Note in passing that the first object-oriented language Simula [9,37] supported coroutines already, and a restricted form known as generators or semi-coroutines has been used in various languages. See e.g. [4] for a recent semantical account of a calculus with coroutines (using a small-step semantics as in the presentation here), and including a type and effect system. Further semantical studies and calculi treating coroutines include [6,7,12,28].

Syntactically, starting a goroutine is similar to deferring code. In both cases, a (function or method) *application* is deferred resp. started asynchronously with the command go. In both cases, while the function may have a return type and return value, it's not handed back to the caller of the deferred code[3] resp. the spawner of the new goroutine. For example, in Listing 1.2 above illustrating stacked defers, one can replace the two defer-commands by two go-commands, letting the functions run asynchronously with the parent goroutine. Since three goroutines are then running concurrently, sharing variable z, the result from f is non-deterministic, depending on the scheduling. However, when a goroutine terminates, all its children terminate, as well. For that example, it means: if the parent goroutine, executing the main function and f terminates before the two child goroutines modify the shared variable z, their update to z will not become effective.[4] It should be noted that if a goroutine is terminated due to its parent's termination, this also prevents the coroutine's already deferred code from happening: deferred code is guaranteed to happen —panicking or not— upon *return* from a call, but this form of aborting of a goroutine precludes any further returns from being executed.

For instance, the deferred function g in Listing 1.3 may or may not be executed, even if the defer-statement itself happens.

Listing 1.3. Termination and defer

```
func g () {
    defer func () {
    } ()
}

func f () {
    go func () {
        defer g()
    } ()
    return
}
func main() {
    go f()
}
```

The semantics therefore needs to account for the parent-child relationship between goroutines. We write $\langle t \rangle$ to denote a goroutine (without child goroutine),

---

[3] With the exception that deferred code can be used to change the value of return parameters declared in the function's signature.

[4] Running the example as is, where the main goroutine does not do much else than spawning two child goroutines, it is practically guaranteed that the parent (and with it the child goroutines) terminates before the children start affecting z.

where t is the term being executed, and use $\parallel$ for the parallel composition. Let G stand for a "set" of goroutines running in parallel, as given as follows.

$$G ::= \circ \mid \langle t \parallel G \rangle \tag{19}$$

As usual, parallel composition $\parallel$ is assumed commutative and associative, and we use $\circ$, representing the empty set of goroutines, as neutral element, i.e., $\langle t \parallel \circ \rangle \equiv \langle t \rangle$. We use $\equiv$ for the induced congruence. Obviously, when stipulating that $\parallel$ is associative, we mean the arrangement of elements inside $\langle t \parallel \ldots \rangle$, the parenthetic structure using the angle brackets represents the parent-child relationship between goroutines and is not associative.

To formulate the steps for configurations of the form $\gamma \vdash G$, we use *evaluation contexts* [16] (also known as reduction contexts [20]) to specify the redex inside G. Since the evaluation strategy is rather trivial —non-deterministically reducing one term of one goroutine in G— the definition of the contexts is likewise rather simple. An evaluation context is basically a syntactic entity, here G, with exactly one hole (written $[\,\cdot\,]$):

$$E ::= [\,\cdot\,] \mid \langle [\,\cdot\,] \parallel G \rangle \mid \langle t \parallel E \rangle. \tag{20}$$

Then $E[t]$ represents the context E with t taking the place of the hole. The global small-step transition relation is then given inductively by the rules of Table 3. Rule R-CONTEXT lifts a local steps to the global level, using the evaluation contexts. Evaluating the go-command spawns asynchronously a new goroutine. The parent-child relationship is captured in that the new goroutine $\langle t \rangle$ runs within the same enclosing angle brackets. Note that goroutines don't carry an identity. Such an identity could be used by the spawning goroutine to obtain back an eventual result, if any, from the asynchronously running code. Such a generalization would correspond to the notion of *futures* [5,21]. Cf. also De Boer's

Table 3. Global transition relation

$$\frac{\gamma_1 \vdash t_1 \rightarrow \gamma_2 \vdash t_2}{\gamma_1 \vdash E[t_1] \rightarrow \gamma_2 \vdash E[t_2]} \text{ R-CONTEXT}$$

$$\frac{}{\gamma \vdash E[\langle (\mathsf{go}\,(t_1);t_2) \parallel G \rangle] \rightarrow \gamma \vdash E[\langle t_2 \parallel \langle t_1 \rangle \parallel G \rangle]} \text{ R-GO}$$

$$\frac{}{\gamma \vdash E[\langle v \parallel G \rangle] \rightarrow \gamma \vdash E[\circ]} \text{ R-TERM}$$

$$\frac{G_1 \equiv G_1' \quad G_1 \equiv G_1' \quad \gamma \vdash \langle G_1 \rangle \rightarrow \gamma \vdash \langle G_2 \rangle}{\gamma \vdash \langle G_1' \rangle \rightarrow \gamma \vdash \langle G_2' \rangle} \text{ R-STRUCT}$$

paper of a proof-theoretic account of a calculus with asynchronous communication using futures [11]). Of course, the functionality of first-class futures can easily be implemented in Go using channels.

3   Conclusion, Discussion, and Future Work

We presented an operational semantics, in particular capturing concurrency and non-standard control-flow using deferred functions, as they have been introduced in the language Go. Concentrating on the mentioned features, the paper obviously left out many others that deserve study. These include references and reference types, which can be treated in a standard manner, namely by introducing references or locations allocated on a heap; their treatment is orthogonal to the aspects covered here. Other interesting data structures include arrays and slices and their iterators.

Concentrating on the run-time behavior and the operational semantics, the presentation leaves out basically all typing aspects. Go claims to be strongly typed. While being strongly typed is nearly as vague an attribute for a programming language as being "modern" or "high-level", Go certainly is light-years ahead when it comes to imposing typing restrictions with meaningful semantics guarantees, compared to its spiritual predecessor C (from which Go otherwise borrows many syntactic conventions). Rather unconventional for most mainstream object-oriented (typed) languages is to do away with *nominal* typing and nominal subtyping (not to mention to do away with classes, class types, and inheritance, ...). Based on record types (or struct types) and interfaces, Go adopts what is known as *structural* (sub-)typing, as alternative to *nominal* subtyping. Nominal subtyping was introduced already in the first object-oriented language Simula [9], and ever since has nominal subtyping been the basis for subtype polymorphism for most general mainstream, class-based object-oriented languages, including Smalltalk, Java, C^{++}and more.

Starting with POOL, a "parallel object-oriented language" [10], Frank de Boer provided semantic studies, proof theories, and verification methods for numerous language features related to object-orientation and concurrency (features like channel communication, multi-threading, objects and object creation, inheritance, futures, active objects ...). It would be interesting to make use of the proof techniques he and his colleagues developed to apply to Go with its new take on combining established language features into an interesting design. While mentioning POOL and as a personal remark: during the early stages of my own PhD, I was working in a group interested in formal methods for concurrency and object-orientation. POOL and its proof theory was one of the works we carefully scrutinized and which influenced our own work as it was one of the few solid theoretical studies on this topic available at that time. Though my concrete thesis work afterwards digressed into type theory for functional (non-concurrent) object-oriented calculi, later my interest repeatedly came back to study aspects of concurrency and object-orientation, an interest which has been sparked by work like Frank's about POOL.

Acknowledgments. I am also grateful for the thorough, insightful, and detailed feedback from the anonymous reviewers which helped improving the paper.

References

1. Ábrahám, E., de Boer, F.S., de Roever, W.-P., Steffen, M.: A deductive proof system for multithreaded Java with exceptions. Fundam. Informaticae **82**(4), 391–463 (2008). (73 pages), An extended version of the 2005 conference contribution to FSEN 2005 and a reworked and shortened version of the University of Kiel, Department of Computer Science Technical report 0303
2. America, P.: Issues in the design of a parallel object-oriented language. Formal Aspects Comput. **1**(4), 366–411 (1989)
3. Ancona, D., Lagorio, G., Zucca, E.: A core calculus for Java exceptions. SIGPLAN Not. **36**, 16–30 (2001)
4. Anton, K., Thiemann, P.: Typing coroutines. In: Page, R., Horváth, Z., Zsók, V. (eds.) TFP 2010. LNCS, vol. 6546, pp. 16–30. Springer, Heidelberg (2011)
5. Baker, H., Hewitt, C.: The incremental garbage collection of processes. ACM Sigplan Not. **12**, 55–59 (1977)
6. Belsnes, D., Østvold, B.M.: Mixing threads and coroutines, Unpublished manuscript (2005)
7. Berdine, J., O'Hearn, P., Reddy, U., Thielecke, H.: Linear continuation-passing. Higher-Order Symbolic Comput. **15**(2–3), 181–208 (2002)
8. Conway, E.M.: Design of a separable transition-diagram compiler. Commun. ACM **6**(7), 396–408 (1963)
9. Dahl, O.-J., Myhrhaug, B., Nygaard, K.: Simula 67, common base language. Technical report S-2, Norsk Regnesentral (Norwegian Computing Center), Oslo, Norway, May 1968
10. de Boer, F.S.: Reasoning about Dynamically Evolving Process Structures. A Proof Theory for the Parallel Object-Oriented Language POOL. Ph.D. thesis, Free University of Amsterdam (1991)
11. de Boer, F.S., Clarke, D., Johnsen, E.B.: A complete guide to the future. In: De Nicola, R. (ed.) ESOP 2007. LNCS, vol. 4421, pp. 316–330. Springer, Heidelberg (2007)
12. de Moura, A.L., Rodriguez, N., Ierusalimschy, R.: Coroutines in Lua. J. Univ. Comput. Sci. **10**, 910–925 (2004)
13. Donovan, A.A.A., Kernighan, B.W.: The Go Programming Language. Addison-Wesley (2015)
14. Evans Jr., A.: PAL – a language designed for teaching programming linguistics. In: Proceedings of the 1968 23rd ACM National Conference, pp. 395–403. ACM, New York (1968)
15. Evans Jr., A.: PAL: pedagogic algorithmic language: a reference manual and primer. Unpublished report, Department of Electrical Engineering, MIT (1968)
16. Felleisen, M., Friedman, D.P.: Control operators, the SECD-machine, and the λ-calculus. In: Wirsing, M. (ed.) Formal Description of Programming Concepts III, pp. 193–217. North-Holland, Amsterdam (1986)
17. Flanagan, C., Sabry, A., Duba, B.F., Felleisen, M.: The essence of compiling with continuations. In: ACM Conference on Programming Language Design and Implementation (PLDI), pp. 237–247. ACM, June 1993. In SIGPLAN Notices 28(6)
18. The Go programming language specification, August 2015. https://golang.org/ref/spec

19. Google. The Go programming language (2014). www.golang.org
20. Gordon, A.D., Hankin, P.D., Lassen, S.B.: Compilation and equivalence of imperative objects. In: Ramesh, S., Sivakumar, G. (eds.) FST TCS 1997. LNCS, vol. 1346, pp. 74–87. Springer, Heidelberg (1997). Full version available as Technical report 429, University of Cambridge Computer Laboratory, June 1997
21. Halstead Jr., R.H.: Multilisp: a language for concurrent symbolic computation. ACM Trans. Program. Lang. Syst. **7**(4), 501–538 (1985)
22. Hoare, C.A.R.: Communicating sequential processes. Commun. ACM **21**(8), 666–677 (1978)
23. Hoare, C.A.R.: Communicating Sequential Processes. Prentice-Hall, Englewood Cliffs (1985)
24. Apple Inc.: Swift. A modern programming language that is safe, fast, and interactive, October 2015. https://developer.apple.com/swift/
25. Jeannin, J.B.: Capsules and closures: a small-step approach. Electron. Notes Theor. Comput. Sci. **276**, 191–293 (2011). Proceedings of the Twenty-seventh Conference on the Mathematical Foundations of Programming Semantics (MFPS XXVII)
26. Jeannin, J.B., Kozen, D.: Computing with capsules. Technical report, Computing and Information Science, Cornell University, January 2011
27. Johnsson, T.: Lambda lifting: transforming programs to recursive equations. In: Jouannaud, J.-P. (ed.) FPCA 1985. LNCS, vol. 201, pp. 190–203. Springer, Heidelberg (1985)
28. Laird, J.: A calculus of coroutines. In: Díaz, J., Karhumäki, J., Lepistö, A., Sannella, D. (eds.) ICALP 2004. LNCS, vol. 3142, pp. 882–893. Springer, Heidelberg (2004)
29. Landin, P.J.: The mechanical evaluation of expressions. Comput. J. **6**(4), 308–320 (1964)
30. Liu, H., Qiu, Z.: Go model and object oriented programming. In: Pardo, A., et al. (eds.) SBLP 2015. LNCS, vol. 9325, pp. 59–74. Springer, Heidelberg (2015). doi:10. 1007/978-3-319-24012-1_5
31. Malayeri, D., Aldrich, J.: Integrating nominal and structural subtyping. In: Vitek, J. (ed.) ECOOP 2008. LNCS, vol. 5142, pp. 260–285. Springer, Heidelberg (2008)
32. Milner, R., Parrow, J., Walker, D.: A calculus of mobile processes, part I/II. Inf. Comput. **100**, 1–77 (1992)
33. Reus, B., Streicher, T.: About hoare logics for higher-order store. In: Caires, L., Italiano, G.F., Monteiro, L., Palamidessi, C., Yung, M. (eds.) ICALP 2005. LNCS, vol. 3580, pp. 1337–1348. Springer, Heidelberg (2005)
34. Steele, G.L., Sussman, G.J., Scheme: an interpreter for the extended lambda calculus. AI Memo 349, MIT Artificial Intelligence Laboratory (1975)
35. Steele, G.L., Sussman, G.J., Scheme: an interpreter for the extended lambda calculus. High.-Order Symbolic Computat. **11**, 405–439 (1998)
36. Summerfield, M.: Programming in Go. Addison-Wesley, Upper Saddle River (2012)
37. Wang, A., Dahl, O.-J.: Coroutine sequencing in a block structured environment. BIT Numer. Meth. **11**(4), 425–449 (1971)

Quicksort Revisited

Verifying Alternative Versions of Quicksort

Razvan Certezeanu[1], Sophia Drossopoulou[1], Benjamin Egelund-Muller[1],
K. Rustan M. Leino[1,2], Sinduran Sivarajan[1], and Mark Wheelhouse[1 (✉)]

[1] Department of Computing, Imperial College London, London, UK
{rc2514,scd,be514,ss7213,mjw03,mark.wheelhouse}@imperial.ac.uk,
leino@microsoft.com
[2] Microsoft Research Redmond, Redmond, USA

Abstract. We verify the correctness of a recursive version of Tony Hoare's `quicksort` algorithm using the Hoare-logic based verification tool Dafny. We then develop a non-standard, iterative version which is based on a stack of pivot-locations rather than the standard stack of ranges. We outline an incomplete Dafny proof for the latter.

Keywords: Automated verification · Algorithms · Quicksort · Program transformation

1 Introduction

In 1959, while working on a project for automated translation from Russian to English, Tony Hoare found a recurring need to be able to sort word sequences into alphabetical order. To tackle this problem he invented an algorithm that was significantly faster than existing alternatives. The publication of this algorithm in 1961 as "Quicksort" [7] revolutionised the way we sort, and more generally, the way we think about and develop algorithms.

Since then, quicksort has inspired practitioners and researchers alike, including the recipient of this Festschrift. The algorithm has been modified and implemented millions of times by experienced programmers and students alike in several programming languages, and has even been choreographed as a Hungarian dance [16]. As well as the fascination for its elegant and succinct presentation, it is also interesting because it involves two inner recursive calls, and thus reasoning and program transformations applied to the algorithm are non-trivial.

In 1971, Foley and Hoare presented a hand-proof of the correctness of quicksort [5], and several proofs have been developed since. Proofs for the recursive as well as the iterative setting have also been proposed by de Boer and his co-authors in [1]. Recently, in his Turing Award lecture, Lamport showed an abstract derivation of iterative quicksort [9]. More recently, and rather surprisingly, de Gouw et al. discovered a subtle bug in Timsort, a sorting algorithm proposed in 2002, and which is the implementation of java.util.Arrays.sort [13]

© Springer International Publishing Switzerland 2016
E. Ábrahám et al. (Eds.): de Boer Festschrift, LNCS 9660, pp. 407–426, 2016.
DOI: 10.1007/978-3-319-30734-3_27

for non-primitive types, and part of the Android platform. They discovered the bug while trying to prove the correctness of `Timsort` using the Hoare-logic based tool Key [2].

In this paper, we reason about the correctness of two versions of quicksort: a recursive version and an iterative version. We too use a Hoare logic-based tool, namely Dafny [10].

Our recursive quicksort method deviates slightly from the standard version presented in the literature, in that we split the array into three sub-arrays, the middle one of length one, and then call the function recursively on the first and third sub-arrays.

Our iterative quicksort method is, to our knowledge, novel, in that rather than storing ranges (i.e. pairs of values) in a stack, we only store the locations of the pivots (i.e. one value), thus saving both space and time.

We have used the tool Dafny to check our implementations. To facilitate the proofs, we have defined and used lemmas in the proof of the code. We have proven some, but not all of these lemmas in Dafny.

1.1 Contributions

The key contributions of our paper are as follows:

- A proof of correctness for our variant of recursive `quicksort` in Dafny.
- A new, iterative version of `quicksort` based on the pivot locations.
- A proof outline for the correctness of our iterative `quicksort` in Dafny.

The complete Dafny code for our work can be found at [3]. To the best of our knowledge, there is no existing proof of imperative recursive quicksort in Dafny before our work. However, Leino has recently developed a proof in Dafny of the standard functional recursive algorithm, as well as an alternative version of the iterative algorithm based on ranges. Both can be found in the Dafny test suite [11]. Also, to the best our knowledge, there is no exiting version of iterative quicksort based on pivots. A comparison of its efficiency with other algorithms is future work.

The rest of this paper is organized as follows:

- Section 2 presents the notation and lemmas we will be using to specify and prove `quicksort`.
- Section 3 shows three recursive versions quicksort:
  (1) Recursive `quicksort` as proposed in Hoare's original paper.
  (2) Recursive `quicksort` as commonly seen in the literature.
  (3) Recursive `quicksort` with the variation that the two sub-ranges are off by one, and an outline of its proof of correctness.
- Section 4 shows two iterative versions of `quicksort`:
  (1) Iterative `quicksort` with a stack simulation of recursion.
  (2) Novel iterative `quicksort` based on a stack of pivot locations, and outline of its proof of correctness.
- Section 5 concludes the paper with an evaluation of our work and an identification of future directions of research.

2 Specifying Quicksort

We now turn to one of the most important parts of automated program verification: specifying the program we wish to implement.

2.1 Sorting – The Task

Let's start by defining the task of sorting the contents of an array.

> Given an array **a** of integers[1] we want to rearrange the array so that the elements of the array are arranged in ascending order. Additionally, we must ensure that no elements are added to or removed from the array.

2.2 Notation, Predicates and Lemmas

Throughout this paper we adopt the Dafny convention of treating arrays as pointers to sequences of values. That is, we think of the array a as a pointer to the sequence $a[0], a[1], a[2], ..., a[|a| - 1]$, where $|a|$ is the length of array a.

More formally, we define a notation for describing a range. For integers i, m and n:

$$i \in [m..n) \equiv_{def} m \leq i < n$$

This notation then has a natural lifting to sequences. For a sequence a, value v and integers m and n:

$$v \in a[m..n) \equiv_{def} \exists i \in [m..n). [0 \leq i < |a| \wedge a[i] = v]$$

where $a[i]$ is the ith value of the sequence. Note above that the range $m..n$ is capped by the length of the sequence to ensure that no invalid dereferences take place. We refer to $a[m..n)$ as a *slice*. A slice is treated as a subsequence of the original sequence and can be dereferenced as follows:

$$a[m..n)[i] = \begin{cases} a[m + i] & \text{if } 0 \leq m + i < |a| \\ \text{undefined} & \text{otherwise} \end{cases}$$

This slice notation allows us to elegantly describe interesting properties about arrays and sequences, such as:

$$a[m..n) \leq x \equiv_{def} \forall v \in a[m..n). v \leq x$$
$$a[m..n) \leq b[p..q) \equiv_{def} \forall v \in a[m..n). \forall v' \in b[p..q). v \leq v'$$

For ease of notation, we introduce the short-hands $a[..)$, $a[..m)$, $a[m..)$ which describe a complete sequence, a sequence up to m and a sequence from m onwards, respectively. That is:

$$a[..) \equiv_{def} a[0..|a|) \qquad a[..m) \equiv_{def} a[0..m) \qquad a[m..) \equiv_{def} a[m..|a|)$$

---

[1] The sorting task can actually be defined for an array of any type that has a less-then-or-equal relation $\leq$.

We further adopt the notation that whenever an array reference a occurs in a context expecting a slice, it should be interpreted as the slice $a[..)$.

Note that Dafny represents sequences with the syntax $a[m..n]$, which is equivalent to the meaning of $a[m..n)$ from our notation. Therefore, whenever the terms `a[m..n]` or `a[..]` appear in our Dafny code, their meaning should be interpreted as $a[m..n)$, or $a[..)$, respectively.

We introduce a notion of *deep equality* on sequences, denoted $\approx$. This describes when two sequences have exactly the same contents. That is:

$$a[..) \approx b[..) \equiv_{def} |a| = |b| \land \forall i \in [0..|a|).\, a[i] = b[i]$$

We define the concatenation of two sequences $a \mathbin{++} b$ such that:

$$|a \mathbin{++} b| = |a| + |b|$$

$$(a \mathbin{++} b)[i] = \begin{cases} a[i] & \text{if } 0 \leq i < |a| \\ b[i - |a|] & \text{if } |a| \leq i < |a| + |b| \\ \text{undefined} & \text{otherwise} \end{cases}$$

We define a predicate that describes when a sequence is sorted. For a sequence a and natural numbers i and j:

$$Sorted(a[i..j)) \equiv_{def} \forall m, n \in [0..|a|).\, [i \leq m \leq n < j \longrightarrow a[m] \leq a[n]]$$

We also define some other useful predicates over sequences and slices. For sequences a and b, integers i, j, m and n and an arbitrary value v:

$$Count(a[i..j), v) \equiv_{def} |\{k \mid k \in [i..j) \land a[k] = v\}|$$
$$a[i..j) \sim b[m..n) \equiv_{def} \forall x.\, Count(a[i..j), x) = Count(b[m..n), x)$$
$$Swapped(a[..), b[..), i, j) \equiv_{def} |a| = |b| \land i, j \in [0..|a|)$$
$$\land\ b[i] = a[j] \land b[j] = a[i]$$
$$\land\ \forall k \in [0..|a|)\backslash\{i,j\}.\, a[k] = b[k]$$

In the above:

- $Count(a[i..j), v)$ tracks the number of times that v occurs in the slice $a[i..j)$.
- $a[i..j) \sim b[m..n)$ states that slice $a[i..j)$ is a *permutation* of slice $b[m..n)$.
- $Swapped(a[..), b[..), i, j)$ states that the sequences $a[..)$ and $b[..)$ are exactly the same except that the elements at positions i and j have been *swapped*.

All the operators and predicates above are available, or can be easily encoded, in Dafny. However, they cannot always be written in infix or symbolic notation.

Finally, we present some useful properties of sequences and their related predicates. The following hold for all sequences a and b and for all integers i, j, k, l, m and n:

Deep Equality:

$$a \approx b \longrightarrow b \approx a \qquad\qquad a \approx b \land b \approx c \longrightarrow a \approx c$$
$$a \approx b \longrightarrow |a| = |b| \qquad\qquad a \approx b \longrightarrow a \sim b$$

Ranges:

$$a \approx b[0..i)\texttt{++}a[i..j)\texttt{++}b[j..|b|) \;\wedge\; m{\leq}i{\leq}j{\leq}n \;\longrightarrow\; a \approx b[0..m)\texttt{++}a[m..n)\texttt{++}b[n..|b|)$$
$$a \approx b[0..i)\texttt{++}a[i..j)\texttt{++}b[j..|b|) \;\wedge\; a[i..j) \sim b[i..j) \;\longrightarrow\; a \sim b$$
$$a \approx a[0..i)\texttt{++}b[i..j)\texttt{++}a[j..|a|) \;\wedge\; b \approx c \;\longrightarrow\; a \approx a[0..i)\texttt{++}c[i..j)\texttt{++}a[j..|a|)$$

Permutation:

$$a \sim b \;\longrightarrow\; b \sim a$$
$$a \sim b \,\wedge\, b \sim c \;\longrightarrow\; a \sim c$$
$$a \sim b \;\longrightarrow\; |a| = |b|$$

Swapping:

$$Swapped(a,\, b,\, i,\, i) \;\longrightarrow\; a \approx b$$
$$Swapped(a,\, b,\, i,\, j) \;\longrightarrow\; a \sim b$$

Sorting:

$$Sorted(\,a[i..j)\,) \,\wedge\, i \leq m \,\wedge\, n \leq j \;\longrightarrow\; Sorted(\,a[m..n)\,)$$

2.3   Specifying Methods

Method specifications consist of a *Precondition*, expected to hold before the method is executed, and a *Postcondition*, that the code must ensure holds after the method terminates. We use the Dafny keywords **requires** and **ensures** to refer to the precondition and postcondition of a method respectively. We use the Dafny keyword **assert** within our code to introduce assertions, or *midconditions*. We also use the Dafny keywords **decreases** and **invariant** to introduce *variants* and *invariants* for loops and recursive methods.

Given some code $\mathbb{C}$ with precondition P and postcondition Q, we adopt the *total correctness* interpretation of such a specification [12], whereby

> For all program states that satisfy the precondition P, the code $\mathbb{C}$ will run without faulting and will terminate in a program state that satisfies the postcondition Q.

Sometimes, in our specifications, we need to refer to both the current and initial values of some variables. For example, in the code snippet x := x+3, the new value of x depends on its previous value. By default, all of our specifications refer to the current values of variables. As in Dafny, we use the keyword *old(.)* to indicate the value before a method call. For example, *old(x)* represents the value of the program variable x before the call to the current method. Notice that arrays are pointers to sequences. So, if we have an array a, the term *old(a)* is the value of the pointer before the call, *old(a)[..]* represents the current contents of the pointer before the call, while *old(a[..])* represents the contents of the array before the call.

When writing specifications we use both Dafny syntax and normal mathematical notation as well as our sequence notation as developed in Sect. 2.2. For example, we write $\forall$ and $\wedge$ rather than **forall** and **&&**.

2.4   The Specification

Sorting is specified as follows

```
method quicksort(a:array<int>)
requires a ≠ null ∧ |a| > 0
ensures  a[..) ~ old( a[..)) ∧ Sorted( a[..))
```

This specification requires that the input be a non-null, non-empty array (to rule out pathological input) and ensures that the resulting array is sorted. Additionally, the specification states that no elements are added to or deleted from the array.

3   Recursive Quicksort

Having identified the task that we need to solve, we now provide several different implementations of quicksort, ranging from classic to more inventive solutions.

The fundamental idea behind the quicksort algorithm is "divide-and-conquer":

1. Choose an element in the list – this element serves as the pivot. Set it aside (e.g. move it to the beginning or end).
2. Partition the array of elements into two sets – those less than the pivot and those greater than or equal to the pivot
3. Repeat steps 1 and 2 on each of the two resulting partitions until each set has one or fewer elements.

3.1   The Original Quicksort

Hoare's original quicksort program, as published in [7], is given as:

```
1  method quicksort(a:array<int>, from:nat, to:nat) {
2    if (from < to) then {
3      var i,j := partition(a, from, to);
4      quicksort(a, from, i);
5      quicksort(a, j, to);
6    }
7  }
```

To sort the whole array, from should be set to 0 and to should be set to |a|.

The code presented above makes use of a variant **partition** method that does not require the caller to provide a pivot value and returns a pair rather than a single value. The pivot value is selected arbitrarily from the range [from..to). The returned pair specifies a range [i..j) of values that are equal to the chosen pivot, with elements in the range [from..i) less than the chosen pivot and [j..to) greater than the chosen pivot. More formally this can be specified as:

$$a[m..i) < a[i..j) < a[j..n) \land \exists v. \, [\, a[i..j) = v \,]$$

The standard version has also been studied in [1]. More recently, the original version is not seen that often. This is perhaps due to the fact that when the array has no duplicate elements, then the middle range will have length 1. i.e. $j = i + 1$. The algorithm then behaves like the "standard" quicksort, which we discuss next.

3.2   The Standard Quicksort

Usually [15], quicksort is presented with a method wrapper and uses a variant of partition which requires a pivot and returns only one value.

```
1  method quicksort(a:array<int>){
2    quicksort(a, 0, a.Length)
3  }
4
5  method quicksort(a:array<int>, from:nat, to:nat) {
6    if (from < to) then {
7      var mid:int := partition(a, from, to, a[from]);
8      quicksort(a, from, mid);
9      quicksort(a, mid, to);
10   }
11 }
```

Partition: The partition method rearranges an array within set bounds according to a pivot value, whilst leaving the rest of the array unmodified. This rearrangement places all elements that are smaller than the pivot before all elements that are greater than or equal to the pivot. The method returns the array index of the first element in the slice which is greater than or equal to the pivot. It is specified as follows:

method partition(a:array<int>, from:nat, to:nat, pivot:int)

returns (r:nat)

requires $a \neq \text{null} \land 0 \le \text{from} \le \text{to} \le |a|$

ensures from $\le r \le$ to

$\land \, a[\text{from}..r) < \text{pivot} \le a[r..\text{to}) \, \land \, a[..) \sim old(\, a[..)\,)$

$\land \, a \approx old(\, a[0..\text{from})\,) ++ a[\text{from}..\text{to}) ++ old(\, a[\text{to}..|a|)\,)$

Note that in the case where all elements in the range are smaller than the pivot, the method will return $r = \text{to}$. Similarly, when all elements in the range are greater than or equal to the pivot, the method will return $r = \text{from}$.

3.3   Quicksort – Our Version

Below we show our version of recursive `quicksort`. In fact, this version was shown to us by Krysia Broda. It is very similar to the standard version, but with a little twist added: our version splits the array into three, rather than two parts: one part that is smaller than, one part that is equal to, and one part that is greater than or equal to, the pivot. Then, the recursive calls need only be called on the first and the third sub-part; the pivot remains where it was placed by `swap` in the current iteration.

Swap: The `swap` method switches the places of two elements within an array, while leaving the rest of the array unmodified. It is specified, making use of our *Swapped* predicate defined in Sect. 2.2, as follows:

$$\text{method swap(a:array<int>, i:nat, j:nat)}$$
$$\text{requires } a \neq \text{null} \land i, j \in [0..|a|)$$
$$\text{ensures } Swapped(\,a[..],\, old(\,a[..]\,)),\, i,\, j)$$

The Code: In the listing below we give assertions about the state of the variables at the corresponding program points, shown in **green**. The full Dafny code for the example below, together with the definitions of all the predicates used can be found at [3].

```
 1  method quicksort(a:array<int>, from:nat, to:nat)
 2  requires a ≠ null ∧ 0 ≤ from ≤ to ≤ |a|
 3  modifies a
 4  ensures a ≈ old( a[0..from) ) ++ a[from..to) ++ old( a[to..|a|) )
 5            ∧ a[..) ~ old( a[..) ) ∧ Sorted( a[from..to) )
 6  decreases to − from
 7  {
 8    var a₀:seq<int> := a[..];
 9    if (from + 1 < to) {
10      var pivot:int := a[from];
11      assert a ≈ a₀ ∧ pivot = a[from] ∧ a[..) ~ old( a[..) )
12
13      var mid:int := partition(a, from + 1, to, pivot);
14      assert from + 1 ≤ mid ≤ to ∧ pivot = a[from]
15            ∧ a[from + 1..mid) < pivot ≤ a[mid..to)
16            ∧ a ≈ a₀[0..from + 1) ++ a[from + 1..to) ++ a[to..|a|)
17            ∧ a[..) ~ old( a[..) )
18
19      swap(a, from, mid - 1);
20      assert from ≤ mid − 1 ≤ to
21            ∧ a[from..mid − 1) < a[mid-1] ≤ a[mid..to)
22            ∧ a ≈ a₀[0..from) ++ a[from..to) ++ a₀[to..|a|)
23            ∧ a[..) ~ old( a[..) )
```

```
24
25      quicksort(a, from, mid - 1);
26      assert from ≤ mid − 1 ≤ to
27              ∧ a[from..mid − 1) < a[mid-1] ≤ a[mid..to)
28              ∧ a ≈ a₀[0..from) ++ a[from..to) ++ a₀[to..|a|)
29              ∧ a[..) ∼ old( a[..) ) ∧ Sorted( a[from..mid − 1) )
30
31      quicksort(a, mid, to);
32      assert a ≈ a₀[0..from) ++ a[from..to) ++ a₀[to..|a|)
33              ∧ a[..) ∼ old( a[..) ) ∧ Sorted( a[from..to) )
34      }
35  }
```

In Fig. 1 we show the assertions at several program points diagrammatically:

- PRE: before the method call (i.e. the precondition)
- MID_2: after the call of **partition** (i.e. at line 14)
- MID_3: after the call of **swap** (i.e. at line 20)
- MID_4: after the first recursive call of **quicksort** (i.e. at line 26)
- MID_5: after the second recursive call of **quicksort** (i.e. at line 32)
- POST: as an implication of the previous assertion (i.e. again at line 32)

We use F, T for **from** and **to**, and K as a shorthand for **mid-1**.

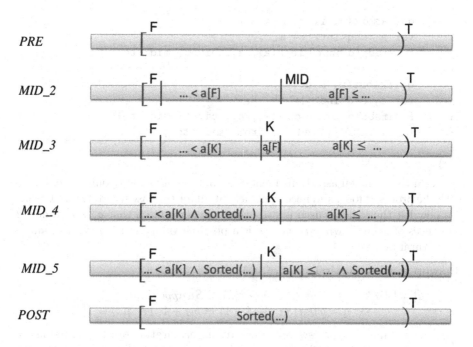

Fig. 1. Diagrammatic assertions for our recursive quicksort program.

Verification: We have verified the above code using Dafny. In order to do this, we defined and used four lemmas. We show below how the verification works: we have included in green the definition of auxiliary variables (lines 8, 12, 17, 21 and 25 below), and the calls of the lemmas (lines 18, 22, 26 and 27 below). The complete Dafny code can be found at [3].

```
1 method quicksort(a:array<int>, from:nat, to:nat)
2   requires a ≠ null ∧ 0 ≤ from ≤ to ≤ |a|
3   modifies a
4   ensures a ≈ old( a[0..from) ) ++ a[from..to) ++ old( a[to..|a|) )
5            ∧ a[..) ∼ old( a[..) ) ∧ Sorted( a[from..to) )
6   decreases to − from
7 {
8   var a₀:seq<int> := a[..];
9   if (from + 1 < to) {
10     var pivot:int := a[from];
11     var mid:int := partition(a, from + 1, to, pivot);
12     var a₁:seq<int> := a[..];
13
14     swap(a, from, mid - 1);
15     var a₂:seq<int> := a[..];
16     L_swap_impl_sameUpTo(a₂, a₁, from, mid -1);
17
18     quicksort(a, from, mid - 1);
19     var a₃:seq<int> := a[..];
20     L_sameUpTo_prsrv_less(a₃, a₂, pivot, mid, to);
21
22     quicksort(a, mid, to);
23     var a₄:seq<int> := a[..];
24     L_sameUpTo_prsrv_grEq(a₄, a₃, pivot, mid, to);
25     L_conc_impl_Sorted(a₄, from, mid, to);
26   }
27 }
```

From the eighteen assertions mentioned in the code, Dafny only needed help with the proofs of four, and needed no help at all for the case where $from+1 \geq to$. We now list the lemmas used above, using the convention that a, b, c stand for sequences of type T, while $elem \in T$ is a possible value, and i, j, k, l, m and n are natural numbers.

L_swap_impl_sameUpTo$(a, b, i, j,)$:

$$|a| = |b| \land i \leq j < |a| \land a[..) \sim b[..) \land Swapped(a, b, i, j)$$
$$\longrightarrow a \approx b[0..i) \mathbin{+\!\!+} a[i..j+1) \mathbin{+\!\!+} b[j+1..) \land a[..) \sim b[..)$$

This lemma says that swapping creates a permutation of the original array, leaving the $[..i)$ and the $[i+1..)$ range unmodified. The proof follows by unfolding the definitions.

L_sameUpTo_prsrv_less(a, b, *elem*, m, n):

$$|a| = |b| \wedge a \approx b[..m) \text{ ++ } a[m..n) \text{ ++ } b[n..) \wedge a[..) \sim b[..)$$
$$\wedge \ b[m..n) < elem$$
$$\longrightarrow \ a[m..n) < elem$$

This lemma says that if an array a is a permutation of an array b, and is identical with b in the ranges $[..m)$ and $[n..)$, then b is smaller than *elem* in the range $[m..n)$, then a is also smaller than *elem* in the range $[m..n)$. The proof follows by establishing that $a[m..m) \sim b[m..m)$.

L_sameUpTo_prsrv_grEq(a, b, *elem*, m, n):

$$|a| = |b| \wedge a \approx b[..m) \text{ ++ } a[m..n) \text{ ++ } b[n..) \wedge a[..) \sim b[..)$$
$$\wedge \ elem \leq b[m..n)$$
$$\longrightarrow \ elem \leq a[m..n)$$

This lemma says that if an array a is a permutation of an array b, and is identical with b in the ranges $[..m)$ and $[n..)$, then b is greater or equal to *elem* in the range $[m..n)$, then a is also greater or equal to *elem* in the range $[m..n)$. The proof follows by establishing that $a[m..m) \sim b[m..m)$.

L_conc_impl_Sorted(a, i, j, k):

$$i < j \leq k \leq |a| \wedge i < |a| \wedge Sorted(\,a[i..j-1)\,) \wedge Sorted(\,a[j..k)\,)$$
$$\wedge \ a[i..j-1) < a[j-1] \leq a[j..)$$
$$\longrightarrow \ Sorted(\,a[i..k)\,)$$

This lemma says that concatenation of two sorted sub-ranges $[i..j-1)$ and $[j..k)$, where the left sub-range contains smaller elements than the element at $a[j-1]$, and where $a[j-1]$ is smaller or equal to the elements at $[j..k)$ produces a sorted range $[i..k)$. The proof follows by unfolding the definitions.

4   Iterative Quicksort

An iterative version of quicksort can be obtained from the recursive one directly by applying the standard transformation of recursion. This is shown in Sect. 4.1. A more interesting (and more efficient) iterative version can be obtained if we observe some properties of the first version. This is shown in Sect. 4.2.

4.1   Iterative Quicksort Version 1 – Simulating Method Arguments

The Code: We use a stack, here called memos, to keep track of the parameters of the recursive method. We simulate the push/pop operations by decrementing/incrementing the value of top. We start by pushing 0 and |a| onto memos (lines 9 and 10). Then, we read the values of from and to iteratively from the stack (lines 13 and 14), until the stack is empty. The first recursive call, `quicksort(a,f,mid-1)`, is represented by pushing the values `from` and `mid − 1` onto the stack (lines 21 and 22), and the second recursive call, `quicksort(a,mid,to)`, is represented by pushing the values `to` and `mid` onto the stack (lines 23 and 24).

```
 1  method quicksort(a:array<int>)
 2  requires a ≠ null ∧ |a| > 0
 3  modifies a
 4  ensures a[..] ∼ old( a[..]) ) ∧ Sorted( a[..] )
 5  {
 6    var len:int := 2 * a.Length
 7    var memos:array<int> := new int[len];
 8    var top:int := len - 2;
 9    memos[top] := 0;
10    memos[top + 1] := a.Length;
11
12    while( top < len ){
13      var from:int := memos[top];
14      var to:int := memos[top + 1];
15      top := top + 2;
16      if (from + 1 < to) {
17        var pivot:int := a[from];
18        var mid:int := partition(a, from + 1, to, pivot);
19        swap(a, from, mid - 1);
20        top := top - 4;
21        memos[top] := from;
22        memos[top + 1] := mid - 1;
23        memos[top + 2] := mid;
24        memos[top + 3] := to;
25      }
26    }
27  }
```

We sketch the loop invariant for this version of `quicksort` in Fig. 2, but do not discuss the verification in more detail.

4.2   Iterative Quicksort Version 2 – Pivot Storage

Preliminaries: We now discuss the second version of iterative `quicksort`, which, to the best of our knowledge, is novel. Rather than just translating the recursion into iteration, as we did in Sect. 4.1, we instead draw inspiration from observing the following two facts about the code from Sect. 4.1: Firstly, neighbouring `to` and `from` values are off by 1 - this can be seen in lines 22 and 23. Secondly, after swapping the array elements at `from` and $(mid − 1)$ (line 19), the contents of the array at $(mid − 1)$ never changes.

This led us to the idea that, rather than pushing and popping the ranges on which we operate (i.e. the values `from` and `to`) we can instead work with the

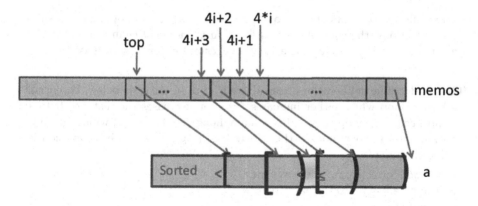

Fig. 2. Invariant sketch for our iterative "simulated recursion" `quicksort` program.

final location of the pivot (`mid − 1`). We know that the contents of the array at this location will not change, and we also know that the next range to operate on will start at the location succeeding the location of the current pivot. Therefore, we use an array of pivot locations, called `pivs`.

We know that `pivs` contains strictly increasing values:

$$\forall i, j \in [0..|\mathtt{pivs}|). \, [\, i < j \rightarrow \mathtt{pivs}[i] < \mathtt{pivs}[j] \,]$$

We also know the pivot locations delineate array segments with increasing values and that the contents of array `a` at location `pivs[i]` will not change in subsequent iterations, since all the values preceding it are smaller, and all values coming after it are greater of equal. We encode these two properties as follows:[2]

$$\forall i \in [\mathtt{top}..|\mathtt{a}|). \, \mathtt{a}[..\mathtt{pivs}[i]) < \mathtt{a}[\mathtt{pivs}[i]] \leq \mathtt{a}[\mathtt{pivs}[i] + 1..)$$

We use the variable `top` with values from the interval $[0..|\mathtt{a}| + 1)$, to range over the indices of the array `pivs`, so that the contents of the slice `pivs[top+1..)` is always defined. We initialize `top` with $|\mathtt{a}|$. We increment `top` in order to pop a pivot location, and decrement it in order to push a pivot location. This gives us the invariant:

$$0 \leq \mathtt{top} \leq |\mathtt{a}|$$

We also use variables `from` and `to` to delineate the range we are currently operating on. We have the invariants that

$$0 \leq \mathtt{top} \leq |\mathtt{a}| \land 0 \leq \mathtt{from} \leq \mathtt{to} = \mathtt{pivs}[\mathtt{top}] \land \mathtt{pivs}[|\mathtt{a}|] = |\mathtt{a}|$$

that the array is sorted up to and including the index `from`, and that all values before `from` are smaller or equal to those starting `from` and onwards:

$$Sorted(\, \mathtt{a}[..\mathtt{from} + 1)\,) \land \mathtt{a}[..\mathtt{from}) \leq \mathtt{a}[\mathtt{from}..)$$

---

[2] The careful reader will notice that the array look-up `a[pivs[i]+1]` is not always defined. Nevertheless, the assertion is well-formed, because it stands for $\forall i \in [\mathtt{top}..|\mathtt{a}|).\forall j \in [0..\mathtt{pivs}[i]).\forall k \in [\mathtt{pivs}[i]+1.. |\mathtt{a}|). \, \mathtt{a}[j] < \mathtt{a}[\mathtt{pivs}[i]] \leq \mathtt{a}[k]$.

Note: while the contents of array a at location pivs[i] will not change in subsequent iterations, the contents of a at location from *might* change at subsequent iterations, as it is possible that $a[\text{from}] > a[\text{from}+k]$ for some $k \in \mathbb{N}$.

The Code: The deliberations from above lead us to the code below. Essentially, we have a loop which either increases from, or decreases the distance between to and from. The loop terminates when $a.\text{Length} - \text{from} \leq 1$, which, given the invariants from above, implies that $Sorted(a[..|a|))$. The loop invariant consists of nine conjuncts.

```
1   method quicksort(a:array<int>)
2   requires a ≠ null ∧ |a| > 0
3   modifies a
4   ensures a[..) ~ old( a[..) ) ∧ Sorted( a[..) )
5   {
6     var pivs:array<int> := new int[a.Length+1];
7     pivs[a.Length] := a.Length;
8     var from, to, top := 0, a.Length, a.Length;
9
10    while (a.Length - from > 1)
11    invariant 0 ≤ top ≤ |a| ∧ 0 ≤ from ≤ to = pivs[top]
12        ∧ pivs[|a|] = |a| ∧ ∀i ∈ [top..|a| + 1).pivs[i] ≤ i + 1
13        ∧ ∀i, j ∈ [top..|a| + 1). [i < j → pivs[i] < pivs[j]]
14        ∧ ∀i ∈ [top..|a|). a[..pivs[i]) < a[pivs[i]] ≤ a[pivs[i]..)
15        ∧ a[..from) ≤ a[from..)
16        ∧ a[..) ~ old( a[..) ) ∧ Sorted( a[..from + 1) )
17    decreases |a| − from, to − from
18    {
19
20      if ( (to - from) <= 1 ) {
21        L_sorted_combine(a, from, to);
22        L_prsrv_pivot(a,to);
23
24        from := to + 1;
25        top := top + 1;
26        to := pivs[top];
27      } else {
28        var a₂:seq<int> := a[..];
29
30        var pivot:int := a[from];
31        var mid:nat := partition(a, from + 1, to, pivot);
32        var a₂:seq<int> := a[..];
33
34        swap(a, from, mid - 1);
35        var a₃:seq<int> := a[..];
36        L_swap_prsrv_less(a₃, a₂, from, mid);
```

```
37        L_sameUpTo_trans(a₃, a₂, a₁, from, to);
38        L_sameUpTo_prsv_sorted(a₃, a₁, from, to);

39
40        top := top - 1;
41        pivs[top] := mid - 1;
42        to := mid - 1;
43      }
44    }
45  }
```

We sketch the loop invariant for this version of `quicksort` in Fig. 3.

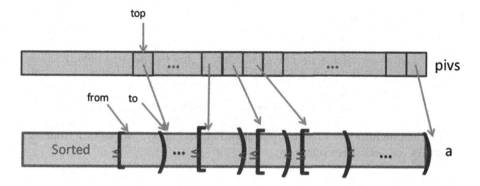

Fig. 3. Invariant sketch for our iterative "pivot storage" `quicksort` program.

Verification: In our Dafny proof we wrote twenty-four `assert` statements to guide the prover, and called five lemmas at the code locations listed above. The lemmas are given below and proven in the next subsection. In the following, a, b and c stand for sequences, while i, j, k, m and n are natural numbers.

L_sorted_combine(a, m, n):

$$m \leq n \leq m + 1 \land Sorted(a[..m+1)) \land a[..n) < a[n] \leq a[n+1..)$$
$$\longrightarrow Sorted(a[..m+2))$$

The lemma above increases the range for which we know that an array a is sorted.

L_prsrv_pivot(a, m):

$$m < |a| \land a[..m) < a[m] \leq a[m+1..) \longrightarrow a[..m+1) \leq a[m+1..)$$

The lemma above increases the range for which we know that elements are smaller than the elements in the remaining array.

L_swap_prsrv_less(a, b, m, n):

$$m < n \leq |b| \wedge b[..m) < b[m..) \wedge b[m+1..n) < b[m] \wedge |a| = |b|$$
$$\wedge\ Swapped(a,\ b,\ m,\ n-1)$$
$$\longrightarrow\ a[..m) < a[m..) \wedge a[m..n-1) < a[n-1]$$

The lemma above asserts that, after swapping, a pivot correctly partitions the array. The left subsequence is smaller than the right subsequence and the middle subsequence is smaller than the element $a[n-1]$.

L_sameUpTo_trans(a, b, c, m, n):

$$|a| = |b| = |c| \wedge m < n \leq |a| \wedge a \approx b[..m) \mathbin{++} a[m..n) \mathbin{++} b[n..)$$
$$\wedge\ a[..) \sim b[..) \wedge b \approx c[..m+1) \mathbin{++} b[m+1..n) \mathbin{++} c[n..)$$
$$\wedge\ b[..) \sim c[..)$$
$$\longrightarrow\ a \approx c[..m) \mathbin{++} a[m..n) \mathbin{++} c[n..) \wedge a[..) \sim c[..)$$

The lemma above asserts that permutation, and array composition from sub-arrays are transitive relations.

L_sameUpTo_prsv_sorted(a, b, i, j):

$$|a| = |b| \wedge i < j \leq |b| \wedge Sorted(b[..i+1)) \wedge a[..i) \leq a[i..)$$
$$\wedge\ a \approx b[..i) \mathbin{++} a[i..j) \mathbin{++} b[j..)$$
$$\longrightarrow\ Sorted(a[..i+1))$$

This lemma ensures that swapping preserves sortedness of sub-ranges of the array.

4.3 Proofs

We now show the proofs of these lemmas.

Proof of L_sorted_combine(a, m, n):

Given
   (1) $m \leq n \leq m+1$
   (2) $Sorted(a[..m+1))$
   (3) $a[..n) < a[n] \leq a[n+1..)$
To show
   (A) $Sorted(a[..m+2))$
From (1), we obtain that either $m = n$ or $m+1 = n$. We proceed by case analysis.

1st Case:
  (4) $m = n$
  Then we have
  (5) $a[..m) < a[m] \leq a[m+1..)$ from (3) and (4)
  (6) $a[m] < a[m+1]$ from (5)
  (A) $Sorted(\,a[..m+2)\,)$ from (2) and (6)

2nd Case:
  (4) $m + 1 = n$
  Then we have
  (5) $a[..m+1) < a[m+1]$ from (3) and (4)
  (A) $Sorted(\,a[..m+2)\,)$ from (2) and (5)

Proof of L_prsrv_pivot(a, m): by unfolding the definitions.

Proof of L_swap_prsrv_less(a, b, m, n):
  Given
  (1) $m < n \leq |b|$
  (2) $b[..m) < b[m..)$
  (3) $b[m+1..n) < b[m] \leq b[n+1..)$
  (4) $|a| = |b|$
  (5) $Swapped(a, b, m, n-1)$
  To Show
  (A) $a[..m) < a[m..)$
  (B) $a[m..n-1) < a[n-1] \leq a[n..)$
  We obtain
  (6) $a[..m) \approx b[..m)$ from (5)
  (7) $a[m] = b[n-1]$ from (5)
  (8) $a[m+1..n-1) \approx b[m+1..n-1)$ from (5)
  (9) $a[n-1] = b[m]$ from (5)
  (10) $a[n..) \approx b[n..)$ from (5)
  (A) $a[..m) < a[m..)$ from $(2), (7)$–(10)
  (11) $a[m..n-1) \approx b[n-1]$ ++ $b[m+1..n-1)$ from (7), (8)
  (12) $a[m..n-1) < b[m]$ from (11), (2) and (3)
  (13) $a[m..n-1) < a[n-1]$ from (12), (9)
  (14) $a[n-1] \leq a[n..)$ from (3), (9) and (10)
  (B) $a[m..n-1) < a[n-1] \leq a[n..)$ from (13) and (14)

Proof of L_sameUpTo_trans(a, b, c, m, n):
  Given
  (1) $|a| = |b| = |c|$
  (2) $m < n \leq |a|$
  (3) $a \approx b[..m)$ ++ $a[m..n)$ ++ $b[n..)$
  (4) $a[..) \sim b[..)$
  (5) $b \approx c[..m+1)$ ++ $b[m+1..n)$ ++ $c[n..)$
  (6) $b[..) \sim [..c)$
  To Show
  (A) $a \approx c[..m)$ ++ $a[m..n)$ ++ $c[n..)$
  (B) $a[..) \sim c[..)$

We obtain

(B) $a[..) \sim c[..)$	from (4) and (6)
(7) $b[..m) \approx c[..m)$	from (5), and by $m < m + 1$
(8) $b[n..) \approx c[n..)$	from (5)
(A) $a \approx c[..m) \mathbin{+\!\!+} a[m..n) \mathbin{+\!\!+} c[n..)$	from (3), (7) and (8)

Proof of L_sameUpTo_prsv_sorted(a, b, i, j):

Given

(1) $|a| = |b|$

(2) $i < j \leq |b|$

(3) $Sorted(b[..i+1))$

(4) $a[..i) \leq a[i..)$

(5) $a \approx b[..i) \mathbin{+\!\!+} a[i..k) \mathbin{+\!\!+} b[k..)$

To Show

(A) $Sorted(a[..i+1))$

We obtain

(6) $Sorted(b[..i))$	from (3) and because $i < i+1$
(7) $Sorted(a[..i))$	from (5) and (6)
(8) $i > 1 \;\rightarrow\; a[i-1] \leq a[i]$	from (4)
(A) $Sorted(a[..i+1))$	from (7) and (8)

5   Experiences, Conclusions and Future Work

Despite extensive testing and hand-written proofs, it was reassuring when Dafny confirmed the correctness of our `quicksort`. We found array-sequence infix operators to be useful in the development of both the algorithm and reasoning.

Dafny was extremely effective in helping us iron out many little, fiddly bugs at the original stages of our work. As we progressed, the process became both slow and addictive. Those of us new to Dafny were often surprised to see that Dafny/Z3 could automatically discharge proof obligations which were, in our opinion, non-trivial, while it was often unable to discharge what we considered trivial ones. This was due to our limited previous understanding of Z3.

We therefore proceeded in a somewhat experimental fashion. We inserted `assume` statements for all the proof obligations, and gradually replaced them by `assert` statements. When the verifier was unable to discharge an obligation, we wrote a lemma, whose validity we checked through hand-written proofs. As a result, the lemmas we have developed do not seem to be the most interesting or intuitive ones, and their choice might have been affected by the particular order in which we happened to require them.

The computational power needed for the proofs to go through was considerable. Therefore, we adopted little tricks to focus the tool on particular aspects of the proof. For example, we would replace part of the code with `assume false`, so that the tool would not need to check validity past this point. We also split the proof of the pivot-based iterative `quicksort` into two: First we replaced the code in the `else` branch by `assume false`. This let us prove that the initialization establishes the loop invariant and that the `then` branch of the loop preserves it. Then we wrote a function whose body consists of `assume` statements for all the loop invariants, followed by the code from the `else` branch of the loop and ending in `assert` statements for all the loop invariants. This let us prove that the `else` branch of the loop also preserves the loop invariant.

The experimental fashion for discovering useful lemmas, and the ticks to focus the tool on certain aspects are often seen in the Verification Corner videos [14]. We believe that Visual Studio should provide more automatic support for steering the proof effort and more help with interactive program and proof development.

As future work, we would like to complete the proofs of the lemmas we have used, complete the proofs of the other two versions of `quicksort`, and try and unify the arguments used in the various proofs. We would also like to run benchmarks to compare the efficiency of our pivot-based algorithm with that of other algorithms in the literature. Finally, we want to port the Dafny proofs to our tool Apollo [4], which maps Java, Haskell code and proof idioms onto Dafny.

Acknowledgments. We thank Krysia Broda for showing us the recursive, non-standard version of `quicksort`, and the anonymous reviewers of this volume for valuable suggestions and pointers.

Razvan Certezeanu, Benjamin Egelund-Muller and Sinduran Sivarajan thank the Department of Computing at Imperial College for funding their Undergraduate Research Opportunities Programme (UROP) Placements, undertaken under Mark Wheelhouse's supervision, which they spent working on Apollo, and this paper.

Sophia Drossopoulou thanks Microsoft Research and Judith Bishop for a research gift and her very warm hospitality at Microsoft Research, and the EU project Upscale, FP7-612985, for supporting part of this work, and for the opportunity to collaborate with Frank S. de Boer, the recipient of this Festschrift.

References

1. Apt, K., Boer, F., Olderog, E.: Verification of Sequential and Concurrent Programs. Springer, Dordrecht (2009)
2. Beckert, B., Hähnle, R., Schmitt, P.H. (eds.): Verification of Object-Oriented Software. The KeY Approach. LNCS (LNAI), vol. 4334. Springer, Heidelberg (2007)
3. Certezeanu, R., Drossopoulou, S., Egelund-Muller, B., Sivarajan, S., Wheelhouse, M., Leino, K.: Dafny Code for Variations on Quicksort. http://www.doc.ic.ac.uk/~mjw03/research/quicksort.html
4. Certezeanu, R., Drossopoulou, S., Egelund-Muller, B., Sivarajan, S., Wheelhouse, M., Leino, K.:Apollo: An interactive Program and Proof development tool for Java and Haskell, based on Dafny (to appear)
5. Foley, M., Hoare, C.: Proof of a recursive program: quicksort. Comput. J. **14**, 391–395 (1971)
6. de Gouw, S., Rot, J., de Boer, F.S., Bubel, R., Hähnle, R.: OpenJDK's Java.utils.Collection.sort() is broken: the good, the bad and the worst case. In: Kroening, D., Păsăreanu, C.S. (eds.) CAV 2015. LNCS, vol. 9206, pp. 273–289. Springer, Heidelberg (2015)
7. Hoare, C.: Algorithm 64: quicksort. Commun. ACM **4**, 321 (1961)

8. Hoare, C.: An axiomatic basis for computer programming. Commun. ACM **12**, 576–580 (1969)
9. Lamort, L.:Thinking Above the Code. https://www.youtube.com/watch?v=-4Yp3j_jk8Q
10. Leino, K.R.M.: Dafny: an automatic program verifier for functional correctness. In: Clarke, E.M., Voronkov, A. (eds.) LPAR-16 2010. LNCS, vol. 6355, pp. 348–370. Springer, Heidelberg (2010)
11. Leino, K.: Dafny: An Automatic Program Verifier for Functional Correctness. http://dafny.codeplex.com
12. Manna, Z.: Mathematical Theory of Computation. McGraw-Hill, New York (1974)
13. Oracle Documentation: Arrays (Java Platform SE 7). http://docs.oracle.com/javase/7/docs/api/java/util/Arrays.html
14. The Verification Corner - Microsoft Research. http://research.microsoft.com/en-us/projects/verificationcorner
15. Wikipedia: Quicksort. https://en.wikipedia.org/wiki/Quicksort
16. YouTube: Quick-sort with Hungarian (Kkllmenti legnyes) folk dance. https://www.youtube.com/watch?v=ywWBy6J5gz8

Author Index

Printed in the United States
By Bookmasters